Conte...

First published in 2007 by

Philip's, a division of Octopus Publishing Group Ltd
2-4 Heron Quays
London E14 4JP

www.philips-maps.co.uk

First edition 2007
First impression 2007

Ordnance Survey® This product includes mapping data licensed from Ordnance Survey®, with the permission of the Controller of Her Majesty's Stationery Office © Crown copyright 2007. All rights reserved. Licence number 100011710.

This product includes mapping data licensed from Ordnance Survey of Northern Ireland® reproduced by permission of the Chief Executive, acting on behalf of the Controller of Her Majesty's Stationery Office. © Crown Copyright 2007 Permit No 60325

All enquiries should be addressed to the Publisher.

To the best of the Publisher's knowledge, the information in this atlas was correct at the time of going to press. No responsibility can be accepted for any errors or their consequences.

The representation in this atlas of any road, drive or track is not evidence of the existence of a right of way.

The mapping on page 212 and the town plans of Edinburgh and London are based on mapping data licenced from Ordnance Survey with the permission of the Controller of Her Majesty's Stationery Office, © Crown copyright 2007. All rights reserved. Licence number 100011710.

The maps of Ireland on pages 26 to 30 and the town plan of Dublin are based on Ordnance Survey Ireland by permission of the Government Permit Number 8186
© Ordnance Survey Ireland and Government of Ireland, and Ordnance Survey Northern Ireland on behalf of the Controller of Her Majesty's Stationery Office © Crown Copyright 2007 Permit Number 60325

Cartography by Philip's
Copyright © Philip's 2007

Printed and bound by Toppan, China

Driving regulations

A national vehicle identification plate is always required when taking a vehicle abroad. It is important for your own safety and that of other drivers to fit headlamp converters or beam deflectors when taking a right-hand drive car to a country where driving is on the right (every country in Europe except the UK and Ireland). When the headlamps are dipped on a right-hand drive car, the lenses of the headlamps cause the beam to shine upwards to the left – and so, when driving on the right, into the eyes of oncoming motorists.

The symbols used are:

🏛 Motorway	△ Warning triangle
⚠ Dual carriageway	➕ First aid kit
⚠ Single carriageway	💡 Spare bulb kit
🚗 Surfaced road	🧯 Fire extinguisher
🚗 Unsurfaced / gravel road	🪖 Motorcycle helmet
🏙 Urban area	📋 Additional documents required
⏱ Speed limit in kilometres per hour (kph)	
🛡 Seat belts	📱 Mobile phones
👶 Children	★ Other information
🍷 Blood alcohol level	

All countries require that you carry a driving licence, green card/insurance documentation, registration document or hire certificate, and passport.

The penalties for infringements of regulations vary considerably from one country to another. In many countries the police have the right to impose on-the-spot fines (you should always request a receipt for any fine paid). Penalties can be severe for serious infringements, particularly for drinking when driving which in some countries can lead to immediate imprisonment. Insurance is important, and you may be forced to take out cover at the frontier if you cannot produce acceptable proof that you are insured.

Please note that driving regulations often change.

Andorra (AND)

🏛	⚠	⚠	🏙
n/a	90	90	50

- 🛡 Compulsory in front seats
- 👶 Over 10 only allowed in front seats if over 150cm
- 🍷 0.05%
- △ Compulsory
- ➕ Recommended
- 💡 Compulsory
- 🧯 Recommended
- 🪖 Compulsory for all riders
- ⊖ 18 (16-18 accompanied)
- 📱 Use not permitted whilst driving

Austria (A)

🏛	⚠	⚠	🏙
130	100	100	50

If towing trailer under 750kg

🏛	⚠	⚠	🏙
100	100	100	50

If towing trailer over 750kg

🏛	⚠	⚠	🏙
100	100	80	50

- 🛡 Compulsory in front seats and rear seats
- 👶 Under 14 and under 150cm in front seats only in child safety seat; under 14 over 150cm must wear adult seat belt
- 🍷 0.05%
- △ Compulsory
- ➕ Compulsory
- 💡 Recommended
- 🧯 Recommended
- 🪖 Compulsory for all riders
- ⊖ 18 (16 for mopeds)
- 📋 Third party insurance
- 📱 Use permitted only with hands-free speaker system
- ★ If you intend to drive on motorways or expressways, a motorway vignette must be purchased at the border. These are available for 10 days, 2 months or 1 year.
- ★ Dipped headlights must be used at all times on motorbikes.

Belarus (BY)

🏛	⚠	⚠	🏙
110	90	90	60

If towing trailer under 750kg

🏛	⚠	⚠	🏙
90	70	70	

Vehicle towing another vehicle 50 kph limit

- 🛡 Compulsory in front seats, and rear seats if fitted
- 👶 Under 12 in front seats only in child safety seat
- 🍷 0.05%
- △ Compulsory

Belgium (B)

🏛	⚠	⚠	🏙
120*	120	90	50

*Minimum speed of 70kph on motorways

If towing trailer

🏛	⚠	⚠	🏙
90	90	60	50

- 🛡 Compulsory in front and rear seats
- 👶 Under 12 in front seats only in child safety seat
- 🍷 0.05%
- △ Compulsory
- ➕ Compulsory
- 💡 Recommended
- 🧯 Compulsory
- 🪖 Compulsory for all riders
- ⊖ 18 (16 for mopeds)
- 📋 Third party insurance
- 📱 Use only allowed with hands-free kit

Bulgaria (BG)

🏛	⚠	⚠	🏙
130	90	90	50

If towing trailer

🏛	⚠	⚠	🏙
100	70	70	50

- 🛡 Compulsory in front and rear seats
- 👶 Under 10 not allowed in front seats
- 🍷 0.05%
- △ Compulsory
- ➕ Compulsory
- 💡 Recommended
- 🧯 Compulsory
- 🪖 Compulsory for all riders
- ⊖ 18 (16 for mopeds)
- 📋 Driving licence with translation or international driving permit, third party insurance
- 📱 Use only allowed with hands-free kit
- ★ Fee at border
- ★ Vignette system in operation, can be purchased from all border-crossing points and available annually, monthly and weekly.

Croatia (HR)

🏛	⚠	⚠	🏙
130	80	80	50

If towing

🏛	⚠	⚠	🏙
110	80	80	50

- 🛡 Compulsory if fitted
- 👶 Under 12 not allowed in front seats
- 🍷 0.00%
- △ Compulsory
- ➕ Compulsory
- 💡 Compulsory
- 🪖 Compulsory for all riders
- ⊖ 18
- 📱 Use only allowed with hands-free kit
- ★ It is compulsory to carry a fluorescent jacket in case of breakdown

Cyprus (CY)

🏛	⚠	⚠	🏙
100	100	80/50	50

If towing

🏛	⚠	⚠	🏙
100	100	80/50	50

- 🛡 Compulsory for front and rear seat passengers (for vehicles manufactured after 01/01/1988)
- 👶 Children under 12 years old or less than 150cm height must be fastened with special fastening belts
- 🍷 0.05% blood, 0.02% breath
- △ Compulsory
- ➕ Compulsory for public vehicles, recommended for the rest
- 💡 N/A
- 🧯 Compulsory for public vehicles, recommended for the rest
- 🪖 Compulsory for all riders
- ⊖ 18 (17 for mopeds)
- 📱 Use only allowed with hands-free kit
- ★ Speed restriction for trucks: 80 kph on motorways and dual carriageways
- ★ No tolls apply but a circulation license is paid according to engine capacity. Trucks pay the circulation license according to the type of suspension and number of axies.

Czech Republic (CZ)

🏛	⚠	⚠	🏙
130	130	90	50

If towing

🏛	⚠	⚠	🏙
80	80	80	50

- 🛡 Compulsory in front seats and, if fitted, in rear
- 👶 Under 12 or under 150cm not allowed in front seats
- 🍷 0.00%

△ Compulsory
✚ Compulsory
💡 Compulsory
⛑ Compulsory for all riders
☸ 18 (16 for motorcycles under 125 cc)
📄 International driving permit
📱 Use only allowed with hands-free kit
★ Vignette needed for motorway driving, available for 1 year, 60 days, 15 days. Toll specific to lorries introduced 2006.

Denmark [DK]

	🛣	⇈	▲	🏙
⊙	110/130	80	80	50
If towing				
⊙	80	70	70	50

💺 Compulsory in front seats and, if fitted, in rear
👶 Under 3 not allowed in front seat except in a child safety seat; in rear, 3 to 7 years in a child safety seat or on a booster cushion
🍸 0.05%
△ Compulsory
✚ Recommended
💡 Recommended
🧯 Recommended
⛑ Compulsory for all riders
☸ 18
📄 Third party insurance
📱 Use only allowed with hands-free kit
★ Dipped headlights must be used at all times

Estonia [EST]

	🛣	⇈	▲	🏙
⊙	n/a	90	70	50

💺 Compulsory in front seats and if fitted in rear seats
👶 Under 12 not allowed in front seats; under 7 must have child safety seat in rear
🍸 0.00%
△ Compulsory
✚ Compulsory
💡 Recommended
🧯 Compulsory
⛑ Compulsory for all riders
☸ 18 (16 for motorcycles, 14 for mopeds)
📄 International driving permit recommended
📱 Use only allowed with hands-free kit

Finland [FIN]

	🛣	⇈	▲	🏙
⊙	120	80*	100/80	30-60
*100 in summer				
If towing				
⊙	80	80	80	30-60

If towing a vehicle by rope, cable or rod, max speed limit 60 kph.

Maximum of 80 kph for vans and lorries

Speed limits are often lowered in winter

💺 Compulsory in front and rear
👶 Children use a safety belt or special child's seat
🍸 0.05%
△ Compulsory
✚ Recommended
💡 Recommended
🧯 Recommended
⛑ Compulsory for all riders
☸ 18
📄 Third party insurance
📱 Use only allowed with hands-free kit
★ Dipped headlights must be used at all times

France [F]

	🛣	⇈	▲	🏙
⊙	130	110	90	50
On wet roads				
⊙	110	90	80	50

50kph on all roads if fog reduces visibility to less than 50m. Licence will be lost and driver fined for exceeding speed limit by over 40kph

💺 Compulsory in front seats and, if fitted, in rear
👶 Under 10 not allowed in front seats unless in approved safety seat facing backwards; in rear, if 4 or under, must have a child safety seat (rear facing if up to 9 months); if 5 to 10 may use a booster seat with suitable seat belt
🍸 0.05%
△ Compulsory unless hazard warning lights are fitted; compulsory for vehicles over 3,500kgs or towing a trailer
✚ Recommended
💡 Recommended
⛑ Compulsory for all riders
☸ 18 (16 for light motorcycles, 14 for mopeds)
📱 Use not permitted whilst driving
★ Tolls on motorways

Germany [D]

	🛣	⇈	▲	🏙
⊙	*	*	100	50
If towing				
⊙	*	*	80	50

*no limit, 130 kph recommended

💺 Compulsory
👶 Children under 12 and under 150cm must have a child safety seat, in front and rear
🍸 0.05%
△ Compulsory
✚ Compulsory
💡 Recommended
🧯 Recommended
⛑ Compulsory for all riders
☸ 18 (motorbikes: 16 if not more than 125cc and limited to 11 kW)
📄 Third party insurance
📱 Use permitted only with hands-free kit – also applies to drivers of motorbikes and bicycles
★ Motorcyclists must use dipped headlights at all times.

Greece [GR]

	🛣	⇈	▲	🏙
⊙	120	110	110	50
If towing				
⊙	90	70	70	40

💺 Compulsory in front seats and, if fitted, in rear
👶 Under 12 not allowed in front seats except with suitable safety seat; under 10 not allowed in front seats
🍸 0.025%
△ Compulsory
✚ Compulsory
💡 Recommended
🧯 Compulsory
⛑ Compulsory for all riders
☸ 18 (16 for low cc motorcycles)
📄 Third party insurance
📱 Use only allowed with hands-free kit

Hungary [H]

	🛣	⇈	▲	🏙
⊙	130	110	90	50
If towing				
⊙	80	70	70	50

💺 Compulsory in front seats and if fitted in rear seats
👶 Under 12 or under 140cm not allowed in front seats
🍸 0.00%
△ Compulsory
✚ Compulsory
💡 Compulsory
🧯 Recommended
⛑ Compulsory for all riders
☸ 18
📄 Third party insurance
📱 Use only allowed with hands-free kit
★ All motorways are toll and operate the vignette system, tickets are available for 4 days, 10 days, 1 month, 1 year
★ Dipped headlights are compulsory during daylight hours (cars exempted in built-up areas)

Iceland [IS]

	🛣	🚗	🚙	🏙
⊙	n/a	90	80	50

💺 Compulsory in front and rear seats
👶 Under 12 or under 140cm not allowed in front seats
🍸 0.00%
△ Compulsory
✚ Compulsory
💡 Compulsory
⛑ Compulsory for all riders
☸ 18
📄 Third party insurance
📱 Use only allowed with hands-free kit
★ Headlights are compulsory at all times
★ Highland roads are not suitable for ordinary cars
★ Driving off marked roads is forbidden

Ireland [IRL]

	🛣	⇈	▲	🏙
⊙	120	100	80	50
If towing				
⊙	80	80	80	50

💺 Compulsory in front seats and if fitted in rear seats. Driver responsible for ensuring passengers under 17 comply.
👶 Under 4 not allowed in front seats unless in a child safety seat or other suitable restraint
🍸 0.08%
△ Recommended
✚ Recommended
💡 Recommended
🧯 Recommended
⛑ Compulsory for all riders
☸ 17 (16 for motorbikes up to 125cc; 18 for over 125cc; 18 for lorries; 21 bus/minibus)
📄 Third party insurance; international driving permit for non-EU drivers
📱 No specific legislation
★ Driving is on the left

Italy [I]

	🛣	⇈	▲	🏙
⊙	130	110	90	50
If towing				
⊙	80	70	70	50

💺 Compulsory in front seats and, if fitted, in rear
👶 Under 12 not allowed in front seats except in child safety seat; children under 3 must have special seat in the back
🍸 0.08%
△ Compulsory
✚ Recommended
💡 Compulsory
🧯 Recommended
⛑ Compulsory for all motorcyclists
☸ 18 (14 for mopeds, 16 for up to 125cc, 20 for up to 350cc)
📄 International Driving Licence unless you have photocard licence
📱 Use only allowed with hands-free kit

Latvia [LV]

	🛣	⇈	▲	🏙
⊙	n/a	90	90	50
If towing				
⊙	n/a	80	80	50

In residential areas limit is 20kph

💺 Compulsory in front seats and if fitted in rear
👶 If under 150cm must use child restraint in front and rear seats
🍸 0.05%
△ Compulsory
✚ Compulsory
💡 Recommended
🧯 Compulsory
⛑ Compulsory for all riders
☸ 18 (14 for mopeds, 16 for up to 125cc, 21 for up to 350cc)
📄 International driving permit if licence is not in accordance with Vienna Convention
📱 Use only allowed with hands-free kit
★ Dipped headlights must be used at all times all year round
★ Cars and minibuses under 3.5 tonnes must have winter tyres from 1Dec-1Mar

Lithuania [LT]

	🛣	⇈	▲	🏙
⊙	130	110	90	60
If towing				
⊙	70	70	70	60

💺 Compulsory in front seats and if fitted in rear seats

- Under 12 not allowed in front seats unless in a child safety seat
- 0.04%
- Compulsory
- Compulsory
- Recommended
- Compulsory
- Compulsory for all riders
- 18 (14 for mopeds)
- Visa
- No legislation
- Dipped headlights must be used day and night from Nov to Mar (all year for motorcyclists) and from 1 to 7 Sept

Luxembourg (L)

130/110	90	90	50
If towing			
90	75	75	50

- Compulsory
- Under 12 or 150cm not allowed in front seats unless in a child safety seat; under 3 must have child safety seat in rear seats; 3 - 11 must have child safety seat or belt if under 150cm
- 0.08%
- Compulsory
- Compulsory (buses)
- Compulsory
- Compulsory (buses, transport of dangerous goods)
- Compulsory for all riders
- 18 (16 for mopeds)
- Third party insurance
- Use permitted only with hands-free speaker system
- Motorcyclists must use dipped headlights at all times.

Macedonia (MK)

120	100	60	60
If towing			
80	70	50	50

- Compulsory in front seats; compulsory if fitted in rear seats
- Under 12 not allowed in front seats
- 0.05%
- Compulsory
- Compulsory
- Compulsory
- Recommended
- Compulsory for all riders
- 18 (mopeds 16)
- International driving permit; visa

- Use not permitted whilst driving
- Headlights must be used at all times

Moldova (MD)

90	90	90	60
If towing or if licence held under 1 year			
70	70	70	60

- Compulsory in front seats and, if fitted, in rear seats
- Under 12 not allowed in front seats
- 0.00%
- Compulsory
- Compulsory
- Recommended
- Compulsory
- Compulsory for all riders
- 18 (mopeds and motorbikes, 16; vehicles with more than eight passenger places, taxis or towing heavy vehicles, 21)
- International driving permit (preferred), third party insurance, vehicle registration papers, visa
- Use only allowed with hands-free kit
- Motorcyclists must use dipped headlights at all times
- Winter tyres recommended from November to February

Montenegro (CG)

n/a	100	80	60

- Compulsory in front and rear seats
- Under 12 not allowed in front seats
- 0.05%
- Compulsory
- Compulsory
- Recommended
- Compulsory
- Compulsory
- 18 (16 for motorbikes less than 125cc; 14 for mopeds)
- International driving permit; visa
- No legislation
- Tolls on some primary roads
- All types of fuel available at petrol stations
- 80km/h speed limit if towing a caravan

Netherlands (NL)

120	80	80	50

- Compulsory in front seats and, if fitted, rear
- Under 12 not allowed in front seats except in child restraint; in rear, 0-3 child safety restraint, 4-12 child restraint or seat belt
- 0.05%
- Recommended
- Recommended
- Recommended
- Recommended
- Compulsory for all riders
- 18 (16 for mopeds)
- Third party insurance
- Use only allowed with hands-free kit

Norway (N)

90	80	80	50
If towing trailer with brakes			
80	80	80	50
If towing trailer without brakes			
60	60	60	50

- Compulsory in front seats and, if fitted, in rear
- Under 4 must have child restraint; over 4 child restraint or seat belt
- 0.02%
- Compulsory
- Recommended
- Recommended
- Recommended
- Compulsory for all riders
- 18 (16 mopeds, heavy vehicles 18/21)
- Use only allowed with hands-free kit
- Dipped headlights must be used at all times
- Tolls apply on some bridges, tunnels and access roads into major cities

Poland (PL)

130	110	90	*50-60

*50kph 06.00–22.00 60kph 23.00–05.00

If towing			
80*	80	60	30

*40kph minimum; 20kph in residential areas

- Compulsory in front seats and, if fitted, in rear
- Under 12 not allowed in front seats unless in a child safety seat or the child is 150cm tall
- 0.02%
- Compulsory
- Recommended
- Recommended
- Compulsory
- Compulsory for all riders
- 18 (mopeds and motorbikes – 16)
- International permit (recommended)
- Use only allowed with hands-free kit
- Between 1 Nov and 1 Mar dipped headlights must be used day and night

Portugal (P)

120*	100	90	50
If towing			
100*	90	80	50

*40kph minimum; 90kph maximum if licence held under 1 year

- Compulsory in front seats; compulsory if fitted in rear seats
- Under 3 not allowed in front seats unless in a child seat; 3 – 12 not allowed in front seats except in approved restraint system
- 0.05%. Imprisonment for 0.12% or more
- Compulsory
- Recommended
- Recommended
- Recommended
- Compulsory for all riders
- 18 (motorcycles under 50cc 16)
- Use only allowed with hands-free kit
- Tolls on motorways

Romania (RO)

Cars			
120	90	90	50
Vehicles seating eight persons or more			
90	80	80	50
Motorcycles			
100	80	80	50

Jeep-like vehicles: 70kph outside built-up areas but 60kph in all areas if diesel

- Compulsory in front seats and, if fitted, in rear
- Under 12 not allowed in front seats
- 0.00%
- Recommended
- Compulsory
- Recommended
- Recommended
- Compulsory for all riders
- 18 (16 for mopeds)
- Visa (only if stay over 30 days for EU citizens); third party insurance
- Use only allowed with hands-free kit
- Tolls on Bucharest to Constanta motorway and bridges over Danube

Russia (RUS)

130	120	110	60

- Compulsory in front seats
- Under 12 not allowed in front seats
- 0.00%
- Compulsory
- Compulsory
- Recommended
- Compulsory
- Compulsory
- 18
- International driving licence with translation; visa
- No legislation

Serbia (SRB)

120	100	80	60

- Compulsory in front and rear seats
- Under 12 not allowed in front seats
- 0.05%
- Compulsory
- Compulsory
- Recommended
- Compulsory
- Compulsory
- 18 (16 for motorbikes less than 125cc; 14 for mopeds)
- International driving permit visa
- No legislation
- Tolls on motorways and some primary roads
- All types of fuel available at petrol stations
- 80km/h speed limit if towing a caravan

Slovak Republic (SK)

130	90	90	60

- Compulsory in front seats and, if fitted, in rear
- Under 12 not allowed in front seats unless in a child safety seat
- 0.0
- Compulsory
- Compulsory
- Compulsory
- Recommended
- Compulsory for motorcyclists
- 18 (15 for mopeds)
- International driving permit

- Use only allowed with hands-free kit
- ★ Tow rope recommended
- ★ Vignette required for motorways, car valid for 1 year, 30 days, 7 days; lorry vignettes carry a higher charge.

Slovenia (SLO)

🏛	⛰	▲	▬
130	100*	90*	50

If towing

🏛	⛰	▲	▬
80	80*	80*	50

*70kph in urban areas

- Compulsory in front seats and, if fitted, in rear
- Under 12 only allowed in the front seats with special seat; babies must use child safety seat
- 0.05%
- Compulsory
- Compulsory
- Compulsory
- Recommended
- Compulsory for all riders
- 18 (motorbikes up to 125cc – 16, up to 350cc – 18)
- Use only allowed with hands-free kit
- ★ Dipped headlights must be used at all times

Spain (E)

🏛	⛰	▲	▬
120	100	90	50

If towing

🏛	⛰	▲	▬
80	80	70	50

- Compulsory in front seats and if fitted in rear seats
- Under 12 not allowed in front seats except in a child safety seat
- 0.05% (0.03% if vehicle over 3,500 kgs or carries more than 9 passengers, and in first two years of driving licence)
- Two compulsory (one for in front, one for behind)
- Recommended
- Compulsory in adverse weather conditions
- Recommended
- Compulsory for all riders
- 18 (18/21 heavy vehicles; 18 for motorbikes over 125cc; 16 for motorbikes up to 125cc; 14 for mopeds up to 75cc)
- Third party insurance
- Use only allowed with hands-free kit
- ★ Tolls on motorways

Sweden (S)

🏛	⛰	▲	▬
110	90	70	50

If towing trailer with brakes

🏛	⛰	▲	▬
80	80	70	50

- Compulsory in front and rear seats
- Under 7 must have safety seat or other suitable restraint
- 0.02%
- Compulsory
- Recommended
- Recommended
- Recommended
- Compulsory for all riders
- 18
- Third party insurance
- No legislation
- ★ Dipped headlights must be used at all times

Switzerland (CH)

🏛	⛰	▲	▬
120	100	80	50/30

If towing up to 1 tonne

🏛	⛰	▲	▬
80	80	80	50/30

If towing over 1 tonne

🏛	⛰	▲	▬
80	80	60	50/30

- Compulsory in front and, if fitted, in rear
- Under 7 not allowed in front seats unless in child restraint; between 7 and 12 must use child restraint or seatbelt
- 0.05%
- Compulsory
- Recommended
- Recommended
- Recommended
- Compulsory for all riders
- 18 (mopeds up to 50cc – 16)
- Third party insurance compulsory
- Use only allowed with hands-free kit
- ★ Motorways are all toll and a vignette must be purchased at the border. Can also be purchased online at www.swisstravelsystem.com/uk, by phone on 020 7420 4900 or freephone 00800 10020030. The vignette costs £18.50 and is valid for one calendar year.

Turkey (TR)

🏛	⛰	▲	▬
120	90	90	50

If towing

🏛	⛰	▲	▬
70	70	70	40

- Compulsory in front seats
- Under 10 not allowed in front seats
- 0.05%
- Two compulsory (one in front, one behind)
- Compulsory
- Compulsory
- Compulsory
- Compulsory for all riders
- 18
- International driving permit advised; note that Turkey is in both Europe and Asia
- Use only allowed with hands-free kit
- ★ Tow rope and tool kit must be carried

Ukraine (UA)

🏛	⛰	▲	▬
130	90	90	60

If towing

🏛	⛰	▲	▬
80	80	80	60

Speed limit in pedestrian zone 20 kph

- Compulsory in front and rear seats
- Under 12 not allowed in front seats
- 0.0%
- Compulsory
- Compulsory
- Optional
- Compulsory
- Compulsory for all riders
- Cars 18; motorbikes 16
- International driving permit; visa
- No legislation
- ★ Tow rope and tool kit recommended

United Kingdom (GB)

🏛	⛰	▲	▬
112	112	96	48

If towing

🏛	⛰	▲	▬
96	96	80	48

- Compulsory in front seats and if fitted in rear seats
- Under 3 not allowed in front seats except with appropriate restraint, and in rear must use child restraint if available; 3–12 and under 150cm must use appropriate restraint or seat belt in front seats, and in rear if available
- 0.08%
- Recommended
- Recommended
- Recommended
- Recommended
- Compulsory for all riders
- 17 (16 for mopeds)
- Use only allowed with hands-free kit
- ★ Driving is on the left

Ski resorts

The resorts listed are popular ski centres, therefore road access to most is normally good and supported by road clearing during snow falls. However, mountain driving is never predictable and drivers should make sure they take suitable snow chains as well as emergency provisions and clothing. Listed for each resort are: the atlas page and grid square; the altitude; the number of lifts; the season start and end dates; the nearest town (with its distance in km) and the telephone number of the local tourist information centre ('00' prefix required for calls from the UK).

Andorra

Pyrenees

Pas de la Casa / Grau Roig 146 B2 2640m 31 lifts Dec–May •Andorra La Vella (30km) ☎+376 801060 🖥http://pas_grau.andor-ramania.com *Access via Envalira Pass (2407m), highest in Pyrenees, snow chains essential.*

Austria

Alps

A 24-hour driving conditions information line is provided by the Tourist Office of Austria www.austria.info +43 1 588 660

Bad Gastein 109 B4 1002m 51 lifts Dec–Apr •Bad Hofgastein (6km) ☎+43 6432 85044 🖥www.skigastein.at *Snow report: +43 6432 64555.*

Bad Hofgastein 109 B4 860m 51 lifts Dec–Apr •Salzburg (90km) ☎+43 6432 33930 🖥www.badhofgastein.com

Bad Kleinkirchheim 109 C4 1100m 32 lifts Dec–Apr •Villach (35km) ☎+43 4240 8212 🖥www.badkleinkirchheim.com *Snowfone:+43 4240 8222. Near Ebene Reichenau.*

Ehrwald 108 B1 1000m 22 lifts Dec–Apr •Imst (30km) ☎+43 5673 20000208 🖥www.tiscover.at/ehrwald *Weather report: +43 5673 3329*

Innsbruck 108 B2 574m 75 lifts Dec–Apr •Innsbruck ☎+43 5125 9850 🖥www.innsbruck-tourismus.com *Motorway normally clear. The motorway through to Italy and through the Arlberg Tunnel West to Austria are both toll roads.*

Ischgl 107 B5 1400m 42 lifts Dec–May •Landeck (25km) ☎+43 5444 52660 🖥www.ischgl.com *Car entry to resort prohibited between 2200hrs and 0600hrs.*

Kaprun 109 B3 800m, 56 lifts Jan–Dec •Zell am See (10km) ☎+43 6542 7700 🖥www.zellkaprun.at *Snow-fone:+43 6547 73684.*

Kirchberg in Tyrol 109 B3 860m 59 lifts Dec–Apr •Kitzbühel (6km) ☎+43 5357 2309 🖥www.kirchberg.at *Easily reached from Munich International Airport (120 km)*

Kitzbühel 109 B3 800m 59 lifts Dec–Apr •Wörgl (40km) ☎+43 5356 777 🖥www.kitzbuehel.com

Lech/Oberlech 107 B5 1450m 84 lifts Dec–Apr •Bludenz (50km) ☎+43 5583 21610 🖥www.Lech.at *Roads normally cleared but keep chains accessible because of altitude. Road conditions report tel +43 5583 1515.*

Mayrhofen 108 B2 630m 29 lifts Dec–Apr •Jenbach (35km) ☎+43 5285 67600 🖥www.mayrhofen.at *Chains rarely required.*

Obertauern 109 B4 1740m 27 lifts Nov–May •Radstadt (20km) ☎+43 6456 7252 🖥www.top-obertauern.com *Roads normally cleared but chains accessibility recommended. Camper vans and caravans not allowed; park these in Radstadt*

Saalbach Hinterglemm 109 B3 1003m 52 lifts Dec–Apr •Zell am See (19km) ☎+43 6541 6800 68 🖥www.saalbach.com *Both village centres are pedestrianised and there is a good ski bus service during the daytime*

St Anton am Arlberg 107 B5 1304m 84 lifts Nov–May •Innsbruck (104km) ☎+43 5446 22690 🖥www.stantonamarlberg.com *Snow report tel +43 5446 2565*

Schladming 109 B4 2708m 86 lifts Nov–Apr •Schladming ☎+43 3687 22777 🖥www.schladming.com

Serfaus 108 B1 1427m 53 lifts Dec–Apr •Landeck (30km) ☎+43 5476 62390 🖥www.serfaus.com *Cars banned from village, use world's only 'hover' powered underground railway.*

Sölden 108 C2 1377m, 32 lifts all year •Imst (50km) ☎+43 5254 5100 🖵www.soelden.com *Roads normally cleared but snow chains recommended because of altitude. The route from Italy and the south over the Timmelsjoch via Obergurgl is closed in the winter and anyone arriving from the south should use the Brenner Pass motorway. Snow information tel +43 5254 2666.*

Zell am See 109 B3 758m 57 lifts Dec–Mar •Zell am See ☎+43 6542 7700 🖵www.zellkaprun.at Snowfone +43 6542 73694 *Low altitude, therefore good access and no mountain passes to cross.*

Zell im Zillertal (Zell am Ziller) 109 B3 580m 47 lifts Dec–Apr •Jenbach (25km) ☎+43 5282 2281 🖵www.tiscover.at/zell Snowfone +43 5282 716526.

Zürs 107 B5 1720m 84 lifts Dec–May •Bludenz (30km) ☎+43 5583 2245 🖵www.lech.at *Roads normally cleared but keep chains accessible because of altitude. Village has garage with 24-hour self-service gas/petrol, breakdown service and wheel chains supply.*

France

Alps

Alpe d'Huez 118 B3 1860m 87 lifts Dec–Apr •Grenoble (63km) ☎+33 4 76 11 44 44 🖵www.alpedhuez.com *Snow chains may be required on access road to resort. Road report tel +33 4 76 11 44 50.*

Avoriaz 118 A3 2277m 38 lifts Dec–May •Morzine (14km) ☎+33 4 50 74 02 11 🖵www.avoriaz.com *Chains may be required for access road from Morzine. Car free resort, park on edge of village. Horse-drawn sleigh service available.*

Chamonix-Mont-Blanc 119 B3 1035m 49 lifts Nov–May •Martigny (38km) ☎+33 4 50 53 00 24 🖵www.chamonix.com

Chamrousse 118 B2 1700m 26 lifts Dec–Apr •Grenoble (30km) ☎+33 4 76 89 92 65 🖵www.chamrousse.com *Roads normally cleared, keep chains accessible because of altitude.*

Châtel 119 A3 2200m 40 lifts Dec–Apr •Thonon Les Bains (35km) ☎+33 4 50 73 22 44 🖵www.chatel.com

Courchevel 118 B3 1850m 185 lifts Dec–Apr •Moûtiers (23km) ☎+33 4 79 08 00 29 🖵www.courchevel.com *Roads normally cleared but keep chains accessible. Traffic 'discouraged' within the four resort bases. Traffic info: +33 4 79 37 73 37.*

Flaine 118 A3 1800m 74 lifts Dec–Apr •Cluses (25km) ☎+33 4 50 90 80 01 🖵www.flaine.com *Keep chains accessible for D6 from Cluses to Flaine. Car access for depositing luggage and passengers only. 1500-space car park outside resort. Road conditions report tel +33 4 50 25 20 50. Near Sixt-Fer-á-Cheval.*

La Clusaz 118 B3 1100m 55 lifts Dec–Apr •Annecy (32km) ☎+33 4 50 32 65 00 🖵www.laclusaz.com *Roads normally clear but keep chains accessible for final road from Annecy.*

La Plagne 118 B3 2100m 110 lifts Dec–Apr Moûtiers (32km) ☎+33 4 79 09 79 79 🖵www.la-plagne.com *Ten different centres up to 2100m altitude. Road access via Bozel, Landry or Aime normally cleared.*

Les Arcs 119 B3 2600m 77 lifts Dec–Apr •Bourg-St-Maurice (15km) ☎+33 4 79 07 12 57 🖵www.lesarcs.com *Three base areas up to 2000 metres; keep chains accessible. Pay parking at edge of each base resort.*

Les Carroz d'Araches 118 A3 1140m 74 lifts Dec–Apr •Cluses (13km) ☎+33 4 50 90 00 04 🖵www.lescarroz.com

Les Deux-Alpes 118 C3 1650m 63 lifts Dec–May •Grenoble (75km) ☎+33 4 76 79 22 00 🖵www.les2alpes.com *Roads normally cleared, however snow chains recommended for D213 up from valley road (N91).*

Les Gets 118 A3 1172m 53 lifts Dec–May •Cluses (18km) ☎+33 4 50 75 80 80 🖵www.lesgets.com

Les Ménuires 118 B3 1815m 197 lifts Dec–Apr •Moûtiers (27km) ☎+33 4 79 00 73 00 🖵www.lesmenuires.com *Keep chains accessible for N515A from Moûtiers.*

Les Sept Laux 118 B3 1350m, 29 lifts Dec–Apr •Grenoble (38km) ☎+33 4 76 08 17 86 🖵www.les7laux.com *Roads normally cleared, however keep chains accessible for mountain road up from the A41 motorway. Near St Sorlin d'Arves.*

Megève 118 B3 2350m 117 lifts Dec–Apr •Sallanches (12km) ☎+33 4 50 21 27 28 🖵www.megeve.com *Horse-drawn sleigh rides available.*

Méribel 118 B3 1400m 197 lifts Dec–May •Moûtiers (18km) ☎+33 4 79 08 60 01 🖵www.meribel.com *Keep chains accessible for 18km to resort on D90 from Moûtiers.*

Morzine 118 A3 1000m 217 lifts, Dec–May •Thonon-Les-Bains (30km) ☎+33 4 50 74 72 72 🖵www.morzine.com

Pra Loup 132 A2 1600m 53 lifts Dec–Apr •Barcelonnette (10km) ☎+33 4 92 84 10 04 🖵www.praloup.com *Roads normally cleared but chains accessibility recommended.*

Risoul 118 C3 1850m 58 lifts Dec–Apr •Briançon (40km) ☎+33 4 92 46 02 60 🖵www.risoul.com *Keep chains accessible. Near Guillestre.*

St Gervais 118 B3 850m 121 lifts Dec–Apr •Sallanches (10km) ☎+33 4 50 47 76 08 🖵www.st-gervais.com

Serre-Chevalier 118 C3 1350m 79 lifts Dec–May •Briançon (10km) ☎+33 4 92 24 98 98 🖵www.serre-chevalier.com *Made up of 13 small villages along the valley road, which is normally cleared.*

Tignes 119 B3 2100m 97 lifts Jan–Dec •Bourg St Maurice (26km) ☎+33 4 79 40 04 40 🖵www.tignes.net *Keep chains accessible because of altitude. Parking information tel +33 4 79 06 39 45.*

Val d'Isère 119 B3 1850m 97 lifts Nov–May •Bourg-St-Maurice (30km) ☎+33 4 79 06 06 60 🖵www.valdisere.com *Roads normally cleared but keep chains accessible.*

Val Thorens 118 B3 2300m 197 lifts Nov–May •Moûtiers (37km) ☎+33 4 79 00 08 08 🖵www.valthorens.com *Chains essential – highest ski resort in Europe. Obligatory paid parking on edge of resort.*

Valloire 118 B3 1430m 36 lifts Dec–May •Modane (20km) ☎+33 4 79 59 03 96 🖵www.valloire.net *Road normally clear up to the Col du Galbier, to the south of the resort, which is closed from 1st November to 1st June.*

Valmeinier 118 B3 2600m 32 lifts Dec–Apr •St Michel de Maurienne (47km) ☎+33 4 79 59 53 69 🖵www.valmeinier.com *Access from north on N9 / N902. Col du Galbier, to the south of the resort closed from 1st November to 1st June. Near Valloire.*

Valmorel 118 B3 1400m 55 lifts Dec–Apr •Moûtiers (15km) ☎+33 4 79 09 85 55 🖵www.valmorel.com *Near St Jean-de-Belleville.*

Vars Les Claux 118 C3 1850m 58 lifts Dec–Apr •Briançon (40km) ☎+33 4 92 46 51 31 🖵www.vars-ski.com *Four base resorts up to 1850 metres. Keep chains accessible. Road and weather information tel +33 4 36 68 02 05 and +33 4 91 78 78 78. Snowfone +33 492 46 51 04*

Villard-de-Lans 118 B2 1050m 29 lifts Dec–Apr •Grenoble (32km) ☎+33 4 76 95 10 38 🖵www.villard-de-lans.com

Pyrenees

Font-Romeu 146 B3 1800m 33 lifts Dec–Apr •Perpignan (87km) ☎+33 4 68 30 68 30 🖵www.fontromeu.com *Roads normally cleared but keep chains accessible.*

St Lary-Soulan 145 B4 830m 32 lifts Dec–Apr •Tarbes (75km) ☎+33 5 62 39 50 81 🖵www.saintlary.com *Access roads constantly cleared of snow.*

Vosges

La Bresse-Hohneck 106 A1 900m 20 lifts Dec–Mar •Cornimont (6km) ☎+33 3 29 25 41 29 🖵www.labresse-remy.com

Germany

Alps

Garmisch-Partenkirchen 108 B2 702m 38 lifts Dec–Apr •Munich (95km) ☎+49 8821 180 700 🖵www.garmisch-partenkirchen.de *Roads usually clear, chains rarely needed.*

Oberaudorf 108 B3 483m 21 lifts Dec–Apr •Kufstein (15km) ☎+49 8033 301 20 🖵www.oberaudorf.de *Motorway normally kep clear. Near Bayrischzell.*

Oberstdorf 107 B5 815m 31 lifts Dec–Apr •Sonthofen (15km) ☎+49 8322 7000 🖵www.oberstdorf.de *Snow information on tel +49 8322 3035 or 1095 or 5757.*

Rothaargebirge

Winterberg 81 A4 700m 55 lifts Dec–Mar •Brilon (30km) ☎+49 2981 925 00 🖵www.winterberg.de *Roads usually cleared, chains rarely required.*

Greece

Central Greece

Mountain Parnassos: Kelaria-Fterolakka 182 E4 1750–1950m 14 lifts Dec–Apr •Amfiklia ☎Kelaria +30 22340 22694, Fterolakka 22340 22373 🖵www.parnassos-ski.gr

Mountain Parnassos: Geron-dovrahos **182 E4** 1800–2390m 3 lifts Dec–Apr •Amfiklia ☎+30 29444 70371

Ipiros

Mountain Pindos: Karakoli **182 D3** 1350–1700m 1 lift Dec–Mar •Metsovo ☎+30 26560 41333

Mountain Pindos: Profitis Ilias **182 D3** 1500–1700m 3 lifts Dec–Mar •Metsovo ☎+30 26560 41095

Peloponnisos

Mountain Helmos: Kalavrita Ski Centre **184 A3** 1650–2340m 7 lifts Dec–Mar •Kalavrita ☎+30 26920 24451/24452 🖳www.kalavrita-ski.gr/en/default.asp

Mountain Menalo: Oropedio Ostrakinos **184 B3** 1600m 3 lifts Dec–Mar •Tripoli ☎+30 27960 22227

Macedonia

Mountain Falakro: Agio Pneuma **183 B6** 1720m 3 lifts Dec–Mar •Drama ☎+30 25210 62224 🖳www.falakro.gr

Mountain Vasilitsa: Vasilitsa **182 C3** 1750m 2 lifts Dec–Mar •Konitsa ☎+30 24620 84850 🖳www.vasilitsa.com

Mountain Vermio: Seli **182 C4** 1500m 4 lifts Dec–Mar •Kozani ☎+30 23310 26237

Mountain Vermio: Tria-Pente Pigadia **182 C3** 1420–2005m 4 lifts Dec–Mar •Ptolemaida ☎+30 23320 44446

Mountain Verno: Vigla **182 C3** 1650–2000m 3 lifts Dec–Mar •Florina ☎+30 23850 22354

Mountain Vrondous: Lailias **183 B5** 1847m 3 lifts Dec–Mar •Serres ☎+30 23210 62400

Thessalia

Mountain Pilio: Agriolefkes **183 D5** 1500m 4 lifts Dec–Mar •Volos ☎+30 24280 73719

Italy

Alps

Bardonecchia **118 B3** 1312m 24 lifts Dec–Apr •Bardonecchia ☎+39 122 99137 Snowfone +39 122 907778 🖳www.bardonecchi-aski.com *Resort reached through the 11km Frejus tunnel from France, roads normally cleared.*

Bórmio **107 C5** 1225m 16 lifts Dec–Apr •Tirano (40km) ☎+39 342 903300 🖳www.bormio.com *Tolls payable in Ponte del Gallo Tunnel, open 0800hrs–2000hrs.*

Breuil-Cervinia **119 B4** 2050m 73 lifts Jan–Dec •Aosta (54km) ☎+39 166 940986 🖳www.breuil-cervinia.it

Snow chains strongly recommended. Bus from Milan airport.

Courmayeur **119 B3** 1224m 27 lifts Dec–Apr •Aosta (40km) ☎+39 165 842370 🖳www.courmayeur.com *Access through the Mont Blanc tunnel from France. Roads constantly cleared.*

Limone Piemonte **133 A3** 1050m 29 lifts Dec–Apr •Cuneo (27km) ☎+39 171 925280 🖳www.limonepiemonte.it *Roads normally cleared, chains rarely required. Snow report tel +39 171 926254.*

Livigno **107 C5** 1816m 33 lifts Dec–May •Zernez (CH) (27km) ☎+39 342 052200 🖳www.aptlivigno.it *Keep chains accessible. La Drosa Tunnel from Zernez, Switzerland, is open only from 0800hrs to 2000hrs.*

Sestrière **119 C3** 2035m 91 lifts Dec–Apr •Oulx (22km) ☎+39 122 755444 🖳www.sestriere.it *One of Europe's highest resorts; although roads are normally cleared keep chains accessible.*

Appennines

Roccaraso – Aremogna **169 B4** 1285m 31 lifts Dec–Apr •Castel di Sangro (7km) ☎+39 864 62210 🖳www.roccaraso.net

Dolomites

Andalo – Fai della Paganella **121 A3** 1042m 22 lifts Dec–Apr •Trento (40km) 🖳www.paganella.net ☎+39 461 585588

Arabba **108 C2** 2500m 30 lifts Dec–Apr •Brunico (45km) ☎+39 436 780019 🖳www.arabba.it *Roads normally cleared but keep chains accessible.*

Cortina d'Ampezzo **108 C3** 1224m 48 lifts Dec–Apr •Belluno (72km) ☎+39 436 866252 🖳www.cortinadampezzo.it *Access from north on route 51 over the Cimabanche Pass may require chains.*

Corvara (Alta Badia) **108 C2** 1568m 54 lifts Dec–Apr •Brunico (38km) ☎+39 471 836176 🖳www.altabadia.it/inverno *Roads normally clear but keep chains accessible.*

Madonna di Campiglio **121 A3** 1550m 60 lifts Dec–Apr •Trento (60km) ☎+39 465 447501 🖳www.campiglio.net *Roads normally cleared but keep chains accessible.*

Moena di Fassa (Sorte/Ronchi) **108 C2** 1184m 29 lifts Dec–Apr •Bolzano (40km) ☎+39 462 602466 🖳www.dolomitisuperski.com

Passo del Tonale **121 A3** 1883m 30 lifts Dec–Aug •Breno (50km) ☎+39 364 903838 🖳www.adamelloski.com *Located*

on high mountain pass; keep chains accessible.

Selva di Val Gardena/Wolkenstein Groden **108 C2** 1563m 82 lifts Dec–Apr •Bolzano (40km) ☎+39 471 792277 🖳www.valgardena.it *Roads normally cleared but keep chains accessible.*

Norway

Hemsedal **47 B5** 650m 16 lifts Nov–May •Honefoss (150km) ☎+47 32 055030 🖳www.hemsedal.com *Be prepared for extreme weather conditions.*

Trysil (Trysilfjellet) **49 A4** 465m 24 lifts Nov–May •Elverum (100km) ☎+47 62 451000 🖳www.trysil.com *Be prepared for extreme weather conditions.*

Slovakia

Chopok **99 C3** 2024m 21 lifts Nov–May •Jasna ☎+421 48 991505 🖳www.jasna.sk

Donovaly **99 C3** 1360m 15 lifts Nov–May •Ruzomberok ☎+421 48 4199900 🖳www.parksnow.sk

Martinske Hole **98 B2** 1456m 7 lifts Nov–May •Zilina ☎+421 41 500 3429 🖳www.martinske-hole.sk

Plejsy **99 C4** 912m 8 lifts Nov–May •Krompachy ☎+421 53 447 1121 🖳www.plejsy.com

Strbske Pleso **99 B4** 1915m 8 lifts Nov–May •Poprad ☎+421 52 449 2343 🖳www.parksnow.sk/tatry-leto

Rohace **99 B3** 1450m 4 lifts Nov–May •Liptovsky Mikulas ☎+421 43 5395320 🖳www.rohace.sk

Slovenia

Julijske Alpe

Kanin **122 A2** 2289m 6 lifts Dec–May •Bovec ☎+386 5 3841 919 🖳www.bovec.si

Kobla **122 A2** 1480m 6 lifts Dec–Apr •Bohinjska Bistrica ☎+386 4 5747 100 🖳www.bohinj.si/kobla

Kranjska Gora **122 A2** 1620m 20 lifts Dec–Apr •Kranjska Gora ☎+386 4 5881 768 🖳www.kranjska-gora.si

Vogel **122 A2** 1800m 9 lifts Dec–Apr •Bohinjska Bistrica ☎+386 4 5724 236 🖳www.vogel.si

Kawiniske Savinjske Alpe

Krvavec **122 A3** 1970m 13 lifts Dec–May •Kranj ☎+386 4 2525 930 🖳www.rtc-krvavec.si *Ski phone tel +386 4 1182 500*

Pohorje

Rogla **123 A4** 1517m 11 lifts

Dec–May •Slovenska Bistrica ☎+386 3 7576 000 🖳www.rogla.si

Spain

Pyrenees

Baqueira/Beret **145 B4** 1500m 24 lifts Dec–Apr •Viella (15km) ☎+34 973 649010 🖳www.baqueira.es *Roads normally clear but keep chains accessible. Snowfone tel +34 973 639025. Near Salardú.*

Sistema Penibetico

Sierra Nevada **163 A4** 2102m 21 lifts Dec–May •Granada (32km) ☎+34 958 249100 🖳www.sierranevadaski.com *Access road designed to be avalanche safe and is snow cleared. Snowfone +34 958 249119.*

Sweden

Idre Fjäll **199 D9** 710m 30 lifts Oct–May •Mora (140km) ☎+46 253 41000 🖳www.idrefjall.se *Be prepared for extreme weather conditions.*

Sälen **49 A5** 360m 101 lifts Nov–Apr •Malung (70km) ☎+46 280 86070 🖳www.skistar.com/english *Be prepared for extreme weather conditions.*

Switzerland

Alps

Adelboden **106 C2** 1353m 50 lifts Dec–Apr •Frutigen (15km) ☎+41 33 673 80 80 🖳www.adelboden.ch

Arosa **107 C4** 1800m 16 lifts Dec–Apr •Chur (30km) ☎+41 81 378 70 20 🖳www.arosa.ch *Roads cleared but keep chains accessible because of high altitude (1800m).*

Crans Montana **119 A4** 1500m 35 lifts Dec–Apr, Jul-Oct •Sierre (15km) ☎+41 27 485 04 04 🖳www.crans-montana.ch *Roads normally cleared, however keep chains accessible for ascent from Sierre.*

Davos **107 C4** 1560m 54 lifts Nov–Apr •Davos ☎+41 81 415 21 21 🖳www.davos.ch

Engelberg **106 C3** 1000m 26 lifts Nov–Jun •Luzern (39km) ☎+41 41 639 77 77 🖳www.engelberg.ch *Straight access road normally cleared.*

Flums (Flumserberg) **107 B4** 1400m 17 lifts Dec–Apr •Buchs (25km) ☎+41 81 720 18 18 🖳www.flumserberg.com *Roads normally cleared, but 1000-metre vertical ascent; keep chains accessible.*

Grindelwald **106 C3** 1034m 30 lifts Dec–Apr •Interlaken (20km) ☎+41 33 854 12 12 🖳www.grindelwald.ch

Gstaad – Saanenland **106 C2** 1050m 66 lifts Dec–Apr •Gstaad ☎+41 33 748 81 81 🖳www.gstaad.ch

Klosters **107 C4** 1191m 61 lifts Dec–Apr •Davos (10km) ☎+41 81 410 20 20 🖳www.klosters.ch *Roads normally clear but keep chains accessable*

Leysin **119 A4** 1263m 19 lifts Dec–Apr •Aigle (6km) ☎+41 24 494 22 44 🖳www.leysin.ch

Mürren **106 C2** 1650m 37 lifts Dec–Apr •Interlaken (18km) ☎+41 33 856 86 86 🖳www.wengen-muerren.ch *No road access. Park in Strechelberg (1500 free places) and take the two-stage cable car.*

Nendaz **119 A4** 1365m 91 lifts Nov–Apr •Sion (16km) ☎+41 27 289 55 89 🖳www.nendaz.ch *Roads normally cleared, however keep chains accessible for ascent from Sion. Near Vex.*

Saas-Fee **119 A4** 1800m 25 lifts Jan–Dec •Brig (35km) ☎+41 27 958 18 58 🖳www.saas-fee.ch *Roads normally cleared but keep chains accessible.*

St Moritz **107 C4** 1856m 58 lifts Nov–May •Chur (89km) ☎+41 81 837 33 33 🖳www.stmoritz.ch *Roads normally cleared but keep chains accessible.*

Samnaun **107 C5** 1846m 42 lifts Dec–May •Scuol (30km) ☎+41 81 868 58 58 🖳www.samnaun.ch *Roads normally cleared but keep chains accessible.*

Verbier **119 A4** 1500m 95 lifts Nov–May, Jun-Jul •Martigny (27km) ☎+41 27 775 38 88 🖳www.verbier.ch *Roads normally cleared.*

Villars **119 A4** 1253m 37 lifts Nov–Apr, Jun-Jul •Montreux (35km) ☎+41 24 495 32 32 🖳www.villars.ch *Roads normally cleared but keep chains accessible for ascent from N9. Near Bex.*

Wengen **106 C2** 1270m 37 lifts Dec–Apr •Interlaken (12km) ☎+41 33 855 14 14 🖳www.wengen-muerren.ch *No road access. Park at Lauterbrunnen and take mountain railway.*

Zermatt **119 A4** 1620m 73 lifts all year •Brig (42km) ☎+41 27 966 81 00 🖳www.zermatt.ch *Cars not permitted in resort, park in Täsch (3km) and use shuttle train.*

Turkey

North Anatolian Mountains

Uludag **186 B4** 2543m 14 lifts Dec–March •Bursa (36km) ☎+90 224 254 22 74 🖳www.guideto-turkey.com/ski_centers

300 greatest sights of Europe

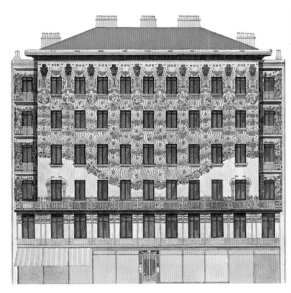

Maholicahaus, Vienna, Austria

Albania Shquipëria

www.albanian.com

Berat
Fascinating old town with picturesque Ottoman Empire buildings and traditional Balkan domestic architecture. **182 C1**

Tirana Tiranë
Capital of Albania. Skanderbeg Square has main historic buildings. Also: 18c Haxhi Ethem Bey Mosque; Art Gallery (Albanian); National Museum of History. Nearby: medieval Krujë; Roman monuments. **182 B1**

Austria Österreich

www.austria-tourism.at

Bregenz
Lakeside town bordering Germany, Liechtenstein, Switzerland. Locals, known as Vorarlbergers, have their own dialect. St Martinsturm 17th century tower, 17th century town hall, Kunsthaus Bregenz gallery of modern art, Vorarlberger Landesmuseum, Festspielhaus www.bregenz.ws **107 B4**

Graz
University town, seat of imperial court to 1619. Historic centre around Hauptplatz. Imperial monuments: Burg; mausoleum of Ferdinand II; towers of 16c schloss; 17c Schloss Eggenburg. Also: 16c Town Hall; Zeughaus; 15c cathedral. Museums: Old Gallery (Gothic, Flemish); New Gallery (good 19–20c). www.graztourismus.at **110 B2**

Innsbruck
Old town is reached by Maria-Theresien-Strasse with famous views. Buildings: Goldenes Dachl (1490s); 18c cathedral; remains of Hofburg imperial residence; 16c Hofkirche (tomb of Maximilian I). www.innsbruck.info **108 B2**

Krems
On a hill above the Danube, medieval quarter has Renaissance mansions. Also: Gothic Piaristenkirche; Wienstadt Museum. www.krems.at **97 C3**

Linz
Port on the Danube. Historic buildings are concentrated on Hauptplatz below the imperial 15c schloss. Notable: Baroque Old Cathedral; 16c Town Hall; New Gallery. www.linz.at **96 C2**

Melk
Set on a rocky hill above the Danube, the fortified abbey is the greatest Baroque achievement in Austria – particularly the Grand Library and abbey church. www.stiftmelk.at **110 A2**

Salzburg
Set in subalpine scenery, the town was associated with powerful 16-17c prince-archbishops. The 17c cathedral has a complex of archiepiscopal buildings: the Residence and its gallery (excellent 16–19c); the 13c Franciscan Church (notable altar). Other sights: Mozart's birthplace; the Hohensalzburg fortress; the Collegiate Church of St Peter (cemetery, catacombs); scenic views from Mönchsberg and Hettwer Bastei. The Grosse Festspielhaus runs the Salzburg festival. www2.salzburg.info **109 B4**

Salzkammergut
Natural beauty with 76 lakes (Wolfgangersee, Altersee, Gosausee, Traunsee, Grundlsee) in mountain scenery. Attractive villages (St Wolfgang) and towns (Bad Ischl, Gmunden) include Hallstatt, famous for Celtic remains. www.salzkammergut.at **109 B4**

Vienna Wien
Capital of Austria. The historic centre lies within the Ring. Churches: Gothic St Stephen's Cathedral; 17c Imperial Vault; 14c Augustine Church; 14c Church of the Teutonic Order (treasure); 18c Baroque churches (Jesuit Church, Franciscan Church, St Peter, St Charles). Imperial residences: Hofburg; Schönbrunn. Architecture of Historicism on Ringstrasse (from 1857). Art Nouveau: Station Pavilions, Postsparkasse, Looshaus, Majolicahaus. Exceptional museums: Art History Museum (antiquities, old masters); Cathedral and Diocesan Museum (15c); Academy of Fine Arts (Flemish); Belvedere (Gothic, Baroque, 19–20c). www.wien.gv.at **111 A3**

Belgium Belgique

www.visitbelgium.com

Antwerp Antwerpen
City with many tall gabled Flemish houses on the river. Heart of the city is Great Market with 16–17c guildhouses and Town Hall. 14–16c Gothic cathedral has Rubens paintings. Rubens also at the Rubens House and his burial place in St Jacob's Church. Excellent museums: Mayer van den Berg Museum (applied arts); Koninklijk Museum of Fine Arts (Flemish, Belgian). www.visitantwerp.be **79 A4**

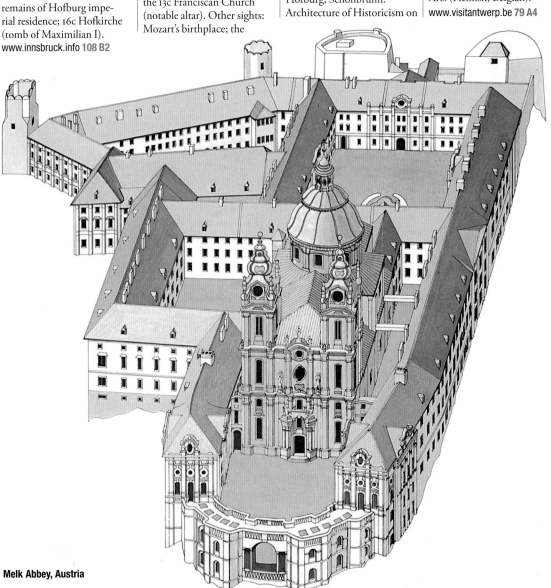

Melk Abbey, Austria

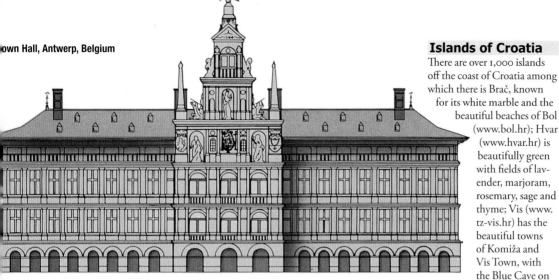
own Hall, Antwerp, Belgium

Bruges Brugge
Well-preserved medieval town with narrow streets and canals. Main squares: the Market with 13c Belfort and covered market; the Burg with Basilica of the Holy Blood and Town Hall. The Groeninge Museum and Memling museum in t Jans Hospital show 15c Flemish masters. The Onze Lieve Vrouwekerk has a famous *Madonna and Child* by Michelangelo www.brugge.be **78 A3**

Brussels Bruxelles
Capital of Belgium. The Lower Town is centred on the enormous Grand Place with Hôtel de Ville and rebuilt guildhouses. Symbols of the city include the 'Manneken Pis' and Atomium (giant model of a molecule). The 13c Notre Dame de la Chapelle is the oldest church. The Upper Town contains: Gothic cathedral; Neoclassical Place Royale; 18c King's Palace; Royal Museums of Fine Arts (old and modern masters). Also: much Art Nouveau (Victor Horta Museum, Hôtel Tassel, Hôtel Solvay); Place du Petit Sablon and Place du Grand Sablon; 19c Palais de Justice. www.brusselsinterna-tional.be **79 B4**

Ghent Gent
Medieval town built on islands surrounded by canals and rivers. Views from Pont t-Michel. The Graslei and Koornlei quays have Flemish guild houses. The Gothic cathedral has famous Van Eyck altarpiece. Also: Belfort; Cloth Market; Gothic Town Hall; Gravensteen. Museums: Bijloke Museum in beautiful abbey (provincial and applied art); Museum of Fine Arts (old masters). www.gent.be **79 A3**

Namur
Reconstructed medieval citadel is the major sight of Namur, which also has a cathedral and provincial museums. www.namur.be **79 B4**

Tournai
The Romanesque-Gothic cathedral is Belgium's finest (much excellent art). Fine Arts Museum has a good collection (15-20c). www.tournai.be **78 B3**

Bulgaria Bulgariya
www.bulgariatravel.org

Black Sea Coast
Beautiful unspoiled beaches (Zlatni Pyasŭtsi). The delightful resort Varna is popular. Nesebŭr is famous for Byzantine churches. Also: Danube Delta in Hungary. **17 D7**

Koprivshtitsa
Beautiful village known both for its half-timbered houses and links with the April Rising of 1876. Six house museums amongst which the Lyutov House and the Oslekov House, plus the birthplaces of Georgi Benkovski, Dimcho Debelyanov, Todor Kableshkov, and Lyuben Karavelov.

Plovdiv
City set spectacularly on three hills. The old town has buildings from many periods: 2c Roman stadium and amphitheatre; 14c Dzumaiya Mosque; 19c Koyumdjioglu House and Museum (traditional objects). Nearby: Bačkovo Monastery (frescoes). www.plovdiv.org **183 A6**

Rila
Bulgaria's finest monastery, set in the most beautiful scenery of the Rila mountains. The church is richly decorated with frescoes.

Sofia Sofiya
Capital of Bulgaria. Sights: exceptional neo-Byzantine cathedral; Church of St Sofia; 4c rotunda of St George (frescoes); Byzantine Boyana Church (frescoes) on panoramic Mount Vitoša. Museums: National Historical Museum (particularly for Thracian artefacts); National Art Gallery (icons, Bulgarian art). www.sofia.bg/en **17 D5**

Veliko Tŭrnovo
Medieval capital with narrow streets. Notable buildings: House of the Little Monkey; Hadji Nicoli Inn; ruins of medieval citadel; Baudouin Tower; churches of the Forty Martyrs and of SS Peter and Paul (frescoes); 14c Monastery of the Transfiguration. www.veliko-tarnovo.net **17 D6**

Croatia Hrvatska
www.croatia.hr

Dalmatia Dalmacija
Exceptionally beautiful coast along the Adriatic. Among its 1185 islands, those of the Kornati Archipelago and Brijuni Islands are perhaps the most spectacular. Along the coast are several attractive medieval and Renaissance towns, most notably Dubrovnik, Split, Šibenik, Trogir, Zadar. www.dalmacija.net **138 B2**

Dubrovnik
Surrounded by medieval and Renaissance walls, the city's architecture dates principally from 15-16c. Sights: many churches and monasteries including Church of St Vlah and Dominican monastery (art collection); promenade street of Stradun, Dubrovnik Museums; Renaissance Rector's Palace; Onofrio's fountain; Sponza Palace. The surrounding area has some 80 16c noblemen's summer villas. www.dubrovnik-online.com **139 C4**

Islands of Croatia
There are over 1,000 islands off the coast of Croatia among which there is Brač, known for its white marble and the beautiful beaches of Bol (www.bol.hr); Hvar (www.hvar.hr) is beautifully green with fields of lavender, marjoram, rosemary, sage and thyme; Vis (www.tz-vis.hr) has the beautiful towns of Komiža and Vis Town, with the Blue Cave on nearby Biševo. **123 & 137-138**

Istria Istra
Peninsula with a number of ancient coastal towns (Rovinj, Poreč, Pula, Piran in Slovene Istria) and medieval hill-top towns (Motovun). Pula has Roman monuments (exceptional 1c amphitheatre). Poreč has narrow old streets; the mosaics in 6c Byzantine basilica of St Euphrasius are exceptional. See also Slovenia. www.istra.com **122 B2**

Plitvička Jezera
Outstandingly beautiful world of water and woodlands with 16 lakes and 92 waterfalls interwoven by canyons. www.np-plitvicka-jezera.hr **123 C4**

Split
Most notable for the exceptional 4c palace of Roman Emperor Diocletian, elements of which are incorporated into the streets and buildings of the town itself. The town also has a cathedral (11c baptistry) and a Franciscan monastery. www.split.hr **138 B2**

Trogir
The 13-15c town centre is surrounded by medieval city walls. Romanesque-Gothic cathedral includes the chapel of Ivan the Blessed. Dominican and Benedictine monasteries house art collections. www.trogir-online.com **138 B2**

Zagreb
Capital city of Croatia with cathedral and Archbishop's Palace in Kaptol and to the west Gradec with Baroque palaces. Donji Grad is home to the Archaological Museum, Art Pavilion, Museum of Arts and Crafts, Ethnographic Museum, Mimara Museum and National Theatre. www.zagreb-touristinfo.hr **124 B1**

Czech Republic Česka Republica
www.czech.cz

Brno
Capital of Moravia. Sights: Vegetable Market and Old Town Hall; Capuchin crypt decorated with bones of dead monks; hill of St Peter with Gothic cathedral; Mies van der Rohe's buildings (Bata, Avion Hotel, Togendhat House). Museums: UPM (modern applied arts); Pražáků Palace (19c Czech art). www.brno.cz **97 B4**

České Budějovice
Famous for Budvar beer, the medieval town is centred on náměsti Přemysla Otokara II. The Black Tower gives fine views. Nearby: medieval Český Krumlov. www.c-budejovice.cz **96 C2**

Kutná Hora
A town with strong silver mining heritage shown in the magnificent Cathedral of sv Barbara which was built by the miners. See also the ossuary with 40,000 complete sets of bones moulded into sculptures and decorations. www.kutnohorsko.cz **97 B3**

Olomouc
Well-preserved medieval university town of squares and fountains. The Upper Square has the Town Hall. Also: 18c Holy Trinity; Baroque Church of St Michael. www.olomoucko.cz **98 B1**

Plzeň
Best known for Plzeňský Prazdroj (Pilsener Urquell), beer has been brewed here since 1295. An industrial town with eclectic architecture shown in the railway stations and the namesti Republiky (main square). www.zcu.cz/plzen **96 B1**

Prague Praha
Capital of Czech Republic and Bohemia. The Castle Quarter has a complex of buildings behind the walls (Royal Castle; Royal Palace; cathedral). The Basilica of St George has a fine Romanesque interior. The Belvedere is the best example of Renaissance architecture. Hradčani Square has aristocratic palaces and the National Gallery. The Little Quarter has many Renaissance (Wallenstein Palace) and Baroque mansions and the Baroque Church of St Nicholas. The Old Town has its centre at the Old Town Square with the Old Town

Hall (astronomical clock),
Art Nouveau Jan Hus monument and Gothic Týn church.
The Jewish quarter has 14c
Staranova Synagogue and
Old Jewish Cemetery. The
Charles Bridge is famous. The
medieval New Town has many
Art Nouveau buildings and is
centred on Wenceslas Square.
www.prague.cz **84 B2**

Spas of Bohemia

Spa towns of Karlovy Vary
(Carlsbad), Márianske Lázně
(Marienbad) and Frantiskovy
Lázně (Franzenbad). **83 B4**

Denmark Danmark

www.visitdenmark.com

Århus

Second largest city in
Denmark with a mixture of
old and new architecture that
blends well, Århus has been
dubbed the culture capital
of Denmark with the Gothic
Domkirke; Latin Quarter;
13th Century Vor Frue
Kirke; Den Gamle By, open
air museum of traditional
Danish life; ARoS, Århus Art
Museum. www.visitaarhus.com
59 B3

Copenhagen
København

Capital of Denmark. Old
centre has fine early 20c Town
Hall. Latin Quarter has 19c
cathedral. 18c Kastellet has
statue of the Little Mermaid
nearby. The 17c Rosenborg
Castle was a royal residence,
as was the Christianborg (now
government offices). Other
popular sights: Nyhavn canal;
Tivoli Gardens. Excellent
art collections: Ny Carlsberg
Glypotek; State Art Museum;
National Museum. www.visitcopenhagen.dk **61 D2**

Hillerød

Frederiksborg is a fine redbrick Renaissance castle set
among three lakes. **61 D2**

Roskilde

Ancient capital of Denmark.
The marvellous cathedral is
a burial place of the Danish
monarchy. The Viking Ship
Museum houses the remains
of five 11c Viking ships excavated in the 1960s. www.visitroskilde.com **61 D2**

Estonia Eesti

www.visitestonia.com

Kuressaare

Main town on the island
of Saaremaa with the 14c
Kuressaare Kindlus. www.
kuressaare.ee **8 C3**

Pärnu

Sea resort with an old town
centre. Sights: 15c Red Tower;
neoclassical Town Hall; St
Catherine's Church. www.
parnu.ee **8 C4**

Tallinn

Capital of Estonia. The old
town is centred on the Town
Hall Square. Sights: 15c Town
Hall; Toompea Castle; Three
Sisters houses. Churches:
Gothic St Nicholas; 14c
Church of the Holy Spirit; St
Olaf's Church. www.tallinn.
ee **8 C4**

Tartu

Historic town with 19c university. The Town Hall Square
is surrounded by neoclassical
buildings. Also: remains of 13c
cathedral; Estonian National
Museum. www.tartu.ee **8 C5**

Finland Suomi

http://virtual.finland.fi

Finnish Lakes

Area of outstanding natural
beauty covering about one
third of the country with
thousands of lakes, of which
Päijänne and Saimaa are the
most important. Tampere,
industrial centre of the region,
has numerous museums,
including the Sara Hildén
Art Museum (modern).
Savonlinna has the medieval
Olavinlinna Castle. Kuopio
has the Orthodox and
Regional Museums. **8 A5**

Helsinki

Capital of Finland. The 19c
neoclassical town planning
between the Esplanade and
Senate Square includes the
Lutheran cathedral. There is
also a Russian
Orthodox
cathedral. The
Constructivist
Stockmann
Department
Store is the
largest in
Europe. The
main railway
station is Art
Nouveau. Gracious
20c buildings in
Mannerheimintie avenue
include Finlandiatalo by
Alvar Aalto. Many good
museums: Art Museum of the
Ateneum (19–20c); National
Museum; Museum of Applied
Arts; Helsinki City Art
Museum (modern Finnish);
Open Air Museum (vernacular architecture); 18c fortress
of Suomenlinna has several
museums.
www.hel.fi **8 B4**

Lappland (Finnish)

Vast unspoiled rural area.
Lappland is home to thousands of nomadic Sámi living
in a traditional way. The capital, Rovaniemi, was rebuilt
after WWII; museums show
Sámi history and culture.
Nearby is the Arctic Circle
with the famous Santa Claus
Village. Inari is a centre of
Sámi culture. See also Norway
and Sweden. www.laplandfinland.com **192–193**

France

www.franceguide.com

Albi

Old town with rosy brick
architecture. The vast
Cathédrale Ste-Cécile (begun
13c) holds some good art.
The Berbie Palace houses the
Toulouse-Lautrec museum.
www.mairie-albi.fr **130 B1**

Alps

Grenoble, capital of the
French Alps, has a good 20c
collection in the Museum of
Painting and Sculpture. The
Vanoise Massif has the greatest
number of resorts (Val d'Isère,
Courchevel). Chamonix has
spectacular views on Mont
Blanc, France's and Europe's
highest peak.
www.thealps.com **118 B2**

Amiens

France's largest Gothic
cathedral has beautiful decoration. The
Museum of Picardy
has unique 16c panel
paintings.
www.amiens.fr **90 B2**

Arles

Ancient, picturesque
town with Roman
relics (1c amphitheatre), 11c cathedral,
Archaeological
Museum (Roman
art). www.tourisme.
ville-arles.fr **131 B3**

Avignon

Medieval papal capital (1309–77) with
14c walls and many
ecclesiastical buildings. Vast Palace of
the Popes has stunning frescoes. The
Little Palace has fine
Italian Renaissance
painting. The 12–13c
Bridge of St Bénézet
is famous. www.
ot-avignon.fr **131 B3**

Bourges

The Gothic Cathedral of St
Etienne, one of the finest in
France, has a superb sculptured choir. Also notable is the
House of Jacques Coeur.
www.bourgestourisme.com
103 B4

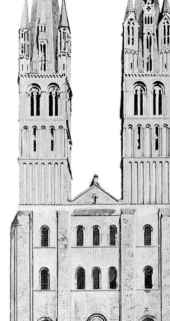

Abbaye aux
Hommes,
Caen, France

Burgundy Bourgogne

Rural wine region with a rich
Romanesque, Gothic and
Renaissance heritage. The
12c cathedral in Autun and
12c basilica in Vézelay have
fine Romanesque sculpture.
Monasteries include 11c
L'Abbaye de Cluny (ruins) an[d]
L'Abbaye de Fontenay. Beaun[e]

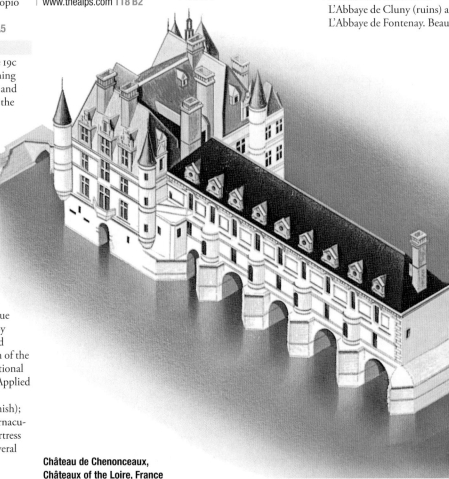

**Château de Chenonceaux,
Châteaux of the Loire, France**

as beautiful Gothic Hôtel-Dieu and 15c Nicolas Rolin hospices. www.burgundy-tourism.com **104 B3**

Brittany Bretagne
Brittany is famous for cliffs, sandy beaches and wild landscape. It is also renowned for megalithic monuments (Carnac) and Celtic culture. Its capital, Rennes, has the Palais de Justice and good collections in the Museum of Brittany (history) and Museum of Fine Arts. Also: Nantes; St-Malo. www.brittany-bretagne.com **100–101**

Caen
City with two beautiful Romanesque buildings: Abbaye aux Hommes; Abbaye aux Dames. The château has two museums (15–20c painting; history). The *Bayeux Tapestry* is displayed in nearby Bayeux. www.ville-caen.fr **89 A3**

Carcassonne
Unusual double-walled fortified town of narrow streets with an inner fortress. The fine Romanesque Church of St Nazaire has superb stained glass. www.carcassonne.org **130 B1**

Chartres
The 12–13c cathedral is an exceptionally fine example of Gothic architecture (Royal Doorway, stained glass, choir screen). The Fine Arts Museum has a good collection. www.chartres.com **90 C1**

Loire Valley
The Loire Valley has many 15–16c châteaux built amid beautiful scenery by French monarchs and members of their courts. Among the most splendid are Azay-le-Rideau, Chenonceaux and Loches. Also: Abbaye de Fontévraud. www.lvo.com **102 B2**

Clermont-Ferrand
The old centre contains the cathedral built out of lava and Romanesque basilica. The Puy de Dôme and Puy de Sancy give spectacular views over some 60 extinct volcanic peaks (*puys*). www.ville-clermont-ferrand.fr **116 B3**

Colmar
Town characterised by Alsatian half-timbered houses. The Unterlinden Museum has excellent German religious art including the famous Isenheim altarpiece. The Dominican church also has a fine altarpiece. www.ot-colmar.fr **106 A2**

Corsica Corse
Corsica has a beautiful rocky coast and mountainous interior. Napoleon's birthplace of Ajaccio has: Fesch Museum with Imperial Chapel and a large collection of Italian art; Maison Bonaparte; cathedral. Bonifacio, a medieval town, is spectacularly set on a rock over the sea. www.visit-corsica.com **180**

Côte d'Azur
The French Riviera is best known for its coastline and glamorous resorts. There are many relics of artists who worked here: St-Tropez has Musée de l'Annonciade; Antibes has 12c Château Grimaldi with the Picasso Museum; Cagnes has the Renoir House and Mediterranean Museum of Modern Art; St-Paul-de-Vence has the excellent Maeght Foundation and Matisse's Chapelle du Rosaire. Cannes is famous for its film festival. Also: Marseille, Monaco, Nice. www.cote.azur.fr **133 B3**

Dijon
Great 15c cultural centre. The Palais des Ducs et des Etats is the most notable monument and contains the Museum of Fine Arts. Also: the Charterhouse of Champmol. www.dijon-tourism.com **105 B4**

Disneyland Paris
Europe's largest theme park follows in the footsteps of its famous predecessors in the United States. www.disneylandparis.com **90 C2**

Le Puy-en-Velay
Medieval town bizarrely set on the peaks of dead volcanoes. It is dominated by the Romanesque cathedral (cloisters). The Romanesque chapel of St-Michel is dramatically situated on the highest rock. www.ot-lepuyenvelay.fr **117 B3**

Lyon
France's third largest city has an old centre and many museums including the Museum of the History of Textiles and the Museum of Fine Arts (old masters). www.lyon-france.com **117 B4**

Marseilles Marseille
Second lagest city in France. Spectacular views from the 19c Notre-Dame-de-la-Garde. The Old Port has 11–12c Basilique St Victor (crypt, catacombs). Cantini Museum has major collection of 20c French art. Château d'If was the setting of Dumas' *The Count of Monte Cristo*. www.marseille-tourisme.com **131 B4**

Mont-St-Michel
Gothic pilgrim abbey (11–12c) set dramatically on a steep rock island rising from mud flats and connected to the land by a road covered by the tide. The abbey is made up of a complex of buildings. www.e-mont-saint-michel.com **101 A4**

Nancy
A centre of Art Nouveau. The 18c Place Stanislas was constructed by dethroned Polish king Stanislas. Museums: School of Nancy Museum (Art Nouveau furniture); Fine Arts Museum. www.ot-nancy.fr **92 C2**

Nantes
Former capital of Brittany, with the 15c Château des ducs de Bretagne. The cathedral has a striking interior. www.nantes-tourisme.com **101 B4**

Nice
Capital of the Côte d'Azur, the old town is centred on the old castle on the hill. The seafront includes the famous 19c Promenade des Anglais. The aristocratic quarter of the Cimiez Hill has the Marc Chagall Museum and the Matisse Museum. Also: Museum of Modern and Contemporary Art (especially neo-Realism and Pop Art). www.nicetourism.com **133 B3**

Paris
Capital of France, one of Europe's most interesting cities. The Île de la Cité area, an island in the River Seine has the 12–13c Gothic Notre Dame (wonderful stained glass) and La Sainte-Chapelle (1240–48), one of the jewels of Gothic art. The Left Bank area: Latin Quarter with the famous Sorbonne university; Museum of Cluny housing medieval art; the Panthéon; Luxembourg Palace and Gardens; Montparnasse, interwar artistic and literary centre; Eiffel Tower; Hôtel des Invalides with Napoleon's tomb. Right Bank: the great boulevards (Avenue des Champs-Élysées joining the Arc de Triomphe and Place de la Concorde); 19c Opéra Quarter; Marais, former aristocratic quarter of elegant mansions (Place des Vosges); Bois de Boulogne, the largest park in Paris; Montmartre, centre of 19c bohemianism, with the Basilique Sacré-Coeur. The Church of St Denis is the first gothic church and the mausoleum of the French monarchy. Paris has three of the world's greatest art collections: The Louvre (to 19c, *Mona Lisa*), Musée d'Orsay (19–20c) and National Modern Art Museum in the Pompidou Centre. Other major museums include: Orangery Museum; Paris Museum of Modern Art; Rodin Museum; Picasso Museum. Notable cemeteries with graves of the famous: Père-Lachaise, Montmartre, Montparnasse. Near Paris are the royal residences of Fontainebleau and Versailles. www.paris.fr **90 C2**

Pyrenees
Beautiful unspoiled mountain range. Towns include: delightful sea resorts of St-Jean-de-Luz and Biarritz; Pau, with access to the Pyrenees National Park; pilgrimage centre Lourdes. www.pyrenees-online.fr **144–145**

Reims
Together with nearby Epernay, the centre of champagne production. The 13c Gothic cathedral is one of the greatest architectural achievements in France (stained glass by Chagall). Other sights: Palais du Tau with cathedral sculpture, 11c Basilica of St Rémi; cellars on Place St-Niçaise and Place des Droits-des-Hommes. www.reims-tourisme.com **91 B4**

Rouen
Old centre with many half-timbered houses and 12–13c Gothic cathedral and the Gothic Church of St Maclou with its fascinating remains of a dance macabre on the former cemetery of Aître St-Maclou. The Fine Arts Museum has a good collection. www.mairie-rouen.fr **89 A5**

St-Malo
Fortified town (much rebuilt) in a fine coastal setting. There is a magnificent boat trip along the river Rance to Dinan, a splendid well-preserved medieval town. www.saint-malo.fr **101 A3**

Strasbourg
Town whose historic centre includes a well-preserved quarter of medieval half-timbered Alsatian houses, many of them set on the canal. The cathedral is one of the best in France. The Palais Rohan contains several museums. www.strasbourg.fr **93 C3**

Toulouse
Medieval university town characterised by flat pink brick (Hôtel Assézat). The Basilique St Sernin, the largest Romanesque church in France, has many art treasures. Marvellous Church of the Jacobins holds the body of St Thomas Aquinas. www.ot-toulouse.fr **129 C4**

Tours
Historic town centred on Place Plumereau. Good collections in the Guilds Museum and Fine Arts Museum. www.tours.fr **102 B2**

Versailles
Vast royal palace built for Louis XIV, primarily by Mansart, set in large formal gardens with magnificent fountains. The extensive and much-imitated state apartments include the famous Hall of Mirrors and the exceptional Baroque chapel. www.chateauversailles.fr **90 C2**

Vézère Valley Caves
A number of prehistoric sites, most notably the cave paintings of Lascaux (some 17,000 years old), now only seen in a duplicate cave, and the cave of Font de Gaume. The National Museum of Prehistory is in Les Eyzies. www.leseyzies.com **129 B4**

Germany Deutschland
www.germany-tourism.de

Northern Germany

Aachen
Once capital of the Holy Roman Empire. Old town around the Münsterplatz with magnificent cathedral. An exceptionally rich treasure is in the Schatzkammer. The Town Hall is on the medieval Market. www.aachen.de **80 B2**

Berlin
Capital of Germany. Sights include: the Kurfürstendamm avenue; Brandenburg Gate, former symbol of the division between East and West Germany; Tiergarten; Unter den Linden; 19c Reichstag. Berlin has many excellent art and history collections. Museum Island includes: Pergamon Museum (classical antiquity, Near and Far East, Islam); Bode Museum (Egyptian, Early Christian, Byzantine and European); Old National Gallery (19–20c German). Dahlem Museums: Picture Gallery (13–18c); Sculpture Collection (13–19c); Prints

and Drawings Collection; Die Brücke Museum (German Expressionism). Tiergarten Museums: New National Gallery (19–20c); Decorative Arts Museum; Bauhaus Archive. In the Kreuzberg area: Berlin Museum; Grupius Building with Jewish Museum and Berlin Gallery; remains of Berlin Wall and Checkpoint Charlie House. Schloss Charlottenburg houses a number of collections including the National Gallery's Romantic Gallery; the Egyptian Museum is nearby. www.berlin-tourist-information.de **74 B2**

Cologne Köln

Ancient city with 13–19c cathedral (rich display of art). In the old town are the Town Hall and many Romanesque churches (Gross St Martin, St Maria im Kapitol, St Maria im Lyskirchen, St Ursula, St Georg, St Severin, St Pantaleon, St Apostolen).

Gothic cathedral, Cologne, Germany

Museums: Diocesan Museum (religious art); Roman-German Museum (ancient history); Wallraf-Richartz/Ludwig Museum (14–20c art). www.koeln.de **80 B2**

Dresden

Historic centre with a rich display of Baroque architecture. Major buildings: Castle of the Electors of Saxony; 18c Hofkirche; Zwinger Palace with fountains and pavilions (excellent old masters); Albertinum with excellent Gallery of New Masters; treasury of Grünes Gewölbe. The Baroque-planned New Town contains the Japanese Palace and Schloss Pillnitz. www.dresden.de **84 A1**

Frankfurt

Financial capital of Germany. The historic centre around the Römerberg Square has 13–15c cathedral, 15c Town Hall, Gothic St Nicholas Church, Saalhof (12c chapel). Museums: Museum of Modern Art (post-war); State Art Institute. www.frankfurt.de **81 B4**

Hamburg

Port city with many parks, lakes and canals. The Kunsthalle has Old Masters and 19-20c German art. Buildings: 19c Town Hall; Baroque St Michael's Church. www.hamburg-tourismus.de **72 A3**

Hildesheim

City of Romanesque architecture (much destroyed). Principal sights: St Michael's Church; cathedral (11c interior, sculptured doors, St Anne's Chapel); superb 15c Tempelhaus on the Market Place. www.hildesheim.de **72 B2**

Lübeck

Beautiful old town built on an island and characterised by Gothic brick architecture. Sights: 15c Holsten Gate; Market with the Town Hall and Gothic brick St Mary's Church; 12–13c cathedral; St Ann Museum. www.luebeck-tourism.de **65 C3**

Mainz

The Electoral Palatinate schloss and Market fountain are Renaissance. Churches: 12c Romanesque cathedral; Gothic St Steven's (with stained glass by Marc Chagall). www.mainz.de **93 A4**

Marburg

Medieval university town with the Market Place and Town Hall, St Elizabeth's Church (frescoes, statues, 13c shrine), 15–16c schloss. www.marburg.de **81 B4**

Münster

Historic city with well-preserved Gothic and Renaissance buildings: 14c Town Hall; Romanesque-Gothic cathedral. The Westphalian Museum holds regional art. www.munster.de **71 C4**

Potsdam

Beautiful Sanssouci Park contains several 18–19c buildings including: Schloss Sanssouci; Gallery (European masters); Orangery; New Palace; Chinese Teahouse. www.potsdam.de **74 B2**

Rhein Valley Rheintal

Beautiful 80km gorge of the Rhein Valley between Mainz and Koblenz with rocks (Loreley), vineyards (Bacharach, Rüdesheim), white medieval towns (Rhens, Oberwesel) and castles. Some castles are medieval (Marksburg, Rheinfles, island fortress Pfalzgrafenstein) others were built or rebuilt in the 19c (Stolzenfles, Rheinstein). www.rheintal.de **80 B3**

Weimar

The Neoclassical schloss, once an important seat of government, now houses a good art collection. Church of SS Peter and Paul has a Cranach masterpiece. Houses of famous people: Goethe, Schiller, Liszt. The famous Bauhaus was founded at the School of Architecture and Engineering www.weimar.de **82 B3**

Southern Germany

Alpine Road Deutsche Alpenstrasse

German Alpine Road in the Bavarian Alps, from Lindau on Bodensee to Berchtesgaden. The setting for 19c fairy-tale follies of Ludwig II of Bavaria (Linderhof, Hohenschwangau, Neuschwanstein), charming old villages (Oberammergau) and Baroque churches (Weiss, Ottobeuren). Garmisch-Partenkirchen has views on Germany's highest peak, the Zugspitze. www.deutsche-alpenstrasse.de **108 B2**

Augsburg

Attractive old city. The Town Hall is one of Germany's finest Renaissance buildings. Maximilianstrasse has several Renaissance houses and Rococo Schaezler Palace (good art collection). Churches:

Romanesque-Gothic cathedral; Renaissance St Anne's Church. The Fuggerei, founded 1519 as an estate for the poor, is still in use. www.augsburg.de **94 C2**

Bamberg
Well-preserved medieval town. The island, connected by two bridges, has the Town Hall and views of Klein Venedig. Romanesque-Gothic cathedral (good art) is on an exceptional square of Gothic, Renaissance and Baroque buildings – Alte Hofhalttung; Neue Residenz with State Gallery (German masters); Ratstube. www.bamberg.info **94 B2**

Black Forest
Schwarzwald
Hilly region between Basel and Karlsruhe, the largest and most picturesque woodland in Germany, with the highest summit, Feldberg, lake resorts (Titisee), health resorts (Baden-Baden) and clock craft (Triberg). Freiburg is regional capital. www.schwarzwald.de **93 C4**

Freiburg
Old university town with system of streams running through the streets. The Gothic Minster is surrounded by the town's finest buildings. Two towers remain of the medieval walls. The Augustine Museum has a good collection. www.freiburg.de **106 B2**

Heidelberg
Germany's oldest university town, majestically set on the banks of the river and romantically dominated by the ruined schloss. The Gothic Church of the Holy Spirit is on the Market Place with the Baroque Town Hall. Other sights include the 16c Knight's House and the Baroque Morass Palace with a museum of Gothic art. www.heidelberg.de **93 B4**

Lake Constance
Bodensee
Lake Constance, with many pleasant lake resorts. Lindau, on an island, has numerous gabled houses. Birnau has an 18c Rococo church. Konstanz (Swiss side) has the Minster set above the Old Town. www.bodensee.de **107 B4**

Munich München
Old town centred on the Marienplatz with 15c Old Town Hall and 19c New Town Hall. Many richly decorated churches: St Peter's (14c tower); Gothic red-brick cathedral; Renaissance St Michael's (royal portraits on the façade); Rococo St Asam's. The Residenz palace consists of seven splendid buildings holding many art objects. Schloss Nymphenburg has a palace, park, botanical gardens and four beautiful pavilions. Superb museums: Old Gallery (old masters), New Gallery (18–19c), Lenbachhaus (modern German). Many famous beer gardens. www.muenchen.de **108 A2**

Nuremberg Nürnberg
Beautiful medieval walled city dominated by the 12c Kaiserburg. Romanesque-Gothic St Sebaldus Church and Gothic St Laurence Church are rich in art. On Hauptmarkt is the famous 14c Schöner Brunnen. Also notable is 15c Dürer House. The German National Museum has excellent German medieval and Renaissance art. www.nuernberg.de **94 B3**

Regensburg
Medieval city set majestically on the Danube. Views from 12c Steinerne Brücke. Churches: Gothic cathedral; Romanesque St Jacob's; Gothic St Blaisius; Baroque St Emmeram. Other sights: Old Town Hall (museum); Haidplatz; Schloss Thurn und Taxis; State Museum. www.regensburg.de **95 B4**

Romantic Road
Romantische Strasse
Romantic route between Aschaffenburg and Füssen, leading through picturesque towns and villages of medieval Germany. The most popular section is the section between Würzburg and Augsburg, centred on Rothenburg ob der Tauber. Also notable are Nördlingen, Harburg Castle, Dinkelsbühl, Creglingen. www.romantischestrasse.de **94 B2**

Rothenburg ob der Tauber
Attractive medieval walled town with tall gabled and half-timbered houses on narrow cobbled streets. The Market Place has Gothic-Renaissance Town Hall, Rattrinke-stubbe and Gothic St Jacob's Church (altarpiece). www.rothenburg.de **94 B2**

Speyer
The 11c cathedral is one of the largest and best Romanesque buildings in Germany. 12c Jewish Baths are well-preserved. www.speyer.de **93 B4**

Stuttgart
Largely modern city with old centre around the Old Schloss, Renaissance Alte Kanzlei, 15c Collegiate Church and Baroque New Schloss. Museums: Regional Museum; post-modern State Gallery (old masters, 20c German). The 1930s Weissenhofsiedlung is by several famous architects. www.stuttgart.de **94 C1**

Trier
Superb Roman monuments: Porta Nigra; Aula Palatina (now a church); Imperial Baths; amphitheatre. The Regional Museum has Roman artefacts. Also, Gothic Church of Our Lady; Romanesque cathedral. www.trier.de **92 B2**

Ulm
Old town with half-timbered gabled houses set on a canal. Gothic 14–19c minster has tallest spire in the world (161m). www.tourismus.ulm.de **94 C1**

Würzburg
Set among vineyard hills, the medieval town is centred on the Market Place with the Rococo House of the Falcon. The 18c episcopal princes' residence (frescoes) is magnificent. The cathedral is rich in art. Work of the great local Gothic sculptor, Riemenschneider, is in Gothic St Mary's Chapel, Baroque New Minster, and the Mainfränkisches Museum. www.wuerzburg.de **94 B1**

Great Britain
www.visitbritain.com

England

Bath
Elegant spa town with notable 18c architecture: Circus, Royal Crescent, Pulteney Bridge, Assembly Rooms; Pump Room. Also: well-preserved Roman baths; superb Perpendicular Gothic Bath Abbey. Nearby: Elizabethan Longleat House; exceptional 18c landscaped gardens at Stourhead. www.visitbath.co.uk **43 A4**

Brighton
Resort with a sea-front of Georgian, Regency and Victorian buildings with the Palace Pier, and an old town of narrow lanes. The main sight is the 19c Royal Pavilion in Oriental styles. www.brighton.co.uk **44 C3**

Bristol
Old port city with the fascinating Floating Harbour. Major sights include Gothic 13–14c Church of St Mary Redcliffe and 19c Clifton Suspension Bridge. www.visitbristol.co.uk **43 A4**

Cambridge
City with university founded in the early 13c. Peterhouse (1284) is the oldest college. Most famous colleges were founded in 14–16c: Queen's, King's (with the superb Perpendicular Gothic 15–16c King's College Chapel), St John's (with famous 19c Bridge of Sighs), Trinity, Clare, Gonville and Caius, Magdalene. Museums: excellent Fitzwilliam Museum (classical, medieval, old masters). Kettle's Yard (20c British). www.visitcambridge.org **45 A4**

Canterbury
Medieval city and old centre of Christianity. The Norman-Gothic cathedral has many sights and was a major medieval pilgrimage site (as related in Chaucer's *Canterbury Tales*). St Augustine, sent to convert the English in 597, founded St Augustine's Abbey, now in ruins. www.canterbury.co.uk **45 B5**

Chatsworth
One of the richest aristocratic country houses in England (largely 17c) set in a large landscaped park. The palatial interior has some 175 richly furnished rooms and a major art collection. www.chatsworth-house.co.uk **40 B2**

Chester
Charming medieval city with complete walls. The Norman-Gothic cathedral has several abbey buildings. www.visitchester.co.uk **38 A4**

Cornish Coast
Scenic landscape of cliffs and sandy beaches (the north coast being a popular surfing destination) with picturesque villages (Fowey, Mevagissey). St Ives has the Tate Gallery with work of the St Ives Group. The island of St Michael's Mount holds a priory. www.cornwalltouristboard.co.uk **42 B1**

Dartmoor
Beautiful wilderness area in Devon with tors and its own breed of wild pony as well as free-ranging cattle and sheep. www.dartmoor-npa.gov.uk **42 B3**

Durham
Historic city with England's finest Norman cathedral and a castle, both placed majestically on a rock above the river. www.durham.gov.uk **37 B5**

Eden Project
Centre showing the diversity of plant life on the planet, built in a disused clay pit. Two biomes, one with Mediterranean and Southern African focus and the larger featuring a waterfall, river and tropical trees plants and flowers. Outdoors also features plantations including bamboo and tea. www.edenproject.com **42 B2**

Hadrian's Wall
Built to protect the northernmost border of the Roman Empire in the 2c AD, the walls originally extended some 120km with castles every mile and 16 forts. Best-preserved walls around Hexam; forts at Housesteads and Chesters. www.hadrians-wall.org **37 A4**

Lake District
Beautiful landscape of lakes (Windermere, Coniston) and England's high peaks (Scafell Pike, Skiddaw, Old Man), famous for its poets, particularly Wordsworth. www.lake-district.gov.uk **36 B3**

Leeds Castle
One of the oldest and most romantic English castles, standing in the middle of a lake. Most of the present appearance dates from 19c. www.leeds-castle.com **45 B4**

Lincoln
Old city perched on a hill with narrow streets, majestically dominated by the Norman-Gothic cathedral and castle. www.visitlincolnshire.com **40 B3**

Liverpool
City on site of port founded in 1207 and focused around 1846 Albert Dock, now a heritage attraction. Croxteth Hall and Country Park; Speke Hall; Sudley House; Royal Liver Building; Liverpool Cathedral; Walker Art Gallery; University of Liverpool Art Gallery. www.visitliverpool.com **38 A4**

London
Capital of UK and Europe's largest city. To the east of the medieval heart of the city – now the largely modern financial district and known as the City of London – is the Tower of London (11c White Tower, Crown Jewels) and 1880s Tower Bridge. The popular heart of the city and its entertainment is the West End, around Piccadilly

Circus, Leicester Square and Trafalgar Square (Nelson's Column). Many sights of political and royal power: Whitehall (Banqueting House, 10 Downing Street, Horse Guards); Neo-Gothic Palace of Westminster (Houses of Parliament) with Big Ben; The Mall leading to Buckingham Palace (royal residence, famous ceremony of the Changing of the Guard). Numerous churches include: 13–16c Gothic Westminster Abbey (many tombs, Henry VII's Chapel); Wren's Baroque St Paul's Cathedral, St Mary-le-Bow, spire of St Bride's, St Stephen Walbrook. Museums of world fame: British Museum (prehistory, oriental and classical antiquity, medieval); Victoria and Albert Museum (decorative arts); National Gallery (old masters to 19c); National Portrait Gallery (historic and current British portraiture); Tate – Britain and Modern; Science Museum; Natural History Museum. Madame Tussaud's waxworks museum is hugely popular. Other sights include: London Eye, Kensington Palace; Greenwich with Old Royal Observatory (Greenwich meridian), Baroque Royal Naval College, Palladian Queen's House; Tudor Hampton Court Palace; Syon House. Nearby: Windsor Castle (art collection, St George's Chapel). www.visitlondon.com 44 B3

Longleat

One of the earliest and finest Elizabethan palaces in England. The palace is richly decorated. Some of the grounds have been turned into a pleasure park, with the Safari Park, the first of its kind outside Africa. www.longleat.co.uk 43 A4

Manchester

Founded on a Roman settlement of 79AD and a main player in the Industrial Revolution. Victorian Gothic Town Hall; Royal Exchange; Cathedral. Many museums including Imperial War Museum North, Lowry Centre and Manchester Art Gallery. www.visitmanchester.com 40 B1

Newcastle

A key player in the Industrial Revolution with 12th century cathedral and many museums as well as strong railway heritage. www.visitnewcastle.co.uk 37 B5

Norwich

Medieval quarter has half-timbered houses. 15c castle keep houses a museum and gallery. Many medieval churches include the Norman-Gothic cathedral. www.visitnorwich.co.uk 41 C5

Oxford

Old university city. Earliest colleges date from 13c: University College; Balliol; Merton. 14–16c colleges include: New College; Magdalen; Christ Church (perhaps the finest). Other buildings: Bodleian Library; Radcliffe Camera; Sheldonian Theatre; cathedral. Good museums: Ashmolean Museum (antiquity to 20c); Museum of Modern Art; Christ Church Picture Gallery (14–17c). Nearby: outstanding 18c Blenheim Palace. www.visitoxford.org 44 B2

Petworth

House (17c) with one of the finest country-house art collections (old masters), set in a huge landscaped park. www.nationaltrust.org.uk 44 C3

Salisbury

Pleasant old city with a magnificent 13c cathedral built in an unusually unified Gothic style. Nearby: Wilton House. www.visitsalisburyuk.com 44 B2

Stonehenge

Some 4000 years old, one of the most famous and haunting Neolithic monuments in Europe. Many other Neolithic sites are nearby. www.english-heritage.org.uk 44 B2

Stourhead

Early 18c palace famous for its grounds, one of the finest examples of neoclassical landscaped gardening, consist-ing of a lake surrounded by numerous temples. www.nationaltrust.org.uk 43 A4

Stratford-upon-Avon

Old town of Tudor and Jacobean half-timbered houses, famed as the birth and burial place of William Shakespeare. Nearby: Warwick Castle. www.shakespeare-country.co.uk 44 A2

Wells

Charming city with beautiful 12–16c cathedral (west facade, scissor arches, chapter house, medieval clock). Also Bishop's Palace; Vicar's Close. 43 A4

Winchester

Historic city with 11–16c cathedral (tombs of early English kings). Also: 13c Great Hall; Winchester College; St Cross almshouses. www.visitwinchester.co.uk 44 B2

York

Attractive medieval city surrounded by well-preserved walls with magnificent Gothic 13–15c Minster. Museums: York City Art Gallery (14–19c); Jorvik Viking Centre. Nearby: Castle Howard. www.york-tourism.co.uk 40 B2

Scotland

Edinburgh

Capital of Scotland, built on volcanic hills. The medieval Old Town is dominated by the castle set high on a volcanic rock (Norman St Margaret's Chapel, state apartments, Crown Room). Holyrood House (15c and 17c) has lavishly decorated state apartments and the ruins of Holyrood Abbey (remains of Scottish monarchs). The 15c cathedral has the Crown Spire and Thistle Chapel. The New Town has good Georgian architecture (Charlotte Square, Georgian House). Excellent museums: Scottish National Portrait Gallery, National Gallery of Scotland; Scottish National Gallery of Modern Art. www.edinburgh.org 35 C4

Glamis Castle

In beautiful, almost flat landscaped grounds, 14c fortress, rebuilt 17c, gives a fairy-tale impression. www.glamis-castle.co.uk 35 B5

Glasgow

Scotland's largest city, with centre around George Square and 13–15c Gothic cathedral. The Glasgow School of Art is the masterpiece of Charles Rennie Mackintosh. Fine art collections: Glasgow Museum and Art Gallery; Hunterian Gallery; Burrell Collection. www.seeglasgow.com 35 C3

Loch Ness

In the heart of the Highlands, the lake forms part of the scenic Great Glen running from Inverness to Fort William. Famous as home of the fabled Loch Ness Monster (exhibition at Drumnadrochit). Nearby: ruins of 14–16c Urquhart Castle. 32 D2 www.loch-ness-scotland.com

Wales

Caernarfon

Town dominated by a magnificent 13c castle, one of a series built by Edward I in Wales (others include Harlech, Conwy, Beaumaris, Caerphilly). www.visitcaernafon.com 38 A2

Cardiff

Capital of Wales, most famous for its medieval castle, restored 19c in Greek, Gothic and Oriental styles. Also: National Museum and Gallery. www.visitcardiff.info 39 C3

Greece Ellas

www.gnto.gr

Athens Athina

Capital of Greece. The Acropolis, with 5c BC sanctuary complex (Parthenon, Propylaia, Erechtheion, Temple of Athena Nike), is the greatest architectural achievement of antiquity in Europe. The Agora was a public meeting place in ancient Athens. Plaka has narrow streets and small Byzantine churches (Kapnikarea). The Olympeum was

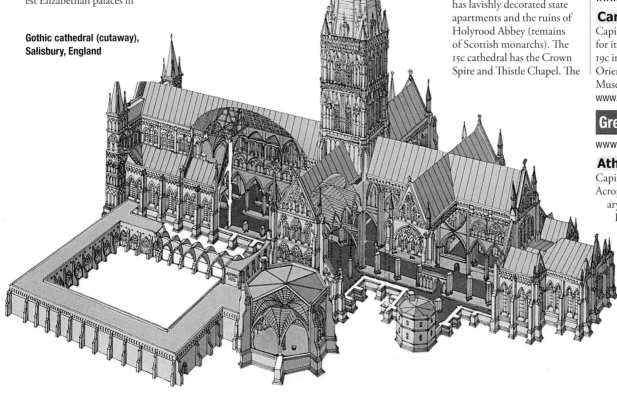

Gothic cathedral (cutaway), Salisbury, England

adcliffe Camera
utaway),
xford, England

e largest temple in Greece.
lso: Olympic Stadium; excel-
nt collections of ancient
rtefacts (Museum of Cycladic
nd Ancient Greek Art;
cropolis Museum; National
rcheological Museum;
enaki Museum).
ww.athens.gr **185 B4**

Corinth Korinthos
ncient Corinth (ruins), with
 BC Temple of Apollo, was in
4 BC made capital of Roman
reece by Julius Caesar. Set
ove the city, the Greek-built
cropolis hill of Acrocorinth
ecame the Roman and
yzantine citadel (ruins).
4 B3

Crete Kriti
argest Greek island, Crete
as home to the great Minoan
vilization (2800–1100
c). The main relics are the
ined Palace of Knossos
nd Malia. Gortys was capi-
l of the Roman province.
icturesque Rethimno has
arrow medieval streets, a
enetian fortress and a former
urkish mosque. Matala has
eautiful beaches and famous
aves cut into cliffs. Iraklio
Heraklion), the capital, has a
ood Archeological Museum.
35 D6

Delphi
t the foot of the Mount
arnassos, Delphi was the

seat of the Delphic Oracle of
Apollo, the most important
oracle in Ancient Greece.
Delphi was also a political
meeting place and the site
of the Pythian Games. The
Sanctuary of Apollo consists
of: Temple of Apollo, led to
by the Sacred Way; Theatre;
Stadium. The museum has a
display of objects from the site
(5c BC Charioteer).
www.delphi.gr **182 E4**

Epidavros
Formerly a spa and reli-
gious centre focused on the
Sanctuary of Asclepius (ruins).
The enormous 4c BC theatre
is probably the finest of all
ancient theatres.
www.ancientepidavros.org
184 B4

Greek Islands
Popular islands with some of
the most beautiful and spectacular beaches in Europe. The
many islands are divided into
various groups and individual
islands: The major groups are
the Kiklades and Dodekanisa
in the Aegean Sea, the largest
islands are Kerkyra (Corfu)
in the Ionian Sea and Kriti.
182–185 & 188

Meteora
The tops of bizarre vertical
cylinders of rock and towering
cliffs are the setting for 14c
Cenobitic monasteries, until

recently only accessible by
baskets or removable ladders.
Mega Meteoro is the grandest
and set on the highest point.
Roussánou has the most
extraordinary site. Varlaám
is one of the oldest and most
beautiful, with the Ascent
Tower and 16c church with
frescoes. Aghiou Nikolaou
also has good frescoes. **182 D3**

Mistras
Set in a beautiful land-
scape, Mistras is the site of
a Byzantine city, now in
ruins, with palaces, frescoed
churches, monasteries and
houses. **184 B3**

Mount Olympus
Oros Olymbos
Mount Olympus, mythical
seat of the Greek gods, is the
highest, most dramatic peak
in Greece. **182 C4**

Mycenae Mikines
The citadel of Mycenae
prospered between 1950 BC
and 1100 BC and consists
of the royal complex of
Agamemnon: Lion Gate, royal
burial site, Royal Palace, South
House, Great Court. **184 B3**

Olympia
In a stunning setting, the
Panhellenic Games were held
here for a millennium. Ruins
of the sanctuary of Olympia
consist of the Doric temples
of Zeus and Hera and the
vast Stadium. There is also
a museum (4c BC figure of
Hermes). **184 B2**

Rhodes
One of the most attractive
islands with wonderful sandy
beaches. The city of Rhodes
has a well-preserved medieval
centre with the Palace of
the Grand Masters and the
Turkish Süleymaniye Mosque
188 C2

Salonica Thessaloniki
Largely modern city with
Byzantine walls and many
fine churches: 8c Aghia Sofia;
11c Panaghia Halkeo; 14c
Dodeka Apostoli; 14c Aghios
Nikolaos Orfanos; 5c Aghios
Dimitrios (largest in Greece,
7c Mosaics).
www.thessalonikicity.gr **183 C5**

Hungary
Magyarorszàg

www.hungarytourism.hu

Balaton
The 'Hungarian sea', famous
for its holiday resorts:
Balatonfüred, Tihany,
Badasconytomaj, Keszthely.
www.balaton.hu **111 C4**

Budapest
Capital of Hungary on River
Danube, with historic area
centring on the Castle Hill of
Buda district. Sights include:
Matthias church; Pest district
with late 19c architecture,
centred on Ferenciek tere;
neo-Gothic Parliament
Building on river; Millennium
Monument. The Royal Castle
houses a number of museums:
Hungarian National Gallery,
Budapest History Museum;
Ludwig Collection. Other
museums: National Museum
of Fine Arts (excellent Old and
Modern masters); Hungarian
National Museum (Hungarian
history). Famous for public
thermal baths: Király and
Rudas baths, both made under
Turkish rule; Gellért baths,
the most visited.
www.budapestinfo.hu **112 B3**

Esztergom
Medieval capital of Hungary
set in scenic landscape. Sights:
Hungary's largest basilica
(completed 1856); royal palace
ruins. www.esztergom.hu
112 B2

Pécs
Attractive old town with
Europe's fifth oldest university
(founded 1367). Famous for
Turkish architecture (Mosque
of Gazi Kasim Pasha, Jakovali
Hassan Mosque).
www.pecs.hu **125 A4**

Sopron
Beautiful walled town with
many Gothic and Renaissance
houses. Nearby: Fertöd with
the marvellous Eszergázy
Palace. www.sopron.hu **111 B3**

Ireland

www.discoverireland.com

Northern Ireland

Antrim Coast
Spectacular coast with diverse
scenery of glens (Glenarm,
Glenariff), cliffs (Murlough
Bay) and the famous Giant's
Causeway, consisting of
some 40,000 basalt columns.
Carrickefergus Castle is the
largest and best-preserved
Norman castle in Ireland.
www.northantrim.com **27 A4**

Belfast
Capital of Northern Ireland.
Sights: Donegall Square
with 18c Town Hall; neo-
Romanesque Protestant cathe-
dral; University Square; Ulster
Museum (European painting).
www.gotobelfast.com **27 B5**

Giant's Causeway
Spectacular and unique rock
formations in the North
Antrim coast, formed by volcanic activity 50–60 million
years ago. World Heritage
Site. www.northantrim.com
27 A4

Republic of Ireland

Aran Islands
Islands with spectacular cliffs
and notable pre-Christian and
Christian sights, especially on
Inishmore.
www.visitaranislands.com **26 B2**

Cashel
Town dominated by the Rock
of Cashel (61m) topped by
ecclesiastical ruins including
13c cathedral; 15c Halls of the
Vicars; beautiful Romanesque
12c Cormac's Chapel (fine
carvings).
www.connemar-tourism.org
29 B4

Connemara
Beautiful wild landscape of
mountains, lakes, peninsulas
and beaches. Clifden is the
capital.
www.connemar-tourism.org
28 A1

Cork
Pleasant city with its centre
along St Patrick's Street and
Grand Parade lined with
fine 18c buildings. Churches:
Georgian St Anne's Shandon
(bell tower); 19c cathedral.
www.corkcorp.ie **29 C3**

County Donegal
Rich scenic landscape of
mystical lakes and glens
and seascape of cliffs (Slieve
League cliffs are the highest in
Europe). The town of Donegal
has a finely preserved Jacobean
castle. www.donegaldirect.ie
26 B2

Dublin
Capital of Ireland. City
of elegant 18c neoclassical
and Georgian architecture
with gardens and parks (St
Stephen's Green, Merrion
Square with Leinster House
– now seat of Irish parliament). City's main landmark,
Trinity College (founded
1591), houses in its Old Library
fine Irish manuscripts (7c
Book of Durrow, 8c Book
of Kells). Two Norman
cathedrals: Christ Church;
St Patrick's. Other buildings:
originally medieval Dublin
Castle with State Apartments;
James Gandon's master-
pieces: Custom House; Four
Courts. Museums: National
Museum (Irish history);
National Gallery (old masters,

Impressionists, Irish painting); Guinness Brewery Museum; Dublin Writers' Museum (Joyce, Wilde, Yeats and others). www.visitdublin.com **30 A2**

Glendalough

Impressive ruins of an important early Celtic (6c) monastery with 9c cathedral, 12c St Kevin's Cross, oratory of St Kevin's Church. www.wicklow. com/glendalough **30 A2**

Kilkenny

Charming medieval town, with narrow streets dominated by 12c castle (restored 19c). The 13c Gothic cathedral has notable tomb monuments. www.kilkenny.ie **30 B1**

Newgrange

One of the best passage graves in Europe, the massive 4500-year-old tomb has stones richly decorated with patterns. www.knowth.com/newgrange **30 A2**

Ring of Kerry

Route around the Iveragh peninsula with beautiful lakes (Lough Leane), peaks overlooking the coastline and islands (Valencia Island, Skelling). Also: Killarney; ruins of 15c Muckross Abbey. www.ringofkerrytourism.com **29 B2**

Italy Italia

www.enit.it

Northern Italy

Alps

Wonderful stretch of the Alps running from the Swiss and French borders to Austria. The region of Valle d'Aosta is one of the most popular ski regions, bordered by the highest peaks of the Alps. www.thealps.com **108–109 & 119–120**

Arezzo

Beautiful old town set on a hill dominated by 13c cathedral. Piazza Grande is surrounded by medieval and Renaissance palaces. Main sight: Piero della Francesca's frescoes in the choir of San Francesco. www.arezzocitta.com **135 B4**

Assisi

Hill-top town that attracts crowds of pilgrims to the shrine of St Francis of Assisi at the Basilica di San Francesco, consisting of two churches, Lower and Upper, with superb frescoes (particularly Giotto's in the Upper). www.assisi.com **136 B1**

Bologna

Elegant city with oldest university in Italy. Historical centre around Piazza Maggiore and Piazza del Nettuno with the Town Hall, Palazzo del Podestà, Basilica di San Petronio. Other churches: San Domenico; San Giacomo Maggiore. The two towers (one incomplete) are symbols of the city. Good collection in the National Gallery (Bolognese). www.commune. bologna.it/bolognaturismo **135 A4**

Dolomites Dolomiti

Part of the Alps, this mountain range spreads over the region of Trentino-Alto Adige, with the most picturesque scenery between Bolzano and Cortina d'Ampezzo. www. dolomiti.it **121 A4**

Ferrara

Old town centre around Romanesque-Gothic cathedral and Palazzo Communale. Also: Castello Estense; Palazzo Schifanoia (frescoes); Palazzo dei Diamanti housing Pinacoteca Nazionale. www. ferraraturismo.it **121 C4**

Florence Firenze

City with exceptionally rich medieval and Renaissance heritage. Piazza del Duomo has:13–15c cathedral (first dome since antiquity); 14c campanile; 11c baptistry (bronze doors). Piazza della Signoria has: 14c Palazzo Vecchio (frescoes); Loggia della Signoria (sculpture); 16c Uffizi Gallery with one of the world's greatest collections (13–18c). Other great paintings: Museo di San Marco; Palatine Gallery in 15–16c

Pitti Palace surrounded by Boboli Gardens. Sculpture: Cathedral Works Museum; Bargello Museum; Academy Gallery (Michelangelo's *David*). Among many other Renaissance palaces: Medici-Riccardi; Rucellai; Strozzi. The 15c church of San Lorenzo has Michelangelo's tombs of the Medici. Many churches have richly frescoed chapels: Santa Maria Novella, Santa Croce, Santa Maria del Carmine. The 13c Ponte Vecchio is one of the most famous sights. www. firenzeturismo.it **135 B4**

Italian Lakes

Beautiful district at the foot of the Alps, most of the lakes with holiday resorts. Many lakes are surrounded by aristocratic villas (Maggiore, Como, Garda). **120–121**

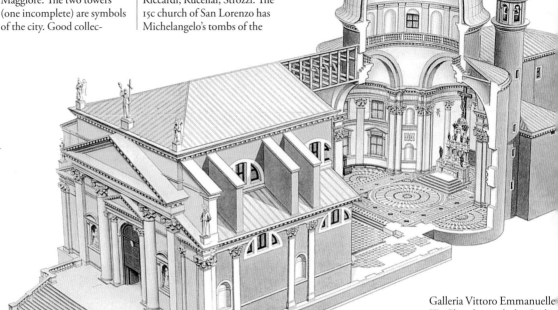

Il Redentore (cutaway), Venice, Italy

Mantua Mántova

Attractive city surrounded by three lakes. Two exceptional palaces: Palazzo Ducale (Sala del Pisanello; Camera degli Sposi, Castello San Giorgio); luxurious Palazzo Tè (brilliant frescoes). Also: 15c Church of Sant'Andrea; 13c law courts. www.mantova.com **121 B3**

Milan Milano

Modern city, Italy's fashion and design capital (Corso and Galleria Vittoro Emmanuelle II). Churches include: Gothic cathedral (1386–1813), the world's largest (4c baptistry); Romanesque St Ambrose; 15c San Satiro; Santa Maria delle Grazie with Leonardo da Vinci's *Last Supper* in the convent refectory. Great art collections, Brera Gallery, Ambrosian Library, Museum of Contemporary Art. Castello Sforzesco (15c, 19c) also has a gallery. The famous La Scala theatre opened in 1778. Nearby: monastery at Pavia. www.milaninfotourist.com **120 B2**

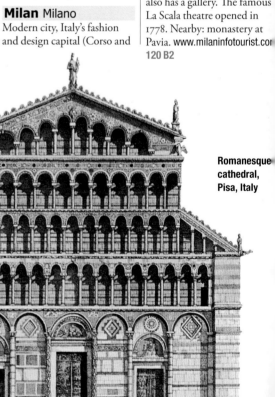

Romanesque cathedral, Pisa, Italy

Padua Pádova

Pleasant old town with arcaded streets. Basilica del Santo is a place of pilgrimage to the tomb of St Anthony. Giotto's frescoes in the Scrovegni chapel are exceptional. Also: Piazza dei Signori with Palazzo del Capitano; vast Palazzo della Ragione; church of the Eremitani (frescoes). www.turismopadova.it **121 B4**

Parma

Attractive city centre, famous for Corregio's frescoes in the Romanesque cathedral and church of St John the Evangelist, and Parmigianino's frescoes in the church of Madonna della Steccata. Their works are also in the National Gallery. www.commune.parma.it **120 C3**

Perúgia

Hill-top town centred around Piazza Quattro Novembre with the cathedral, Fontana Maggiore and Palazzo dei Priori. Also: Collegio di Cambio (frescoes); National Gallery of Umbria; many churches. www.perugiaonline.com **136 B1**

Pisa

Medieval town centred on the Piazza dei Miracoli. Sights: famous Romanesque Leaning Tower, Romanesque cathedral (excellent façade, Gothic pulpit); 12–13c Baptistry; 13c Camposanto cloistered cemetery (fascinating 14c frescoes). www.commune.pisa.it **134 B3**

Ravenna

Ancient town with exceptionally well-preserved Byzantine mosaics. The finest are in 5c Mausoleo di Galla Placidia and 6c Basilica di San Vitale. Good mosaics also in the basilicas of Sant'Apollinare in Classe and Sant'Apollinare Nuovo. www.turismo.ravenna.it **135 A5**

Siena

Outstanding 13–14c medieval town centred on beautiful Piazza del Campo with Gothic Palazzo Publico (frescoes of secular life). Delightful Romanesque-Gothic Duomo (Libreria Piccolomini, baptistry, art works). Many other richly decorated churches. Fine Sienese painting in Pinacoteca Nazionale and Museo dell'Opera del Duomo. www.terresiena.it **135 B4**

Turin Torino

City centre has 17-18c Baroque layout dominated by twin Baroque churches. Also: 15c cathedral (holds Turin Shroud); Palazzo Reale; 18c Superga Basilica; Academy of Science with two museums (Egyptian antiquities; European painting). www.commune.torino.it **119 B4**

Urbino

Set in beautiful hilly landscape, Urbino's heritage is mainly due to the 15c court of Federico da Montefeltro at the magnificent Ducal Palace (notable Studiolo), now also a gallery. www.turismo.pesaurbino.it **136 B1**

Venice Venezia

Stunning old city built on islands in a lagoon, with some 150 canals. The Grand Canal is crossed by the famous 16c Rialto Bridge and is lined with elegant palaces (Gothic Ca'd'Oro and Ca'Foscari, Renaissance Palazzo Grimani, Baroque Rezzonico). The district of San Marco has the core of the best known sights and is centred on Piazza San Marco with 11c Basilica di San Marco (bronze horses, 13c mosaics); Campanile (exceptional views) and Ducal Palace (connected with the prison by the famous Bridge of Sighs). Many churches (Santa Maria Gloriosa dei Frari, Santa Maria della Salute, Redentore, San Giorgio Maggiore, San Giovanni e Paolo) and scuole (Scuola di San Rocco, Scuola di San Giorgio degli Schiavoni) have excellent works of art. The Gallery of the Academy houses superb 14–18c Venetian art. The Guggenheim Museum holds 20c art. http://english.comune.venezia.it **122 B1**

Verona

Old town with remains of 1c Roman Arena and medieval sights including the Palazzo degli Scaligeri; Arche Scaligere; Romanesque Santa Maria Antica; Castelvecchio; Ponte Scaliger. The famous 14c House of Juliet has associations with *Romeo and Juliet*. Many churches with fine art works (cathedral; Sant'Anastasia; basilica di San Zeno Maggiore). www.tourism.verona.it **121 B4**

Vicenza

Beautiful town, famous for the architecture of Palladio, including the Olympic Theatre (extraordinary stage), Corso Palladio with many of his palaces, and Palazzo Chиericati. Nearby: Villa Rotonda, the most influential of all Palladian buildings. www.vicenzae.org **121 B4**

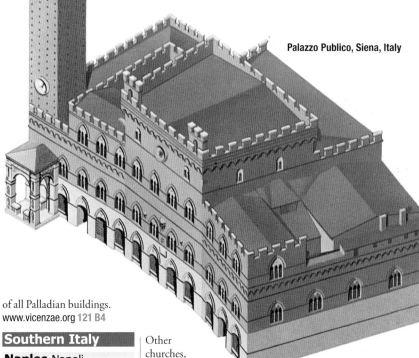

Palazzo Publico, Siena, Italy

Southern Italy

Naples Napoli

Historical centre around Gothic cathedral (crypt). Spaccanapoli area has numerous churches (bizarre Cappella Sansevero, Gesù Nuovo, Gothic Santa Chiara with fabulous tombs). Buildings: 13c Castello Nuovo; 13c Castel dell'Ovo; 15c Palazzo Cuomo. Museums: National Archeological Museum (artefacts from Pompeii and Herculaneum); National Museum of Capodimonte (Renaissance painting). Nearby: spectacular coast around Amalfi; Pompeii; Herculaneum. www.inaples.it **170 C2**

Orvieto

Medieval hill-top town with a number of monuments including the Romanesque-Gothic cathedral (façade, frescoes). www.commune.orvieto.tr.it **168 A2**

Rome Roma

Capital of Italy, exceptionally rich in sights from many eras. Ancient sights: Colosseum; Arch of Constantine; Trajan's Column; Roman and Imperial fora; hills of Palatino and Campidoglio (Capitoline Museum shows antiquities); Pantheon; Castel Sant'Angelo; Baths of Caracalla). Early Christian sights: catacombs (San Calisto, San Sebastiano, Domitilla); basilicas (San Giovanni in Laterano, Santa Maria Maggiore, San Paolo Fuori le Mura). Rome is known for richly decorated Baroque churches: il Gesù, Sant'Ignazio, Santa Maria della Vittoria, Chiesa Nuova. Other churches, often with art treasures: Romanesque Santa Maria in Cosmedin, Gothic Santa Maria Sopra Minerva, Renaissance Santa Maria del Popolo, San Pietro in Vincoli. Several Renaissance and Baroque palaces and villas house superb art collections (Palazzo Barberini, Palazzo Doria Pamphilj, Palazzo Spada, Palazzo Corsini, Villa Giulia, Galleria Borghese) and are beautifully frescoed (Villa Farnesina). Fine Baroque public spaces with fountains: Piazza Navona; Piazza di Spagna with the Spanish Steps; also Trevi Fountain. Nearby: Tivoli; Villa Adriana. Rome also contains the Vatican City (Città del Vaticano). www.romaturismo.com **168 B2**

Volcanic Region

Region from Naples to Sicily. Mount Etna is one of the most famous European volcanoes. Vesuvius dominates the Bay of Naples and has at its foot two of Italy's finest Roman sites, Pompeii and Herculaneum, both destroyed by its eruption in 79ad. Stromboli is one of the beautiful Aeolian Islands.

Sardinia Sardegna

Sardinia has some of the most beautiful beaches in Italy (Alghero). Unique are the nuraghi, some 7000 stone constructions (Su Nuraxi, Serra Orios), the remains of an old civilization (1500–400 BC). Old towns include Cagliari and Sássari. www.sardi.it **178–179**

Sicily Sicilia

Surrounded by beautiful beaches and full of monuments of many periods, Sicily is the largest island in the Mediterranean. Taormina with its Greek theatre has one of the most spectacular beaches, lying under the mildly active volcano Mount Etna. Also: Agrigento; Palermo, Siracusa. www.regione.sicilia.it/turismo/web_turismo **176–177**

Agrigento

Set on a hill above the sea and famed for the Valley of the Temples. The nine originally 5c BC Doric temples are Sicily's best-preserved Greek remains. www.agrigento-sicilia.it **176 B2**

Palermo

City with Moorish, Norman and Baroque architecture, especially around the main squares (Quattro Canti, Piazza Pretoria, Piazza Bellini). Sights: remains of Norman palace (12c Palatine Chapel); Norman cathedral; Regional

Gallery (medieval); some 8000 preserved bodies in the catacombs of the Cappuchin Convent. Nearby: 12c Norman Duomo di Monreale. www.commune.palermo.it **176 A2**

Syracuse Siracusa

Built on an island connected to the mainland by a bridge, the old town has a 7c cathedral, ruins of the Temple of Apollo; Fountain of Arethusa; archaeological museum. On the mainland: 5c BC Greek theatre with seats cut out of rock; Greek fortress of Euralus; 2c Roman amphitheatre; 5–6c Catacombs of St John. www.apt-siracusa.it **177 B4**

Latvia Latvija

www.lv

Riga

Well-preserved medieval town centre around the cathedral. Sights: Riga Castle; medieval Hanseatic houses; Great Guild Hall; Gothic Church of St Peter; Art Nouveau buildings in the New Town. Nearby: Baroque Rundale Castle. www.riga.lv **8 D4**

Lithuania Lietuva

www.tourism.lt

Vilnius

Baroque old town with fine architecture including: cathedral; Gediminas Tower; university complex; Archbishop's Palace; Church of St Anne. Also: remains of Jewish life; Vilnius Picture Gallery (16–19c regional); Lithuanian National Museum. www.vilnius.lt **13 A6**

Luxembourg

www.ont.lu

Luxembourg

Capital of Luxembourg, built on a rock with fine views. Old town is around the Place d'Armes. Buildings: Grand Ducal Palace; fortifications of Rocher du Bock; cathedral. Museum of History and Art holds an excellent regional collection. www.ont.lu **92 B2**

Macedonia Makedonija

www.macedonia.org

Skopje

Historic town with Turkish citadel, fine 15c mosques, oriental bazaar, ancient bridge.

Superb Byzantine churches nearby. www.skopjeonline.com. mk **182 A3**

Ohrid

Old town, beautifully set by a lake, with houses of wood and brick, remains of a Turkish citadel, many churches (two cathedrals; St Naum south of the lake). www.ohrid.org.mk **182 B2**

Malta

www.visitmalta.com

Valletta

Capital of Malta. Historic walled city, founded in 16c by the Maltese Knights, with 16c Grand Master's Palace and a richly decorated cathedral. **175 C3**

Monaco

www.visitmonaco.com

Monaco

Major resort area in a beautiful location. Sights include: Monte Carlo casino, Prince's Palace at Monaco-Ville; 19c cathedral; oceanographic museum. www.visitmonaco.com **133 B3**

The Netherlands Nederland

www.visitholland.com

Amsterdam

Capital of the Netherlands. Old centre has picturesque canals lined with distinctive elegant 17–18c merchants' houses. Dam Square has 15c New Church and Royal Palace. Other churches include Westerkerk. The Museumplein has three

Westerkerk, Amsterdam, Netherlands

world-famous museums: Rijksmuseum (several art collections including 15–17c painting); Van Gogh Museum; Municipal Museum (art from 1850 on). Other museums: Anne Frank House; Jewish Historical Museum; Rembrandt House. www.visitamsterdam.nl **70 B1**

Delft

Well-preserved old Dutch town with gabled red-roofed houses along canals. Gothic churches: New Church; Old Church. Famous for Delftware (two museums). www.delft.nl **70 B1**

The Hague Den Haag

Seat of Government and of the royal house of the Netherlands. The 17c Mauritshuis houses the Royal Picture Gallery (excellent 15–18c Flemish and Dutch). Other good collections: Prince William V Gallery; Hesdag Museum; Municipal Museum www.denhaag.nl **70 B1**

Haarlem

Many medieval gabled houses centred on the Great Market with 14c Town Hall and 15c Church of St Bavon. Museums: Frans Hals Museum; Teylers Museum. www.haarlem.nl **70 B1**

Het Loo

Former royal palace and gardens set in a vast landscape (commissioned by future Queen of England, Mary Stuart). www.paleishetloo.nl **70 B2**

Keukenhof

Landscaped gardens, planted with bulbs of many varieties, are the largest flower gardens in the world. www.keukenhof.nl **70 B1**

Leiden

University town of beautiful gabled houses set along canals. The Rijksmuseum Van Oudheden is Holland's most important home to archaeological artefacts from the Antiquity. The 16c Hortus Botanicus is one of the oldest botanical gardens in Europe. The Cloth Hall with van Leyden's *Last Judgement*. www.leidenpromotie.nl **70 B1**

Rotterdam

The largest port in the world. The Boymans-van Beuningen Museum has a huge and excellent decorative and fine art

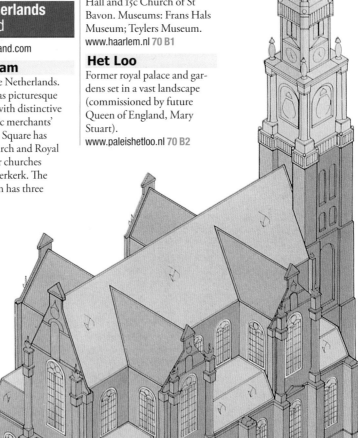

collection (old and modern). Nearby: 18c Kinderdijk with 19 windmills. www.rotterdam.nl **79 A4**

Utrecht

Delightful old town centre along canals with the Netherlands' oldest university and Gothic cathedral. Good art collections: Central Museum; National Museum. www.utrecht.nl **70 B2**

Norway Norge

www.norway.no

Bergen

Norway's second city in a scenic setting. The Quay has many painted wooden medieval buildings. Sights: 12c Romanesque St Mary's Church; Bergenhus fortress with 13c Haakon's Hall; Rosenkrantztårnet; Grieghallen; Rasmus Meyer Collection (Norwegian art); Bryggens Museum. www.visitbergen.com **46 B2**

Lappland (Norwegian)

Vast land of Finnmark is home to the Sámi. Nordkapp is the northern point of Europe. Also Finland, Sweden. www.lappland.no **192–193**

Norwegian Fjords

Beautiful and majestic landscape of deep glacial valleys filled by the sea. The most thrilling fjords are between Bergen and Ålesund. www.fjords.com **46 & 198**

Oslo

Capital of Norway with a modern centre. Buildings: 17c cathedral; 19c city hall, 19c royal palace; 19c Stortinget (housing parliament); 19c University; 13c Akershus (castle); 12c Akerskirke (church). Museums: National Gallery; Munch Museum; Viking Ship Museum; Folk Museum (reconstructed buildings). www.visitoslo.com **48 C2**

Stavkirker

Wooden medieval stave churches of bizarre pyramidal structure, carved with images from Nordic mythology. Best preserved in southern Norway.

Tromsø

Main arctic city of Norway with a university and two cathedrals. www.destinasjontromso.no **192 C3**

Trondheim

Set on the edge of a fjord, a modern city with the superb Nidaros cathedral (rebuilt 19c). Also: Stiftsgaard (royal

sidence); Applied Arts Museum.
ww.trondheim.com 199 B7

Poland Polska

ww.poland.pl

Częstochowa
Centre of Polish Catholicism, ith the 14c monastery of sna Góra a pilgrimage te to the icon of the Black Madonna for six centuries. 6 B3

Gdańsk
Medieval centre with: 14c own Hall (state rooms); Gothic brick St Mary's Church, Poland's largest; Long Market has fine buildings Artus Court); National Art Museum. www.gdansk.pl 69 A3

Kraków
Old university city, rich in rchitecture, centred on uperb 16c Marketplace with Gothic-Renaissance Cloth Hall containing the Art Gallery (19c Polish), Clock ower, Gothic red-brick St Mary's Church (altarpiece). Czartoryski Palace has ity's finest art collection. Wawel Hill has the Gothic athedral and splendid Renaissance Royal Palace. he former Jewish ghetto in Kazimierz district has 16c Old ynagogue, now a museum. ww.krakow.pl 99 A3

Poznań
own centred on the Old quare with Renaissance Town Hall and Baroque mansions. Also: medieval castle; Gothic athedral; National Museum European masters). www.plot. oznan.pl 76 B1

Tatry
One of Europe's most delightul mountain ranges with many beautiful ski resorts Zakopane). Also in Slovakia. 9 B3

Warsaw Warszawa
Capital of Poland, with many istoric monuments in the Old Town with the Royal Castle (museum) and Old own Square surrounded y reconstructed 17–18c merchants' houses. Several hurches including: Gothic athedral; Baroque Church f the Nuns of Visitation. Richly decorated royal palaces nd gardens: Neoclassical azienki Palace; Baroque palce in Wilanów. The National Museum has Polish and European art. ww.warsawtour.pl 7 C6

Wrocław
Historic town centred on the Market Square with 15c Town Hall and mansions. Churches: Baroque cathedral; St Elizabeth; St Adalbert. National Museum displays fine art. Vast painting of Battle of Racławice is specially housed. www.wroclaw.pl 85 A5

Portugal

www.visitportugal.pt

Alcobaça
Monastery of Santa Maria, one of the best examples of a Cistercian abbey, founded in 1147 (exterior 17–18c). The church is Portugal's largest (14c tombs). 154 A1

Algarve
Modern seaside resorts among picturesque sandy beaches and rocky coves (Praia da Rocha). Old towns: Lagos; Faro. www.rtalgarve.pt 160 B1

Batalha
Abbey is one of the masterpieces of French Gothic and Manueline architecture (tombs, English Perpendicular chapel, unfinished pantheon). 154 A2

Braga
Historic town with cathedral and large Archbishop's Palace. www.cm-braga.com.pt 148 A1

Coimbra
Old town with narrow streets set on a hill. The Romanesque cathedral is particularly fine (portal). The university (founded 1290) has a fascinating Baroque library. Also: Museum of Machado de Castro; many monasteries and convents. 148 B1

Évora
Centre of the town, surrounded by walls, has narrow streets of Moorish character and medieval and Renaissance architecture. Churches: 12–13c Gothic cathedral; São Francisco with a chapel decorated with bones of some 5000 monks; 15c Convent of Dos Lóis. The Jesuit university was founded in 1559. Museum of Évora holds fine art (particularly Flemish and Portugese). 154 B3

Guimarães
Old town with a castle with seven towers on a vast keep. Churches: Romanesque chapel of São Miguel; São Francisco. Alberto Sampaio Museum and Martins Sarmento Museum are excellent. 148 A1

Lisbon Lisboa
Capital of Portugal. Baixa is the Neoclassical heart of Lisbon with the Praça do Comércio and Rossío squares. São Jorge castle (Visigothic, Moorish, Romanesque) is surrounded by the medieval quarters. Bairro Alto is famous for *fado* (songs). Monastery of Jerónimos is exceptional. Churches: 12c cathedral; São Vicente de Fora; São Roque (tiled chapels); Torre de Belém; Convento da Madre de Deus. Museums: Gulbenkian Museum (ancient, oriental, European), National Museum of Antique Art (old masters), Modern Art Centre; Azulejo Museum (decorative tiles). Nearby: palatial monastic complex Mafra; royal resort Sintra. www.cm-lisboa.pt 154 B1

Porto
Historic centre with narrow streets. Views from Clérigos Tower. Churches: São Francisco; cathedral. Soares dos Reis Museum holds fine and decorative arts (18–19c). The suburb of Vila Nova de Gaia is the centre for port wine. www.portoturismo.pt 148 A1

Tomar
Attractive town with the Convento de Cristo, founded in 1162 as the headquarters of the Knights Templar (Charola temple, chapter house, Renaissance cloisters). 154 A2

Romania

www.turism.ro

Bucovina
Beautiful region in northern Romanian Moldova renowned for a number of 15–16c monasteries and their fresco cycles. Of particular note are Moldovita, Voroneț and Sucevița. 17 B6

Bucharest Bucureşti
Capital of Romania with the majority of sites along the Calea Victoriei and centring on Piaţa Revoluţiei with 19c Romanian Athenaeum and 1930s Royal Palace housing the National Art Gallery. The infamous 1980s Civic Centre with People's Palace is a symbol of dictatorial aggrandisement. www.bucuresti.ro 17 C7

Carpathian Mountains Carpaţii
The beautiful Carpathian Mountains have several ski resorts (Sinaia) and peaks noted for first-rate mountaineering (Făgăraşuiui, Rodnei).

Danube Delta Europe's largest marshland, a spectacular nature reserve. Travel in the area is by boat, with Tulcea the starting point for visitors. The Romanian Black Sea Coast has a stretch of resorts (Mamaia, Eforie) between Constantaţ and the border, and well-preserved Roman remains in Histria. 17 B6

Transylvania Transilvania
Beautiful and fascinating scenic region of medieval citadels (Timişoara, Sibiu) provides a setting for the haunting image of the legendary Dracula (Sighişoara, Braşov, Bran Castle). Cluj-Napoca is the main town. 17 B5

Russia Rossiya

www.russia.com

Moscow Moskva
Capital of Russia, with many monuments. Within the Kremlin's red walls are: 15c Cathedral of the Dormition; 16c Cathedral of the Archangel; Cathedral of the Annunciation (icons), Armour Palace. Outside the walls, Red Square has the Lenin Mausoleum and 16c St Basil's Cathedral. There are a number of monasteries (16c Novodevichi). Two superb museums: Tretiakov Art Gallery (Russian); Pushkin Museum of Fine Art (European). Kolomenskoe, once a royal summer retreat, has the Church of the Ascension. The VDNKh is a symbol of the Stalinist era. www.moscow-guide.ru 9 E10

Novgorod
One of Russia's oldest towns, centred on 15c Kremlin with St Sophia Cathedral (iconostasis, west door). Two other cathedrals: St Nicholas; St George. Museum of History, Architecture and Art has notable icons and other artefacts. www.novgorod.ru 9 C7

Petrodvorets
Grand palace with numerous pavilions (Monplaisir) set in beautiful parkland interwoven by a system of fountains, cascades and waterways connected to the sea. www.petrodvorets.ru 9 C6

Pushkin
(Tsarskoye Selo) Birthplace of Alexander Pushkin, with the vast Baroque Catherine Palace – splendid state apartments, beautiful gardens and lakes. www.pushkin-town.net 9 C7

Saint Petersburg Sankt Peterburg
Founded in 1703 with the SS Peter and Paul Fortress and its cathedral by Peter the Great, and functioning as seat of court and government until 1918. Many of the most famous sights are around elegant Nevski Prospekt. The Hermitage, one of the world's largest and finest art collections, is housed in five buildings including the Baroque Winter and Summer palaces. The Mikhailovsky Palace houses the Russian Museum (Russian art). Other sights: neoclassical Admiralty; 19c St Isaac's Cathedral and St Kazan Cathedral; Vasilievsky Island with 18c Menshikov Palace; Alexander Nevsky Monastery; 18c Smolny Convent. www. spb.ru 9 C7

Sergiev Posad
(Zagorsk) Trinity St Sergius monastery with 15c cathedral. www.musobl.divo.ru 9 D11

Serbia Srbija

www.serbia-tourism.org

Belgrade Beograd
Capital of Serbia. The largely modern city is set between the Danube and Sava rivers. The National Museum holds European art. To the south there are numerous fascinating medieval monasteries, richly embellished with frescoes. www.belgradetourism.org.yu 127 C2

Spain España

www.spaintour.com

Ávila
Medieval town with 2km-long 11c walls. Pilgrimage site to shrines to St Teresa of Ávila (Convent of Santa Teresa, Convent of the Incarnation). www.avila.world-guides.com 150 B3

Barcelona
Showcase of Gothic ('Barri Gòtic': cathedral; Santa María del Mar; mansions on Carrer de Montcada) and *modernista* architecture ('Eixample' area with Manzana de la Discòrdia; Sagrada Familia, Güell Park, La Pedrera). Many elegant boulevards (La Rambla, Passeig de Gràcia). Museums: Modern Catalan Art; Picasso Museum, Miró Museum; Tàpies Museum. Nearby: monastery of Montserrat (Madonna); Figueres (Dali Museum). www.barcelonaturisme.com 147 C3

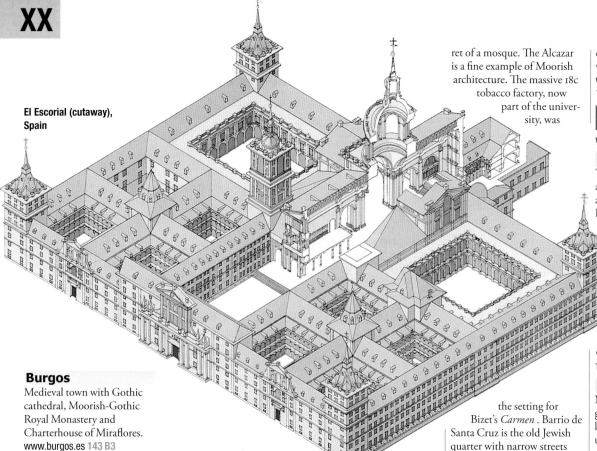

El Escorial (cutaway), Spain

Burgos
Medieval town with Gothic cathedral, Moorish-Gothic Royal Monastery and Charterhouse of Miraflores. www.burgos.es **143 B3**

Cáceres
Medieval town surrounded by originally Moorish walls and with several aristocratic palaces with solars. www.caceres.es **155 A4**

Córdoba
Capital of Moorish Spain with a labyrinth of streets and houses with tile-decorated patios. The 8–10c Mezquita is the finest mosque in Spain. A 16c cathedral was added at the centre of the building and a 17c tower replaced the minaret. The old Jewish quarter has 14c synagogue www.cordoba.es **156 C3**

El Escorial
Immense Renaissance complex of palatial and monastic buildings and mausoleum of the Spanish monarchs. www.patrimonionacional.es/escorial/escorial.htm **151 B3**

Granada
The Alhambra was hill-top palace-fortress of the rulers of the last Moorish kingdom and is the most splendid example of Moorish art and architecture in Spain. The complex has three principal parts: Alcazaba fortress (11c); Casa Real palace (14c, with later Palace of Carlos V); Generalife gardens. Also: Moorish quarter; gypsy quarter; Royal Chapel with good art in the sacristy. www.granadatur.com **163 A4**

León
Gothic cathedral has notable stained glass. Royal Pantheon commemorates early kings of Castile and León. **142 B1**

Madrid
Capital of Spain, a mainly modern city with 17–19c architecture at its centre around Plaza Mayor. Sights: Royal Palace with lavish apartments; Descalzas Reales Convent (tapestries and other works); Royal Armoury museum. Spain's three leading galleries: Prado (15–18c); Queen Sofía Centre (20c Spanish, Picasso's *Guernica*); Thyssen-Bornemisza Museum (medieval to modern). www.munimadrid.es **151 B4**

Oviedo
Gothic cathedral with 12c sanctuary. Three Visigoth (9c) churches: Santullano, Santa María del Naranco, San Miguel de Lillo. www.ayto-oviedo.es **141 A5**

Palma
Situated on Mallorca, the largest and most beautiful of the Balearic islands, with an impressive Gothic cathedral. www.a-palma.es **166 B2**

Picos de Europa
Mountain range with river gorges and peaks topped by Visigothic and Romanesque churches. **142 A2**

Pyrenees
Unspoiled mountain range with beautiful landscape and villages full of Romanesque architecture (cathedral of Jaca). The Ordesa National Park has many waterfalls and canyons. **144–145**

Salamanca
Delightful old city with some uniquely Spanish architecture: Renaissance Plateresque is famously seen on 16c portal of the university (founded 1215); Baroque Churrigueresque on 18c Plaza Mayo; both styles at the Convent of San Esteban. Also: Romanesque Old Cathedral; Gothic-Plateresque New Cathedral; House of Shells. www.salamanca.com **150 B2**

Santiago di Compostela
Medieval city with many churches and religious institutions. The famous pilgrimage to the shrine of St James the Apostle ends here in the magnificent cathedral, originally Romanesque with many later elements (18c Baroque façade). www.santiagoturismo.com **140 B2**

Segovia
Old town set on a rock with a 1c Roman aqueduct. Also: 16c Gothic cathedral; Alcázar (14–15c, rebuilt 19c); 12-sided 13c Templar church of Vera Cruz. www.viasegovia.com **151 B3**

Seville Sevilla
City noted for festivals and flamenco. The world's largest Gothic cathedral (15c) retains the Orange Court and minaret of a mosque. The Alcazar is a fine example of Moorish architecture. The massive 18c tobacco factory, now part of the university, was the setting for Bizet's *Carmen* . Barrio de Santa Cruz is the old Jewish quarter with narrow streets and white houses. Casa de Pilatos (15–16c) has a fine domestic patio. Hospital de la Caridad has good Spanish painting. Nearby: Roman Italica with amphitheatre. www.sevilla.org **162 A2**

Tarragona
The city and its surroundings have some of the best-preserved Roman heritage in Spain. Also: Gothic cathedral (cloister); Archaeological Museum. www.tarragona.es **147 C2**

Toledo
Historic city with Moorish, Jewish and Christian sights. The small 11c mosque of El Cristo de la Luz is one of the earliest in Spain. Two synagogues have been preserved: Santa María la Blanca; El Tránsito. Churches: San Juan de los Reyes; Gothic cathedral (good artworks). El Greco's *Burial of the Count of Orgaz* is in the Church of Santo Tomé. More of his works are in the El Greco house and, with other art, in Hospital de Santa Cruz. www.toledo.es **151 C3**

Valencia
The old town has houses and palaces with elaborate façades. Also: Gothic cathedral and Lonja de la Seda church. www.comunitatvalenciana.com **159 B3**

Zaragoza
Town notable for Moorish architecture (11c Aljafería Palace). The Basilica de Nuestra Señora del Pilar, one of two cathedrals, is highly venerated. www.zaragoza-ciudad.com **153 A3**

Slovenia Slovenija
www.slovenia-tourism.si

Istria Istra
Two town centres, Koper and Piran, with medieval and Renaissance squares and Baroque palaces. See also Croatia. www.slo-istra.com **122 B2**

Julian Alps
Julijske Alpe
Wonderfully scenic section of the Alps with lakes (Bled, Bohinj), dee valleys (Planica, Vrata) and ski resorts (Kranjska Gora, Bohinjska Bistrica). **122 A2**

Karst Caves
Numerous caves with huge galleries, extraordinary stalactites and stalagmites, and underground rivers. The mos spectacular are Postojna (the most famous, with Predjamsk Castle nearby) and Škocjan. www.postojnska-jama.si **123 B3**

Ljubljana
Capital of Slovenia. The old town, dominated by the castle (good views), is principally between Prešeren Square and Town Hall (15c, 18c), with the Three Bridges and colonnaded market. Many Baroque churches (cathedral, St Jacob, St Francis, Ursuline) and palaces (Bishop's Palace, Seminary, Gruber Palace). Also: 17c Križanke church an monastery complex; National Gallery and Modern Gallery show Slovene art. www.ljubljana.si **123 A3**

Slovakia Slovenska Republika
www.slovenska-republika.com

Bratislava
Capital of Slovakia, dominated by the castle (Slovak National Museum, good views). Old Town centred on the Main Square with Old Town Hall and Jesuit Church Many 18–19c palaces (Mirbac Palace, Pálffy Palace, Primate's Palace), churches (Gothic cathedral, Corpus Christi Chapel) and museums (Slova National Gallery). www.bratislava.sk **111 A4**

Košice
Charming old town with many Baroque and neoclassical buildings and Gothic cathedral. www.kosice.sk **12 D**

Spišské Podhradie
region, east of the Tatry, full of picturesque medieval towns (Levoča, Kežmarok, Prešov) and architectural monuments (Spišský Castle). **99 B4**

Tatry
beautiful mountain region. Poprad is an old town with 19c villas. Starý Smokovec is a popular ski resort. See also Poland. www.tatry.sk **99 B3**

Sweden Sverige
www.sweden.se

Abisko
popular resort in the Swedish part of Lapland set in an inspiring landscape of lakes and mountains.
www.abisko.nu **194 B9**

Gothenburg Göteborg
largest port in Sweden, the historic centre has 17–18c Dutch architectural character (Kronhuset). The Art Museum has interesting Swedish works.
www.goteborg.com **60 B1**

Gotland
island with Sweden's most popular beach resorts (Ljugarn) and unspoiled countryside with churches in Baltic Gothic style (Dahlem, Lunge). Visby is a pleasant walled medieval town.
www.gotland.se **57 C4**

Lappland (Swedish)
Swedish part of Lappland with 18c Arvidsjaur the old-est preserved Sámi village. Jokkmokk is a Sámi cultural centre, Abisko a popular resort in fine scenery. Also Finland, Norway. www.lappland.se **192–193**

Lund
charming university city with medieval centre and a fine 12c Romanesque cathedral (14c astronomical clock, carved tombs). www.lund.se **61 D3**

Malmö
Old town centre set among canals and parks dominated by a red-brick castle (museums) and a vast market square with Town Hall and Gothic Church of St Peter.
www.malmo.se **61 D3**

Mora
Delightful village on the shores of Siljan Lake in the heart of the Dalarna region, home to folklore and traditional crafts.
www.mora.se **50 A1**

Stockholm
Capital of Sweden built on a number of islands. The Old Town is largely on three islands with 17–18c houses, Baroque Royal Castle (apartments and museums), Gothic cathedral, parliament. Riddarholms church has tombs of the monarchy. Museums include: Modern Gallery (one of world's best modern collections); Nordiska Museet (cultural history); open-air Skansen (Swedish houses). Baroque Drottningholm Castle is the residence of the monarchy.
www.stockholm.se
57 A4

Swedish Lakes
Beautiful region around the Vättern and Vänern Lakes. Siljan Lake is in the Dalarna region where folklore and crafts are preserved (Leksand, Mora, Rättvik).
55 B4

Uppsala
Appealing university town with a medieval centre around the massive Gothic cathedral.
www.uppsala.se **51 C4**

Switzerland Schweiz
www.myswitzerland.com

Alps
The most popular Alpine region is the Berner Oberland with the town of Interlaken a starting point for exploring the large number of picturesque peaks (Jungfrau). The valleys of the Graubünden have famous ski resorts (Davos, St Moritz). Zermatt lies below the highest and most recognizable Swiss peak, the Matterhorn.
www.thealps.com **119 A4**

Basle Basel
Medieval university town with Romanesque-Gothic cathedral (tomb of Erasmus). Superb collections: Art Museum; Museum of Contemporary Art. www.baseltourismus.ch
106 B2

Bern
Capital of Switzerland. Medieval centre has fountains, characteristic streets (Spitalgasse) and tower-gates. The Bärengraben is famed for its bears. Also: Gothic cathedral; good Fine Arts Museum.
www.berne.ch
106 C2

Geneva Genève
Wonderfully situated on the lake with the world's highest fountain. The historic area is centred on the Romanesque cathedral and Place du Bourg du Four. Excellent collections: Art and History Museum;

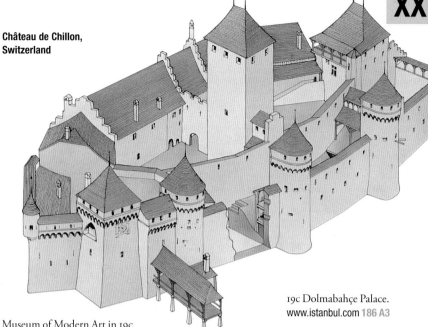

Château de Chillon,
Switzerland

Museum of Modern Art in 19c Petit Palais. On the lake shore: splendid medieval Château de Chillon.
www.geneva-tourism.ch **118 A3**

Interlaken
Starting point for excursions to the most delightful part of the Swiss Alps, the Bernese Oberland, with Grindelwald and Lauterbrunnen – one of the most thrilling valleys leading up to the ski resort of Wengen with views on the Jungfrau.
www.interlakentourism.ch
106 C2

Lucerne Luzern
On the beautiful shores of Vierwaldstättersee, a charming medieval town of white houses on narrow streets and of wooden bridges (Kapellbrücke, Spreuerbrücke). It is centred on the Kornmarkt with the Renaissance Old Town Hall and Am Rhyn-Haus (Picasso collection). www.luzern.org
106 C1

Zürich
Set on Zürichsee, the old quarter is around Niederdorf with 15c cathedral. Gothic Fraumünster has stained glass by Chagall. Museums: Swiss National Museum (history); Art Museum (old and modern masters); Bührle Foundation (Impressionists, Post-impressionists). www.zuerich.com
107 B3

Turkey Türkiye
www.tourismturkey.org

Istanbul
Divided by the spectcular Bosphorus, the stretch of water that separates Europe from Asia, the historic district is surrounded by the Golden Horn, Sea of Marmara and the 5c wall of Theodosius. Major sights: 6c Byzantine church of St Sophia (converted first to a mosque in 1453 and then a museum in 1934); 15c Topkapi Palace; treasury and Archaeological Museum; 17c Blue Mosque; 19c Bazaar; 16c Süleymaniye Mosque; 12c Kariye Camii; European district with Galata Tower and 19c Dolmabahçe Palace.
www.istanbul.com **186 A3**

Ukraine Ukraina
www.ukraine.com

Kiev Kyїv
Capital of Ukraine, known for its cathedral (11c, 17c) with Byzantine frescoes and mosaics. The Monastery of the Caves has churches, monastic buildings and catacombs.
www.uazone.net/kiev **13 C9**

Vatican City
Città del Vaticano
www.vatican.va

Vatican City
Città del Vaticano
Independent state within Rome. On Piazza San Pietro is the 15–16c Renaissance-Baroque Basilica San Pietro (Michelangelo's dome and *Pietà*), the world's most important Roman Catholic church. The Vatican Palace contains the Vatican Museums with many fine art treasures including Michelangelo's frescoes in the Sistine Chapel.
www.vatican.va **168 B2**

The facade of Basilica San Pietro, Vatican City

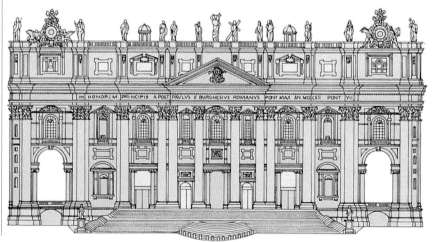

History and culture of Europe

The following definitions describe some of the key terms in the timeline below.

Aegean civilization Bronze Age cultures, chiefly Minoan (on Crete, at its height c.1700BC–c.1100BC) and Mycenaean (at its height c.1580BC–c.1120BC).

Baroque Style of art and architecture which at its best was a blend of light, colour, and movement calculated to overwhelm through emotional appeal. Buildings were heavily decorated with ornament and free-standing sculpture. Baroque became increasingly complex and florid. The term is often used to describe the period in history as well as the style.

Byzantine Empire Christian, Greek-speaking, Eastern Roman Empire that outlasted the Western Empire by nearly 1000 years. The area of the Byzantine Empire varied greatly, and its history from c.600 was marked by continual military crisis and recovery.

Carolingian period Cultural revival in France and Italy beginning under the encouragement of Charlemagne, who gathered notable educators and artists to his court at Aachen.

Counter-Reformation Revival of the Roman Catholic Church in Europe, beginning as a reaction to the Reformation. The reforms were largely conservative, trying to remove many of the abuses of the late medieval church and win new prestige for the papacy. The Council of Trent (1545-63) generated many of the key decisions and doctrines.

Dark Ages Term that at one time historians used to imply cultural and economic backwardness, but now is used mainly to indicate our ignorance of the period due to lack of historical evidence.

Enlightenment (Age of Reason) Philosophical movement that influenced many aspects of 18th-century society. It was inspired by the scientific and philosophical revolutions of the late 17th century and stressed the use of reason and the rational side of human nature.

Gothic Architecture and painting characterized by the pointed arch and ribbed vault. Religious in inspiration, its greatest expression was the cathedral. Gothic sculpture was elegant and more realistic than Romanesque. The Gothic style was also well expressed in manuscript illumination.

High Renaissance Brief period regarded as the height of Italian (particularly Roman) Renaissance art, brought to an end by the sack of Rome by the troops of Charles V.

Historicism, 19th-century Revival of past architectural styles. Ancient Greek and Gothic forms were constructed in a wide range of styles, including Renaissance, Romanesque, and baroque.

Holy Roman Empire Empire centred on Germany, which aimed to echo ancient Rome. It was founded when Otto I was crowned in Rome (some date it from the coronation of Charlemagne). The Emperor claimed to be the worldly sovereign of Christendom ruling in co-operation with

1500

c.1250-1200 Trojan War

Bronze age to c.1000 | Aegean civilization to c.1200

Treasury of Atreus, Mycenae, c.1325

1000

776 First Olympic Games held in Greece

753 Traditional date for the foundation of Rome by Romulus and Remus

c1000 Ancient Greek civilisation c.27 | c.900 Etruscans | c.753 Early Romans c.500 | c.800 Carthaginian power 146 | c.500 Rise of Roman power c.27

c.750 *Odyssey* and *Iliad* complete in known forms

Erechtheion, part of the Acropolis, Athens, 421-405

582?-500? Pythagoras

500

336-323 Alexander the Great's campaigns

218 Hannibal crosses Alps with elephants

58-51 Romans conquer Gaul

43 Romans invade Britain

27BC Pax Romana AD180 | 27BC Imperial Rome AD476

428?-347? Plato
384-322 Aristotle
356-323 Alexander the Great
c.140 Venus de Milo sculpted
100-44 Julius Caesar
69-30 Cleopatra
63BC-14AD Augustus
37-68 Nero
c.58 St Paul's Letter to the Corinthians
75-80 Coliseum built in Rome
53-117 Trajan

BC

AD

79 Vesuvius erupts burying Pompeii and Herculaneum

Arch of Titus, Rome, 81

Pantheon, Rome, 120-124

100

101–2, 105–6 Trajan's Dacian campaigns (recounted on Trajan's Column)

c.150 Major Slavic invasions of eastern Europe c.900 | 180 Germanic (barbarian) tribes invade Roman empire 476

121-126 Hadrian's wall built across northern England

121-180 Marcus Aurelius

200

285 Byzantine empire 1453

285 Roman Empire first split – Rome in the West and Byzantium (Constantinople) in the East

245-313 Diocletian
c.274-337 Constantine the Great

Temple of Vesta, Rome, 205

300

313 Edict of Milan: tolerance of Christianity in Empire
330 Constantinople founded
391 Christianity official religion of Roman Empire
395 Final division of Roman Empire into E and W

313-315 Arch of Constantine
c.329-379 St Basil
354-430 St Augustine

Palace of Diocletian, Split, Croatia, c.300

400

410 Visigoths sack Rome

455 Vandals sack Rome

476 Last Western Roman emperor overthrown

476 Middle Ages c.1400 | 476 Dark Ages c.1000 | c.481 Frankish power in western Europe 962

465-511 Clovis I, Frankish (Merovingian) king

483-565 Justinian I, ruler in first Byzantine Golden Age

San Apollinare Nuovo, Ravenna, Italy, detail of apse mosaic, 6th century

500

527–530 Slavs cross Danube

c.550 Major outbreak of bubonic plague in Europe

c.550 Height of Byzantine power and art

532-37 Church of Santa Sophia (Hagia Sophia) built in Constantinople

532-37 Church of San Vitale, Ravenna, built

San Apollinare in Classe, Ravenna, Italy, begun 532

600

603 Slavs invade Balkans

c.679–1018 First Bulgarian Empire

700

711-718 Muslims invade Spain

732 Franks defeat Muslims in Spain, preventing further conquests

742-814 Charlemagne

790-800 Palatine Chapel at Aachen

Great Mosque, Cordoba, Spain, detail of arches, begun 785

800

800 Charlemagne crowned Emperor by Pope

835-71 Danes establish settlements in England

c.860 Vikings raiders reach Mediterranean

c.800 Vikings raid… | c.800 Carolingian period 962

900

911 Vikings take control of Normandy

962 Holy Roman Empire founded

972 Hungarian state established

476 Middle Ages c.1400 | 476 Dark Ages c.1000 | 285 Byzantine empire 1453 | c.800 Vikings raid many parts of Europe c.1050

1000

1054 Church splits into Roman Catholic and Eastern Orthodox

1066 Norman conquest of England begins

1094 El Cid takes Valencia from the Moors

c.1000 Romanesque c.1180

1100

1130 Normans take control of Sicily, having conquered much of southern Italy

1186–1393 Second Bulgarian Empire

c.1135 Gothic period c.1450 | 1096 Crusades 1291

1200

1204 Fourth Crusade and sack of Constantinople

1209-1229 Wars against Albigensians in France

1209 St Francis of Assisi establishes rules for Franciscans

1236 Christian forces take Córdoba from Moors

1237-1241 Tartar Golden Horde ravage Russia and much of north-east Europe

1250

1261-1431 Paleologue age in Byzantium

1265 First English parliament in Westminster Hall, London

1271 Marco Polo's first visit to China

1282 Sicilian Vespers massacre of French in Sicily

c.1290 Invention of spectacles

1291 Swiss Confederation formed

1300

c.1300 Gunpowder appears in Europe

1309-77 Papacy moves from Rome to Avignon

1337 Hundred Years War…

1347-50 Worst outbreaks of plague (the Black Death), which kill about a quarter of Europe's population

912-973 Otto I, first Holy Roman Emperor

Durham Cathedral, England, 1093-c.1130

1050 Work begins on St Marks, Venice
1063 Pisa Romanesque cathedral started

Worms Cathedral, Germany, c.1110-81

c.1077-97 White Tower of the Tower of London begun

1140 First gothic cathedral, St Denis near Paris, begun

1194-1250 Frederick II Barbarossa Holy Roman Emperor and King of Sicily

Chartres Cathedral France, 1194-1280

Angel Choir, Lincoln Cathedral, England, 1256-1280

1265-1321 Dante Alighieri

c.1266-1337 Giotto

Salisbury Cathedral, England, 1220-1380

1304-74 Francesco Petrarch

1309 Doge's Palace, Venice, started

1313-1321 Dante works on the *Divine Comedy*

Church of the Holy Apostles, Salonica, Greece, an Orthodox continuation of the Byzantine style, 1312-15

Gothic window tracery

the Pope. After 1648 the Empire became a loose confederation, containing hundreds of virtually independent states. It was abolished by Napoleon I.

Imperial Rome Period of Roman history starting when Augustus declared himself emperor, ending the Roman republic. Most of the empire had already been conquered.

International Gothic Style of painting characterized by naturalistic detail, elegant elongated figures and jewel-like colour.

Mannerism Loose term applied to the art and architecture of Italy between the High Renaissance and the Baroque. A self-conscious style, it aimed to exceed earlier work in emotional impact. Painting is characterized by elongated figures in distorted poses,

often using lurid colours.

Middle Ages Period between the disintegration of the Roman Empire and the Renaissance. The Middle Ages were, above all, the age of the Christian church and of the social structure known as the feudal system.

Modern Art Loose term that describes painting and sculpture that breaks from traditions going back to the Renaissance. There have been many movements, including fauvism, cubism, surrealism and expressionism.

Neoclassicism Movement in art and architecture that grew out of the Enlightenment. Exponents admired and imitated the order and clarity of ancient Greek and Roman art.

Pax Romana Period when ancient Rome was so powerful that its authority could not be challenged by outside forces and peace was maintained in the empire.

Reformation Sixteenth-century movement that sought reform of the Catholic Church and resulted in the development of Protestantism. The starting date is often given as 1517, when Martin Luther nailed his 95 theses to the door of the Schlosskirche in Wittenburg, Germany, protesting against abuses of the clergy. In Zurich, the Reformation was led by Ulrich Zwingli and then by John Calvin.

Renaissance Period of rapid cultural and economic development. An important element in this was humanism, which involved

a revival of interest in classical learning and emphasis on the philosophical and moral importance of the human individual. There was a great flowering of all the arts. Architectural and artistic style emerged in Italy and was heavily influenced by Greek and Roman models and by humanism. There was development of perspective, increasing use of secular and pagan subjects, a rise of portraiture, constant experimentation, and growing concern for the expression of the individual artist. The ideas spread and were emulated with national variations.

Rococo Playful, light style of art, architecture and decoration that developed from baroque. Rococo brought to interior decoration swirls, scrolls, shells and arabesques.

It was also applied to furniture, porcelain and silverware.

Romanesque Medieval architectural style preceding gothic. It was characterized by heavy round arches and massive walls, often decorated with carving or, originally, painted scenes.

Romanticism Movement that valued individual experience and intuition, rather than the orderly, structured universe of neoclassicism. An emphasis on nature was also a characteristic. In music, the term refers to the rather later period from c.1800–1910.

1350

1353 First Ottoman (Turkish) invasion of Europe

1378-81 War of Chioggia – Venice takes control of Mediterranean

1378-1417 Great Schism in the Papacy between Rome and Avignon

1389 Battle of Kosovo - Turks gain firm foothold in the Balkans

476 Middle Ages c.1400
c.1135 Gothic period c.1400
285 Byzantine empire 1453
1337 Hundred Years War between England and Franc 1453
c.1370 International Gothic style c.1450

1353 Giovanni Boccaccio writes the *Decameron*

1377-1446 Filippo Brunelleschi
1378-1455 Lorenzo Ghiberti
1386-1466 Donatello
1387/1400-55 Fra Angelico
c.1390-1441 Jan van Eyck
1386-1400 Geoffrey Chaucer's *Canterbury Tales*

Church of the Holy Cross, Schwabish-Gemund, Germany, begun c.1350

1400

c.1400 onward Full plate armour begins to be used instead of chain main

1414 Discovery of Vitruvius' ancient treatise on architecture

1415 Introduction of oil paints by Jan and Hubert van Eyck in the Netherlands

1434-94 Medici family gain power in Florence

1431 Joan of Arc executed at Rouen

c.1440 Gutenberg invents moveable type allowing large-scale printing

c.1400 Renaissance c.1600

c.1400-1464 Rogier van der Weyden
1401-c1428 Masaccio
Foundling Hospital, Florence, Italy, from 1429

1404-72 Leon Battista Alberti
1415-92 Piero della Francesca
c.1420 Work begins on dome of Florence Cathedral
1434 Van Eyck paints the *Arnolfini Marriage*
c.1445-1510 Sandro Botticelli

Town Hall, Louvain, Belgium, 1448-63

1450

1453 Turks capture Constantinople

1479 Aragon and Castile unite to become Spain
1479 Start of Spanish Inquisition
1492 Christopher Columbus reaches the Americas; Spanish and Portuguese colonization begins
1494 Spanish take Granada, the last Moorish stronghold
1499 Portuguese discover sea route to India

c.1450 Late Gothic period c.1550
c.1480 Great age of European discovery c.1580

c.1450-1516 Hieronymus Bosch
1452-1519 Leonardo da Vinci
1466?-1536 Erasmus of Rotterdam
1471-1528 Albrecht Dürer
1475-1564 Michelangelo Buonarotti
1473-1543 Nicolaus Copernicus
1483-1512 Raphael Sanzio
c.1487-1576 Titian
1492/9-1546 Giuliano Romano
1497/8-1543 Hans Holbein the Younger
c.1480 Botticelli paints *The Birth of Venus*

St Georges Chapel, Windsor Castle, England, 1481-1528

St Maria Novella, Florence, Italy, from 1458

1500

1506 Antique statue of the Laocöon discovered near Rome, sparking increased interest in the forms of Hellenistic sculpture
1517 Martin Luther publishes his 95 Theses in Wittenberg
1522 Magellan's expedition completes circumnavigation of the globe
1527 Sack of Rome by Imperial troops
1541 John Calvin founds church in Geneva
1543 Copernicus publishes idea that Earth revolves around the Sun

1495 High Renaissance 1527
1517 Reformation c.1600
c.1480 Great age of European discovery c.1580
c.1520 Mannerism c.1610

1500 Bosch paints *The Garden of Earthly Delights*
1503 Leonardo da Vinci paints *Mona Lisa*
1504 Michelangelo sculpts *David*
1506 St Peter's, Rome, begun on Bramante's plan
1508-1512 Michelangelo paints Sistine Chapel
1508-80 Andrea Palladio
1513 Machiavelli's *The Prince*
1541-1614 El Greco
1547 Ivan IV (the Terrible) Tsar of Russia

Palazzo Strozzi, Florence, Italy, from 1490

Bibliotecha Laurenziana, door to library, Florence, Italy, from 1524

1550

1545-63 Council of Trent
1562 Netherlands revolt against Spanish rule
1562-98 Wars of Religion in France; end with religious tolerance under Edict of Nantes
1557-82 Livonia War between Sweden and its Baltic neighbours
1571 Ottoman Turk navy defeated by Holy League at Battle of Lepanto
1572 St Bartholomew's Day Massacre in Paris
1572-1648 Dutch revolt against Spanish rule
1581 Independence of United Provinces (Netherlands)
1588 English fleet defeats Spanish Armada

c.1400 Renaissance c.1600
1545 Counter Reformation 1648
c.1520 Mannerism c.1610
c.1480 Great age of European discovery c.1580

1600

1607 First English colony in North America at Jamestown
1618 Defenestration of Prague starts Thirty Years' War
1630 Sweden enters Thirty Year's War
1635 Peace of Prague ends German involvement in Thirty Years' War
1635 France enters Thirty Years' War
1642-5 English Civil War
1648 Treaty of Westphalia ends Thirty Years' War
1649 Execution of Charles I of England

c.1600 Baroque c.1750
1618 Thirty Years' War 1648

1650

1652-3, 1665-7, 1672-4 1st, 2nd and 3rd Anglo-Dutch wars
1660 Restoration of English monarchy
1666 Great Fire of London
1671 Spain and United Provinces ally against France
1671 Hungarian Revolt and Reign of Terror
1682 Spain and Holy Roman Empire ally against France
1683 Turks besiege Vienna
1685 Edict of Nantes revoked and Huguenots leave France
1689 English Parliament passes Bill of Rights
1699 Habsburgs recover Hungary from Turks

1700

1700-21 Great Northern War between Sweden and Russia and its allies
1702-1713 War of Spanish Succession (ends with Peace of Utrecht)
1703 St Petersburg founded
1704 "Grand Alliance" of Holland, England and Austria defeat France at Blenheim
1707 Act of Union between England and Scotland
1730 Methodism founded by John and Charles Wesley
1740-86 Prussia under Frederick the Great
1740-8 War of Austrian Succession

c.1700 Rococo c.1750
c.1700 Age of Enlightenment 1789
c.1730 Gothic Revival c.1780

1558-1603 Elizabeth I Queen of England
1564-1616 William Shakespeare
1571-1610 Michelangelo Merisi da Caravaggio
1573-1652 Inigo Jones
1577-1640 Peter Paul Rubens
1581/5-1666 Frans Hals
1594-1665 Nicolas Poussin
1598-1680 Gianlorenzo Bernini
1599-1660 Diego Velazquez
1599-1641 Sir Anthony Van Dyck
1598-1666 François Mansart

Palace of Charles V, Granada, Spain, detail, begun 1526

S. Georgio Maggiore, Venice, Italy, begun 1566

1600-92 Claude Lorraine
1603 *Hamlet* written by Shakespeare
1606-69 Rembrandt van Rijn
1624 Frans Hals paints *The Laughing Cavalier*
1624 Palace of Versailles started
1627-1725 Peter I, the Great, of Russia
1632-75 Jan Vermeer
1632-1723 Sir Christopher Wren
1633 Galileo tried for heresy
1642 Rembrandt paints *The Night Watch*

Mauritzhuis, The Hague, Netherlands, c.1633

1661 Louis XIV takes power in France
1667 John Milton, *Paradise Lost*
1667-70 Main façade of Louvre
1687 Isaac Newton publishes *Principia Mathematica*
1696 Peter I, the Great, becomes Tsar of Russia
1696-1770 Giovanni Battista Tiepolo

S. Carlo alle Quatro Fontane, Rome, Italy, detail, begun 1633

Troja Palace, Prague, Czech Republic, 1679-96

1719 Daniel Defoe, *Robinson Crusoe*
1720 J.S.Bach *Brandenburg Concertos*
1726 Jonathan Swift, *Gulliver's Travels*
1728-92 Robert Adam
1742 Handel's *Messiah*
1746-1828 Goya
1748-1825 Jacques-Louis David
1749-1832 Johann Wolfgang von Goethe

Baroque interior, St John Nepomuk, Munich, Germany 1732-46

Amalienburg Palace, near Munich, Rococo detail and decoration, 1734

1750

1755 Earthquake destroys Lisbon

1756-63 Britain defeats France in Seven Years' War (ends with Treaty of Paris)

1772 Partition of Poland between Austria and Russia

1776 Britain's North American colonies declare indepence (gained 1783)

1783 Montgolfier brothers ascend in hot-air balloon

1789-99 French Revolution

1797 Fall of Venetian Republic to forces of Napoleon

1799 Napoleon Bonaparte seizes power in France

1800

1803-1815 Napoleonic Wars

1805 Battle of Trafalgar

1806 End of Holy Roman Empire

1812 Napoleon invades Russia

1815 Battle of Waterloo

1820-28 War of Greek Independence

c.1825 Joseph Niépce produces first known photograph

1830 July Revolution in France

1830 Independence of Belgium from Netherlands

1845 Irish potato famine

1848 Revolutions all round Europe, particularly France, Germany, Hungary, Italy

1850

1853-6 Crimean War

1860 Garibaldi's Expedition of the Thousand leads to founding of Kingdom of Italy (1861)

1870-1 Franco-Prussian War

1871-1940 Third Republic in France

1885 Karl Benz in Germany builds first car with internal combustion engine

1893 Lumiére brothers invent cinematograph

1897-9 Marconi demonstrates radio communication

1900

1903 Wright brothers make first powered flight

1914-1918 World War I

1917 Russian Revolution

1919 Treaty of Versailles

1922 USSR established

1922 Mussolini in power in Italy

1923 Hitler leads Munich Putsch

1929 Wall Street Crash heralds Great Depression of the 1930s

1933 Hitler becomes Chancellor of Germany

1936-39 Spanish Civil War

1939 Germany invades Poland, provoking World War II

1950

1957 Treaty of Rome establishes European Economic Community (EEC)

1961 Soviet authorities build Berlin Wall

1967 EEC become European Community (EC)

1968 Soviet invasion ends 'Prague Spring'

1989 Berlin Wall dismantled

1992 Maastrict Treaty establishes European Union (EU)

1999 Birth of the Euro

1999 NATO intervenes in Kosovo

c.1730 Gothic Revival **c.1780**

c.1760 Greek Revival **c.1830**

c.1780 Romanticism **c.1850**

c.1750 Neoclassicism **c.1810**

c.1870 Modern art

c.1890 Art Nouveau **1914**

c.1925 Art Deco **1939**

c.1700 Age of Enlightenment **c.1900**

c.1800 Historicism in architecture **c.1900**

from 1863 Modern art

from c.1905 Modernism in architecture

from c.1950 Post-modernism in architecture

c.1760 Industrial Revolution **c.1900**

1789

1867 Austro-Hungarian Empire **1918**

c.1880 Height of European Imperialism **1914**

from c.1910 Abstract art

from c.1960 Conceptual art

Impressionism c.1890

1762-96 Catherine the Great Empress of Russia

1769-1821 Napoleon Bonaparte

1775-1851 JMW Turner

1780-1867 Jean Auguste Dominique Ingres

Kedleston Hall, England, 1757-70

1781 Kant *Critique of Pure Reason*

1798 Wordsworth and Coleridge *Lyrical Ballads*

1799 Beethoven's First Symphony

Pantheon, Paris, France, 1757-80

1821 Constable *The Hay Wain*

1830-40 Helsinki Cathedral

1832-83 Edouard Manet

1834-96 William Morris

1834-1917 Edgar Degas

1839 Dickens *Oliver Twist*

1839-1906 Paul Cezanne

1840-1917 Auguste Rodin

1840-1926 Claude Monet

1841-1919 Pierre Auguste Renoir

1848 Marx and Engels *Communist Manifesto*

Crystal Palace, London England, 1851

1848-55 Pre-Raphaelites (style continues later)

1848-1903 Paul Gauguin

1853 Verdi *La Traviata*

1853-90 Vincent van Gogh

1859 Charles Darwin *The Origin of Species*

1859-91 Georges Seurat

1863 Manet paints *Dejeuner sur l'Herbe*, often regarded as the first modern painting

1863-1944 Edvard Munch

1865-69 Tolstoy *War and Peace*

1867 Marx *Das Kapital*

1869-1954 Henri Matisse

1874 First Impressionist exhibition in Paris

1878-1953 Stalin

1875 Bizet *Carmen*

1898-1976 Alvar Aalto

Votivkirche, Vienna 1856-79

1900 Sigmund Freud *The Interpretation of Dreams*

1902 Edvard Munch *The Scream* exhibited

1904-89 Salvador Dali

1905 Einstein publishes special theory of relativity

Bauhaus, Dessau, Germany, 1925

1907 First cubist exhibition

1913 Stravinsky *The Rite of Spring*

1916 Einstein publishes general theory of relativity

1919 Bauhaus movement founded

Gruntvig Church, Copenhagen, Denmark, 1920-40

1932 Aldous Huxley *Brave New World*

1937 Pablo Picasso *Guernica*

1953 Crick and Watson discover structure of DNA

1905–1989 Samuel Beckett

1936– Vaclav Havel

1959 Günter Grass *The Tin Drum*

1961–70 The Beatles

1997 JK Rowling *Harry Potter and the Philosopher's Stone*

1997 Guggenheim Museum, Bilbao

The Roman empire, AD 100–300
- Imperial frontier AD 106
- Important provincial capital
- Territory occupied after AD 106
- Defence works
- African fortifications
- Main Roman road
- Boundary between the Eastern and Western Empire 3rd century AD
- Legionary base
- Naval base

Europe c.1400
- Boundary of the Holy Roman Empire
- Habsburg territories
- Luxembourg territories
- Crown of Aragon
- Burgundian territories
- Angevin territories
- Union of Kalmar 1397
- Union of Krewo 1385/6
- Ottoman Empire
- Ottoman advance

European alliances 1914
- Triple Alliance
- Triple Entente
- Ally of Central Powers 1914
- Future ally of Central Powers
- Ally of Entente Powers 1914
- Future ally of Entente Powers

European politics and economics

EUROPEAN UNION MEMBERSHIP

1957 Founder members, Belgium, France, Italy, Germany, Luxembourg, Netherlands

1973 Denmark, Ireland, UK

1981 Greece

1986 Portugal, Spain

1990 East Germany, following German reunification

1995 Austria, Finland, Sweden

2004 Czech Republic, Cyprus, Estonia, Hungary, Latvia, Lithuania, Malta, Poland, Slovakia, Slovenia

Future candidates for EU membership

Eurozone countries are outlined in yellow

Albania *Shqipëria*

Area 28,748 sq km (11,100 sq miles)
Population 3,563,112
Capital Tirana / Tiranë (380,400)
Languages Albanian (official), Greek, Vlach, Romani and Slavic
GDP 2005 US$4,900
Currency Lek = 100 Quindars
Government multiparty republic
Head of state President Alfred Moisiu, 2002
Head of government Prime Minister Ali Berisha, Democratic Party, 2005
Website www.parlament.al
Events In the 2005 general elections, the Democratic Party and its allies won a decisive victory on pledges of reducing crime and corruption, promoting economic growth, and decreasing the size of government. The election, and particularly the orderly transition of power, was considered an important step forward.
Economy Although the economy continues to grow, it is still one of the poorest in Europe. It is continuing to work toward joining NATO and the EU. With troops in Iraq and Afghanistan, it has been a strong supporter of the global war on terrorism. 56% of the workforce are engaged in agriculture. Private ownership of land has been encouraged since 1991.

Andorra
Principat d'Andorra

Area 468 sq km (181 sq miles)
Population 70,549
Capital Andorra la Vella (20,300)
Languages Catalan (official), French, Castilian and Portuguese
GDP 2005 US$26,800
Currency Euro = 100 cents
Government independent state and co-principality
Head of state co-princes: Joan Enric Vives Sicilia, Bishop of Urgell, 2003 and Jacques Chirac (see France), 1995
Head of government Chief Executive Albert Pintat, 2005
Website www.andorra.ad
Events In 1993 a new democratic constitution was adopted that reduced the roles of the President of France and the Bishop of Urgell to purely constitutional figureheads.
Economy Tourism accounts for more than 80% of GDP with an estimated 11.6 million visiting annually, attracted by duty-free status and its summer and winter resorts. Agricultural production is limited (2% of the land is arable) and most food has to be imported. The principal livestock activity is sheep raising. Manufacturing output consists mainly of cigarettes, cigars, and furniture.

Austria *Österreich*

Area 83,859 sq km (32,377 sq miles)
Population 8,184,691
Capital Vienna / Wien (1,807,000)
Languages German (official)
GDP 2005 US$32,900
Currency Euro = 100 cents
Government federal republic
Head of state President Heinz Fischer, Social Democrats, 2004
Head of government Federal Chancellor Wolfgang Schüssel, People's Party, 2000
Website www.austria.gv.at
Events In general elections in 1999, the extreme right Freedom Party, under Jörg Haider, made gains at the expense of the Social Democrats. He subsequently resigned as leader. People's Party electoral win in 2002 wasn't sufficient to form a government so a new government coalition was formed with the Freedom Party after failure of talks with the Social Democrats and the Greens. In July 2004 President Fischer's predecessor Thomas Klestil died of a heart attack one day before Heinz Fischer was due to take his place. The Freedom Party split in April 2005 when its former leader Jörg Haider left to set up the Alliance for Austria's Future.
Economy Has a well-developed market economy and high standard of living. The leading economic activity is the manufacture of metals and tourism. Dairy and livestock farming are the principal agricultural activities. To meet increased competition from both EU and Central European countries, particularly the new EU members, Austria will need to continue restructuring, emphasising knowledge-based sectors of the economy and encouraging greater labour flexibility.

Belarus

Area 207,600 sq km (80,154 sq miles)
Population 10,300,483
Capital Minsk (1,717,000)
Languages Belarusian, Russian (both official)
GDP 2005 US$7,600
Currency Belarussian ruble = 100 kopek
Government Republic
Head of state President Alexander Lukashenko, 1994
Head of government Prime Minister Sergei Sidorsky, 2003
Website http://government.by/eng/sovmin/index.htm
Events Belarus attained its independence in 1991. As a result of a referendum in 1996 the president increased his power at the expense of parliament. In 1997, Belarus signed a Union Treaty committing it to political and economic integration with Russia. Since his election in July 1994 as the country's first president, Alexander Lukashenko, has steadily consolidated his power through authoritarian means. Government restrictions on freedom of speech, the press and religion continue.
Economy Belarus continues to receive heavily discounted oil and natural gas from Russia. Agriculture, especially meat and dairy farming, is important.

Belgium *Belgique*

Area 30,528 sq km (11,786 sq miles)
Population 10,364,388
Capital Brussels/Bruxelles (964,000)
Languages Dutch, French, German (all official)
GDP 2005 US$31,800
Currency Euro = 100 cents
Government federal constitutional monarchy
Head of state King Albert II, 1993
Head of government Prime Minister Guy Verhofstadt, Flemish Liberal Democrats, 1999
Website www.belgium.be
Events In 1993 Belgium adopted a federal system of government, each of the regions having its own parliament. The socialist and liberal parties have two

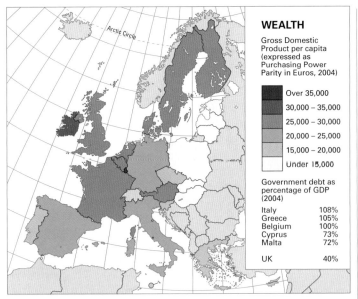

WEALTH

Gross Domestic
Product per capita
(expressed as
Purchasing Power
Parity in Euros, 2004)

Over 35,000
30,000 – 35,000
25,000 – 30,000
20,000 – 25,000
15,000 – 20,000
Under 15,000

Government debt as
percentage of GDP
(2004)

Italy	108%
Greece	105%
Belgium	100%
Cyprus	73%
Malta	72%
UK	40%

thirds of the seats in parliament, each main party is split into two – half for the Flemish and half for the Walloons.
Economy Belgium is a major trading nation with a modern, private-enterprise economy. The leading activity is manufacturing i.e. steel and chemicals. With few natural resources, it imports substantial quantities of raw materials and export a large volume of manufactures. Belgium began circulating the euro currency in January 2002.

Bosnia-Herzegovina
Bosna i Hercegovina

Area 51,197 sq km
(19,767 sq miles)
Population 4,025,476
Capital Sarajevo (737,350)
Languages Bosnian/Croatian/Serbian
GDP 2005 US$2,600
Currency Convertible Marka =
100 convertible pfenniga
Government federal republic
Head of state Chairman of the Presidency Ivo Miro Jovic, Croatian Democratic Union, 2005
Head of government Chairman of the Council of Ministers Adnan Terzic, Muslim Party of Democratic Action, 2002
Website www.fbihvlada.gov.ba
Events In 1992 a referendum approved independence from the Yugoslav federation. The Bosnian Serb population was against independence and in the resulting war occupied over two-thirds of the land. Croat forces seized other parts of the country. The 1995 Dayton Peace Accord ended the war and set up the Bosnian Muslim/Croat Federation and the Bosnian Serb Republic, each with their own president, government, parliament, military and police, there is also a central Bosnian government and rotating presidency the other members of which are Sulejman Tihic (Muslim Party of Democratic Action) and Borislav Paravac (Serb Democratic Party). The office of High Representative has the power to

impose decision where the authorities are unable to agree or where political or economic interests are affected. In 2005, Paddy Ashdown sacked Ivo Jovic's predecessor Dragan Covic. Eufor troops took over from the NATO-led force as peacekeepers in 2004.
Economy Excluding Macedonia, Bosnia was the least developed of the former republics of Yugoslavia. Currently receiving substantial aid, though this will be reduced.

Bulgaria *Bulgariya*

Area 110,912 sq km
(42,822 sq miles)
Population 7,450,349
Capital Sofia (1,187,000)
Languages
Bulgarian (official), Turkish
GDP 2005 US$9,000
Currency Lev = 100 stotinki
Government multiparty republic
Head of state
President Georgi Purvanov, Bulgarian Socialist Party, 2002
Head of government Prime Minister Sergei Stanishev, Bulgarian Socialist Party, 2005
Website www.president.bg/en
Events In 1990 the first non-communist president for 40 years, Zhelyu Zhelev, was elected. A new constitution in 1991 saw the adoption of free-market reforms. Former king Simeon Saxe-Coburg-Gotha was the first ex-monarch in post-communist eastern Europe to return to power. He leads a coalition government, has gained membership of NATO for Bulgaria and signed an accession treaty with the EU in April 2005 allowing for EU membership in 2007 subject to reforms being satisfactory. Parliament voted in early 2005 to withdraw troops from Iraq by the end of 2005. Elections in June 2005 were inclusive. Sergei Stanishev's Socialist Party was originally asked to form a government but after parliament rejected his choice of ministers,

the president asked the NMS to form a coalition.
Economy Bulgaria has experienced macroeconomic stability and strong growth since 1996 when a major economic downturn led to the fall of the then socialist government. Bulgaria has averaged 4% growth since 2000 and has begun to attract significant amounts of foreign direct investment. Manufacturing is the leading economic activity but has outdated technology.
The main products are chemicals, metals, machinery and textiles. The valleys of the Maritsa are ideal for winemaking, plums and tobacco. Tourism is increasing rapidly.

Croatia *Hrvatska*

Area 56,538 sq km
(21,829 sq miles)
Population 4,495,904
Capital Zagreb (1,067,000)
Languages Croatian
GDP 2005 US$11,600
Currency Kuna = 100 lipas
Government
multiparty republic
Head of state
President Stjepan Mesic, 2000
Head of government
Prime Minister Ivo Sanader, Croatian Democratic Union, 2003
Website www.croatia.hr
Events A 1991 referendum voted overwhelmingly in favour of independence. Serb-dominated areas took up arms to remain in the federation. Serbia armed Croatian Serbs, war broke out between Serbia and Croatia, and Croatia lost much territory. In 1992 United Nations peacekeeping troops were deployed. Following the Dayton Peace Accord of 1995, Croatia and Yugoslavia established diplomatic relations. An agreement between the Croatian government and Croatian Serbs provided for the eventual reintegration of Krajina into Croatia in 1998. PM Sanader leads a minority government with the support of many smaller parties. Croatia is a partner-country with NATO and applied for EU membership in 2003. The start-date for accession talks has been postponed because of the lack of progress in arresting some war crimes suspects, particularly Gen Ante Gotvina.
Economy The wars have badly disrupted Croatia's relatively prosperous economy but it emerged from a mild recession in 2000 with tourism, banking, and public investments leading the way. Unemployment remains high, at about 18%, with structural factors slowing its decline. Croatia has a wide range of manufacturing industries, such as steel, chemicals, oil refining, and wood products. Agriculture is the principal employer. Crops include maize, soya beans, sugar beet and wheat.

Czech Republic
Česká Republica

Area 78,864 sq km
(30,449 sq miles)
Population 10,241,138
Capital Prague/Praha (1,203,000)
Languages Czech (official), Moravian
GDP 2005 US$18,100
Currency Czech Koruna = 100 haler
Government multiparty republic
Head of state President Václav Klaus, 2003
Head of government Prime Minister Jiri Paroubek, Czech Social Democratic Party, 2005
Website www.czech.cz
Events In 1992 the government agree to the secession of the Slovak Republic, and on 1 January 1993 the Czech Republic was created. The Czech Republic was granted full membership of NATO in 1999 and joined the EU in May 2004. The opposition Civic Democratic Party, with their agenda of not ceding too much power to the EU, were the winners in the European elections of June 2004, as a result of which Prime Minist Vladimir Spidla resigned, to be replace by Stanislav Gross, who then resigned in April 2005 over a financial scandal. An election to the Chamber of Deputies took place in June 2006, producing an evenly balanced result. Forming a stabl government that will last four years wi be difficult.
Economy The country has deposits of coal, uranium, iron ore, tin and zinc. Industries include chemicals, beer, iron and steel. Private ownership of land is gradually being restored. Agriculture employs 12% of the workforce. Inflation is under control. Privatisation of the state-owned telecommunications firm Cesky Telecom took place in 2005. Intensified restructuring among large enterprises, improvements in the financial sector, and effective use of availabl EU funds should strengthen output growth. Prague is now a major tourist destination.

Denmark *Danmark*

Area 43,094 sq km
(16,638 sq miles)
Population 5,432,335
Capital Copenhagen /
København (1,332,000)
Languages Danish (official)
GDP 2005 US$33,500
Currency Krone = 100 øre
Government parliamentary monarchy
Head of state Queen Margrethe II, 1972
Head of government Prime Minister Anders Fogh Rasmussen, Venstre (Left) Party, 2001
Website www.denmark.dk
Events In 1992 Denmark rejected the Maastricht Treaty, but reversed the

decision in a 1993 referendum. In 1998 the Amsterdam Treaty was ratified by a further referendum. Currency pegged to Euro but still independent. The government is a coalition formed with the Conservative Party. Anti-immigration policies are backed by the well-supported far-right Danish People's Party. The opposition Social Democrats were clear winners in the European elections of June 2004, though this could be down to opposition to the government's support for the war in Iraq, and snap elections in February 2005 gave Rasmussen's Venstre Party a second term in power.

Economy Danes enjoy a high standard of living with a thoroughly modern market economy featuring high-tech agriculture, up-to-date small-scale and corporate industry, comfortable living standards and a stable currency. Economic growth gained momentum in 2004 and the upturn accelerated through 2005. Denmark is self-sufficient in oil and natural gas. Services, including tourism, form the largest sector (63% of GDP). Farming employs only 4% of the workforce but is highly productive. Fishing is also important.

Estonia *Eesti*

Area 45,100 sq km
(17,413 sq miles)
Population 1,332,893
Capital Tallinn (392,000)
Languages Estonian (official), Russian
GDP 2005 US$16,400
Currency Kroon = 100 sents
Government multiparty republic
Head of state President Arnold Rüütel, Estonian People's Union, 2001
Head of government Prime Minister Andrus Ansip, Reform Party 2005
Website www.riik.ee/en
Events In 1992 Estonia adopted a new constitution and multiparty elections were held. Estonia joined NATO in March 2004 and the EU in May 2004. In June 2004 the value of the Kroon was fixed against the Euro with a view to joining in 2007.
Economy Privatisation and free-trade reforms have increased foreign investment and trade with the EU. Chief natural resources are oil shale and forests. The economy benefits from strong electronics and telecommunications sectors. The state budget is essentially in balance and public debt is low. Manufactures include petrochemicals, fertilisers and textiles.

Finland *Suomi*

Area 338,145 sq km
(130,557 sq miles)
Population 5,223,442
Capital Helsinki (558,000)
Languages Finnish, Swedish (both official)
GDP 2005 US$30,300
Currency Euro = 100 cents
Government multiparty republic
Head of state President Tarja Kaarina Halonen, 2000
Head of government Prime Minister Matti Vanhanen, Centre Party, 2003
Website www.government.fi
Events In 1986 Finland became a member of EFTA, and in 1995 joined the EU. A new constitution was established in March 2000. A coalition was set up between the Social Democrats and the Swedish Peoples' Party after a close election result in 2003.
Economy Forests are Finland's most valuable resource, with wood and paper products accounting for 35% of exports. Engineering, shipbuilding and textile industries have grown. Finland excels in high-tech exports and is a leading light in the telecoms industry. Farming employs 9% of the workforce. High unemployment is a persistent problem.

France

Area 551,500 sq km
(212,934 sq miles)
Population 60,656,178
Capital Paris (9,630,000)
Languages French (official), Breton, Occitan
GDP 2005 US$29,900
Currency Euro = 100 cents
Government multiparty republic
Head of state President Jacques Chirac, Assembly for the Republic, 1995
Head of government Prime Minister Dominique de Villepin, Democratie Liberale, 2005
Website www.elysee.fr
Events In 2002 voter apathy led to FN leader Jean-Marie Le Pen reaching second round of voting in presidential elections above Lionel Jospin, who resigned as PM after the presidential elections which Jacques Chirac won with 82% of the vote. As a result of their opposition to the 2003 war in Iraq, France and Germany have forged closer ties while relations with the UK and the US have been put under some strain. The US believes that France is being ungrateful for their assistance in WWII some 60 years before. The resounding 'no' vote in the referendum on the European constitution in May 2005 led both to the resignation of PM Jean-Pierre Raffarin and further decline in the relationship between Jacques Chirac and Tony Blair over the UK's rebate and Common Agricultural Policy subsidies for French farmers. Riots in October and November 2005 led to strong debates about integration and discrimination in France.
Economy France is a leading industrial nation. It is the world's fourth-largest manufacturer of cars. Industries include chemicals and steel. It is the leading producer of farm products in western Europe. Livestock and dairy farming are

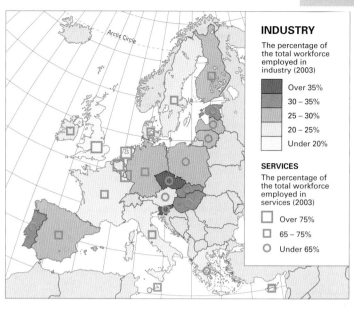

INDUSTRY
The percentage of the total workforce employed in industry (2003)

- Over 35%
- 30 – 35%
- 25 – 30%
- 20 – 25%
- Under 20%

SERVICES
The percentage of the total workforce employed in services (2003)

- Over 75%
- 65 – 75%
- Under 65%

vital sectors. It is the world's second-largest producer of cheese and wine. Tourism is a major industry.

Germany *Deutschland*

Area 357,022 sq km
(137,846 sq miles)
Population 82,431,390
Capital Berlin (3,387,000)
Languages German (official)
GDP 2005 US$29,700
Currency Euro = 100 cents
Government federal multiparty republic
Head of state President Horst Köehler, Christian Democratic Union, 2004
Head of government Chancellor Angela Merkel in coalition with SPD
Website www.deutschland.de
Events Germany is a major supporter of the European Union, and former chancellor Helmut Köhl was the driving force behind the creation of the Euro. During 2002, state elections in the former German Democratic Republic saw massive losses for the Social Democrats. As a result of their opposition to the 2003 war in Iraq Germany and France have forged closer ties. In July 2005, Schröder triggered early general elections, which took place in September 2005. The opposition Christian Democratic Union (CDU) and its sister party, the Christian Social Union (CSU), significantly lost momentum during the campaign and ultimately won only 1% more votes. Exit polls showed clearly that neither coalition group had won a majority of seats. On October 10, 2005, officials indicated that negotiations had concluded successfully and that the participating parties would form a Grand Coalition with Angela Merkel as Chancellor.
Economy Germany is one of the world's greatest economic powers. Services form the largest economic sector. Machinery and transport equipment account for 50% of exports. It is the world's third-largest car producer. Other major products: ships, iron, steel, petroleum, tyres. It has the world's second-largest lignite mining industry. Other minerals: copper, potash, lead, salt, zinc, aluminium. Germany is the world's second-largest producer of hops and beer, and fifth-largest of wine. Other products: cheese and milk, barley, rye, pork.

Greece *Ellas*

Area 131,957 sq km
(50,948 sq miles)
Population 10,668,354
Capital Athens / Athina (3,116,000)
Languages Greek (official)
GDP 2005 US$22,800
Currency Euro = 100 cents
Government multiparty republic
Head of state President Karolos Papoulias, Panhellenic Socialist Movement (PASOK), 2005
Head of government Prime Minister Konstandinos Karamanlis, New Democracy Party, 2004
Website www.greece.gr
Events In 1981 Greece joined the EU and Andreas Papandreou became Greece's first socialist prime minister, 1981-89 and 1993-96. PM Costas Karamanlis is the nephew of former Greek president Constantine Karamanlis. The issue of Cyprus is still contentious in Greece's relations with Turkey, with the southern two-thirds still being Greek Cypriot and no agreement on unification yet reached. In July 2004 Greece unexpectedly won the European football championships. The 28th Olympiad took place in Greece in August 2004. Karolos Papoulias was nominated President by the PM in 2005.
Economy Greece is one of the poorest members of the European Union. Manufacturing is important. Products: textiles, cement, chemicals, metallurgy. Minerals: lignite, bauxite, chromite. Farmland covers 33% of Greece, grazing land 40%.

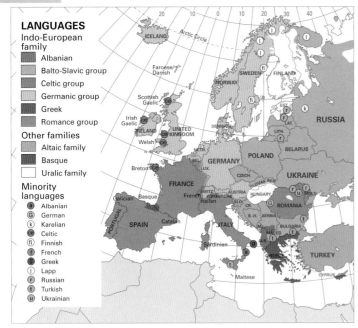

LANGUAGES
Indo-European family
- Albanian
- Balto-Slavic group
- Celtic group
- Germanic group
- Greek
- Romance group

Other families
- Altaic family
- Basque
- Uralic family

Minority languages
- (a) Albanian
- (G) German
- (k) Karelian
- (ce) Celtic
- (fi) Finnish
- (f) French
- (GI) Greek
- (l) Lapp
- (r) Russian
- (t) Turkish
- (u) Ukrainian

Major crops: tobacco, olives, grapes, cotton, wheat. Livestock are raised. Tourism provides 15% of GDP.

Hungary *Magyarorszàg*

Area 93,032 sq km (35,919 sq miles)
Population 10,006,835
Capital Budapest (1,819,000)
Languages Hungarian (official)
GDP 2005 US$15,900
Currency Forint = 100 filler
Government multiparty republic
Head of state President Laszlo Solyom, 2005
Head of government Prime Minister Ferenc Gyurcsany, 2004
Website www.magyarorszag.hu/angol
Events In 1990 multiparty elections were won by the conservative Democratic Forum. In 1999 Hungary joined NATO. Former PM Peter Medgyessy narrowly avoided having to resign in 2002 when he admitted to having worked for the secret services in the late 70s/early 80s, but denied working for the KGB. He oversaw Hungary's accession to the European Union in May 2004 but resigned later in the year after arguments over a cabinet reshuffle with coalition co-members the Free Democrats. Hungary still has problems with discrimination against the Roma community, though in the European elections of 2004 a member of this ethnic group was elected for the first time. Hungary is aiming to adopt the Euro in 2010.
Economy Since the early 1990s, Hungary has adopted market reforms and privatisation programmes. Inflation has declined from 14% in 1998 to 3.7% in 2005. Germany is by far Hungary's largest economic partner. The manufacture of machinery and transport is the most valuable sector. Hungary's resources

include bauxite, coal and natural gas. Major crops include grapes for wine-making, maize, potatoes, sugar beet and wheat. Tourism is a growing sector.

Iceland *Ísland*

Area 103,000 sq km (39,768 sq miles)
Population 296,737
Capital Reykjavik (114,500)
Languages Icelandic
GDP 2005 US$34,600
Currency Krona = 100 aurar
Government multiparty republic
Head of state President Olafur Ragnar Grimsson, 1996
Head of government Prime Minister Halldor Asgrimsson, Progressive Party, 2004
Website http://government.is
Events In 1944, a referendum decisively voted to sever links with Denmark, and Iceland became a fully independent republic. In 1946 it joined NATO. The USA maintained military bases on Iceland after WWII. In 1970 Iceland joined the European Free Trade Association. The extension of Iceland's fishing limits in 1958 and 1972 precipitated the "Cod War" with the UK. In 1977, the UK agreed not to fish within Iceland's 370km fishing limits. The continuing US military presence remains a political issue. David Oddson leader of the Independence Party stood down as PM in September 2004 and the leader of coalition partner the Progressive Party Halldor Asgrimsson took over the premiership.
Economy The economy remains sensitive to declining fish stocks as well as to fluctuations in world prices for its main exports: fish and fish products, aluminum, and ferrosilicon. There is low unemployment, and remarkably even distribution of income.

Ireland, Republic of *Eire*

Area 70,273 sq km (27,132 sq miles)
Population 4,015,676
Capital Dublin (985,000)
Languages Irish, English (both official)
GDP 2005 US$34,100
Currency Euro = 100 cents
Government multiparty republic
Head of state President Mary McAleese, 1997
Head of government Taoiseach Bertie Ahern, Fianna Fáil, 1997
Website www.irlgov.ie
Events In 1948 Ireland withdrew from the British Commonwealth and joined the European Community in 1973. The Anglo-Irish Agreement (1985) gave Ireland a consultative role in the affairs of Northern Ireland. Following a 1995 referendum, divorce was legalised. Abortion remains a contentious political issue. In 1997 elections Bertie Ahern became taoiseach and Mary McAleese became president. In the Good Friday Agreement of 1998 the Irish Republic gave up its constitutional claim to Northern Ireland and a North-South Ministerial Council was established. Sinn Fein got its first seats in the European elections of June 2004.
Economy Ireland has benefited greatly from its membership of the European Union. It joined in circulating the euro in 2002. Grants have enabled the modernisation of farming, which employs 14% of the workforce. Major products include cereals, cattle and dairy products, sheep, sugar beet and potatoes. Fishing is important. Traditional sectors, such as brewing, distilling and textiles, have been supplemented by high-tech industries, such as electronics. Tourism is the most important component of the service industry. The economy has also benefited from a rise in consumer spending, construction, and business investment.

Italy *Italia*

Area 301,318 sq km (116,338 sq miles)
Population 58,103,033
Capital Rome / Roma (2,649,000)
Languages Italian (official)
GDP 2005 US$28,300
Currency Euro = 100 cents
Government social democracy
Head of state President Giorgio Napolitano, 2006
Head of government Romano Prodi, L'Unione, 2006
Website www.enit.it
Events In the 2006 general election, prime minister Silvio Berlusconi, leader of the centre-right House of Freedoms, was closely defeated by Romano Prodi, leader of the centre-left The Union. Prodi declared victory on 11 April. Berlusconi

was Italy's longest serving premier in half a century. The mandate of President Ciampi came to an end in May 2006, he declined to run again. Giorgio Napolitano was elected and his term officially started with a swearing-in ceremony on 15 May.
Economy Italy's main industrial region is the north-western triangle of Milan, Turin and Genoa. It is the world's eighth-largest car and steel producer. Machinery and transport equipment account for 37% of exports. Agricultural production is important. Italy is the world's largest producer of wine. Tourism is a vital economic sector. The economy experienced almost no growth in 2005 and unemployment remained at a high level.

Latvia *Latvija*

Area 64,589 sq km (24,942 sq miles)
Population 2,290,237
Capital Riga (811,000)
Languages Latvian (official), Russian
GDP 2005 US$12,800
Currency Lats = 100 santims
Government multiparty republic
Head of state President Vaira Vike-Freiberga, 1999
Head of government Prime Minister Aigars Kalvitis, People's Party, 2004
Website www.lv
Events In 1993 Latvia held its first multiparty elections. President Vaira Vike-Freiberga was re-elected for a second four-year term in June 2003. Latvia became a member of NATO and the EU in spring 2004. People applying for citizenship are now required to pass a Latvian language test, which has caused much upset amongst the one third of the population who are Russian speakers. As a result many are without citizenship, much like their compatriots in Estonia. PM Indulis Emsis was chosen as a result of the resignation of his predecessor just before Latvia's accession to the EU. After the resignation of the ruling minority coalition in October 2004 following rejection of Indulis Emsis' budget for 2005, a new 4-party coalition was approved by parliament in December.
Economy Latvia is a lower-middle-income country. The country has to import many of the materials needed for manufacturing. Latvia produces only 10% of the electricity it needs, and the rest has to be imported from Belarus, Russia and Ukraine. Manufactures include electronic goods, farm machinery and fertiliser. Farm exports include beef, dairy products and pork. The majority of companies, banks, and real estate have been privatised.

Liechtenstein

Area 157 sq km
(61 sq miles)
Population 33,717
Capital Vaduz (5,200)
Languages German (official)
GDP 2005 US$25,000
Currency Swiss franc = 100 centimes
Government independent principality
Head of state Prince Alois, 2004
Head of government Prime Minister Ottmar Hasler, Progressive Citizens Party, 2001
Website www.liechtenstein.li/en
Events Women finally got the vote in 1984. The principality joined the UN in 1990. In 2003 the people voted in a referendum to give Prince Hans Adam II new political powers, rendering the country Europe's only absolute monarchy with the prince having power of veto over the government. Its status as a tax haven has been criticised as it has been alleged that many billions are laundered there each year. The law has been reformed to ensure that anonymity is no longer permitted when opening a bank account. In August 2004 Prince Hans Adam II transferred the day-to-day running of the country to his son Prince Alois, though he did not abdicate and remains titular head of state. Following elections in 2005, the government is made up of 3 ministers from the Progressive Citizens Party and 2 from the People's Union.
Economy Liechtenstein is the fourth-smallest country in the world and one of the richest per capita. Since 1945 it has rapidly developed a specialised manufacturing base. It imports more than 90% of its energy requirements. The economy is widely diversified with a large number of small businesses. Tourism is increasingly important.

Lithuania *Lietuva*

Area 65,200 sq km
(25,173 sq miles)
Population 3,596,617
Capital Vilnius (542,000)
Languages Lithuanian (official), Russian, Polish
GDP 2005 US$13,700
Currency Litas = 100 centai
Government multiparty republic
Head of state President Valdas Adamkus, 2004
Head of government Premier Algirdas Mykolas Brazauskas, Social Democratic Party, 2001
Website www.lithuania.lt
Events The Soviet Union recognised Lithuania as independent in September 1991. Valdas Adamkus regained the presidency from Rolandus Paksas after the latter was impeached in April 2004 after being found guilty of leaking classified material and unlawfully granting citizenship to a Russian businessman who had funded his election campaign. His successor was also his predecessor. Lithuania joined NATO in March 2004 and the EU in May 2004. In June 2004 Lithuania fixed the value of the Litas against the Euro with a view to joining in 2007.
Economy Lithuania is dependent on Russian raw materials. Manufacturing is the most valuable export sector and major products include chemicals, electronic goods and machine tools. Dairy and meat farming and fishing are also important activities. More than 80% of enterprises have been privatised.

Luxembourg

Area 2,586 sq km
(998 sq miles)
Population 468,571
Capital Luxembourg (76,300)
Languages Luxembourgian / Letzeburgish (official), French, German
GDP 2005 US$62,700
Currency Euro = 100 cents
Government constitutional monarchy (or grand duchy)
Head of state Grand Duke Henri, 2000
Head of government Prime Minister Jean-Claude Juncker, Christian Social People's Party, 1995
Website www.luxembourg.lu/en
Events Following 1994 elections, the Christian Social People's Party (CD) and the Luxembourg Socialist Workers' Party (SOC) formed a coalition government, which lasted until 1999 and was followed by a 5-year coalition with the Democratic Party. Grand Duke Jean abdicated in favour of his son Prince Henri in October 2000. In general elections in 2004, the CD held on to power, again in coalition with the SOC. In 2005 the people voted for the European constitution.
Economy It has a stable, high-income economy, benefiting from its proximity to France, Germany and Belgium. The city of Luxembourg is a major centre of European administration and finance. Its strict laws on secrecy in banking have meant that tax evasion and fraud are prevalent. There are rich deposits of iron ore, and is a major producer of iron and steel. Other industries include chemicals, textiles, tourism, banking and electronics.

Former Yugoslav Republic of Macedonia *Makedonija*

Area 25,713 sq km
(9,927 sq miles)
Population 2,045,262
Capital Skoplje (477,400)
Languages Macedonian (official), Albanian
GDP 2005 US$7,400
Currency Denar = 100 deni
Government multiparty republic
Head of state President Branko Crvenkovski, Social Democrat Union, 2004
Head of government Vlado Buckovski, Social Democrats, 2004
Website www.vlada.mk
Events In 1993 the UN accepted the new republic as a member. Still retains the FYR prefix due to Greek fears that the name implies territorial ambitions towards the Greek region named Macedonia. President Branko Crvenovski was elected in April 2004 as a result of the death in a plane crash of Boris Trajkovski. He aims to continue the improvement of the country with EU membership as the goal. The government is a coalition of Social Democrat Union and Democratic Union for Integration (Albanian community). In August 2004, proposed expansion of rights and local autonomy for Albanians provoked riots by Macedonian nationalists, but the ensuing referendum was rendered invalid by a low turnout and the measures went through.
Economy Macedonia is a developing country. The poorest of the six former republics of Yugoslavia, its economy was devastated by UN trade damaged by sanctions against Yugoslavia and by the Greek embargo. The GDP is increasing each year and successful privatisation in 2000 boosted the country's reserves to over $700 Million. Manufactures, especially metals, dominate exports. Agriculture employs 17% of the workforce. Major crops include cotton, fruits, maize, tobacco and wheat.

Malta

Area 316 sq km
(122 sq miles)
Population 398,534
Capital Valetta (6,700)
Languages Maltese, English (both official)
GDP 2005 US$18,800
Currency Maltese lira = 100 cents
Government multiparty republic
Head of state President Edward Fenech Adami, Christian Democratic Nationalist Party, 2004
Head of government Prime Minister Lawrence Gonzi, Christian Democratic Nationalist Party, 2004
Website www.gov.mt
Events In 1990 Malta applied to join the EU. In 1997 the newly elected Malta Labour Party pledged to rescind the application. The Christian Democratic Nationalist Party, led by the pro-European Edward Fenech Adami, regained power in 1998 elections. Malta joined the EU in May 2004.
Economy Malta produces only about 20% of its food needs, has limited fresh water supplies and has few domestic energy sources. Machinery and transport equipment account for more than 50% of exports. Malta's historic naval dockyards are now used for commercial shipbuilding and repair. Manufactures include chemicals, electronic equipment and textiles. The largest sector is services, especially tourism. Privatisation of state-controlled companies and liberalisation of markets is still a contentious issue.

Moldova

Area 33,851 sq km
(13,069 sq miles)
Population 4,455,421
Capital Chisinau (623,600)
Languages Moldovan / Romanian (official)
GDP 2005 US$2,100
Currency Leu = 100 bani
Government multiparty republic
Head of state President Vladimir Voronin, Communist Party, 2001

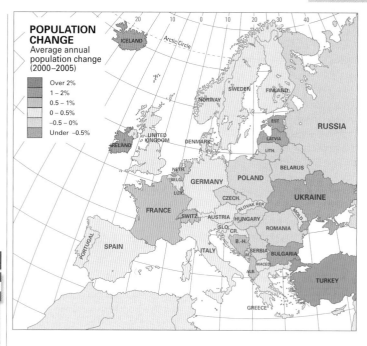

POPULATION CHANGE
Average annual population change (2000–2005)

- Over 2%
- 1 – 2%
- 0.5 – 1%
- 0 – 0.5%
- –0.5 – 0%
- Under –0.5%

Head of government Prime Minister Vasile Tarlev, Communist Party, 2001

Website www.parliament.md/en.html

Events In 1994 a referendum rejected reunification with Romania and Parliament voted to join the CIS. A new constitution established a presidential parliamentary republic. In 2001 Vladimir Voronin was elected president - the first former Soviet state to elect a Communist as its president. The Transnistria region mainly inhabited by Russian and Ukrainian speakers declared independence from Moldova in 1990 fearing the impact of closer ties with Romania, this independence has never been recognised. Relations with Moscow have cooled in the last few years and Voronin is now actively seeking ties with the west.

Economy There is a favourable climate and good farmland but no major mineral deposits. Agriculture is important and major products include fruits and grapes for wine-making. Farmers also raise livestock, including dairy cattle and pigs. Moldova has to import materials and fuels for its industries. Exports include food, wine, tobacco and textiles. The economy remains vulnerable to higher fuel prices and poor agricultural weather.

Monaco

Area 1.5 sq km (0.6 sq miles)
Population 32,409
Capital Monaco-Ville (970)
Languages French (official), Italian, Monegasque
GDP 2005 US$27,000
Currency Euro = 100 cents
Government principality
Head of state Prince Albert II, 2005
Head of government
Minister of State Jean-Paul Proust, 2005
Website www.monaco.gouv.mc

Events Monaco has been ruled by the Grimaldi family since the end of the 13th century and been under the protection of France since 1860.

Economy The chief source of income is tourism. The state retains monopolies in tobacco, the telephone network and the postal service. There is some light industry, including printing, textiles and postage stamps. Also a major banking centre, residents live tax free. The state has been accused of tolerating money laundering.

Montenegro *Crna Gora*

Area 13,812 sq km (5,333 sq miles)
Population 680,158
Capital Podgorica (160,100)
Languages Serbian (of the Ijekavian dialect)
GDP 2005 US$3,100
Currency Euro = 100 cents
Government federal republic

Head of state President of Montenegro Filip Vujanovic, 2003

Head of government Prime Minister Milo Djukanovic, Democratic Party of Socialists, 2002

Website www.montenegro.yu

Events In 1992 Montenegro went into federation with Serbia, first as Federal Republic of Yugoslavia, then as a looser State Union of Serbia and Montenegro. Montenegro formed its own economic policy and adopted the Deutschmark as its currency in 1999. It currently uses the euro, though it is not formally part of the Eurozone. In 2002, Serbia and Montenegro came to a new agreement regarding continued cooperation. On 21 May 2006, the status of the union was decided as 55.54% of voters voted for independence of Montenegro, narrowly passing the 55% threshold needed to validate the referendum under rules set by the EU. On 3 June 2006 the Parliament of Montenegro declared independence, formally confirming the result of the referendum on independence. Montenegro has begun the process of seeking international recognition as well as a seat at international organisations.

Economy A rapid period of urbanisation and industrialisation was created within the communism era of Montenegro. During 1993, two thirds of the Montenegrin population lived below the poverty line. Financial losses under the effects of the UN sanctions on the economy of Montenegro are estimated to be $6.39 billion - the second highest hyperinflation in the history of humankind. Today there is faster and more efficient privatisation, introduction of VAT and usage of the euro.

The Netherlands *Nederland*

Area 41,526 sq km (16,033 sq miles)
Population 16,407,491
Capital Amsterdam (1,105,000); administrative capital 's-Gravenhage (The Hague) (440,000)
Languages Dutch (official), Frisian
GDP 2005 US$30,500
Currency Euro = 100 cents
Government constitutional monarchy
Head of state Queen Beatrix, 1980
Head of government
Prime Minister Jan Peter Balkenende, Christian Democrats, 2002
Website www.holland.com

Events A founding member of NATO and the EU. In 2002 Pim Fortuyn, leader of right wing anti-immigrant party Lijst Pim Fortuyn was assassinated. Subsequently Wim Kok lost power to Jan Peter Balkenende who formed a coalition cabinet with the Democrats-66 and VVD (Peoples' Party for Freedom and Democracy). Like the French, the Dutch voters rejected the proposed European constitution in 2005.

Economy The Netherlands has prospered through its close European ties. Private enterprise has successfully combined with progressive social policies. It is highly industrialised. Products include aircraft, chemicals, electronics and machinery. Agriculture is intensive and mechanised, employing only 5% of the workforce. Dairy farming is the leading agricultural activity. It continues to be one of the leading European nations for attracting foreign direct investment.

Norway *Norge*

Area 323,877 sq km (125,049 sq miles)
Population 4,593,041
Capital Oslo (779,000)
Languages Norwegian (official), Lappish, Finnish
GDP 2005 US$42,400
Currency Krone = 100 øre
Government constitutional monarchy
Head of state King Harald V, 1991
Head of government
Prime Minister Jens Stoltenberg, Labour, 2005
Website www.norge.no

Events In referenda in 1972 and 1994 Norway rejected joining the EU. A centre-left coalition, the Labour-led 'Red-Green Alliance' won closely contested elections in September 2005.

Economy Norway has one of the world's highest standards of living. Discovery of oil and gas in adjacent waters in the late 1960s boosted its economic fortunes, with its chief exports now oil and natural gas. Per capita, it is the world's largest producer of hydroelectricity. It is possible oil and gas will begin to run out in Norway in the next two decades but it has been saving its oil budget surpluses and is invested abroad in a fund, now valued at more than $150 billion. Major manufactures include petroleum products, chemicals, aluminium, wood pulp and paper. The chief farming activities are dairy and meat production, but Norway has to import food.

Poland *Polska*

Area 323,250 sq km (124,807 sq miles)
Population 38,635,144
Capital Warsaw / Warszawa (1,626,000)
Languages Polish (official)
GDP 2005 US$12,700
Currency Zloty = 100 groszy
Government multiparty republic
Head of state President Lech Kaczynski, Law and Justice (PiS), 2005
Head of government Prime Minister Kazimierz Marcinkiewicz, Law and Justice (PiS), 2005
Website www.poland.pl

Events In 1996 Poland joined the Organisation for Economic Cooperation and Development. Poland joined NATO in 1999 and the EU in May 2004. The 2005 elections brought in President Kaczynski of the right-wing Law and Justice party – the party was established in 2001 by the Kaczynski twins. Poland sent about 2,000 troops to Iraq in support of the US, the new President stating these troops could continue their mission in Iraq beyond the current timetable.

Economy Of the workforce, 27% is employed in agriculture and 37% in industry. The GDP per capita roughly equals that of the three Baltic states. Poland is the world's fifth-largest producer of lignite and ships. Copper ore is also a vital resource. Manufacturing accounts for 24% of exports. Agriculture remains important. Major crops include barley, potatoes and wheat. Economic growth is slowly returning.

Portugal

Area 88,797 sq km (34,284 sq miles)
Population 10,566,212
Capital Lisbon / Lisboa (3,861,000)
Languages Portuguese (official)
GDP 2005 US$18,400
Currency Euro = 100 cents
Government multiparty republic
Head of state President Jorge Sampaio, Socialist Party, 1996
Head of government Jose Socrates, Socialist Party, 2005
Website www.portugal.gov.pt

Events In 1986 Portugal joined the EU. In 2002 the Social Democrat Party won the election and formed a coalition government with the Popular Party. The opposition Socialist Party were clear victors in European elections of June 2004, a result attributed in part to the ruling party's support for the war in Iraq. Portugal hosted the Euro 2004 football championships. PM Barroso was chosen as president of EU Commission in July 2004 and consequently resigned his premiership. President Sampaio chose Lisbon mayor Pedro Santana Lopes to succeed him. The leader of the Socialists Eduardo Ferro Rodrigues then resigned in protest saying Sampaio should have ordered elections. In the general election in February 2005, the Socialists won an outright majority under their new leader Jose Socrates.

Economy Portugal's commitment to the EU has seen the economy emerge from recession, but a poor educational system, in particular, has been an obstacle to greater productivity and growth. Manufacturing accounts for 33% of exports. Textiles, footwear and clothing are major exports. Portugal is the world's fifth-largest producer of tungsten and eighth-largest producer of wine. Olives, potatoes and wheat are also grown. Tourism is very important.

omania

ea 238,391 sq km
2,042 sq miles)
pulation 22,329,977
apital Bucharest / Bucuresti
,001,000)
nguages Romanian (official), Hun-
rian
DP 2005 U$8,300
rrency Romanian leu = 100 bani
overnment multiparty republic
ead of state President Traian Basescu,
04
ead of government Calin Popescu-
riceanu, 2004
ebsite www.gov.ro/engleza
ents A new constitution was intro-
ced in 1991. Ion Iliescu, a former com-
unist official, was re-elected in 2000,
t barred from standing again in 2004,
en he was replaced by Traian Basescu.
riceanu's government is a centrist
alition. Romania joined NATO in
arch 2004 and signed its EU accession
eaty in April 2005 and could become a
ember in 2007/08, depending on the
ce of reform. The Romany minority still
ffers from discrimination.
onomy In 2005, confidence in the
onomic process was emphasised
enthe government re-valued its cur-
ncy, making 10,000 'old' Lei equal to
new' Lei.

ussia *Rossiya*

ea 17,075,000 sq km
592,800 sq miles)
pulation 143,420,309
apital Moscow / Moskva (8,367,000)
nguages Russian (official),
d many others
DP 2005 US$10,700
rrency Russian ruble = 100 kopeks
vernment federal multiparty repub-

ad of state
esident Vladimir Putin, 2000
ead of government Premier Mikail
dkov, 2004
ebsite www.president.kremlin.ru/eng/
ents In 1992 the Russian Federation
came a co-founder of the CIS (Com-
onwealth of Independent States). A
w Federal Treaty was signed between
e central government and the autono-
ous republics within the Russian Fed-
ation, Chechnya refused to sign and
clared independence. In December
93 a new democratic constitution
is adopted. From 1994 to 1996, Rus-
 fought a costly civil war in Chechnya
ich flared up again in 1999. Tycoons
o have capitalised on the change
a capitalist system find themselves
der criminal investigation. Putin
elected March 2004, much criticism
the west of media bias towards him
t left opponents little opportunity to
adcast their views, this also applied

to parliamentary elections of December
2003. Putin has a very high level of control over parliament and appointed the
PM Fradkov. The only privately owned
national television station was closed in
2003. Moscow-backed Chechen president Kadryov assassinated in May 2004.
In September 2004 Chechen separatists
stormed a school in North Ossetia taking
over 1000 children and adults hostage.
Hundreds died when bombs were set off
and a gun battle ensued.
Economy In 1993 mass privatisation
began. By 1996, 80% of the Russian
economy was in private hands. A major
problem remains the size of Russia's foreign debt. It is reliant on world oil prices
to keep its economy from crashing.
Industry employs 46% of the workforce
and contributes 48% of GDP. Mining is
the most valuable activity. Russia is the
world's leading producer of natural gas
and nickel, the second largest producer
of aluminium and phosphates. and the
third-largest of crude oil, lignite and
brown coal. Most farmland is still gov-
ernment-owned or run as collectives,
with important products barley, oats, rye,
potatoes, beef and veal.

San Marino

Area 61 sq km (24 sq miles)
Population 28,880
Capital San Marino (4,600)
Languages Italian (official)
GDP 2005 US$34,600
Currency Euro = 100 cents
Government multiparty republic
Head of state co-Chiefs of State: Cap-
tain Regent Gian Franco Terenzi and
Captain Regent Loris Francini
Head of government Secretary of
State for Foreign and Political Affairs
Fabio Berardi, 2003
Website www.omniway.sm
Events World's smallest republic and
perhaps Europe's oldest state, San
Marino's links with Italy led to the adop-
tion of the Euro. Its 60-member Great
and General Council is elected every
five years and headed by two captains-
regent, who are elected by the council
every six months.
Economy The economy is largely agricultural. Tourism is vital to the state's
income, contributing over 50% of GDP.
Also a tax haven used by many non-
residents.

Serbia *Srbija*

Area 88,412 sq km
(34,137 sq miles)
Population 9,981,929
Capital Belgrade / Beograd (1,113,500)
Languages Serbian
GDP 2005 US$3,200
Currency Dinar = 100 paras
Government federal republic
Head of state President of Serbia Boris
Tadic, Democratic Party, 2004

Head of government Prime Minister
Vojislav Kostunica, Democratic Party,
2004
Website www.serbia-tourism.org
Events In 1989 Slobodan Milosevic
became president of Serbia and called
for the creation of a "Greater Serbia".
Serbian attempts to dominate the Yugoslav federation led to the secession of
Slovenia and Croatia in 1991 and to Bos-
nia-Herzegovina's declaration of independence in March 1992. Serbian aid to
the Bosnian Serb campaign of "ethnic
cleansing" in the civil war in Bosnia led
the UN to impose sanctions on Serbia. In
1995 Milosevic signed the Dayton Peace
Accord, which ended the Bosnian war.
In 1997 Milosevic became president of
Yugoslavia. In 1999, following the forced
expulsion of Albanians from Kosovo,
NATO bombed Yugoslavia, forcing with-
drawal of Serbian forces from Kosovo.
Kostunica won the elections of September 2000, but Milosevic refused to hand
over power. After a week of civil unrest
and increased support for Kostunica,
Milosevic was finally ousted. From 2003
to 2006, Serbia was part of the State
Union of Serbia and Montenegro. On 21
May 2006 Montenegro held a referendum to determine whether to terminate
its union with Serbia. On 22 May state-
certified results showed voters favouring
independence. On 3 June, the Parliament
of Montenegro declared Montenegro
independent of the State Union, and on
5 June the National Assembly of Serbia
declared Serbia the successor to the
State Union.
Economy The lower-middle income
economy was devastated by war and
economic sanctions. Industrial production collapsed. Natural resources include
bauxite, coal and copper. There is some
oil and natural gas. Manufacturing
includes aluminium, cars, machinery,
plastics, steel and textiles. Agriculture is
important.

Slovakia
Slovenska Republika

Area 49,012 sq km
(18,923 sq miles)
Population 5,431,363
Capital Bratislava (422,400)
Languages Slovak (official), Hungarian
GDP 2005 US$15,700
Currency Koruna = 100 halierov
Government multiparty republic
Head of state President Ivan
Gasparovic, 2004
Head of government Prime Minister
Mikulás Dzurinda, Democratic & Chris-
tian Union, 1998
Website www.slovakia.org
Events Slovakia joined NATO in March
2004 and the EU in May 2004. There is
still a problem with the Romany popula-
tion being deprived. The 17% turn-out

for the European elections in June 2004
was the lowest of all 25 members.
Economy The transition from communism to private ownership has been
painful with industrial output falling,
unemployment and inflation rising. In
1995 the privatisation programme was
suspended but major privatisations are
nearly now complete with the banking
sector almost completely in foreign
hands. Manufacturing employs 33% of
the workforce. Bratislava and Košice are
the chief industrial cities. Major products
include ceramics, machinery and steel.
Farming employs 12% of the workforce.
Crops include barley and grapes. Tourism
is growing.

Slovenia *Slovenija*

Area 20,256 sq km
(7,820 sq miles)
Population 2,011,070
Capital Ljubljana (254,100)
Languages Slovene
GDP 2005 US$20,900
Currency Tolar = 100 stotin
Government multiparty republic
Head of state President Janez
Drnovsek, Liberal Democrats of Slovenia,
2002
Head of government Prime Minister
Janez Jansa, Slovenian Democratic Party,
2004
Website www.gov.si
Events In 1990 Slovenia declared itself
independent, which led to brief fighting
between Slovenes and the federal army.
In 1992 the EU recognised Slovenia's
independence. Janez Drnovsek was
elected president in December 2002 and
immediately stepped down as prime
minister. Slovenia joined NATO in March
2004 and the EU in May 2004. In June
2004 the value of the Tolar was fixed
against the Euro with a view to joining in
2007. Their reputation as a liberal nation
has been somewhat scarred by the
recent referendum overturning a parliamentary bill that restored citizenship of
Slovenia to resident nationals of other
former Yugoslav countries. The 2004
general election resulted in a coalition
government of the Slovenian Democratic
Party, New Slovenia, the People's Party
and the Democratic Party of Pensioners.
Economy The transformation of a cen-
trally planned economy and the fighting
in other parts of former Yugoslavia have
caused problems for Slovenia. Manufacturing is the leading activity. Major manufactures include chemicals, machinery,
transport equipment, metal goods and
textiles. Major crops include maize, fruit,
potatoes and wheat.

Spain *España*

Area 497,548 sq km
(192,103 sq miles)
Population 40,341,462
Capital Madrid (3,017,000)
Languages Castilian Spanish (official),
Catalan, Galician, Basque
GDP 2005 US$25,100
Currency Euro = 100 cents
Government constitutional monarchy
Head of state King Juan Carlos, 1975
Head of government Prime Minister
Jose Luis Rodriguez Zapatero, Socialist
Party, 2004
Website www.la-moncloa.es
Events From 1959 the militant Basque
organization ETA waged a campaign
of terror but announced a ceasefire in
1998. Basque separatist party Batasuna
was permanently banned in 2003 as
it is thought to be the political wing
of ETA. In March 2004 terrorist bombs
exploded in Madrid killing 191 people,
this was deemed to be the work of al
Qaeda, though the then government
were keen to persuade the people that it
was the work of ETA. The country went
to the polls three days later and voted
Aznar out, largely seen as a reaction
to his support of the US in Iraq and the
sending of troops which was to blame
for the bombing some three days earlier.
The new PM subsequently withdrew all
troops from Iraq. Although the ruling
Socialist Party are short of a majority,
Zapatero has pledged to govern through
dialogue with others rather than form
a coalition. In a referendum in 2005,
Spanish voters voted for the proposed
European constitution.
Economy Spain has rapidly transformed
from a largely poor, agrarian society into
a prosperous industrial nation. Agriculture now employs only 10% of the workforce. Spain is the world's third-largest
wine producer. Other crops include citrus
fruits, tomatoes and olives. Industries:
cars, ships, chemicals, electronics, metal
goods, steel, textiles.

Sweden *Sverige*

Area 449,964 sq km
(173,731 sq miles)
Population 9,001,774
Capital Stockholm (1,612,000)
Languages Swedish (official), Finnish
GDP 2005 US$29,600
Currency Swedish krona = 100 ore
Government constitutional monarchy
Head of state King Carl XVI Gustaf,
1973
Head of government Prime Minister
Göran Persson, Social Democratic Work-
ers' Party (SSA), 1996
Website www.sweden.gov.se
Events In 1995 Sweden joined the
European Union. The cost of maintain-
ing Sweden's extensive welfare services
has become a major political issue. In

September 2003 Sweden was shocked
by the murder of popular minister Anna
Lindh (a pro-Euro campaigner), reignit-
ing discussion over the relaxed attitude
to security. Days later Sweden said no to
the Euro. Brand new Euro-sceptic party
Junilistan came third in the European
elections, exceeding all expectations
and underlining Swedish ambivalence
towards Europe.
Economy Sweden is a highly developed
industrial country. It has rich iron ore
deposits. Privately owned firms account
for about 90% of industrial output. Steel
is a major product, used to manufacture
aircraft, cars, machinery and ships. For-
estry and fishing are important. Agriculture accounts for only 2% of GDP and of
jobs. The Swedish central bank focuses
on price stability with its inflation target
of 2%.

Switzerland *Schweiz*

Area 41,284 sq km
(15,939 sq miles)
Population 7,489,370
Capital Bern (120,500)
Languages French, German, Italian,
Romansch (all official)
GDP 2005 US$35,000
Currency Swiss Franc = 100 centimes
Government federal republic
Head of state President Samuel
Schmid, 2005
Website www.gov.ch
Events Priding itself on their neutral-
ity, Swiss voters rejected membership
of the UN in 1986 and the EU in 1992
and 2001. However, Switzerland finally
became a partner country of NATO in
1997 and joined the UN in 2002. The
federal council is made up of seven federal ministers from whom the president
is chosen on an annual basis. Prior to
2003 the allocation of posts was fixed
between Free Democrats (2), Social
Democrats (2), Christian Democrats (2)
and Swiss People's Party (SVP) (1), however this changed after the elections of
2003 when the SVP increased their share
of the vote to 28%, thereby becoming
the largest party. The allocation was subsequently changed (after much debate)
with the SVP taking an extra seat and
the Christian Democrats losing one.
Economy Switzerland is wealthy and a
stable modern market economy with low
unemployment. Manufactures include
chemicals, electrical equipment, machinery, precision instruments, watches and
textiles. Livestock raising, notably dairy
farming, is the chief agricultural activity.
Tourism is important, and Swiss banks
remain a safehaven for investors.

Turkey *Türkiye*

Area 774,815 sq km
(299,156 sq miles)
Population 69,660,559
Capital Ankara (3,203,000)

Languages Turkish (official), Kurdish
GDP 2005 US$7,900
Currency New Turkish lira = 100 kurus
Government multiparty republic
Head of state President Ahmet Necdet
Sezer, 2000
Head of government Prime Minister
Recep Tayyip Erdogan, Justice and Development Party (AK), 2003
Website www.tourismturkey.org
Events The president is interested in
greater freedom of expression. The PM is
leader of the Islamist Justice & Development Party, though claims to be commit-
ted to secularism.
Economy Turkey is a lower-middle
income developing country. Agriculture
employs 47% of the workforce. Turkey is
a leading producer of citrus fruits, barley,
cotton, wheat, tobacco and tea. It is a
major producer of chromium and phos-
phate fertilisers. Tourism is a vital source
of foreign exchange. In January 2005,
the New Turkish lira was introduced
at a rate of 1 to 1,000,000 old Turkish
lira. Privatisation sales are currently
approaching $21 billion.

Ukraine *Ukraina*

Area 603,700 sq km
(233,088 sq miles)
Population 47,425,336
Capital Kiev / Kyviv (2,621,000)
Languages
Ukrainian (official), Russian
GDP 2005 US$6,800
Currency Hryvnia = 100 kopiykas
Government multiparty republic
Head of state
President Viktor Yushchenko, 2005
Head of government Prime Minister
Yuriy Yekhanurov, 2005
Website www.mfa.gov.ua/mfa/en
Events The Chernobyl disaster of 1986
contaminated large areas of Ukraine.
Final independence was achieved in
1991 with the dissolution of the USSR.
Leonid Kuchma was elected president
in 1994. He continued the policy of
establishing closer ties with the West
and sped up the pace of privatisation.
Ukraine is pushing for membership
of NATO though reforms are required
before this can happen. The election of
November 2004 was thrown into turmoil
after opposition presidential candidate
Yushchenko was poisoned with dioxins
and the result was declared as a victory
for former PM, and pro-Russian, Viktor
Yanukovich leading to accusations of
electoral fraud and widespread dem-
onstrations. After 10 days the Supreme
Court declared the vote invalid and the
elections were re-run, resulting in victory
for the pro-west Yushchenko. In September 2005, bitter in-fighting, widespread
accusations of corruption and lack of
progress on economic reform led Mr
Yushchenko to sack the entire cabinet
and appoint Yuri Yekhanurov as acting

Prime Minister, subject to parliamentar
approval.
Economy Ukraine is a lower-middle-
income economy. Agriculture is important. It is the world's leading producer
sugar beet, the second-largest produce
of barley, and a major producer of
wheat. Ukraine has extensive raw mate
rials, including coal (though many mine
are exhausted), iron ore and manganes
ore. Ukraine is reliant on oil and natura
gas imports. The privatization of the Kr
voryzhstal steelworks in late 2005 pro-
duced $4.8 billion in windfall revenue f
the government. Some of the proceeds
were used to finance the budget defici
some to recapitalize two state banks,
some to retire public debt, and the rest
may be used to finance future deficits.

United Kingdom

Area 241,857 sq km
(93,381 sq miles)
Population 60,441,457
Capital London (8,089,000)
Languages English (official),
Welsh (also official in Wales), Gaelic
GDP 2005 US$30,900
Currency Sterling (pound) = 100 penc
Government constitutional monarchy
Head of state Queen Elizabeth II, 195
Head of government
Prime Minister Tony Blair, Labour Party,
1997
Website www.parliament.uk
Events The United Kingdom of Great
Britain and Northern Ireland is a union
of four countries – England, Northern
Ireland, Scotland and Wales. In 1997
referenda on devolution saw Scotland
and Wales gain their own legislative
assemblies. The Scottish assembly was
given tax-varying power. The Good Friday Agreement of 1998 offered the bes
chance of peace in Northern Ireland fo
generation. In 2005 the IRA announce
a permanent cessation of hostilities.
Tony Blair controversially gave full sup
port to Bush over the war in Iraq in 200
The 2005 general election resulted in a
reduced majority for Labour. Widesprea
delight at London's winning the 2012
Olympics was shattered the following day when four suicide bombers hit
the city's transport network killing 57
people.
Economy The UK is a major industrial
and trading nation. The economy has
become more service-centred and high
technology industries have grown in
importance. A producer of oil, petroleu
products, natural gas, potash, salt and
lead. Agriculture employs only 2% of t
workforce. Financial services and tourism are the leading service industries.

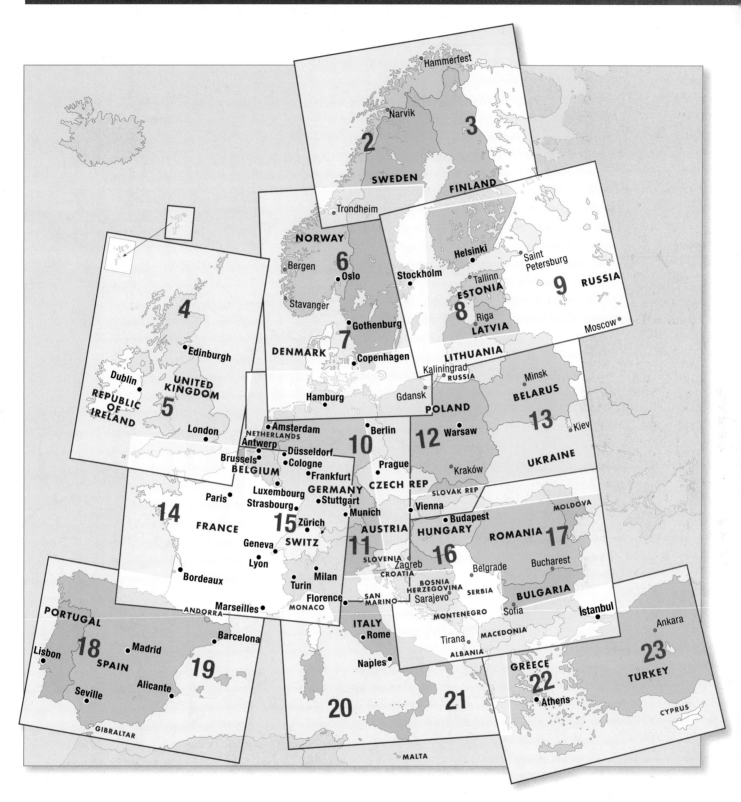

North Sea

100 miles
80
60
40
20
0

160 km
120
80
40
0

BERGEN

Shetland Is. (U.K.)

Unst
Fetlar
Yell
Mainland
Lerwick
Foula
Sumburgh Hd.
Fair Isle

TÓRSHAVN
SEYDISFJÖRDUR

STAVANGER
HAUGESUND
BERGEN

ZEEBRUGGE

Orkney Is.
Westray
Sanday
Stronsay
Kirkwall
South Ronaldsay
Mainland
Stromness
Hoy
Pentland Firth

C. Wrath

North Minch

Rubha Robhanais
Stornoway
Tairbeart

Eilean Leodais

Na Hearadh

Uibhist a Tuath
Loch nam Madadh
Beinn na Faoghla
Loch Baghasdail
Bagh a Chaisteil
Eilean Bharraigh
Uibhist a Deas

Outer Hebrides

St. Kilda

John o' Groats
Wick
Helmsdale
Golspie
Tain
Thurso
Tongue
Lairg
Loch Shin
Invergordon
Dingwall
Inverness
Moray Firth
Buckie
Elgin
Nairn
Forres
Banff
Huntly
Fraserburgh
Ratray Hd.
Peterhead
Aberdeen
Stonehaven
Montrose
Brechin
Arbroath
Forfar
Blairgowrie
Dundee
St. Andrews
Glenrothes
Kirkcaldy
North Berwick
Dunbar
Berwick-upon-Tweed
Coldstream
Alnwick

Ullapool
Lochinver
Kyle of Lochalsh
Portree
Uig
Skye
Raasay
Mallaig
Eigg
Rum
Coll
Tobermory
Mull
Colonsay
Jura
Islay
Port Askaig
Port Ellen
Tiree

Inner Hebrides

West Highlands
North Highlands
Fort Augustus
Newtonmore
Aviemore
Ballater
Braemar
Ben Nevis
Fort William
Ballachulish
Oban
Loch Lomond
Loch nam
Tarbert
Ardrossan
Brodick
Arran
Campbeltown
Rothesay
Dunoon
Greenock
Dumbarton
Stirling
Glasgow
Paisley
East Kilbride
Hamilton
Irvine
Kilmarnock
Ayr
Cumnock
Lochgilphead
Port

SCOTLAND
Grampian Mts.
Ben
Pitlochry
Perth
Dunfermline
Edinburgh
Peebles
Galashiels
Jedburgh
Hawick
Moffat

Firth of Forth

Aberfeldy
Loch Tay
L. Tay

Loch Ness
L. Ness

Firth of Clyde

Malin Hd.

Norway numbers: 90, 947, 97, 96, 98, 165, 9, 195, 9, 836, 836, 897, 838, 835, 890, 896, 832, 830, 828, 1342, 87, 1182, 90, 85, 887, 45, 90, 96, 965, 1311, 1214, 973, 135, 82, 811, 737, 84, 71, 77, 78, 815, 816, 205, 78, 708, 701, 702, 840, 68, 90, 92, 91, 145, 93, 185, 932, 836, 789, 882

Føroyar (Danmark)
Færoe Islands (Denmark)

Norðoyar
Klaksvík
Eysturoy
Streymoy
Mykines
Vágar
Tórshavn
Sandoy
Suðuroy
Slættaratindur
882

SEYDISFJÖRDUR
HANSTHOLM
LERWICK BERGEN

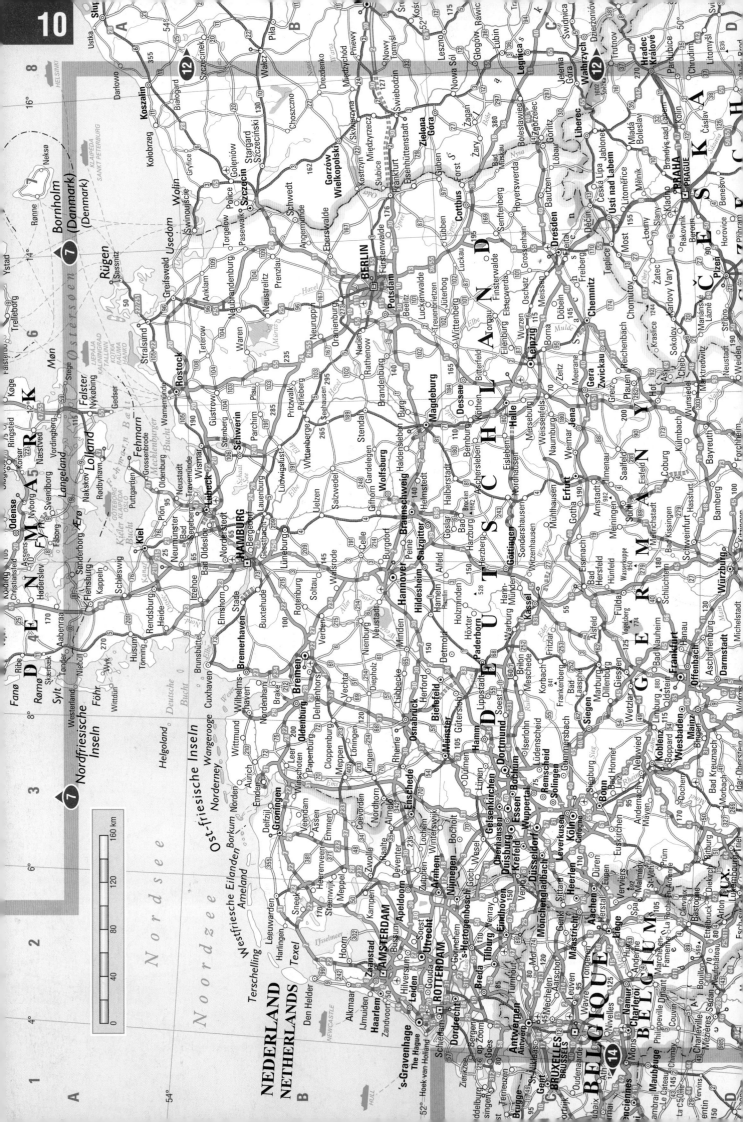

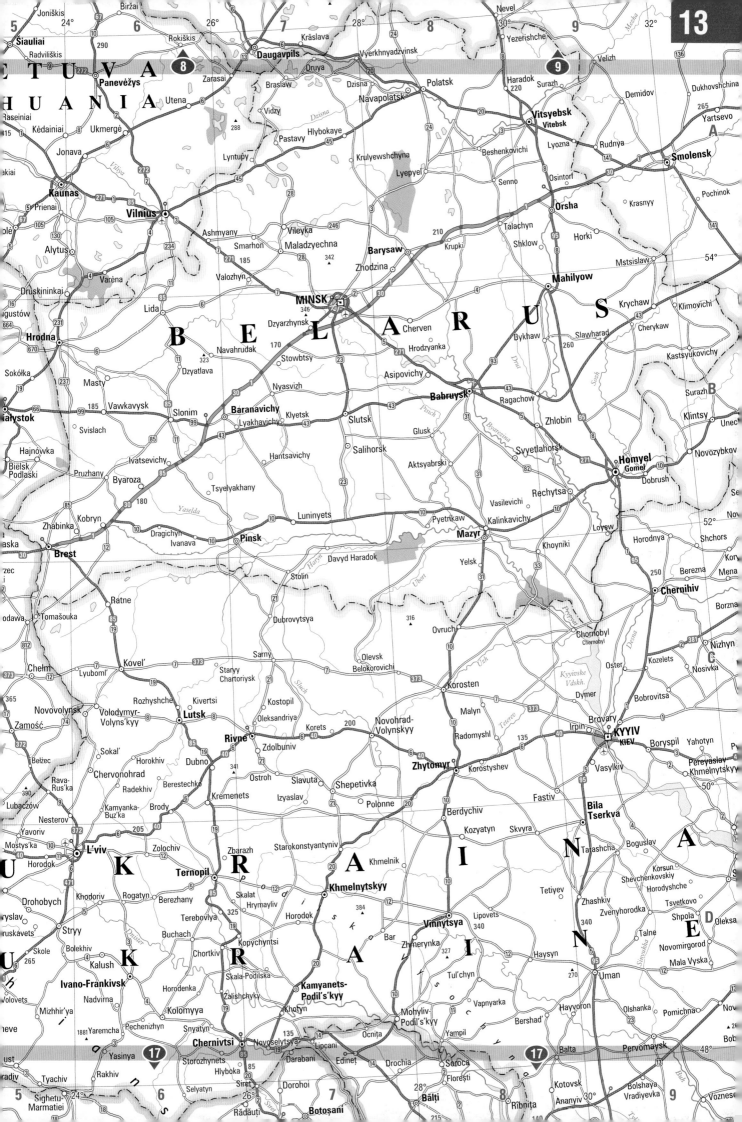

ENGLISH Channel

La Manche

PARIS

F R A N C E

Bay of Biscay

Golfe de Gascogne

G. de St.-Malo

CÔTE D'EMERAUDE

CÔTE DE CORNOUAILLE

CÔTE D'AMOUR

CÔTE DE JADE

CÔTE DES LANDES

CÔTE D'ARGENT

CÔTE BASQUE

COSTA VASCA

COSTA MONTAÑESA

Baie de la Seine

CÔTE DE NACRE

Channel Is. (U.K.)

Isle of Wight

Major place names:

Barnstaple, Minehead, Bideford, Bridgwater, Taunton, Shaftesbury, Salisbury, Andover, Basingstoke, Woking, Dorking, Guildford, Reigate, Crawley, Maidstone, Canterbury, Ramsgate, North Foreland, Dover, De Panne, Dunkerque, Calais, Folkestone, Ashford, Tonbridge, Royal Tunbridge Wells, Hastings, Bexhill, Eastbourne, Newhaven, Brighton, Worthing, Havant, Portsmouth, Gosport, Bournemouth, Poole, Newport, Swanage, Weymouth, Exmouth, Sidmouth, Bridport, Dorchester, Winchester, Southampton, Yeovil, Glastonbury, Exeter, Newton Abbot, Torquay, Torbay, Dartmouth, Plymouth, Launceston, Okehampton, Bude, Bodmin, Newquay, Redruth, St. Austell, Truro, Falmouth, Penzance, Land's End, Lizard Pt., Start Pt., Portland Bill

Boulogne-sur-Mer, Le Touquet-Paris-Plage, Berck, Abbeville, Amiens, Le Tréport, Dieppe, Fécamp, Le Havre, Honfleur, Deauville, Bolbec, Yvetot, Rouen, Beauvais, Gisors, Versailles, Créteil, Evry, Étampes, Nemours, Pithiviers, Orléans, Chartres, Rambouillet, Dreux, Évreux, Bernay, Lisieux, Caen, Bayeux, St.-Lô, Coutances, Granville, Avranches, Cherbourg, Valognes, Carentan, Ste-Mère-Église, Barfleur, Le Mont-St-Michel, Dinard, St.-Malo, Dinan, Lamballe, St.-Brieuc, Paimpol, Lannion, Perros-Guirec, Roscoff, Morlaix, Landivisiau, Brest, Le Conquet, Crozon, Douarnenez, Audierne, Quimper, Concarneau, Quimperlé, Lorient, Auray, Vannes, Carnac, Quiberon, Belle-Île, Le Palais, St.-Nazaire, La Baule, Savenay, Nantes, Rennes, Laval, Mayenne, Alençon, Argentan, Falaise, Flers, L'Aigle, Verneuil-sur-Avre, Nonancourt, Mantes-la-Jolie, Pontoise, St.-Denis, St.-Germain, Le Mans, Sablé-sur-Sarthe, La Flèche, Vendôme, Blois, Amboise, Tours, Châteaudun, Angers, Saumur, Cholet, Ancenis, Châteaubriant, Redon, Ploërmel, Loudéac, Pontivy, Carhaix-Plouguer, Mur-de-Bretagne, Guingamp, Vitré, Fougères, Domfront, Mortain, Châtellerault, Poitiers, Niort, La Rochelle, Île de Ré, Île d'Oléron, Rochefort, Saintes, Cognac, Angoulême, Royan, Bordeaux, Libourne, Bergerac, Périgueux, Brantôme, Limoges, St-Junien, Confolens, Ruffec, Civray, Montmorillon, Guéret, Aubusson, Montluçon, Châteauroux, Issoudun, Bourges, Vierzon, Valençay, Loches, Chinon, Thouars, Bressuire, Parthenay, Fontenay-le-Comte, Luçon, Les Sables-d'Olonne, La Roche-sur-Yon, Challans, Île de Noirmoutier, Île d'Yeu, St-Gilles-Croix-de-Vie, Montaigu, Clisson, Pornic

Arcachon, C. Ferret, Le Verdon-sur-Mer, Blaye, Langon, Marmande, Agen, Moissac, Montauban, Toulouse, Auch, Tarbes, Lourdes, Pau, Oloron-Ste-Marie, Bayonne, Biarritz, St.-Jean-de-Luz, Donostia-San Sebastián, Irún, Bilbao, Barakaldo, Santander, Torrelavega, Reinosa, Llanes, San Vicente de la Barquera, Laredo, Castro Urdiales, Gernika-Lumo, Durango, Eibar, Vitoria-Gasteiz, Pamplona, Carcassonne, Foix, St-Girons, Pamiers

Scale:

0 — 20 — 40 — 60 — 80 — 100 miles

0 — 40 — 80 — 120 — 160 km

Key to road map pages

● **Florence** **City plan**
  Firenze

□ **İstanbul** **City approach map**

■ **Milan** **City plan and approach map**
  Milano See pages 201–224 for city plans
  and approach maps

97 Map pages at 1:750 000

182 Map pages at 1:1 500 000

ICELAND
190 ÍSLAND 191
Reykjavik

Hammerfest
192 193
Tromsö

194
Narvik

195 196 197 FINLAND
SUOMI

Oulu

198 199 200
Trondheim Umeå
Vaasa
NORWAY
NORGE SWEDEN
SVERIGE
Turku Saint Petersburg
Sankt Peterburg

31 32 33
Inverness Aberdeen

46 47 48 49 50 51
Bergen Gävle
Oslo Stockholm Tallinn ESTONIA
EESTI RUSSIA
ROSSIYA

52 53 Örebro
Stavanger 54 55 56 57
Kristiansand

34 35
Glasgow
Edinburgh

58 Gothenburg Göteborg
60 62
Ålborg LATVIA
61 Riga LATVIJA

26 27 Belfast
36 37
REPUBLIC
OF IRELAND UNITED 59 DENMARK
28 Dublin KINGDOM DANMARK 63 LITHUANIA
29 Cork 30 Esbjerg Copenhagen LIETUVA
38 Manchester København
Liverpool Malmö
40 41 Kaliningrad RUSSIA Vilnius Minsk
39 Birmingham 64 Kiel 65 66 67 Gdansk ROSSIYA
Cardiff 68 69 BELARUS
42 43 Bristol London 70 71 Hamburg Szczecin
44 45 NETHERLANDS Bremen 72 73 Berlin Poznan 76 77 Warsaw
Plymouth NEDERLAND Hanover 74 75 Warszawa
Calais Amsterdam Hannover POLAND Brest
78 Antwerp 80 81 GERMANY POLSKA
89 Antwerpen Düsseldorf DEUTSCHLAND 84 85 86 87 UKRAINE
79 Brussels 82 83 Dresden UKRAINA
Bruxelles Cologne Frankfurt Leipzig Wrocław
BELGIUM Köln Prague Kraków Lviv
Le Havre BELGIQUE Praha
88 89 90 91 LUXEMBOURG 92 93 Nuremberg 94 95 CZECH REPUBLIC 96 97 Brno SLOVAK REP MOLDOVA
Brest Luxembourg Nürnberg ČESKÁ REPUBLIKA SLOVENSKÁ REP 98 99
101 Paris Strasbourg Stuttgart Munich Vienna Wien
Rennes 92 93 München 96 Bratislava Budapest
100 102 103 104 105 106 107 Salzburg AUSTRIA 111 112 113 ROMÂNIA
Nantes Dijon LIECHTENSTEIN ÖSTERREICH Graz HUNGARY Szeged
FRANCE Bern Zürich Innsbruck 108 109 110 MAGYARORSZAG 126 Timişoara
Geneva SWITZERLAND SLOVENIA Zagreb Belgrade
114 115 Genève SCHWEIZ 108 109 110 Ljubljana 124 125 CROATIA Beograd Bucharest
116 117 SLOVENIJA HRVATSKA 127 Bucureşti
Clermont- Lyon 118 119 120 121 122 123 BOSNIA
Ferrand Milan Venice HERZEGOVINA SERBIA BULGARIA
128 129 Turin Milano Venézia BOSNA I SRBIJA BULGARIYA
Bordeaux Torino Bologna HERCEGOVINA
130 131 Genoa 134 135 SAN Split Sarajevo 138 139 Sofia
A Coruña Nice Génova MARINO Sofiya
140 141 Toulouse MONACO 136 137 MONTENEGRO
Vigo Marseilles 132 133 Florence CRNA GORA Skopje
142 143 Marseille Firenze MACEDONIA
Porto 144 145 146 ITALY 170 171 Bari MAKEDONIJA Salonica
PORTUGAL Bilbao ANDORRA 180 ITALIA 169 Naples 172 173 Tirana Thessaloniki
148 149 SPAIN Zaragoza 147 Ajaccio Rome Nápoli Táranto Tiranë
Valladolid ESPAÑA Barcelona Roma 174 ALBANIA 182 183
154 155 Madrid 150 151 152 153 SHQIPËRIA
Lisbon 178 168 175 GREECE
Lisboa Valencia ELLAS
156 157 158 159 179
Seville Cordoba 166 167 Cágliari Palermo Patras
160 161 162 Alicante 176 177 Catània Patra Athens
Granada 164 165 Athina
Málaga 184 185
GIBRALTAR MALTA

Amsterdam

548	**Dublin**	Dublin ▶ Göteborg = 477 km
726 346	**Edinburgh**	
575 1123 1301	**Frankfurt**	
1342 477 176 1067	**Göteborg**	
760 477 1486 485 582	**Hamburg**	

000 = _ _ _🚢_ _

2945 **Athina**

1505 3192 **Barcelona**

1484 3742 2803 **Bergen**

650 2412 1863 1309 **Berlin**

197 2895 1308 1586 764 **Bruxelles**

2245 1219 2644 3037 1707 2181 **Bucuresti**

1420 1530 1999 2212 882 1358 852 **Budapest**

367 3100 1269 1783 956 215 2398 1573 **Calais**

533 3630 1817 270 1504 763 3021 2196 548 **Dublin**

1093 3826 1995 176 1696 941 3124 2299 726 346 **Edinburgh**

441 2499 1313 1508 550 383 1804 979 575 1123 1301 **Frankfurt**

1029 3080 2362 819 668 1145 1734 1550 1342 477 176 1067 **Göteborg**

447 2719 1780 1023 286 563 2014 1189 760 477 1486 485 582 **Hamburg**

1560 2539 2338 1063 475 1239 1834 1009 1431 1318 1236 1598 505 1113 **Helsinki**

2756 1145 2990 3653 2223 2706 690 1341 2911 3537 3657 2314 2891 2530 2350 **İstanbul**

965 2782 2090 1103 370 1081 2077 1252 1278 752 479 795 284 518 803 2593 **København**

256 2684 1376 1427 566 198 1983 1158 390 938 1116 180 986 404 1517 2499 714 **Köln**

2331 4460 1268 3723 2869 3141 3917 3222 2069 2617 2795 2400 3282 2700 3817 4342 3014 2339 **Lisboa**

480 3200 1387 458 1074 333 2591 1766 118 430 608 693 122 878 1991 3107 1188 508 2187 **London**

406 2661 1190 1613 749 209 2052 1227 424 972 1150 240 1172 590 1703 2472 900 186 2160 542 **Luxembourg**

1790 3809 617 3183 2364 1600 3262 2622 1528 1634 2254 1930 2742 2160 3276 3589 2473 1798 651 1646 1628 **Madrid**

1210 2683 509 2435 1541 1030 2154 1505 1063 1588 1789 1023 1994 1412 2525 2479 1722 1006 1777 1182 822 1126 **Marseille**

1085 2182 1038 2141 1060 890 1668 992 1072 1620 1798 683 1700 1118 1535 1993 1428 868 2315 1190 679 1655 538 **Milano**

2457 2930 3655 2223 1821 2585 1761 2099 2800 3348 3526 2312 1665 2115 1160 2605 2325 2387 4875 2918 2852 4224 3270 3027 **Moskva**

839 2106 1340 1788 594 789 1497 672 994 1524 1720 398 1347 765 1069 1907 969 580 2545 1094 555 2010 1011 473 2305 **München**

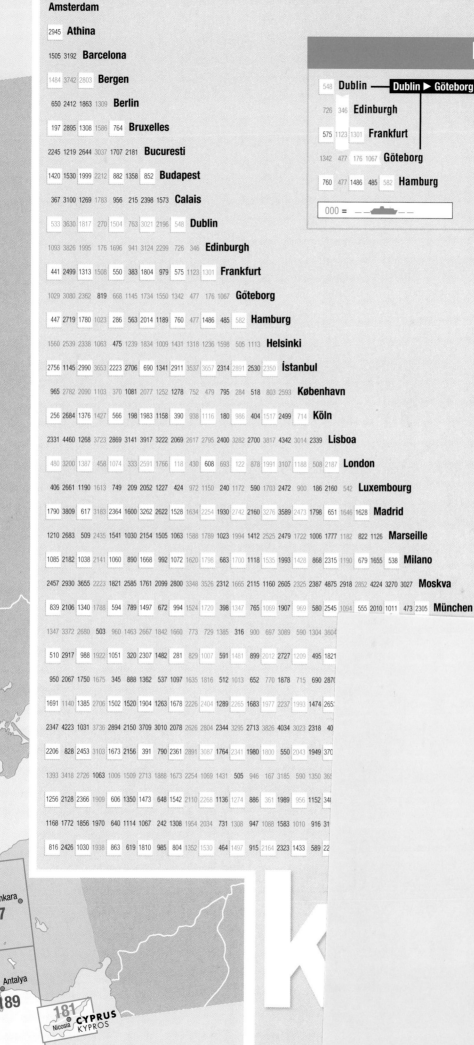

1347 3372 2680 503 960 1463 2667 1842 1660 773 729 1385 316 900 697 3089 590 1304 3604

510 2917 988 1922 1051 320 2307 1482 281 829 1007 591 1481 899 2012 2727 1209 495 1821

950 2067 1750 1675 345 888 1362 537 1097 1635 1816 512 1013 652 770 1878 715 690 287(

1691 1140 1385 2706 1502 1520 1904 1263 1678 2226 2404 1289 2265 1683 1977 2237 1993 1474 265

2347 4223 1031 3736 2894 2150 3709 3010 2078 2626 2804 2344 3295 2713 3826 4034 3023 2318 40

2206 828 2453 3103 1673 2156 391 790 2361 2891 3087 1764 2341 1980 1800 550 2043 1949 370

1393 3418 2726 1063 1006 1509 2713 1888 1673 2254 1069 1431 505 946 167 3185 590 1350 363

1256 2128 2366 1909 606 1350 1473 648 1542 2110 2268 1136 1274 886 361 1989 956 1152 34

1168 1772 1856 1970 640 1114 1067 242 1308 1954 2034 731 1308 947 1088 1583 1010 916 31

816 2426 1030 1938 863 619 1810 985 804 1352 1530 464 1497 915 2164 2323 1433 589 22

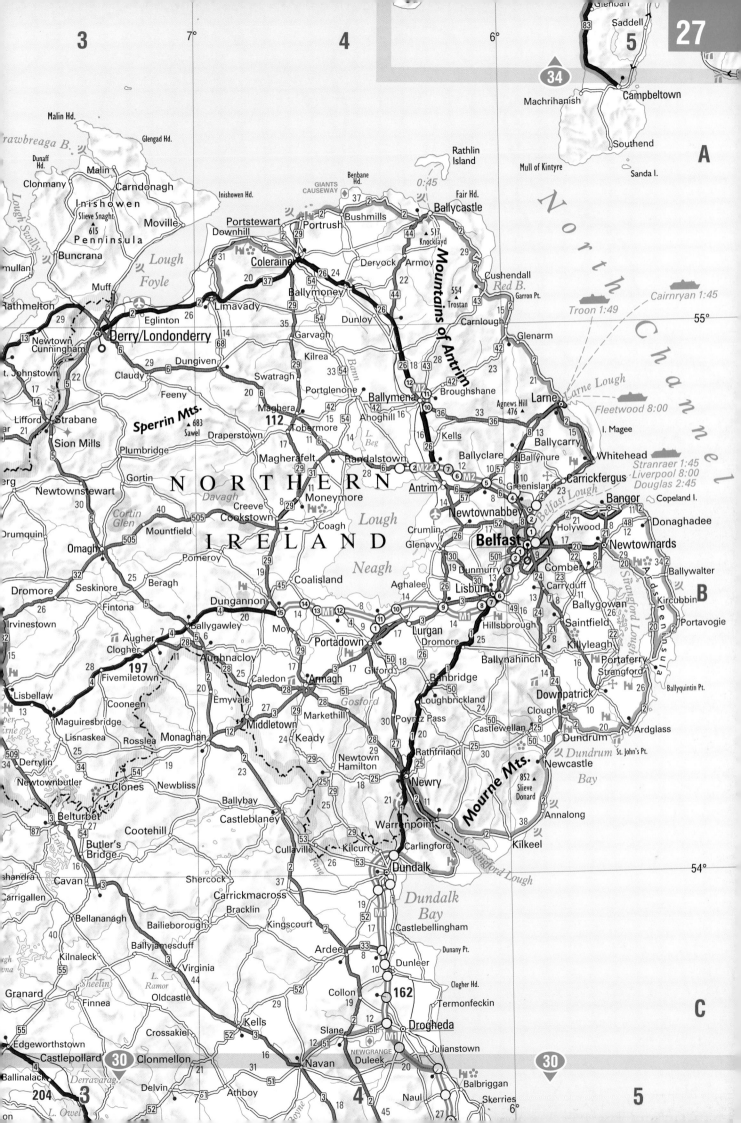

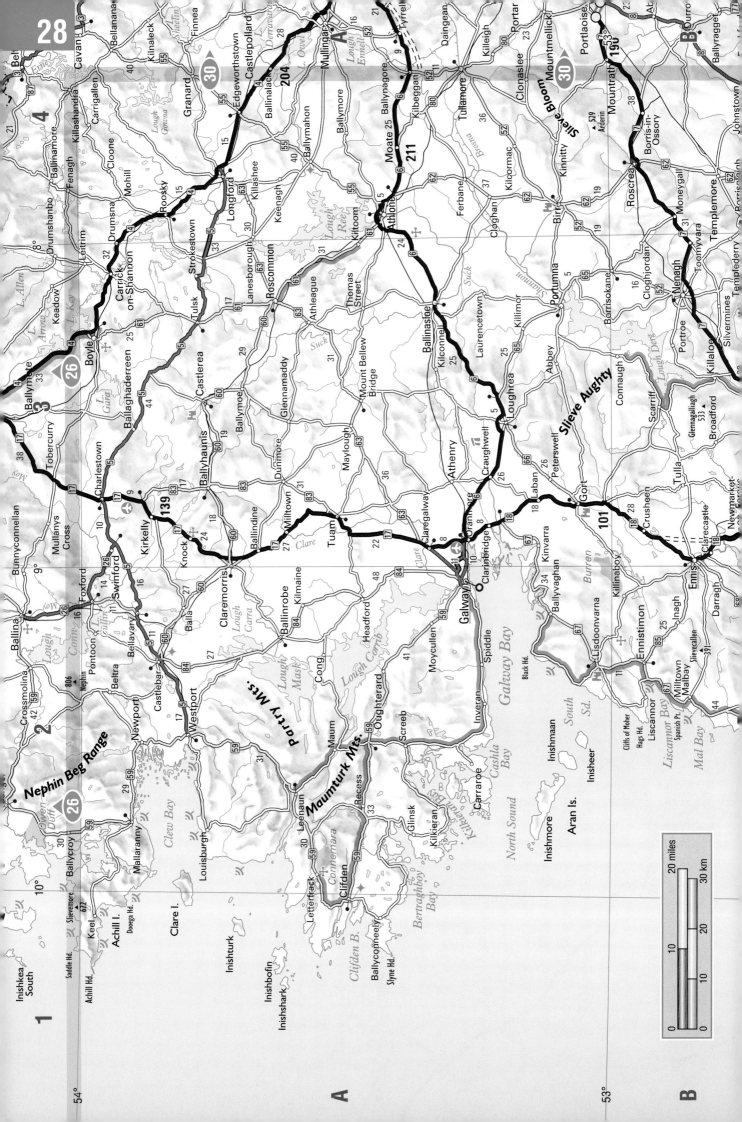

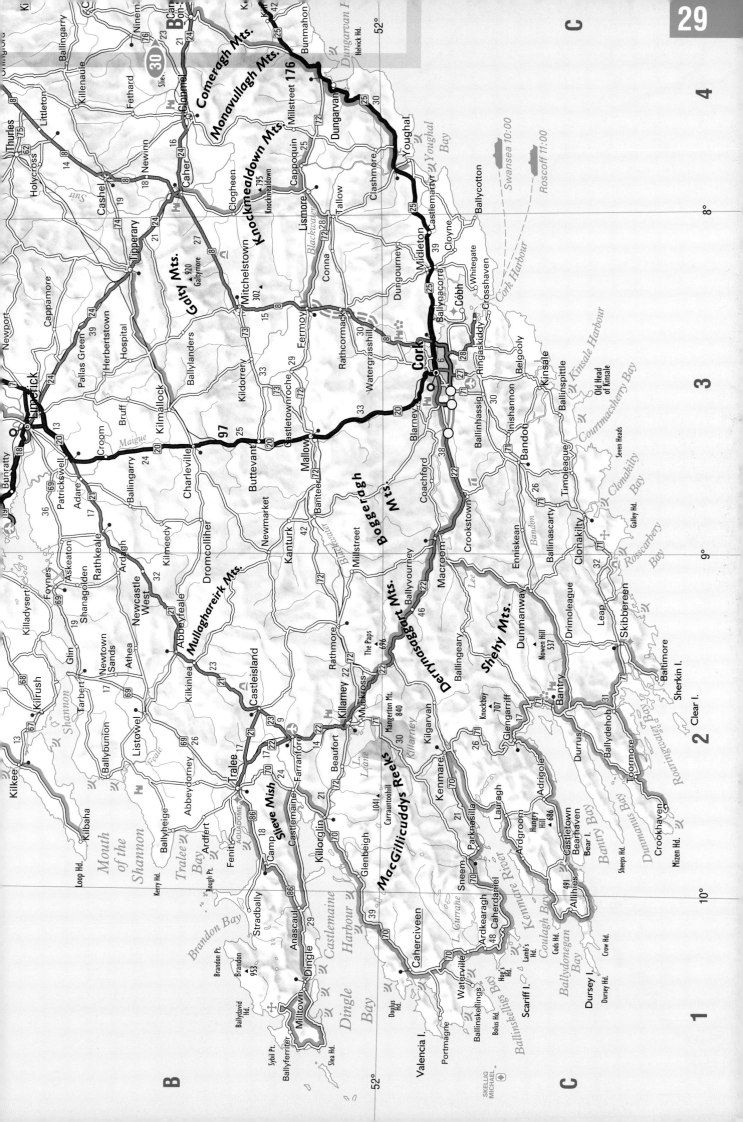

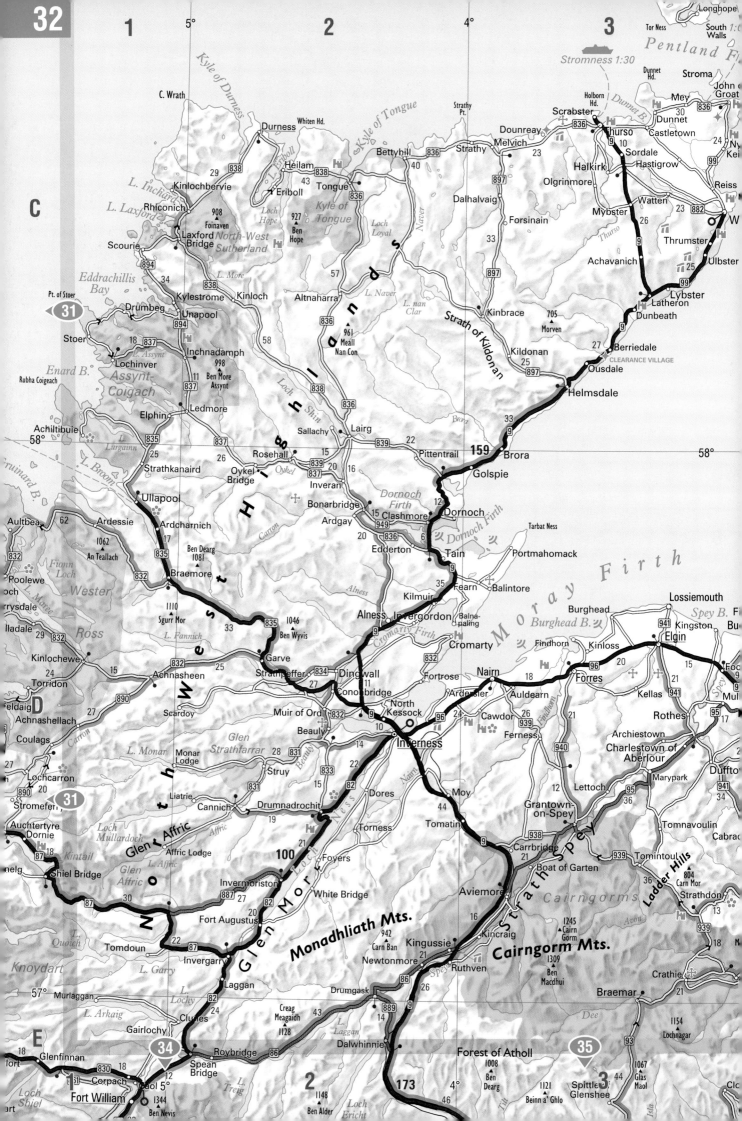

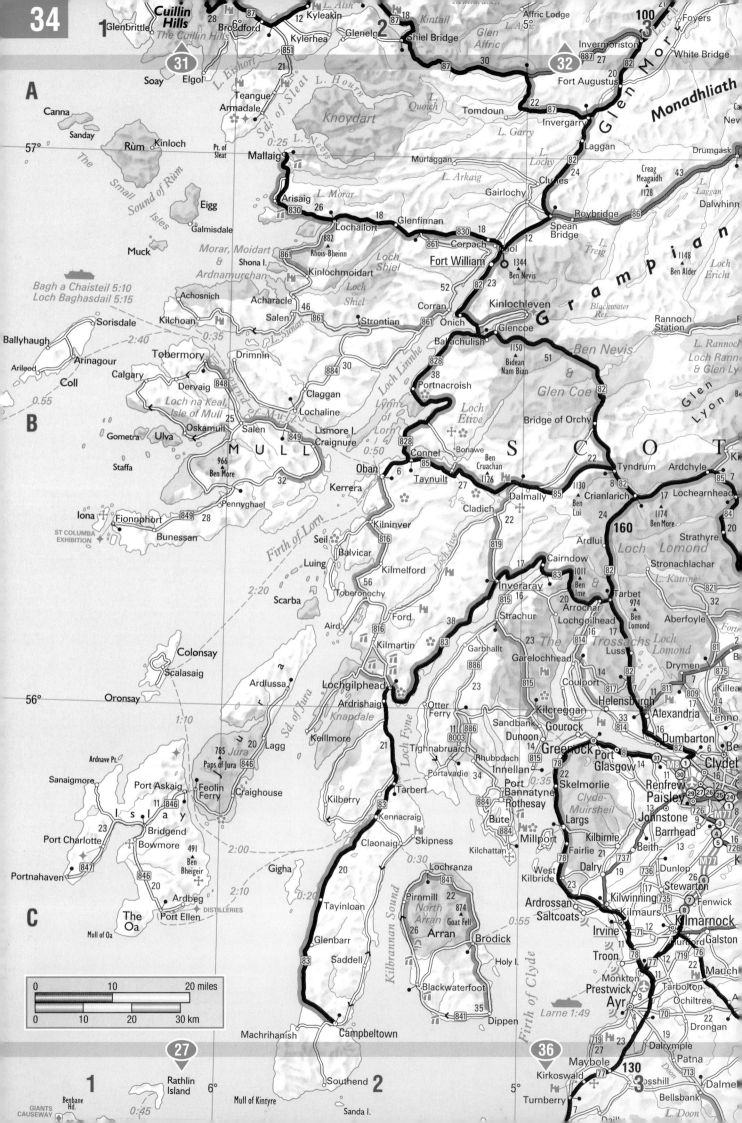

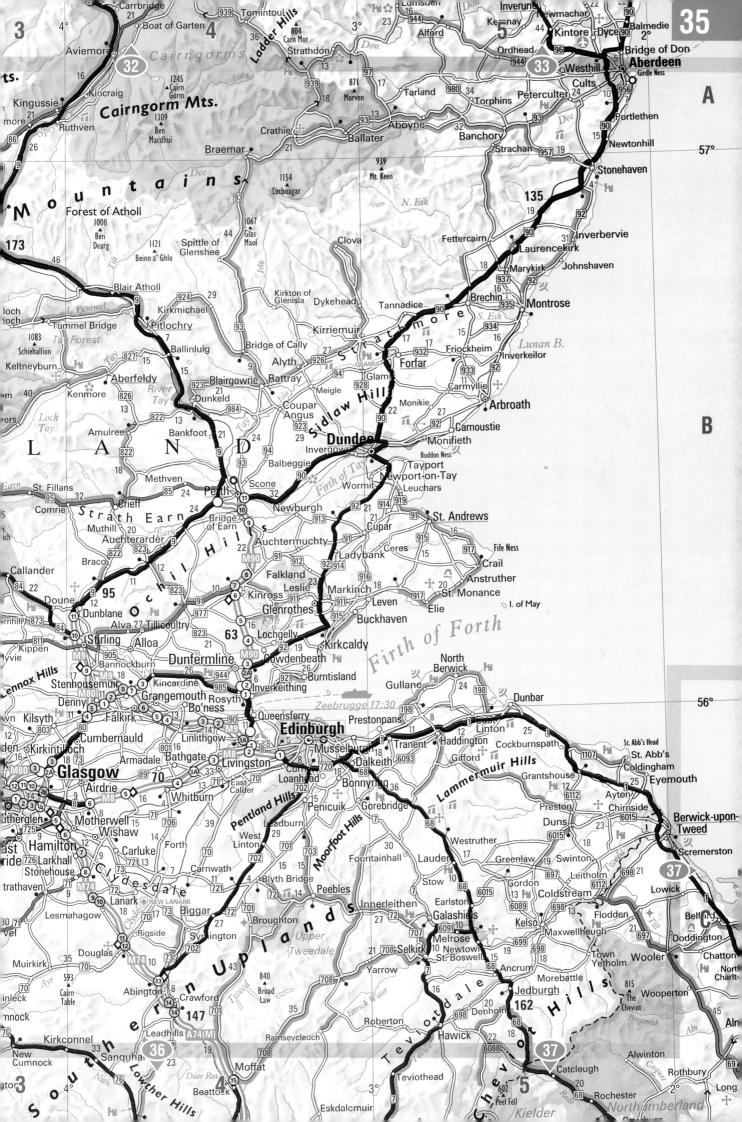

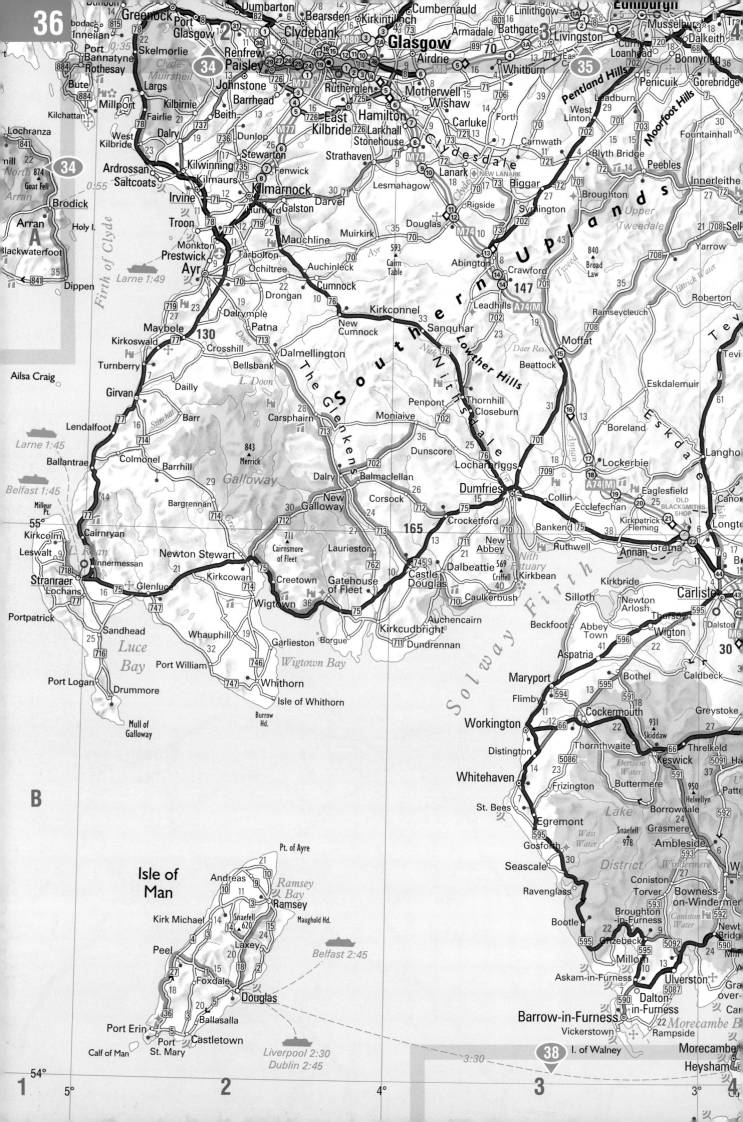

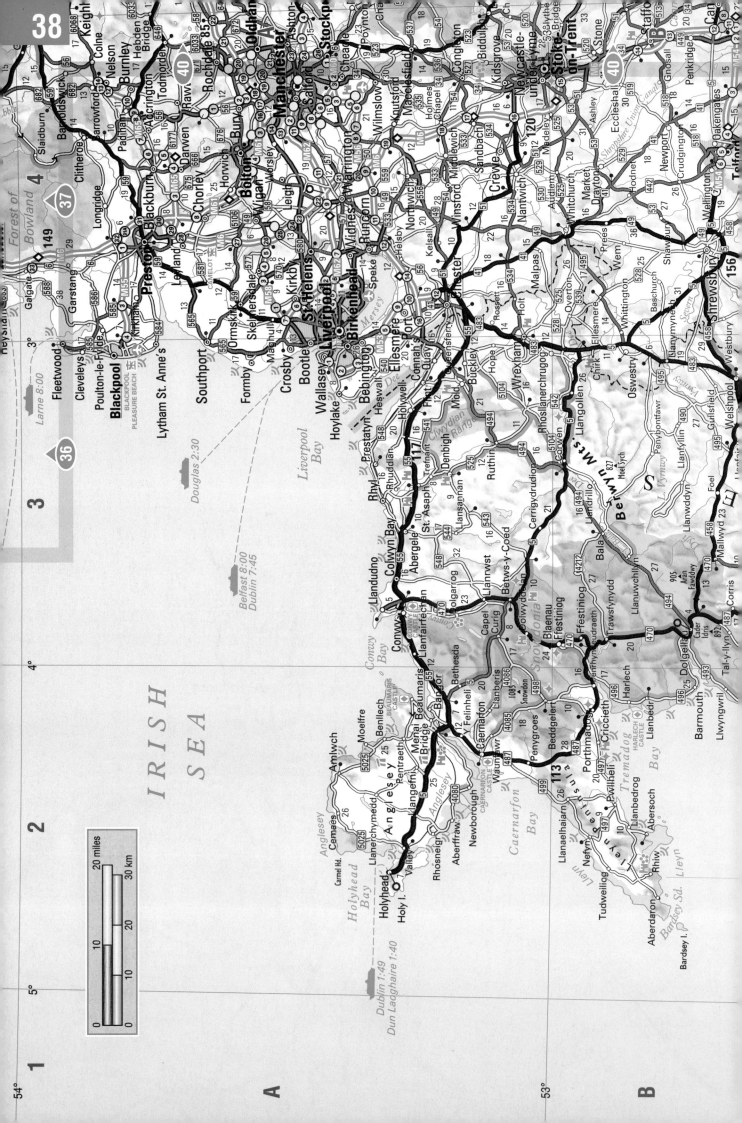

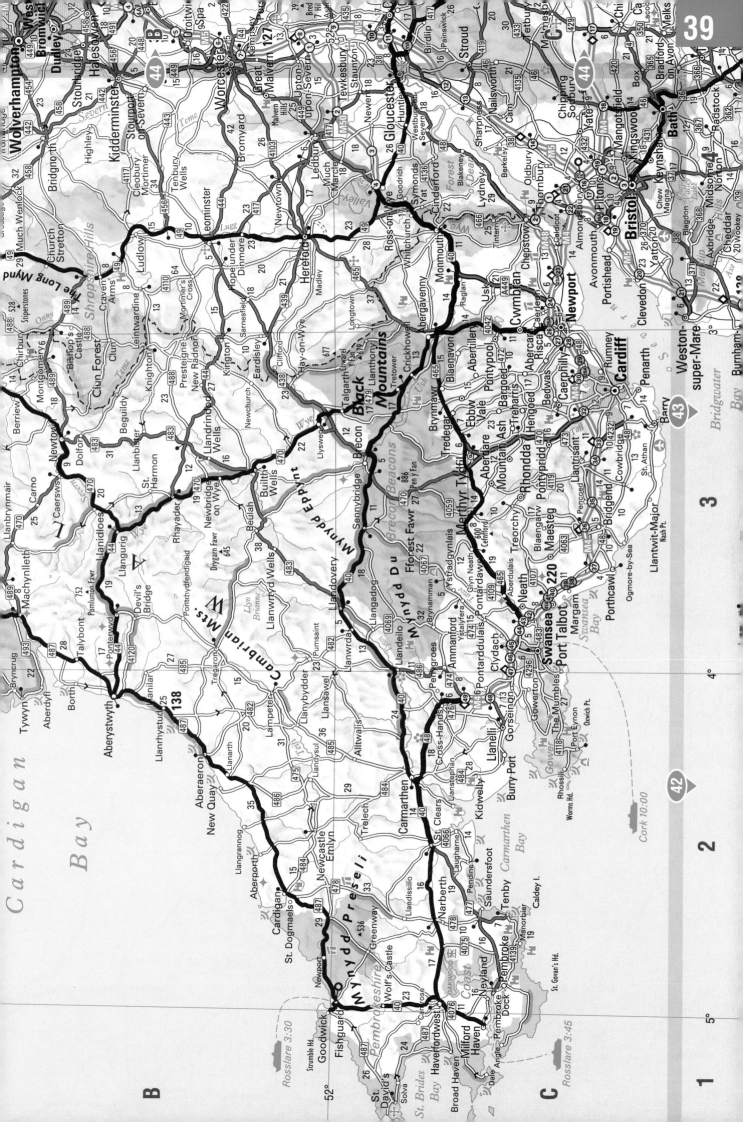

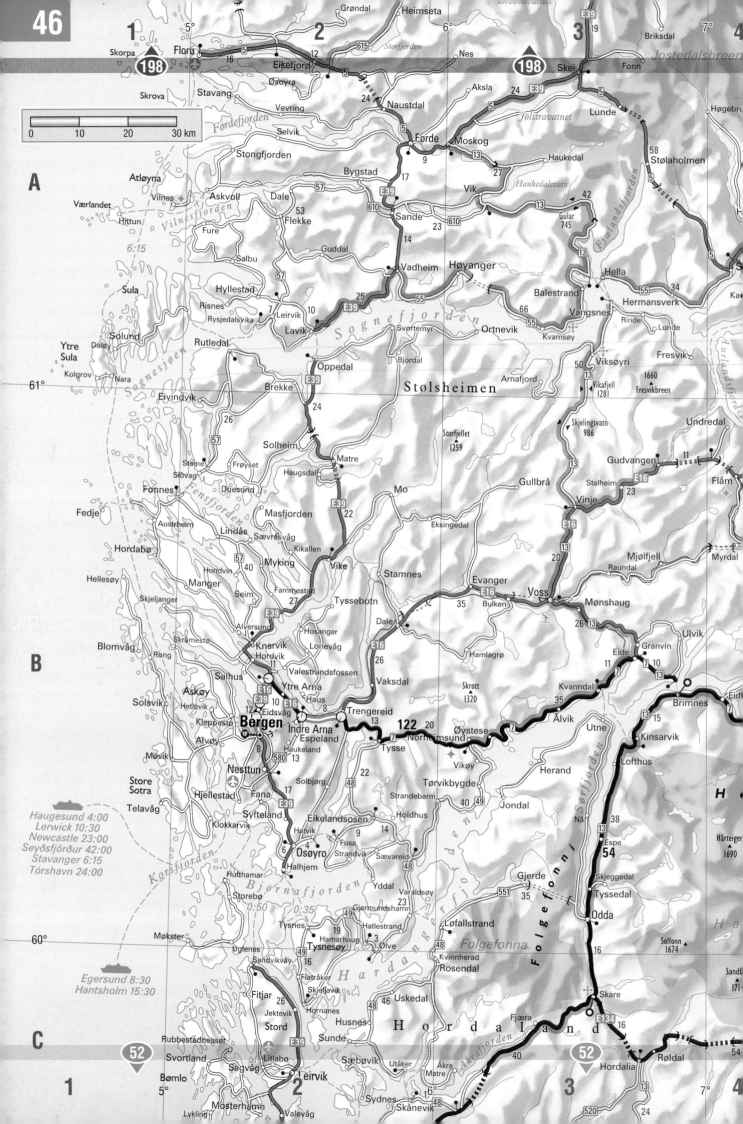

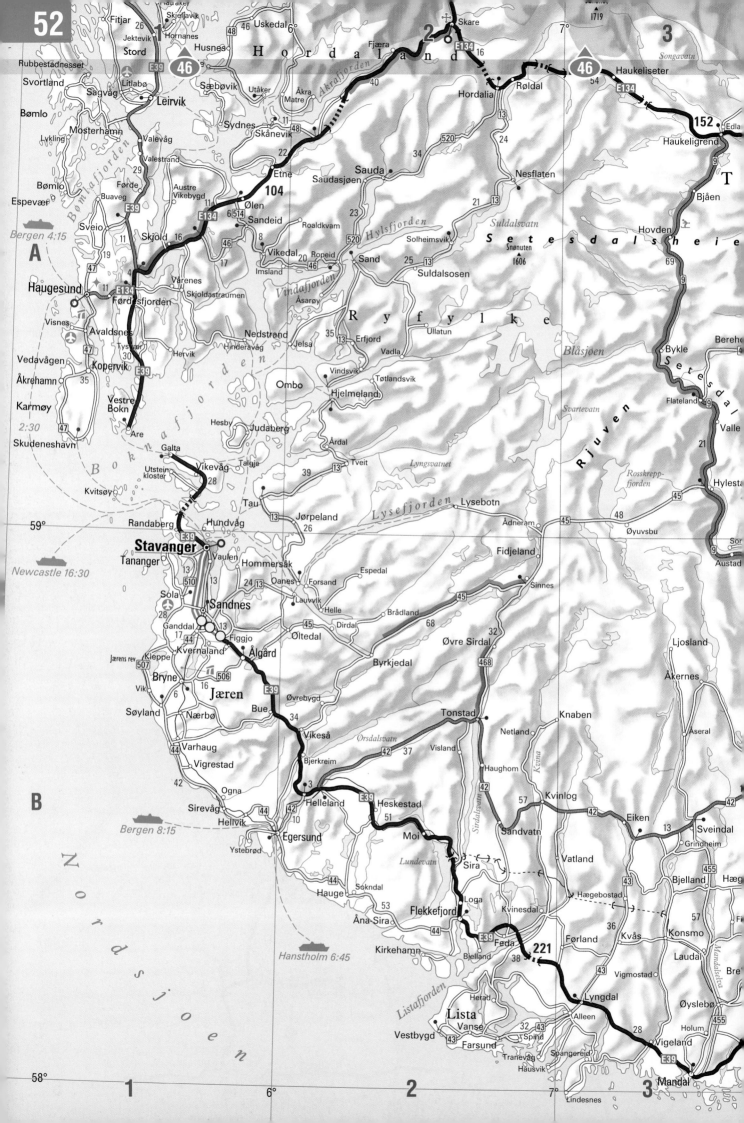

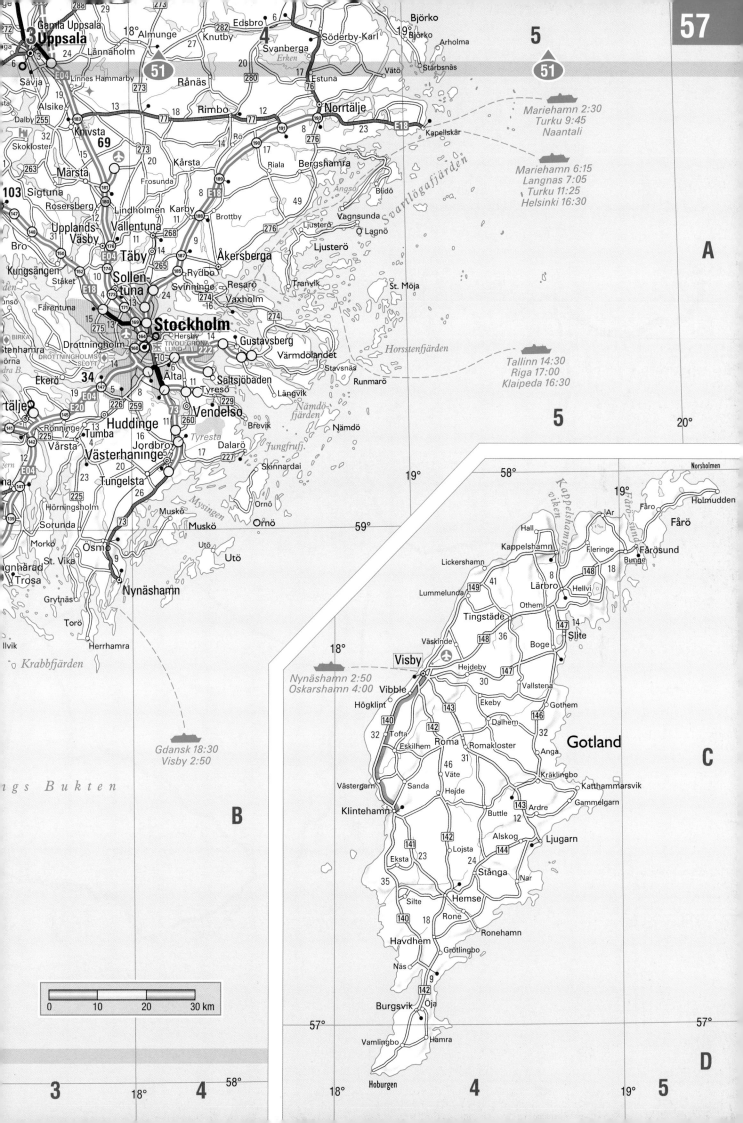

3 Gamla Uppsala
Uppsala
18° Almunge
Lännäholm
288 29 273
Edsbro 282
6
Knutby
Söderby-Karl
7
Björko
19° Björko
Arholma
Stärbsnäs
4
Svanberga
Erken
5
51

24
Linnes Hammarby
Rånäs
273
280
Svanberga
Vätö
51

19
Sävja
E04
Alsike
Dalby 255
183
Knivsta
13
18
Rimbo
12
77
77
Rö
190
191
Estuna
76
Norrtälje
193
23
E18
Kapellskär

Mariehamn 2:30
Turku 9:45
Naantali

32
Skokloster
69
15
263
Märsta
181
Frosunda
273
20
Kårsta
189
Riala
Bergshamra
276

Mariehamn 6:15
Langnas 7:05
Turku 11:25
Helsinki 16:30

103 Sigtuna
Rosersberg
180
Lindholmen
Karby
8
E18
188
Brottby
49
Ljusterö
O. Lagnö
Ljusterö
Svartlögafjärden
Ångsö
Blidö

147
148
Bro
150
Upplands
Väsby
12
176
268
9
276
Vagnsunda
St. Möja

Kungsängen
Stäket
152
174
Vallentuna
11
Täby
265
187
Åkersberga
Ljusterö

Ångsö
A

Färentuna
173
171
Sollen-tuna
185
Rydbo
Svinninge
Resarö
274
Vaxholm
16
St. Möja

15
275
169
13
Hersby
274
Stockholm
14
Gustavsberg
Horsstenfjärden

Drottningholm
160
164
TIVOLI GRÖNA LUND
222
Värmdölandet

DROTTNINGHOLMS SLOTT
Ekerö
34
147
5
8
10
Älta
11
Saltsjöbaden
Längvik
Stavsnäs
Runmarö
Tallinn 14:30
Riga 17:00
Klaipeda 16:30

19
226
259
73
260
Vendelso
Brevik
Nämdö-fjärden
Nämdö
5
20°

E20
145
Rönninge
Huddinge
11
Tyresö
Tyresta
Dalarö
229
227
Skinnardai
Jungfruj.

141
142
Vårsta
Tumba
16
Jordbro
Västerhaninge
17
Örnö
58°
19°
Norsholmen

12
E04
225
Tungelsta
26
Mysingen
Muskö
Ornö
Ornö
59°
Kappelshamns-viken
19°
Fårö
Holmudden

141
139
Hörningsholm
Sorunda
73
Muskö
Utö
18°
Hall
Kappelshamn
Ar
Fleringe
Fårö
Fårö

Morko
St. Vika
9
Ösmo
Utö
Lickershamn
148
8
Hellvi
18
Bunge
Fårösund

gnhärad
Trosa
Grytnäs
Torö
Nynäshamn
Lummelunda
149
41
Lärbro
147
14
Slite

Ilvik
Herrhamra
Krabbfjärden
Tingstäde
148
36
Othem
Boge
147

Väskinde
Visby
Hejdeby
30
Vallstena
146
Gothem
Gotland
C

Nynäshamn 2:50
Oskarshamn 4:00
Vibble
Högklint
143
Ekeby
Dalhem
32
Anga

Gdansk 18:30
Visby 2:50
140
Tofta
142
Roma
46
31
Romakloster
Kräklingbo
Katthammarsvik

ngs Bukten
32
Eskilhem
Väte
Hejde
143
Ardre
Gammelgarn
141
142
Västergarn
Sanda
Alskog
12
Ljugarn

B
Klintehamn
141
23
Lojsta
24
144
Stånga
Nar

35
Eksta
Silte
Hemse
Rone

140
18
Havdhem
Ronehamn

Näs
Grötlingbo
Burgsvik
Öja
142
9
D

0 10 20 30 km

Vamlingbo
Hamra
57°
57°

3
18°
4
58°
18°
4
19°
5

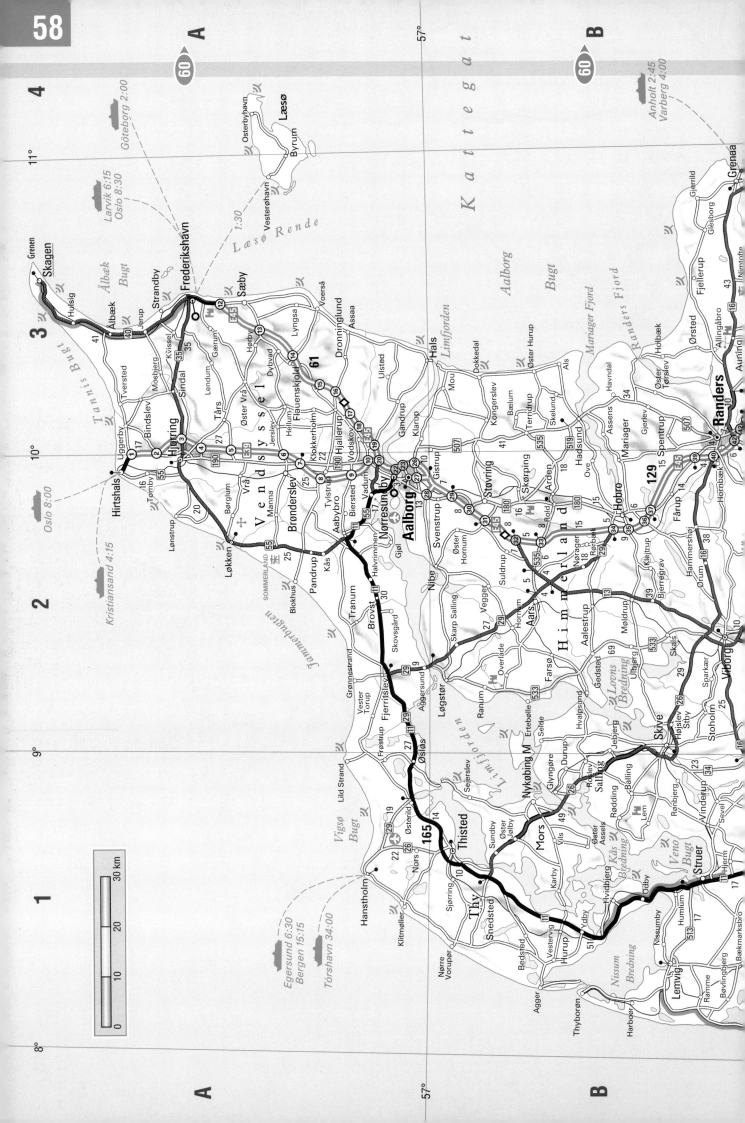

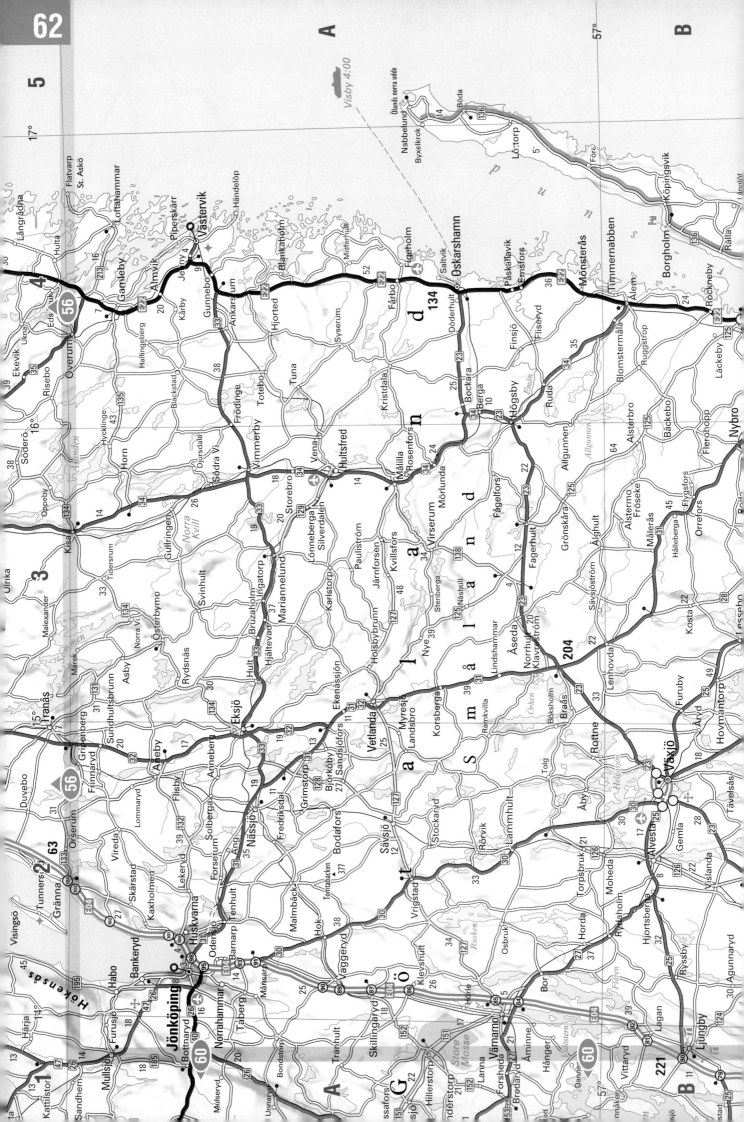

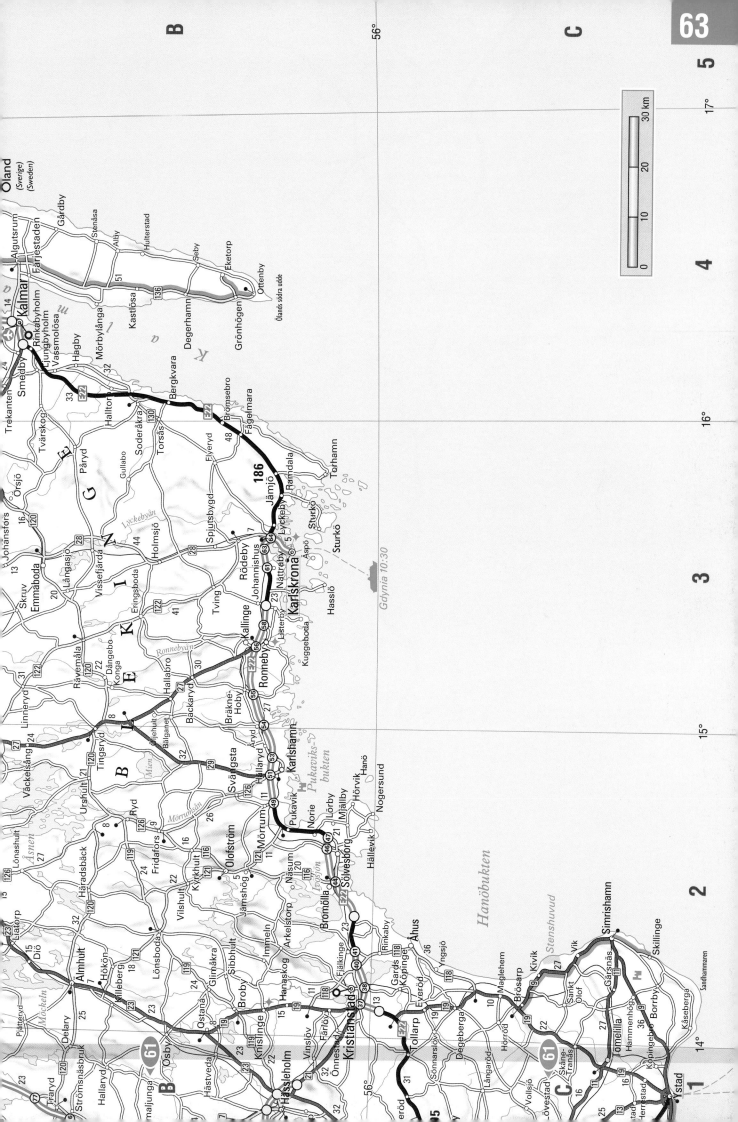

5

4

3

2

1

A

B

C

17°

16°

15°

14°

56°

56°

30 km

20

10

0

Öland
(Sverige)
(Sweden)

Kalmar

Smedby

Trekanten

Tvärskog

Örsjö

Johansfors

Skruv

Emmaboda

Lönashult

Liatorp

Älmhult

Diö

Hökön

Delary

Osby

Hässleholm

Kristianstad

Ystad

Simrishamn

Karlskrona

Ronneby

Karlshamn

Sölvesborg

Olofström

Bromölla

Åhus

Gårdby

Stenåsa

Alby

Hulterstad

Seby

Eketorp

Ottenby

Grönhögen

Degerhamn

Kastlösa

Mörbylånga

Färjestaden

Rinkabyholm

Ljungbyholm

Vassmolösa

Hagby

Bergkvara

Halltorp

Söderåkra

Torsås

Flyeryd

Brömsebro

Fågelmara

Jämjö

Ramdala

Torhamn

Sturkö

Aspö

Hasslö

Nättraby

Johannishus

Rödeby

Spjutsbygd

Holmsjö

Tving

Hallabro

Bräkne-Hoby

Backaryd

Eringsboda

Långasjö

Vissefjärda

Rävemåla

Dångebo

Konga

Linneryd

Väckelsång

Urshult

Ryd

Tingsryd

Vilshult

Jämshög

Näsum

Kyrkhult

Kvarkhult

Fridafors

Häradsbäck

Lönsboda

Glimåkra

Broby

Hanaskog

Immeln

Arkelstorp

Fjälkinge

Köpinge

Everöd

Degeberga

Maglehem

Brösarp

Kivik

Vik

Gärsnäs

Skillinge

Borrby

Tomelilla

Lövestad

Tollarp

Vinslöv

Önnestad

Hästveda

Krislinge

Färlöv

Ostanå

Sandhammaren

Kåseberga

Käglebro

Ölands södra udde

Mörbylånga

Gdynia 10:30

Hanöbukten

Pukaviksbukten

Lyckebyån

Ronnebyån

Mörrumsån

Åsnen

Möckeln

Mien

Stenshuvud

61

61

E22

E22

E22

E22

E22

186

136

130

120

120

120

120

120

120

120

121

121

119

119

116

116

116

126

126

126

122

122

28

28

28

33

32

51

51

48

44

41

30

27

27

Hällevik

Nogersund

Hörvik

Hanö

Mjällby

Lörby

Norje

Pukavik

Mörrum

Svängsta

Hällaryd

Kallinge

Listerby

Kuggeboda

Åryd

Svängsta

Ateryd

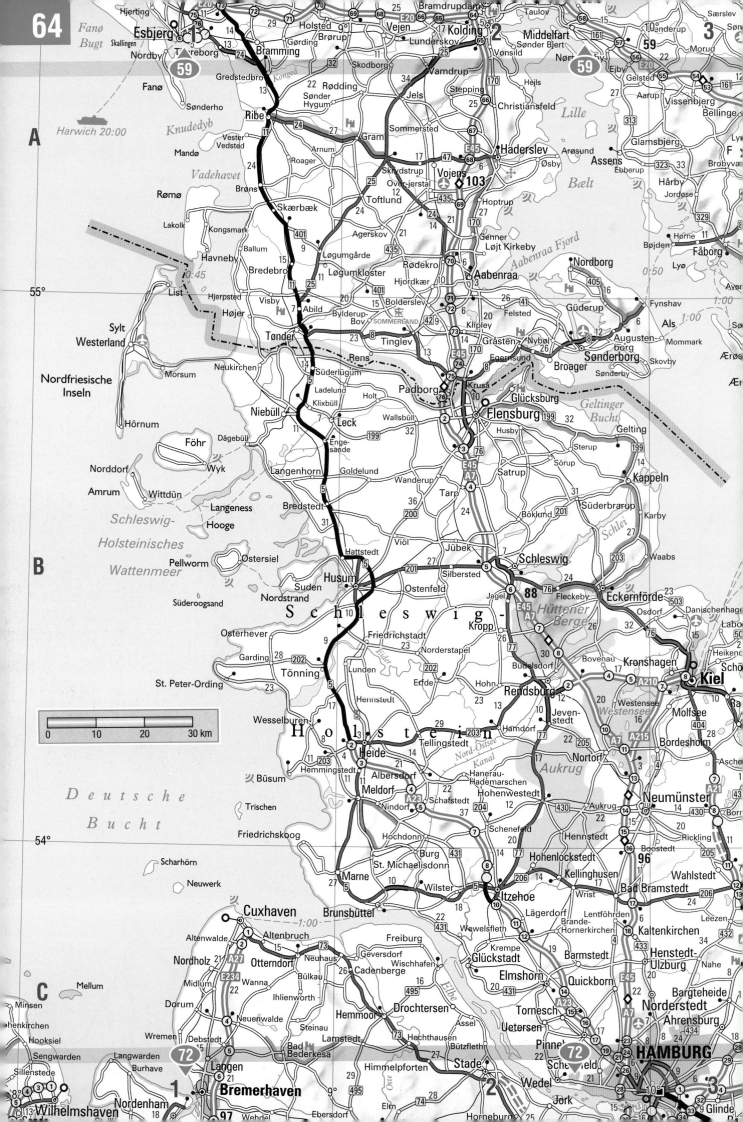

3 15° 4 16° 5

A

tenshuvud

Simrishamn

killinge

Wik

Holmsgattet

Ertholmene

Hammeren

Sandvig-Allinge

Tejn

Bornholm
(Danmark)
(Denmark)

Gudhjem

Rø

Hasle

Klemensker

Nyker

Svaneke

Øster-marie

København 6:00

Rønne

Nylars

Åkirkeby

28

38

Neksø

Pedersker

Snogebaek

55°

5:15

København 9:00
Malmö 9:00
Ystad 6:30

Jaroslawiec

J.

J. Kopań

B

64 *Wieprza*

203

Darłowo

Stary Jaroslaw

Dąbki

Sławno

Łazy *J. Bukowo*

68

203

32 Ostrowiec

Mielno *J. Jamno*

Jamno

E28 6

Sarbinowo

Jamno

Lejkowo

Ustronie Morskie

42

11

Sianów

Mrzeżyno

Kołobrzeg

11

Koszalin

6

206

35 Nacław

5

Dygowo

Dobrzyca

Bonin

Manowo

Wrzosowo

26

Biesiekierz

Niedalino

Rosnowo

Mostowo

Niechorze

102

162

27

163

31

167

37

11

Radew

Rewal

21

Gościno

19

Karlino

166

12

Dargiń

54°

Pobierowo

102 31

103

Cerkwica

18

Gorawino

Rymań

E28

16

Białogard

19

163

25

Bobolice

Dziwnów

109

Rega

169

Międzywodzie

Swierzno

17

105

Rzeszńikowo

Sławoborze

Tychowo

171

8 **Kamień Pomorski**

102 32 Kolczewo

12

Mechowo

Gryfice

219

33

Rabino

Tychówka

167

29 Grzmiąca

Wolinski

11

Międzyzdroje

107

15

13

Ząbrowo

162

17

Białowąs

23

C

scie

3 21

18

Gołczewo

108

20 Płoty

E28

Rusinowo

Sława

21

15

Połczyn-Zdrój

24 172

Lubin

E65

75

106

Resko

152

Starogard

4

Świdwin

Bierzwnica

75

Barwice

172 18

Wolin

r Haff

Zalew Szczeciński

Przybiernów

15

Żabowo

18

Radowo Wielkie

Brzeźno

151

16°

163

Ostropole

Nowe Warpno

3

4

Drawski

27

171

0 10 20 30 km

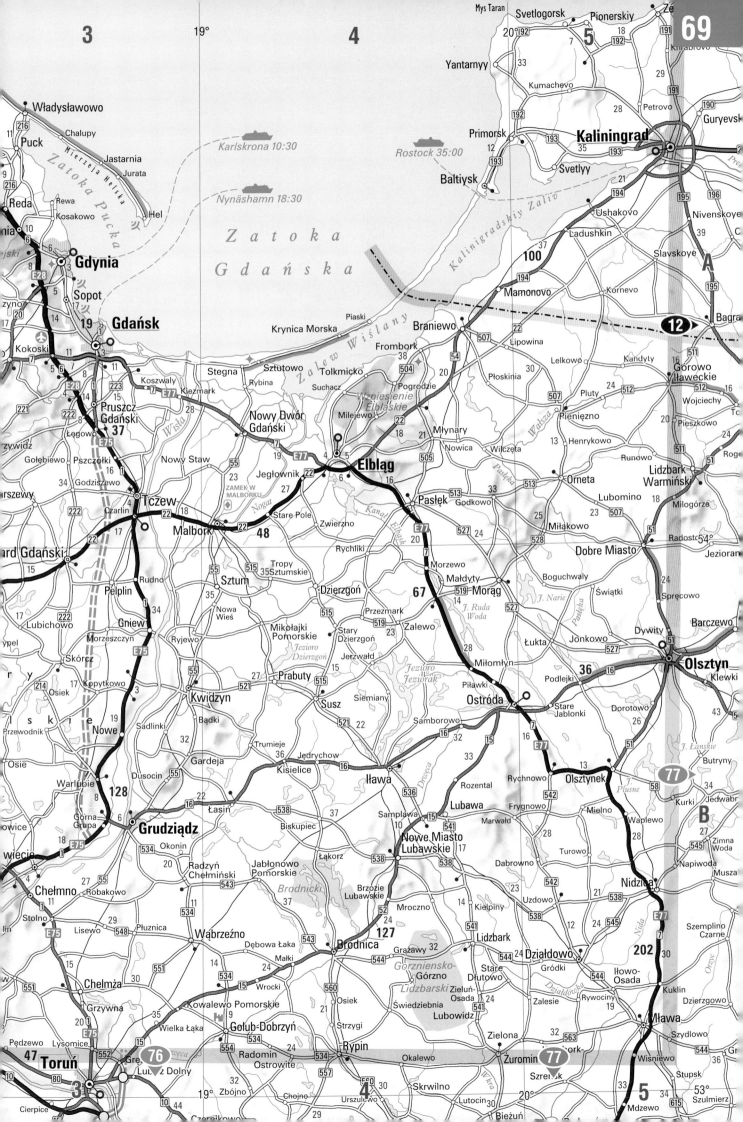

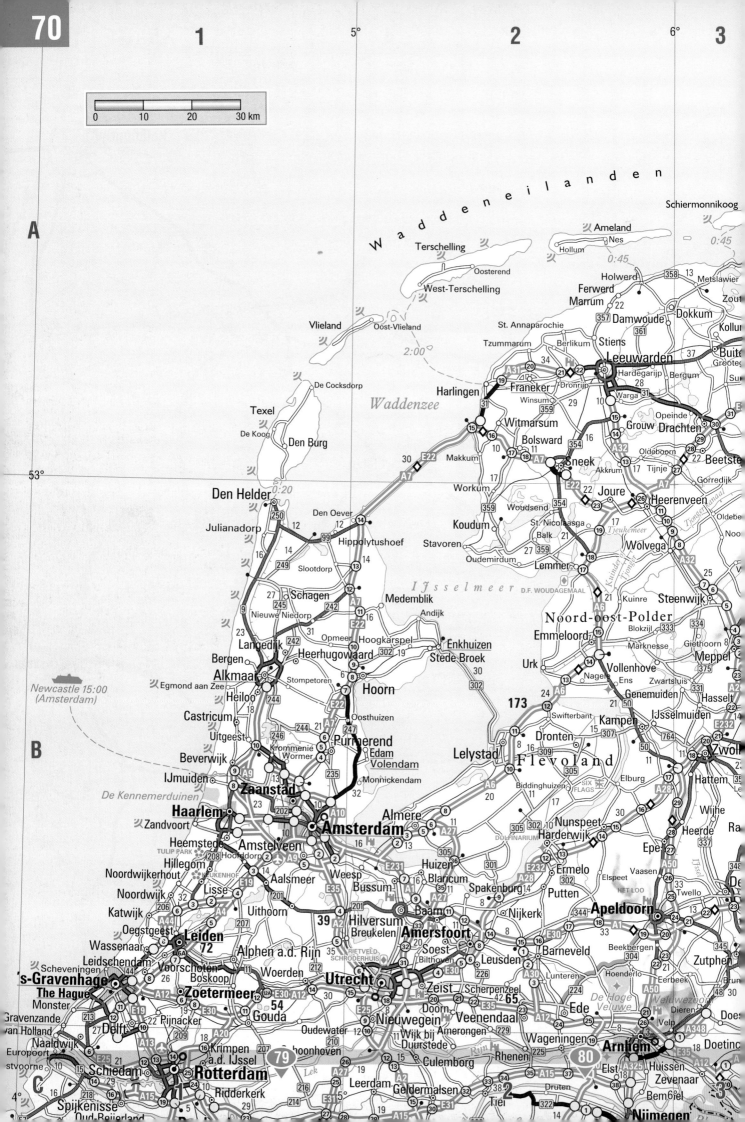

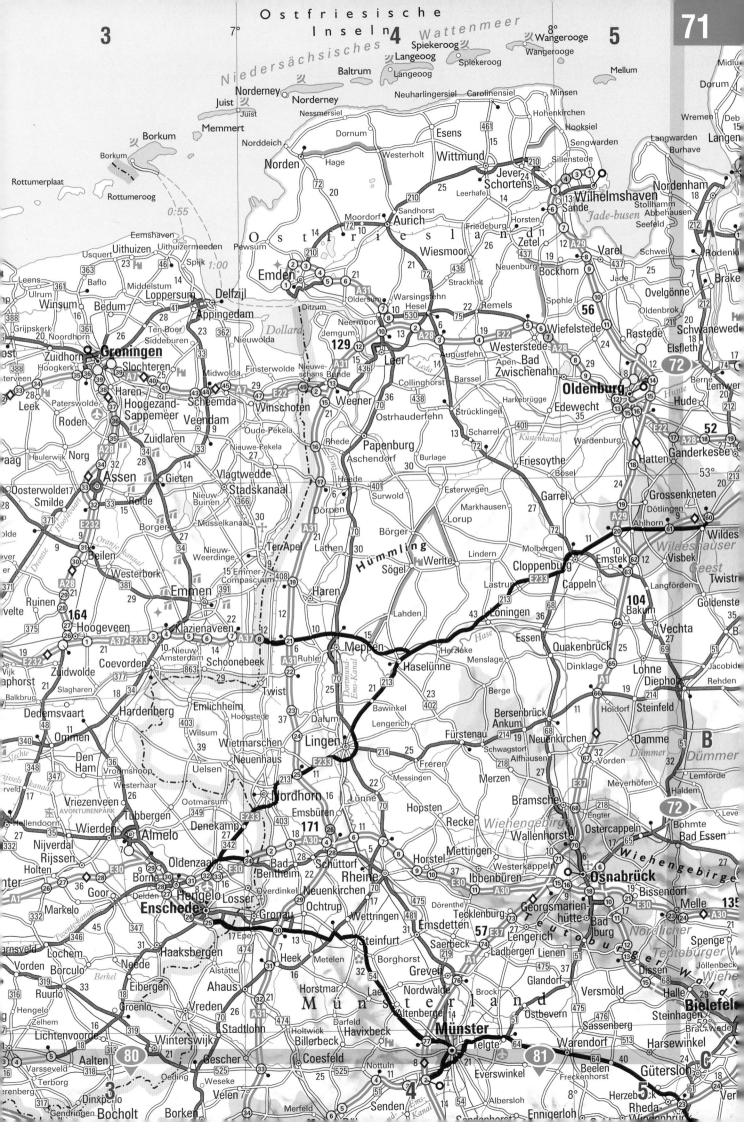

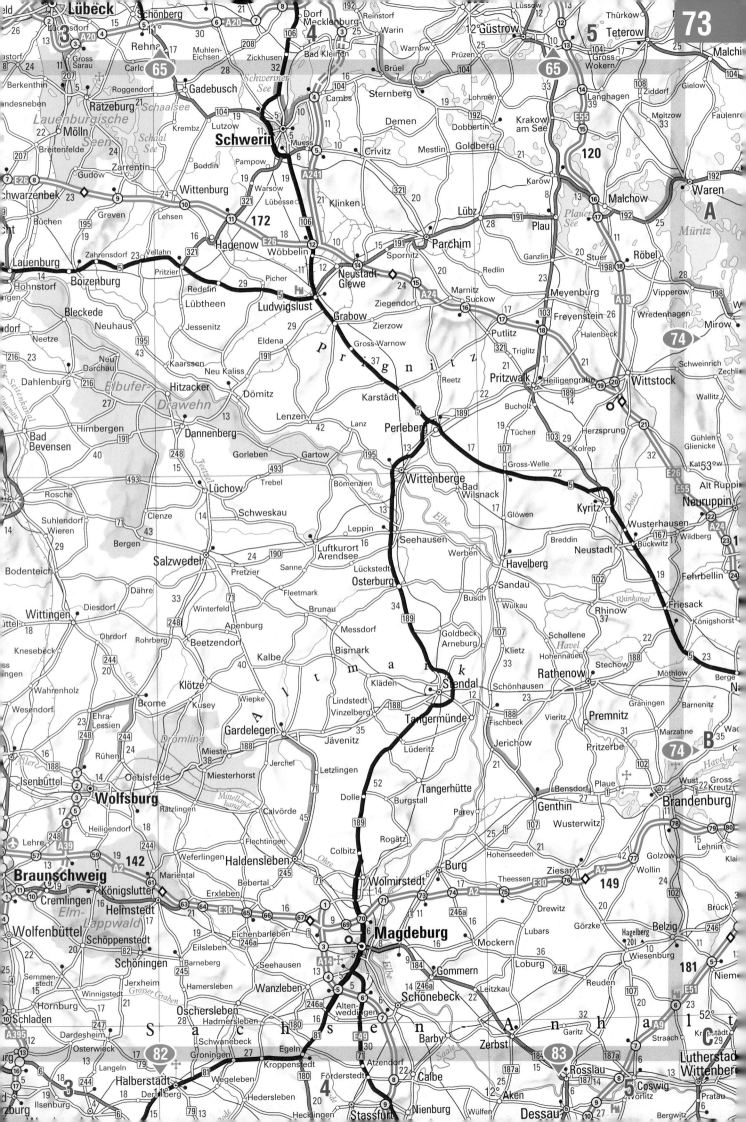

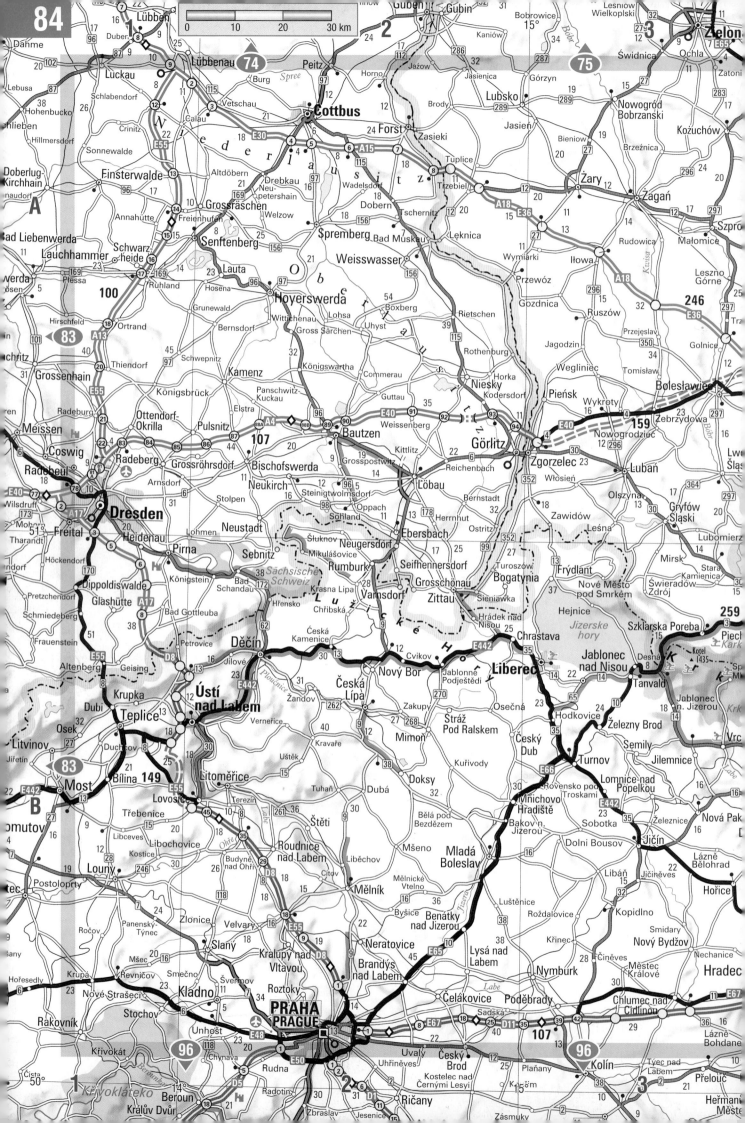

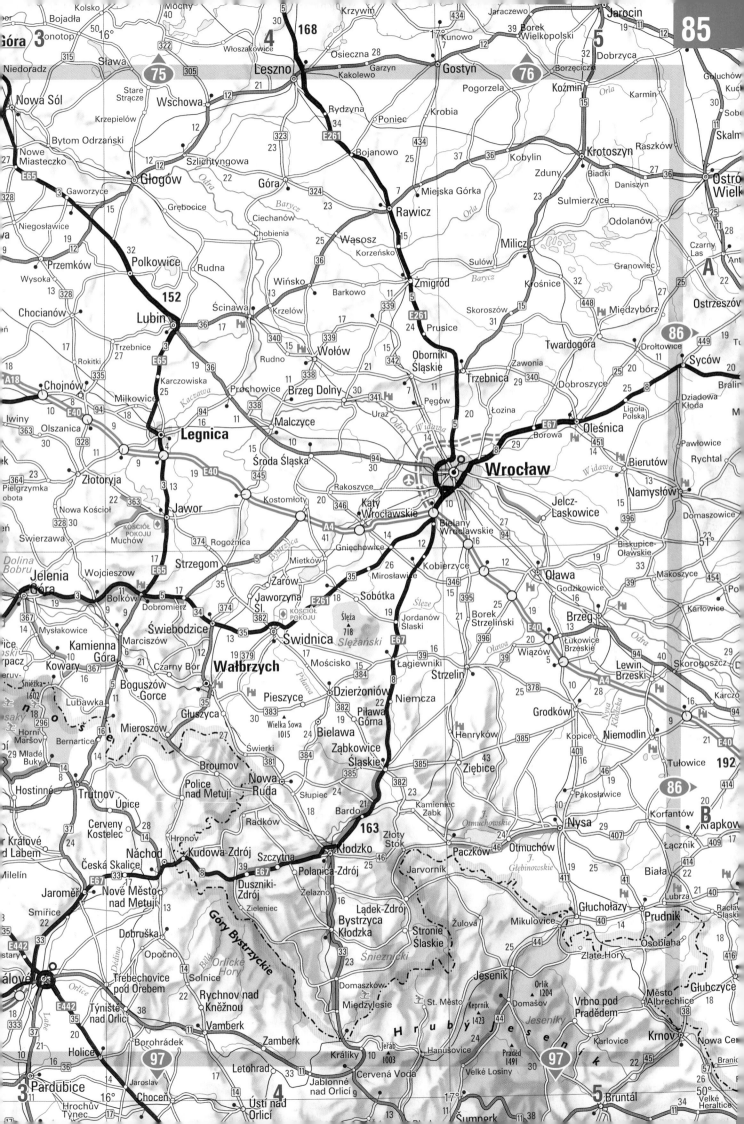

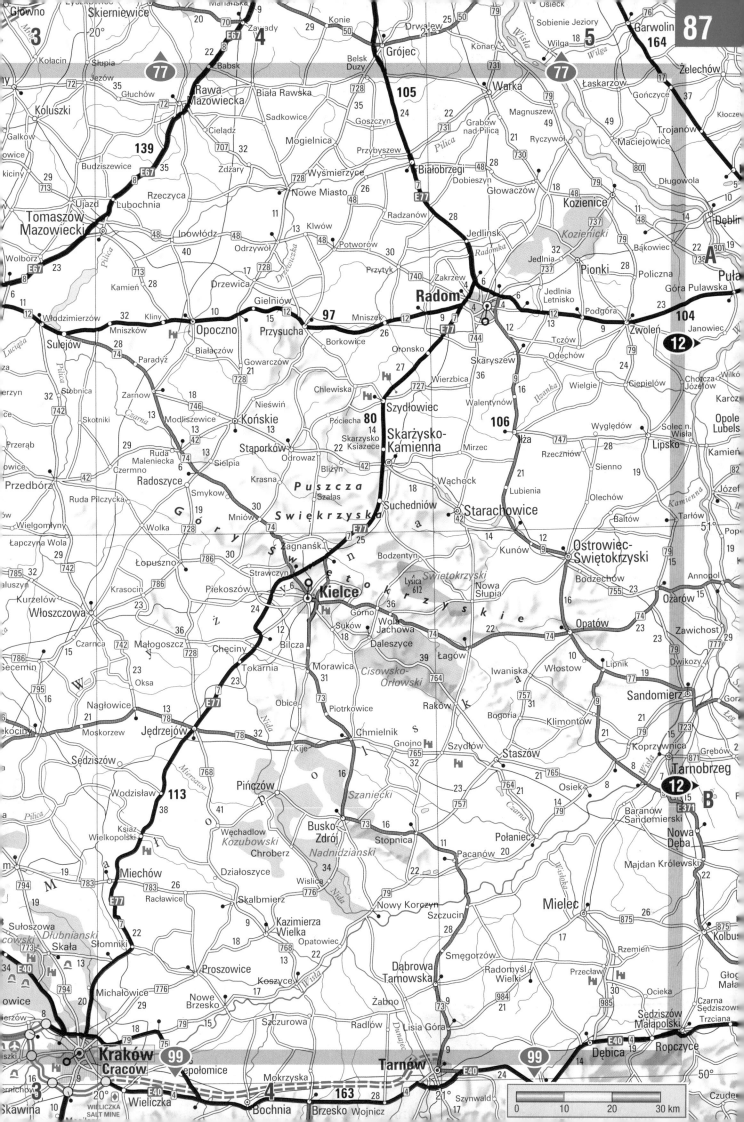

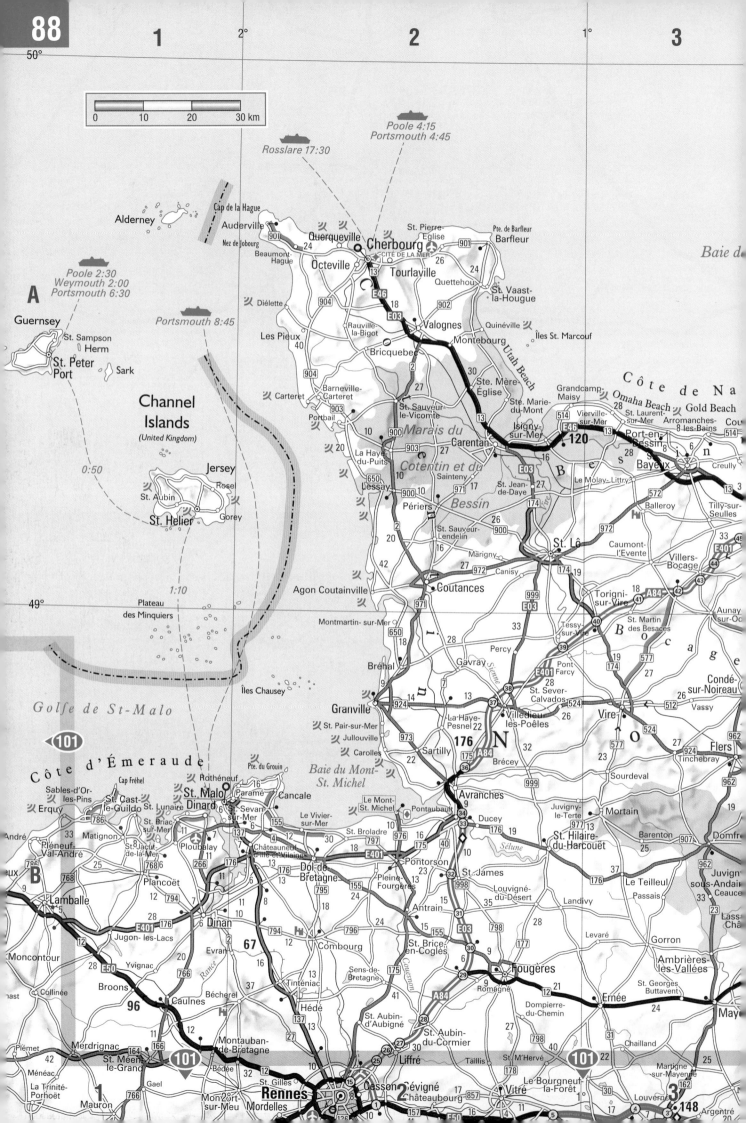

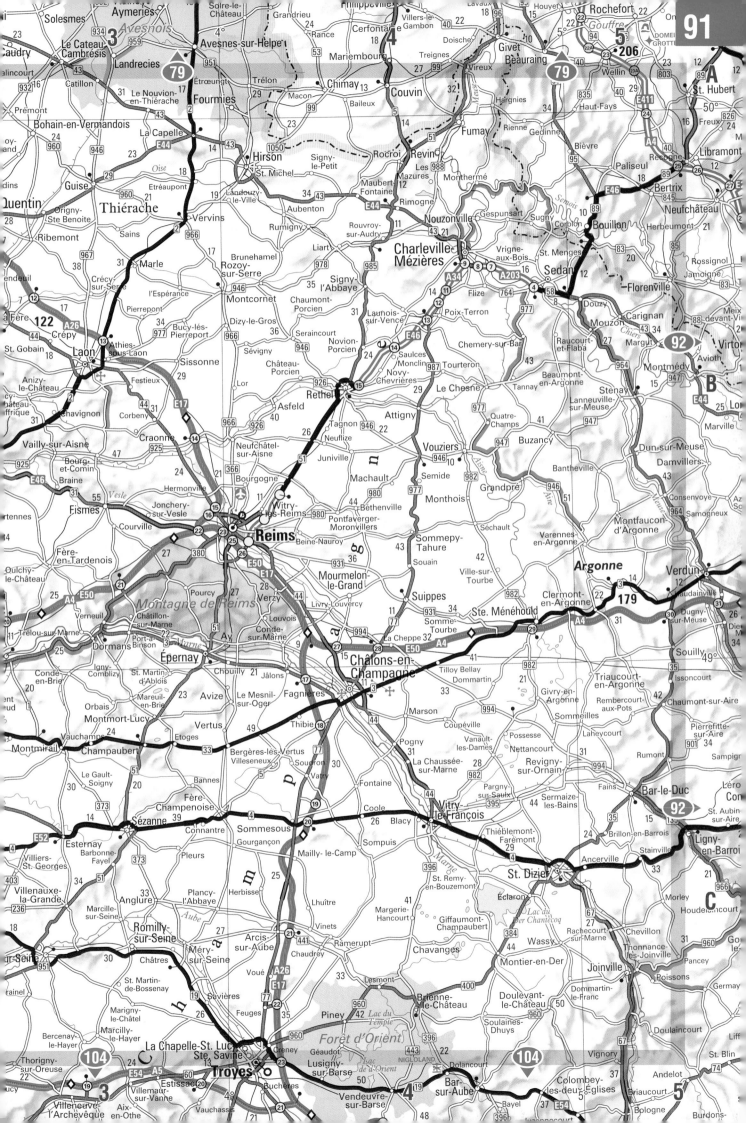

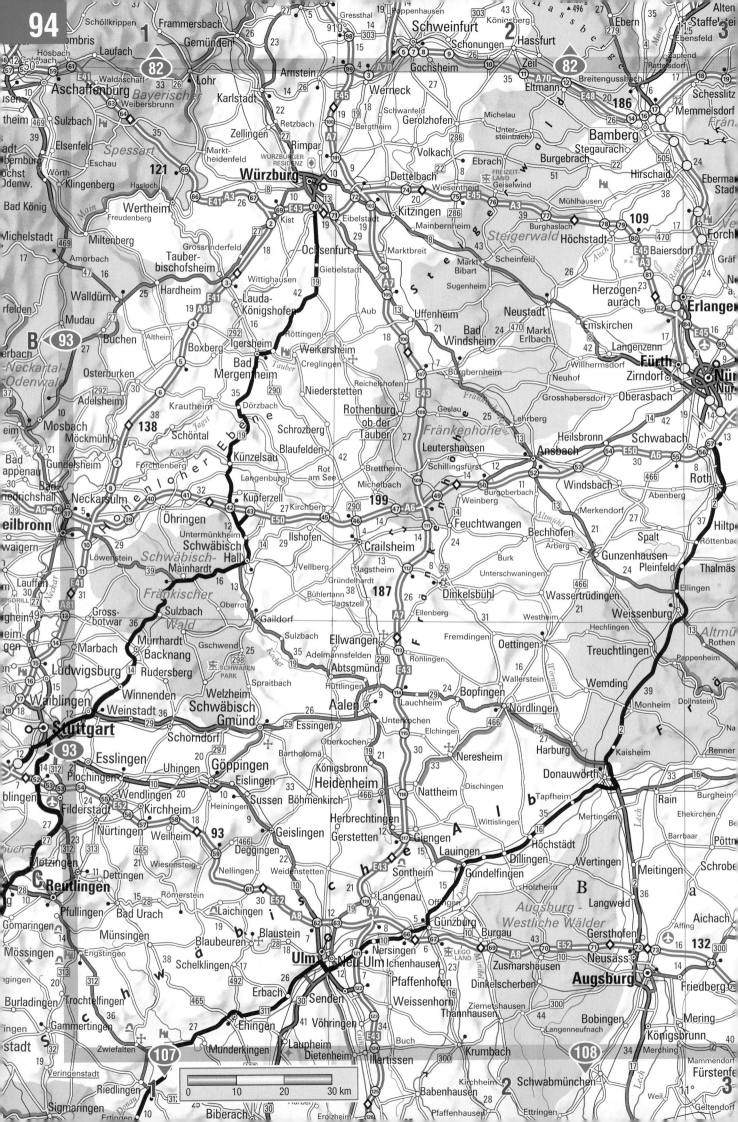

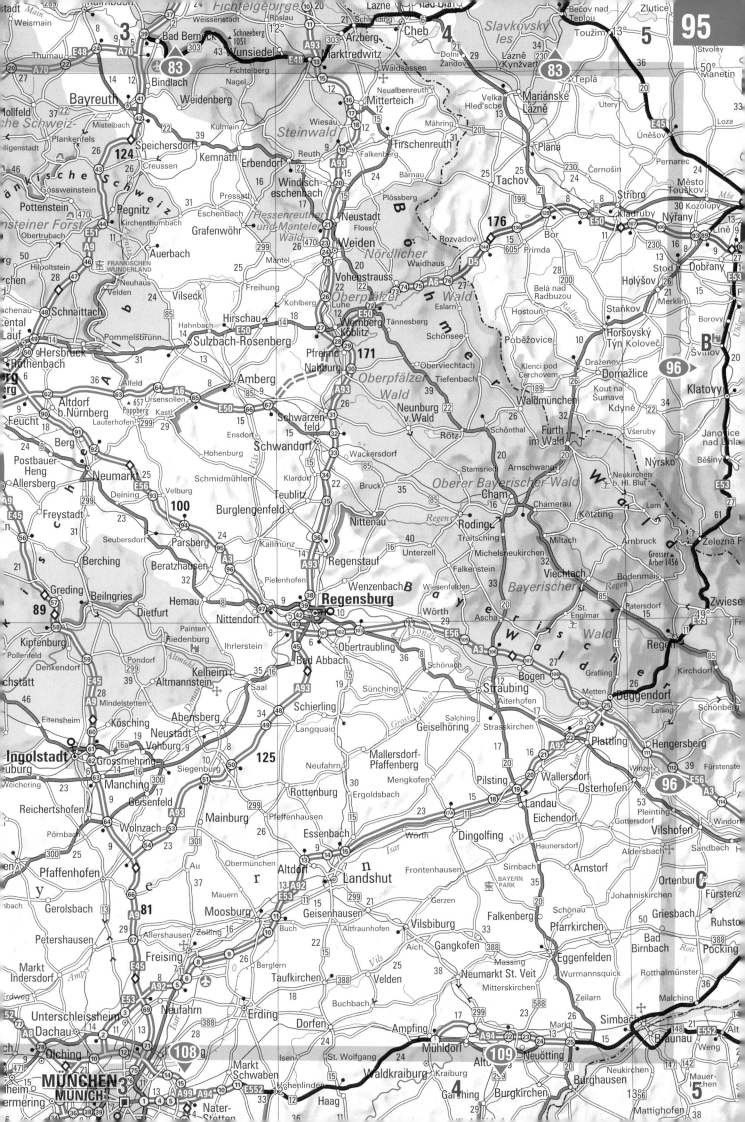

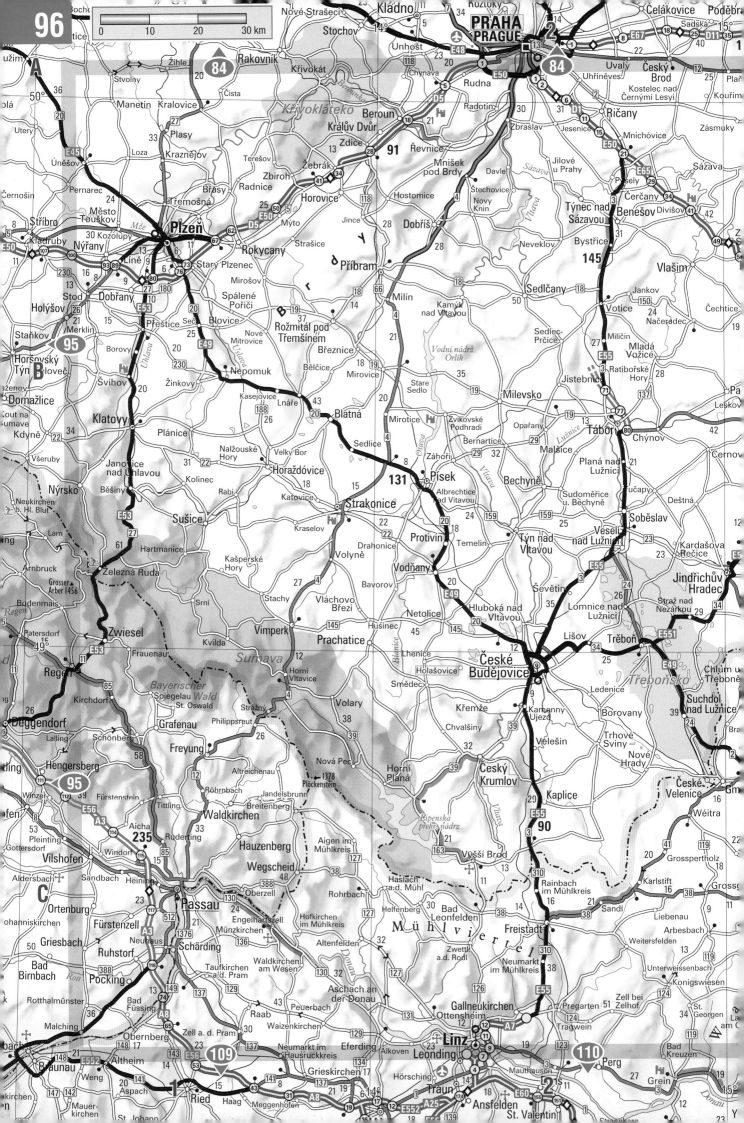

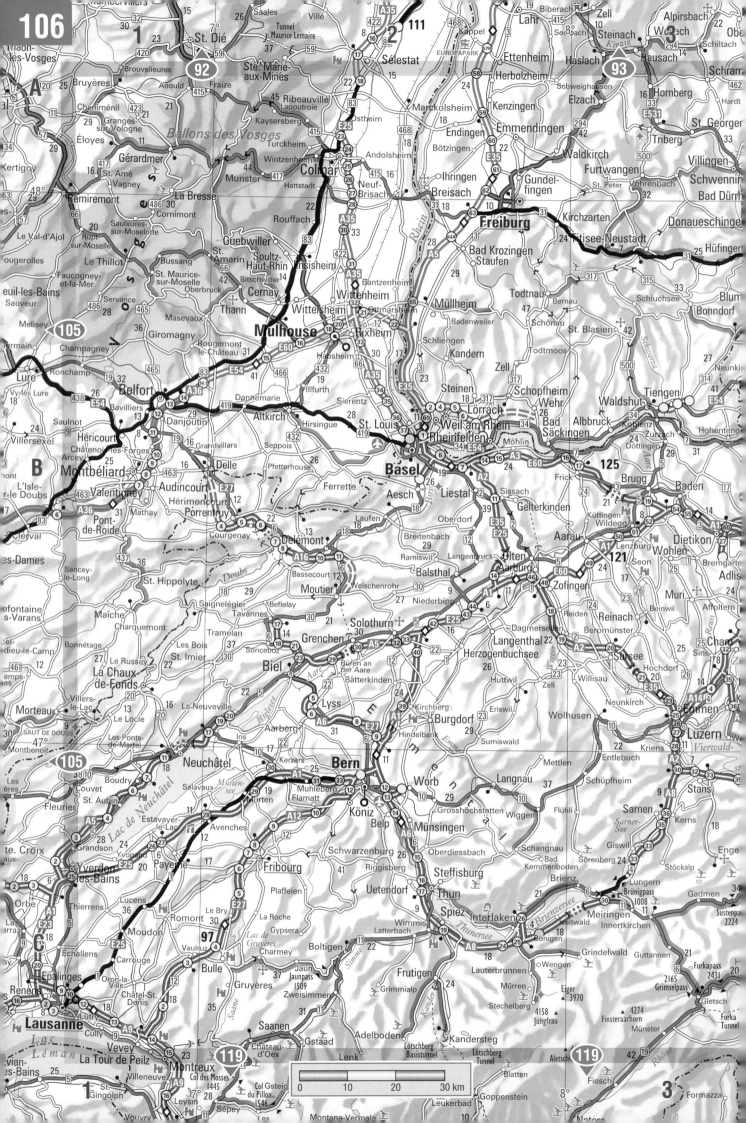

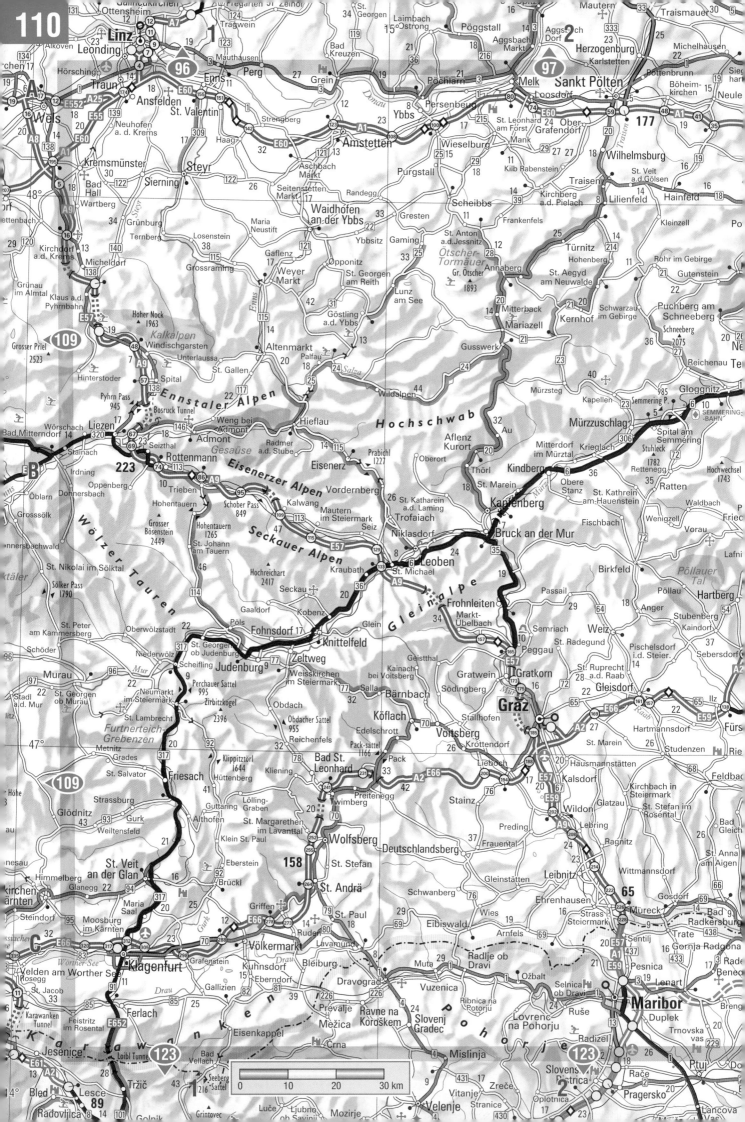

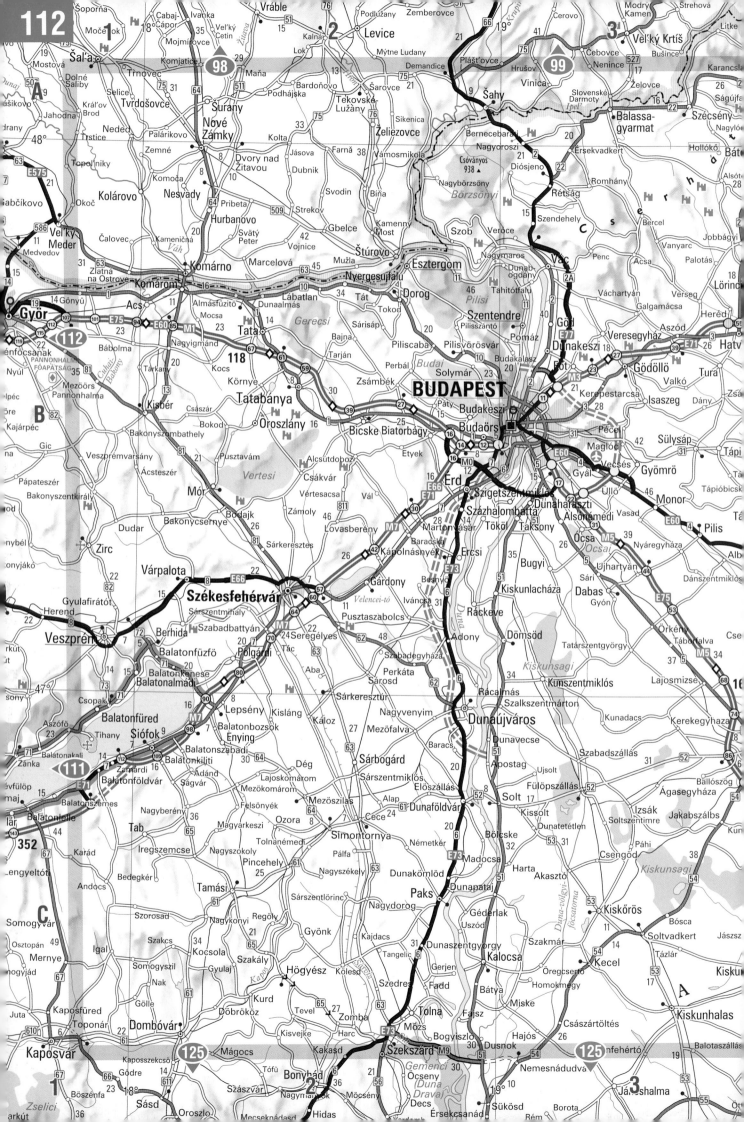

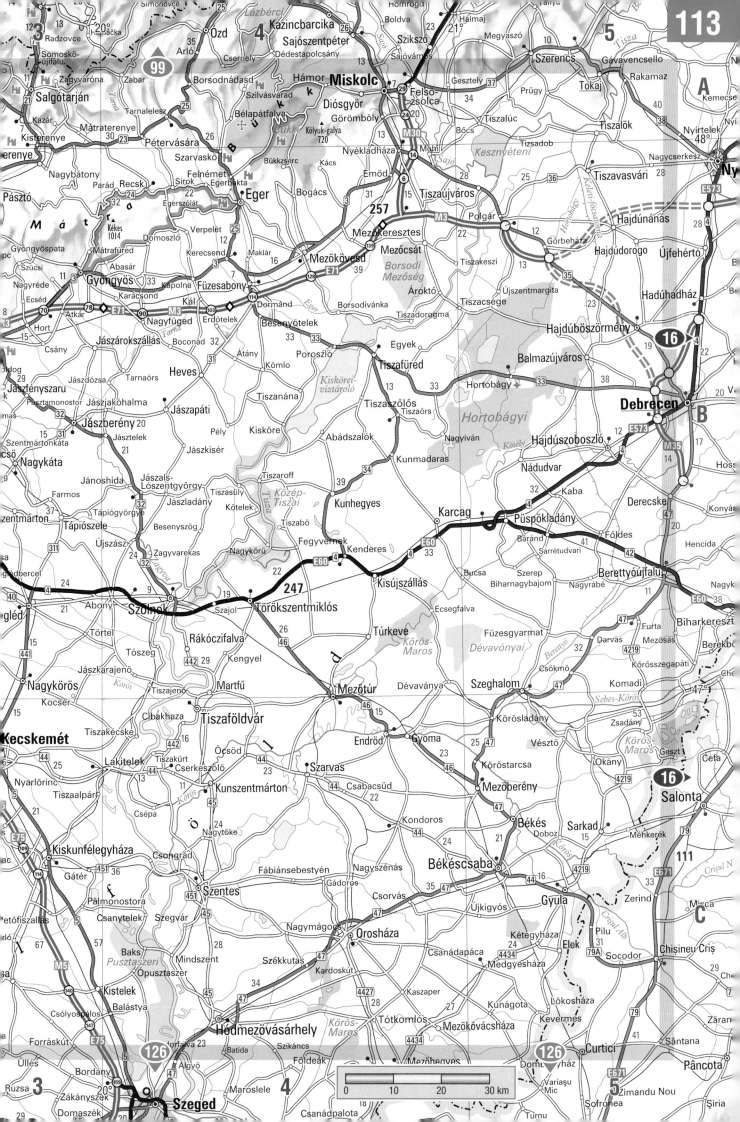

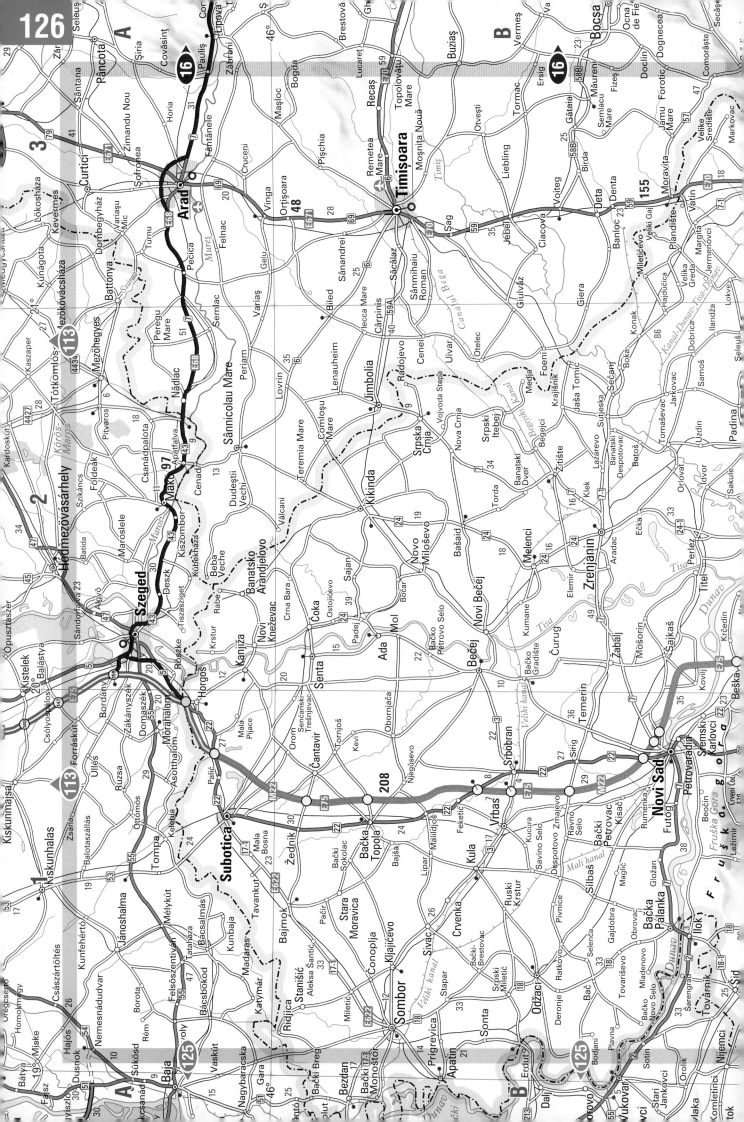

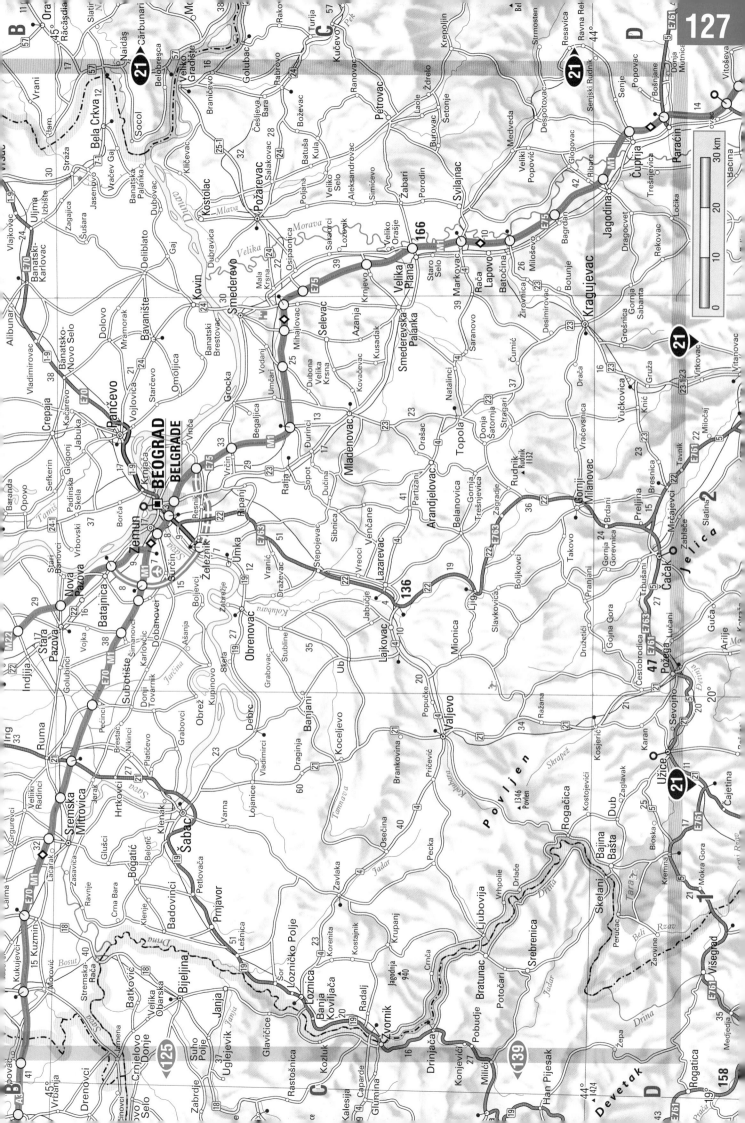

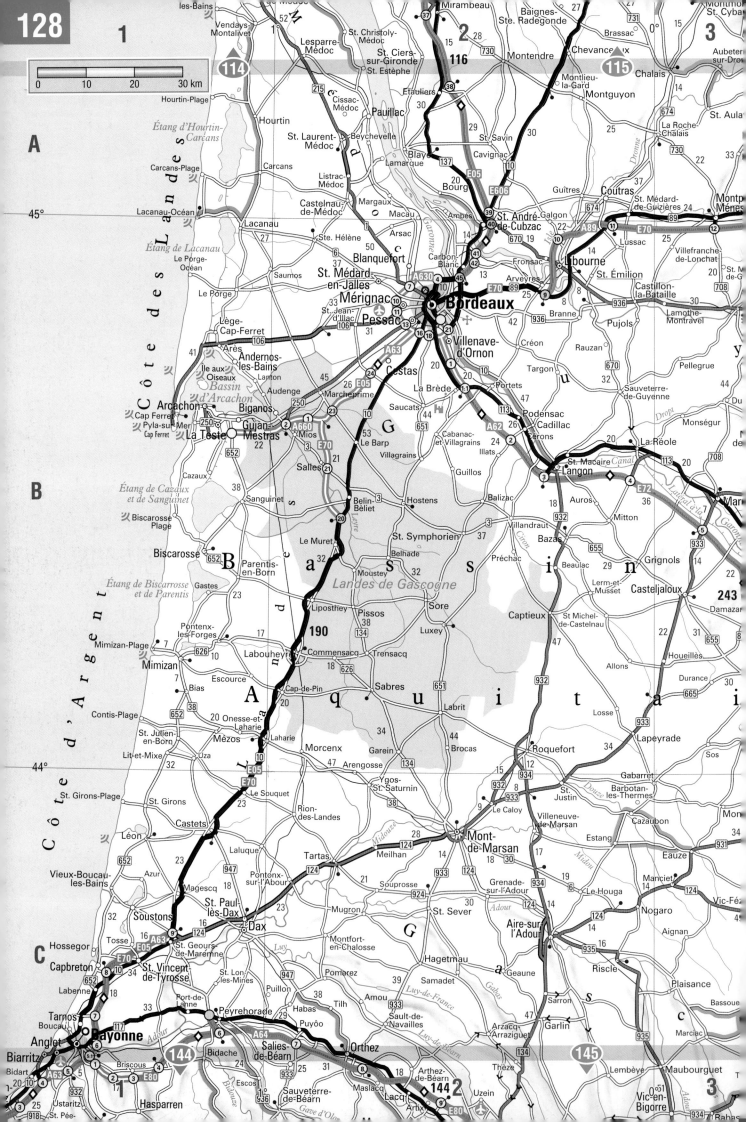

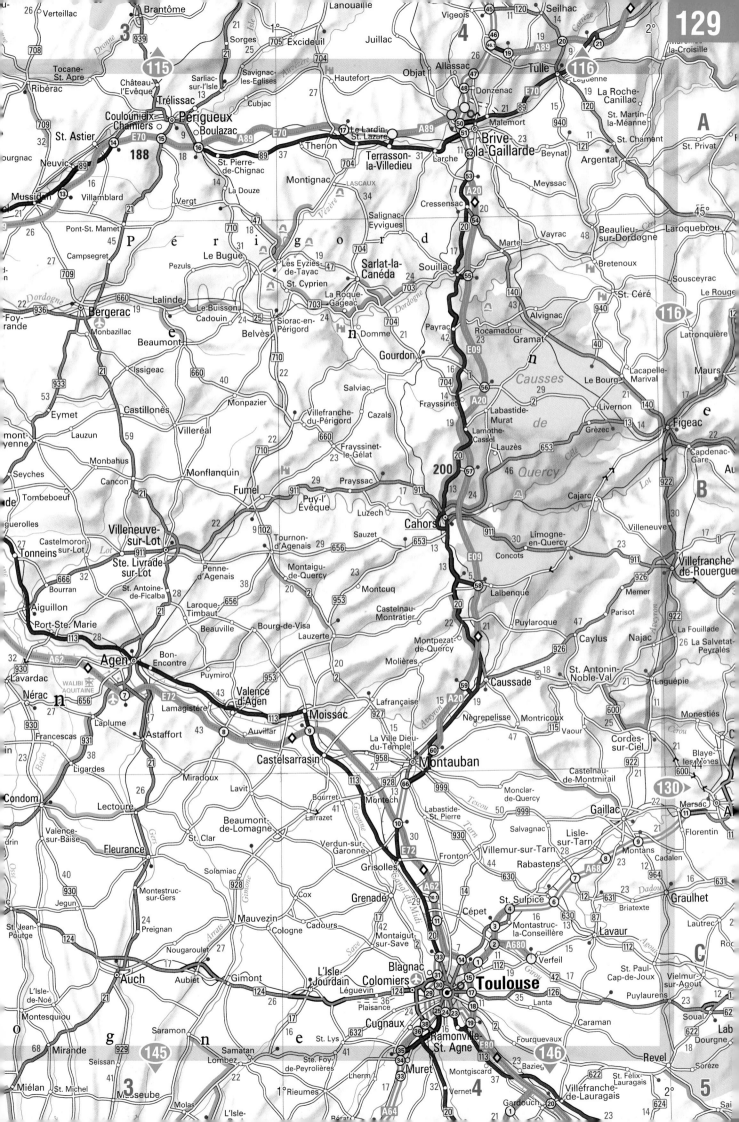

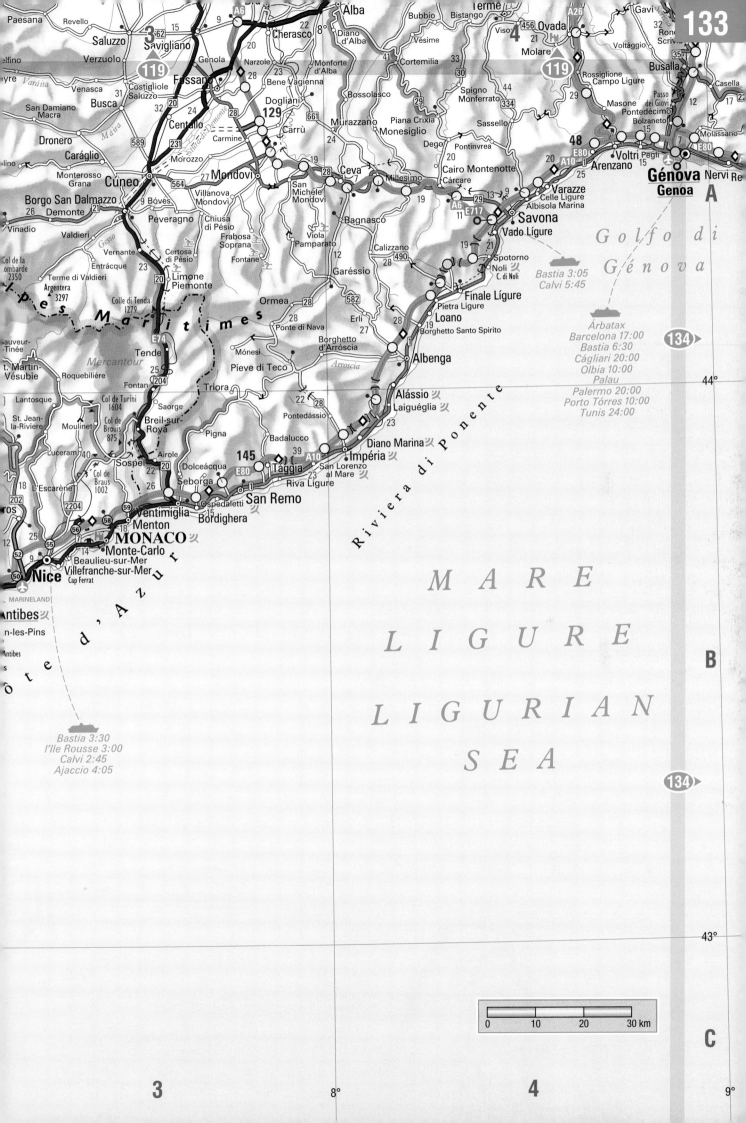

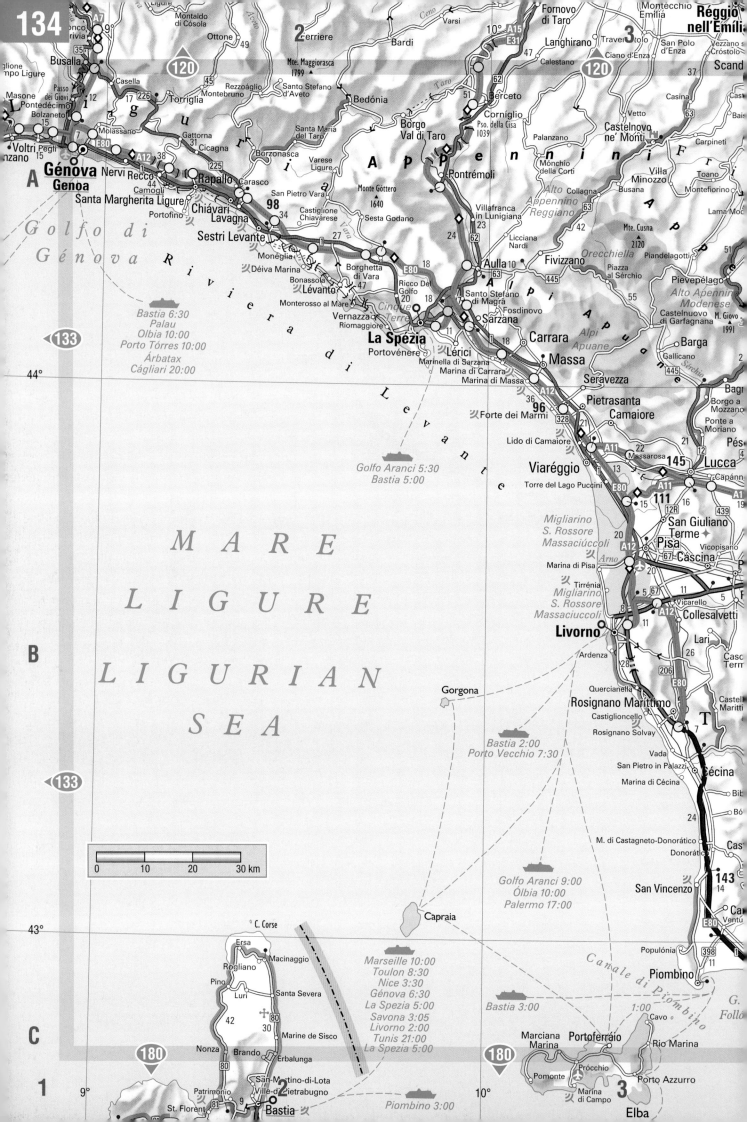

Unije
Nerezine
Čunski
3
Pula 3:00

Mali Lošinj
Veli Lošinj
123
1:30

Susak

Silba
Premuda
Olib
Ist
Molat 2:15

Virsko more

Ancona 6:00

Sestrunj
Petrčane
1:20

Božava
Uglijan
Preko
Kali
Brbinj

Dugi Otok

Kukljica

dar 6:00

Šibenik 8:30
Split 4:30
Starigrad 9:30
Vis 8:00
Hvar 5:00
Vela Luka 6:20
Ubli 7:30
Bar 32:00
Durrës 18:00

Pašman
Zaglav
Pašman
Sali
Žut
Telašćica
Kornati
Kornat
Tkon

Split 5:15

Murter
Žirje
Ancona 8:30

Jabucka

Svetac

A D R I A T I C   S E A

Tronto

Prizna
15°
Novalja
Stara
Novalja
Cesarica
Karlobag
E65
928
25
Metajna
Pag
Gorica
Barič Draga
Tribanj
Kruščica
Paklenica
Starigrad-
Paklenica

Pag

Vir
Povljana
Vir
Ražanac

Privlaka
Vrsi
Nin
Poličnik
8
Jasenice 54
17
E65
8
Posedarje
Novigrad

Murvica
Zadar
18
502
13
Zemunik Donji
56
21
Bibinje
Sukošan
17
Benkovac
26
Miranje
A1
Turanj
27
Biograd na Moru
Pakoštane
Stankovci
Vransko
Jezero
39
8
E65
Pirovac
27
Prokljansko
Jezero
Murter
Tisno
37
Vodice
8
Zablaće
149
Krapanj
Primošten
Rogoznica

Klanac
Lički
Osik
odlapača
4
Gospić
389
Vrebac
123
Udbina
Brušane
29
Bilaj
Lukovo
Šugorje
28
50
22
Gornja
Ploča
17
Medak
Vaganski
vrh
1757
Raduč
Sveti Rok
Velebit
A1
50
21
Gračac
27
Zrmanja
Obrovac
16
18
Medvide
10
Kaštel
Zegarski
23
Ervenik
138
Đevrske
44°
Krka
Skradin
Žablaće
33
Šibenik
138

Josan
Donj
389
A
Kremen
1591
Mazin
Bruvno
33
1
Otr
1
Mokro
Polj

43°
Biševo

0   10   20   30 km

3
15°
4
C

egli Abruzzi

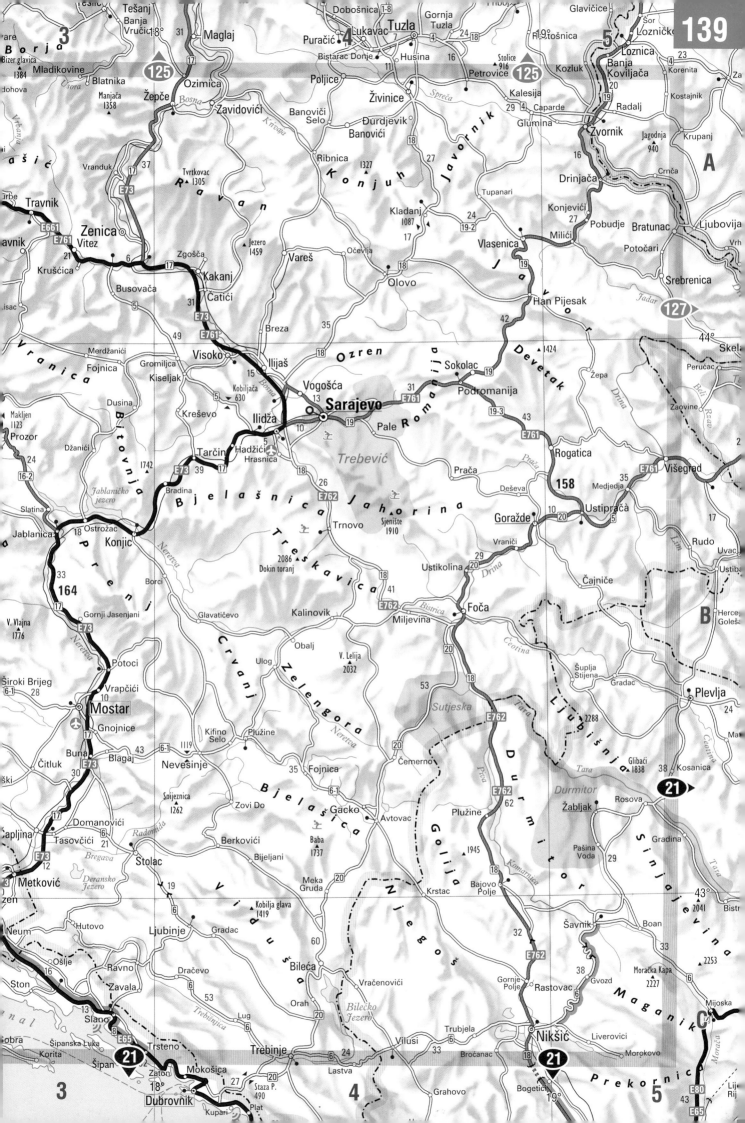

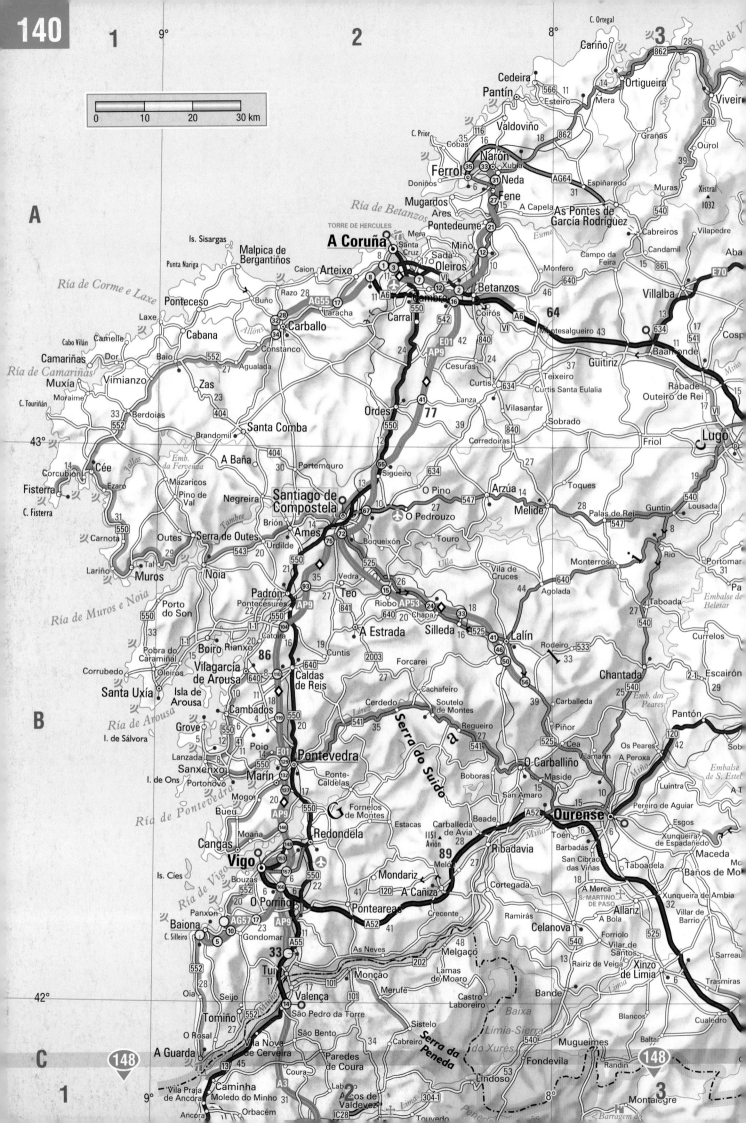

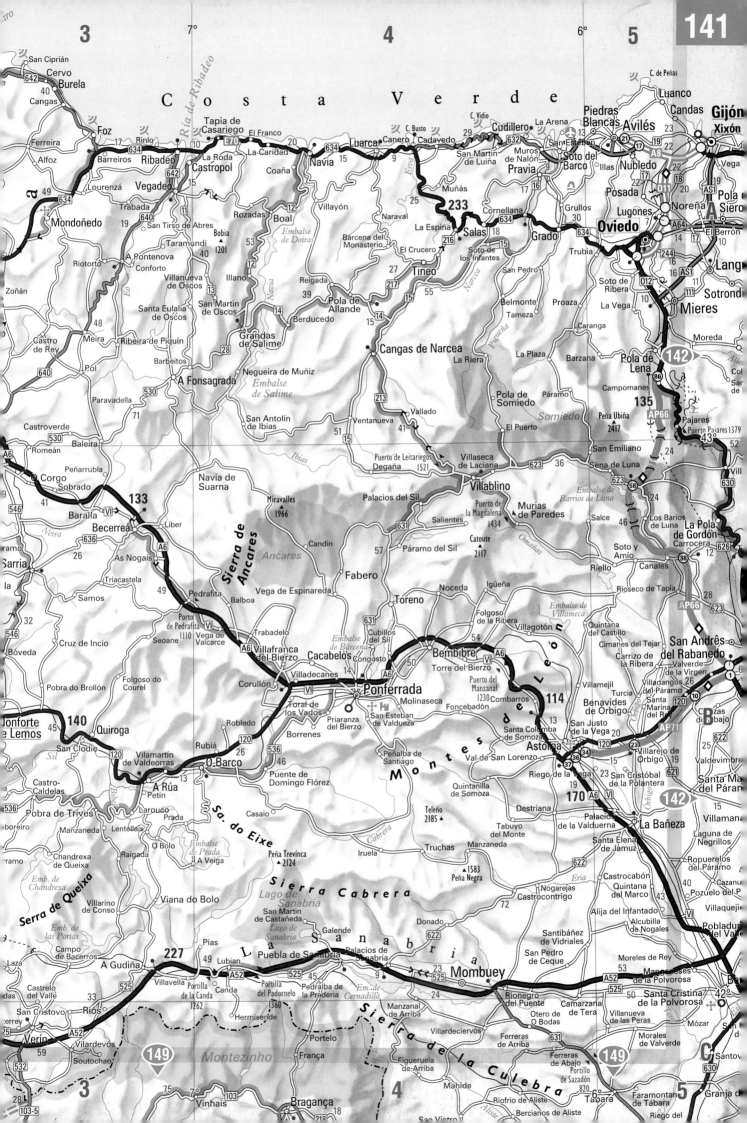

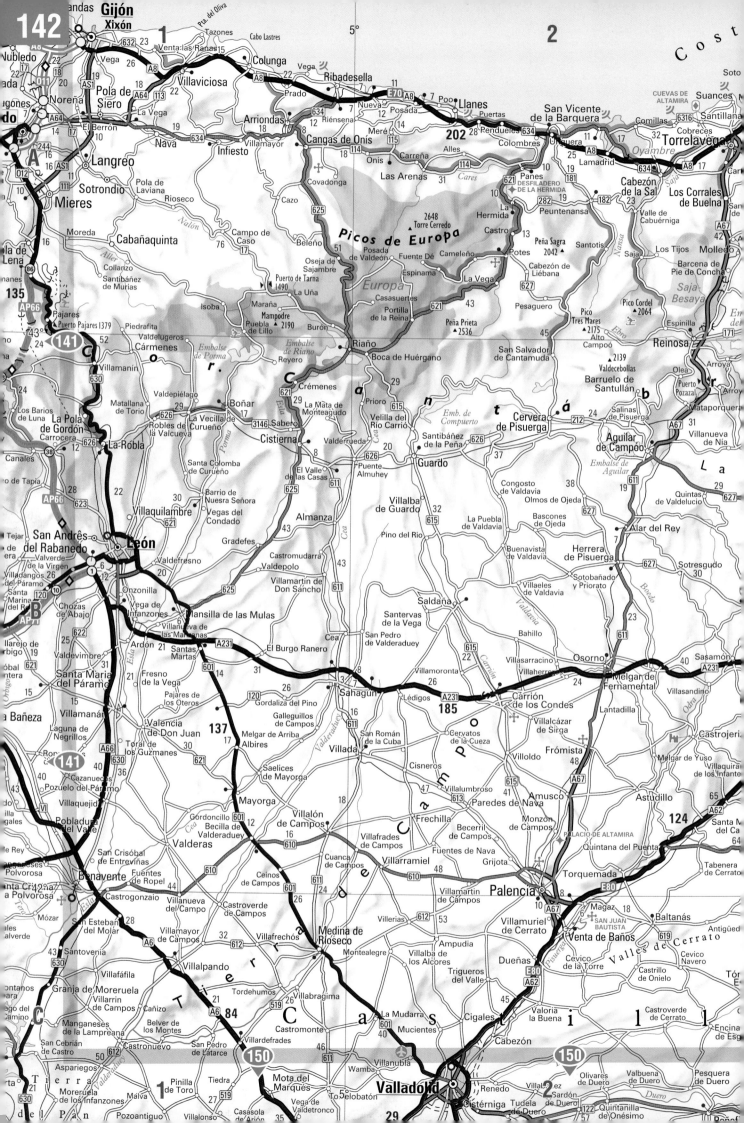

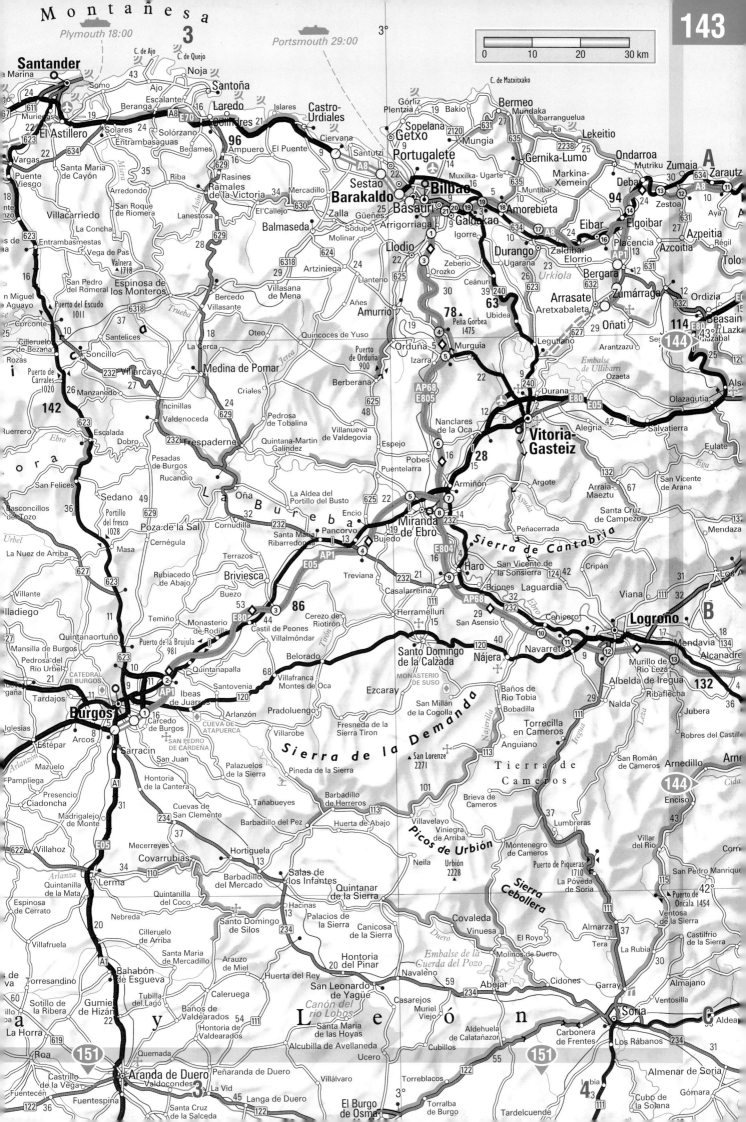

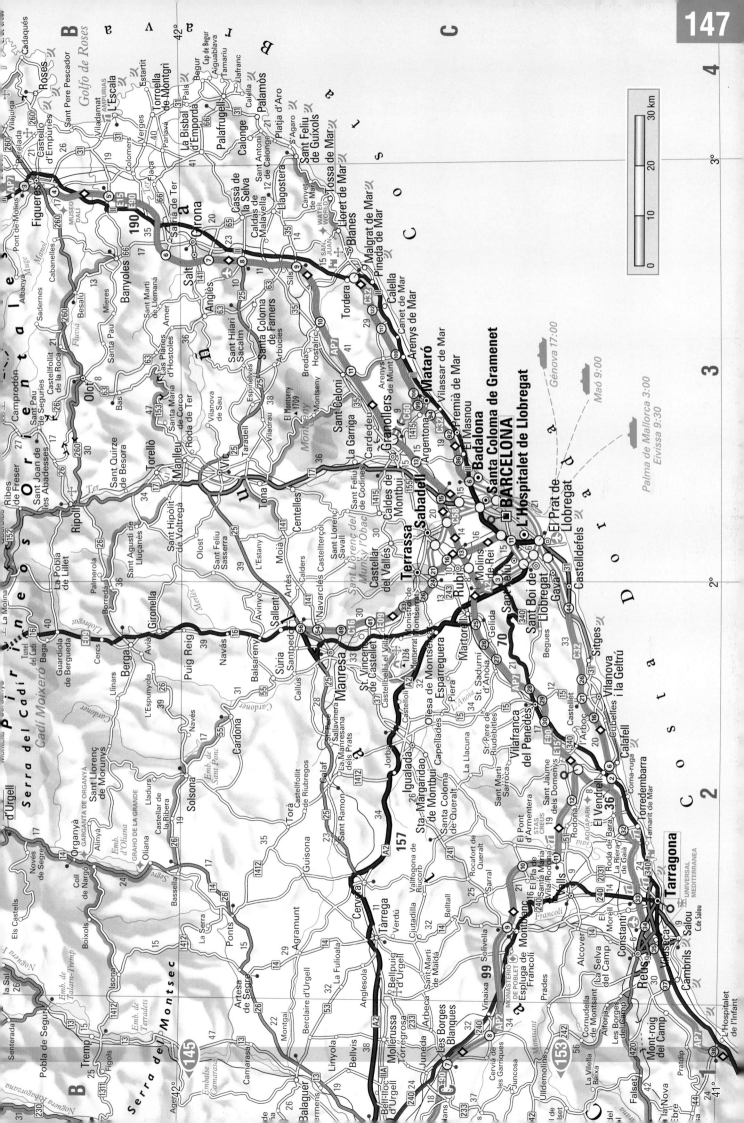

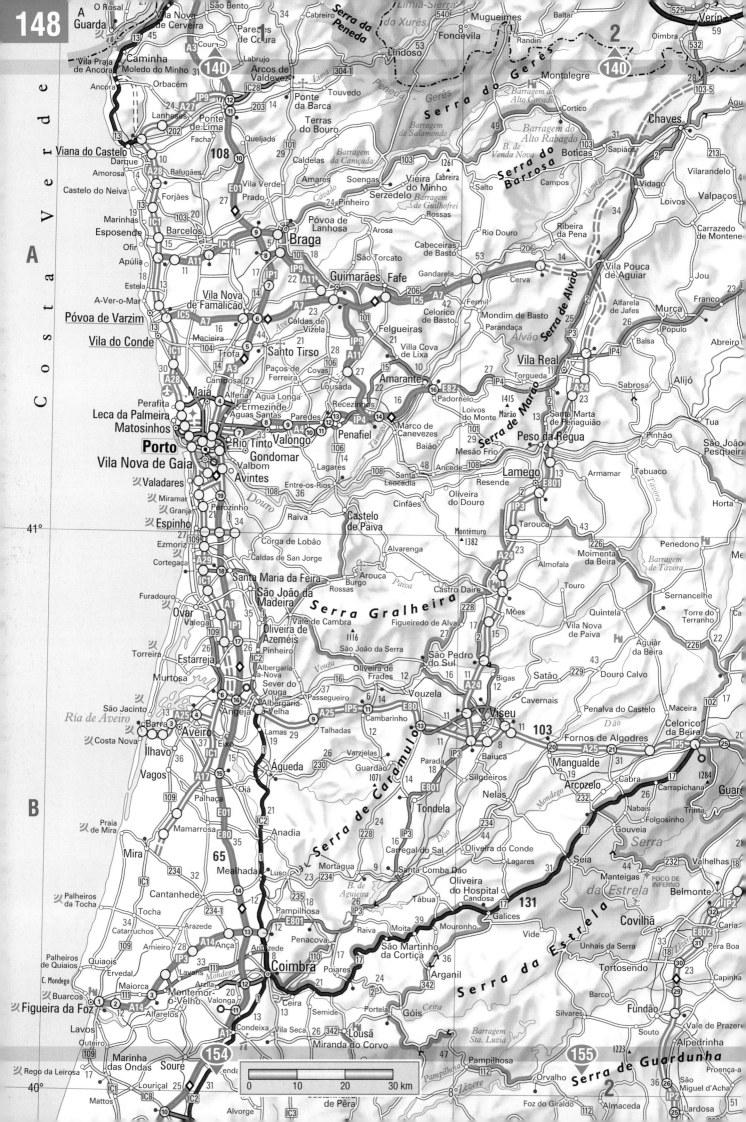

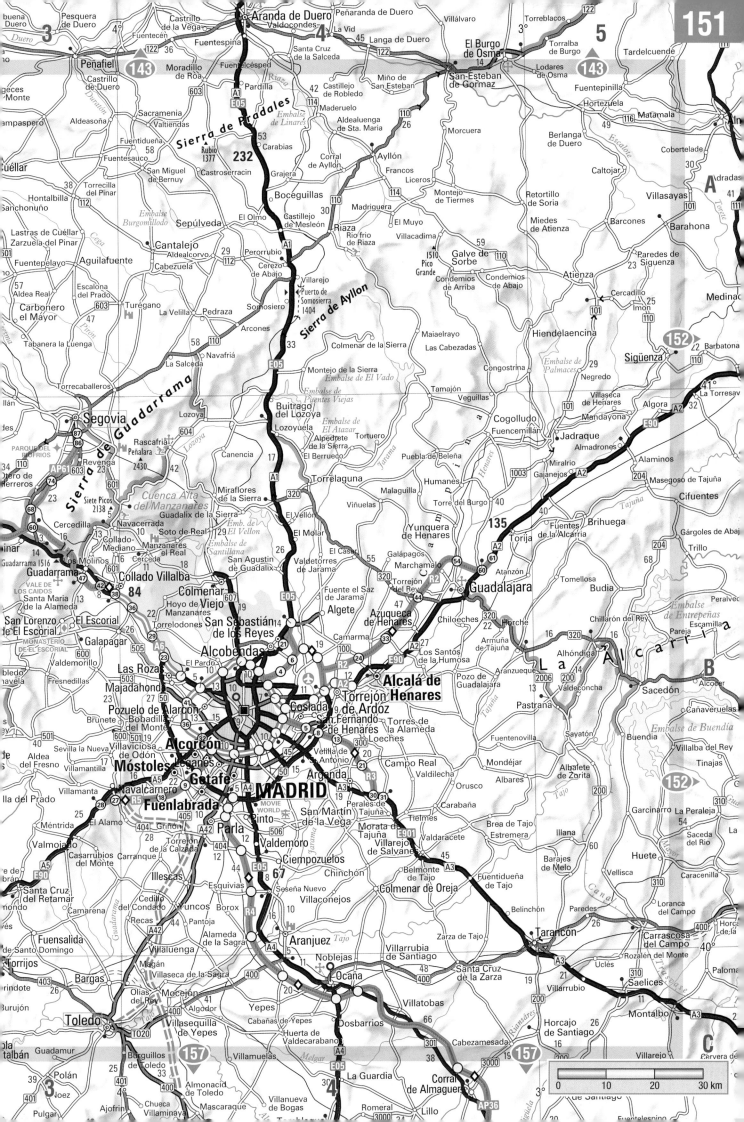

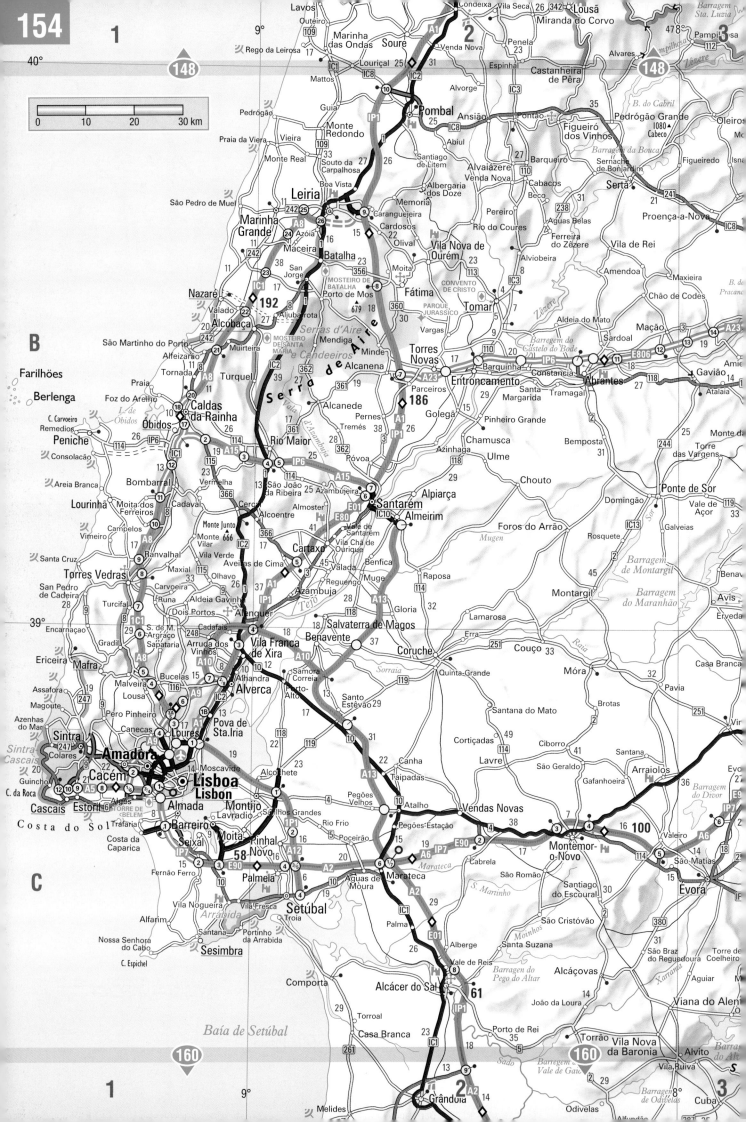

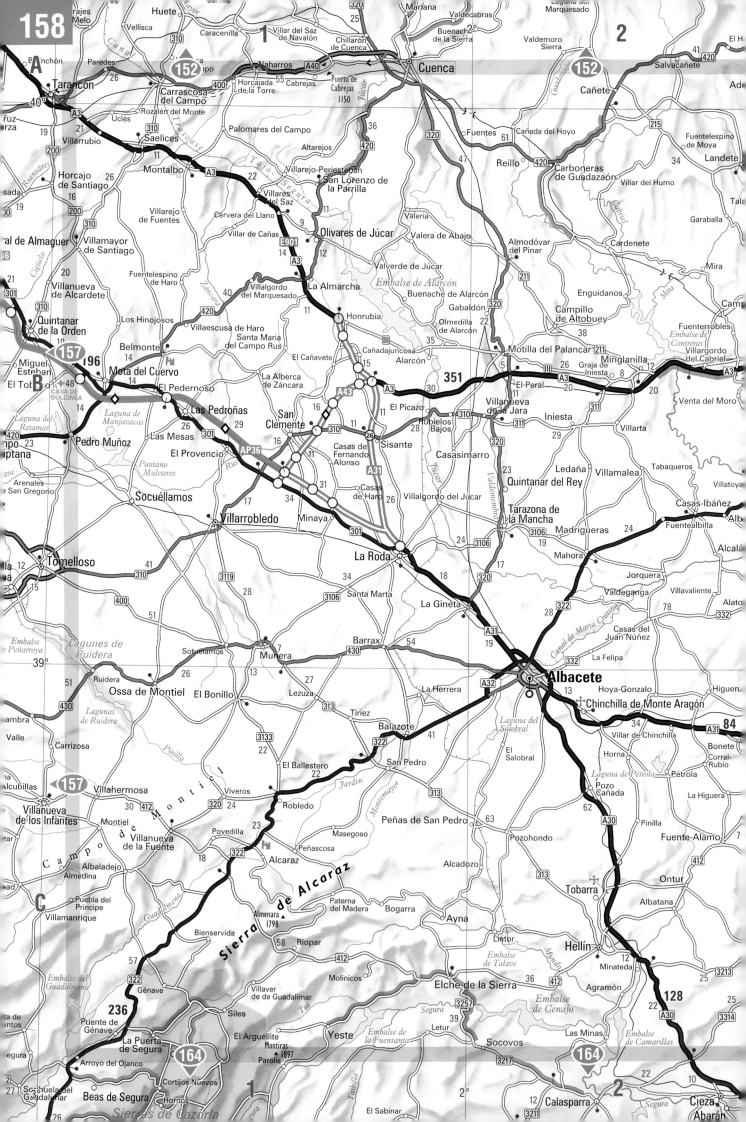

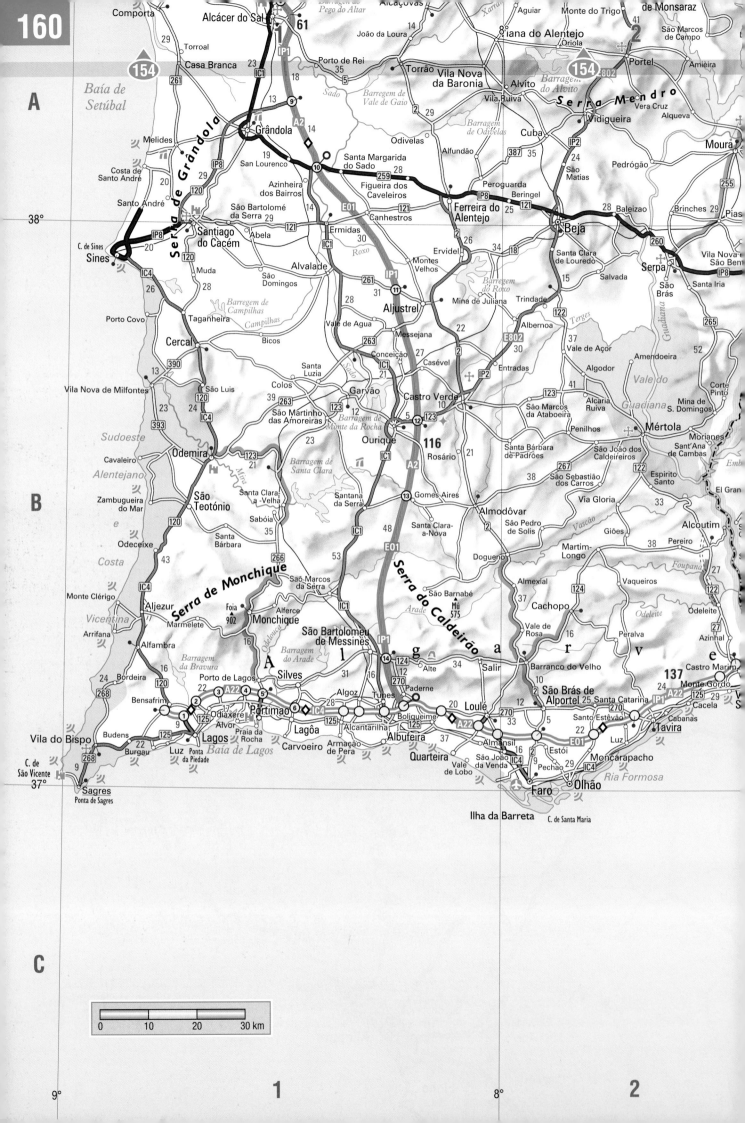

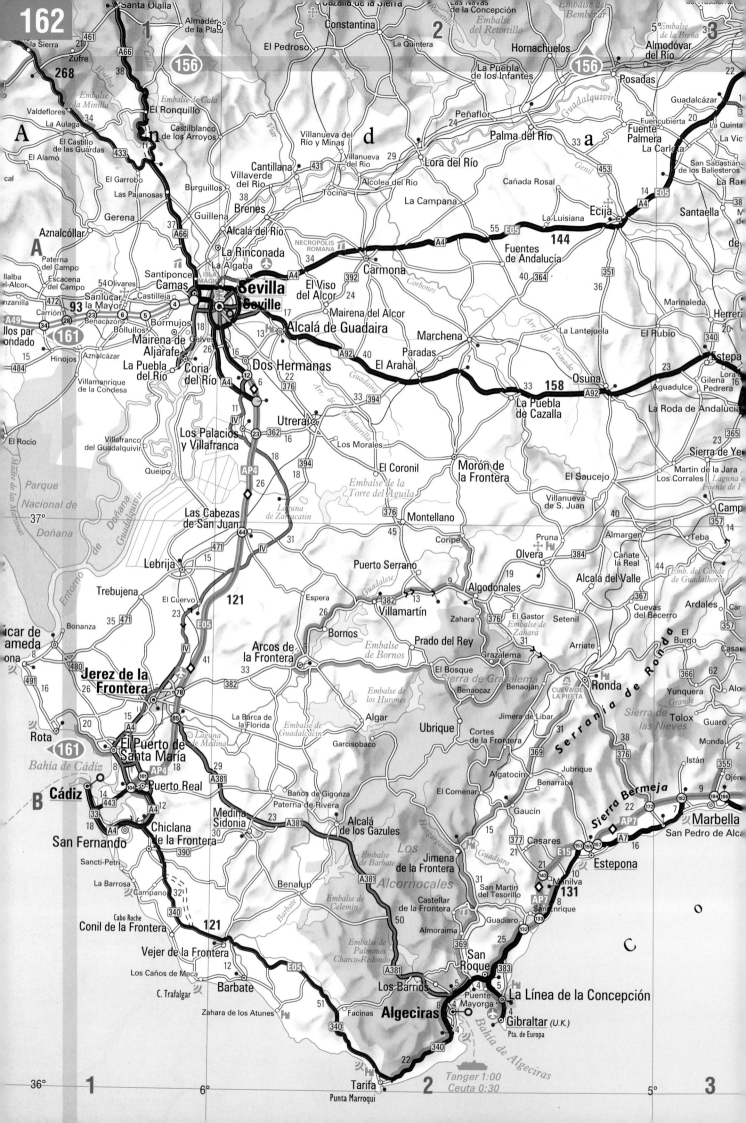

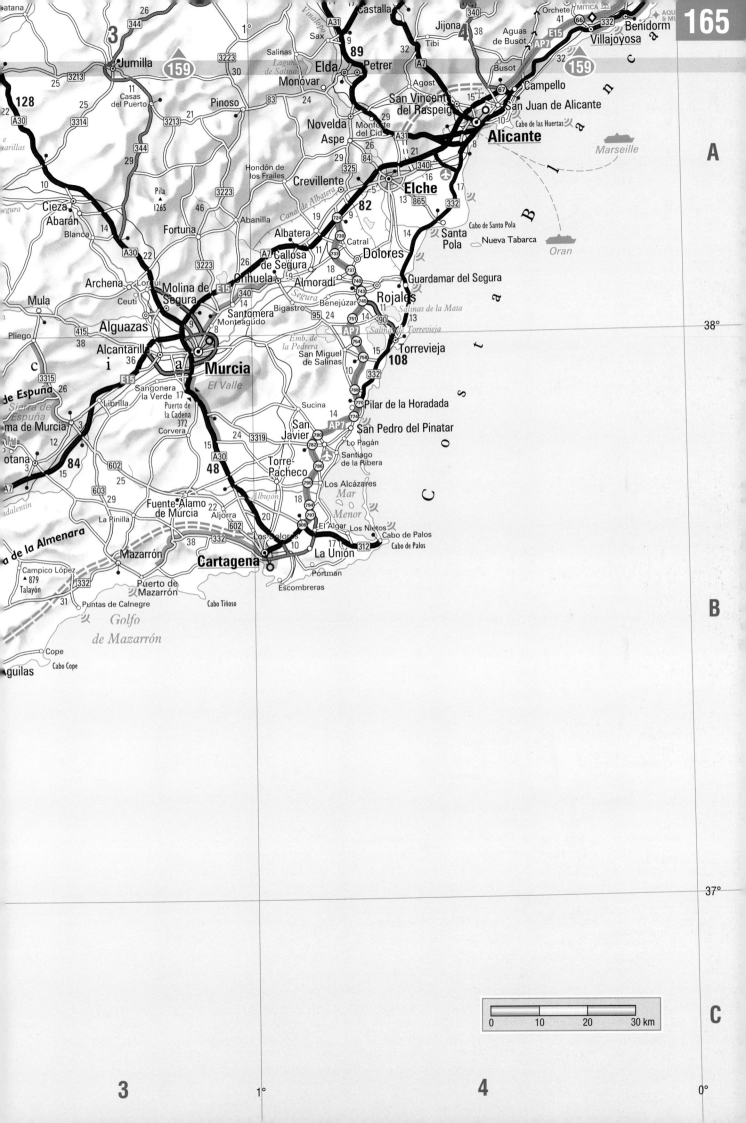

A

1   2°   2

40°

Islas
Columbretes
(Espana)
(Spain)

40°

*Islas
Columbretes*

1°

B

ISLAS
BALEARES
BALEARIC
ISLANDS

Port de Sóller
Fo
Sóller
Deia
Tunel.d
Sóller
Valldemossa
Alar
Banyalbufar
25
Bunyo
Estellencs
39
Esporles
711
Puigpunyent
Marratxi.
12
Sa Dragonera
710
Palma de
Mallorca
Andratx
Calvià
PM1
6
10
Port d'Andratx
15
719
13
12
PM1
Peguera
Palma
Can
Nova
Pastilla
Santa Ponça
Magaluf
S'Arenal
Cap Enderrocat
Barcelona 3:00
Cap de Cala Figuera
Bahía
de Palma
Maó 6:30
Valencia 6:00
Mallorca
Cap
Eivissa 2:15
Majorca
Denia 9:00

C

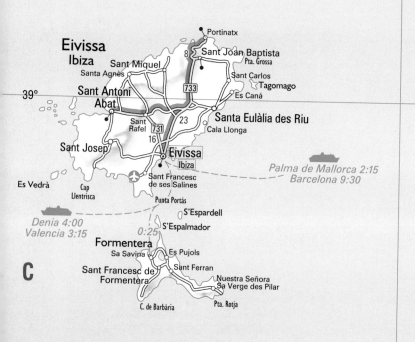

Portinatx
Eivissa
Ibiza
8
Sant Joan Baptista
Sant Miquel
Pta. Grossa
Santa Agnès
Sant Carlos
733
Tagomago
Sant Antoni
Es Caná
39°
Abat
23
Santa Eulàlia des Riu
Sant
Rafel
731
Cala Llonga
16
Sant Josep
Eivissa
Ibiza
Palma de Mallorca 2:15
Barcelona 9:30
Es Vedrà
Cap
Sant Francesc
Llentrisca
de ses Salines
Punta Portás
Denia 4:00
S'Espardell
Valencia 3:15
S'Espalmador
0:25
Formentera
Es Pujols
Sa Savina
Sant Ferran
Sant Francesc de
Nuestra Señora
Formentera
Sa Verge des Pilar
C. de Barbària
Pta. Rotja

1   2°   2

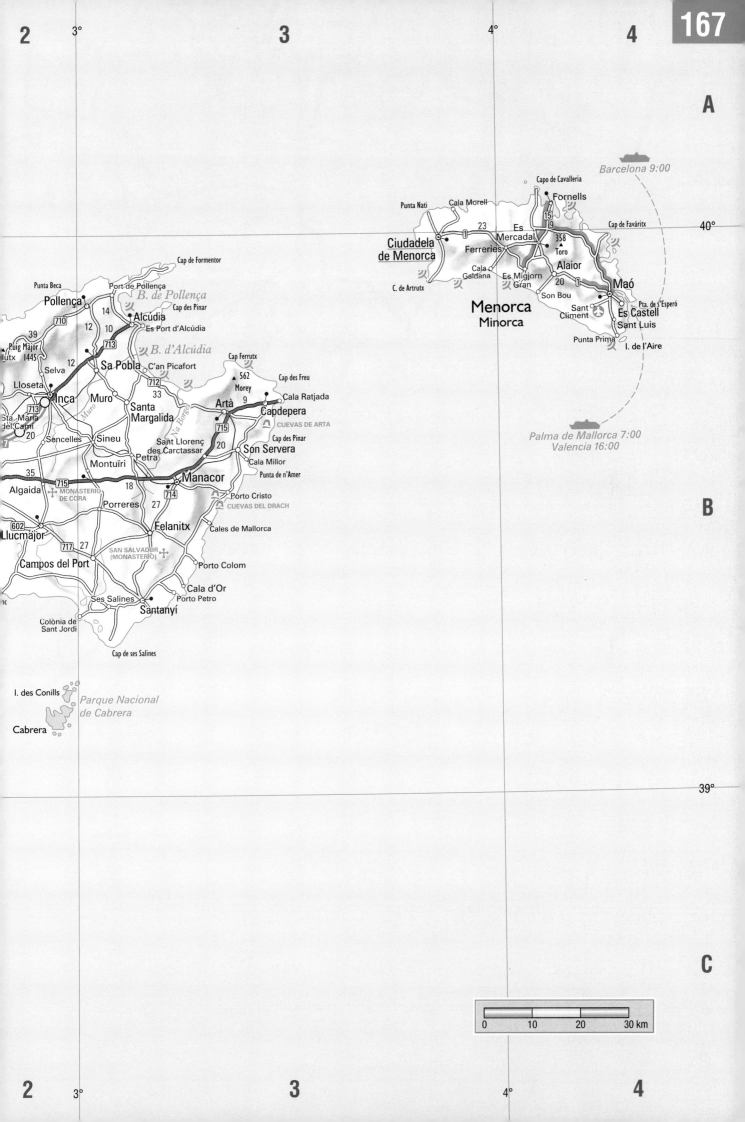

2 3° 3 4° 4

A

Capo de Cavalleria
Barcelona 9:00
Punta Nati Cala Morell Fornells
23 Es Mercadal 15 9 Cap de Favàritx 40°
Ciudadela de Menorca Ferreries 358 Toro Alaior Maó
Cala Galdana Es Migjorn Gran 20 1 Pta. de s'Esperó
Menorca Son Bou Sant Es Castell
Minorca C. de Artrutx Climent Sant Luis
Punta Prima
Palma de Mallorca 7:00 I. de l'Aire
Valencia 16:00

Cap de Formentor
Punta Beca
Pollença 14 Port de Pollença B. de Pollença
710 12 10 Alcúdia Cap des Pinar
39 713 Es Port d'Alcúdia
Puig Major B. d'Alcúdia
1445 12 Sa Pobla C'an Picafort Cap Ferrutx
Selva 712 562 Cap des Freu
Lloseta 33 Morey
Inca Muro Artà 9 Cala Ratjada
Sta. Maria Santa Margalida 715 Capdepera
del Camí 20 Sencelles Sineu Sant Llorenç 20 CUEVAS DE ARTA
Petra des Carctassar Son Servera Cap des Pinar
Montuïri 18 Cala Millor
35 715 MONASTERIO Manacor Punta de n'Amer
Algaida DE CORA 714 Porto Cristo
602 Porreres 27 CUEVAS DEL DRACH
Llucmàjor Felanitx Cales de Mallorca
717 27 SAN SALVADOR Porto Colom
Campos del Port (MONASTERIO) Cala d'Or
Ses Salines Porto Petro
Colònia de Santanyí
Sant Jordi
Cap de ses Salines

I. des Conills
Parque Nacional
de Cabrera
Cabrera

B

39°

C

0 10 20 30 km

2 3° 3 4° 4

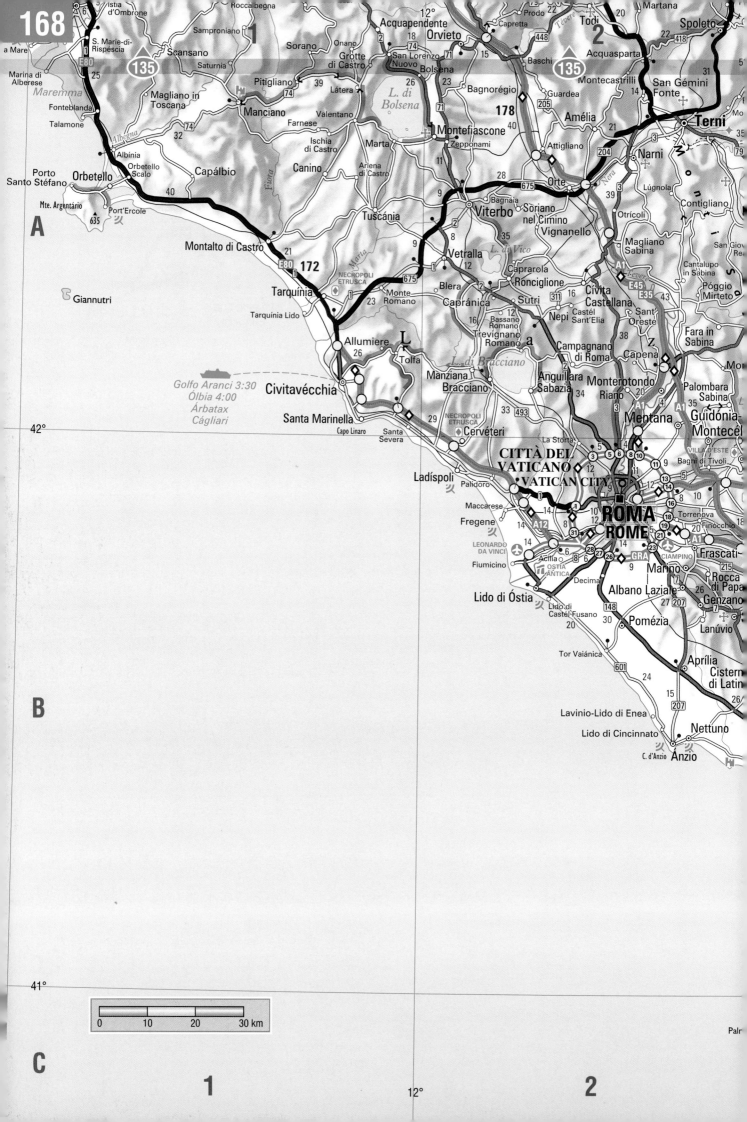

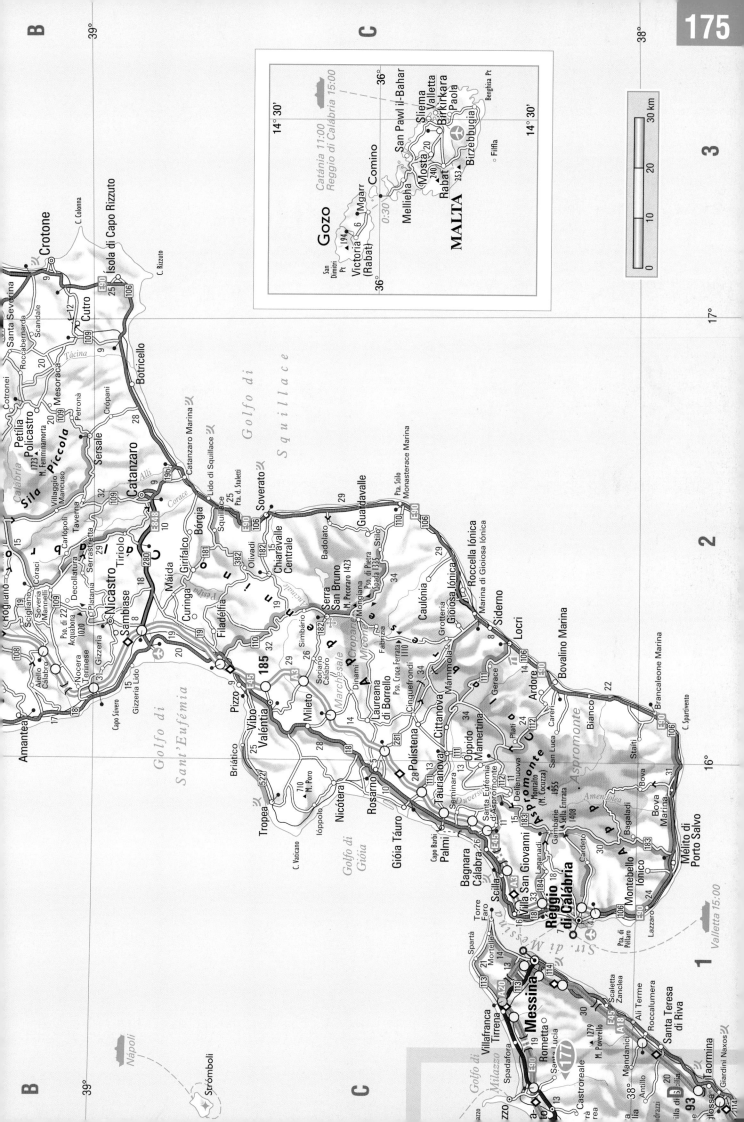

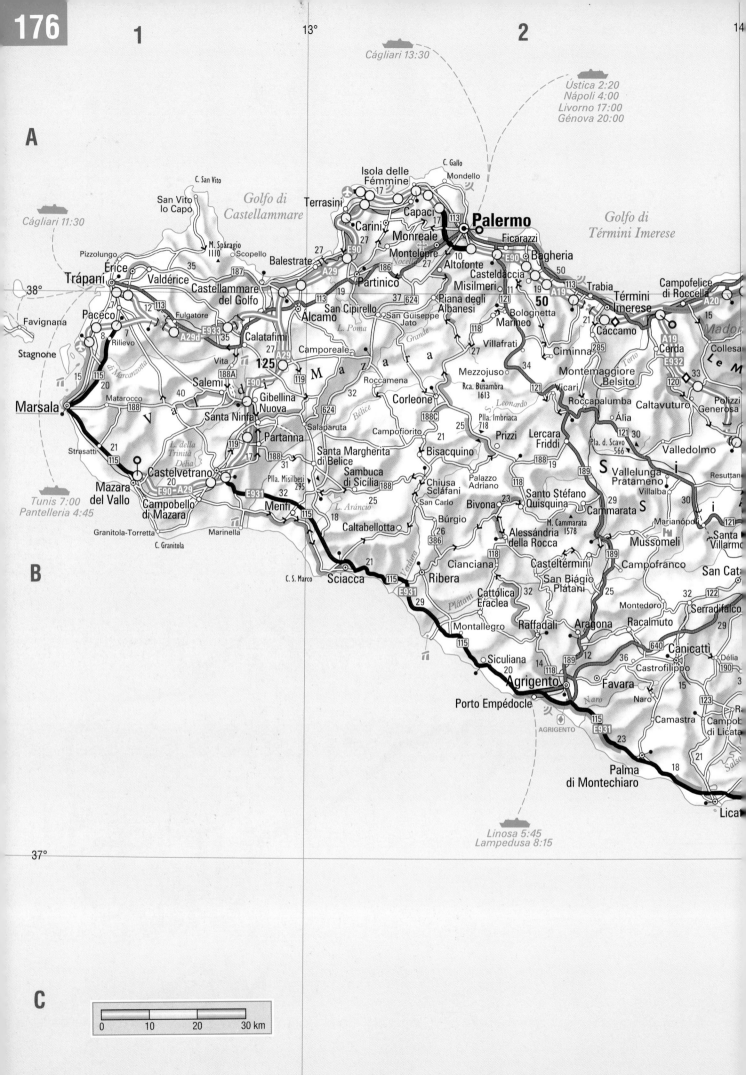

1   13°   2   14

A

Cágliari 13:30

Ústica 2:20
Nápoli 4:00
Livorno 17:00
Génova 20:00

C. San Vito

San Vito
lo Capo

Golfo di
Castellammare

C. Gallo
Mondello

Isola delle
Fémmine   17

Terrasini

Capaci   17
113

Palermo

Golfo di
Términi Imerese

Cágliari 11:30

Pizzolungo

M. Spáragio
1110   Scopello

Carini   27

Monreale
Montelepre

Ficarazzi

Bagheria

Érice   35

Valdérice

Castellammare
del Golfo

Balestrate   27

E90   10

Altofonte

Casteldáccia

50

Trápani   38°

187

A29

Partinico   19

186   Nocella   27

Misilmeri

Trabia

Campofelice
di Roccella

113   San Cipirello   624

Piana degli
Albanesi

11   19   A19   113   Términi
Imerese   A20

Paceco   7   113   12

Fulgatore

113

37   37

50

15

Favignana   8   7
Rilievo

A29d   E933   35

Calatafimi   27

Álcamo

San Güiseppe
Jato

Bolognetta

121

Cáccamo   21

Cerda

A19

Collesa
Le M

Stagnone   di Marcanzotta

Vita

188A   125

A29   119   M a z a r a   Camporeale

L. Poma   Grande

Marineo

Villafrati   27

118

E932

Madon

15   115   20

Salemi   40   di   188   V a l   d i

Gibellina
Nuova

Roccamena   32

Corleone

Mezzojuso   34

Vicari

Montemaggiore
Belsito

120   33

Polizzi
Generosa

Marsala   188

Matarocco   21

Santa Ninfa

624

Rca. Busambra
1613

Leonardo

121

Roccapalumba   Caltavuturo

Álía

285   121   30

Strasatti   21   119   17

Partanna   188   31

Salaparuta

Bélice   188C

Campofiorito   21

Bisacquino   25   718

Prizzi

Lercara
Friddi   188   19

S   Vallelunga
Pratameno

Villalba   30

Valledolmo

115   Castelvetrano

E90 A29   E931

Plla. Misilbesi
295   32

Santa Margherita
di Belice

Sambuca
di Sicília   188

Chiusa
Sclafani

Palazzo
Adriano   118

Santo Stéfano
Quisquina   23

189   Cammarata   29

Marianópoli

121   Santa
Villarmo

Tunis 7:00
Pantelleria 4:45

Mazara
del Vallo

Campobello
di Mazara

Menfi   32

L. Aráncio   25

San Carlo

Bivona   23   M. Cammarata
1578

Mussomeli

Campofranco

San Cat

Granitola-Torretta   Marinella

115   18

Caltabellotta   26   386

Búrgio

Alessándria
della Rocca

189

Serradifalco   122

C. Granitola   C. S. Marco   21   Sciacca

E931

115   29

Plátani   Ribera   Cianciana

Verdura   Cattólica
Eráclea   32

San Biágio
Plátani

Casteltérmini   118   25

Montedoro   29

115   Montallegro

Raffadali   Aragona

Racalmuto   640

Canicattì   Délia   190

Siculiana   20   14   118   189   12   36   Castrofilippo   15   3

Agrigento

Favara   Naro   123   R.
Campob
di Licata

Porto Empédocle   Naro   Camastra

AGRIGENTO   E931   23

Palma
di Montechiaro   18   Salso

Lica

Linosa 5:45
Lampedusa 8:15

37°

B

C

0   10   20   30 km

3   15°   4

Canneto
Lípari
Lípari
Vulcano

A

Sspartà
Torre
Mortelle   Faro
Villafranca   21
Tirrena   113   14
Capo di Milazzo   Golfo di   A20   13
Milazzo   Spadafora   113
Milazzo   E90   19   **Messina**
Golfo di Patti   Barcellona-   Rometta
Gioiosa Marea   Pozzo di Gotto   Santa Lucia   114
Broto   22   C. Calavá   Falcone   20   del Mela   13
C. d'Orlando   113   Mazzarrà   Castroreale
Naso   26   Patti   S. Andrea   1279   30
Sant'Ágata   21   San Piero-Patti   14   M. Poverello
Militello   15   Longi   Montalbano   185
Alcara   28   19   Ucria   Elicona   Novara
Caronia   il Fúsi   116   Floresta   di Sicília   Mandanici
Santo Stéfano   E90   San   Tortorici   28   Antillo   Alì Terme
Cefalù   25   di Camastra   Fratello   Santa Doménica   39   Roccalumera
113   24   A20   20   Vittória   Francavilla di Sicília   Santa Teresa
E90   21 Tusa   **176**   **Monti Nébrodi**   Plla. di Zoppo   di Riva
Castelbuono   Mistretta   289   1264   Plla. Mandrazzi
1979   286   117   M. Soro   1125   Castiglione   **93**
Carbonara   1847   Nébrodi   di Sicília   Taormina
Geraci Sículo   Colle del   Randazzo   25   Linguaglossa   6
32   Capizzi   Contrasto   120   Passopisciaro   120   Giardini Naxos
Gangi   18   1107   L. di Ancipa   Cesarò   114
Petralia   120   35   Cerami   Maletto   Piedimonte Etneo
Sottana   1147   29   Troina   284   Fiumefreddo di Sicília
120   Pella. Madonnuzza   Gagliano   Bronte   Etna   Máscali
29   Sperlinga   Castelferrato   575   3323   Riposto
Alimena   Nicosia   27   11   Giarre
21   117   L. di   Adrano   Zafferana   E45
Salso   20   Pozzillo   17   Etnea   31   A18
Leonforte   Centúripe   Biancavilla   Nicolosi   Acireale
Villarosa   14   Agira   Santa Maria   Trecastagni   Aci Catena
122   Calascibetta   Ássoro   di Licodia   Belpasso   Aci Castello
11   121   192   **156**   28   A19   Paternò   121   11
6   **Enna**   Pergusa   Catenanuova   E932   33   16   9   **Catánia**
12   122   117   13   Valguarnera   192   Misterbianco   12
18   Caropepe   Raddusa   Castel   16   417   10   114
Caltanissetta   Plla Grottacalda   di Iúdica   Gerbini   9
Pietraperzia   647   Ramacca   Golfo di
191   11   30   Catánia
626   Aidone   288   Gornalunga   Valletta 11:00
18   Piazza Armerina   31   Lago di
24   Barrafranca   VILLA ROMANA   Lentini   E45
Riesi   DEL CASALE   Mirabella Imbáccari   Palagonía   114
190   Mazzarino   117   24   385   Lentini   13   114
Butera   124   San Michele di Ganzaria   Scordia   10   Augusta
32   20   417   34   Villasmundo   Capo S. Croce
12   385   Militello in   Golfo di Augusta
E931   Niscemi   Mineo   Val di Catánia   Melilli
115   117   Grammichele   Francofonte   Priolo
10   20   194   21   Gargallo
Maróglio   10   Sortino
Gela   Vizzini   Ferla   Ánapo
San Pietro   124   Buccheri   124   Solarino
Acate   Licodía   Floridía   5   **Siracusa**
E45   32   Eubéa   M. Lauro   32
Golfo di Gela   30   Monterosso   986   A18
115   Chiaramonte   514   Almo   Canicattini   C. Murro
Vittória   Gulfi   Giarratana   Palazzolo   Bagni   di Porco
16   Cómiso   36   194   Acréide   28   31
Scoglitti   8   5   Cassíbile   37°
Santa Croce   **Ragusa**   24   115
Camerina   115   11   17   20
C. Scarámia   18   **Módica**   Noto   **Ávola**
Marina di Ragusa   Irmínio   21   Rosolini   E45   Golfo di
Donnalucata   Scicli   115   A18   Noto
Sampieri   Íspica   19
Pozzallo   Marzamemi
  Pachino
  C. Passero
  Portopalo di
  C. Passero

Reggio di Calábr

Villa San
A3   184
18   33
16
Scilla
Str. di Messina
175
Pta. di   106
Péllaro   38°   Monte
E90   Ió
Lazzaro   24
Valletta 15:00

Ravenna 35:00   **B**

C

3   15°   4

1
2
3
4
A
B
8°
9°
10°
41°
180
Bonifacio
C. Pertusato
Île. de Cavallo
Bouches de Bonifacio
1:00
Génova
Porto-Vecchio
Marseille 14:15
Toulon 9:30
Propriano 3:30
Génova 10:00
Livorno 9:00
La Spezia 5:30
Civitavécchia 3:30
Génova 10:00
Livorno 10:00
Civitavécchia 4:00
Árbatax
Santa Teresa
Gallura
C. Testa
Arcipélago
Maddalena
de la Maddalena
la Maddalena
Caprera
Palau
C. Ferro
Costa
Smeralda
Porto
Cervo
Arzachena
San Pantaleo
Golfo Aranci
C. Figari
G. di
Ólbia
Ólbia
Tavolara
Molara
C. Coda Cavallo
Pta. Caprara
Asinara
La Reale
Fornelli
C. del Falcone
Stintino
Golfo
dell'Asinara
Castelsardo
Porto
Tórres
Platamona
Lido
Pozzo
San Nicola
Sorso
Sénnori
Nulvi
Ósilo
Sássari
Argentiera
C. dell'Argentiera
Palmádula
M. Forte
464
Santa Maria
la Palma
Olmedo
Usini
Ossi
Codrongianos
Tramariglio
GROTTA DI
NETTUNO
Capo Cáccia
Alghero
Serra
Mannu
Íttiri
Villanova
Monteleone
Romana
M. Minerva
644
Padria
Pozzomaggiore
Montresta
Capo Marárgiu
Bosa
Temo
Tresnurághes
Suni
Sindia
Macomer
Cúglieri
Santu
Lussurgiu
M. Urtigu
1050
Bonárcado
Santa Caterina
di Pittinuri
Séneghe
NURAGHE
LOSA
Paulilátino
Ghilarza
Sédilo
Bórore
Dualchi
L.
Omodeo
Aústis
Valledoria
Sédini
Pérfugas
Mártis
Chiaramonti
L. del
Coghinas
Tula
Ploaghe
Ardara
Bonnánaro
Thiesi
Móres
Ittireddu
Ozieri
Pattada
Trinità
d'Agultu
Ággius
Lúras
Tempio
Pausánia
la Variante
676
M. Limbara
1359
Berchidda
Oschiri
Monti di Alá
Bassacutena
Aglientu
Luogosanto
L. di
Líscia
Líscia
G A L L U R A
Sant'Antonio-
di-Gallura
Calangiánus
Telti
S. Simone
Monti
Lóiri
Padru
Straulas
Budoni
Tanaunella
Posada
Torpè
La Caletta
Siniscóla
C. Comino
Monte Albo
Monti Remule
Alà dei Sardi
Buddusò
Lodè
Osidda
Nule
Bitti
Lula
Foresta
di Búrgos
M. Rasu
1259
Bono
Bonorva
Bolótana
Silánus
Tirso
Orotelli
Ottana
Orune
Isalle
Núoro
Irgoli
Galtellì
Orosei
Cedrino
Dorgali
Cala
Gonone
Golfo
di Orosei
Oliena
Orgósolo
Mamoiada
Orani
Gavoi
Fonni
Pso. di Caravai
1118
Ovodda
Urzulei
Golfo Orosei e
del Gennargentu
Flumineddu
Taloro
C. di Monte Santu
Sardegna
Logudoro
(I t a l i a)
E25
E840
118
132
125
133
200
131
134
672
127
291
597
199
392
389
128
292
129

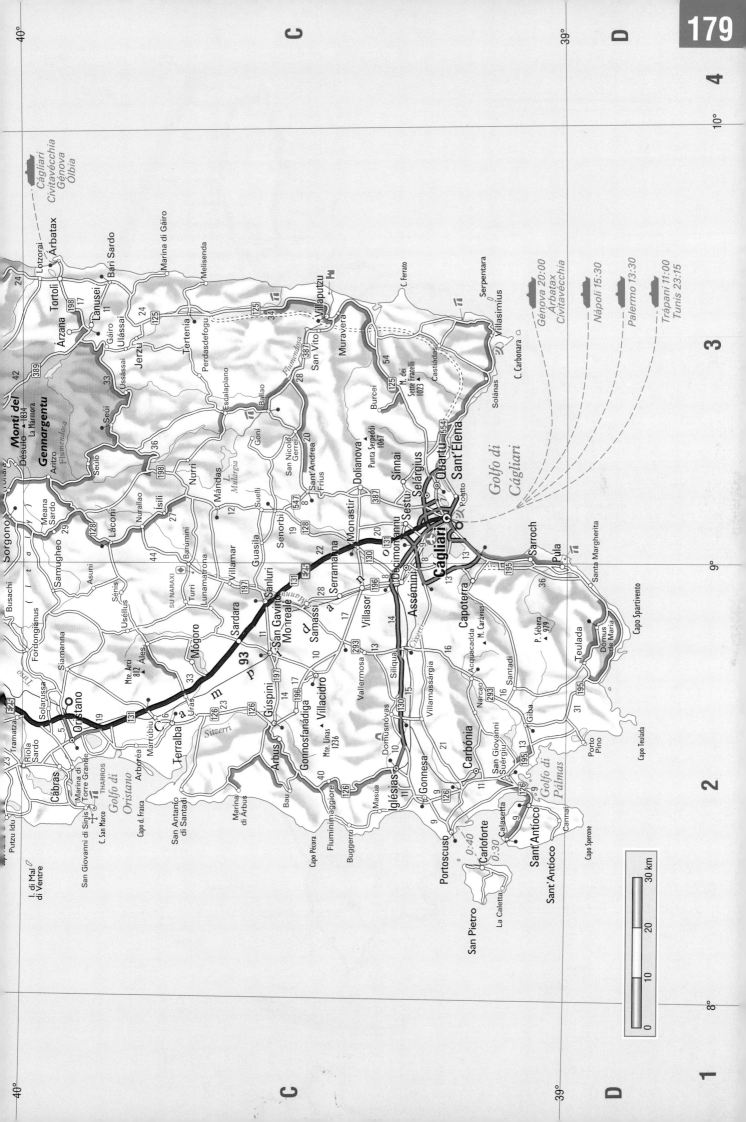

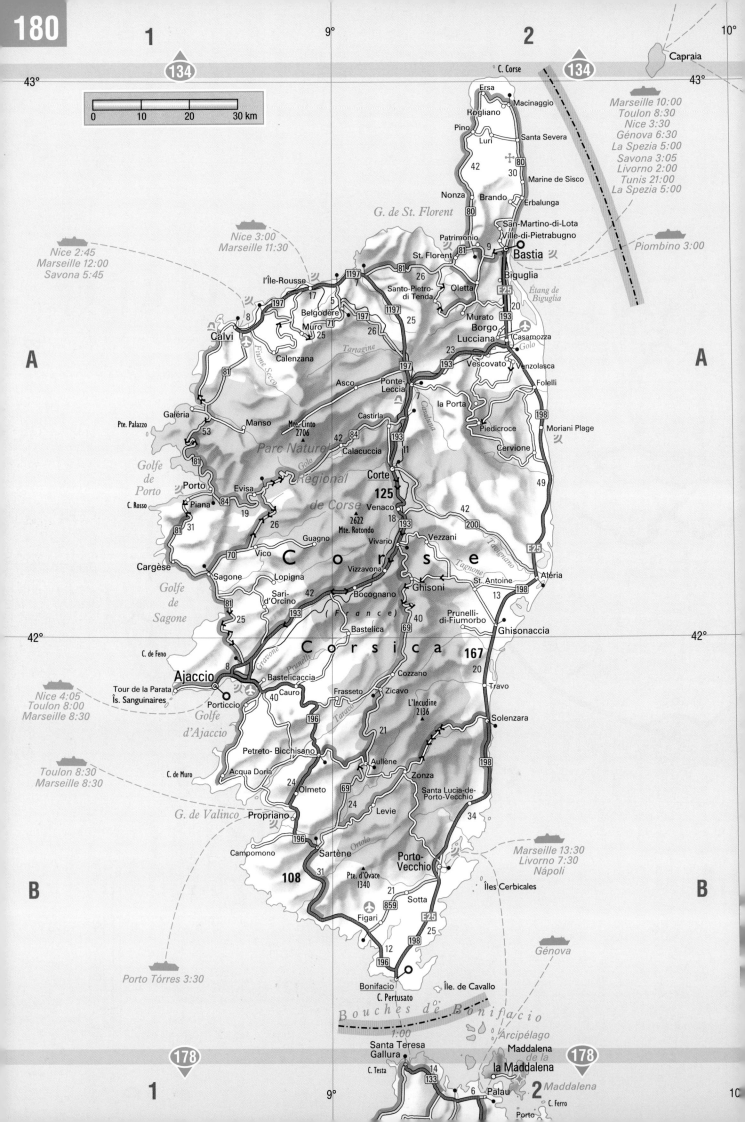

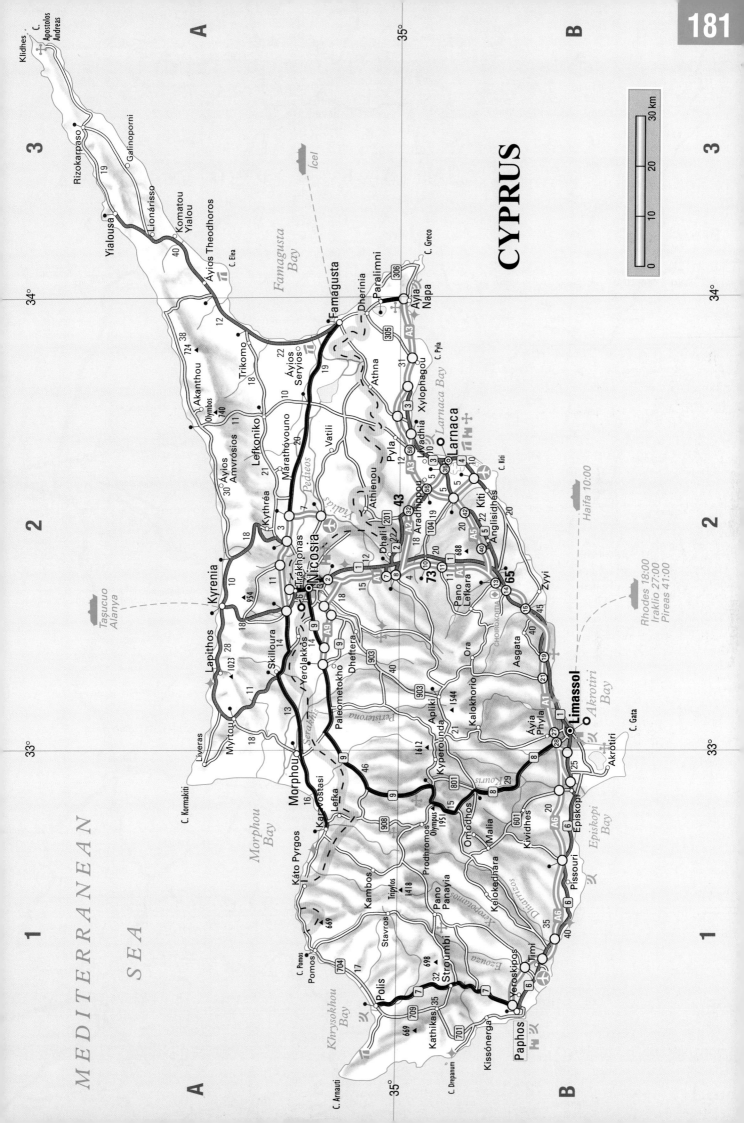

CYPRUS

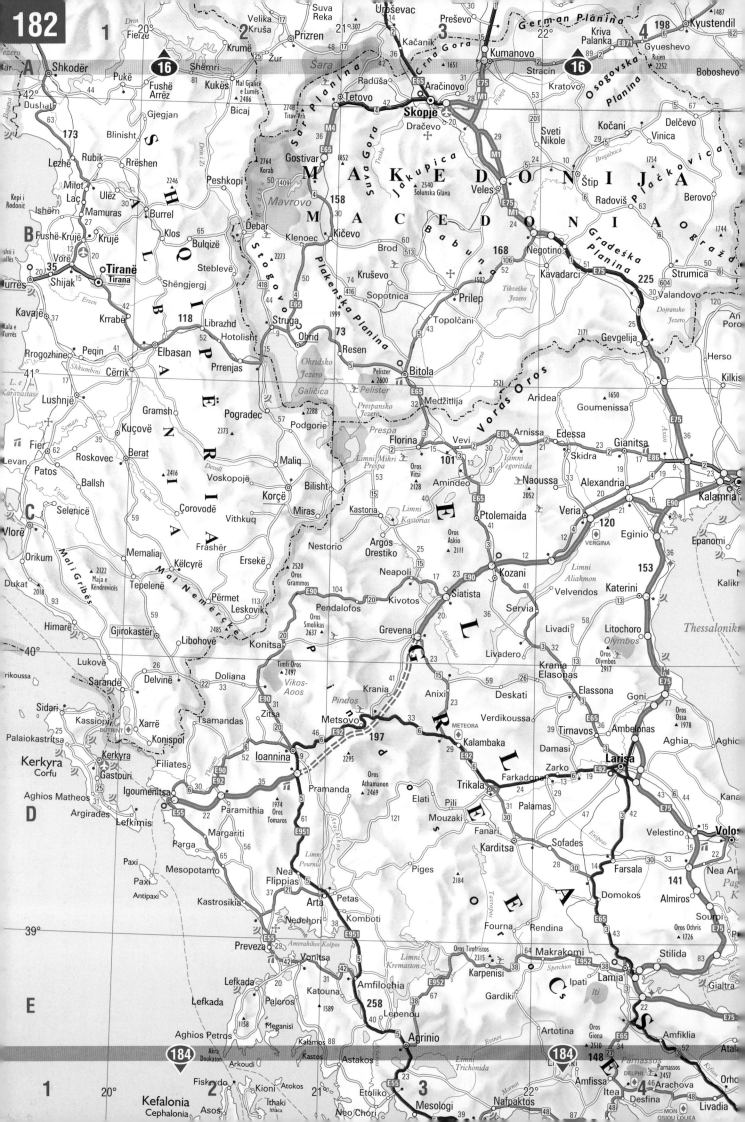

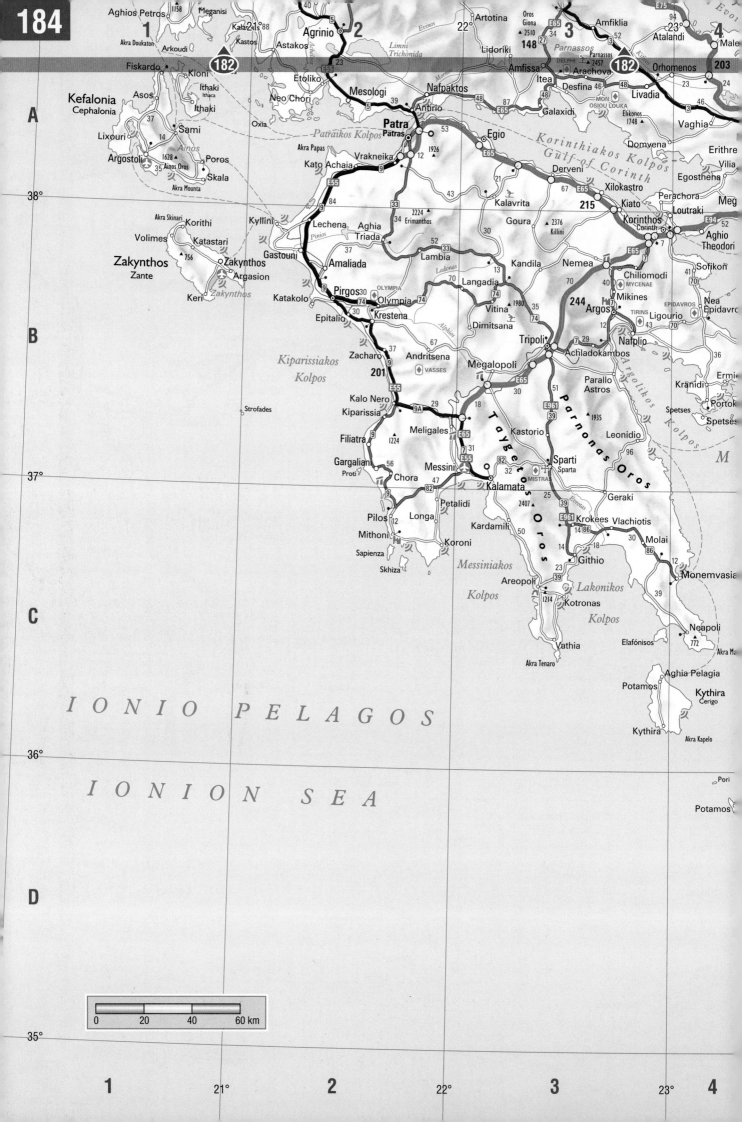

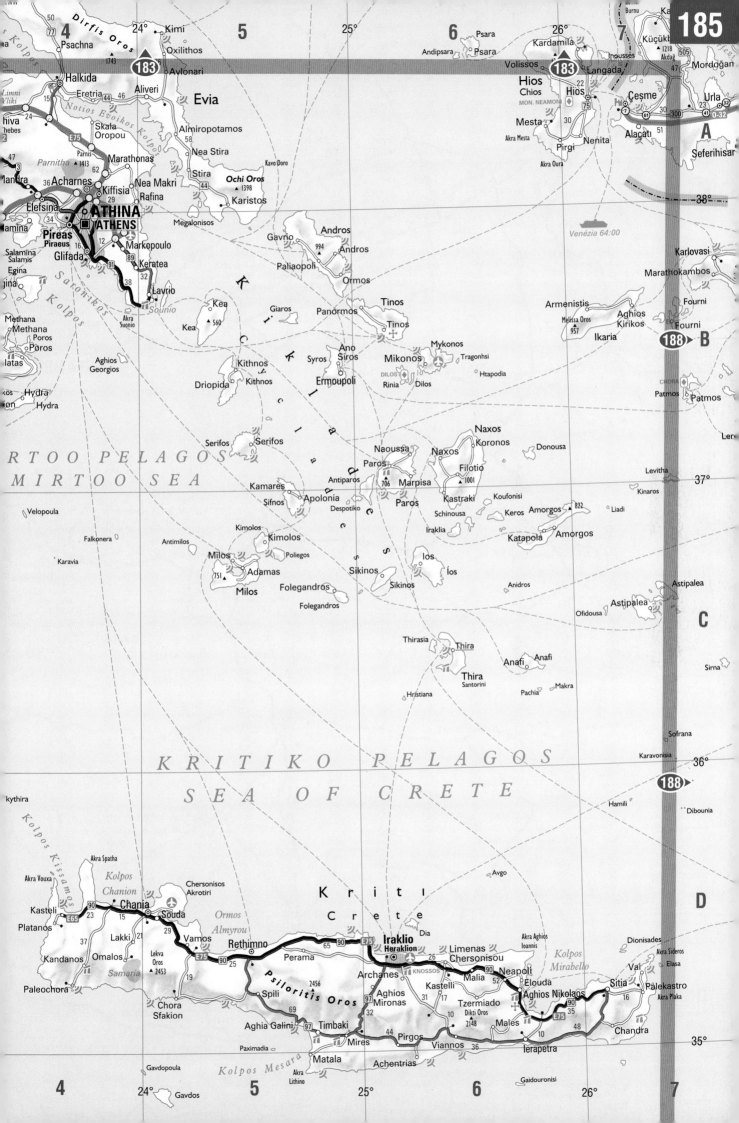

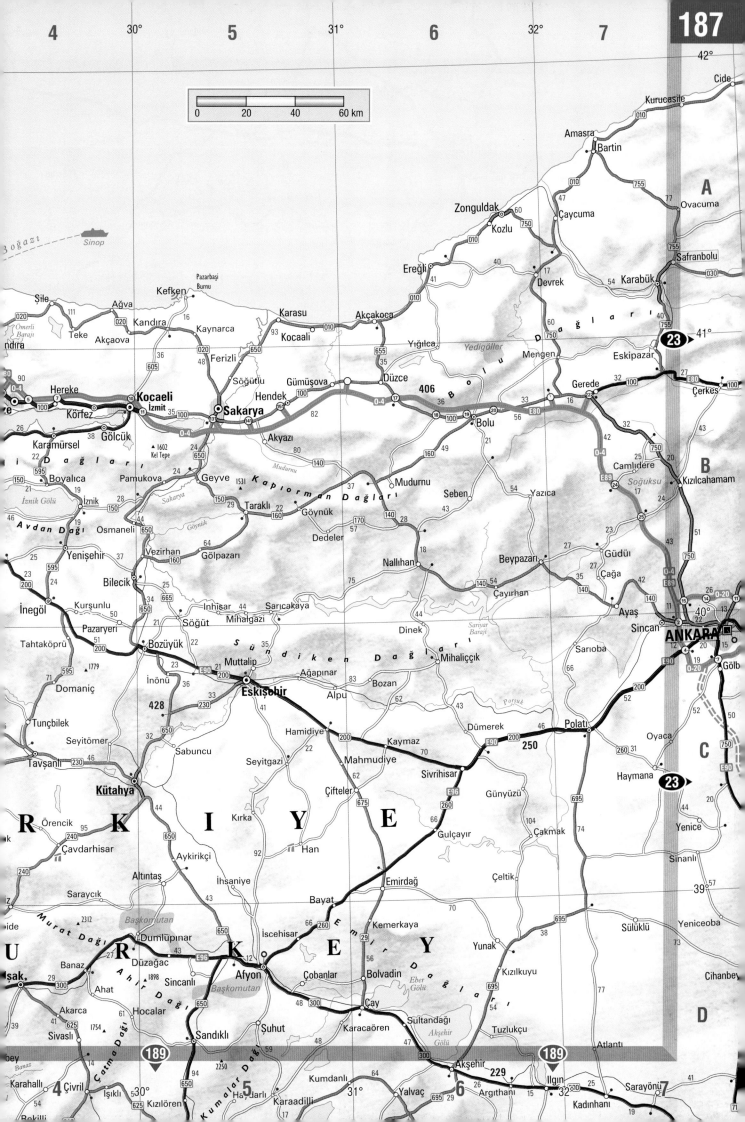

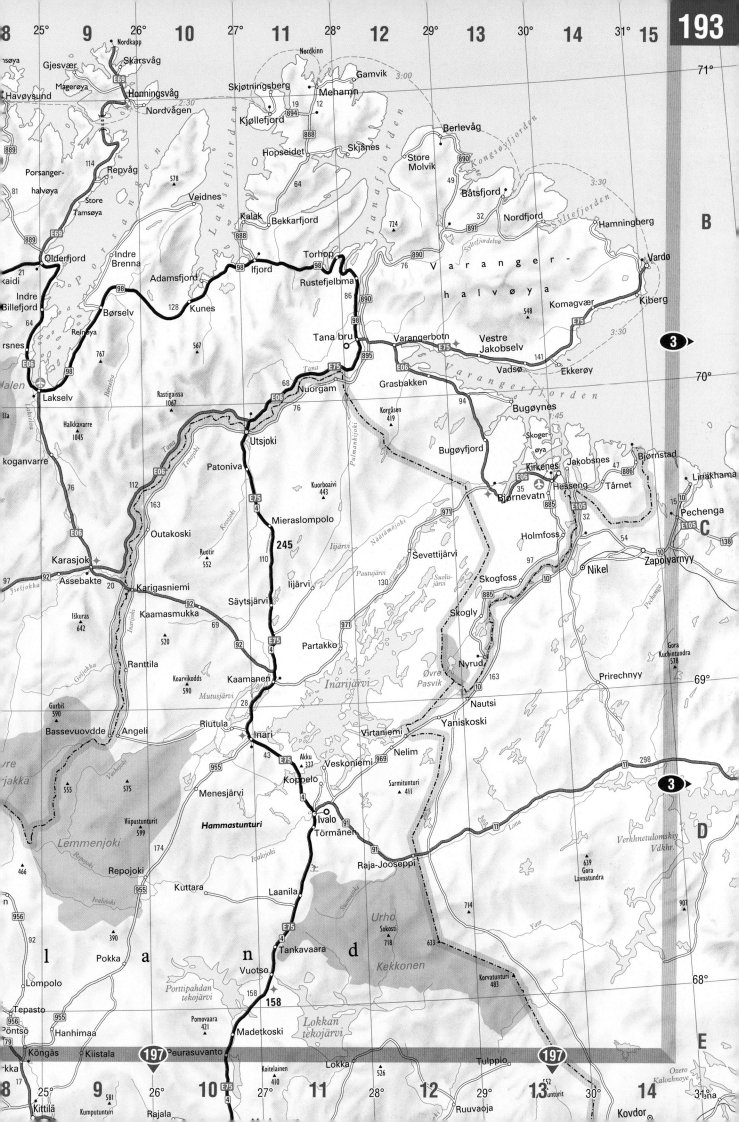

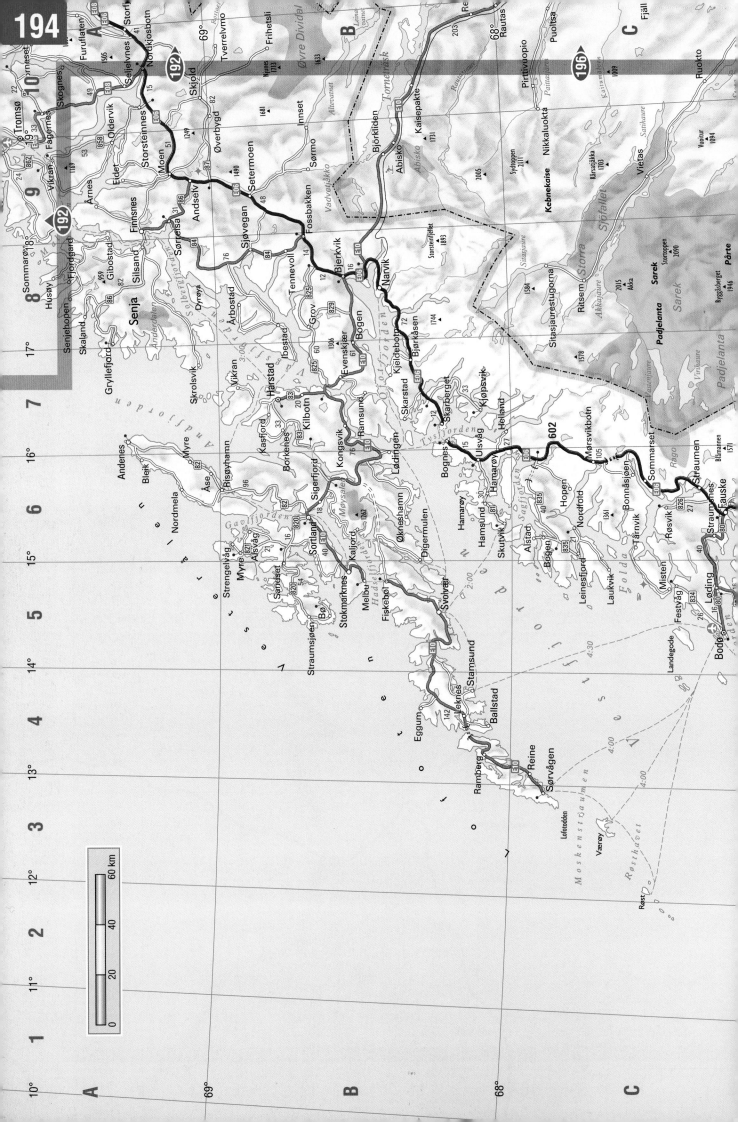

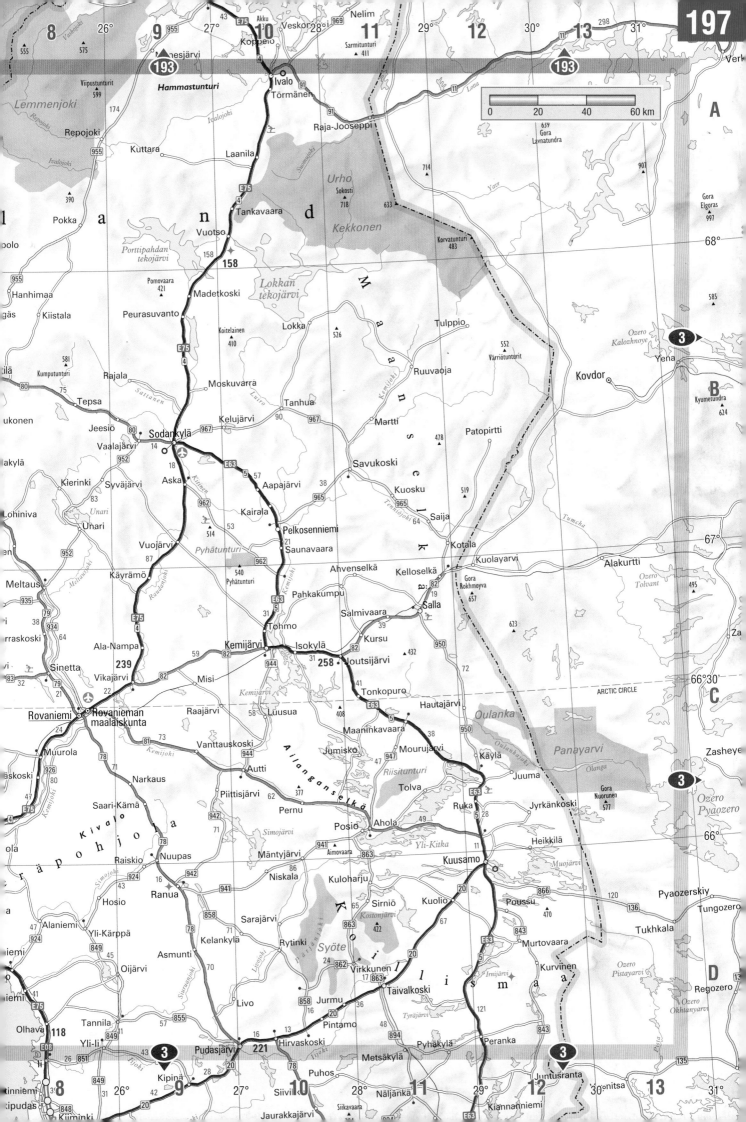

City plans • Plans de villes
Stadtpläne • Piante di città

Motorway	Autoroute	Autobahn	Autostrada		
Major through route	Route principale majeur	Hauptstrecke	Strada di grande communicazione		
Through route	Route principale	Schnellstrasse	Strada d'importanza regionale		
Secondary road	Route secondaire	Nebenstrasse	Strada d'interesse locale		
Dual carriageway	Chaussées séparées	Zweispurig Schnellstrasse	Strada a carreggiate doppie		
Other road	Autre route	Nebenstrecke	Altra strada		
Tunnel	Tunnel	Tunnel	Galleria stradale		
Limited access / pedestrian road	Rue réglementée / rue piétonne	Beschränkter Zugang/ Fussgängerzone	Strada pedonale / a accesso limitato		
One-way street	Sens unique	Einbahnstrasse	Senso unico		
Parking	Parc de stationnement	Parkplatz	Parcheggio		
Motorway number A7	Numéro d'autoroute	Autobahnnummer A7	Numero di autostrada		
National road number 447	Numéro de route nationale	Nationalstrassen-nummer 447	Numero di strada nazionale		
European road number E45	Numéro de route européenne	Europäische Strassennummer E45	Numero di strada europea		
Destination GENT	Destination	Ziel GENT	Destinazione		
Car ferry	Bac passant les autos	Autofähre	Traghetto automobili		
Railway	Chemin de fer	Eisenbahn	Ferrovia		
Rail/bus station	Gare / gare routière	Bahnhof / Busstation	Stazione ferrovia / pullman		
Underground, metro station	Station de métro	U-Bahnstation	Metropolitano		
Cable car	Téléférique	Drahtseilbahn	Funivia		
Abbey, cathedral	Abbaye, cathédrale	Abtei, Kloster, Kathedrale	Abbazia, duomo		
Church of interest	Église intéressante	Interessante Kirche	Chiesa da vedere		
Synagogue	Synagogue	Synagoge	Sinagoga		
Hospital	Hôpital	Krankenhaus	Ospedale		
Police station	Police	Polizeiwache	Polizia		
Post office	Bureau de poste	Postamt	Ufficio postale		
Tourist information	Office de tourisme	Informationsbüro	Ufficio informazioni turistiche		
Place of interest	Autre curiosité	Sonstige Sehenswürdigkeit	Luogo da vedere		

Approach maps • Agglomérations
Carte régionale • Regionalkarte

Toll motorway – with motorway number A10	Autoroute à péage – avec numéro d'autoroute	Gebührenpflichtige Autobahn – mit Autobahnnummer A10	Autostrada a pedaggio – con numero		
Toll-free motorway – with European road number E51	Autoroute – avec numéro de route européenne	Gebührenfreie Autobahn – E51 Europäische Strassennummer	Autostrada – con numero di strada europea		
Pre-pay motorway – vignette required	Autoroute – 'vignette'	Autobahn – 'vignette'	Autostrada – 'vignette'		
Motorway services	Aire de service	Autobahnservice	Area di servizio autostradale		
Motorway junction – full/restricted 24	Échangeur d'autoroute – accès libre/ accès reglémenté	Autobahnkreuz – voller/begrenzter Zugang 24	Raccordi autostradali – completo/parziali		
Under construction	En construction	Im Bau	In construzione		
Tunnel	Tunnel	Tunnel	Galleria stradale		
Major route dual carriageway 14 single carriageway 14	Route principale chausées séparées chausée sans séparation	Hauptstrecke	Strada di grande communicazione		
Secondary route dual carriageway 96 single carriageway 96	Route secondaire chaussées séparées chausée sans séparation	zweispurige 14 Schnellstrasse 14	carreggiata doppia carreggiata unica		
Other road	Autre route	Nebenstrasse	Strada d'interesse locale		
Car ferry	Bac passant les autos	zweispurige 96 Schnellstrasse 96	carreggiata doppia carreggiata unica		
Destination GIRONA	Destination	Nebenstrecke	Altra strada		
Railway	Chemin de fer	Autofähre	Traghetto automobili		
Railway station Estación Central	Gare	Ziel GIRONA	Destinazione		
Height above sea level – in metres 234	Altitude – en mètres	Eisenbahn	Ferrovia		
Airport	Aéroport principal	Hauptbahnhof Estación Central	Stazione ferrovia		
Airfield	Autre aéroport	Höhe über dem Meeresspiegel 234	Altezza in metri		
City plan coverage area	Région de plan de ville	Flughafen	Aeroporto		
		Flugplatz	Aerodromo/campo d'aviazione		
		Vom Stadtplan abgedecktes Gebiet	Area della pianta della città		

Alicante
0   km   0.5

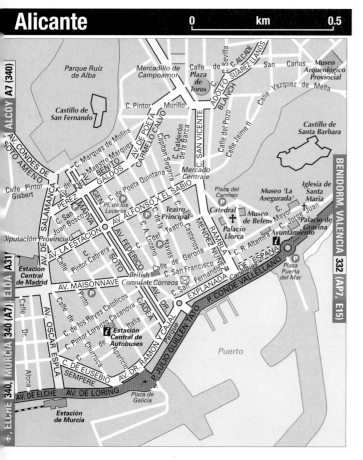

Antwerpen Antwerp
0   km   1

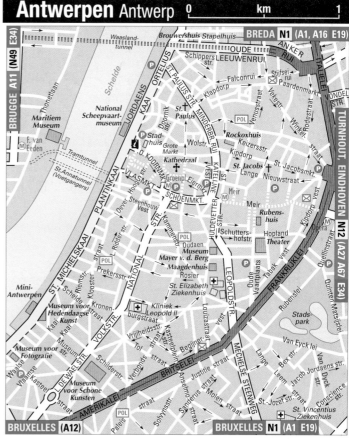

Amsterdam

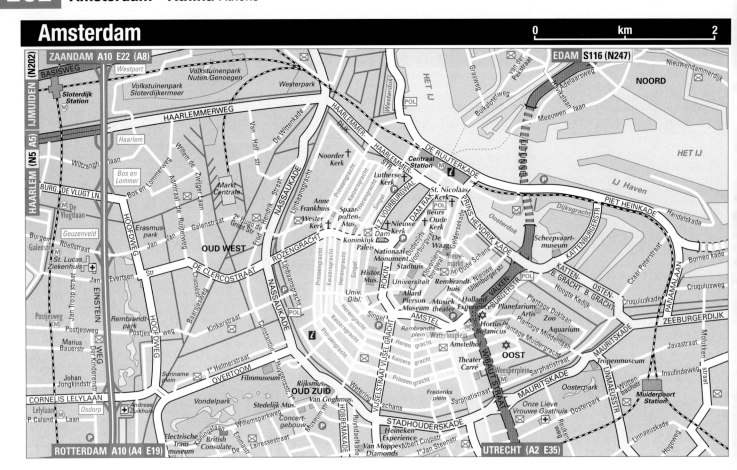

Athina Athens

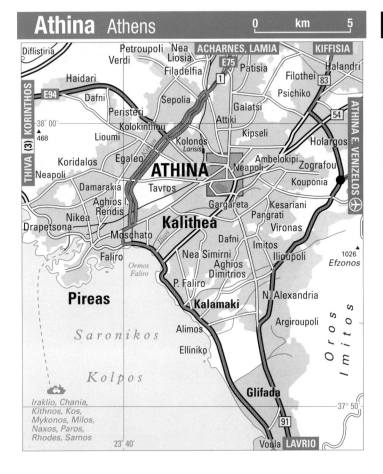

Athina Athens

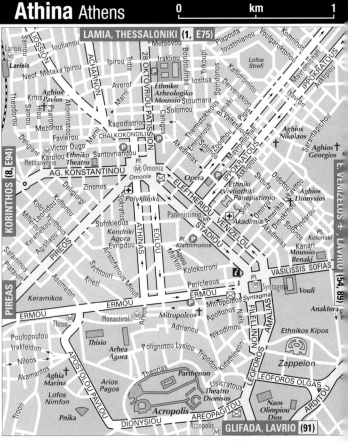

Barcelona

Barcelona

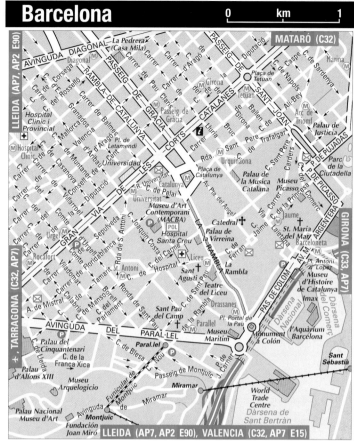

Bruxelles Brussels

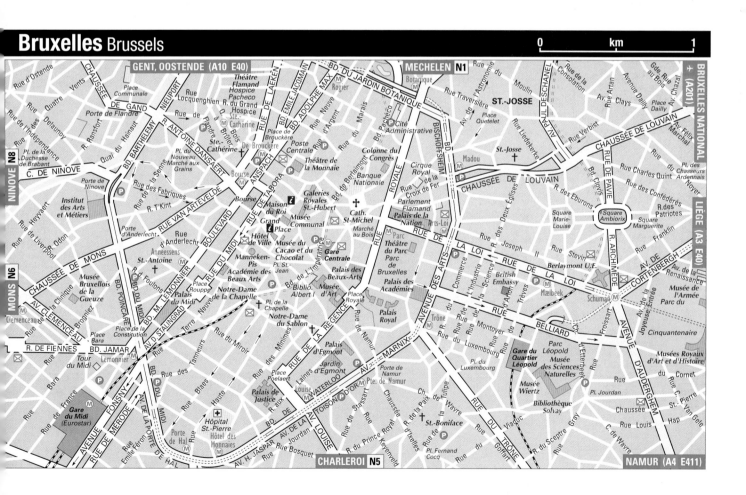

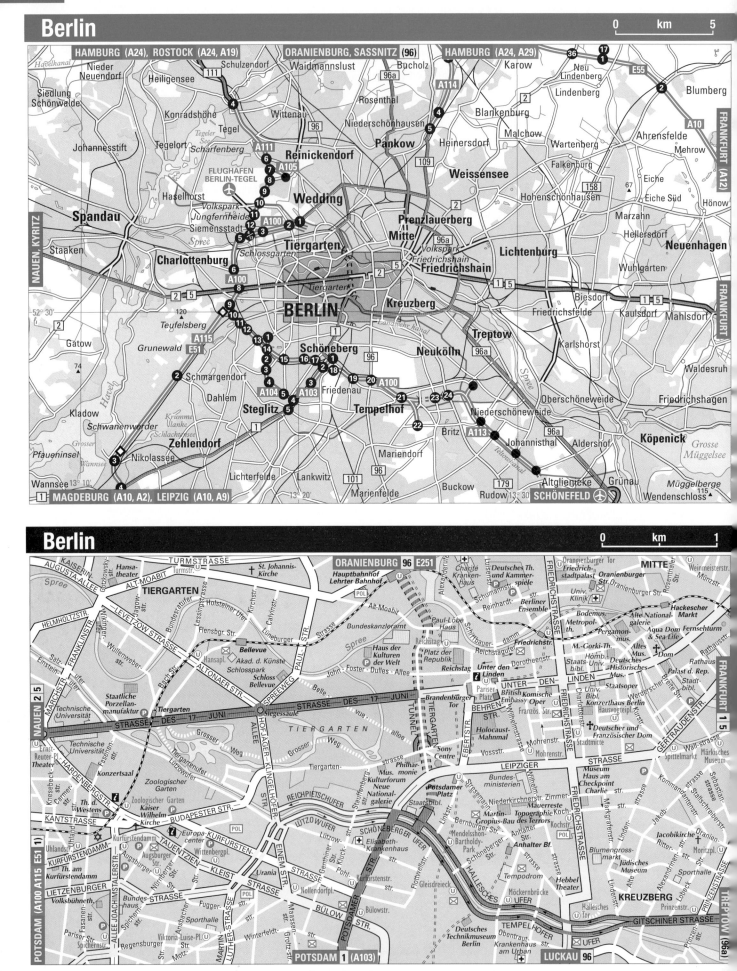

Bordeaux

0 km 5

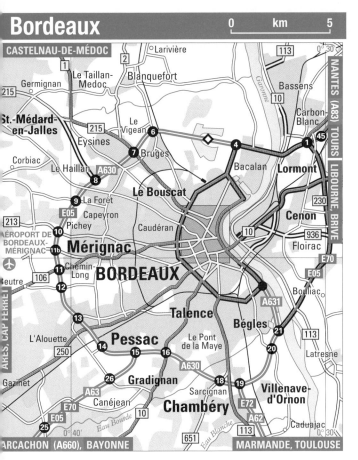

Bordeaux

0 km 1

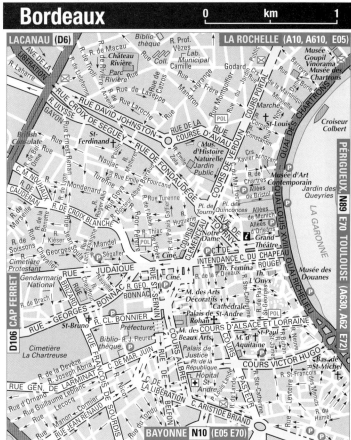

Budapest

0 km 1

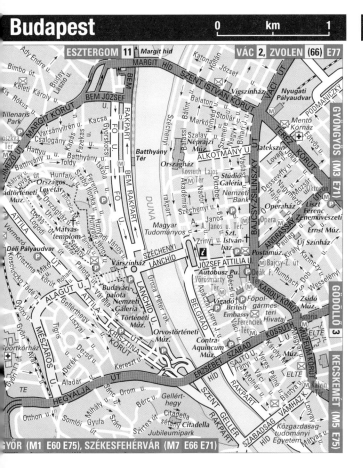

Dublin

0 km 0,5

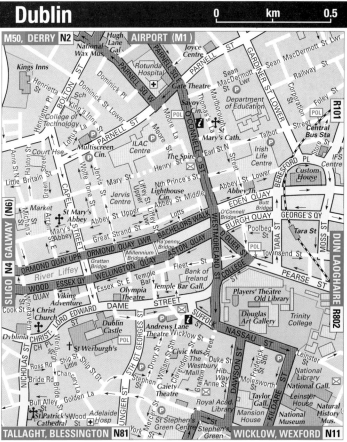

For **Cologne** see page 211
For **Copenhagen** see page 210

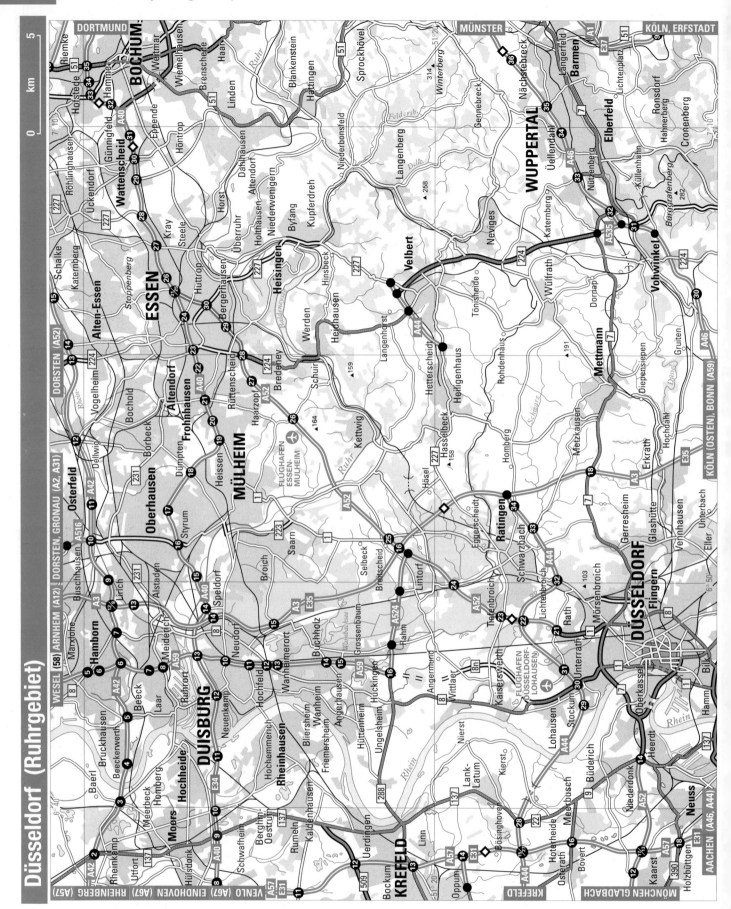

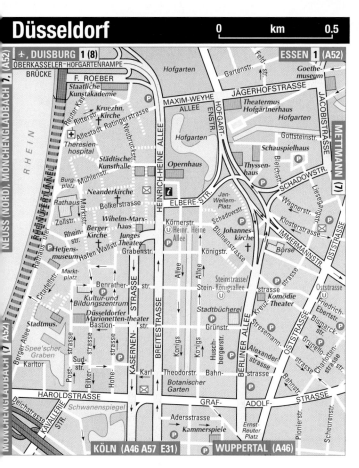
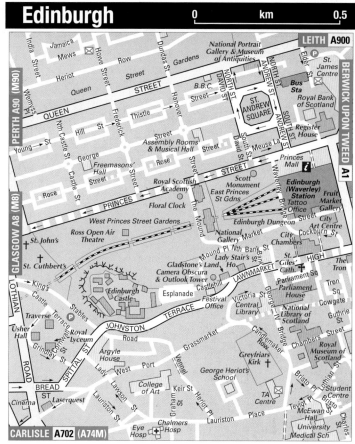
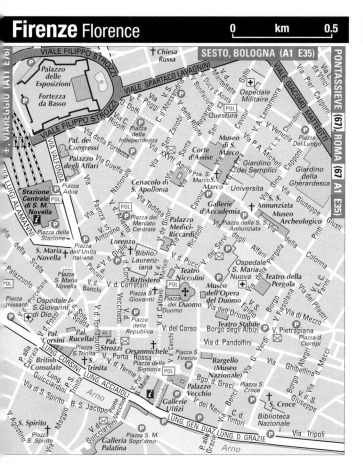
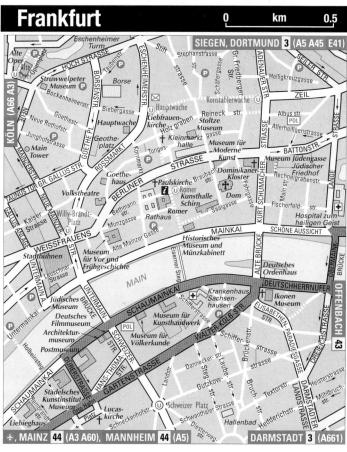

Genève Geneva

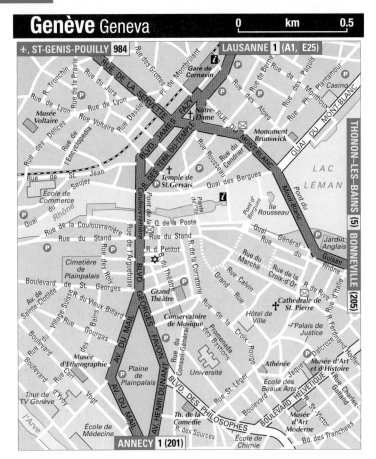

Göteborg Gothenburg

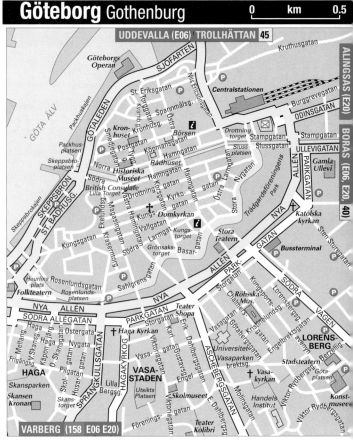

Hamburg

Hamburg

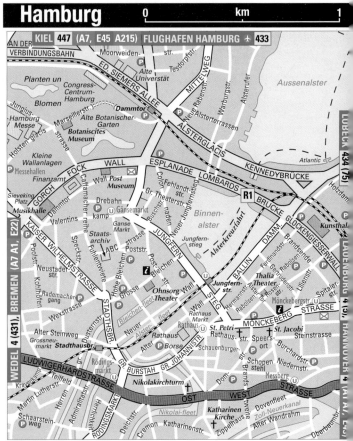

Helsinki

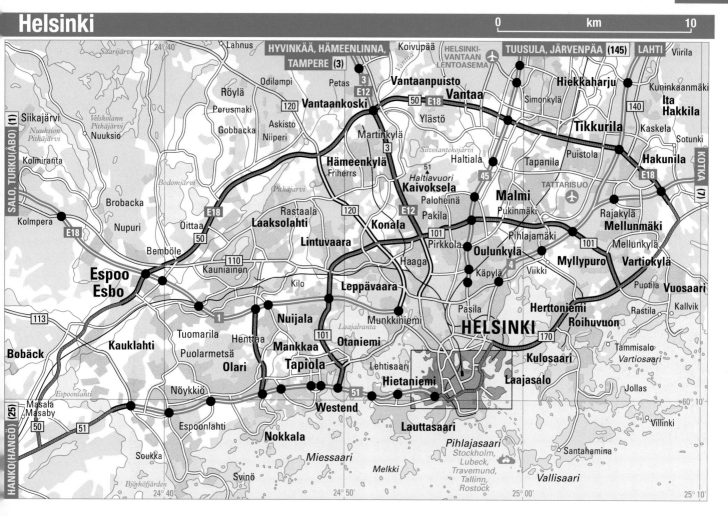

Helsinki

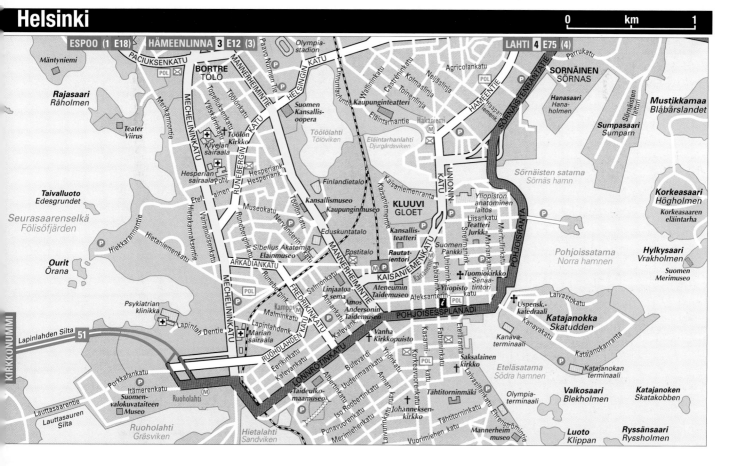

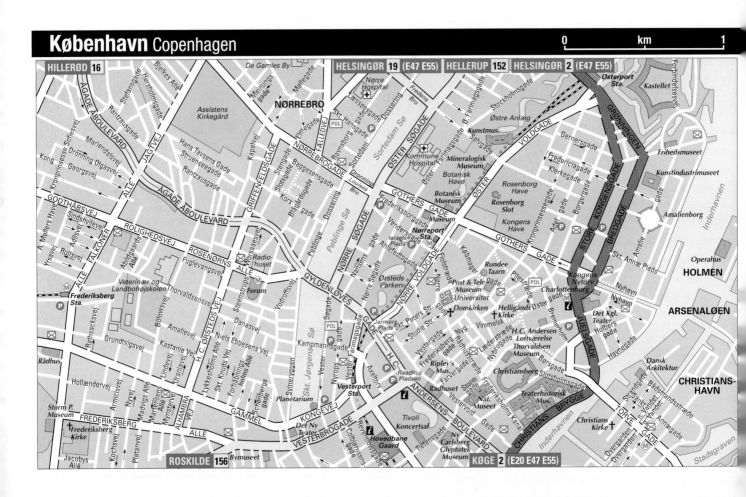

Köln Cologne

0 — km — 0.5

Luxembourg

0 — km — 0.5

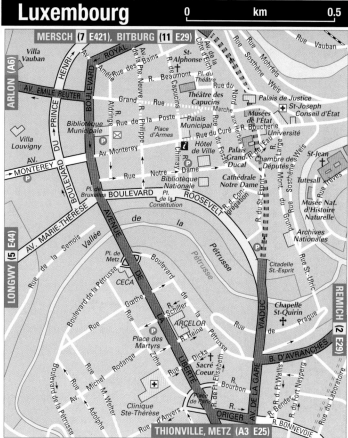

Lisboa Lisbon

0 — km — 5

Lisboa Lisbon

0 — km — 1

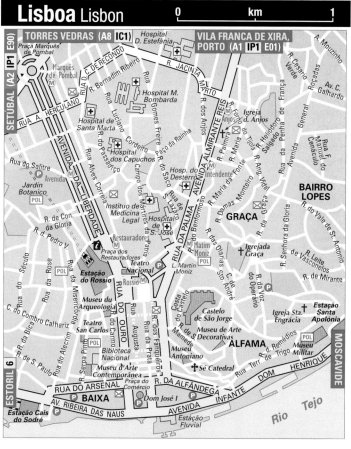

London

0   km   10

London

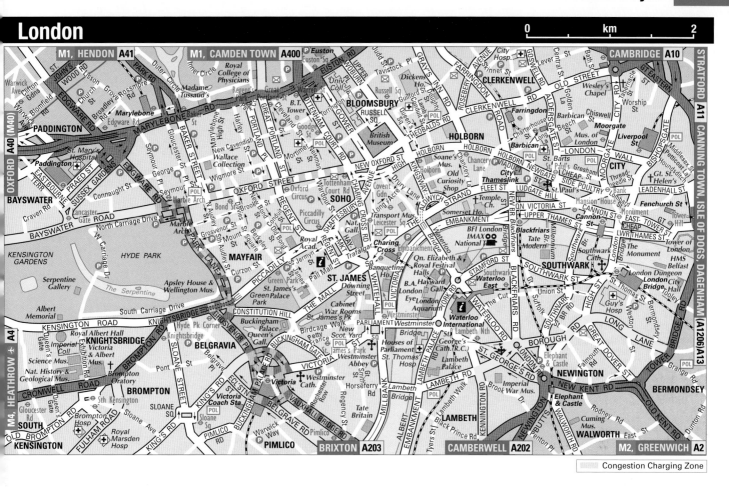

Congestion Charging Zone

Lyon

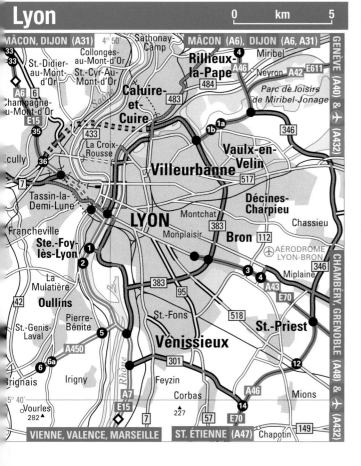

Lyon

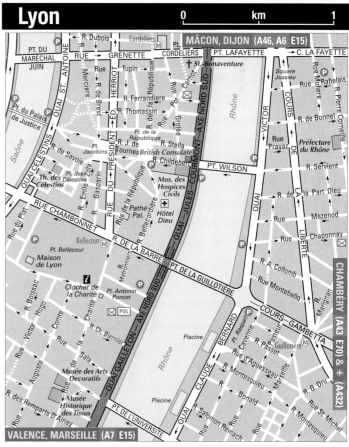

Madrid

0   km   5

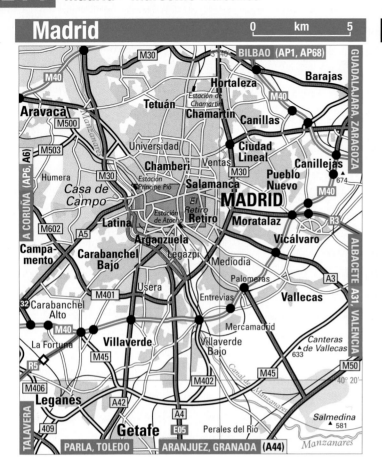

Marseille Marseilles

0   km   0.5

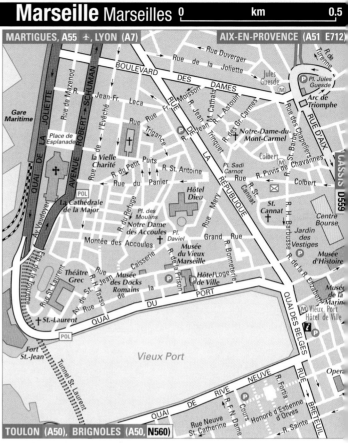

Madrid

0   km   1

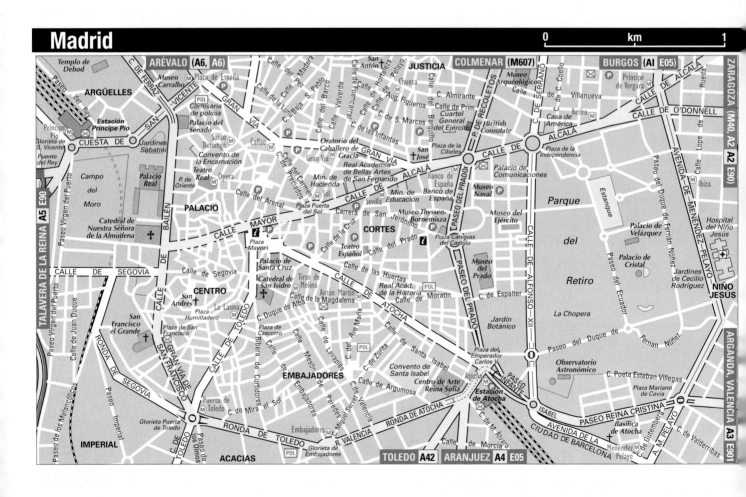

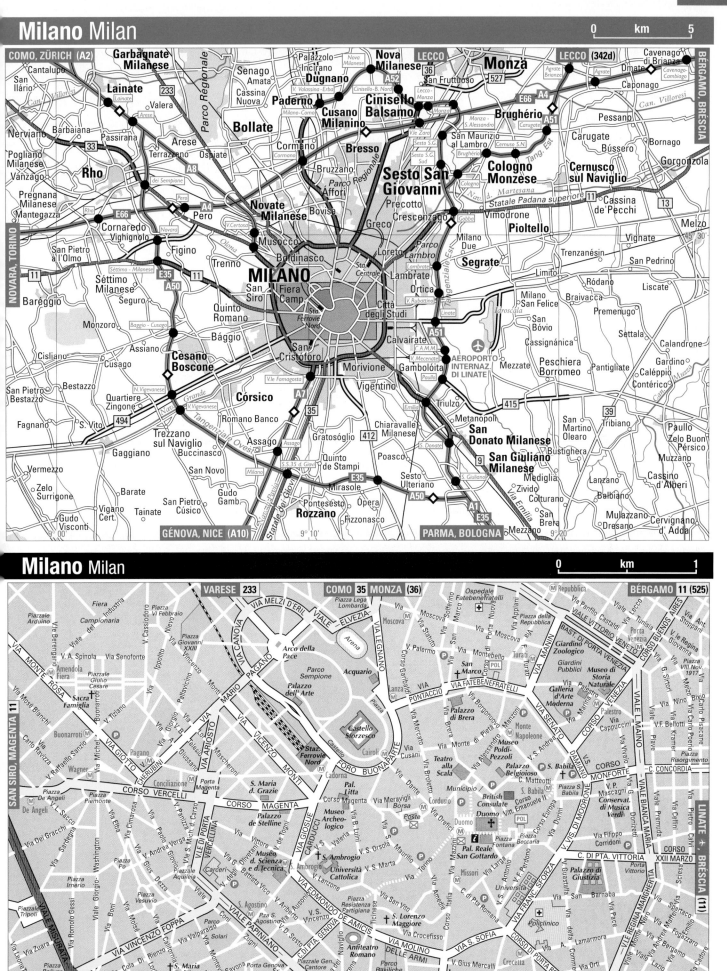

Milano Milan

0 km 5

COMO, ZÜRICH (A2)

LECCO

LECCO (342d)

BÉRGAMO, BRÉSCIA

Cantalupo
San Ilário
Garbagnate Milanese
Lainate
Lainate
233
Valera
Arese
Nerviano
Barbaiana
Passirana
33
Pogliano Milanese
Vánzago
Rho
Pregnana Milanese
Mantegazza
E66
Cornaredo
Vighignolo
San Pietro all'Olmo
Figino
11
Baréggio
Séttimo Milanese
E35
A50
11
Monzoro
Quinto Romano
Bággio
Assiano
Cisliano
Cúsago
Bestazzo
Cesano Boscone
San Pietro Bestazzo
Fagnano
S. Vito
Quartiere Zingone
494
Córsico
Romano Banco
35
Trezzano sul Naviglio
Assago
Vermezzo
Zelo Surrigone
Gaggiano
Buccinasco
San Novo
Barate
Vigano Cert.
Tainate
Gudo Gamb.
Gudo Visconti
S.S.35 d. Giov.
Mirasole
E35
Rozzano
Fizzonasco
Opera
Poasco
Pontesesto
Quinto de Stampi
Gratosóglio
412
Chiaravalle Milanese
S. Donato
Sesto Ulteriano

Senago
Amata
Cassina Nuova
Bollate
Arese
Pero
dei Sempione
Novate Milanese
Musocco
Boldinasco
Trenno
MILANO
San Siro
Il Fiera Camp.
Sta. Ferrovie Nord
San Cristóforo
V.le Famagosta
Morivione
Vigentino

Palazzolo Incirano
V. Valassina-Erba
Paderno
Cusano Milanino
Cormáno
Cormano
Bruzzano
Parco Regionale
Affori
Bovisa
Sta. Centrale
Città degli Studi
Calvairate
C.A.M.M.
Gambolóita
Paullo
Triulzo
Metanópoli
San Donato Milanese
San Giuliano Milanese
9
Mezzano

Nova Milanese
Dugnano
36
A52
Cinisello Balsamo
Bresso
Sesto San Giovanni
Precotto
Greco
Loreto
Lambrate
Ortica
V. Rubattino

Nova Milanese
San Fruttuoso
Monza
Lecco-Monza
V.le Zara
Sesto S.G.
Sesto S.G. Sud
Cológno
Parco Lambro
Milano Due
Milano San Felice
San Bóvio
Idroscalo
AEROPORTO INTERNAZ. DI LINATE
Mezzate
Zivido
Colturano
S. Brera

Monzá
527
San Maurizio al Lambro
Monza - S. Alessandro
Brughério
Carugate
Cernuso S.N.
Tang. Est
Cológno Monzese
Martesana
Statale Padana superiore
11
Vimodrone
Pioltello
Segrate
Milano
Limito
Ródano
Liscate
Settala
Peschiera Borromeo
415
San Martino Olearo
Mediglia
Bustighera
Cólturano

Agrate Brianze
E66
A4
Agrate
A51
Carugate
Brughério
Cernusco sul Naviglio
Cassina de' Pecchi
13
Vignate
Trenzanésin
San Pedrino
Braivacca
Premenugo
Cassignánica
Calándrone
Gardino
Caléppio
Contérico
Mulazzano
Dresano
Cervignano d'Adda

Cavenago di Brianza
Dmate
Cavenago-Cambiago
Caponago
Pessano
Bússero
Bornago
Gorgonzola
Melzo
Pantigliate
39
Tribiano
Zelo Buon Pérsico
Lanzano
Balbiano
Cassino d'Alberi
Muzzano

NOVARA, TORINO

GÉNOVA, NICE (A10)

PARMA, BOLOGNA

Milano Milan

0 km 1

VARESE 233

COMO 35 MONZA (36)

BÉRGAMO 11 (525)

Milano Milan

SAN SIRO, MAGENTA 11

LINATE BRÉSCIA (11)

GÉNOVA (A7 E62)

LODI 9 PARMA (A51, A1)

München Munich
0 km 5

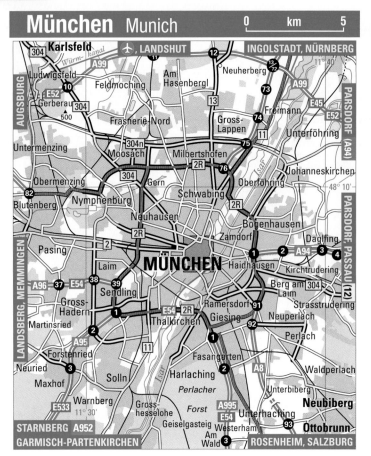

München Munich
0 km 1

Nápoli Naples
0 km 5

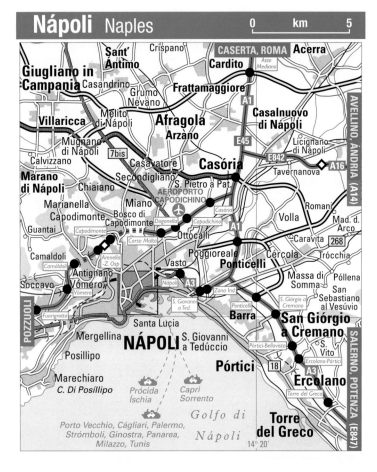

Nápoli Naples
0 km 1

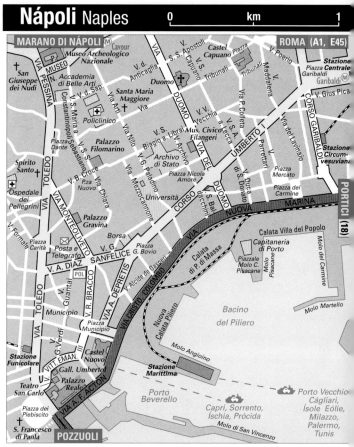

Oslo

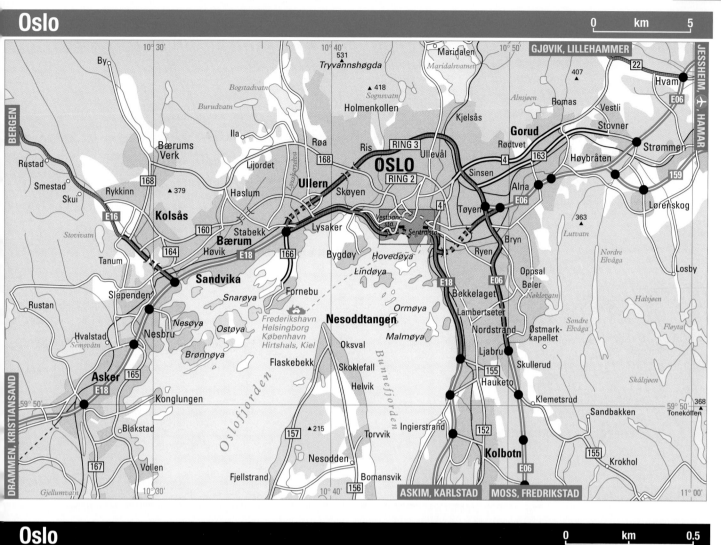

BERGEN

GJØVIK, LILLEHAMMER

JESSHEIM, HAMAR

By

Rustad

Smestad
Skui

Rykkinn

▲ 379

Kolsås

E16

Bærums
Verk

Ila

Lijordet

Haslum

Stabekk

168

Bærum

Høvik

E18

166

164

160

Tanum

Stovivatn

Sandvika

Slependen

Rustan

Hvalstad
Semsvatn

Nesøya

Nesbru

Ostøya

Brønnøya

165

Asker

E18

167

Konglungen

Blakstad

Vollen

Gjellumvatn

Bogstadvatn

Burudvatn

Tryvannshøgda
531

▲ 418

Holmenkollen

Røa

Ris

Ullern

Skøyen

Lysaker

Snarøya

Fornebu

Bygdøy

Frederikshavn
Helsingborg
København
Hirtshals, Kiel

Lindøya

Hovedøya

Nesoddtangen

Flaskebekk

Oksval

Skoklefall

Helvik

Nesodden

Fjellstrand

157

▲ 215

156

Bomansvik

Torvvik

Oslofjorden

Maridalen

Maridalsvatnet

Sognsvatn

Kjelsås

RING 3

Ulleväl

OSLO

RING 2

168

Sinsen

Tøyen

Ormøya

Malmøya

Bunnefjorden

Ingierstrand

ASKIM, KARLSTAD

22

Hvam

407

Romas

Vestli

Stovner

Gorud

Rødtvet

Høybråten

Strømmen

163

4

E06

Alna

Bryn

Ryen

E18

E06

Bekkelaget

Lambertseter

Nordstrand

Østmark-
kapellet

Ljabru

Skullerud

155

Hauketo

152

Klemetsrud

Kolbotn

E06

Krokhol

155

Sandbakken

368
Tonekollen

E06

Lørenskog

159

Losby

Nordre
Elvåga

Lutvatn
363
▲

Søndre
Elvåga

Oppsal
Bøler
Nøklevatn

Halsjøen

Fløyta

Sondre

Skålsjøen

MOSS, FREDRIKSTAD

Oslo

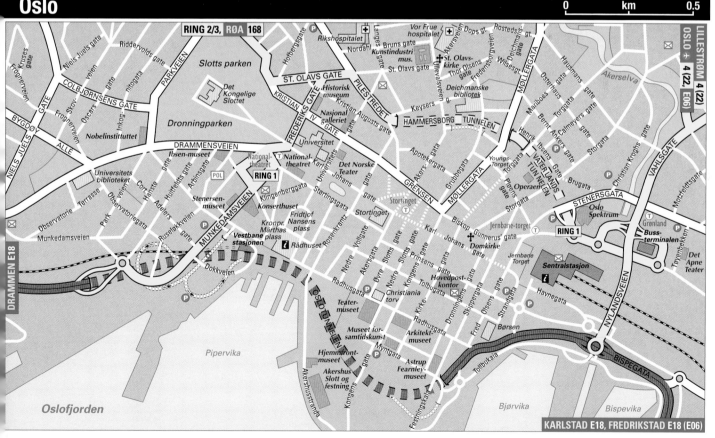

RING 2/3, RØA 168

LILLESTRØM 4 (22)
OSLO 4 (22, E06)

DRAMMEN E18

Oslofjorden

Pipervika

Bjørvika

Bispevika

KARLSTAD E18, FREDRIKSTAD E18 (E06)

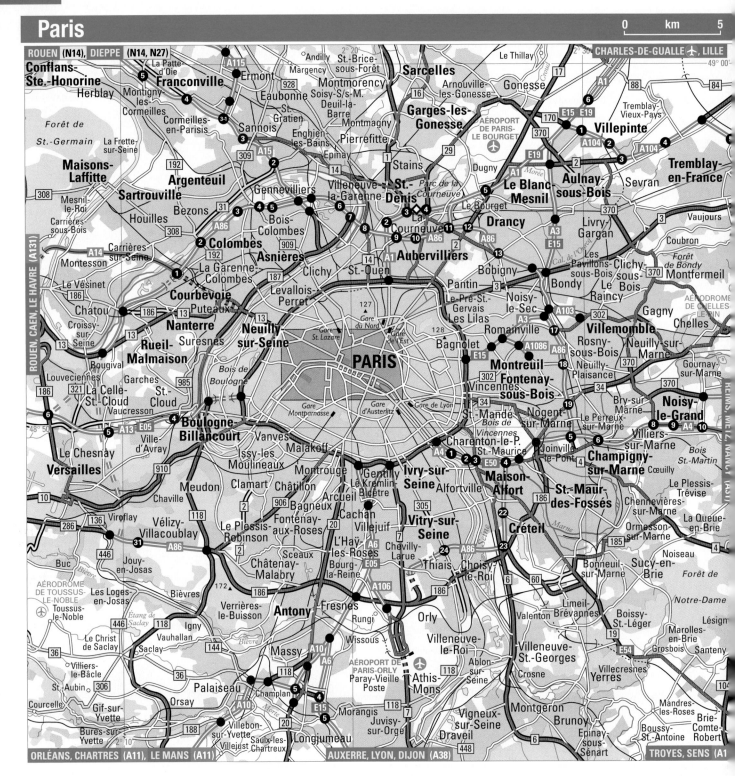

Paris

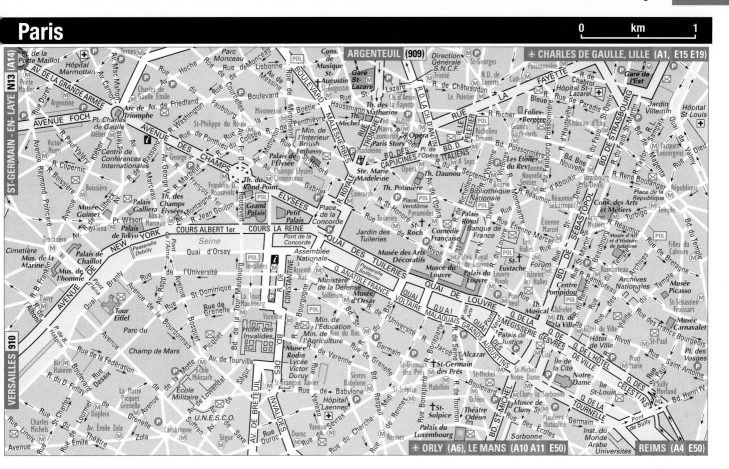

0 km 1

Praha Prague

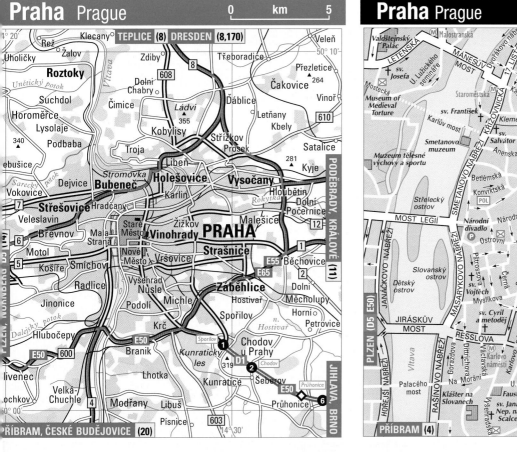

0 km 5

Praha Prague

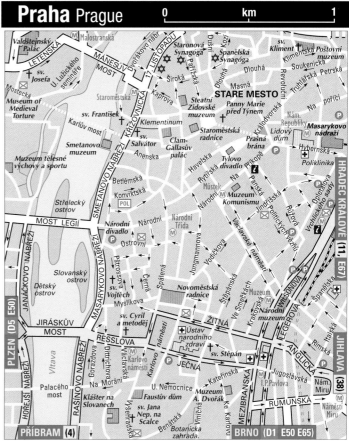

0 km 1

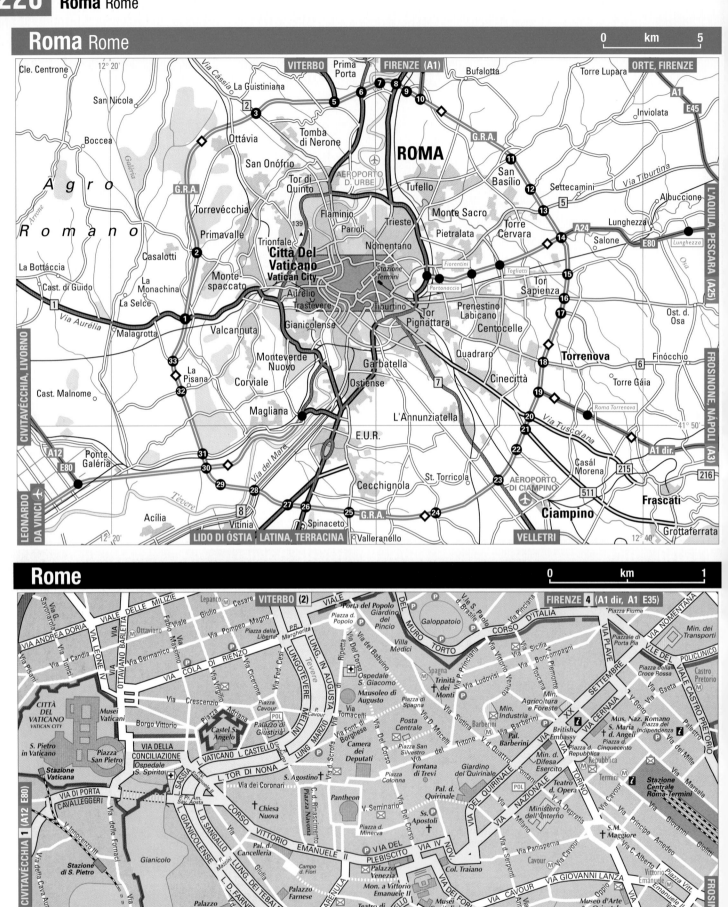

Roma Rome

0 km 5

Rome

0 km 1

Stockholm

0   km   5

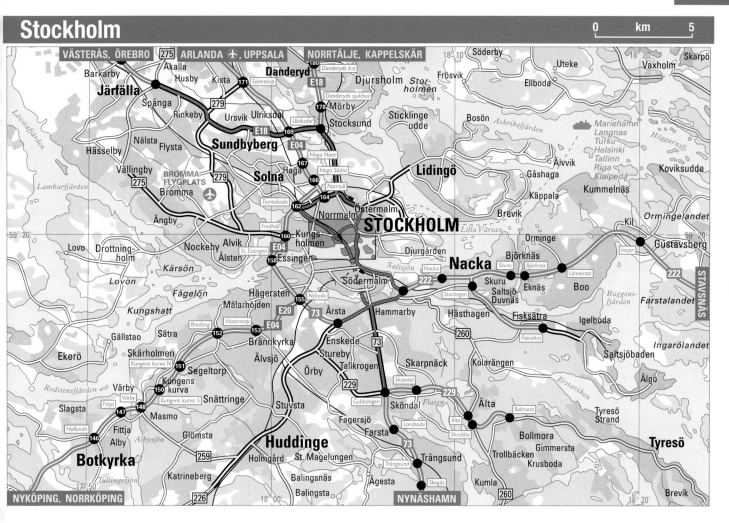

Stockholm

0   km   1

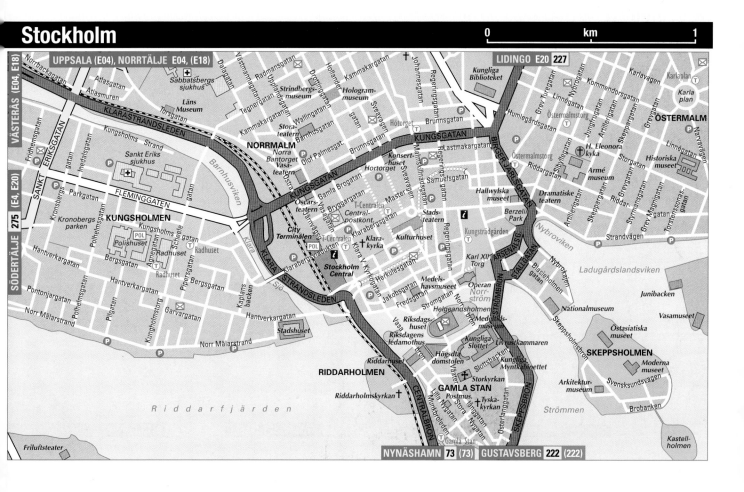

Strasbourg

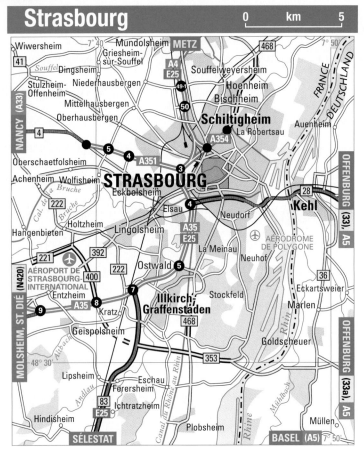

Strasbourg

Sevilla Seville

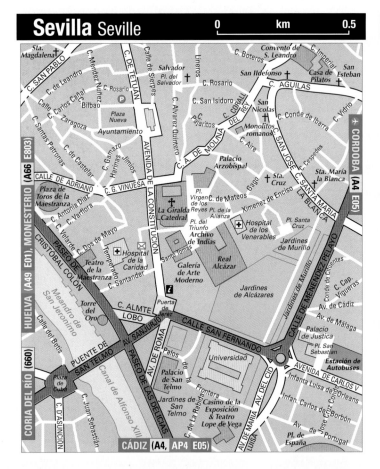

Stuttgart

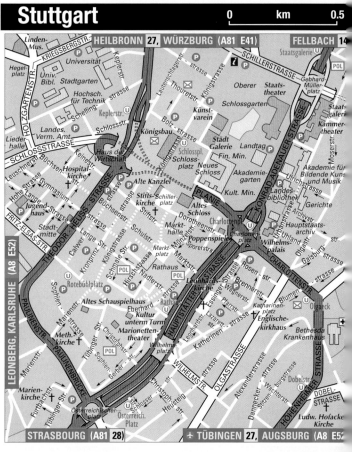

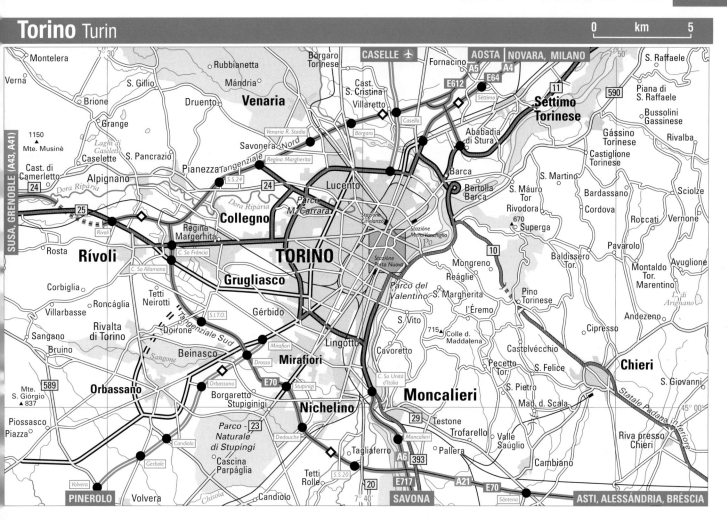

Torino Turin

0   km   5

Montelera
Verná
Brione
S. Gillio
Rubbianetta
Mándria
Bórgaro Torinese
CASELLE ✈
Fornacino
AOSTA **NOVARA, MILANO**
S. Raffaele
A5 | A4
E612 | E64
Piana di S. Raffaele
Druento
Venaria
Cast. S. Cristina Villaretto
Casello
11
Séttimo
590
Bussolini Gassinese
Verná
Grange
1150 ▲ Mte. Musinè
Laghi di Caselette
S. Pancrazio
Savonera Nord
Venaria R. Stadio
Bórgaro
Ababadia di Stura
Settimo Torinese
Gássino Torinese
Rivalba
Cast. di Camerletto
Alpignano
Pianezza
Tangenziale
Regina Margherita
S.S.24
Barca
Castiglione Torinese
Cordova
24
Dora Riparia
25
Rivoli
Regina Margherita
C. So Fráncia
24
Lucento
Parco M. Carrara
Dora Riparia
Stazione Cinisanzo
Bertolla Barca
S. Máuro Tor.
Rivodora
670 Superga
Roccati
Vernone
SUSA, GRENOBLE (A43, A41)
Rosta
Rívoli
Collegno
TORINO
Stazione Metro Vanchiglia
Po
S. Martino
Pavarolo
Corbiglia
Villarbasse
Roncáglia
Tetti Neirotti
Doirone
Grugliasco
Gérbido
S.I.T.O.
Stazione Porta Nuova
Mongreno
Reáglie
Baldissero Tor.
10
Montaldo Tor. Marentino
Avuglione
Sangano
Bruino
Rivalta di Torino
Tangenziale Sud
Drosso
Mirafiori
Mirafiori
Lingotto
Parco del Valentino
S. Margherita
l'Éremo
Pino Torinese
Andezeno
Cipresso
Mte. S. Giórgio ▲ 837
589
Orbassano
Orbassano
E70
Stupinigi
Borgaretto Stupiginigi
Nichelino
29
Cavoretto
S. Vito
715 ▲ Colle d. Maddalena
Cascina Parpáglia
Piossasco Piazza
Parco Naturale di Stupinigi
23
Candiolo
Dedouche
Tagliaferro
A6
393
Testone
Trofarello
S. Felice
S. Pietro
Mad. d. Scala
Castelvécchio
Pecetto Tor.
Chieri
S. Giovanni
Volera
PINEROLO
Volvera
Candiolo
Tetti Rolle
S.S.20
20
E717
SAVONA
Séntena
A21
E70
Moncalieri
Pallera
Valle Sáuglio
Cambiano
Riva presso Chieri
ASTI, ALESSÁNDRIA, BRÉSCIA
Moncalieri

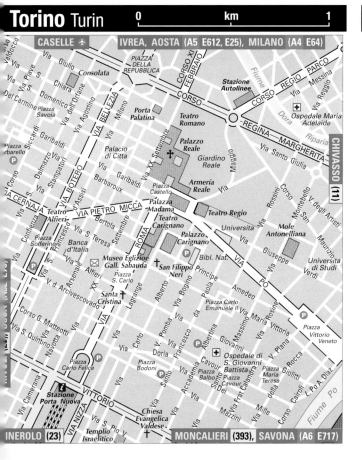

Torino Turin

0   km   1

CASELLE ✈   **IVREA, AOSTA (A5 E612, E25), MILANO (A4 E64)**

INEROLO (23)   **MONCALIERI (393), SAVONA (A6 E717)**

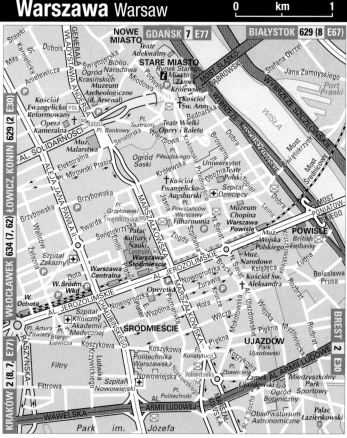

Warszawa Warsaw

0   km   1

NOWE MIASTO   **GDAŃSK** 7 E77   **BIAŁYSTOK** 629 (8) E67

KRAKÓW 2 (8, 7 E77) | **WŁOCŁAWEK 634 (7, 62)** | **ŁOWICZ, KONIN 629 (2) E30** | **BREST 2 E30**

For **Vienna** see page 224

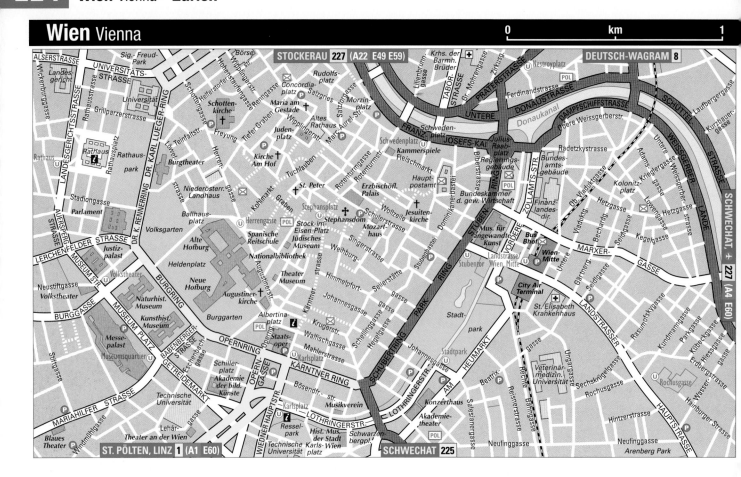

Wien Vienna

0 km 1

STOCKERAU **227** (A22 E49 E59)

DEUTSCH-WAGRAM **8**

SCHWECHAT, ✈ **227** (A4 E60)

ST. PÖLTEN, LINZ **1** (A1 E60)

SCHWECHAT **225**

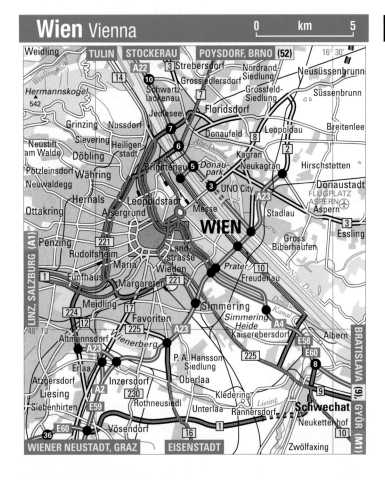

Wien Vienna

0 km 5

TULIN STOCKERAU POYSDORF, BRNO (52)

Weidling
A22
14
10
3 Strebersdorf
Nordrand-Siedlung
Neusüssenbrunn
Hermannskogel 542
Schwartz-lackenau
7
Grossiedlersdorf
Grossfeld-Siedlung
Süssenbrunn
Grinzing Nussdorf
Jedlesee
Floridsdorf
Sievering
Heiligenstadt
7
Donaufeld
8
Leopoldau
Breitenlee
Neustift am Walde
Döbling
6
Brigittenau
Donaupark
Kagran
2
Hirschstetten
Pötzleinsdorf
Währing
5
Donau-park
Neukagran
Neuwaldegg
3 UNO City
Donaustadt
Hernals
Leopoldstadt
A23
FLUGPLATZ ASPERN
Ottakring
Alsergrund
Messe
Aspern
WIEN
Stadlau
3
Penzing
Land-strasse
Gross Biberhaufen
Essling
221
Maria
Wieden
Prater
10
Rudolfsheim
Fünfhaus
Margareten
221
Freudenau
1
Meidling
17
224
225
Simmering
Simmering Heide
A23
A4
12
Favoriten
Kaiserebersdorf
E58
Altmannsdorf
A23
Wienerberg
225
Albern
E60
Erlaa
A2
P. A. Hansson Siedlung
8
Atzgersdorf
230
Oberlaa
9
Liesing
Inzersdorf
Kledering
Siebenhirten
Rothneusiedl
Liesing
Unterlaa
Rannersdorf
Schwechat
36
E60
Vösendorf
16
1
Neukettenhof
10
Zwölfaxing
WIENER NEUSTADT, GRAZ
EISENSTADT
LINZ, SALZBURG (A1)
BRATISLAVA (9), GYÖR (M1)

16° 30'
48° 10'

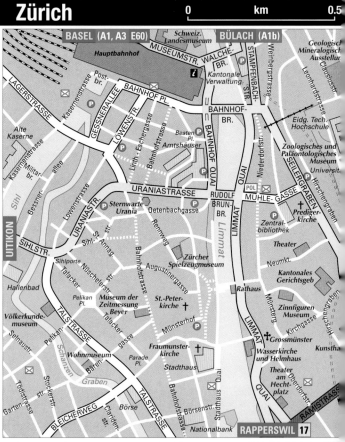

Zürich

0 km 0.5

BASEL (A1, A3 E60)

BÜLACH (A1b)

Schweiz. Landesmuseum
MUSEUMSTR. WALCHE-
Geologisch Mineralogisch Ausstellur
Hauptbahnhof
Postbr.
Kantonale Verwaltung
Weinbergstr.
STAMPFENBACH-STR.
Kasernenstrasse
BAHNHOF PL.
Leonhardstr.
LAGERSTRASSE
LÖWENSTR.
Bahnhofstrasse
BAHNHOF-BR.
Eidg. Tech. Hochschule
Alte Kaserne
Beaten Pl.
Eschergasse
Amtshäuser
Zoologisches und Paläontologisches Museum
Universit.
Kasernen-Militär-br.
Linth- Escherg.
BAHNHOF QUAI
Niederdorfstr.
Sihl
Löwenstr.
Gessner-
Rennweg
RUDOLF BRUN-BR.
QUAI
Hirschengraben
UTIKON
URANIASTRASSE
POL
MÜHLE-GASSE
Predigerkirche
Sternwarte Urania
Oetenbachgasse
Limmat
Zentralbibliothek
SIHLSTR.
Sihl-2
Augustinergasse
Zürcher Spielzeugmuseum
Theater
Sihlporte
Rathaus
Neumkt.
Pelikan Pl.
St.-Peter-kirche
Münsterg.
Kantonales Gerichtsgeb
Hallenbad
Museum der Zeitmessung Beyer
Zinnfiguren Museum
TALSTRASSE
Talacker
Münsterhof
Kirchgasse
Völkerkunde-museum
Fraumünster-kirche
Grossmünster
Wohnmuseum
Parade Pl.
Wasserkirche und Helmhaus
LIMMAT QUAI
Bären-
Stadthaus
Theater am Hecht-platz
Graben
Schanzen
Börse
Börsenstr.
BLEICHERWEG
Bahnhofstr.
Nationalbank
RAMISTRASSE
RAPPERSWIL **17**

GB	F	D	I
Ⓐ Austria	Autriche	Österreich	Austria
ⒶⓁ Albania	Albanie	Albanien	Albania
ⒶⓃⒹ Andorra	Andorre	Andorra	Andorra
Ⓑ Belgium	Belgique	Belgien	Belgio
ⒷⒼ Bulgaria	Bulgarie	Bulgarien	Bulgaria
ⒷⒾⒽ Bosnia-Herzegovina	Bosnie-Herzegovine	Bosnien-Herzegowina	Bosnia-Herzogovina
ⒷⓎ Belarus	Belarus	Weissrussland	Bielorussia
ⒸⒼ Montenegro	Monténégro	Montenegro	Montenegro
ⒸⒽ Switzerland	Suisse	Schweiz	Svizzera
ⒸⓎ Cyprus	Chypre	Zypern	Cipro
ⒸⓏ Czech Republic	République Tchèque	Tschechische Republik	Repubblica Ceca
Ⓓ Germany	Allemagne	Deutschland	Germania
ⒹⓀ Denmark	Danemark	Dänemark	Danimarca
Ⓔ Spain	Espagne	Spanien	Spagna
ⒺⓈⓉ Estonia	Estonie	Estland	Estonia
Ⓕ France	France	Frankreich	Francia
ⒻⒾⓃ Finland	Finlande	Finnland	Finlandia
ⒻⓁ Liechtenstein	Liechtenstein	Liechtenstein	Liechtenstein
ⒻⓄ Faeroe Islands	Îles Féroé	Färöer-Inseln	Isole Faroe
ⒼⒷ United Kingdom	Royaume Uni	Grossbritannien und Nordirland	Regno Unito
ⒼⒷⓏ Gibraltar	Gibraltar	Gibraltar	Gibilterra
ⒼⓇ Greece	Grèce	Greichenland	Grecia
Ⓗ Hungary	Hongrie	Ungarn	Ungheria
ⒽⓇ Croatia	Croatie	Kroatien	Croazia
Ⓘ Italy	Italie	Italien	Italia
ⒾⓇⓁ Ireland	Irlande	Irland	Irlanda
ⒾⓈ Iceland	Islande	Island	Islanda
Ⓛ Luxembourg	Luxembourg	Luxemburg	Lussemburgo
ⓁⓉ Lithuania	Lituanie	Litauen	Lituania
ⓁⓋ Latvia	Lettonie	Lettland	Lettonia
Ⓜ Malta	Malte	Malta	Malta
ⓂⒸ Monaco	Monaco	Monaco	Monaco
ⓂⒹ Moldova	Moldavie	Moldawien	Moldavia
ⓂⓀ Macedonia	Macédoine	Makedonien	Macedonia
Ⓝ Norway	Norvège	Norwegen	Norvegia
ⓃⓁ Netherlands	Pays-Bas	Niederlande	Paesi Bassi
Ⓟ Portugal	Portugal	Portugal	Portogallo
ⓅⓁ Poland	Pologne	Polen	Polonia
ⓇⓄ Romania	Roumanie	Rumanien	Romania
ⓇⓈⓂ San Marino	Saint-Marin	San Marino	San Marino
ⓇⓊⓈ Russia	Russie	Russland	Russia
Ⓢ Sweden	Suède	Schweden	Svezia
ⓈⓀ Slovak Republic	République Slovaque	Slowak Republik	Repubblica Slovacca
ⓈⓁⓄ Slovenia	Slovénie	Slowenien	Slovenia
ⓈⓇⒷ Serbia	Serbie	Serbien	Serbia
ⓉⓇ Turkey	Turquie	Türkei	Turchia
ⓊⒶ Ukraine	Ukraine	Ukraine	Ucraina

A

Amurrio E 143 A4
Amusco E 142 B2
An t-Ob GB 31 B1
Åna-Sira N 52 B2
Anacapri I 170 C2
Anadia P 148 B1
Anadon E 152 B2
Anafi GR 185 C6
Anagni I 169 B3
Anamur TR 23 C7
Ananyiv UA 17 B8
Anascaul IRL 29 B1
Ånäset S 2 D7
Anastażewo PL 76 B3
Anaya de Alba E 150 B2
Ança P 148 B1
Ancaster GB 40 C3
Ancede P 148 A1
Ancenis F 101 B4
Ancerville F 91 C5
Anchuras E 156 A3
Ancona I 136 B2
Ancora P 148 A1
Ancrum GB 35 C5
Ancy-le-Franc F 104 B3
Andalo I 121 A3
Åndalsnes N 198 C4
Andance F 117 B4
Andau A 111 B4
Andebu N 53 A6
Andeer CH 107 C4
Andelfingen CH 107 B3
Andelot F 105 A4
Andelot-en-Montagne F 105 C4
Andenes N 194 A7
Andenne B 79 B5
Anderlues B 79 B4
Andermatt CH 107 C3
Andernach D 80 B3
Andernos-les-Bains F 128 B1
Anderslöv S 66 A2
Anderstorp S 60 B3
Andijk NL 70 B2
Andoain E 144 A1
Andocs H 112 C1
Andolsheim F 106 A2
Andorra E 153 B3
Andorra La Vella AND 146 B2
Andosilla E 144 B2
Andover GB 44 B2
Andratx E 166 B2
Andreapol RUS 9 D8
Andreas GB 36 B2
Andréspol PL 86 A3
Andrest F 145 A4
Andretta I 172 B1
Andrezieux-Bouthéon F 117 B4
Ándria I 171 B4
Andrijevica CG 16 D3
Andritsena GR 184 B2
Andros GR 185 B5
Andrychów PL 99 B3
Andselv N 194 A9
Andújar E 157 B3
Anduze F 131 A2
Åneby N 48 B2
Aneby S 62 A2
Añes E 143 A3
Anet F 90 C1
Anfo I 121 B3
Ang S 62 A2
Anga S 57 C4
Angaïs F 145 A3
Ånge, *Jämtland* S 199 B11
Ånge, *Västernorrland* S 200 D1
Angeja P 148 B1
Ängelholm S 61 C2
Angeli FIN 193 D9
Ängelsberg S 50 C3
Anger A 110 B2
Angera I 120 B1
Angermünde D 74 A3
Angern A 97 C4
Angers F 102 B1
Angerville F 90 C2
Anghiari I 135 B5
Angle GB 39 C1
Anglès E 147 C3
Anglés, *Tarn* F 130 B1
Angles, *Vendée* F 114 B2
Angles sur l'Anglin F 115 B4
Anglesola E 147 C2
Anglet F 128 C1
Anglisidhes CY 181 B2
Anglure F 91 C3
Angoulême F 115 C4
Angoulins F 114 B2
Angsö S 56 A2
Angueira P 149 A3
Angües E 145 B3
Anguiano E 143 B4
Anguillara Sabazia I 168 A2
Anguillara Véneta I 121 B4
Anhée B 79 B4
Anholt DK 60 C1
Aniane F 130 B2
Aniche F 78 B3
Ånimskog S 54 B3
Anina RO 16 C4
Anixi GR 182 D3
Anizy-le-Château F 91 B3
Anjalankoski FIN 8 B5
Anjan S 199 B9
Ankara TR 187 C7
Ankaran SLO 122 B2
Ankarsrum S 62 A4
Ankerlia N 192 C4
Anklam D 66 C2
Ankum D 71 B4
Anlauftal A 109 B4
Anlezy F 104 C2
Ånn S 199 B9
Annaberg A 110 B2
Annaberg-Buchholz D 83 B5
Annaberg im Lammertal A 109 B4
Annaburg D 83 A5
Annahütte D 84 A1
Annalong GB 27 B5
Annan GB 36 B3
Anndalsvågen N 195 E3
Anneberg, *Halland* S 60 B2
Anneberg, *Jönköping* S 62 A2
Annecy F 118 B3
Annelund S 60 B3
Annemasse F 118 A3
Annenskiy Most RUS 9 B10
Annerstad S 60 C3
Annestown IRL 30 B1
Annevoie-Rouillon B 79 B4
Annonay F 117 B4
Annot F 132 B2
Annweiler D 93 B3
Ano Poroia GR 183 B5
Ano Siros GR 185 B5
Añora E 156 B3
Anould F 106 A1
Anquela del Ducado E 152 B1
Anröchte D 81 A4
Ans DK 59 B2
Ansager DK 59 C1
Ansbach D 94 B2
Anse F 117 B4
Anserœuil B 79 B3
Ansfelden A 110 A1
Ansião P 154 B2
Ansó E 144 B3
Ansoain E 144 B2
Anstruther GB 35 B5
Antalya TR 189 C5
Antas E 164 B3
Antegnate I 120 B2
Antequera E 163 A3
Anterselva di Mezzo I 108 C3
Antibes F 132 B3
Antigüedad E 142 C2
Antillo I 177 B4
Antirio GR 184 A2
Antnäs S 196 D4
Antoing B 79 B3
Antonin PL 86 A1
Antrain F 88 B2
Antrim GB 27 B4
Antrodoco I 169 A3
Antronapiana I 119 A5
Anttis S 196 B5
Antuzede P 148 B1
Antwerp = Antwerpen B 79 A4
Antwerpen = Antwerp B 79 A4
Anversa d'Abruzzi I 169 B3
Anvin F 78 B2
Anzat-le-Luguet F 116 B3
Anzi I 172 B1
Ánzio I 168 B2
Anzola d'Emilia I 135 A4
Anzón E 144 C2
Aoiz E 144 B2
Aosta I 119 B4
Apalhão P 155 B3
Apátfalva H 126 A2
Apatin SRB 125 B5
Apatity RUS 3 C13
Apc H 112 B3
Apécchio I 136 B1
Apeldoorn NL 70 B2
Apen D 71 A4
Apenburg D 73 B4
Apensen D 72 A2
Apiro I 136 B2
Apliki CY 181 B2
Apolda D 82 A3
Apolonia GR 185 C5
Apostag H 112 C2
Äppelbo S 49 B6
Appennino I 136 C2
Appenzell CH 107 B4
Appiano I 108 C2
Appingedam NL 71 A3
Appleby-in-Westmorland GB 37 B4
Applecross GB 31 B3
Appledore GB 42 A2
Appoigny F 104 B2
Apremont-la-Forêt F 92 C1
Aprica I 120 A3
Apricena I 171 B3
Aprigliano I 174 B2
Aprília I 168 B2
Apt F 131 B4
Apúlia P 148 A1
Aquiléia I 122 B2
Aquilónia I 172 B1
Aquino I 169 B3
Ar S 57 C4
Arabayona E 150 A2
Arabba I 108 C2
Araç TR 23 A7
Aracena E 161 B3
Arachova GR 184 A3
Aračinovo MK 182 A3
Arad RO 126 A3
Aradac SRB 126 B2
Aradhippou CY 181 B2
Aragnouet F 145 B4
Aragona I 176 B2
Aramits F 144 A3
Aramon F 131 B3
Aranda de Duero E 143 C3
Aranda de Moncayo E 152 A2
Arandjelovac SRB 127 C2
Aranjuez E 151 B4
Arantzazu E 143 B4
Aranzueque E 151 B4
Aras de Alpuente E 159 B2
Arauzo de Miel E 143 C3
Arazede P 148 B1
Arbas F 145 B4
Árbatax I 179 C3
Arbeca E 147 C1
Arberg D 94 B2
Arbesbach A 96 C2
Arboga S 56 A1
Arbois F 105 C4
Arbon CH 107 B4
Arboréa I 179 C2
Arbório I 119 B5
Årbostad N 194 B8
Arbrå S 50 A3
Arbroath GB 35 B5
Arbúcies E 147 C3
Arbuniel E 163 A4
Arbus I 179 C2
Arc-en-Barrois F 105 B3
Arc-et-Senans F 105 B4
Arc-lès-Gray F 105 B4
Arc-sur-Tille F 105 B4
Arcachon F 128 B1
Arce I 169 B3
Arcen NL 80 A2
Arces-Dilo F 104 A2
Arcévia I 136 B1
Arcey F 106 B1
Archanes GR 185 D6
Archangelos GR 188 C3
Archena E 165 A3
Archez E 163 B4
Archiac F 115 C3
Archidona E 163 A3
Archiestown GB 32 D3
Archivel E 164 A3
Arcidosso I 135 C4
Arcille I 135 C4
Arcis-sur-Aube F 91 C4
Arco I 121 B3
Arcones E 151 A4
Arcos E 143 B3
Arcos de Jalón E 152 A1
Arcos de la Frontera E 162 B2
Arcos de la Sierra E 152 B1
Arcos de las Salinas E 159 B2
Arcos de Valdevez P 148 A1
Arcozelo P 148 B2
Arcusa E 145 B4
Arcy-sur-Cure F 104 B2
Ardagh IRL 29 B2
Årdal N 52 A2
Ardala S 55 B4
Ardales E 162 B3
Årdalstangen N 47 A4
Ardara I 178 B2
Ardara IRL 26 B2
Ardarroch GB 31 B3
Ardbeg GB 34 C1
Ardcharnich GB 32 D1
Ardchyle GB 34 B3
Ardee IRL 27 C4
Arden DK 58 B2
Ardentes F 103 C3
Ardenza I 134 B3
Ardersier GB 32 D2
Ardes F 116 B3
Ardessie GB 32 D1
Ardez CH 107 C5
Ardfert IRL 29 B2
Ardgay GB 32 D2
Ardglass GB 27 B5
Ardgroom IRL 29 C2
Ardhasig GB 31 B2
Ardino BG 183 B7
Ardisa E 144 B3
Ardkearagh IRL 29 C1
Ardlui GB 34 B3
Ardlussa GB 34 B2
Ardón E 142 B1
Ardooie B 78 B3
Ardore I 175 C2
Ardre S 57 C4
Ardres F 78 B1
Ardrishaig GB 34 B2
Ardrossan GB 34 C3
Are N 52 A1
Åre S 199 B10
Areia Branca P 154 B1
Aremark N 54 A2
Arenales de San Gregorio E 157 A4
Arenas E 163 B3
Arenas de Iguña E 142 A2
Arenas de San Juan E 157 A4
Arenas de San Pedro E 150 B2
Arenas del Rey E 163 B4
Arendal N 53 B4
Arendonk B 79 A5
Arengosse F 128 B2
Arentorp S 55 B3
Arenys de Mar E 147 C3
Arenys de Munt E 147 C3
Arenzano I 133 A4
Areo E 146 B2
Areopoli GR 184 C3
Ares E 140 A2
Arès F 128 B1
Ares del Maestrat E 153 B3
Aresvika N 198 B5
Arette F 144 A3
Aretxabaleta E 143 A4
Arevalillo E 150 B2
Arévalo E 150 A3
Arez P 155 B3
Arezzo I 135 B4
Arfeuilles F 117 A3
Argalasti GR 183 D5
Argallón E 156 B2
Argamasilla de Alba E 157 A4
Argamasilla de Calatrava E 157 B3
Arganda E 151 B4
Arganil P 148 B1
Argasion GR 184 B1
Argegno I 120 B2
Argelès-Gazost F 145 A3
Argelès-sur-Mer F 146 B4
Argent-sur-Sauldre F 103 B4
Argenta I 121 C4
Argentan F 89 B3
Argentat F 116 B1
Argentera I 132 A2
Argenteuil F 90 C2
Argenthal D 93 B3
Argentiera I 178 B2
Argenton-Château F 102 C1
Argenton-sur-Creuse F 103 C3
Argentona E 147 C3
Argentré F 102 A1
Argentré-du-Plessis F 101 A4
Argıthanı TR 189 A6
Argirades GR 182 D1
Argos GR 184 B3
Argos Orestiko GR 182 C3
Argostoli GR 184 A1
Argote E 143 B4
Arguedas E 144 B2
Argueil F 90 B1
Arholma S 51 C6
Århus DK 59 B3
Ariano Irpino I 170 B3
Ariano nel Polésine I 121 C5
Aribe E 144 B2
Aridea GR 182 C4
Arienzo I 170 B2
Arild S 61 C2
Arileod GB 34 B1
Arinagour GB 34 B1
Ariño E 153 A3
Arinthod F 118 A2
Arisaig GB 34 B2
Arisgotas E 157 A4
Aritzo I 179 C3
Ariza E 152 A1
Årjäng S 54 A3
Arjeplog S 195 D8
Arjona E 157 C3
Arjonilla E 157 C3
Arkasa GR 188 D2
Arkelstorp S 63 B2
Arklow IRL 30 B2
Arkösund S 56 B2
Ärla S 56 A2
Arlanc F 117 B3
Arlanzón E 143 B3
Arlebosc F 117 B4
Arlena di Castro I 168 A1
Arles F 131 B3
Arles-sur-Tech F 146 B3
Arló H 113 A4
Arlon B 92 B1
Armação de Pera P 160 B1
Armadale, *Highland* GB 31 B3
Armadale, *West Lothian* GB 35 C4
Armagh GB 27 B4
Armamar P 148 A2
Armenistis GR 185 B7
Armeno I 119 B5
Armenteros E 150 B2
Armentières F 78 B2
Armilla E 163 A4
Armiñón E 143 B4
Armoy GB 27 A4
Armuña de Tajuña E 151 B4
Armutlu, *Bursa* TR 186 B3
Armutlu, *İzmir* TR 188 A2
Arnac-Pompadour F 115 C5
Arnafjord N 46 A3
Arnage F 102 B2
Arnas F 117 A4
Årnäs S 55 B4
Arnay-le-Duc F 104 B3
Arnborg DK 59 B2
Arnbruck D 95 B4
Arnea GR 183 C5
Arneberg, *Hedmark* N 48 A2
Arneberg, *Hedmark* N 49 B4
Arneburg D 73 B5
Arnedillo E 144 B1
Arnedo E 144 B1
Arneguy F 144 A2
Arnés E 153 B4
Árnes IS 190 A4
Årnes, *Akershus* N 48 B3
Årnes, *Troms* N 194 A9
Arnfels A 110 C2
Arnhem NL 70 C2
Arnissa GR 182 C3
Arno S 56 B3
Arnold GB 40 B2
Arnoldstein A 109 C4
Arnsberg D 81 A4
Arnschwang D 95 B4
Arnsdorf D 84 A1
Årnset N 198 B6
Arnside GB 37 B4
Arnstadt D 82 B2
Arnstein D 94 B1
Arnstorf D 95 C4
Arnum DK 59 C1
Aroche E 161 B3
Ároktő H 113 B4
Arolla CH 119 A4
Arolsen D 81 A5
Arona I 119 B5
Åros N 54 A1
Arosa CH 107 C4
Arosa P 148 A1
Arøsund DK 59 C2
Arouca P 148 B1
Årøysund N 54 A1
Arpajon F 90 C2
Arpajon-sur-Cère F 116 C2
Arpela FIN 196 C7
Arpino I 169 B3
Arquata del Tronto I 136 C2
Arques F 78 B2
Arques-la-Bataille F 89 A5
Arquillos E 157 B4
Arraia-Maeztu E 143 B4
Arraiolos P 154 C2
Arrancourt F 92 C2
Arras F 78 B2
Arrasate E 143 A4
Årre DK 59 C1
Arreau F 145 B4
Arredondo E 143 A3
Arrens-Marsous F 145 B3
Arriate E 162 B2
Arrifana P 160 B1
Arrigorriaga E 143 A4
Arriondas E 142 A1
Arroba de los Montes E 157 A3
Arrochar GB 34 B3
Arromanches-les-Bains F 88 A3
Arronches P 155 B3
Arroniz E 144 B1
Arrou F 103 A3
Arroya E 142 B2
Arroya de Cuéllar E 150 A3
Arroyal E 142 B2
Arroyo de la Luz E 155 B4
Arroyo de San Servan E 155 C4
Arroyo del Ojanco E 164 A2
Arroyomolinos de León E 161 A3
Arroyomolinos de Montánchez E 156 A1
Arruda dos Vinhos P 154 C1
Ars-en-Ré F 114 B2
Ars-sur-Moselle F 92 B2
Arsac F 128 B2
Arsiè I 121 B4
Arsiero I 121 B4
Årslev DK 59 C3
Ársoli I 169 A3
Årsunda S 50 B3
Artà E 167 B3
Arta GR 182 D3
Artajona E 144 B2
Artegna I 122 A2
Arteixo E 140 A2
Artemare F 118 B2
Arten I 121 A4
Artena I 169 B2
Artenay F 103 A3
Artern D 82 A3
Artés E 147 C2
Artesa de Segre E 147 C2
Arth CH 107 B3
Arthez-de-Béarn F 145 A3
Arthon-en-Retz F 101 B4
Arthurstown IRL 30 B2
Artieda E 144 B3
Artix F 145 A3
Artotina GR 182 E4
Artsyz UA 17 B8
Artziniega E 143 A3
Arudy F 145 A3
Arundel GB 44 C3
Årup DK 59 C3
Arveyres F 128 B2
Arvidsjaur S 196 D2
Arvieux F 118 C3
Arvika S 54 A3
Åryd, *Blekinge* S 63 B3
Åryd, *Kronoberg* S 62 B2
Arzachena I 178 A3
Arzacq-Arraziguet F 128 C2
Árzana I 179 C3
Arzano F 100 B2
Aržano HR 138 B2
Arzberg D 95 A4
Arzignano I 121 B4
Arzila P 148 B1
Arzl im Pitztal A 108 B1
Arzúa E 140 B2
As B 80 A1
Aš CZ 83 B4
Ås N 54 A1
As Neves E 140 B2
As Nogais E 141 B3
As Pontes de García Rodríguez E 140 A3
Åsa S 60 B2
Aşağıçiğil TR 189 A6
Ašanja SRB 127 C2
Åsarna S 199 C11
Åsarøy N 52 A2
Åsarp S 55 B4
Asasp F 145 A3
Åsbro S 55 A6
Asby CH 107 C4
Åsby, *Halland* S 60 B2
Åsby, *Östergötland* S 62 A3
Ásbygri IS 191 A9
Ascain F 144 A2
Ascea I 172 B1
Ascha D 95 B4
Aschach an der Donau A 96 C2
Aschaffenburg D 93 B5
Aschbach Markt A 110 A1
Ascheberg, *Nordrhein-Westfalen* D 81 A3
Ascheberg, *Schleswig-Holstein* D 65 B3
Aschendorf D 71 A4
Aschersleben D 82 A3
Asciano I 135 B4
Ascó E 153 A4
Asco F 180 A2
Áscoli Piceno I 136 C2
Áscoli Satriano I 171 B3
Ascona CH 120 A1
Ascot GB 44 B3
Ascoux F 103 A4
Åse N 194 A6
Åseda S 62 A3
Åsele S 200 B3
Åsen N 199 B8
Åsen S 49 A5
Asendorf D 72 B2
Asenovgrad BG 183 A6
Åsensbruk S 54 B3
Åseral N 52 B3
Asfeld F 91 B4
Ásgarður IS 190 B1
Åsgårdstrand N 54 A1
Asgate CY 181 B2
Ash, *Kent* GB 45 B5
Ash, *Surrey* GB 44 B3
Åshammar S 50 B3
Ashbourne GB 40 B2
Ashbourne IRL 30 A2
Ashburton GB 43 B3
Ashby-de-la-Zouch GB 40 C2
Ashchurch GB 44 B1
Åsheim N 199 D8
Ashford GB 45 B4
Ashington GB 37 A5
Ashley GB 38 B4
Ashmyany BY 13 A6
Ashton Under Lyne GB 40 B1
Ashwell GB 44 A3
Asiago I 121 B4
Asipovichy BY 13 B8
Aska FIN 197 B9
Askam-in-Furness GB 36 B3
Askeaton IRL 29 B3
Asker N 48 C2

Balatonederics H 111 C4
Balatonfenyves H 111 C4
Balatonföldvár H 112 C1
Balatonfüred H 112 C1
Balatonfűzfő H 112 B2
Balatonkenese H 112 B2
Balatonkiliti H 112 C2
Balatonlelle H 111 C4
Balatonszabadi H 112 C2
Balatonszemes H 111 C4
Balatonszentgyörgy H 111 C4
Balazote E 158 C1
Balbeggie GB 35 B4
Balbigny F 117 B4
Balboa E 141 B4
Balbriggan IRL 30 A2
Balchik BG 17 D8
Balçova TR 188 A2
Baldock GB 44 B3
Bale HR 122 B2
Baleira E 141 A3
Baleizao P 160 A2
Balen B 79 A5
Balerma E 164 C2
Balestrand N 46 A3
Balestrate I 176 A2
Balfour GB 33 B4
Bälganet S 63 B3
Balıkesir TR 186 C2
Balıklıçeşme TR 186 B2
Bälinge S 51 C4
Balingen D 107 A3
Balingsta S 56 A3
Balintore GB 32 D3
Balizac F 128 B2
Balk NL 70 B2
Balkbrug NL 71 B3
Balla IRL 28 A2
Ballachulish GB 34 B2
Ballaghaderreen IRL 26 C2
Ballancourt-sur-Essonne F 90 C2
Ballantrae GB 36 A2
Ballao I 179 C3
Ballasalla GB 36 B2
Ballater GB 32 D3
Ballen DK 59 C3
Ballenstedt D 82 A3
Ballerias E 145 C3
Balleroy F 88 A3
Ballerup DK 61 D2
Ballesteros de Calatrava E 157 B4
Ballı TR 186 B2
Ballina IRL 26 B1
Ballinalack IRL 30 A1
Ballinamore IRL 26 B3
Ballinascarty IRL 29 C3
Ballinasloe IRL 28 A3
Ballindine IRL 28 A3
Balling DK 58 B1
Ballingarry, *Limerick* IRL 29 B3
Ballingarry, *Tipperary* IRL 30 B1
Ballingeary IRL 29 C2
Ballinhassig IRL 29 C3
Ballinluig GB 35 B4
Ballino I 121 B3
Ballinrobe IRL 28 A2
Ballinskellings IRL 29 C1
Ballinspittle IRL 29 C3
Ballintra IRL 26 B2
Ballivor IRL 30 A2
Ballobar E 153 A4
Ballon F 102 A2
Ballon IRL 30 B2
Ballószög H 112 C3
Ballsh AL 182 C1
Ballstad N 194 B4
Ballum DK 64 A1
Ballybay IRL 27 B4
Ballybofey IRL 26 B3
Ballybunion IRL 29 B2
Ballycanew IRL 30 B2
Ballycarry GB 27 B5
Ballycastle GB 27 A4
Ballycastle IRL 26 B1
Ballyclare GB 27 B5
Ballyconneely IRL 28 A1
Ballycotton IRL 29 C3
Ballycroy IRL 26 B1
Ballydehob IRL 29 C2
Ballyferriter IRL 29 B1
Ballygawley GB 27 B3
Ballygowan GB 27 B5
Ballyhaunis IRL 28 A3
Ballyheige IRL 29 B2
Ballyjamesduff IRL 27 C3
Ballylanders IRL 29 B3
Ballylynan IRL 30 B1
Ballymahon IRL 28 A4
Ballymena GB 27 B4
Ballymoe IRL 28 A3
Ballymoney GB 27 A4
Ballymore IRL 28 A4
Ballymote IRL 26 B2
Ballynacorra IRL 29 C3
Ballynagore IRL 30 A1
Ballynahinch GB 27 B5
Ballynure GB 27 B5
Ballyragget IRL 30 B1
Ballysadare IRL 26 B2
Ballyshannon IRL 26 B2
Ballyvaghan IRL 28 A2
Ballyvourney IRL 29 C2
Ballywalter GB 27 B5
Balmaclellan GB 36 A2
Balmaseda E 143 A3
Balmazújváros H 113 B5
Balme I 119 B4
Balmedie GB 33 D4
Balmuccia I 119 B5
Balna-paling GB 32 D2
Balneario de Panticosa E 145 B3
Balotaszállás H 126 A1
Balsa P 148 A2
Balsareny E 147 C2
Balsorano-Nuovo I 169 B3
Bålsta S 57 A3
Balsthal CH 106 B2
Balta UA 17 A8
Baltanás E 142 C2
Baltar E 140 C3
Baltasound GB 33 A6
Bălţi MD 17 B7
Baltimore IRL 29 C2
Baltinglass IRL 30 B2
Baltiysk RUS 69 A4
Baltów PL 87 A5
Balugães P 148 A1
Balve D 81 A3
Balvi LV 8 D5
Balvicar GB 34 B2
Balya TR 186 C2
Balzo I 136 C2
Bamberg D 94 B2
Bamburgh GB 37 A5
Banatska Palanka SRB 127 C3
Banatski Brestovac SRB 127 C2
Banatski Despotovac SRB 126 B2
Banatski Dvor SRB 126 B2
Banatski-Karlovac SRB 127 B3
Banatsko Arandjelovo SRB 126 A2
Banatsko-Novo Selo SRB 127 C2
Banaz TR 187 D4
Banbridge GB 27 B4
Banbury GB 44 A2
Banchory GB 33 D4
Bande B 79 B5
Bande E 140 B3
Bandholm DK 65 B4
Bandırma TR 186 B2
Bandol F 132 B1
Bandon IRL 29 C3
Bañeres E 159 C3
Banff GB 33 D4
Bangor F 100 B2
Bangor, *Down* GB 27 B5
Bangor, *Gwynedd* GB 38 A2
Bangor IRL 26 B1
Bangsund N 199 A8
Banie PL 74 A3
Banja Koviljača SRB 127 C1
Banja Luka BIH 124 C3
Banja Vručica BIH 125 C3
Banjaloka SLO 123 B3
Banjani SRB 127 C1
Banka SK 98 C1
Bankekind S 56 B1
Bankend GB 36 A3
Bankeryd S 62 A2
Bankfoot GB 35 B4
Banloc RO 126 B3
Bannalec F 100 B2
Bannes F 91 C3
Bannockburn GB 35 B4
Bañobárez E 149 B3
Bañon E 152 B2
Banon F 132 A1
Baños E 149 B4
Baños de Gigonza E 162 B2
Baños de la Encina E 157 B4
Baños de Molgas E 140 B3
Baños de Rio Tobia E 143 B4
Baños de Valdearados E 143 C3
Bánov CZ 98 C1
Banova Jaruga HR 124 B2
Bánovce nad Bebravou SK 98 C2
Banovići BIH 139 A4
Banoviči Selo BIH 139 A4
Bánréve H 99 C4
Bansin D 66 C3
Banská Belá SK 98 C2
Banská Bystrica SK 99 C3
Banská Štiavnica SK 98 C2
Bansko BG 183 B5
Banstead GB 44 B3
Banteer IRL 29 B3
Bantheville F 91 B5
Bantry IRL 29 C2
Bantzenheim F 106 B2
Banyalbufar E 166 B2
Banyoles E 147 B3
Banyuls-sur-Mer F 146 B4
Bapaume F 90 A2
Bar CG 16 D3
Bar UA 13 D7
Bar-le-Duc F 91 C5
Bar-sur-Aube F 104 A3
Bar-sur-Seine F 104 A3
Barabhas GB 31 A2
Barači BIH 138 A2
Baracs H 112 C2
Baracska H 112 B2
Barahona E 151 A5
Barajes de Melo E 151 B5
Barakaldo E 143 A4
Baralla E 141 B3
Barañain E 144 B2
Baranavichy BY 13 B7
Báránd H 113 B5
Baranda SRB 127 B2
Baranello I 170 B2
Baranów Sandomierski PL 87 B5
Baraqueville F 130 A1
Barasoain E 144 B2
Barbacena P 155 C3
Barbadás E 140 B3
Barbadillo E 149 B4
Barbadillo de Herreros E 143 B3
Barbadillo del Mercado E 143 B3
Barbadillo del Pez E 143 B3
Barban HR 123 B3
Barbarano Vicento I 121 B4
Barbariga HR 122 C2
Barbaros TR 186 B2
Barbastro E 145 B4
Barbate E 162 B2
Barbatona E 152 A1
Barbâtre F 114 B1
Barbazan F 145 A4
Barbeitos E 141 A3
Barbentane F 131 B3
Barberino di Mugello I 135 A4
Barbezieux-St. Hilaire F 115 C3
Barbonne-Fayel F 91 C3
Barbotan-les-Thermes F 128 C2
Barby D 73 C4
Barca de Alva P 149 A3
Bárcabo E 145 B4
Barcarrota E 155 C4
Barcellona-Pozzo di Gotto I 177 A4
Barcelona E 147 C3
Barcelonette F 132 A2
Barcelos P 148 A1
Barcena de Pie de Concha E 142 A2
Bárcena del Monasterio E 141 A4
Barchfeld D 82 B2
Barcin PL 76 B2
Barcino PL 68 A1
Bárcis I 122 A1
Barco P 148 B2
Barcones E 151 A5
Barcs H 124 B3
Barcus F 144 A3
Bardejov SK 12 D4
Bårdesø DK 59 C3
Bardi I 120 C2
Bardney GB 40 B3
Bardo PL 85 B4
Bardolino I 121 B3
Bardonécchia I 118 B3
Bardoňovo SK 112 A2
Barèges F 145 B4
Barenstein D 83 B5
Barentin F 89 A4
Barenton F 88 B3
Barevo BIH 138 A3
Barfleur F 88 A2
Barga I 134 A3
Bargas E 151 C3
Barge I 119 C4
Bargemon F 132 B2
Barghe I 120 B3
Bargoed GB 39 C3
Bargrennan GB 36 A2
Bargteheide D 64 C3
Barham GB 45 B5
Bari I 173 A2
Bari Sardo I 179 C3
Barič Draga HR 137 A4
Barilović HR 123 B4
Barisciano I 169 A3
Barjac F 131 A3
Barjols F 132 B1
Barjon F 105 B3
Bårkåker N 54 A1
Barkald N 199 D7
Barkowo, *Dolnośląskie* PL 85 A4
Barkowo, *Pomorskie* PL 68 B2
Bârlad RO 17 B7
Barles F 132 A2
Barletta I 171 B4
Barlinek PL 75 B4
Barmouth GB 38 B2
Barmstedt D 64 C2
Barnard Castle GB 37 B5
Barnarp S 62 A2
Bärnau D 95 B4
Bärnbach A 110 B2
Barneberg D 73 B4
Barnenitz D 74 B1
Barnet GB 44 B3
Barnetby le Wold GB 40 B3
Barneveld NL 70 B2
Barneville-Carteret F 88 A2
Barnoldswick GB 40 B1
Barnowko PL 75 B3
Barnsley GB 40 B2
Barnstädt D 83 A3
Barnstaple GB 42 A2
Barnstorf D 72 B1
Barntrup D 72 C2
Baron F 90 B2
Baronissi I 170 C2
Barqueiro P 154 B2
Barquinha P 154 B2
Barr F 93 C3
Barr GB 36 A2
Barra P 148 B1
Barracas E 159 A3
Barraco E 150 B3
Barrado E 150 B2
Barrafranca I 177 B3
Barranco do Velho P 160 B2
Barrancos P 161 A3
Barrax E 158 B1
Barrbaar D 94 C2
Barre-des-Cevennes F 130 A2
Barreiro P 154 C1
Barreiros E 141 A3
Barrême F 132 B2
Barret-le-Bas F 132 A1
Barrhead GB 34 C3
Barrhill GB 36 A2
Barrio de Nuesra Señora E 142 B1
Barrow-in-Furness GB 36 B3
Barrow upon Humber GB 40 B3
Barrowford GB 40 B1
Barruecopardo E 149 A3
Barruelo de Santullán E 142 B2
Barruera E 145 B4
Barry GB 39 C3
Bårse DK 65 A4
Barsinghausen D 72 B2
Barssel D 71 A4
Barth D 66 B1
Bartholomä D 94 C1
Bartin TR 187 A7
Barton upon Humber GB 40 B3
Barúmini I 179 C2
Baruth D 74 B2
Barvaux B 80 B1
Barver D 72 B1
Barwatd PL 99 B3
Barwice PL 68 B1
Barysaw BY 13 A8
Barzana E 141 A5
Bârzava RO 16 B4
Bárzio I 120 B2
Bas E 147 B3
Bašaid SRB 126 B2
Basaluzzo I 120 C1
Basarabeasca MD 17 B8
Basauri E 143 A4
Baschi I 168 A2
Baschurch GB 38 B4
Basconcillos del Tozo E 143 B3
Bascones de Ojeda E 142 B2
Basécles B 79 B3
Basel CH 106 B2
Basélice I 170 B2
Basildon GB 45 B4
Basingstoke GB 44 B2
Baška CZ 98 B2
Baška HR 123 C3
Baška Voda HR 138 B2
Bäsksjö S 200 B3
Baslow GB 40 B2
Başmakçı TR 189 B5
Basovizza I 122 B2
Bassacutena I 178 A3
Bassano del Grappa I 121 B4
Bassano Romano I 168 A2
Bassecourt CH 106 B2
Bassella E 147 B2
Bassevuovdde N 193 D9
Bassou F 104 B2
Bassoues F 128 C3
Bassum D 72 B1
Båstad S 61 C2
Bastardo I 136 C1
Bastelica F 180 A2
Bastelicaccia F 180 B1
Bastia F 180 A2
Bastia I 136 B1
Bastogne B 92 A1
Baston GB 40 C3
Bastuträsk S 200 B6
Bata H 125 A4
Batajnica SRB 127 C2
Batak BG 183 B6
Batalha P 154 B2
Bátaszék H 125 A4
Batea E 153 A4
Batelov CZ 97 B3
Bath GB 43 A4
Bathgate GB 35 C4
Batida H 126 A2
Batignano I 135 C4
Batina HR 125 B4
Bátka SK 99 C4
Batković BIH 125 C5
Batley GB 40 B2
Batnfjordsøra N 198 C4
Batočina SRB 127 C3
Bátonyterenye H 113 B3
Batrina HR 125 B3
Båtsfjord N 193 B13
Båtskärsnäs S 196 D6
Battaglia Terme I 121 B4
Bätterkinden CH 106 B2
Battice B 80 B1
Battipáglia I 170 C2
Battle GB 45 C4
Battonya H 126 A3
Batuša SRB 127 C3
Bátya H 112 C2
Bau I 179 C2
Baud F 100 B2
Baudour B 79 B3
Baugé F 102 B1
Baugy F 103 B4
Bauma CH 107 B3
Baume-les-Dames F 105 B5
Baumholder D 93 B3
Baunatal D 81 A5
Baunei I 178 B3
Bauska LV 8 D4
Bautzen D 84 A2
Bavanište SRB 127 C2
Bavay F 79 B3
Bavilliers F 106 B1
Bavorov CZ 96 B2
Bawdsey GB 45 A5
Bawinkel D 71 B4
Bawtry GB 40 B2
Bayat TR 187 D5
Bayel F 105 A3
Bayeux F 88 A3
Bayındır TR 188 A2
Bayon F 92 C2
Bayonne F 128 C1
Bayons F 132 A2
Bayramiç TR 186 C1
Bayreuth D 95 B3
Bayrischzell D 108 B3
Baza E 164 B2
Bazas F 128 B2
Baziege F 146 A2
Bazoches-les-Gallerandes F 103 A4
Bazoches-sur-Hoëne F 89 B4
Bazzano I 135 A4
Beaconsfield GB 44 B3
Beade E 140 B2
Beadnell GB 37 A5
Beaminster GB 43 B4
Bearsden GB 34 C3
Beas E 161 B3
Beas de Segura E 164 A2
Beasain E 144 A1
Beattock GB 36 A3
Beaubery F 117 A4
Beaucaire F 131 B3
Beaufort F 118 B3
Beaufort IRL 29 B2
Beaufort-en Vallée F 102 B1
Beaugency F 103 B3
Beaujeu, *Alpes-de-Haute-Provence* F 132 A2
Beaujeu, *Rhône* F 117 A4
Beaulac F 128 B2
Beaulieu F 103 B4
Beaulieu GB 44 C2
Beaulieu-sous-la-Roche F 114 B2
Beaulieu-sur-Dordogne F 129 B4
Beaulieu-sur-Mer F 133 B3
Beaulon F 104 C2
Beauly GB 32 D2
Beaumaris GB 38 A2
Beaumesnil F 89 A4
Beaumetz-lès-Loges F 78 B2
Beaumont B 79 B4
Beaumont F 129 B3
Beaumont-de-Lomagne F 129 C3
Beaumont-du-Gâtinais F 103 A4
Beaumont-en-Argonne F 91 B5
Beaumont-Hague F 88 A2
Beaumont-la-Ronce F 102 B2
Beaumont-le-Roger F 89 A4
Beaumont-sur-Oise F 90 B2
Beaumont-sur-Sarthe F 102 A2
Beaune F 105 B3
Beaune-la-Rolande F 103 A4
Beaupréau F 101 B5
Beauraing B 91 A4
Beaurepaire F 117 B5
Beaurepaire-en-Bresse F 105 C4
Beaurières F 132 A1
Beauvais F 90 B2
Beauval F 90 A2
Beauville F 129 B3
Beauvoir-sur-Mer F 114 B1
Beauvoir-sur-Niort F 114 B3
Beba Veche RO 126 A2
Bebertal D 73 B4
Bebington GB 38 A3
Bebra D 82 B1
Bebrina HR 125 B3
Beccles GB 45 A5
Becedas E 150 B2
Beceite E 153 B4
Bečej SRB 126 B2
Becerreá E 141 B3
Becerril de Campos E 142 B2
Bécherel F 101 A4
Bechhofen D 94 B2
Bechyně CZ 96 B2
Becilla de Valderaduey E 142 B1
Beckfoot GB 36 B3
Beckingham GB 40 B3
Beckum D 81 A4
Beco P 154 B2
Bécon-les-Granits F 102 B1
Bečov nad Teplou CZ 83 B4
Becsehely H 111 C3
Bedale GB 37 B5
Bedames E 143 A3
Bédar E 164 B3
Bédarieux F 130 B2
Bédarrides F 131 A3
Bedburg D 80 B2
Beddgelert GB 38 A2
Beddingestrand S 66 A2
Bédée F 101 A4
Bedegkér H 112 C2
Beden TR 189 C7
Bedford GB 44 A3
Będków PL 87 A3
Bedlington GB 37 A5
Bedlno PL 77 B4
Bedmar E 163 A4
Bédoin F 131 A4
Bedónia I 134 A2
Bedretto CH 107 C3
Bedsted DK 58 B1
Bedum NL 71 A3
Bedwas GB 39 C3
Bedworth GB 40 C2
Będzin PL 86 B3
Beek en Donk NL 80 A1
Beekbergen NL 70 B2
Beelen D 71 C5
Beelitz D 74 B1
Beer GB 43 B3
Beerfelde D 74 B3
Beerfelden D 93 B4
Beernem B 78 A3
Beeskow D 74 B3
Beetsterzwaag NL 70 A3
Beetzendorf D 73 B4
Beflelay CH 106 B2
Begaljica SRB 127 C2
Bégard F 100 A2
Begejci SRB 126 B2
Begijar E 157 C4
Begijnendijk B 79 A4
Begndal N 48 B1
Begues E 147 C2
Beguildy GB 39 B3
Begur E 147 C4
Beho B 80 B1
Behringen D 82 A2
Beilen NL 71 B3
Beilngries D 95 B3
Beine-Nauroy F 91 B4
Beinwil CH 106 B3
Beiseförth D 82 A1
Beith GB 34 C3
Beitostølen N 47 A5
Beiuş RO 16 B5
Beja P 160 A2
Béjar E 149 B4
Bekçiler TR 189 C4
Békés H 113 C5
Békéscsaba H 113 C5
Bekilli TR 189 A4
Bekkarfjord N 193 B11
Bela SK 98 B2
Bela Crkva SRB 127 C3
Belá nad Radbuzou CZ 95 B4
Bělá Pod Bezdězem CZ 84 B2
Bélâbre F 115 B5
Belalcázar E 156 B2
Belanovica SRB 127 C2
Bélapátfalva H 113 A4
Belcaire F 146 B2
Bełchatów PL 86 A3
Belchite E 153 A3
Bělčice CZ 96 B1

Blachownia PL 86 B2
Blackburn GB 38 A4
Blackpool GB 38 A3
Blackstad S 62 A4
Blackwater IRL 30 B2
Blackwaterfoot GB 34 C2
Blacy F 91 C4
Bladåker S 51 B5
Blaenau Ffestiniog GB 38 B3
Blaenavon GB 39 C3
Blaengarw GB 39 C3
Blagaj BIH 124 B2
Blagaj BIH 139 B3
Blagdon GB 43 A4
Blagnac F 129 C4
Blagoevgrad BG 183 A5
Blaichach D 107 B5
Blain F 101 B4
Blainville-sur-l'Eau F 92 C2
Blair Atholl GB 35 B4
Blairgowrie GB 35 B4
Blajan F 145 A4
Blakeney GB 39 C4
Blakstad N 53 B4
Blâmont F 92 C2
Blanca E 165 A3
Blancos E 140 C3
Blandford Forum GB 43 B4
Blanes E 147 C3
Blangy-sur-Bresle F 90 B1
Blankaholm S 62 A4
Blankenberge B 78 A3
Blankenburg D 82 A2
Blankenfelde D 74 B2
Blankenhain D 82 B3
Blankenheim D 80 B2
Blanquefort F 128 B2
Blansko CZ 97 B4
Blanzac F 115 C4
Blanzy F 104 C3
Blaricum NL 70 B2
Blarney IRL 29 C3
Blascomillán E 150 B2
Blascosancho E 150 B3
Błaszki PL 86 A2
Blatná CZ 96 B1
Blatné SK 111 A4
Blatnice CZ 98 C1
Blatnika BIH 139 A3
Blato HR 138 C2
Blato na Cetini HR 138 B2
Blatten CH 119 A4
Blattnicksele S 195 E8
Blatzheim D 80 B2
Blaubeuren D 94 C1
Blaufelden D 94 B1
Blaustein D 94 C1
Blaydon GB 37 B5
Blaye F 128 A2
Blaye-les-Mines F 130 A1
Blázquez E 156 B2
Bleckede D 73 A3
Blecua E 145 B3
Bled SLO 123 A3
Bleiburg A 110 C1
Bleichenbach D 81 B5
Bleicherode D 82 A2
Bleik N 194 A6
Bleikvassli N 195 E4
Bléneau F 104 B1
Blentarp S 61 D3
Blera I 168 A2
Blérancourt F 90 B3
Bléré F 102 B2
Blesle F 116 B3
Blessington IRL 30 A2
Blet F 103 C4
Bletchley GB 44 B3
Bletterans F 105 C4
Blidö S 57 A4
Blidsberg S 60 B3
Blieskastel D 92 B3
Bligny-sur-Ouche F 104 B3
Blikstorp S 55 B5
Blinisht AL 182 B1
Blinja HR 124 B2
Blizanówek PL 76 C3
Bliżyn PL 87 A4
Blois F 103 B3
Blokhus DK 58 A2
Blokzijl NL 70 B2
Blombacka S 55 A4
Blomberg D 72 C2
Blomskog S 54 A3
Blomstermåla S 62 B4
Blomvåg N 46 B1
Blönduós IS 190 B5
Błonie PL 77 B5
Blonville-sur-Mer F 89 A4
Blötberget S 50 B2
Blovice CZ 96 B1
Bloxham GB 44 A2
Blšany CZ 83 B5
Bludenz A 107 B4
Bludov CZ 97 B4
Blumberg D 107 B3
Blyberg S 49 A6
Blyth, *Northumberland* GB 37 A5
Blyth, *Nottinghamshire* GB 40 B2
Blyth Bridge GB 35 C4
Blythburgh GB 45 A5
Blythe Bridge GB 40 C1
Bø, *Nordland* N 194 B5
Bø, *Telemark* N 53 A5
Boa Vista P 154 B2
Boal E 141 A4
Boan CG 139 C5
Boario Terme I 120 B3
Boat of Garten GB 32 D3
Boba H 111 B4
Bobadilla, *Logroño* E 143 B4
Bobadilla, *Málaga* E 163 A3
Bobadilla del Campo E 150 A2
Bobadilla del Monte E 151 B4
Bóbbio I 120 C2
Bóbbio Pellice I 119 C4
Bobigny F 90 C2
Bobingen D 94 C2
Böblingen D 93 C5
Bobolice PL 68 B1
Boboras E 140 B2
Boboshevo BG 182 A4
Bobowa PL 99 B4
Bobrová CZ 97 B4
Bobrovitsa UA 13 C9
Bobrowice PL 75 C4
Bobrówko PL 75 B4
Boca de Huérgano E 142 B2
Bocairent E 159 C3
Bočar SRB 126 B2
Bocchigliero I 174 B2
Boceguillas E 151 A4
Bochnia PL 99 B4
Bocholt B 80 A1
Bocholt D 80 A2
Bochov CZ 83 B5
Bochum D 80 A3
Bockara S 62 A4
Bockenem D 72 B3
Bockfliess A 97 C4
Bockhorn D 71 A5
Bočna SLO 123 A3
Bocognano F 180 A2
Boconád H 113 B4
Bőcs H 113 A4
Boczów PL 75 B3
Boda, *Dalarnas* S 50 A2
Böda, *Öland* S 62 A5
Boda, *Stockholm* S 51 B5
Boda, *Värmland* S 55 A4
Boda, *Västernorrland* S 200 D2
Boda Glasbruk S 63 B3
Bodafors S 62 A2
Bodajk H 112 B2
Boddam, *Aberdeenshire* GB 33 D5
Boddam, *Shetland* GB 33 B5
Boddin D 73 A4
Bödefeld-Freiheit D 81 A4
Boden S 196 D4
Bodenmais D 95 B5
Bodenteich D 73 B3
Bodenwerder D 72 C2
Bodiam GB 45 B4
Bodinnick GB 42 B2
Bodio CH 120 A1
Bodjani SRB 125 B5
Bodmin GB 42 B2
Bodø N 194 C5
Bodonal de la Sierra E 161 A3
Bodrum TR 188 B2
Bodstedt D 66 B1
Bodträskfors S 196 C3
Bodzanów PL 77 B5
Bodzanowice PL 86 B2
Bodzechów PL 87 B5
Bodzentyn PL 87 B4
Boecillo E 150 A3
Boëge F 118 A3
Boën F 117 B3
Bogács H 113 B4
Bogadmindszent H 125 B4
Bogajo E 149 B3
Bogarra E 158 C1
Bogarre E 163 A4
Bogatić SRB 127 C1
Bogatynia PL 84 B2
Boğazkale TR 23 A8
Boğazlıyan TR 23 B8
Bogda RO 126 B3
Bogdaniec PL 75 B4
Boge S 57 C4
Bogen D 95 C4
Bogen, *Nordland* N 194 B7
Bogen, *Nordland* N 194 C6
Bogen S 49 B4
Bogense DK 59 C3
Bognanco Fonti I 119 A5
Bognelv N 192 B6
Bognes N 194 B7
Bogno CH 120 A2
Bognor Regis GB 44 C3
Bogoria PL 87 B5
Bograngen S 49 B4
Boguchwaly PL 69 B5
Bogumiłowice PL 86 A3
Boguslav UA 13 D9
Boguszów-Gorce PL 85 B4
Bogyiszló H 112 C2
Bohain-en-Vermandois F 91 B3
Böheimkirchen A 110 A2
Bohinjska Bistrica SLO 122 A2
Böhlen D 83 A4
Böhmenkirch D 94 C1
Bohmte D 71 B5
Bohonal de Ibor E 150 C2
Böhönye H 124 A3
Bohumin CZ 98 B2
Boiro E 140 B2
Bois-d'Amont F 105 C5
Boisseron F 131 B3
Boitzenburg D 74 A2
Boixols E 147 B2
Boizenburg D 73 A3
Bojadła PL 75 C4
Bojano I 170 B2
Bojanowo PL 85 A4
Bøjden DK 64 A3
Bojkovice CZ 98 B1
Bojná SK 98 C2
Bojnice SK 98 C2
Boka SRB 126 B2
Böklund D 64 B2
Bokod H 112 B2
Böksholm S 62 A2
Boksitogorsk RUS 9 C8
Bol HR 138 B2
Bolaños de Calatrava E 157 B4
Bolayır TR 186 B1
Bolbec F 89 A4
Bölcske H 112 C2
Bolderslev DK 64 B2
Boldog H 112 B3
Boldva H 113 A4
Böle S 196 D4
Bolea E 145 B3
Bolekhiv UA 13 D5
Bolesławiec PL 84 A3
Boleszkowice PL 74 B3
Bolewice PL 75 B5
Bólgheri I 134 B3
Bolhrad UA 17 C8
Boliden S 200 B6
Bolimów PL 77 B5
Boliqueime P 160 B1
Boljevci SRB 127 C2
Boljkovci SRB 127 C2
Bolków PL 85 B4
Bollebygd S 60 B2
Bollène F 131 A3
Bólliga E 152 B1
Bollnäs S 50 A3
Bollstabruk S 200 D3
Bollullos E 161 B3
Bollullos par del Condado E 161 B3
Bologna I 135 A4
Bologne F 105 A4
Bolognetta I 176 B2
Bolognola I 136 C2
Bologoye RUS 9 D9
Bolótana I 178 B2
Bolsena I 168 A1
Bolshaya Vradiyevka UA 17 B9
Bolsover GB 40 B2
Bolstad S 54 B3
Bolsward NL 70 A2
Boltaña E 145 B4
Boltenhagen D 65 C4
Boltigen CH 106 C2
Bolton GB 38 A4
Bolu TR 187 B6
Bolungavík IS 190 A2
Bolvadin TR 187 D6
Bóly H 125 B4
Bolzaneto I 133 A4
Bolzano I 108 C2
Bomba I 169 A4
Bombarral P 154 B1
Bömenzien D 73 B4
Bomlitz D 72 B2
Bømlo N 52 A1
Bøn N 48 B3
Bon-Encontre F 129 B3
Bona F 104 B2
Bonaduz CH 107 C4
Bonanza E 161 C3
Boñar E 142 B1
Bonarbridge GB 32 D2
Bonárcado I 178 B2
Bonares E 161 B3
Bonäs S 50 A1
Bonassola I 134 A2
Bonawe GB 34 B2
Bondal N 53 A4
Bondeno I 121 C4
Bondorf D 93 C4
Bondstorp S 60 B3
Bo'ness GB 35 B4
Bonete E 158 C2
Bonifacio F 180 B2
Bonigen CH 106 C2
Bonin PL 67 B5
Bonn D 80 B3
Bonnánaro I 178 B2
Bonnåsjøen N 194 C6
Bonnat F 116 A1
Bonndorf D 106 B3
Bonnétable F 102 A2
Bonnétage F 106 B1
Bonneuil-les-Eaux F 90 B2
Bonneuil-Matours F 115 B4
Bonneval F 103 A3
Bonneval-sur-Arc F 119 B4
Bonneville F 118 A3
Bonnières-sur-Seine F 90 B1
Bonnieux F 131 B4
Bönnigheim D 93 B5
Bonny-sur-Loire F 103 B4
Bonnyrigg GB 35 C4
Bono E 145 B4
Bono I 178 B3
Bonorva I 178 B2
Bønsnes N 48 B2
Bonyhád H 125 A4
Boom B 79 A4
Boos F 89 A5
Boostedt D 64 B3
Bootle, *Cumbria* GB 36 B3
Bootle, *Merseyside* GB 38 A3
Bopfingen D 94 C2
Boppard D 81 B3
Boqueixón E 140 B2
Bor CZ 95 B4
Bor S 62 A2
Bor SRB 16 C5
Bor TR 23 C8
Boran-sur-Oise F 90 B2
Borås S 60 B2
Borba P 155 C3
Borbona I 169 A3
Borča SRB 127 C2
Borci BIH 139 B4
Borculo NL 71 B3
Bordány H 126 A1
Bordeaux F 128 B2
Bordeira P 160 B1
Bordesholm D 64 B3
Borðeyri IS 190 B4
Bordighera I 133 B3
Bording DK 59 B2
Bordón E 153 B3
Bore I 120 C2
Borehamwood GB 44 B3
Borek Strzeliński PL 85 B5
Borek Wielkopolski PL 76 C2
Boreland GB 36 A3
Borello I 135 A5
Borensberg S 56 B1
Borgafjäll S 199 A12
Borgarnes IS 190 C4
Borgentreich D 81 A5
Börger D 71 B4
Borger NL 71 B3
Borggård S 56 B1
Borghamn S 55 B5
Borghetta di Vara I 134 A2
Borghetto d'Arróscia I 133 A3
Borghetto Santo Spirito I 133 A4
Borgholm S 62 B4
Borghorst D 71 B4
Bórgia I 175 C2
Borgloon B 79 B5
Børglum DK 58 A2
Borgo F 180 A2
Borgo a Mozzano I 134 B3
Borgo alla Collina I 135 B4
Borgo Pace I 135 B5
Borgo San Dalmazzo I 133 A3
Borgo San Lorenzo I 135 B4
Borgo Val di Taro I 134 A2
Borgo Valsugana I 121 A4
Borgo Vercelli I 119 B5
Borgoforte I 121 B3
Borgofranco d'Ivrea I 119 B4
Borgomanero I 119 B5
Borgomasino I 119 B4
Borgonovo Val Tidone I 120 B2
Borgorose I 169 A3
Borgosésia I 119 B5
Borgstena S 60 B3
Borgue GB 36 B2
Borgund N 47 A4
Borgvik S 55 A3
Borja E 144 C2
Bork D 80 A3
Borken D 80 A2
Borkenes N 194 B7
Børkop DK 59 C2
Borkowice PL 87 A4
Borkowo PL 77 B5
Borkum D 71 A3
Borlänge S 50 B2
Borlu TR 186 D3
Bormes-les-Mimosas F 132 B2
Bórmio I 107 C5
Bormujos E 161 B3
Borna D 83 A4
Borne NL 71 B3
Borne Sulinowo PL 68 B1
Bornes P 149 A2
Bornheim D 80 B2
Bornhöved D 64 B3
Börnicke D 74 B1
Bornos E 162 B2
Borobia E 152 A2
Borodino RUS 9 E9
Borohrádek CZ 85 B4
Boronów PL 86 B2
Bórore I 178 B2
Borosźow PL 86 B2
Borota H 126 A1
Boroughbridge GB 40 A2
Borovany CZ 96 C2
Borovichi RUS 9 C8
Borovnica SLO 123 B3
Borovo HR 125 B4
Borovsk RUS 9 E10
Borovy CZ 96 B1
Borowa PL 85 A5
Borox E 151 B4
Borrby S 66 A3
Borre DK 65 B5
Borre N 54 A1
Borredá E 147 B2
Borrenes E 141 B4
Borriol E 159 A3
Borris DK 59 C1
Borris IRL 30 B2
Borris-in-Ossory IRL 28 B4
Borrisokane IRL 28 B3
Borrisoleigh IRL 28 B4
Borrowdale GB 36 B3
Børrud N 49 C4
Borşa RO 17 B6
Borsdorf D 83 A4
Børselv N 193 B9
Borsfa H 111 C3
Borský Mikuláš SK 98 C1
Borsodivánka H 113 B4
Borsodnádasd H 113 A4
Bort-les-Orgues F 116 B2
Börte N 53 A3
Borth GB 39 B2
Börtnan S 199 C10
Børtnes N 47 B6
Boruja Kościelne PL 75 B5
Borup DK 61 D1
Boryslav UA 13 D5
Boryspil UA 13 C9
Boryszyn PL 75 B4
Borzęciczki PL 85 A5
Borzęcin PL 77 B5
Borzonasca I 134 A2
Borzyszkowy PL 68 A2
Borzytuchom PL 68 A2
Bosa I 178 B2
Bošáca SK 98 C1
Bosanci HR 123 B4
Bosanska Dubica BIH 124 B2
Bosanska Gradiška BIH 124 B3
Bosanska Kostajnica BIH 124 B2
Bosanska Krupa BIH 124 C2
Bosanski Brod BIH 125 B3
Bosanski Novi BIH 124 B2
Bosanski Petrovac BIH 124 C2
Bosanski Šamac BIH 125 B4
Bosansko Grahovo BIH 138 A2
Bošany SK 98 C2
Bösárkány H 111 B4
Bosau D 65 B3
Bósca H 112 C3
Boscastle GB 42 B2
Bosco I 120 C1
Bosco Chiesanuova I 121 B4
Bösdorf D 65 B3
Bösel D 71 A4
Bosham GB 44 C3
Bösingfeld D 72 B2
Bosjön S 49 C5
Boskoop NL 70 B1
Boskovice CZ 97 B4
Bošnjaci HR 125 B4
Bošnjane SRB 127 D3
Bossast E 145 B4
Bossolasco I 133 A4
Boštanj SLO 123 A4
Boston GB 41 C3
Bostrak N 53 A4
Böszénfa H 125 A3
Bot E 153 A4
Botajica BIH 125 C4
Bøte By DK 65 B4
Bothel GB 36 B3
Boticas P 148 A2
Botilsäter S 55 A4
Botngård N 198 B6
Botoš SRB 126 B2
Botoşani RO 17 B7
Botricello I 175 C2
Botsmark S 200 B6
Bottendorf D 81 A4
Bottesford GB 40 C3
Bottnaryd S 60 B3
Bottrop D 80 A2
Botunje SRB 127 C3
Bötzingen D 106 A2
Bouaye F 101 B4
Bouça P 149 A2
Boucau F 128 C1
Bouchain F 78 B3
Bouchoir F 90 B2
Boudreville F 105 B3
Boudry CH 106 C1
Bouesse F 103 C3
Bouguenais F 101 B4
Bouhy F 104 B2
Bouillargues F 131 B3
Bouillon B 91 B5
Bouilly F 104 A2
Bouin F 114 B2
Boulay-Moselle F 92 B2
Boulazac F 129 A3
Boule-d'Amont F 146 B3
Bouligny F 92 B1
Boulogne-sur-Gesse F 145 A4
Boulogne-sur-Mer F 78 B1
Bouloire F 102 B2
Bouquemaison F 78 B2
Bourbon-Lancy F 104 C2
Bourbon-l'Archambault F 104 C2
Bourbonne-les-Bains F 105 B4
Bourbourg F 78 B2
Bourbriac F 100 A2
Bourcefranc-le-Chapus F 114 C2
Bourdeaux F 131 A4
Bouresse F 115 B4
Bourg F 128 A2
Bourg-Achard F 89 A4
Bourg-Argental F 117 B4
Bourg-de-Péage F 117 B5
Bourg-de-Thizy F 117 A4
Bourg-de-Visa F 129 B3
Bourg-en-Bresse F 118 A2
Bourg-et-Comin F 91 B3
Bourg-Lastic F 116 B2
Bourg-Madame F 146 B2
Bourg-St. Andéol F 131 A3
Bourg-St. Maurice F 119 B3
Bourganeuf F 116 B1
Bourges F 103 B4
Bourgneuf-en-Retz F 114 A2
Bourgogne F 91 B4
Bourgoin-Jallieu F 118 B2
Bourgtheroulde F 89 A4
Bourgueil F 102 B2
Bourmont F 105 A4
Bourne GB 40 C3
Bournemouth GB 43 B5
Bourneville F 89 A4
Bournezeau F 114 B2
Bourran F 129 B3
Bourret F 129 C4
Bourron-Marlotte F 90 C2
Bourton-on-The-Water GB 44 B2
Boussac F 116 A2
Boussens F 145 A4
Boutersem B 79 B4
Bouttencourt F 90 B1
Bouvières F 131 A4
Bouvron F 101 B4
Bouxwiller F 93 C3
Bouzas E 140 B2
Bouzonville F 92 B2
Bova I 175 D1
Bova Marina I 175 D1
Bovalino Marina I 175 C2
Bovallstrand S 54 B2
Bovec SLO 122 A2
Bóveda E 141 B3
Bóvegno I 120 B3
Bovenau D 64 B2
Bovenden D 82 A1
Bøverdal N 198 D5
Bóves I 133 A3
Bovey Tracey GB 43 B3
Bovino I 171 B3
Bøvlingbjerg DK 58 B1
Bovolenta I 121 B4
Bovolone I 121 B4
Bowes GB 37 B5
Bowmore GB 34 C1
Bowness-on-Windermere GB 36 B4
Box GB 43 A4
Boxberg, *Baden-Württemberg* D 94 B1
Boxberg, *Sachsen* D 84 A2
Boxholm S 55 B6
Boxmeer NL 80 A1
Boxtel NL 79 A5
Boyabat TR 23 A8
Boyalıca TR 187 B4
Boyle IRL 26 C2
Bozan TR 187 C6
Božava HR 137 A3
Bozburun TR 188 C3
Bozcaada TR 186 C1
Bozdoğan TR 188 B3
Bożepole Wielkie PL 68 A2
Boževac SRB 127 C3
Boži Dar CZ 83 B4
Božice CZ 97 C4
Bozkır TR 189 B7

Ciechanów, *Mazowieckie* PL 77 B5
Ciechocinek PL 76 B3
Cielądz PL 87 A4
Ciemnik PL 75 A4
Ciempozuelos E 151 B4
Ciepielów PL 87 A5
Čierny Balog SK 99 C3
Cierp F 145 B4
Cierpice PL 76 B3
Ciervana E 143 A3
Cierznie PL 68 B2
Cieslé PL 77 B5
Cieszyn PL 98 B2
Cieutat F 145 A4
Cieza E 165 A3
Cifer SK 98 C1
Çifteler TR 187 C6
Cifuentes E 151 B5
Cigales E 142 C2
Cigliano I 119 B5
Cihanbeyli TR 23 B7
Cillas E 152 B2
Cilleros E 149 B3
Cilleruelo de Arriba E 143 C3
Cilleruelo de Bezana E 143 B3
Cimalmotto CH 119 A5
Cimanes del Tejar E 141 B5
Ciminna I 176 B2
Cimişlia MD 17 B8
Cimoláis I 122 A1
Cîmpulung RO 17 C6
Cinctorres E 153 B3
Cinderford GB 39 C4
Çine TR 188 B3
Činěves CZ 84 B3
Ciney B 79 B5
Cinfães P 148 A1
Cingia de Botti I 120 B3
Cingoli I 136 B2
Cinigiano I 135 C4
Cinobaňa SK 99 C3
Cinq-Mars-la-Pile F 102 B2
Cinquefrondi I 175 C2
Cintegabelle F 146 A2
Cintruénigo E 144 B2
Ciółkowo PL 77 B4
Ciperez E 149 B3
Cirat E 153 B3
Cirella I 174 B1
Cirencester GB 44 B2
Cirey-sur-Vezouze F 92 C2
Ciria E 152 A2
Ciriè I 119 B4
Cirigliano I 174 A2
Cirò I 174 B3
Cirò Marina I 174 B3
Ciry-le-Noble F 104 C3
Cislău RO 17 C7
Cismon del Grappa I 121 B4
Cisneros E 142 B2
Cissac-Médoc F 128 A2
Čistá CZ 96 A1
Cisterna di Latina I 169 B2
Cistérniga E 150 A3
Cisternino I 173 B3
Cistierna E 142 B1
Čitluk BIH 139 B3
Cítov CZ 84 B2
Cittá del Vaticano = Vatican City I 168 B2
Città della Pieve I 135 C5
Città di Castello I 135 B5
Città Sant'Angelo I 169 A4
Cittadella I 121 B4
Cittaducale I 169 A2
Cittanova I 175 C2
Ciudad Real E 157 B4
Ciudad Rodrigo E 149 B3
Ciudadela de Menorca E 167 B3
Cividale del Friuli I 122 A2
Cívita I 169 A3
Cívita Castellana I 168 A2
Civitanova Alta I 136 B2
Civitanova Marche I 136 B2
Civitavécchia I 168 A1
Civitella di Romagna I 135 A4
Civitella di Tronto I 136 C2
Civitella Roveto I 169 B3
Civray F 115 B4
Çivril TR 189 A4
Cizur Mayor E 144 B2
Cjutadilla E 147 C2
Clabhach GB 34 B1
Clachan GB 31 B2
Clachan na Luib GB 31 B1
Clacton-on-Sea GB 45 B5
Cladich GB 34 B2
Claggan GB 34 B2
Clairvaux-les-Lacs F 105 C4
Clamecy F 104 B2
Claonaig GB 34 C2
Clarecastle IRL 28 B3
Claregalway IRL 28 A3
Claremorris IRL 28 A2
Clarinbridge IRL 28 A3
Clashmore GB 32 D2
Clashmore IRL 29 B4
Claudy GB 27 B3
Clausthal-Zellerfeld D 82 A2
Cláut I 122 A1
Clay Cross GB 40 B2
Claye-Souilly F 90 C2
Cléder F 100 A1
Cleethorpes GB 41 B3
Clefmont F 105 A4
Cléguérec F 100 A2
Clelles F 118 C2
Clenze D 73 B3
Cleobury Mortimer GB 39 B4
Cléon-d'Andran F 117 C4
Cléré-les-Pins F 102 B2
Clères F 89 A5
Clermont F 90 B2
Clermont-en-Argonne F 91 B5
Clermont-Ferrand F 116 B3
Clermont-l'Hérault F 130 B2
Clerval F 105 B5
Clervaux L 92 A2
Clèry-St. André F 103 B3
Cles I 121 A4
Clevedon GB 43 A4
Cleveleys GB 38 A3
Cley GB 41 C5
Clifden IRL 28 A1
Clifford GB 39 B3
Clisson F 101 B4
Clitheroe GB 40 B1
Clogh IRL 30 B1
Cloghan, *Donegal* IRL 26 B3
Cloghan, *Offaly* IRL 28 A4
Clogheen IRL 29 B4
Clogher GB 27 B3
Cloghjordan IRL 28 B3
Clohars-Carnoët F 100 B2
Clonakilty IRL 29 C3
Clonaslee IRL 30 A1
Clondalkin IRL 30 A2
Clones IRL 27 B3
Clonmany IRL 27 A3
Clonmel IRL 29 B4
Clonmellon IRL 30 A1
Clonord IRL 30 A1
Clonroche IRL 30 B2
Cloone IRL 26 C3
Cloppenburg D 71 B5
Closeburn GB 36 A3
Clough GB 27 B5
Clova GB 35 B4
Clovelly GB 42 B2
Clowne GB 40 B2
Cloyes-sur-le-Loir F 103 B3
Cloyne IRL 29 C3
Cluis F 103 C3
Cluj-Napoca RO 17 B5
Clun GB 39 B3
Clunes GB 34 B3
Cluny F 117 A4
Cluses F 118 A3
Clusone I 120 B2
Clydach GB 39 C3
Clydebank GB 34 C3
Coachford IRL 29 C3
Coagh GB 27 B4
Coalisland GB 27 B4
Coalville GB 40 C2
Coaña E 141 A4
Çobanlar TR 187 D5
Cobas E 140 A2
Cobertelade E 151 A5
Cobeta E 152 B1
Cóbh IRL 29 C3
Cobreces E 142 A2
Coburg D 82 B2
Coca E 150 A3
Cocentaina E 159 C3
Cochem D 80 B3
Cockburnspath GB 35 C5
Cockermouth GB 36 B3
Codigoro I 121 C5
Codogno I 120 B2
Codos E 152 A2
Codróipo I 122 B1
Codrongianos I 178 B2
Coelhoso P 149 A3
Coesfeld D 71 C4
Coevorden NL 71 B3
Cofrentes E 159 B2
Cogeces del Monte E 150 A3
Coggeshall GB 45 B4
Cognac F 115 C3
Cogne I 119 B4
Cognin F 118 B2
Cogolin F 132 B2
Cogollos de Guadix E 164 B1
Cogollos-Vega E 163 A4
Cogolludo E 151 B4
Coimbra P 148 B1
Coín E 163 B3
Coirós E 140 A2
Čoka SRB 126 B2
Col SLO 123 B3
Colares P 154 C1
Cölbe D 81 B4
Colbitz D 73 B4
Colchester GB 45 B4
Coldingham GB 35 C5
Colditz D 83 A4
Coldstream GB 35 C5
Colebrooke GB 43 B3
Colera E 146 B4
Coleraine GB 27 A4
Colfiorito I 136 B1
Cólico I 120 A2
Coligny F 118 A2
Colindres E 143 A3
Coll de Nargó E 147 B2
Collado-Mediano E 151 B3
Collado Villalba E 151 B4
Collagna I 134 A3
Collanzo E 142 A1
Collat F 117 B3
Colle di Val d'Elsa I 135 B4
Colle Isarco I 108 C2
Colle Sannita I 170 B2
Collécchio I 120 C3
Colledimezzo I 169 B4
Colleferro I 169 B3
Collelongo I 169 B3
Collepasso I 173 B4
Collepepe I 136 C1
Collesalvetti I 134 B3
Collesano I 176 B2
Colli a Volturno I 169 B4
Collin GB 36 A3
Collinée F 101 A3
Collingham, *Nottinghamshire* GB 40 B2
Collingham, *West Yorkshire* GB 40 B3
Collinghorst D 71 A4
Cóllio I 120 B3
Collobrières F 132 B2
Collon IRL 27 C4
Collooney IRL 26 B2
Colmar F 106 A2
Colmars F 132 A2
Colmenar E 163 B3
Colmenar de la Sierra E 151 A4
Colmenar de Oreja E 151 B4
Colmenar Viejo E 151 B4
Colmonel GB 36 A2
Colne GB 40 B1
Colobraro I 174 A2
Cologna Véneta I 121 B4
Cologne F 129 C3
Cologne = Köln D 80 B2
Cologne al Serio I 120 B2
Colombey-les-Belles F 92 C1
Colombey-les-deux-Églises F 105 A3
Colombres E 142 A2
Colomera E 163 A4
Colomers E 147 B3
Colomiers F 129 C4
Colònia de Sant Jordi E 167 B3
Colorno I 120 C3
Colos P 160 B1
Cölpin D 74 A2
Colpy GB 33 D4
Colsterworth GB 40 C3
Coltishall GB 41 C5
Colunga E 142 A1
Colwell GB 37 A4
Colwyn Bay GB 38 A3
Colyford GB 43 B3
Coma-ruga E 147 C2
Comácchio I 121 C5
Combarros E 141 B4
Combeaufontaine F 105 B4
Comber GB 27 B5
Comblain-au-Pont B 80 B1
Combloux F 118 B3
Combourg F 88 B2
Combronde F 116 B3
Comeglians I 109 C3
Comillas E 142 A2
Comines F 78 B3
Cómiso I 177 C3
Comloşu Mare RO 126 B2
Commensacq F 128 B2
Commentry F 116 A2
Commerau D 84 A2
Commercy F 92 C1
Como I 120 B2
Cómpeta E 163 B4
Compiègne F 90 B2
Comporta P 154 C2
Comps-sur-Artuby F 132 B2
Comrat MD 17 B8
Comrie GB 35 B4
Comunanza I 136 C2
Cona, *Emilia Romagna* I 121 C4
Cona, *Veneto* I 121 B5
Concarneau F 100 B2
Conceição P 160 B1
Conches-en-Ouche F 89 B4
Concordia Sagittária I 122 B1
Concordia sulla Sécchia I 121 C3
Concots F 129 B4
Condat F 116 B2
Condé-en-Brie F 91 C3
Condé-sur-l'Escaut F 79 B3
Conde-sur-Marne F 91 B4
Condé-sur-Noireau F 88 B3
Condeixa P 148 B1
Condemios de Abajo E 151 A4
Condemios de Arriba E 151 A4
Condino I 121 B3
Condom F 129 C3
Condove I 119 B4
Condrieu F 117 B4
Conegliano I 122 B1
Conflans-sur-Lanterne F 105 B5
Confolens F 115 B4
Conforto E 141 A3
Cong IRL 28 A2
Congleton GB 40 B1
Congosto E 141 B4
Congosto de Valdavia E 142 B2
Congostrina E 151 A4
Conil de la Frontera E 162 B1
Coningsby GB 41 B3
Coniston GB 36 B3
Conlie F 102 A1
Conliège F 105 C4
Conna IRL 29 B3
Connah's Quay GB 38 A3
Connantre F 91 C3
Connaugh IRL 28 B3
Connaux F 131 A3
Connel GB 34 B2
Connerré F 102 A2
Cononbridge GB 32 D2
Čonoplja SRB 126 B1
Conques F 116 C2
Conques-sur-Orbiel F 146 A3
Conquista E 157 B3
Conquista de la Sierra E 156 A2
Consándolo I 121 C4
Consélice I 135 A4
Conselve I 121 B4
Consenvoye F 91 B5
Consett GB 37 B5
Consolacão P 154 B1
Constancia P 154 B2
Constanco E 140 A2
Constanţa RO 17 C8
Constanti E 147 C2
Constantina E 162 A2
Consuegra E 157 A4
Consuma I 135 B4
Contarina I 122 B1
Contay F 90 B2
Conthey CH 119 A4
Contigliano I 168 A2
Contis-Plage F 128 B1
Contrada I 170 C2
Contres F 103 B3
Contrexéville F 105 A4
Controne I 172 B1
Contursi Termi I 172 B1
Conty F 90 B2
Conversano I 173 B3
Conwy GB 38 A3
Cookstown GB 27 B4
Coole F 91 C4
Coolgreany IRL 30 B2
Cooneen GB 27 B3
Cootehill IRL 27 B3
Cope E 165 B3
Copenhagen = København DK 61 D2
Copertino I 173 B4
Copparo I 121 C4
Coppenbrugge D 72 B2
Corabia RO 17 D6
Córaci I 175 B2
Coralići BIH 124 C1
Corato I 171 B4
Coray F 100 A2
Corbeil-Essonnes F 90 C2
Corbeny F 91 B3
Corbera E 159 B3
Corbie F 90 B2
Corbigny F 104 B2
Corbion B 91 B4
Corbridge GB 37 B4
Corby GB 40 C3
Corconte E 143 A3
Corcubión E 140 B1
Corcumello I 169 A3
Cordenòns I 122 B1
Cordes-sur-Ciel F 129 B4
Córdoba E 156 C3
Cordobilla de Lácara E 155 B4
Cordovado I 122 B1
Corella E 144 B2
Coreses E 150 A2
Corfe Castle GB 43 B4
Corga de Lobão P 148 B1
Cori I 169 B2
Coria E 155 B4
Coria del Río E 162 A1
Corigliano Cálabro I 174 B2
Corinaldo I 136 B1
Corinth = Korinthos GR 184 B3
Cório I 119 B4
Coripe E 162 B2
Cork IRL 29 C3
Corlay F 100 A2
Corleone I 176 B2
Corleto Monforte I 172 B1
Corleto Perticara I 174 A2
Çorlu TR 186 A2
Cormainville F 103 A3
Cormatin F 104 C3
Cormeilles F 89 A4
Cormery F 102 B2
Cormòns I 122 B2
Cormoz F 118 A2
Cornago E 144 B1
Cornberg D 82 A1
Cornellana E 141 A4
Corneşti MD 17 B8
Corníglio I 134 A3
Cornimont F 106 B1
Corniolo I 135 B4
Cornuda I 121 B5
Cornudella de Montsant E 147 C1
Cornudilla E 143 B3
Cornus F 130 B2
Çorovodë AL 182 C2
Corpach GB 34 B2
Corps F 118 C2
Corps Nuds F 101 B4
Corral de Almaguer E 157 A4
Corral de Ayllon E 151 A4
Corral de Calatrava E 157 B3
Corral-Rubio E 158 C2
Corrales E 149 A4
Corran GB 34 B2
Corredoiras E 140 A2
Corréggio I 121 C3
Corrèze F 116 B1
Corridónia I 136 B2
Corris GB 38 B3
Corrubedo E 140 B1
Córsico I 120 B2
Corsock GB 36 A3
Corte F 180 A2
Corte de Peleas E 155 C4
Corte Pinto P 160 B2
Corteconcepción E 161 B3
Cortegaca P 148 B1
Cortegada E 140 B2
Cortegana E 161 B3
Cortemaggiore I 120 B2
Cortemilia I 133 A4
Cortes E 144 C2
Cortes de Aragón E 153 B3
Cortes de Arenoso E 153 B3
Cortes de Baza E 164 B2
Cortes de la Frontera E 162 B2
Cortes de Pallás E 159 B3
Cortiçadas P 154 C2
Cortico P 148 A2
Cortijo de Arriba E 157 A3
Cortijos Nuevos E 164 A2
Cortina d'Ampezzo I 108 C3
Corton GB 41 C5
Cortona I 135 B4
Coruche P 154 C2
Corullón E 141 B4
Çorum TR 23 A8
Corvara in Badia I 108 C2
Corvera E 165 B3
Corwen GB 38 B3
Cosenza I 174 B2
Cosham GB 44 C2
Coslada E 151 B4
Cosne-Cours-sur-Loire F 104 B1
Cosne d'Allier F 103 C4
Cospeito E 140 A3
Cossato I 119 B5
Cossaye F 104 C2
Cossé-le-Vivien F 101 B5
Cossonay CH 105 C5
Costa da Caparica P 154 C1
Costa de Santo André P 160 A1
Costa Nova P 148 B1
Costalpino I 135 B4
Costaros F 117 C3
Costeşti RO 17 C6
Costigliole d'Asti I 119 C5
Costigliole Saluzzo I 133 A3
Coswig, *Sachsen-Anhalt* D 83 A4
Coswig, *Sachsen* D 83 A5
Cotherstone GB 37 B5
Cotronei I 175 B2
Cottbus D 84 A2
Cottenham GB 45 A4
Cottingham GB 40 B3
Coublanc F 105 B4
Couches F 104 C3
Couço P 154 C2
Coucouron F 117 C3
Coucy-le-Château-Auffrique F 90 B3
Couëron F 101 B4
Couflens F 146 B2
Couhé F 115 B4
Couiza F 146 B3
Coulags GB 31 B3
Coulanges F 104 C2
Coulanges-la-Vineuse F 104 B2
Coulanges-sur-Yonne F 104 B2
Couleuvre F 104 C1
Coulmier-le-Sec F 104 B3
Coulommiers F 90 C3
Coulonges-sur-l'Autize F 114 B3
Coulounieix-Chamiers F 129 A3
Coulport GB 34 B3
Coupar Angus GB 35 B4
Coupéville F 91 C4
Couptrain F 89 B3
Cour-Cheverny F 103 B3
Cour-et-Buis F 117 B4
Coura P 140 C2
Courcelles B 79 B4
Courcelles-Chaussy F 92 B2
Courchevel F 118 B3
Courcôme F 115 C4
Courçon F 114 B3
Courgenay CH 106 B2
Courmayeur I 119 B3
Courniou F 130 B1
Cournon-d'Auvergne F 116 B3
Cournonterral F 130 B2
Courpière F 117 B3
Cours-la-Ville F 117 A4
Coursan F 130 B2
Courseulles-sur-Mer F 89 A3
Courson-les-Carrières F 104 B2
Courtalain F 103 A3
Courtenay F 104 A2
Courtomer F 89 B4
Courville, *Eure-et-Loire* F 89 B5
Courville, *Marne* F 91 B3
Coussac-Bonneval F 115 C5
Coutances F 88 A2
Couterne F 89 B3
Coutras F 128 A2
Couvet CH 106 C1
Couvin B 91 A4
Couzon F 104 C2
Covadonga E 142 A1
Covaleda E 143 C4
Covarrubias E 143 B3
Covas P 148 A1
Cove GB 31 B3
Coventry GB 44 A2
Coverack GB 42 B1
Covigliáio I 135 A4
Covilhã P 148 B2
Cowbridge GB 39 C3
Cowdenbeath GB 35 B4
Cowes GB 44 C2
Cox F 129 C4
Cózar E 157 B4
Cozes F 114 C3
Cozzano F 180 B2
Craco I 174 A2
Craibstone GB 33 D4
Craighouse GB 34 C2
Craignure GB 34 B2
Crail GB 35 B5
Crailsheim D 94 B2
Craiova RO 17 C5
Cramlington GB 37 A5
Cranleigh GB 44 B3
Craon F 101 B5
Craonne F 91 B3
Craponne F 117 B4
Craponne-sur-Arzon F 117 B3
Crathie GB 32 D3
Crato P 155 B3
Craughwell IRL 28 A3
Craven Arms GB 39 B4
Crawford GB 36 A3
Crawinkel D 82 B2
Crawley GB 44 B3
Creag Ghoraidh GB 31 B1
Crecente E 140 B2
Crèches-sur-Saône F 117 A4
Crécy-en-Ponthieu F 78 B1
Crécy-la-Chapelle F 90 C2
Crécy-sur-Serre F 91 B3
Crediton GB 43 B3
Creeslough IRL 26 A3
Creetown GB 36 B2

Eberstein A 110 C1
Eberswalde D 74 B2
Ebnat-Kappel CH 107 B4
Éboli I 170 C3
Ebrach D 94 B2
Ebreichsdorf A 111 B3
Ebreuil F 116 A3
Ebstorf D 72 A3
Ecclefechan GB 36 A3
Eccleshall GB 40 C1
Eceabat TR 186 B1
Echallens CH 106 C1
Echauri E 144 B2
Echinos GR 183 B7
Echiré F 114 B3
Échirolles F 118 B2
Echourgnac F 128 A3
Echt NL 80 A1
Echte D 82 A2
Echternach L 92 B2
Ecija E 162 A2
Ečka SRB 126 B2
Eckartsberga D 82 A3
Eckelshausen D 81 B4
Eckental D 94 B3
Eckernförde D 64 B2
Eckerö FIN 51 B6
Eckington GB 40 B2
Éclaron F 91 C4
Écommoy F 102 B2
Écouché F 89 B3
Ecouis F 90 B1
Ecséd H 113 B3
Ecsegfalva H 113 B4
Écueillé F 103 B4
Ed S 54 B2
Eda S 49 C4
Eda glasbruk S 49 C4
Edam NL 70 B2
Edane S 55 A3
Edderton GB 32 D2
Ede NL 70 B2
Edebäck S 49 B5
Edebo S 51 B5
Edelény H 99 C4
Edelschrott A 110 B2
Edemissen D 72 B3
Edenbridge GB 45 B4
Edenderry IRL 30 A1
Edenkoben D 93 B4
Edesheim D 93 B4
Edessa GR 182 C4
Edewecht D 71 A4
Edgeworthstown IRL 30 A1
Edinburgh GB 35 C4
Edineţ MD 17 A7
Edirne TR 186 A1
Edland N 52 A3
Edolo I 120 A3
Edøy N 198 B5
Edremit TR 186 C2
Eds bruk S 56 B2
Edsbro S 51 C5
Edsbyn S 50 A2
Edsele S 200 C2
Edsleskog S 54 A3
Edsvalla S 55 A4
Eekloo B 79 A3
Eemshaven NL 71 A3
Eerbeek NL 70 B3
Eersel NL 79 A5
Eferding A 96 C2
Effiat F 116 A3
Efteløt N 53 A5
Egeln D 73 C4
Eger H 113 B4
Egerbakta H 113 B4
Egernsund DK 64 B2
Egersund N 52 B2
Egerszólát H 113 B4
Egervár H 111 C3
Egg A 107 B4
Egg D 107 A5
Eggby S 55 B4
Eggedal N 47 B6
Eggenburg A 97 C4
Eggenfelden D 95 C4
Eggesin D 74 A3
Eggum N 194 B4
Egham GB 44 B3
Éghezée B 79 B4
Egiertowo PL 68 A3
Egilsstaðir IS 191 B11
Egina GR 185 B4
Eginio GR 182 C4
Egio GR 184 A3
Égletons F 116 B2
Egling D 108 B2
Eglinton GB 27 A3
Eglisau CH 107 B3
Égliseneuve-d'Entraigues F 116 B2
Eglofs D 107 B4
Egmond aan Zee NL 70 B1
Egna I 121 A4
Egosthena GR 184 A4
Egremont GB 36 B3
Eğridir TR 189 B5
Egtved DK 59 C2
Eguilles F 131 B4
Eguilly-sous-Bois F 104 A3
Éguzon-Chantôme F 103 C3
Egyek H 113 B4
Egyházasrádóc H 111 B3
Ehekirchen D 94 C3
Ehingen D 94 C1
Ehra-Lessien D 73 B3
Ehrang D 92 B2
Ehrenfriedersdorf D 83 B4
Ehrenhain D 83 B4
Ehrenhausen A 110 C2
Ehringshausen D 81 B4
Ehrwald A 108 B1
Eibar E 143 A4
Eibelstadt D 94 B2
Eibenstock D 83 B4
Eibergen NL 71 B3
Eibiswald A 110 C2
Eichenbarleben D 73 B4
Eichendorf D 95 C4
Eichstätt D 95 C3
Eickelborn D 81 A4
Eide, *Hordaland* N 46 B3
Eide, *Møre og Romsdal* N 198 C4
Eidet N 194 A9
Eidfjord N 46 B4
Eidsberg N 54 A2
Eidsbugarden N 47 A5
Eidsdal N 198 C4
Eidsfoss N 53 A6
Eidskog N 49 B4
Eidsvåg, *Hordaland* N 46 B2
Eidsvåg, *Møre og Romsdal* N 198 C5
Eidsvoll N 48 B3
Eikefjord N 46 A2
Eikelandsosen N 46 B2
Eiken N 52 B3
Eikesdal N 198 C5
Eikstrand N 53 A5
Eilenburg D 83 A4
Eilsleben D 73 B4
Eina N 48 B2
Einbeck D 82 A1
Eindhoven NL 79 A5
Einsiedeln CH 107 B3
Einville-au-Jard F 92 C2
Eisenach D 82 B2
Eisenberg, *Rheinland-Pfalz* D 93 B4
Eisenberg, *Thüringen* D 83 B3
Eisenerz A 110 B1
Eisenhüttenstadt D 74 B3
Eisenkappel A 110 C1
Eisenstadt A 111 B3
Eisentratten A 109 C4
Eisfeld D 82 B2
Eisleben D 82 A3
Eislingen D 94 C1
Eitensheim D 95 C3
Eiterfeld D 82 B1
Eitorf D 80 B3
Eivindvik N 46 B2
Eivissa = Ibiza E 166 C1
Eixo P 148 B1
Ejby DK 59 C2
Ejea de los Caballeros E 144 B2
Ejstrupholm DK 59 C2
Ejulve E 153 B3
Eke B 79 B3
Ekeby, *Gotland* S 57 C4
Ekeby, *Skåne* S 61 D2
Ekeby, *Uppsala* S 51 B5
Ekeby-Almby S 56 A1
Ekenäs S 55 B4
Ekenässjön S 62 A3
Ekerö S 57 A3
Eket S 61 C3
Eketorp S 63 B4
Ekevik S 56 B2
Ekkerøy N 193 B14
Ekshärad S 49 B5
Eksingedal N 46 B2
Eksjö S 62 A2
Eksta S 57 C4
Ekträsk S 200 B5
El Alamo, *Madrid* E 151 B4
El Alamo, *Sevilla* E 161 B3
El Algar E 165 B4
El Almendro E 161 B2
El Alquián E 164 C2
El Arahal E 162 A2
El Arenal E 150 B2
El Arguellite E 164 A2
El Astillero E 143 A3
El Ballestero E 158 C1
El Barco de Ávila E 150 B2
El Berrón E 142 A1
El Berrueco E 151 B4
El Bodón E 149 B3
El Bonillo E 158 C1
El Bosque E 162 B2
El Bullaque E 157 A3
El Burgo E 162 B3
El Burgo de Ebro E 153 A3
El Burgo de Osma E 151 A4
El Burgo Ranero E 142 B1
El Buste E 144 C2
El Cabaco E 149 B3
El Callejo E 143 A3
El Campillo E 161 B3
El Campillo de la Jara E 156 A2
El Cañavete E 158 B1
El Carpio E 157 C3
El Carpio de Tajo E 150 C3
El Casar E 151 B4
El Casar de Escalona E 150 B3
El Castillo de las Guardas E 161 B3
El Centenillo E 157 B4
El Cerro E 149 B4
El Cerro de Andévalo E 161 B3
El Comenar E 162 B2
El Coronil E 162 A2
El Crucero E 141 A4
El Cubo de Tierra del Vino E 149 A4
El Cuervo E 162 B1
El Ejido E 164 C2
El Escorial E 151 B3
El Espinar E 151 B3
El Frago E 144 B3
El Franco E 141 A4
El Frasno E 152 A2
El Garrobo E 161 B3
El Gastor E 162 B2
El Gordo E 150 C2
El Grado E 145 B4
El Granado E 161 B2
El Grao de Castelló E 159 B4
El Grau E 159 C3
El Higuera E 163 A3
El Hijate E 164 B2
El Hontanar E 152 B2
El Hoyo E 157 B4
El Madroño E 161 B3
El Maillo E 149 B3
El Masnou E 147 C3
El Mirón E 150 B2
El Molar E 151 B4
El Molinillo E 157 A3
El Morell E 147 C2
El Muyo E 151 A4
El Olmo E 151 A4
El Palo E 163 B3
El Pardo E 151 B4
El Payo E 149 B3
El Pedernoso E 158 B1
El Pedroso E 162 A2
El Peral E 158 B2
El Perelló, *Tarragona* E 153 B4
El Perelló, *Valencia* E 159 B3
El Picazo E 158 B1
El Pinell de Bray E 153 A4
El Piñero E 150 A2
El Pla de Santa Maria E 147 C2
El Pobo E 153 B3
El Pobo de Dueñas E 152 B2
El Pont d'Armentera E 147 C2
El Port de la Selva E 147 B4
El Port de Llançà E 146 B4
El Port de Sagunt E 159 B3
El Prat de Llobregat E 147 C3
El Provencio E 158 B1
El Puente E 143 A3
El Puente del Arzobispo E 150 C2
El Puerto E 141 A4
El Puerto de Santa María E 162 B1
El Real de la Jara E 161 B3
El Real de San Vincente E 150 B3
El Robledo E 157 A3
El Rocio E 161 B3
El Rompido E 161 B2
El Ronquillo E 161 B3
El Royo E 143 C4
El Rubio E 162 A3
El Sabinar E 164 A2
El Saler E 159 B3
El Salobral E 158 C2
El Saucejo E 162 A2
El Serrat AND 146 B2
El Temple E 144 C3
El Tiemblo E 150 B3
El Toboso E 157 A5
El Tormillo E 145 C3
El Torno E 149 B4
El Valle de las Casas E 142 B1
El Vellón E 151 B4
El Vendrell E 147 C2
El Villar de Arnedo E 144 B1
El Viso E 156 B3
El Viso del Alcor E 162 A2
Élancourt F 90 C1
Elassona GR 182 D4
Elati GR 182 D3
Elbasan AL 182 B2
Elbeuf F 89 A4
Elbingerode D 82 A2
Elbląg PL 69 A4
Elburg NL 70 B2
Elche E 165 A4
Elche de la Sierra E 158 C1
Elchingen D 94 C2
Elda E 159 C3
Eldena D 73 A4
Eldingen D 72 B3
Elefsina GR 185 A4
Elek H 113 C5
Elemir SRB 126 B2
Eleutheroupoli GR 183 C6
Elgå N 199 C8
Elgin GB 32 D3
Elgoibar E 143 A4
Elgol GB 31 B2
Elgshøa N 49 A4
Elie GB 35 B5
Elizondo E 144 A2
Ełk PL 12 B5
Elkhovo BG 17 D7
Ellenberg D 94 B2
Ellesmere GB 38 B4
Ellesmere Port GB 38 A4
Ellezelles B 79 B3
Ellingen D 94 B2
Ellmau A 109 B3
Ellon GB 33 D4
Ellös S 54 B2
Ellrich D 82 A2
Ellwangen D 94 C2
Elm CH 107 C4
Elm D 72 A2
Elmadağ TR 23 B7
Elmalı TR 189 C4
Elmshorn D 64 C2
Elmstein D 93 B3
Elne F 146 B3
Elnesvågen N 198 C4
Elorrio E 143 A4
Elöszállás H 112 C2
Elouda GR 185 D6
Éloyes F 105 A5
Elphin GB 32 C1
Els Castells E 147 B2
Elsdorf D 80 B2
Elsenfeld D 93 B5
Elsfleth D 72 A1
Elspeet NL 70 B2
Elst NL 70 C2
Elstead GB 44 B3
Elster D 83 A4
Elsterberg D 83 B4
Elsterwerda D 83 A5
Elstra D 84 A2
Eltmann D 94 B2
Eltville D 93 A4
Elvas P 155 C3
Elvebakken N 192 C7
Elven F 101 B3
Elverum N 48 B3
Elvington GB 40 B3
Elxleben D 82 A2
Ely GB 45 A4
Elzach D 106 A3
Elze D 72 B2
Emådalen S 50 A1
Embleton GB 37 A5
Embonas GR 188 C2
Embrun F 132 A2
Embún E 144 B3
Emden D 71 A4
Emecik TR 188 C2
Emet TR 186 C4
Emirdağ TR 187 C6
Emlichheim D 71 B3
Emmaboda S 63 B3
Emmaljunga S 61 C3
Emmeloord NL 70 B2
Emmen CH 106 B3
Emmen NL 71 B3
Emmendingen D 106 A2
Emmer-Compascuum NL 71 B4
Emmerich D 80 A2
Emmern D 72 B2
Emöd H 113 B4
Émpoli I 135 B3
Emsbüren D 71 B4
Emsdetten D 71 B4
Emsfors S 62 A4
Emskirchen D 94 B2
Emstek D 71 B5
Emsworth GB 44 C3
Emyvale IRL 27 B4
Enafors S 199 B9
Enånger S 51 A4
Encamp AND 146 B2
Encarnaçao P 154 C1
Encinas de Abajo E 150 B2
Encinas de Esgueva E 142 C2
Encinas Reales E 163 A3
Encinasola E 161 A3
Encio E 143 B3
Enciso E 144 B1
Enden N 199 D7
Endingen D 106 A2
Endrinal E 149 B4
Endröd H 113 C4
Enebakk N 54 A2
Eneryda S 63 B2
Enese H 111 B4
Enez TR 183 C8
Enfield IRL 30 A2
Eng A 108 B2
Enge-sande D 64 B1
Engelberg CH 106 C3
Engelhartszell A 96 C1
Engelskirchen D 80 B3
Engen D 107 B3
Enger N 48 B2
Engerdal N 199 D8
Engerneset N 49 A4
Engesvang DK 59 B2
Enghien B 79 B4
Engstingen D 94 C1
Engter D 71 B5
Enguera E 159 C3
Enguidanos E 158 B2
Enkenbach D 93 B3
Enkhuizen NL 70 B2
Enklinge FIN 51 B7
Enköping S 56 A3
Enna I 177 B3
Ennezat F 116 B3
Ennigerloh D 81 A4
Enningdal N 54 B2
Ennis IRL 28 B3
Enniscorthy IRL 30 B2
Enniskean IRL 29 C3
Enniskillen GB 27 B3
Ennistimon IRL 28 B2
Enns A 110 A1
Eno FIN 9 A7
Enontekiö FIN 196 A6
Ens NL 70 B2
Enschede NL 71 B3
Ensdorf D 95 B3
Ensisheim F 106 B2
Enstaberga S 56 B2
Enstone GB 44 B2
Entlebuch CH 106 B3
Entrácque I 133 A3
Entradas P 160 B1
Entrains-sur-Nohain F 104 B2
Entrambasaguas E 143 A3
Entrambasmestas E 143 A3
Entraygues-sur-Truyère F 116 C2
Entre-os-Rios P 148 A1
Entrevaux F 132 B2
Entrin Bajo E 155 C4
Entroncamento P 154 B2
Entzheim F 93 C3
Envermeu F 89 A5
Enviken S 50 B2
Enying H 112 C2
Enzingerboden A 109 B3
Enzklösterle D 93 C4
Épagny F 90 B3
Epalinges CH 106 C1
Epannes F 114 B3
Epanomi GR 182 C4
Epe D 71 B4
Epe NL 70 B2
Épernay F 91 B3
Épernon F 90 C1
Epfig F 93 C3
Epierre F 118 B3
Épila E 152 A2
Épinac F 104 C3
Épinal F 105 A5
Episcopia I 174 A2
Episkopi CY 181 B1
Epitalio GR 184 B2
Epoisses F 104 B3
Eppenbrunn D 93 B3
Eppendorf D 83 B5
Epping GB 45 B4
Eppingen D 93 B4
Epsom GB 44 B3
Epworth GB 40 B3
Eraclea I 122 B1
Eraclea Mare I 122 B1
Erba I 120 B2
Erbach, *Baden-Württemberg* D 94 C1
Erbach, *Hessen* D 93 B4
Erbalunga F 180 A2
Erbendorf D 95 B4
Érchie I 173 B3
Ercolano I 170 C2
Ercsi H 112 B2
Érd H 112 B2
Erdek TR 186 B2
Erdemli TR 23 C8
Erdevik SRB 126 B1
Erding D 95 C3
Erdötelek H 113 B4
Erdut HR 125 B5
Erdweg D 95 C3
Ereğli, *Konya* TR 23 C8
Ereğli, *Zonguldak* TR 187 A6
Erenkaya TR 189 B7
Eresfjord N 198 C5
Eresos GR 183 D7
Eretria GR 185 A4
Erfde D 64 B2
Erfjord N 52 A2
Erfstadt D 80 B2
Erfurt D 82 B3
Ērgli LV 8 D4
Ergoldsbach D 95 C4
Eriboll GB 32 C2
Érice I 176 A1
Ericeira P 154 C1
Eriksberg S 195 E6
Eriksmåla S 62 B3
Eringsboda S 63 B3
Eriswil CH 106 B2
Erithres GR 185 A4
Erkelenz D 80 A2
Erkner D 74 B2
Erkrath D 80 A2
Erla E 144 B3
Erlangen D 94 B3
Erli I 133 A4
Erlsbach A 109 C3
Ermelo NL 70 B2
Ermenak TR 23 C7
Ermenonville F 90 B2
Ermezinde P 148 A1
Ermidas P 160 A1
Ermioni GR 184 B4
Ermoupoli GR 185 B5
Ermsleben D 82 A3
Erndtebrück D 81 B4
Ernée F 88 B3
Ernestinovo HR 125 B4
Ernstbrunn A 97 C4
Erolzheim D 107 A5
Erquelinnes B 79 B4
Erquy F 101 A3
Erra P 154 C2
Erratzu E 144 A2
Errindlev DK 65 B4
Erro E 144 B2
Ersa F 180 A2
Érsekcsanád H 125 A4
Ersekë AL 182 C2
Érsekvadkert H 112 B3
Ersmark S 200 C6
Erstein F 93 C3
Erstfeld CH 107 C3
Ertebølle DK 58 B2
Ertingen D 107 A4
Ervedal, *Coimbra* P 148 B1
Ervedal, *Portalegre* P 154 B3
Ervenik HR 138 A1
Ervidel P 160 B1
Ervy-le-Châtel F 104 A2
Erwitte D 81 A4
Erxleben D 73 B4
Erzsébet H 125 A4
Es Caná E 166 B1
Es Castell E 167 B4
Es Mercadal E 167 B4
Es Migjorn Gran E 167 B4
Es Port d'Alcúdia E 167 B3
Es Pujols E 166 C1
Es Soleràs E 153 A4
Esbjerg DK 59 C1
Esbly F 90 C2
Escacena del Campo E 161 B3
Escairón E 140 B3
Escalada E 143 B3
Escalante E 143 A3
Escalaplano I 179 C3
Escalona E 150 B3
Escalona del Prado E 151 A3
Escalonilla E 150 C3
Escalos de Baixo P 155 B3
Escalos de Cima P 155 B3
Escamilla E 152 B1
Escañuela E 157 C3
Escatrón E 153 A3
Esch-sur-Alzette L 92 B1
Esch-sur-Sûre L 92 B1
Eschach D 107 B4
Eschau D 94 B1
Eschede D 72 B3
Eschenau D 95 B3
Eschenbach D 95 B3
Eschenz CH 107 B3
Eschershausen D 72 C2
Eschwege D 82 A2
Eschweiler D 80 B2
Escobasa de Almazán E 152 A1
Escoeuilles F 78 B1
Escombreras E 165 B4
Escos F 144 A2
Escource F 128 B1
Escragnolles F 132 B2
Escrick GB 40 B2
Escurial E 156 A2
Escurial de la Sierra E 149 B4
Esens D 71 A4
Esgos E 140 B3
Esher GB 44 B3
Eskdalemuir GB 36 A3
Eskifjörður IS 191 B12
Eskilhem S 57 C4
Eskilsäter S 55 B4
Eskilstrup DK 65 B4
Eskilstuna S 56 A2
Eskipazar TR 187 B7
Eskişehir TR 187 C5
Eslarn D 95 B4
Eslava E 144 B2
Eslida E 159 B3
Eslohe D 81 A4
Eslöv S 61 D3
Eşme TR 188 A3
Espa N 48 B3
Espalion F 130 A1
Esparragalejo E 155 C4
Esparragosa del Caudillo E 156 B2
Esparragossa de la Serena E 156 B2
Esparreguera E 147 C2
Esparron F 132 B1

Foiano della Chiana I 135 B4
Foix F 146 B2
Fojnica BIH 139 B3
Fojnica BIH 139 B4
Fokstua N 198 C6
Földeák H 126 A2
Foldereid N 199 A9
Főldes H 113 B5
Folegandros GR 185 C5
Folelli F 180 A2
Folgaria I 121 B4
Folgosinho P 148 B2
Folgoso de la Ribera E 141 B4
Folgoso do Courel E 141 B3
Foligno I 136 C1
Folkärna S 50 B3
Folkestad N 198 C3
Folkestone GB 45 B5
Follafoss N 199 B8
Folldal N 198 C6
Follebu N 48 A2
Follina I 121 B5
Föllinge S 199 B11
Follónica I 135 C3
Fölsbyn S 54 A3
Foncebadón E 141 B4
Foncine-le-Bas F 105 C5
Fondevila E 140 C2
Fondi I 169 B3
Fondo I 121 A4
Fonelas E 164 B1
Fonfría, *Teruel* E 152 B2
Fonfría, *Zamora* E 149 A3
Fonn N 46 A3
Fonnes N 46 B1
Fonni I 178 B3
Font-Romeu F 146 B3
Fontaine F 91 C4
Fontaine de Vaucluse F 131 B4
Fontaine-Française F 105 B4
Fontaine-le-Dun F 89 A4
Fontainebleau F 90 C2
Fontan F 133 A3
Fontanarejo E 157 A3
Fontane I 133 A3
Fontanélice I 135 A4
Fontanières F 116 A2
Fontanosas E 157 B3
Fonteblanda I 168 A1
Fontenay-le-Comte F 114 B3
Fontenay-Trésigny F 90 C2
Fontevrault-l'Abbaye F 102 B2
Fontiveros E 150 B3
Fontoy F 92 B1
Fontpédrouse F 146 B3
Fontstown IRL 30 A2
Fonyód H 111 C4
Fonz E 145 B4
Fonzaso I 121 A4
Fóppolo I 120 A2
Föra S 62 A4
Forbach D 93 C4
Forbach F 92 B2
Forcall E 153 B3
Forcalquier F 132 B1
Forcarei E 140 B2
Forchheim D 94 B3
Forchtenau A 111 B3
Forchtenberg D 94 B1
Ford GB 34 B2
Førde, *Hordaland* N 52 A1
Førde, *Sogn og Fjordane* N 46 A2
Förderstedt D 83 A3
Førdesfjorden N 52 A1
Fordham GB 45 A4
Fordingbridge GB 44 C2
Fordon PL 76 A3
Fordongiánus I 179 C2
Forenza I 172 B1
Foresta di Búrgos I 178 B2
Forfar GB 35 B5
Forges-les-Eaux F 90 B1
Foria I 172 B1
Forío I 170 C1
Forjães P 148 A1
Førland N 52 B3
Forlì I 135 A5
Forlimpopoli I 135 A5
Formazza I 119 A5
Formby GB 38 A3
Formerie F 90 B1
Fórmia I 169 B3
Formígine I 135 A3
Formigliana I 119 B5
Formiguères F 146 B3
Fornalutx E 166 B2
Fornåsa S 56 B1
Fornelli I 178 B2
Fornells E 167 A4
Fornelos de Montes E 140 B2
Fornes E 163 B4
Forneset N 192 C3
Forni Avoltri I 109 C3
Forni di Sopra I 122 A1
Forni di Sotto I 122 A1
Forno, *Piemonte* I 119 B4
Forno, *Piemonte* I 119 B5
Forno Alpi-Gráie I 119 B4
Forno di Zoldo I 121 A5
Fornos de Algodres P 148 B2
Fornovo di Taro I 120 C3
Foros do Arrão P 154 B2
Forráskút H 126 A1
Forres GB 32 D3
Forriolo E 140 B3
Fors S 50 B3
Forsand N 52 B2
Forsbacka S 51 B3
Forserum S 62 A2
Forshaga S 55 A4
Forsheda S 60 B3
Forsinain GB 32 C3
Førslev DK 65 A4
Förslöv S 61 C2
Forsmark, *Uppsala* S 51 B5
Forsmark, *Västerbotten* S 195 E6
Forsmo S 200 C3
Forsnäs S 195 D9
Forsnes N 198 B5
Forssa FIN 8 B3
Forssjöbruk S 56 B2
Forst D 84 A2
Forsvik S 55 B5
Fort Augustus GB 32 D2
Fort-Mahon-Plage F 78 B1
Fort William GB 34 B2
Fortanete E 153 B3
Forte dei Marmi I 134 B3
Fortezza I 108 C2
Forth GB 35 C4
Fortrie GB 33 D4
Fortrose GB 32 D2
Fortun N 47 A4
Fortuna E 165 A3
Fortuneswell GB 43 B4
Forvik N 195 E3
Fos F 145 B4
Fos-sur-Mer F 131 B3
Fosdinovo I 134 A3
Foss N 47 B6
Fossacésia I 169 A4
Fossano I 133 A3
Fossato di Vico I 136 B1
Fossbakken N 194 B8
Fosse-la-Ville B 79 B4
Fossombrone I 136 B1
Fot H 112 B3
Fouchères F 104 A3
Fouesnant F 100 B1
Foug F 92 C1
Fougères F 88 B2
Fougerolles F 105 B5
Foulain F 105 A4
Fountainhall GB 35 C5
Fouras F 114 C2
Fourchambault F 104 B2
Fourmies F 91 A4
Fourna GR 182 D3
Fournels F 116 C3
Fourni GR 188 B1
Fournols F 117 B3
Fourques F 146 B3
Fourquevaux F 146 A2
Fours F 104 C2
Fowey GB 42 B2
Foxdale GB 36 B2
Foxford IRL 26 C1
Foyers GB 32 D2
Foynes IRL 29 B2
Foz E 141 A3
Foz do Arelho P 154 B1
Foz do Giraldo P 155 B3
Foza I 121 B4
Frabosa Soprana I 133 A3
Frades de la Sierra E 149 B4
Fraga E 153 A4
Fragagnano I 173 B3
Frailes E 163 A4
Fraire B 79 B4
Fraize F 106 A1
Framlingham GB 45 A5
Frammersbach D 94 A1
Framnes N 54 A1
França P 141 C4
Francaltroff F 92 C2
Francavilla al Mare I 169 A4
Francavilla di Sicília I 177 B4
Francavilla Fontana I 173 B3
Francavilla in Sinni I 174 A2
Francescas F 129 B3
Franco P 148 A2
Francofonte I 177 B3
Francos E 151 A4
Frändefors S 54 B3
Franeker NL 70 A2
Frangy F 118 A2
Frankenau D 81 A4
Frankenberg, *Hessen* D 81 A4
Frankenberg, *Sachsen* D 83 B5
Frankenburg A 109 A4
Frankenfels A 110 B2
Frankenmarkt A 109 B4
Frankenthal D 93 B4
Frankfurt, *Brandenburg* D 74 B3
Frankfurt, *Hessen* D 81 B4
Frankrike S 199 B10
Fränsta S 200 D2
Františkovy Lázně CZ 83 B4
Franzburg D 66 B1
Frascati I 168 B2
Frasdorf D 109 B3
Fraserburgh GB 33 D4
Frashër AL 182 C2
Frasne F 105 C5
Frasnes-lez-Anvaing B 79 B3
Frasseto F 180 B2
Frastanz A 107 B4
Fratel P 155 B3
Fratta Todina I 135 C5
Frauenau D 96 C1
Frauenfeld CH 107 B3
Frauenkirchen A 111 B3
Frauenstein D 83 B5
Frauental A 110 C2
Frayssinet F 129 B4
Frayssinet-le-Gélat F 129 B4
Frechas P 149 A2
Frechen D 80 B2
Frechilla E 142 B2
Freckenhorst D 71 C4
Fredeburg D 81 A4
Fredelsloh D 82 A1
Fredeng N 48 B2
Fredensborg DK 61 D2
Fredericia DK 59 C2
Frederiks DK 59 B2
Frederikshavn DK 58 A3
Frederikssund DK 61 D2
Frederiksværk DK 61 D2
Fredrika S 200 B4
Fredriksberg S 50 B1
Fredriksdal S 62 A2
Fredrikstad N 54 A1
Fregenal de la Sierra E 161 A3
Fregene I 168 B2
Freiberg D 83 B5
Freiburg, *Baden-Württemberg* D 106 B2
Freiburg, *Niedersachsen* D 64 C2
Freienhagen D 81 A5
Freienhufen D 84 A1
Freiensteinau D 81 B5
Freihung D 95 B3
Freilassing D 109 B3
Freisen D 92 B3
Freising D 95 C3
Freistadt A 96 C2
Freital D 84 A1
Freixedas P 149 B2
Freixo de Espada à Cinta P 149 A3
Fréjus F 132 B2
Fremdingen D 94 C2
Frenštát pod Radhoštěm CZ 98 B2
Freren D 71 B4
Freshford IRL 30 B1
Freshwater GB 44 C2
Fresnay-sur-Sarthe F 89 B4
Fresne-St. Mamès F 105 B4
Fresneda de la Sierra E 152 B1
Fresneda de la Sierra Tiron E 143 B3
Fresnedillas E 151 B3
Fresnes-en-Woevre F 92 B1
Fresno Alhandiga E 150 B2
Fresno de la Ribera E 150 A2
Fresno de la Vega E 142 B1
Fresno de Sayago E 149 A4
Fresnoy-Folny F 90 B1
Fresnoy-le-Grand F 91 B3
Fressenville F 90 A1
Fresvik N 46 A3
Fréteval F 103 B3
Fretigney F 105 B4
Freudenberg, *Baden-Württemberg* D 94 B1
Freudenberg, *Nordrhein-Westfalen* D 81 B3
Freudenstadt D 93 C4
Freux B 92 B1
Frévent F 78 B2
Freyburg D 83 A3
Freyenstein D 73 A5
Freyming-Merlebach F 92 B2
Freystadt D 95 B3
Freyung D 96 C1
Frias de Albarracin E 152 B2
Fribourg CH 106 C2
Frick CH 106 B3
Fridafors S 63 B2
Fridaythorpe GB 40 A3
Friedberg A 111 B3
Friedberg, *Bayern* D 94 C2
Friedberg, *Hessen* D 81 B4
Friedeburg D 71 A4
Friedewald D 82 B1
Friedland, *Brandenburg* D 74 B3
Friedland, *Mecklenburg-Vorpommern* D 74 A2
Friedland, *Niedersachsen* D 82 A1
Friedrichroda D 82 B2
Friedrichsdorf D 81 B4
Friedrichshafen D 107 B4
Friedrichskoog D 64 B1
Friedrichstadt D 64 B2
Friedrichswalde D 74 A2
Friesach A 110 C1
Friesack D 73 B5
Friesenheim D 93 C3
Friesoythe D 71 A4
Friggesund S 200 E2
Frigiliana E 163 B4
Frihetsli N 192 D3
Frillesås S 60 B2
Frinnaryd S 62 A2
Frinton-on-Sea GB 45 B5
Friockheim GB 35 B5
Friol E 140 A3
Fristad S 60 B2
Fritsla S 60 B2
Fritzlar D 81 A5
Frizington GB 36 B3
Frödinge S 62 A4
Froges F 118 B2
Frohburg D 83 A4
Frohnhausen D 81 B4
Frohnleiten A 110 B2
Froissy F 90 B2
Frombork PL 69 A4
Frome GB 43 A4
Frómista E 142 B2
Fröndenberg D 81 A3
Fronsac F 128 B2
Front I 119 B4
Fronteira P 155 B3
Frontenay-Rohan-Rohan F 114 B3
Frontenhausen D 95 C4
Frontignan F 130 B2
Fronton F 129 C4
Fröseke S 62 B3
Frosinone I 169 B3
Frosolone I 170 B2
Frosta N 199 B7
Frøstrup DK 58 A1
Frosunda S 57 A4
Frouard F 92 C2
Frövi S 56 A1
Frøyset N 46 B2
Fruges F 78 B2
Frutigen CH 106 C2
Frýdek-Místek CZ 98 B2
Frýdlant CZ 84 B3
Frydlant nad Ostravicí CZ 98 B2
Frygnowo PL 77 A5
Fryšták CZ 98 B1
Fucécchio I 135 B3
Fuencaliente, *Ciudad Real* E 157 A4
Fuencaliente, *Ciudad Real* E 157 B3
Fuencemillán E 151 B4
Fuendejalón E 144 C2
Fuengirola E 163 B3
Fuenlabrada E 151 B4
Fuenlabrada de los Montes E 156 A3
Fuensalida E 151 B3
Fuensanta E 164 B3
Fuensanta de Martos E 163 A4
Fuente al Olmo de Iscar E 150 A3
Fuente-Alamo E 158 C2
Fuente-Álamo de Murcia E 165 B3
Fuente Dé E 142 A2
Fuente de Cantos E 155 C4
Fuente de Santa Cruz E 150 A3
Fuente del Arco E 156 B2
Fuente del Conde E 163 A3
Fuente del Maestre E 155 C4
Fuente el Fresno E 157 A4
Fuente el Saz de Jarama E 151 B4
Fuente el Sol E 150 A3
Fuente Obejuna E 156 B2
Fuente Palmera E 162 A2
Fuente-Tójar E 163 A3
Fuente Vaqueros E 163 A4
Fuentealbilla E 158 B2
Fuentecén E 151 A4
Fuenteguinaldo E 149 B3
Fuentelapeña E 150 A2
Fuentelcésped E 151 A4
Fuentelespino de Haro E 158 B1
Fuentelespino de Moya E 158 B2
Fuentenovilla E 151 B4
Fuentepelayo E 151 A3
Fuentepinilla E 151 A5
Fuenterroble de Salvatierra E 150 B2
Fuenterrobles E 158 B2
Fuentes E 158 B1
Fuentes de Andalucía E 162 A2
Fuentes de Ebro E 153 A3
Fuentes de Jiloca E 152 A2
Fuentes de la Alcarria E 151 B5
Fuentes de León E 161 A3
Fuentes de Nava E 142 B2
Fuentes de Oñoro E 149 B3
Fuentes de Ropel E 142 B1
Fuentesauco, *Segovia* E 151 A3
Fuentesaúco, *Zamora* E 150 A2
Fuentespalda E 153 B4
Fuentespina E 151 A4
Fuentidueña E 151 A4
Fuentidueña de Tajo E 151 B4
Fuerte del Rey E 157 C4
Fügen A 108 B2
Fuglebjerg DK 65 A4
Fuglevik N 54 A1
Fuhrberg D 72 B2
Fulda D 82 B1
Fulgatore I 176 B1
Fully CH 119 A4
Fulnek CZ 98 B1
Fülöpszállás H 112 C3
Fulpmes A 108 B2
Fulunäs S 49 A5
Fumay F 91 B4
Fumel F 129 B3
Funäsdalen S 199 C9
Fundão P 148 B2
Funzie GB 33 A6
Furadouro P 148 B1
Fure N 46 A2
Fürstenau, *Niedersachsen* D 71 B4
Furstenau, *Nordrhein-Westfalen* D 81 A5
Fürstenberg D 74 A2
Fürstenfeld A 111 B3
Fürstenfeldbruck D 108 A2
Fürstenstein D 96 C1
Fürstenwalde D 74 B3
Fürstenwerder D 74 A2
Fürstenzell D 96 C1
Furta H 113 B5
Fürth, *Bayern* D 94 B2
Fürth, *Hessen* D 93 B4
Furth im Wald D 95 B4
Furtwangen D 106 A3
Furuby S 62 B3
Furudal S 50 A2
Furuflaten N 192 C4
Furulund S 61 D3
Furusjö S 60 B3
Fusa N 46 B2
Fuscaldo I 174 B2
Fusch an der Grossglocknerstrasse A 109 B3
Fushë Arrëz AL 182 A2
Fushë-Krujë AL 182 B1
Fusina I 122 B1
Fusio CH 107 C3
Füssen D 108 B1
Fustiñana E 144 B2
Futog SRB 126 B1
Futrikelv N 192 C3
Füzesabony H 113 B4
Füzesgyarmat H 113 B5
Fužine HR 123 B3
Fyllinge S 61 C2
Fynshav DK 64 B2
Fyresdal N 53 A4

G

Gaaldorf A 110 B1
Gabaldón E 158 B2
Gabarret F 128 C2
Gabčíkovo SK 111 B4
Gąbin PL 77 B4
Gabriac F 130 A1
Gabrovo BG 17 D6
Gaby I 119 B4
Gacé F 89 B4
Gacko BIH 139 B4
Gäddede S 199 A11
Gadebusch D 65 C4
Gadmen CH 106 C3
Gádor E 164 C2
Gádoros H 113 C4
Gael F 101 A3
Gærum DK 58 A3
Găeşti RO 17 C6
Gaeta I 169 B3
Gafanhoeira P 154 C2
Gaflenz A 110 B1
Gagarin RUS 9 E9
Gaggenau D 93 C4
Gagliano Castelferrato I 177 B3
Gagliano del Capo I 173 C4
Gagnet S 50 B2
Gaibanella I 121 C4
Gaildorf D 94 B1
Gaillac F 129 C4
Gaillefontaine F 90 B1
Gaillon F 89 A5
Gainsborough GB 40 B3
Gairloch GB 31 B3
Gairlochy GB 34 B3
Gáiro I 179 C3
Gaj HR 124 B3
Gaj SRB 127 C3
Gaja-la-Selve F 146 A2
Gajanejos E 151 B5
Gajary SK 97 C4
Gajdobra SRB 126 B1
Galan F 145 A4
Galanta SK 111 A4
Galapagar E 151 B3
Galápagos E 151 B4
Galaroza E 161 B3
Galashiels GB 35 C5
Galatas GR 185 B4
Galaţi RO 17 C8
Galatina I 173 B4
Galatista GR 183 C5
Galátone I 173 B4
Galaxidi GR 184 A3
Galdakao E 143 A4
Galeata I 135 B4
Galende E 141 B4
Galera E 164 B2
Galéria F 180 A1
Galgamácsa H 112 B3
Galgate GB 38 A4
Galgon F 128 B2
Galices P 148 B2
Galinduste E 150 B2
Galinoporni CY 181 A3
Galisteo E 155 B4
Galków PL 87 A3
Gallarate I 120 B1
Gallardon F 90 C1
Gallegos de Argañán E 149 B3
Gallegos del Solmirón E 150 B2
Galleguillos de Campos E 142 B1
Galleno I 135 B3
Galliate I 120 B1
Gallicano I 134 A3
Gállio I 121 B4
Gallípoli I 173 B3
Gallipoli = Gelibolu TR 186 B1
Gällivare S 196 B3
Gallizien A 110 C1
Gallneukirchen A 96 C2
Gällö S 199 C12
Gallocanta E 152 B2
Gällstad S 60 B3
Gallur E 144 C2
Galmisdale GB 31 C2
Galmpton GB 43 B3
Galston GB 36 A2
Galta N 52 A1
Galtelli I 178 B3
Galten DK 59 B2
Galtür A 107 C5
Galve de Sorbe E 151 A4
Galveias P 154 B2
Gálvez E 157 A3
Galway IRL 28 A2
Gamaches F 90 B1
Gámbara I 120 B3
Gambárie I 175 C1
Gambassi Terme I 135 B3
Gambatesa I 170 B2
Gambolò I 120 B1
Gaming A 110 B2
Gamla Uppsala S 51 C4
Gamleby S 62 A4
Gamlingay GB 44 A3
Gammelgarn S 57 C4
Gammelstad S 196 D5
Gammertingen D 107 A4
Gams CH 107 B4
Gamvik, *Finnmark* N 192 B6
Gamvik, *Finnmark* N 193 A12
Gan F 145 A3
Gáname E 149 A3
Ganda di Martello I 108 C1
Gandarela P 148 A1
Gandal N 52 B1
Ganderkesee D 72 A1
Gandesa E 153 A4
Gandía E 159 C3
Gandino I 120 B2
Gandrup DK 58 A3
Ganges F 130 B2
Gånghester S 60 B3
Gangi I 177 B3
Gangkofen D 95 C4

Gannat F 116 A3
Gannay-sur-Loire F 104 C2
Gänserdorf A 97 C4
Ganzlin D 73 A5
Gap F 132 A2
Gara H 125 A5
Garaballa E 158 B2
Garaguso I 172 B2
Garbayuela E 156 A2
Garbhallt GB 34 B2
Garbsen D 72 B2
Garching D 109 A3
Garciaz E 156 A2
Garcihernández E 150 B2
Garcillán E 151 B3
Garcinarro E 151 B5
Garcisobaco E 162 B2
Garda I 121 B3
Gardanne F 131 B4
Gärdås S 49 B5
Gårdby S 63 B4
Gardeja PL 69 B3
Gardelegen D 73 B4
Gardermoen N 48 B3
Gardiki GR 182 E3
Garding D 64 B1
Gardone Riviera I 121 B3
Gardone Val Trómpia I 120 B3
Gárdony H 112 B2
Gardouch F 146 A2
Gards Köpinge S 63 C2
Gårdsjö S 55 B5
Gårdskär S 51 B4
Garein F 128 B2
Garelochhead GB 34 B3
Garéoult F 132 B2
Garešnica HR 124 B2
Garéssio I 133 A4
Garforth GB 40 B2
Gargaliani GR 184 B2
Gargaligas E 156 A2
Gargallo E 153 B3
Garganta la Olla E 150 B2
Gargantiel E 156 B3
Gargellen A 107 C4
Gargilesse-Dampierre F 103 C3
Gargnano I 121 B3
Gargnäs S 195 E8
Gárgoles de Abajo E 152 B1
Gargrave GB 40 B1
Garitz D 73 C5
Garlasco I 120 B1
Garlieston GB 36 B2
Garlin F 128 C2
Garlitos E 156 B2
Garmisch-Partenkirchen D 108 B2
Garnat-sur-Engièvre F 104 C2
Garpenberg S 50 B3
Garphyttan S 55 A5
Garray E 143 C4
Garrel D 71 B5
Garriguella E 146 B4
Garrison GB 26 B2
Garrovillas E 155 B4
Garrucha E 164 B3
Gars-a-Kamp A 97 C3
Garsås S 50 B1
Garsdale Head GB 37 B4
Gärsnäs S 63 C2
Garstang GB 38 A4
Gartow D 73 A4
Gartz D 74 A3
Garvagh GB 27 B4
Garvão P 160 B1
Garve GB 32 D2
Garwolin PL 12 C4
Garz D 66 B2
Garzyn PL 85 A4
Gąsawa PL 76 B2
Gåsborn S 49 C6
Gaschurn A 107 C5
Gascueña E 152 B1
Gasny F 90 B1
Gąsocin PL 77 B5
Gastes F 128 B1
Gastouni GR 184 B2
Gastouri GR 182 D1
Gata E 149 B3
Gata HR 138 B2
Gata de Gorgos E 159 C4
Gătaia RO 126 B3
Gatchina RUS 9 C7
Gatehouse of Fleet GB 36 B2
Gátér H 113 C3
Gateshead GB 37 B5
Gátova E 159 B3
Gattendorf A 111 A3
Gatteo a Mare I 136 A1
Gattinara I 119 B5
Gattorna I 134 A2
Gaucín E 162 B2
Gaulstad N 199 B9
Gaupne N 47 A4
Gautefall N 53 A4
Gauting D 108 A2
Gauto S 195 D7
Gava E 147 C3
Gavardo I 121 B3
Gavarnie F 145 B3
Gávavencsello H 113 A5
Gavi I 120 C1
Gavião P 154 B3
Gavirate I 120 B1
Gävle S 51 B4
Gavoi I 178 B3
Gavorrano I 135 C3
Gavray F 88 B2
Gavrio GR 185 B5
Gävunda S 49 B6
Gaweinstal A 97 C4
Gaworzyce PL 85 A3
Gawroniec PL 75 A5
Gaydon GB 44 A2
Gayton GB 41 C4
Gazipaşa TR 189 C7
Gazoldo degli Ippoliti I 121 B3
Gazzuolo I 121 B3
Gbelce SK 112 B2
Gdańsk PL 69 A3
Gdinj HR 138 B2
Gdov RUS 8 C5
Gdów PL 99 B4
Gdynia PL 69 A3
Gea de Albarracin E 152 B2
Geary GB 31 B2
Géaudot F 91 C4
Geaune F 128 C2
Gebesee D 82 A2
Gebiz TR 189 B5
Gebze TR 187 B4
Géderlak H 112 C2
Gedern D 81 B5
Gedinne B 91 B4
Gediz TR 187 D4
Gèdre F 145 B4
Gedser DK 65 B4
Gedsted DK 58 B2
Geel B 79 A4
Geesthacht D 72 A3
Geetbets B 79 B5
Gefell D 83 B3
Gehrden D 72 B2
Gehren D 82 B3
Geilenkirchen D 80 B2
Geilo N 47 B5
Geinsheim D 93 B4
Geisa D 82 B1
Geiselhöring D 95 C4
Geiselwind D 94 B2
Geisenfeld D 95 C3
Geisenhausen D 95 C4
Geisenheim D 93 B4
Geising D 84 B1
Geisingen D 107 B3
Geislingen D 94 C1
Geistthal A 110 B2
Geiterygghytta N 47 B4
Geithain D 83 A4
Geithus N 48 C1
Gela I 177 B3
Geldermalsen NL 79 A5
Geldern D 80 A2
Geldrop NL 80 A1
Geleen NL 80 B1
Gelembe TR 186 C2
Gelendost TR 189 A6
Gelibolu = Gallipoli TR 186 B1
Gelida E 147 C2
Gelnhausen D 81 B5
Gelnica SK 99 C4
Gelsa E 153 A3
Gelse H 111 C3
Gelsenkirchen D 80 A3
Gelsted DK 59 C2
Geltendorf D 108 A2
Gelterkinden CH 106 B2
Gelting D 64 B2
Gelu RO 126 A3
Gelves E 162 A1
Gembloux B 79 B4
Gemeaux F 105 B4
Gémenos F 132 B1
Gemerská Poloma SK 99 C4
Gemerská Ves SK 99 C4
Gemert NL 80 A1
Gemla S 62 B2
Gemlik TR 186 B4
Gemmenich B 80 B1
Gemona del Friuli I 122 A2
Gémozac F 114 C3
Gemund D 80 B2
Gemünden, *Bayern* D 94 A1
Gemünden, *Hessen* D 81 B4
Gemünden, *Rheinland-Pfalz* D 93 B3
Genappe B 79 B4
Génave E 164 A2
Genazzano I 169 B2
Gençay F 115 B4
Gencsapáti H 111 B3
Gendringen NL 80 A2
Genelard F 104 C3
Genemuiden NL 70 B3
Generalski Stol HR 123 B4
Geneva = Genève CH 118 A3
Genevad S 61 C3
Genève = Geneva CH 118 A3
Genevriéres F 105 B4
Gengenbach D 93 C4
Genillé F 103 B3
Genk B 80 B1
Genlis F 105 B4
Gennep NL 80 A1
Genner DK 64 A2
Gennes F 102 B1
Genoa = Génova I 134 A1
Genola I 133 A3
Génova = Genoa I 134 A1
Genowefa PL 76 B3
Gensingen D 93 B3
Gent = Ghent B 79 A3
Genthin D 73 B5
Gentioux F 116 B1
Genzano di Lucánia I 172 B2
Genzano di Roma I 168 B2
Georgenthal D 82 B2
Georgsmarienhütte D 71 B5
Gera D 83 B4
Geraards-bergen B 79 B3
Gerace I 175 C2
Geraci Siculo I 177 B3
Geraki GR 184 C3
Gérardmer F 106 A1
Geras A 97 C3
Gerbéviller F 92 C2
Gerbini I 177 B3
Gerbstedt D 83 A3
Gerði IS 191 C9
Gerede TR 187 B7
Gerena E 161 B3
Geretsried D 108 B2
Gérgal E 164 B2
Gergy F 105 C3
Gerindote E 150 C3
Gerjen H 112 C2
Gerlos A 108 B3
Germay F 92 C1
Germencik TR 188 B2
Germering D 108 A2
Germersheim D 93 B4
Gernika-Lumo E 143 A4
Gernrode D 82 A3
Gernsbach D 93 C4
Gernsheim D 93 B4
Geroda D 82 B1
Gerola Alta I 120 A2
Geroldsgrun D 83 B3
Gerolsbach D 95 C3
Gerolstein D 80 B2
Gerolzhofen D 94 B2
Gerovo HR 123 B3
Gerpinnes B 79 B4
Gerrards Cross GB 44 B3
Gerri de la Sal E 147 B2
Gersfeld D 82 B1
Gerstetten D 94 C2
Gersthofen D 94 C2
Gerstungen D 82 B2
Gerswalde D 74 A2
Gerzat F 116 B3
Gerze TR 23 A8
Gerzen D 95 C4
Gescher D 71 C4
Geseke D 81 A4
Geslau D 94 B2
Gespunsart F 91 B4
Gesté F 101 B4
Gestorf D 72 B2
Gesualda I 170 C3
Gesunda S 50 B1
Gesztely H 113 A4
Geta FIN 51 B6
Getafe E 151 B4
Getinge S 60 C2
Getxo E 143 A4
Geversdorf D 64 C2
Gevgelija MK 182 B4
Gevora del Caudillo E 155 C4
Gevrey-Chambertin F 105 B3
Gex F 118 A3
Gey D 80 B2
Geyikli TR 186 C1
Geysir IS 190 C5
Geyve TR 187 B5
Gföhl A 97 C3
Ghedi I 120 B3
Ghent = Gent B 79 A3
Gheorgheni RO 17 B6
Ghigo I 119 C4
Ghilarza I 178 B2
Ghisonaccia F 180 A2
Ghisoni F 180 A2
Gialtra GR 182 E4
Gianitsa GR 182 C4
Giardinetto Vécchio I 171 B3
Giardini Naxos I 177 B4
Giarratana I 177 B3
Giarre I 177 B4
Giat F 116 B2
Giaveno I 119 B4
Giazza I 121 B4
Giba I 179 C2
Gibellina Nuova I 176 B1
Gibostad N 194 A9
Gibraleón E 161 B3
Gibraltar GBZ 162 B2
Gic H 111 B4
Gideå S 200 C5
Gideåkroken S 200 B3
Gidle PL 86 B3
Giebelstadt D 94 B1
Gieboldehausen D 82 A2
Gielniów PL 87 A4
Gielow D 74 A1
Gien F 103 B4
Giengen D 94 C2
Giens F 132 B2
Giera RO 126 B2
Gieselwerder D 81 A5
Giessen D 81 B4
Gieten NL 71 A3
Giethoorn NL 70 B3
Giffaumont-Champaubert F 91 C4
Gifford GB 35 C5
Gifhorn D 73 B3
Gige H 125 A3
Gignac F 130 B2
Gijón E 142 A1
Gilena E 162 A3
Gilford GB 27 B4
Gillberga S 55 A3
Gilleleje DK 61 C2
Gilley F 105 B5
Gilley-sur-Loire F 104 C2
Gillingham, *Dorset* GB 43 A4
Gillingham, *Medway* GB 45 B4
Gilocourt F 90 B2
Gilserberg D 81 B5
Gilsland GB 37 B4
Gilze NL 79 A4
Gimåt S 200 C4
Gimo S 51 B5
Gimont F 129 C3
Ginasservis F 132 B1
Gingelom B 79 B5
Gingst D 66 B2
Ginosa I 171 C4
Ginzling A 108 B2
Giões P 160 B2
Gióia dei Marsi I 169 B3
Gióia del Colle I 173 B2
Gióia Sannitica I 170 B2
Gióia Táuro I 175 C1
Gioiosa Iónica I 175 C2
Gioiosa Marea I 177 A3
Giosla GB 31 A2
Giovinazzo I 171 B4
Girifalco I 175 C2
Giromagny F 106 B1
Girona E 147 C3
Gironcourt-sur-Vraine F 92 C1
Gironella E 147 B2
Gironville-sous-les-Côtes F 92 C1
Girvan GB 36 A2
Gislaved S 60 B3
Gislev DK 59 C3
Gisors F 90 B1
Gissi I 170 A2
Gistad S 56 B1
Gistel B 78 A2
Gistrup DK 58 B3
Giswil CH 106 C3
Githio GR 184 C3
Giugliano in Campania I 170 C2
Giulianova I 136 C2
Giulvăz RO 126 B2
Giurgiu RO 17 D6
Give DK 59 C2
Givet F 91 A4
Givors F 117 B4
Givry B 79 B4
Givry F 104 C3
Givry-en-Argonne F 91 C4
Givskud DK 59 C2
Giżalki PL 76 B2
Gizeux F 102 B2
Giżycko PL 12 A4
Gizzeria I 175 C2
Gizzeria Lido I 175 C2
Gjedved DK 59 C2
Gjegjan AL 182 B2
Gjendesheim N 47 A5
Gjerde N 46 B3
Gjerlev DK 58 B3
Gjermundshamn N 46 B2
Gjerrild DK 58 B3
Gjerstad N 53 B5
Gjesås N 49 B4
Gjesvær N 193 A9
Gjirokastër AL 182 C2
Gjøfjell N 54 A1
Gjøl DK 58 A2
Gjøra N 198 C6
Gjøvik N 48 B2
Gladbeck D 80 A2
Gladenbach D 81 B4
Gladstad N 195 E2
Glamis GB 35 B4
Glamoč BIH 138 A2
Glamsbjerg DK 59 C3
Gland CH 105 C5
Glandorf D 71 B4
Glanegg A 110 C1
Glanshammar S 56 A1
Glarus CH 107 B4
Glasgow GB 35 C3
Glashütte, *Bayern* D 108 B2
Glashütte, *Sachsen* D 84 B1
Glastonbury GB 43 A4
Glatzau A 110 C2
Glauchau D 83 B4
Glava S 54 A3
Glavatičevo BIH 139 B4
Glavičice BIH 127 C1
Glein A 110 B1
Glein N 195 D3
Gleinstätten A 110 C2
Gleisdorf A 110 B2
Glenamoy IRL 26 B1
Glenarm GB 27 B5
Glenavy GB 27 B4
Glenbarr GB 34 C2
Glenbeigh IRL 29 B2
Glenbrittle GB 31 B2
Glencoe GB 34 B2
Glencolumbkille IRL 26 B2
Glendalough IRL 30 A2
Glenealy IRL 30 B2
Glenelg GB 31 B3
Glenfinnan GB 34 B2
Glengarriff IRL 29 C2
Glenluce GB 36 B2
Glennamaddy IRL 28 A3
Glenrothes GB 35 B4
Glenties IRL 26 B2
Glesborg DK 58 B3
Glesien D 83 A4
Gletsch CH 106 C3
Glewitz D 66 B1
Glifada GR 185 B4
Glimåkra S 63 B2
Glin IRL 29 B2
Glina HR 124 B2
Glinde D 72 A3
Glinojeck PL 77 B5
Glinsk IRL 28 A2
Gliwice PL 86 B2
Glödnitz A 109 C5
Gloggnitz A 110 B2
Głogoczów PL 99 B3
Glogonj SRB 127 C2
Glogovac SRB 127 C3
Głogów PL 85 A4
Głogówek PL 86 B1
Glomel F 100 A2
Glomfjord N 195 D4
Glommen S 60 C2
Glommersträsk S 196 D2
Glonn D 108 B2
Glorenza I 108 C1
Gloria P 154 B2
Glosa GR 183 D5
Glossop GB 40 B2
Gloucester GB 39 C4
Głowaczów PL 87 A5
Główczyce PL 68 A2
Glöwen D 73 B5
Głowno PL 77 C4
Gložan SRB 126 B1
Głubczyce PL 86 B1
Głuchołazy PL 85 B5
Głuchów PL 87 A4
Głuchowo PL 75 B5
Glücksburg D 64 B2
Glückstadt D 64 C2
Glumina BIH 139 A5
Glumsø DK 65 A4
Glušci SRB 127 C1
Glusk BY 13 B8
Głuszyca PL 85 B4
Glyn Neath GB 39 C3
Glyngøre DK 58 B1
Gmünd, *Karnten* A 109 C4
Gmünd, *Nieder Östereich* A 96 C2
Gmund D 108 B2
Gmunden A 109 B4
Gnarp S 200 D3
Gnarrenburg D 72 A2
Gnesau A 109 C4
Gnesta S 56 A3
Gnięchowice PL 85 A4
Gniew PL 69 B3
Gniewkowo PL 76 B3
Gniezno PL 76 B2
Gnoien D 66 C1
Gnojnice BIH 139 B3
Gnojno PL 87 B4
Gnosall GB 40 C1
Gnosjö S 60 B3
Göbel TR 186 B3
Göçbeyli TR 186 C2
Goch D 80 A2
Gochsheim D 94 A2
Göd H 112 B3
Godalming GB 44 B3
Godby FIN 51 B6
Goddelsheim D 81 A4
Gódega di Sant'Urbano I 122 B1
Godegård S 56 B1
Godelheim D 81 A5
Goderville F 89 A4
Goðdalir IS 190 B6
Godiasco I 120 C2
Godič SLO 123 A3
Godkowo PL 69 A4
Godmanchester GB 44 A3
Gödöllö H 112 B3
Gödre H 125 A3
Godshill GB 44 C2
Godzikowice PL 85 B5
Godziszewo PL 69 A3
Goes NL 79 A3
Goetzenbrück F 93 C3
Góglio I 119 A5
Gogolin PL 86 B2
Göhren D 66 B2
Goirle NL 79 A5
Góis P 148 B1
Góito I 121 B3
Goizueta E 144 A2
Gojna Gora SRB 127 D2
Gójsk PL 77 B4
Gökçedağ TR 186 C3
Gökçen TR 188 A2
Gökçeören TR 188 A3
Gökçeyazı TR 186 C2
Göktepe TR 188 B3
Gol N 47 B5
Gola HR 124 A3
Gola N 48 A1
Gołańcz PL 76 B2
Gölbaşı TR 23 B7
Gölby FIN 51 B6
Gölcük, *Kocaeli* TR 187 B4
Gölcük, *Niğde* TR 23 B8
Golčův Jenikov CZ 97 B3
Gołczewo PL 67 C3
Goldach CH 107 B4
Goldbach D 93 A5
Goldbeck D 73 B4
Goldberg D 73 A5
Goldelund D 64 B2
Goldenstedt D 72 B1
Gołębiewo PL 69 A3
Golegã P 154 B2
Goleniów PL 75 A3
Golfo Aranci I 178 B3
Gölhisar TR 189 B4
Golina PL 76 B3
Gölle H 112 C2
Göllersdorf A 97 C4
Golling an der Salzach A 109 B4
Gölmarmara TR 186 D2
Golnice PL 84 A3
Golnik SLO 123 A3
Gölova TR 189 C5
Gölpazarı TR 187 B5
Gols A 111 B3
Golspie GB 32 D3
Golssen D 74 C2
Golub-Dobrzyń PL 77 A4
Golubinci SRB 127 C2
Goluchów PL 86 A1
Golymin-Ośrodek PL 77 B5
Golzow D 73 B5
Gomagoi I 108 C1
Gómara E 152 A1
Gomaringen D 93 C5
Gömbe TR 189 C4
Gömeç TR 186 C1
Gomel = Homyel BY 13 B9
Gomes Aires P 160 B1
Gómezserracin E 150 A3
Gommern D 73 B4
Gomulin PL 86 A3
Gonäs S 50 B2
Goncelin F 118 B2
Gończyce PL 87 A5
Gondomar E 140 B2
Gondomar P 148 A1
Gondrecourt-le-Château F 92 C1
Gondrin F 128 C3
Gönen, *Balıkesir* TR 186 B2
Gönen, *Isparta* TR 189 B5
Gonfaron F 132 B2
Goñi E 144 B2
Goni GR 182 D4
Goni I 179 C3
Gonnesa I 179 C2
Gonnosfanádiga I 179 C2
Gönyü H 111 B4
Gonzaga I 121 C3
Goodrich GB 39 C4
Goodwick GB 39 B1
Gooik B 79 B4
Goole GB 40 B3
Goor NL 71 B3
Göpfritz an der Wild A 97 C3
Goppenstein CH 119 A4
Göppingen D 94 C1
Gor E 164 B2
Góra, *Dolnośląskie* PL 85 A4
Góra, *Mazowieckie* PL 77 B5
Gorafe E 164 B1
Gorawino PL 67 C4
Goražde BIH 139 B4
Gőrbeháza H 113 B5
Gordaliza del Pino E 142 B1
Gördes TR 186 D3
Gørding DK 59 C1
Górdola CH 120 A1
Gordon GB 35 C5
Gordoncillo E 142 B1
Gorebridge GB 35 C4
Gorenja Vas SLO 123 A3
Gorenje Jelenje HR 123 B3
Gorey GB 88 A1
Gorey IRL 30 B2
Gorgonzola I 120 B2
Gorica HR 137 A4
Gorican HR 124 A2

Gorinchem NL 79 A4
Goring GB 44 B2
Goritsy RUS 9 D10
Göritz D 74 A2
Gorízia I 122 B2
Górki PL 77 B4
Gorleben D 73 A4
Gorleston-on-sea GB 41 C5
Gørlev DK 61 D1
Görlitz D 84 A2
Górliz E 143 A4
Görmin D 66 C2
Górna Grupa PL 69 B3
Gorna Oryakhovitsa BG 17 D6
Gornja Gorevnica SRB 127 D2
Gornja Ploča HR 137 A4
Gornja Radgona SLO 110 C2
Gornja Sabanta SRB 127 D3
Gornja Trešnjevica SRB 127 C2
Gornja Tuzla BIH 125 C4
Gornje Polje CG 139 C4
Gornje Ratkovo BIH 124 C2
Gornji Grad SLO 123 A3
Gornji Humac HR 138 B2
Gornji Jasenjani BIH 139 B3
Gornji Kamengrad BIH 124 C2
Gornji Kneginec HR 124 A2
Gornji Kosinj HR 123 C4
Gornji Milanovac SRB 127 C2
Gornji Podgradci BIH 124 B3
Gornji Ravno BIH 138 B3
Gornji Sjenicak HR 124 B1
Gornji Vakuf BIH 138 B3
Górno PL 87 B4
Görömböly H 113 A4
Górowo Iławeckie PL 69 A5
Gorran Haven GB 42 B2
Gorredijk NL 70 A3
Gorron F 88 B3
Gorseinon GB 39 C2
Gort IRL 28 A3
Gortin GB 27 B3
Görzke D 73 B5
Gorzkowice PL 86 A3
Górzno, *Kujawsko-Pomorskie* PL 77 A4
Górzno, *Zachodnio-Pomorskie* PL 75 A4
Gorzów Śląski PL 86 A2
Gorzów Wielkopolski PL 75 B4
Górzyca PL 74 B3
Gorzyce PL 98 B2
Górzyn, *Lubuskie* PL 84 A2
Gorzyń, *Wielkopolskie* PL 75 B4
Gorzyno PL 68 A2
Gosaldo I 121 A4
Gosau A 109 B4
Gosberton GB 41 C3
Gościcino PL 68 A3
Gościęcin PL 86 B2
Gościm PL 75 B4
Gościno PL 67 B4
Gosdorf A 110 C2
Gosforth GB 36 B3
Goslar D 82 A2
Goslice PL 77 B4
Gospič HR 137 A4
Gosport GB 44 C2
Goss Ilsede D 72 B3
Gössäter S 55 B4
Gossau CH 107 B4
Gössnitz D 83 B4
Gössweinstein D 95 B3
Gostivar MK 182 B2
Gostkow PL 77 C4
Göstling an der Ybbs A 110 B1
Gostomia PL 75 A5
Gostycyn PL 76 A2
Gostyń PL 85 A5
Gostynin PL 77 B4
Goszczyn PL 87 A4
Göta S 54 B3
Göteborg = Gothenburg S 60 B1
Götene S 55 B4
Gotha D 82 B2
Gothem S 57 C4
Gothenburg = Göteborg S 60 B1
Gotse Delchev BG 183 B5
Gottersdorf D 95 C4
Göttingen D 82 A1
Gottne S 200 C4
Götzis A 107 B4
Gouarec F 100 A2
Gouda NL 70 B1
Goudhurst GB 45 B4
Goumenissa GR 182 C4
Goura GR 184 B3
Gourdon F 129 B4
Gourgançon F 91 C4
Gourin F 100 A2
Gournay-en-Bray F 90 B1
Gourock GB 34 C3
Gouveia P 148 B2
Gouvy B 80 B1
Gouzeacourt F 90 A3
Gouzon F 116 A2
Govedari HR 138 C3
Govérnolo I 121 B3
Gowarczów PL 87 A4
Gowerton GB 39 C2
Gowidlino PL 68 A2
Gowran IRL 30 B1
Goyatz D 74 B3
Göynük, *Antalya* TR 189 C5
Göynük TR 187 B5
Gozdnica PL 84 A3
Gozdowo PL 77 B4
Gozee B 79 B4
Graal-Müritz D 65 B5
Grabenstätt D 109 B3
Grabhair GB 31 A2
Gråbo S 60 B2
Grabovac HR 138 B2
Grabovac SRB 127 C2
Grabovci SRB 127 C1
Grabow D 73 A4
Grabów PL 77 B4
Grabow nad Pilicą PL 87 A5
Grabów nad Prosną PL 86 A2
Grabowno PL 76 A2
Grabs CH 107 B4
Gračac HR 138 A1
Gračanica BIH 125 C4
Graçay F 103 B3
Grad SLO 111 C3
Gradac BIH 139 C4
Gradac CG 139 B5
Gradac HR 138 B3
Gradačac BIH 125 C4
Gradec HR 124 B2
Gradefes E 142 B1
Grades A 110 C1
Gradil P 154 C1
Gradina CG 139 B5
Gradina HR 124 B3
Gradisca d'Isonzo I 122 B2
Gradište HR 125 B4
Grado E 141 A4
Grado I 122 B2
Grærup Strand DK 59 C1
Græsted DK 61 C2
Grafenau D 96 C1
Gräfenberg D 95 B3
Gräfenhainichen D 83 A4
Grafenschlag A 97 C3
Grafenstein A 110 C1
Gräfenthal D 82 B3
Grafentonna D 82 A2
Grafenwöhr D 95 B3
Grafing D 108 A2
Grafling D 95 C4
Gräfsnäs S 54 B3
Gragnano I 170 C2
Grahovo SLO 122 A2
Graiguenamanagh IRL 30 B2
Grain GB 45 B4
Grainau D 108 B2
Graja de Iniesta E 158 B2
Grajera E 151 A4
Gram DK 59 C2
Gramais A 108 B1
Gramat F 129 B4
Gramatneusiedl A 111 A3
Grambow D 74 A3
Grammichele I 177 B3
Gramsh AL 182 C2
Gramzow D 74 A3
Gran N 48 B2
Granada E 163 A4
Granard IRL 27 C3
Grañas E 140 A3
Granátula de Calatrava E 157 B4
Grancey-le-Château F 105 B4
Grand-Champ F 100 B3
Grand Couronne F 89 A5
Grand-Fougeray F 101 B4
Grandas de Salime E 141 A4
Grandcamp-Maisy F 88 A2
Grândola P 160 A1
Grandpré F 91 B4
Grandrieu B 79 B4
Grandrieu F 117 C3
Grandson CH 106 C1
Grandvillars F 106 B1
Grandvilliers F 90 B1
Grañén E 145 C3
Grangärde S 50 B1
Grange IRL 26 B2
Grange-over-Sands GB 36 B4
Grangemouth GB 35 B4
Granges-de Crouhens F 145 B4
Granges-sur-Vologne F 106 A1
Grängesberg S 50 B1
Gräningen D 73 B5
Granitola-Torretta I 176 B1
Granja, *Évora* P 155 C3
Granja, *Porto* P 148 A1
Granja de Moreruela E 142 C1
Granja de Torrehermosa E 156 B2
Gränna S 55 B5
Grannäs, *Västerbotten* S 195 E7
Grannäs, *Västerbotten* S 195 E8
Granö S 200 B5
Granollers E 147 C3
Granowiec PL 85 A5
Granowo PL 75 B5
Gransee D 74 A2
Gransherad N 53 A5
Grantham GB 40 C3
Grantown-on-Spey GB 32 D3
Grantshouse GB 35 C5
Granville F 88 B2
Granvin N 46 B3
Gräsås S 60 C2
Grasbakken N 193 B12
Grasberg D 72 A2
Grasmere GB 36 B3
Gräsmyr S 200 C5
Grasö S 51 B5
Grassano I 172 B2
Grassau D 109 B3
Grasse F 132 B2
Grassington GB 40 A2
Gråsten DK 64 B2
Grästorp S 54 B3
Gratkorn A 110 B2
Gråträsk S 196 D2
Gratwein A 110 B2
Graulhet F 129 C4
Graus E 145 B4
Grávalos E 144 B2
Gravberget N 49 B4
Grave NL 80 A1
Gravedona I 120 A2
Gravelines F 78 A2
Gravellona Toce I 119 B5
Gravendal S 50 B1
Gravens DK 59 C2
Gravesend GB 45 B4
Graveson F 131 B3
Gravina in Púglia I 172 B2
Gray F 105 B4
Grayrigg GB 37 B4
Grays GB 45 B4
Grayshott GB 44 B3
Graz A 110 B2
Grazalema E 162 B2
Grążawy PL 69 B4
Grazzano Visconti I 120 C2
Greåker N 54 A2
Great Dunmow GB 45 B4
Great Malvern GB 39 B4
Great Torrington GB 42 B2
Great Waltham GB 45 B4
Great Yarmouth GB 41 C5
Grebbestad S 54 B2
Grebenstein D 81 A5
Grębocice PL 85 A4
Grębocin PL 76 A3
Greding D 95 B3
Gredstedbro DK 59 C1
Greenhead GB 37 B4
Greenisland GB 27 B5
Greenlaw GB 35 C5
Greenock GB 34 C3
Greenway GB 39 C2
Greenwich GB 45 B4
Grefrath D 80 A2
Greifenburg A 109 C4
Greiffenberg D 74 A2
Greifswald D 66 B2
Grein A 110 A1
Greipstad N 53 B3
Greiz D 83 B4
Grenaa DK 58 B3
Grenade F 129 C4
Grenade-sur-l'Adour F 128 C2
Grenchen CH 106 B2
Grendi N 53 B3
Grenivík IS 191 B7
Grenoble F 118 B2
Gréoux-les-Bains F 132 B1
Gresenhorst D 66 B1
Gressoney-la-Trinité I 119 B4
Gressoney-St.-Jean I 119 B4
Gressthal D 82 B2
Gressvik N 54 A1
Gresten A 110 B2
Gretna GB 36 B3
Greussen D 82 A2
Greve in Chianti I 135 B4
Greven, *Mecklenburg-Vorpommern* D 73 A3
Greven, *Nordrhein-Westfalen* D 71 B4
Grevena GR 182 C3
Grevenbroich D 80 A2
Grevenbrück D 81 A4
Grevenmacher L 92 B2
Grevesmühlen D 65 C4
Grevestrand DK 61 D2
Grevie S 61 C2
Greystoke GB 36 B4
Greystones IRL 30 A2
Grez-Doiceau B 79 B4
Grez-en-Bouère F 102 B1
Grèzec F 129 B4
Grezzana I 121 B4
Grgar SLO 122 A2
Grgurevci SRB 127 B1
Gries A 108 B2
Gries in Sellrain A 108 B2
Griesbach D 96 C1
Griesheim D 93 B4
Grieskirchen A 109 A4
Griffen A 110 C1
Grignan F 131 A3
Grignano I 122 B2
Grigno I 121 A4
Grignols F 128 B2
Grignon F 118 B3
Grijota E 142 B2
Grijpskerk NL 71 A3
Grillby S 56 A3
Grimaud F 132 B2
Grimbergen B 79 B4
Grimma D 83 A4
Grimmen D 66 B2
Grimmialp CH 106 C2
Grimsås S 60 B3
Grimsby GB 41 B3
Grimslöv S 62 B2
Grímsstaðir IS 191 B9
Grimstad N 53 B4
Grimstorp S 62 A2
Grindavík IS 190 D3
Grindelwald CH 106 C3
Grindheim N 52 B3
Grindsted DK 59 C1
Griñón E 151 B4
Gripenberg S 62 A2
Gripsholm S 56 A3
Grisolles F 129 C4
Grisslehamn S 51 B5
Gritley GB 33 C4
Grizebeck GB 36 B3
Grndina BIH 124 C2
Gröbming A 109 B4
Gröbzig D 83 A3
Grocka SRB 127 C2
Gröditz D 83 A5
Gródki PL 77 A5
Grodków PL 85 B5
Grodziec PL 76 B3
Grodzisk Mazowiecki PL 77 B5
Groenlo NL 71 B3
Groesbeek NL 80 A1
Grohote HR 138 B2
Groitzsch D 83 A4
Groix F 100 B2
Grójec PL 77 C5
Grom PL 77 A5
Gromiljca BIH 139 B4
Grömitz D 65 B3
Gromnik PL 99 B4
Gromo I 120 B2
Gronau, *Niedersachsen* D 72 B2
Gronau, *Nordrhein-Westfalen* D 71 B4
Grønbjerg DK 59 B1
Grönenbach D 107 B5
Grong N 199 A9
Grönhögen S 63 B4
Groningen D 73 C4
Groningen NL 71 A3
Grønnestrand DK 58 A2
Grono CH 120 A2
Grönskåra S 62 A3
Grootegast NL 71 A3
Gropello Cairoli I 120 B1
Grorud N 48 C2
Grósio I 120 A3
Grošnica SRB 127 D2
Gross Beeren D 74 B2
Gross Berkel D 72 B2
Gross-botwar D 94 C1
Gross-Dölln D 74 A2
Gross-Gerau D 93 B4
Gross-hartmansdorf D 83 B5
Gross Kreutz D 74 B1
Gross Lafferde D 72 B3
Gross Leutheb D 74 B3
Gross Muckrow D 74 B3
Gross Oesingen D 72 B3
Gross Reken D 80 A3
Gross Sarau D 65 C3
Gross Särchen D 84 A2
Gross Schönebeck D 74 B2
Gross Umstadt D 93 B4
Gross Warnow D 73 A4
Gross-Weikersdorf A 97 C3
Gross-Welle D 73 A5
Gross Wokern D 65 C5
Grossalmerode D 82 A1
Grossarl A 109 B4
Grossbodungen D 82 A2
Grossburgwedel D 72 B2
Grosschönau D 84 B2
Grossenbrode D 65 B4
Grossenehrich D 82 A2
Grossengottern D 82 A2
Grossenhain D 83 A5
Grossenkneten D 71 B5
Grossenlüder D 81 B5
Grossensee D 72 A3
Grossenzersdorf A 111 A3
Grosseto I 135 C4
Grossgerungs A 96 C2
Grossglobnitz A 97 C3
Grosshabersdorf D 94 B2
Grossharras A 97 C4
Grosshöchstetten CH 106 C2
Grosskrut A 97 C4
Grosslohra D 82 A2
Grossmehring D 95 C3
Grossostheim D 93 B5
Grosspertholz A 96 C2
Grosspetersdorf A 111 B3
Grosspostwitz D 84 A2
Grossraming A 110 B1
Grossräschen D 84 A2
Grossrinderfeld D 94 B1
Grossröhrsdorf D 84 A2
Grossschirma D 83 B5
Grossschweinbarth A 97 C4
Grosssiegharts A 97 C3
Grosssölk A 109 B4
Grosswarasdorf A 111 B3
Grosswilfersdorf A 110 B2
Grostenquin F 92 C2
Grosuplje SLO 123 B3
Grotli N 198 C4
Grötlingbo S 57 C4
Grottáglie I 173 B3
Grottaminarda I 170 B3
Grottammare I 136 C2
Grotte di Castro I 168 A1
Grotteria I 175 C2
Gróttole I 172 B2
Grouw NL 70 A2
Grov N 194 B8
Grova N 53 A4
Grove E 140 B2
Grua N 48 B2
Grube D 65 B4
Grubišno Polje HR 124 B3
Grude BIH 138 B3
Grudovo BG 17 D7
Grudusk PL 77 A5
Grudziądz PL 69 B3
Grue N 49 B4
Gruissan F 130 B2
Grullos E 141 A4
Grumo Áppula I 171 B4
Grums S 55 A4
Grünau im Almtal A 109 B4
Grünberg D 81 B4
Grünburg A 110 B1
Grundarfjörður IS 190 C2
Gründau D 81 B5
Gründelhardt D 94 B1
Grundforsen S 49 A4
Grundlsee A 109 B4
Grundsund S 54 B2
Grunewald D 84 A1
Grungedal N 53 A3
Grunow D 74 B3
Grünstadt D 93 B4
Gruvberget S 50 A3
Gruyères CH 106 C2
Gruža SRB 127 D2
Grybów PL 99 B4
Grycksbo S 50 B2
Gryfice PL 67 C4
Gryfino PL 74 A3
Gryfów Śląski PL 84 A3
Gryllefjord N 194 A8
Grymyr N 48 B2
Gryt S 56 B2
Grytgöl S 56 B1
Grythyttan S 55 A5
Grytnäs S 57 B3
Grzmiąca PL 68 B1
Grzybno PL 74 A3
Grzywna PL 76 A3
Gschnitz A 108 B2
Gschwend D 94 C1
Gstaad CH 106 C2
Gsteig CH 119 A4
Guadahortuna E 163 A4
Guadalajara E 151 B4
Guadalaviar E 152 B2
Guadalcanal E 156 B2
Guadalcázar E 162 A3
Guadalix de la Sierra E 151 B4
Guadálmez E 156 B3
Guadalupe E 156 A2
Guadamur E 151 C3
Guadarrama E 151 B3
Guadiaro E 162 B2
Guadix E 164 B1
Guagnano I 173 B3
Guagno F 180 A1
Guajar-Faragüit E 163 B4
Gualchos E 163 B4
Gualdo Tadino I 136 B1
Gualtieri I 121 C3
Guarcino I 169 B3
Guarda P 149 B2
Guardamar del Segura E 165 A4
Guardão P 148 B1
Guardavalle I 175 C2
Guardea I 168 A2
Guárdia I 172 B1
Guárdia Sanframondi I 170 B2
Guardiagrele I 169 A4
Guardiarégia I 170 B2
Guardias Viejas E 164 C2
Guardiola de Bergueda E 147 B2
Guardo E 142 B2
Guareña E 156 B1
Guaro E 162 B3
Guarromán E 157 B4
Guasila I 179 C3
Guastalla I 121 C3
Gubbhögen S 199 A12
Gúbbio I 136 B1
Guben D 74 C3
Gubin PL 74 C3
Gudå N 199 B8
Gudavac BIH 124 C2
Guddal N 46 A2
Güderup DK 64 B2
Gudhem S 55 B4
Gudhjem DK 67 A3
Gudovac HR 124 B2
Gudow D 73 A3
Güdül TR 187 B7
Gudvangen N 46 B3
Guebwiller F 106 B2
Guéjar-Sierra E 163 A4
Guéméné-Penfao F 101 B4
Guéméné-sur-Scorff F 100 A2
Güeñes E 143 A3
Guer F 101 B3
Guérande F 101 B3
Guéret F 116 A1
Guérigny F 104 B2
Guesa E 144 B2
Gueugnon F 104 C3
Guglionesi I 170 B2
Gühlen Glienicke D 74 A1
Guia P 154 B2
Guichen F 101 B4
Guidizzolo I 121 B3
Guidónia-Montecélio I 168 B2
Guiglia I 135 A3
Guignes F 90 C2
Guijo E 156 B3
Guijo de Coria E 149 B3
Guijo de Santa Bábera E 150 B2
Guijuelo E 150 B2
Guildford GB 44 B3
Guillaumes F 132 A2
Guillena E 162 A1
Guillestre F 118 C3
Guillos F 128 B2
Guilsfield GB 38 B3
Guilvinec F 100 B1
Guimarães P 148 A1
Guincho P 154 C1
Guînes F 78 B1
Guingamp F 100 A2
Guipavas F 100 A1
Guisborough GB 37 B5
Guiscard F 90 B3
Guiscriff F 100 A2
Guise F 91 B3
Guisona E 147 C2
Guitiriz E 140 A3
Guîtres F 128 A2
Gujan-Mestras F 128 B1
Gulbene LV 8 D5
Gulçayır TR 187 C6
Guldborg DK 65 B4
Gullabo S 63 B3
Gullane GB 35 B5
Gullbrå N 46 B3
Gullbrandstorp S 61 C2
Gulleråsen S 50 A2
Gullhaug N 53 A6
Gullringen S 62 A3
Gullspång S 55 B5
Gullstein N 198 B5
Güllük TR 188 B2
Gülnar TR 23 C7
Gülpınar TR 186 C1
Gülşehir TR 23 B8
Gulsvik N 48 B1
Gülübovo BG 183 A7
Gumiel de Hizán E 143 C3
Gummersbach D 81 A3
Gümüldür TR 188 A2
Gümüşhaciköy TR 23 A8
Gümüşova TR 187 B5
Gundel-fingen D 106 A2
Gundelfingen D 94 C2
Gundelsheim D 93 B5
Gunderschoffen F 93 C3
Gundertshausen A 109 A3
Gundinci HR 125 B4
Gündoğmuş TR 189 C7
Güney, *Burdur* TR 189 B4
Güney, *Denizli* TR 188 A4
Gunja HR 125 C4
Günlüce TR 188 C3
Gunnarn S 195 E8
Gunnarsbyn S 196 C4
Gunnarskog S 49 C4
Gunnebo S 62 A4
Gunnislake GB 42 B2
Günselsdorf A 111 B3
Guntersblum D 93 B4
Guntersdorf A 97 C4

Guntin E 140 B3
Günyüzü TR 187 C6
Günzburg D 94 C2
Gunzenhausen D 94 B2
Güre, *Balıkesir* TR 186 C1
Güre, *Uşak* TR 186 D4
Gurk A 110 C1
Gurrea de Gállego E 144 B3
Gürsu TR 186 B4
Gušće HR 124 B2
Gusev RUS 12 A5
Gúspini I 179 C2
Gusselby S 56 A1
Güssing A 111 B3
Gusswerk A 110 B2
Gustav Adolf S 49 B5
Gustavsberg S 57 A4
Gustavsfors S 54 A3
Güstrow D 65 C5
Gusum S 56 B2
Gutcher GB 33 A5
Gutenstein A 110 B2
Gütersloh D 81 A4
Guttannen CH 106 C3
Guttaring A 110 C1
Guttau D 84 A2
Güttingen CH 107 B4
Gützkow D 66 C2
Guzów PL 77 B5
Gvardeysk RUS 12 A4
Gvarv N 53 A5
Gvozd CG 139 C5
Gvozdansko HR 124 B2
Gwda Wielka PL 68 B1
Gwennap GB 42 B1
Gy F 105 B4
Gyál H 112 B3
Gyarmat H 111 B4
Gyé-sur-Seine F 104 A3
Gyékényes H 124 A3
Gyljen S 196 C5
Gylling DK 59 C3
Gyoma H 113 C4
Gyömöre H 111 B4
Gyömrö H 112 B3
Gyón H 112 B3
Gyöngyfa H 125 B3
Gyöngyös H 113 B3
Gyöngyöspata H 113 B3
Gyönk H 112 C2
Györ H 111 B4
Györszemere H 111 B4
Gypsera CH 106 C2
Gysinge S 51 B3
Gyttorp S 55 A5
Gyula H 113 C5
Gyulafirátót H 112 B1
Gyulaj H 112 C2

H

Haacht B 79 B4
Haag, *Nieder Östereich* A 110 A1
Haag, *Ober Östereich* A 109 A4
Haag D 108 A3
Haaksbergen NL 71 B3
Haamstede NL 79 A3
Haan D 80 A3
Haapajärvi FIN 3 E9
Haapsalu EST 8 C3
Haarlem NL 70 B1
Habas F 128 C2
Habay B 92 B1
Habo S 62 A2
Håbol S 54 B3
Habry CZ 97 B3
Habsheim F 106 B2
Hachenburg D 81 B3
Hacıbektaş TR 23 B8
Hacılar TR 23 B8
Hacinas E 143 C3
Hackås S 199 C11
Hacketstown IRL 30 B2
Hackthorpe GB 37 B4
Hadamar D 81 B4
Hädanberg S 200 C4
Haddington GB 35 C5
Hadersdorf am Kamp A 97 C3
Haderslev DK 59 C2
Haderup DK 59 B1
Hadım TR 23 C7
Hadleigh, *Essex* GB 45 B4
Hadleigh, *Suffolk* GB 45 A4
Hadlow GB 45 B4
Hadmersleben D 73 B4
Hadsten DK 59 B3
Hadsund DK 58 B3
Hadžići BIH 139 B4
Hægebostad N 52 B3
Hægeland N 53 B3
Hafnarfjörður IS 190 C4
Hafnir IS 190 D3
Hafslo N 47 A4
Haganj HR 124 B2
Hagby S 63 B4
Hage D 71 A4
Hagen, *Niedersachsen* D 72 A1
Hagen, *Nordrhein-Westfalen* D 80 A3
Hagenbach D 93 B4
Hagenow D 73 A4
Hagetmau F 128 C2
Hagfors S 49 B5
Häggenås S 199 B11
Hagondange F 92 B2
Hagsta S 51 B4
Haguenau F 93 C3
Hahnbach D 95 B3
Hahnslätten D 81 B4
Hahót H 111 C3
Haiger D 81 B4
Haigerloch D 93 C4
Hailsham GB 45 C4
Hainburg A 111 A3
Hainfeld A 110 A2
Hainichen D 83 B5
Hajdúböszörmény H 113 B5
Hajdučica SRB 126 B2
Hajdúdorogo H 113 B5
Hajdúnánás H 113 B5
Hajdúszoboszló H 113 B5
Hajnáčka SK 113 A3
Hajnówka PL 13 B5
Hajós H 112 C3
Håkafot S 199 A11
Hakkas S 196 C4
Håksberg S 50 B2
Halaszi H 111 B4
Halberstadt D 82 A3
Halberton GB 43 B3
Hald Ege DK 58 B2
Haldem D 71 B5
Halden N 54 A2
Haldensleben D 73 B4
Halenbeck D 73 A5
Halesowen GB 40 C1
Halesworth GB 45 A5
Halfing D 109 B3
Halhjem N 46 B2
Håliden S 49 B5
Halifax GB 40 B2
Häljelöt S 56 B2
Halkida GR 185 A4
Halkirk GB 32 C3
Hall S 57 C4
Hall in Tirol A 108 B2
Hälla S 200 C3
Hallabro S 63 B3
Hällabrottet S 56 A1
Halland GB 45 C4
Hällaryd, *Blekinge* S 63 B2
Hallaryd, *Kronoberg* S 61 C3
Hällberga S 56 A2
Hällbybrunn S 56 A2
Halle B 79 B4
Halle, *Nordrhein-Westfalen* D 72 B1
Halle, *Sachsen-Anhalt* D 83 A3
Hålleberga S 62 B3
Hällefors S 55 A5
Hälleforsnäs S 56 A2
Hallein A 109 B4
Hällekis S 55 B4
Hallen, *Jämtland* S 199 B11
Hållen, *Uppsala* S 51 B4
Hallenberg D 81 A4
Hällestad S 56 B1
Hällevadsholm S 54 B2
Hällevik S 63 B2
Hälleviksstrand S 54 B2
Hallingby N 48 B2
Hallingeberg S 62 A4
Hallingen N 47 B6
Hällnäs, *Norrbotten* S 195 D9
Hållnäs, *Uppsala* S 51 B4
Hällnäs, *Västerbotten* S 200 B5
Hallormsstaður IS 191 B11
Hallsberg S 56 A1
Hållsta S 56 A2
Hallstahammar S 56 A2
Hallstatt A 109 B4
Hallstavik S 51 B5
Halltorp S 63 B4
Halluin F 78 B3
Hallviken S 199 B12
Hallworthy GB 42 B2
Halmstad S 61 C2
Hals DK 58 A3
Halsa N 198 B5
Halstead GB 45 B4
Haltdalen N 199 C8
Haltern D 80 A3
Haltwhistle GB 37 B4
Halvarsgårdarna S 50 B2
Halver D 80 A3
Halvrimmen DK 58 A2
Ham F 90 B3
Hamar N 48 B3
Hamarhaug N 46 B2
Hamarøy N 194 B6
Hambach F 92 B3
Hambergen D 72 A1
Hambergsund S 54 B2
Hambledon GB 44 C2
Hambuhren D 72 B2
Hamburg D 72 A3
Hamdibey TR 186 C2
Hamdorf D 64 B2
Hämeenlinna FIN 8 B4
Hameln = Hamlin D 72 B2
Hamersleben D 73 B4
Hamidiye TR 187 C5
Hamilton GB 36 A2
Hamina FIN 8 B5
Hamlagrø N 46 B3
Hamlin = Hameln D 72 B2
Hamm D 81 A3
Hammar S 55 B5
Hammarland FIN 51 B6
Hammarö S 55 A4
Hammarstrand S 200 C2
Hamme B 79 A4
Hammel DK 59 B2
Hammelburg D 82 B1
Hammelspring D 74 A2
Hammenhög S 66 A3
Hammerdal S 199 B12
Hammerfest N 192 B7
Hammershøj DK 58 B2
Hammerum DK 59 B2
Hamminkeln D 80 A2
Hamnavoe GB 33 A5
Hamneda S 60 C3
Hamningberg N 193 B14
Hamoir B 80 B1
Hamont B 80 A1
Hámor H 113 A4
Hamra, *Gävleborg* S 199 D12
Hamra, *Gotland* S 57 D4
Hamrångefjärden S 51 B4
Hamstreet GB 45 B4
Hamsund N 194 B6
Han TR 187 C5
Han Knežica BIH 124 B2
Han Pijesak BIH 139 A4
Hanaskog S 61 C4
Hanau D 81 B4
Händelöp S 62 A4
Handlová SK 98 C2
Hanerau-Hademarschen D 64 B2
Hånger S 60 B3
Hanhimaa FIN 197 B8
Hanken S 55 B5
Hankensbüttel D 73 B3
Hanko FIN 8 C3
Hannover D 72 B2
Hannut B 79 B5
Hansnes N 192 C3
Hanstedt D 72 A3
Hanstholm DK 58 A1
Hantsavichy BY 13 B7
Hanušovice CZ 85 B4
Haparanda S 196 D7
Haradok BY 13 A8
Harads S 196 C4
Häradsbäck S 63 B2
Häradsbygden S 50 B2
Harbo S 51 B4
Harboør DK 58 B1
Harburg, *Bayern* D 94 C2
Harburg, *Hamburg* D 72 A2
Hårby DK 59 C3
Harc H 112 C2
Hardegarijp NL 70 A2
Hardegsen D 82 A1
Hardelot Plage F 78 B1
Hardenbeck D 74 A2
Hardenberg NL 71 B3
Harderwijk NL 70 B2
Hardheim D 94 B1
Hardt D 106 A3
Hareid N 198 C3
Haren D 71 B4
Haren NL 71 A3
Harestua N 48 B2
Harfleur F 89 A4
Harg S 51 B5
Hargicourt F 90 B3
Hargnies F 91 A4
Hargshamn S 51 B5
Härja S 55 B4
Harkány H 125 B4
Härkeberga S 56 A3
Harkebrügge D 71 A4
Harlech GB 38 B2
Harleston GB 45 A5
Hårlev DK 65 A5
Harlingen NL 70 A2
Harlösa S 61 D3
Harlow GB 45 B4
Harmancık TR 186 C4
Harmånger S 200 E3
Härnevi S 56 A3
Härnösand S 200 D3
Haro E 143 B4
Haroldswick GB 33 A6
Háromfa H 124 A3
Haroué F 92 C2
Harpenden GB 44 B3
Harplinge S 60 C2
Harpstedt D 72 B1
Harrogate GB 40 A2
Harrow GB 44 B3
Härryda S 60 B2
Harsefeld D 72 A2
Harsewinkel D 71 C5
Hârşova RO 17 C7
Harstad N 194 B7
Harsum D 72 B2
Harsvik N 199 A7
Harta H 112 C3
Hartberg A 110 B2
Hartburn GB 37 A5
Hartennes F 90 B3
Hartest GB 45 A4
Hartha D 83 A4
Hartland GB 42 B2
Hartlepool GB 37 B5
Hartmanice CZ 96 B1
Hartmannsdorf A 110 B2
Harvassdal N 195 E5
Harwell GB 44 B2
Harwich GB 45 B5
Harzgerode D 82 A3
Häselgehr A 108 B1
Haselünne D 71 B4
Hasköy TR 186 A1
Haslach D 106 A3
Haslach an der Mühl A 96 C2
Hasle DK 67 A3
Haslemere GB 44 B3
Haslev DK 65 A4
Hasloch D 94 B1
Hasparren F 144 A2
Hassela S 200 D2
Hasselfelde D 82 A2
Hasselfors S 55 A5
Hasselt B 79 B5
Hasselt NL 70 B3
Hassfurt D 94 A2
Hassleben D 74 A2
Hässleholm S 61 C3
Hasslö S 63 B3
Hassloch D 93 B4
Hästbo S 51 B4
Hastersboda FIN 51 B7
Hästholmen S 55 B5
Hastière-Lavaux B 79 B4
Hastigrow GB 32 C3
Hastings GB 45 C4
Hästveda S 61 C3
Hasvik N 192 B6
Hatfield, *Hertfordshire* GB 44 B3
Hatfield, *South Yorkshire* GB 40 B3
Hatherleigh GB 42 B2
Hathersage GB 40 B2
Hatlestrand N 46 B2
Hattem NL 70 B3
Hatten D 71 A5
Hatten F 93 C3
Hattfjelldal N 195 E4
Hatting DK 59 C2
Hattingen D 80 A3
Hattstadt F 106 A2
Hattstedt D 64 B2
Hatvan H 112 B3
Hatvik N 46 B2
Hau D 80 A2
Haudainville F 92 B1
Hauganes IS 191 B7
Haugastøl N 47 B4
Hauge N 52 B2
Haugesund N 52 A1
Haughom N 52 B2
Haugsdal N 46 B2
Haugsdorf A 97 C4
Haukedal N 46 A3
Haukeland N 46 B2
Haukeligrend N 52 A3
Haukeliseter N 52 A3
Haukipudas FIN 3 D9
Haulerwijk NL 71 A3
Haunersdorf D 95 C4
Haus N 46 B2
Hausach D 106 A3
Hausham D 108 B2
Hausmannstätten A 110 C2
Hausvik N 52 B2
Haut-Fays B 91 A5
Hautajärvi FIN 197 C12
Hautefort F 129 A4
Hauterives F 117 B5
Hauteville-Lompnès F 118 B2
Hautmont F 79 B3
Hautrage B 79 B3
Hauzenberg D 96 C1
Havant GB 44 C3
Havdhem S 57 C4
Havdrup DK 61 D2
Havelange B 79 B5
Havelberg D 73 B5
Havelte NL 70 B3
Haverfordwest GB 39 C2
Haverhill GB 45 A4
Havering GB 45 B4
Håverud S 54 B3
Havířov CZ 98 B2
Havixbeck D 71 C4
Havlíčkův Brod CZ 97 B3
Havndal DK 58 B3
Havneby DK 64 A1
Havnebyen DK 61 D1
Havnsø DK 61 D1
Havøysund N 193 A8
Havran TR 186 C2
Havrebjerg DK 61 D1
Havsa TR 186 A1
Havstenssund S 54 B2
Havza TR 23 A8
Hawes GB 37 B4
Hawick GB 35 C5
Hawkhurst GB 45 B4
Hawkinge GB 45 B5
Haxey GB 40 B3
Hay-on-Wye GB 39 B3
Hayange F 92 B2
Haydarlı TR 189 A5
Haydon Bridge GB 37 B4
Hayle GB 42 B1
Haymana TR 187 C7
Hayrabolu TR 186 A2
Haysyn UA 13 D8
Hayvoron UA 13 D8
Haywards Heath GB 44 C3
Hazebrouck F 78 B2
Hazlov CZ 83 B4
Heacham GB 41 C4
Headcorn GB 45 B4
Headford IRL 28 A2
Heanor GB 40 B2
Héas F 145 B4
Heathfield GB 45 C4
Hebden Bridge GB 40 B1
Heberg S 60 C2
Heby S 51 C3
Hechingen D 93 C4
Hechlingen D 94 C2
Hecho E 144 B3
Hechtel B 79 A5
Hechthausen D 72 A2
Heckelberg D 74 B2
Heckington GB 41 C3
Hecklingen D 82 A3
Hed S 56 A1
Hedalen N 48 B1
Hedared S 60 B2
Heddal N 53 A5
Hédé F 101 A4
Hede S 199 C10
Hedekas S 54 B2
Hedemora S 50 B2
Hedenäset S 196 C6
Hedensted DK 59 C2
Hedersleben D 82 A3
Hedesunda S 51 B4
Hedge End GB 44 C2
Hedon GB 41 B3
Heede D 71 B4
Heek D 71 B4
Heemstede NL 70 B1
Heerde NL 70 B3
Heerenveen NL 70 B2
Heerhugowaard NL 70 B1
Heerlen NL 80 B1
Heeze NL 80 A1
Heggenes N 47 A6
Hegra N 199 B8
Hegyeshalom H 111 B4
Hegyközség H 111 B3
Heia N 199 A9
Heide D 64 B2
Heidelberg D 93 B4
Heiden D 80 A2
Heidenau D 84 B1
Heidenheim D 94 C2
Heidenreichstein A 97 C3
Heikendorf D 64 B3
Heikkilä FIN 197 C12
Heilam GB 32 C2
Heiland N 53 B4
Heilbad Heiligenstadt D 82 A2
Heilbronn D 93 B5
Heiligenblut A 109 B3
Heiligendamn D 65 B4
Heiligendorf D 73 B3
Heiligengrabe D 73 A5
Heiligenhafen D 65 B3
Heiligenhaus D 80 A2
Heiligenkreuz A 111 C3
Heiligenstadt D 94 B3
Heiloo NL 70 B1
Heilsbronn D 94 B2
Heim N 198 B6
Heimburg D 82 A2
Heimdal N 199 B7
Heinerscheid L 92 A2
Heinersdorf D 74 B3
Heining D 96 C1
Heiningen D 94 C1
Heinola FIN 8 B5
Heinsberg D 80 A2
Heist-op-den-Berg B 79 A4
Hejde S 57 C4
Hejdeby S 57 C4
Hejls DK 59 C2
Hejnice CZ 84 B3
Hel PL 69 A3
Helchteren B 79 A5
Heldburg D 82 B2
Heldrungen D 82 A3
Helechosa E 156 A3
Helensburgh GB 34 B3
Helfenberg A 96 C2
Helgen N 53 A5
Helgeroa N 53 B5
Hella IS 190 D5
Hella N 46 A3
Helland N 194 B7
Hellas S 55 B3
Helle N 52 B2
Helleland N 52 B2
Hellendoorn NL 71 B3
Hellenthal D 80 B2
Hellesøy N 46 B1
Hellesylt N 198 C3
Hellevoetsluis NL 79 A4
Helligskogen N 192 C4
Hellín E 158 C2
Hellissandur IS 190 C2
Hellnar IS 190 C2
Hellum DK 58 A3
Hellvi S 57 C4
Hellvik N 52 B1
Helm-brechts D 83 B3
Helmond NL 80 A1
Helmsdale GB 32 C3
Helmsley GB 37 B5
Helmstedt D 73 B3
Hel'pa SK 99 C3
Helsa D 82 A1
Helsby GB 38 A4
Helsingborg S 61 C2
Helsinge DK 61 C2
Helsingør DK 61 C2
Helsinki FIN 8 B4
Helston GB 42 B1
Hemau D 95 B3
Hemavan S 195 E6
Hemel Hempstead GB 44 B3
Hemer D 81 A3
Héming F 92 C2
Hemmet DK 59 C1
Hemmingstedt D 64 B2
Hemmoor D 64 C2
Hemnes N 54 A2
Hemnesberget N 195 D4
Hemse S 57 C4
Hemsedal N 47 B5
Hemslingen D 72 A2
Hemsworth GB 40 B2
Hen N 48 B2
Henån S 54 B2
Hendaye F 144 A2
Hendek TR 187 B5
Hendungen D 82 B2
Henfield GB 44 C3
Hengelo, *Gelderland* NL 71 B3
Hengelo, *Overijssel* NL 71 B3
Hengersberg D 95 C5
Hengoed GB 39 C3
Hénin-Beaumont F 78 B2
Henley-on-Thames GB 44 B3
Hennan S 200 D1
Henne Strand DK 59 C1
Henneberg D 82 B2
Hennebont F 100 B2
Hennigsdorf D 74 B2
Hennset N 198 B5
Hennstedt, *Schleswig-Holstein* D 64 B2
Hennstedt, *Schleswig-Holstein* D 64 B2
Henrichemont F 103 B4
Henryków PL 85 B5
Henrykowo PL 69 A5
Henså s N 47 A5
Henstedt-Ulzburg D 64 C2
Heppenheim D 93 B4
Herad, *Buskerud* N 47 B6
Herad, *Vest-Agder* N 52 B2
Heradsbygd N 48 B3
Heraklion = Iraklio GR 185 D6
Herálec CZ 97 B4
Herand N 46 B3
Herbault F 103 B3
Herbern D 81 A3
Herbertstown IRL 29 B3
Herbeumont B 91 B5
Herbignac F 101 B3
Herbisse F 91 C4
Herbitzheim F 92 B3
Herbolzheim D 106 A2
Herborn D 81 B4
Herbrechtingen D 94 C2
Herby PL 86 B2
Herceg-Novi CG 16 D3
Hercegovać HR 124 B3
Hercegszántó H 125 B4
Herchen D 80 B3
Heréd H 112 B3
Hereford GB 39 B4
Herefoss N 53 B4
Hereke TR 187 B4
Herencia E 157 A4
Herend H 111 B4
Herent B 79 B4
Herentals B 79 A4
Hérépian F 130 B2
Herfølge DK 61 D2
Herford D 72 B1
Herguijuela E 156 A2
Héric F 101 B4
Héricourt F 106 B1
Héricourt-en-Caux F 89 A4
Hérimoncourt F 106 B1
Heringsdorf D 65 B4
Herisau CH 107 B4
Hérisson F 103 C4
Herk-de-Stad B 79 B5
Herlufmagle DK 65 A4
Hermagor A 109 C4
Hermannsburg D 72 B3
Hermansverk N 46 A3
Heřmanův Městec CZ 97 B3

Herment F 116 B2
Hermeskeil D 92 B2
Hermisende E 141 C4
Hermonville F 91 B3
Hermsdorf D 83 B3
Hernani E 144 A2
Hernansancho E 150 B3
Herne D 80 A3
Herne Bay GB 45 B5
Hernes N 48 B3
Herning DK 59 B1
Herøya N 53 A5
Herramelluri E 143 B3
Herräng S 51 B5
Herre N 53 A5
Herrenberg D 93 C4
Herrera E 162 A3
Herrera de Alcántara E 155 B3
Herrera de los Navarros E 152 A2
Herrera de Pisuerga E 142 B2
Herrera del Duque E 156 A2
Herrerias E 161 B2
Herreros del Suso E 150 B2
Herrestad S 54 B2
Herrhamra S 57 B3
Herritslev DK 65 B4
Herrlisheim F 93 C3
Herrljunga S 55 B4
Herrnhut D 84 A2
Herrsching D 108 A2
Hersbruck D 95 B3
Hersby S 57 A4
Herscheid D 81 A3
Herselt B 79 A4
Herso GR 182 B4
Herstal B 80 B1
Herstmonceux GB 45 C4
Herten D 80 A3
Hertford GB 44 B3
Hervás E 149 B4
Hervik N 52 A1
Herxheim D 93 B4
Herzberg, *Brandenburg* D 74 B1
Herzberg, *Brandenburg* D 83 A5
Herzberg, *Niedersachsen* D 82 A2
Herzebrock D 81 A4
Herzfelde D 74 B2
Herzlake D 71 B4
Herzogenaurach D 94 B2
Herzogenbuchsee CH 106 B2
Herzogenburg A 110 A2
Herzsprung D 73 A5
Hesby N 52 A1
Hesdin F 78 B2
Hesel D 71 A4
Heskestad N 52 B2
Hessdalen N 199 C8
Hesselager DK 65 A3
Hesseng N 193 C13
Hessisch Lichtenau D 82 A1
Hessisch-Oldendorf D 72 B2
Hestra S 60 B3
Heswall GB 38 A3
Hetlevik N 46 B2
Hettange-Grande F 92 B2
Hetton-le-Hole GB 37 B5
Hettstedt D 82 A3
Heuchin F 78 B2
Heudicourt-sous-les-Côtes F 92 C1
Heunezel F 105 A5
Heuqueville F 89 A4
Heves H 113 B4
Héviz H 111 C4
Hexham GB 37 B4
Heysham GB 36 B4
Heytesbury GB 43 A4
Hidas H 125 A4
Hieflau A 110 B1
Hiendelaencina E 151 A5
Hiersac F 115 C4
High Bentham GB 37 B4
High Hesket GB 37 B4
High Wycombe GB 44 B3
Highclere GB 44 B2
Highley GB 39 B4
Higuera de Arjona E 157 C4
Higuera de Calatrava E 163 A3
Higuera de la Serena E 156 B2
Higuera de la Sierra E 161 B3
Higuera de Vargas E 155 C4
Higuera la Real E 161 A3
Higuers de Llerena E 156 B1
Higueruela E 158 C2
Híjar E 153 A5
Hilchenbach D 81 A4
Hildburghausen D 82 B2
Hilden D 80 A2
Hilders D 82 B1
Hildesheim D 72 B2
Hilgay GB 41 C4
Hillared S 60 B3
Hille D 72 B1
Hillegom NL 70 B1
Hillerød DK 61 D2
Hillerstorp S 60 B3
Hillesheim D 80 B2
Hillestad N 53 A6
Hillmersdorf D 83 A5
Hillsborough GB 27 B4
Hillswick GB 33 A5
Hilpoltstein D 95 B3
Hiltpoltstein D 94 B3
Hilvarenbeek NL 79 A5
Hilversum NL 70 B2
Himarë AL 182 C1
Himbergen D 73 A3
Himesháza H 125 A4
Himmelberg A 109 C5
Himmelpforten D 72 A2
Himód H 111 B4
Hinckley GB 40 C2
Hindås S 60 B2
Hindelang D 108 B1
Hindelbank CH 106 B2
Hinderavåg N 52 A1
Hindhead GB 44 B3
Hinjosa del Valle E 156 B1
Hinnerup DK 59 B3
Hinneryd S 61 C3
Hinojal E 155 B4
Hinojales E 161 B3
Hinojos E 161 B3
Hinojosa del Duque E 156 B2
Hinojosas de Calatrava E 157 B3
Hinterhornbach A 108 B1
Hinterriss A 108 B2
Hintersee A 109 B4
Hintersee D 74 A3
Hinterstoder A 110 B1
Hintertux A 108 B2
Hinterweidenthal D 93 B3
Hinwil CH 107 B3
Hios GR 185 A7
Hippolytushoef NL 70 B1
Hirschaid D 94 B2
Hirschau D 95 B3
Hirschfeld D 83 A5
Hirschhorn D 93 B4
Hirsingue F 106 B2
Hirson F 91 B4
Hirtshals DK 58 A2
Hirvaskoski FIN 197 D10
Hirzenhain D 81 B5
Hisarcık TR 186 C4
Hishult S 61 C3
Hissjön S 200 C6
Hitchin GB 44 B3
Hitra N 198 B5
Hittarp S 61 C2
Hittisau A 107 B4
Hittun N 46 A1
Hitzacker D 73 A4
Hjallerup DK 58 A3
Hjällstad S 49 B5
Hjältevad S 62 A3
Hjärnarp S 61 C2
Hjartdal N 53 A4
Hjellestad N 46 B2
Hjelmeland N 52 A2
Hjelset N 198 C4
Hjerkinn N 198 C6
Hjerm DK 58 B1
Hjerpsted DK 64 A1
Hjerting DK 59 C1
Hjo S 55 B5
Hjordkær DK 64 A2
Hjørring DK 58 A2
Hjorted S 62 A4
Hjortkvarn S 56 B1
Hjortnäs S 50 B1
Hjortsberga S 62 B2
Hjukse N 53 A5
Hjuksebø N 53 A5
Hjulsjö S 55 A5
Hliník nad Hronom. SK 98 C2
Hlinsko CZ 97 B3
Hlío IS 191 A10
Hlohovec SK 98 C1
Hluboká nad Vltavou CZ 96 B2
Hlučín CZ 98 B2
Hlyboka UA 17 A6
Hlybokaye BY 13 A7
Hniezdne SK 99 B4
Hnilec SK 99 C4
Hnúšťa SK 99 C3
Hobol H 125 A3
Hobro DK 58 B2
Hobscheid L 92 B1
Hocalar TR 189 A4
Hochdonn D 64 B2
Hochdorf CH 106 B3
Hochfelden F 93 C3
Hochspeyer D 93 B3
Höchst im Odenwald D 93 B5
Höchstadt, *Bayern* D 94 B2
Höchstädt, *Bayern* D 94 C2
Hochstenbach D 81 B3
Höckendorf D 83 B5
Hockenheim D 93 B4
Hoddesdon GB 44 B3
Hodejov SK 99 C3
Hodenhagen D 72 B2
Hodkovice CZ 84 B3
Hódmezövásárhely H 113 C4
Hodnet GB 38 B4
Hodonín CZ 98 C1
Hodslavice CZ 98 B2
Hoedekenskerke NL 79 A3
Hoegaarden B 79 B4
Hoek van Holland NL 79 A4
Hoenderlo NL 70 B2
Hof D 83 B3
Hof N 53 A6
Hofbieber D 82 B1
Hoff GB 37 B4
Hofgeismar D 81 A5
Hofheim, *Bayern* D 82 B2
Hofheim, *Hessen* D 93 A4
Hofkirchen im Mühlkreis A 96 C1
Höfn IS 191 C10
Hofors S 50 B3
Hofsós IS 190 B6
Hofstad N 199 A7
Höganäs S 61 C2
Högbo S 51 B3
Hogdal S 54 A2
Høgebru N 46 A4
Högfors S 50 C2
Högklint S 57 C4
Högsäter S 54 B3
Högsby S 62 A4
Högsjö S 56 A1
Hogstad S 55 B6
Högyész H 112 C2
Hohen Neuendorf D 74 B2
Hohenau A 97 C4
Hohenberg A 110 B2
Hohenbucko D 83 A5
Hohenburg D 95 B3
Hohendorf D 66 B1
Hohenems A 107 B4
Hohenhameln D 72 B3
Hohenhausen D 72 B1
Hohenkirchen D 71 A4
Hohenlinden D 108 A2
Hohenlockstedt D 64 C2
Hohenmölsen D 83 A4
Hohennauen D 73 B5
Hohenseeden D 73 B5
Hohentauern A 110 B1
Hohentengen D 106 B3
Hohenwepel D 81 A5
Hohenwestedt D 64 B2
Hohenwutzen D 74 B3
Hohenzieritz D 74 A2
Hohn D 64 B2
Hohne D 72 B3
Hohnstorf D 73 A3
Højer DK 64 B1
Højslev Stby DK 58 B2
Hok S 62 A2
Hökerum S 60 B3
Hökhuvud S 51 B5
Hokksund N 53 A5
Hökön S 63 B2
Hol N 47 B5
Hólar IS 190 B6
Holašovice CZ 96 C2
Holbæk, *Aarhus Amt.* DK 58 B3
Holbæk, *Vestsjællands Amt.* DK 61 D1
Holbeach GB 41 C4
Holdenstedt D 73 B3
Holdhus N 46 B2
Holdorf D 71 B5
Holeby DK 65 B4
Hølen N 54 A1
Hølervasseter N 47 B6
Holešov CZ 98 B1
Holguera E 155 B4
Holíč SK 98 C1
Holice CZ 97 A3
Holice SK 111 B4
Höljes S 49 B4
Hollabrunn A 97 C4
Hollandstoun GB 33 B4
Høllen N 53 B3
Hollfeld D 95 B3
Hollókő H 112 B3
Hollstadt D 82 B2
Hollum NL 70 A2
Höllviksnäs S 66 A1
Holm N 195 E3
Hólmavík IS 190 B4
Holmbukt N 192 B5
Holme-on-Spalding-Moor GB 40 B3
Holmedal S 54 A2
Holmegil N 54 A2
Holmen N 48 B2
Holmes Chapel GB 38 A4
Holmestrand N 54 A1
Holmfirth GB 40 B2
Holmfoss N 193 C14
Holmsbu N 54 A1
Holmsjö S 63 B3
Holmsund S 200 C6
Holmsveden S 50 A3
Holmudden S 57 C5
Hölö S 57 A3
Holøydal N 199 C8
Holsbybrunn S 62 A3
Holseter N 48 A1
Holsljunga S 60 B2
Holstebro DK 59 B1
Holsted DK 59 C1
Holsworthy GB 42 B2
Holt D 64 B2
Holt, *Norfolk* GB 41 C5
Holt, *Wrexham* GB 38 A4
Holt IS 190 D6
Holt N 53 B4
Holten NL 71 B3
Holtwick D 71 B4
Holum N 52 B3
Holwerd NL 70 A2
Holycross IRL 29 B4
Holyhead GB 38 A2
Holýšov CZ 95 B5
Holywell GB 38 A3
Holywood GB 27 B5
Holzdorf D 83 A5
Holzhausen D 72 B1
Holzheim D 94 C2
Holzkirchen D 108 B2
Holzminden D 81 A5
Holzthaleben D 82 A2
Homberg, *Hessen* D 81 A5
Homberg, *Hessen* D 81 B5
Homburg D 93 B3
Hommelstø N 195 E3
Hommersåk N 52 B1
Homokmegy H 112 C3
Homokszentgyörgy H 124 A3
Homyel = Gomel BY 13 B9
Honaz TR 188 B4
Hondarribia E 144 A2
Hondón de los Frailes E 165 A4
Hondschoote F 78 B2
Hönebach D 82 B1
Hønefoss N 48 B2
Honfleur F 89 A4
Høng DK 61 D1
Honiton GB 43 B3
Hönningen D 80 B2
Honningsvåg N 193 B9
Hönö S 60 B1
Honrubia E 158 B1
Hontalbilla E 151 A3
Hontheim D 92 A2
Hontianske-Nemce SK 98 C2
Hontoria de la Cantera E 143 B3
Hontoria de Valdearados E 143 C3
Hontoria del Pinar E 143 C3
Hoofddorp NL 70 B1
Hoogerheide NL 79 A4
Hoogeveen NL 71 B3
Hoogezand-Sappemeer NL 71 A3
Hoogkarspel NL 70 B2
Hoogkerk NL 71 A3
Hoogstede D 71 B3
Hoogstraten B 79 A4
Hook GB 44 B3
Hooksiel D 71 A5
Höör S 61 D3
Hoorn NL 70 B2
Hope GB 38 A3
Hope under Dinmore GB 39 B4
Hopen N 194 C6
Hopfgarten A 108 B3
Hopfgarten in Defereggen A 109 C3
Hopseidet N 193 B11
Hopsten D 71 B4
Hoptrup DK 59 C2
Hora Svatého Sebestiána CZ 83 B5
Horažďovice CZ 96 B1
Horb am Neckar D 93 C4
Horbelev DK 65 B5
Hørby DK 58 A3
Hörby S 61 D3
Horcajada de la Torre E 158 A1
Horcajo de los Montes E 156 A3
Horcajo de Santiago E 151 C4
Horcajo-Medianero E 150 B2
Horche E 151 B4
Horda S 62 A2
Hordabø N 46 B1
Hordalia N 52 A2
Hordvik N 46 B2
Hořesedly CZ 83 B5
Horezu RO 17 C6
Horgen CH 107 B3
Horgoš SRB 126 A1
Horia RO 126 A3
Hořice CZ 84 B3
Horjul SLO 123 A3
Horka D 84 A2
Hörken S 50 B1
Horki BY 13 A9
Hörle S 60 B4
Horn A 97 C3
Horn D 81 A4
Horn N 48 B2
Horn S 62 A3
Horna E 158 C2
Horná Mariková SK 98 B2
Horná Streda SK 98 C1
Horná Štrubna SK 98 C2
Horná Súča SK 98 C1
Hornachos E 156 B1
Hornachuelos E 162 A2
Hornanes N 46 C2
Hornbæk, *Aarhus Amt.* DK 58 B2
Hornbæk, *Frederiksværk* DK 61 C2
Hornberg D 106 A3
Hornburg D 73 B3
Horncastle GB 41 B3
Horndal S 50 B3
Horndean GB 44 C2
Horne, *Fyns Amt.* DK 64 A3
Horne, *Ribe Amt.* DK 59 C1
Hörnebo S 55 B5
Horneburg D 72 A2
Hörnefors S 200 C5
Horní Bečva CZ 98 B2
Horni Benešov CZ 98 B1
Horni Cerekev CZ 97 B3
Horní Jiřetín CZ 83 B5
Horní Lomná CZ 98 B2
Horni Maršov CZ 85 B3
Horní Planá CZ 96 C2
Horni Slavkov CZ 83 B4
Horni Vltavice CZ 96 C1
Hornindal N 198 D3
Hørning DK 59 B3
Hörningsholm S 57 A3
Hornnes N 53 B3
Horno D 84 A2
Hornos E 164 A2
Hornoy-le-Bourg F 90 B1
Hornsea GB 41 B3
Hornsjø N 48 A2
Hornslet DK 59 B3
Hornstein A 111 B3
Hörnum D 64 B1
Hornum DK 58 B2
Horný Tisovnik SK 99 C3
Horodenka UA 13 D6
Horodnya UA 13 C9
Horodok, *Khmelnytskyy* UA 13 D7
Horodok, *Lviv* UA 13 D5
Horokhiv UA 13 C6
Horovice CZ 96 B1
Horred S 60 B2
Hörröd S 61 D4
Hörsching A 110 A1
Horsens DK 59 C2
Horsham GB 44 B3
Hørsholm DK 61 D2
Horslunde DK 65 B4
Horšovský Týn CZ 95 B4
Horst NL 80 A2
Horstel D 71 B4
Horsten D 71 A4
Horstmar D 71 B4
Hort H 113 B3
Horta P 148 A2
Horten N 54 A1
Hortezuela E 151 A5
Hortiguela E 143 B3
Hortobágy H 113 B5
Horton in Ribblesdale GB 37 B4
Hørve DK 61 D1
Hörvik S 63 B2
Horwich GB 38 A4
Hosanger N 46 B2
Hösbach D 93 A5
Hosena D 84 A2
Hosenfeld D 81 B5
Hosingen L 92 A2
Hosio FIN 197 D8
Hospental CH 107 C3
Hospital IRL 29 B3
Hossegor F 128 C1
Hosszuhetény H 125 A4
Hostal de Ipiés E 145 B3
Hošťálkova CZ 98 B1
Hostalric E 147 C3
Hostens F 128 B2
Hostěradice CZ 97 C4
Hostinné CZ 85 B3
Hostomice CZ 96 B2
Hostouň CZ 95 B4
Hotagen S 199 B11
Hoting S 200 B2
Hotolisht AL 182 B2
Hotton B 79 B5
Houdain F 78 B2
Houdan F 90 C1
Houdelaincourt F 92 C1
Houeillès F 128 B3
Houffalize B 92 A1
Houghton-le-Spring GB 37 B5
Houlberg DK 59 B2
Houlgate F 89 A3
Hounslow GB 44 B3
Hourtin F 128 A1
Hourtin-Plage F 128 A1
Houthalen B 79 A5
Houyet B 79 B4
Hov DK 59 C3
Hov N 48 B2
Hova S 55 B5
Høvåg N 53 B4
Hovborg DK 59 C1
Hovda N 47 B6
Hovden N 52 A3
Hove GB 44 C3
Hovedgård DK 59 C2
Hovelhof D 81 A4
Hoven DK 59 C1
Hovet N 47 B5
Hovingham GB 40 A3
Hovmantorp S 62 B3
Hovsta S 56 A1
Howden GB 40 B3
Howe D 72 A3
Höxter D 81 A5
Hoya D 72 B2
Hoya de Santa Maria E 161 B3
Hoya-Gonzalo E 158 C2
Høyanger N 46 A3
Hoyerswerda D 84 A2
Høyjord N 53 A6
Hoylake GB 38 A3
Høylandet N 199 A9
Hoym D 82 A3
Høymyr N 47 C6
Hoyo de Manzanares E 151 B4
Hoyo de Pinares E 150 B3
Hoyocasero E 150 B3
Hoyos E 149 B3
Hoyos del Espino E 150 B2
Hrabusiče SK 99 C4
Hradec Králové CZ 85 B3
Hradec nad Moravicí CZ 98 B1
Hrádek CZ 97 C4
Hrádek nad Nisou CZ 84 B2
Hradište SK 98 C2
Hrafnagil IS 191 B7
Hrafnseyri IS 190 B2
Hranice, *Severomoravský* CZ 98 B1
Hranice, *Západočeský* CZ 83 B4
Hranovnica SK 99 C4
Hrasnica BIH 139 B4
Hrastnik SLO 123 A4
Hřensko CZ 84 B2
Hriňová SK 99 C3
Hrisoupoli GR 183 C6
Hrochov CZ 97 B4
Hrochův Tynec CZ 97 B3
Hrodna BY 13 B5
Hrodzyanka BY 13 B8
Hronov CZ 85 B4
Hronský Beňadik SK 98 C2
Hrotovice CZ 97 B4
Hrtkovci SRB 127 C1
Hrun IS 190 A5
Hrušov SK 112 A3
Hrušovany nad Jevišovkou CZ 97 C4
Hřuštin SK 99 B3
Hrvaćani BIH 124 C3
Hrvace HR 138 B2
Hrymayliv UA 13 D7
Huben A 109 C3
Hückel-hoven D 80 A2
Hückeswagen D 80 A3
Hucknall GB 40 B2
Hucqueliers F 78 B1
Huddersfield GB 40 B2
Huddinge S 57 A3
Huddunge S 51 B3
Hude D 72 A1
Hudiksvall S 200 E3
Huélago E 163 A4
Huélamo E 152 B2
Huelgoat F 100 A2
Huelma E 163 A4
Huelva E 161 B3
Huéneja E 164 B2
Huércal de Almeria E 164 C2
Huércal-Overa E 164 B3
Huerta de Abajo E 143 B3
Huerta de Valdecarabanos E 151 C4
Huerta del Rey E 143 C3
Huertahernando E 152 B1
Huesa E 164 B1
Huesca E 145 B3
Huéscar E 164 B2
Huete E 151 B5
Huétor Tájar E 163 A3
Hüfingen D 106 B3
Hufthamar N 46 B2
Hugh Town GB 42 B1
Huglfing D 108 B2
Huissen NL 70 C2
Huittinen FIN 8 B3
Huizen NL 70 B2
Hulín CZ 98 B1
Hüls D 80 A2
Hulsig DK 58 A3
Hulst NL 79 A4

Hult S 62 A3
Hulta S 56 B2
Hulteby S 55 A5
Hulterstad S 63 B4
Hultsfred S 62 A3
Humanes E 151 B4
Humberston GB 41 B3
Humble DK 65 B3
Humenné SK 12 D4
Humilladero E 163 A3
Humlebæk DK 61 D2
Humlum DK 58 B1
Hummelsta S 56 A2
Humpolec CZ 97 B3
Humshaugh GB 37 A4
Hundåla N 195 E3
Hundested DK 61 D1
Hundorp N 48 A1
Hundvåg N 52 A1
Hundvin N 46 B2
Hunedoara RO 17 C5
Hünfeld D 82 B1
Hungen D 81 B4
Hungerford GB 44 B2
Hunndalen N 48 B2
Hunnebostrand S 54 B2
Hunstanton GB 41 C4
Huntingdon GB 44 A3
Huntley GB 39 C4
Huntly GB 33 D4
Hünxe D 80 A2
Hurbanovo SK 112 B2
Hürbel D 107 A4
Hurdal N 48 B3
Hurezani RO 17 C5
Hurlford GB 36 A2
Hurstbourne Tarrant GB 44 B2
Hurstpierpoint GB 44 C3
Hürth D 80 B2
Hurum N 47 A5
Hurup DK 58 B1
Húsafell IS 190 C5
Húsavík IS 191 A8
Husbands Bosworth GB 44 A2
Husby D 64 B2
Husby DK 59 B1
Husey IS 191 B11
Huşi RO 17 B8
Husina BIH 139 A4
Husinec CZ 96 B1
Husinish GB 31 B1
Huskvarna S 62 A2
Husnes N 46 C2
Husøy N 194 A8
Hustad N 198 C4
Hüsten D 81 A3
Hustopeče CZ 97 C4
Hustopeče nad Bečvou CZ 98 B1
Husum D 64 B2
Husum S 200 C5
Husvika N 195 E3
Huta PL 75 B5
Hutovo BIH 139 C3
Hüttenberg A 110 C1
Hüttlingen D 94 C2
Huttoft GB 41 B4
Hutton Cranswick GB 40 B3
Hüttschlag A 109 B4
Huttwil CH 106 B2
Huy B 79 B5
Hüyük TR 189 B6
Hval N 48 B2
Hvåle N 47 B6
Hvaler N 54 A2
Hvalpsund DK 58 B2
Hvammstangi IS 190 B5
Hvammur IS 190 B6
Hvanneyri IS 190 C4
Hvar HR 138 B2
Hvarnes N 53 A5
Hveragerði IS 190 D4
Hvidbjerg DK 58 B1
Hvide Sande DK 59 C1
Hvittingfoss N 53 A6
Hvolsvöllur IS 190 D5
Hybe SK 99 B3
Hycklinge S 62 A3
Hydra GR 185 B4
Hyen N 198 D2
Hyères F 132 B2
Hyéres Plage F 132 B2
Hylestad N 52 A3
Hylke DK 59 C2
Hyllestad N 46 A2
Hyllstofta S 61 C3
Hyltebruk S 60 B3
Hynnekleiv N 53 B4
Hythe, *Hampshire* GB 44 C2
Hythe, *Kent* GB 45 B5
Hyvinkää FIN 8 B4

I

Iam RO 127 B3
Iaşi RO 17 B7
Iasmos GR 183 B7
Ibahernando E 156 A2
Ibarranguelua E 143 A4
Ibbenbüren D 71 B4
Ibeas de Juarros E 143 B3
Ibestad N 194 B8
Ibi E 159 C3
Ibiza = Eivissa E 166 C1
İbradı TR 189 B6
İbriktepe TR 186 A1
Ibros E 157 B4
Ibstock GB 40 C2
İçel TR 23 C8
Ichenhausen D 94 C2
Ichtegem B 78 A3
Ichtershausen D 82 B2
Idanha-a-Novo P 155 B3
Idar-Oberstein D 93 B3
Idd N 54 A2
Idiazábal E 144 B1
Idivuoma S 196 A4
Idkerberget S 50 B2
Idön S 51 B5
Idre S 199 D9
Idrija SLO 123 A3
Idritsa RUS 9 D6
Idstein D 81 B4
Idvor SRB 126 B2
Iecca Mare RO 126 B2
Ielsi I 170 B2
Ieper = Ypres B 78 B2
Ierapetra GR 185 D6
Ierissos GR 183 C5
Iesi I 136 B2
Ifjord N 193 B11
Ig SLO 123 B3
Igal H 112 C1
Igea E 144 B1
Igea Marina I 136 A1
Igelfors S 56 B1
Igersheim D 94 B1
Iggesund S 200 E3
Iglesias E 143 B3
Iglésias I 179 C2
Igls A 108 B2
İğneada TR 186 A2
Igny-Comblizy F 91 B3
Igorre E 143 A4
Igoumenitsa GR 182 D2
Igries E 145 B3
Igualada E 147 C2
Igüeña E 141 B4
Iguerande F 117 A4
Iharosberény H 124 A3
Ihl'any SK 99 B4
Ihlienworth D 64 C1
Ihringen D 106 A2
Ihrlerstein D 95 C3
İhsaniye TR 187 C5
Ii FIN 197 D8
Iijärvi FIN 193 C11
Iisalmi FIN 3 E10
IJmuiden NL 70 B1
IJsselmuiden NL 70 B2
IJzendijke NL 79 A3
Ikast DK 59 B2
Ikervár H 111 B3
il Castagno I 135 B3
Ilandža SRB 126 B2
Ilanz CH 107 C4
Ilava SK 98 C2
Iława PL 69 B4
Ilche E 145 C4
Ilchester GB 43 B4
Ilfeld D 82 A2
Ilfracombe GB 42 A2
Ilgaz TR 23 A7
Ilgın TR 189 A6
Ílhavo P 148 B1
Ilica TR 186 C2
Ilidža BIH 139 B4
Ilijaš BIH 139 B4
Ilirska Bistrica SLO 123 B3
Ilkeston GB 40 C2
Ilkley GB 40 B2
Illana E 151 B5
Illano E 141 A4
Illar E 164 C2
Illas E 141 A5
Illats F 128 B2
Ille-sur-Têt F 146 B3
Illertissen D 94 C2
Illescas E 151 B4
Illfurth F 106 B2
Illichivsk UA 17 B9
Illiers-Combray F 89 B5
Illkirch-Graffenstaden F 93 C3
Illmersdorf D 74 C2
Illmitz A 111 B3
Íllora E 163 A4
Illueca E 152 A2
Ilmajoki FIN 8 A3
Ilmenau D 82 B2
Ilminster GB 43 B4
Ilok HR 126 B1
Ilomantsi FIN 9 A7
Iłow PL 77 B5
Iłowa PL 84 A3
Iłowo-Osada PL 77 A5
Ilsenburg D 82 A2
Ilshofen D 94 B1
Ilz A 110 B2
Iłża PL 87 A5
Imatra FIN 9 B6
Imielin PL 86 B3
Imingen N 47 B5
Immeln S 63 B2
Immenhausen D 81 A5
Immenstadt D 107 B5
Immingham GB 41 B3
Ímola I 135 A4
Imon E 151 A5
Imotski HR 138 B3
Impéria I 133 B4
Imphy F 104 C2
İmroz TR 183 C7
Imsland N 52 A1
Imst A 108 B1
Inagh IRL 28 B2
Inari FIN 193 D10
Inca E 167 B2
Inchnadamph GB 32 C2
Incinillas E 143 B3
Indal S 200 D3
Indjija SRB 127 B2
Indre Arna N 46 B2
Indre Billefjord N 193 B9
Indre Brenna N 193 B9
İnebolu TR 23 A7
İnecik TR 186 B2
İnegöl TR 187 B4
Inerthal CH 107 B3
Infiesto E 142 A1
Ingatorp S 62 A3
Ingedal N 54 A2
Ingelheim D 93 B4
Ingelmunster B 78 B3
Ingelstad S 62 B2
Ingleton GB 37 B4
Ingolfsland N 47 C5
Ingolstadt D 95 C3
Ingrandes, *Maine-et-Loire* F 101 B5
Ingrandes, *Vienne* F 102 C2
Ingwiller F 93 C3
Inhisar TR 187 B5
Iniesta E 158 B2
Inishannon IRL 29 C3
Inishcrone IRL 26 B1
Inke H 124 A3
Inndyr N 195 C5
Innellan GB 34 C3
Innerleithen GB 35 C4
Innermessan GB 36 B2
Innertkirchen CH 106 C3
Innervillgraten A 109 C3
Innsbruck A 108 B2
Innset N 194 B9
Innvik N 198 D3
İnönü TR 187 C5
Inowłódz PL 87 A4
Inowrocław PL 76 B3
Ins CH 106 B2
Insch GB 33 D4
Insjön S 50 B2
Ińsko PL 75 A4
Instow GB 42 A2
İntepe TR 186 B1
Interlaken CH 106 C2
Intragna CH 120 A1
Introbio I 120 B2
Inverallochy GB 33 D5
Inveran GB 32 D2
Inveran IRL 28 A2
Inveraray GB 34 B2
Inverbervie GB 35 B5
Invergarry GB 32 D2
Invergordon GB 32 D2
Invergowrie GB 35 B4
Inverkeilor GB 35 B5
Inverkeithing GB 35 B4
Invermoriston GB 32 D2
Inverness GB 32 D2
Inveruno I 120 B1
Inverurie GB 33 D4
Ioannina GR 182 D2
Iolanda di Savoia I 121 C4
Ion Corvin RO 17 C7
Ióppolo I 175 C1
Ios GR 185 C6
Ipati GR 182 E4
Ipsala TR 186 B1
Ipswich GB 45 A5
Iraklia GR 183 B5
Iraklio = Heraklion GR 185 D6
Irdning A 110 B1
Iregszemcse H 112 C2
Irgoli I 178 B3
Irig SRB 127 B1
Ironbridge GB 39 B4
Irpin UA 13 C9
Irrel D 92 B2
Irsina I 172 B2
Irthlingborough GB 44 A3
Iruela E 141 B4
Irún E 144 A2
Irurita E 144 A2
Irurzun E 144 B2
Irvine GB 36 A2
Irvinestown GB 27 B3
Is-sur-Tille F 105 B4
Isaba E 144 B3
Isabela E 157 B4
Ísafjörður IS 190 A3
Isane N 198 D2
Isaszeg H 112 B3
Isbister GB 33 A5
Iscar E 150 A3
İscehisar TR 187 D5
Ischgl A 107 B5
Íschia I 170 C1
Ischia di Castro I 168 A1
Ischitella I 171 B3
Isdes F 103 B4
Ise N 54 A2
Iselle I 119 A5
Iseltwald CH 106 C2
Isen D 108 A3
Isenbüttel D 73 B3
Iseo I 120 B3
Iserlohn D 81 A3
Isérnia I 170 B2
Isfjorden N 198 C4
Ishëm AL 182 B1
Işıklı TR 189 A4
Isigny-sur-Mer F 88 A2
Ísili I 179 C3
İskilip TR 23 A8
Isla Canela E 161 B2
Isla Cristina E 161 B2
Islares E 143 A3
Isle Of Whithorn GB 36 B2
Isleham GB 45 A4
Ismaning D 108 A2
Isna P 154 B3
Isnestoften N 192 B6
Isny D 107 B5
Isoba E 142 A1
Isokylä FIN 197 C10
Isokylä S 196 B5
Isola F 132 A3
Isola del Gran Sasso d'Itália I 169 A3
Ísola del Liri I 169 B3
Ísola della Scala I 121 B4
Isola delle Fémmine I 176 A2
Ísola di Capo Rizzuto I 175 C3
Isona E 147 B2
Ispagnac F 130 A2
Isparta TR 189 B5
Isperikh BG 17 D7
Íspica I 177 C3
Isselburg D 80 A2
Issigeac F 129 B3
Issogne I 119 B4
Issoire F 116 B3
Issoncourt F 91 C5
Issoudun F 103 C4
Issum D 80 A2
Issy-l'Evêque F 104 C2
Istán E 162 B3
İstanbul TR 186 A3
Istebna PL 98 B2
Ístia d'Ombrone I 135 C4
Istiea GR 183 E5
Istres F 131 B3
Istvándi H 125 A3
Itea GR 184 A3
Ithaki GR 184 A1
Itoiz E 144 B2
Ítrabo E 163 B4
Itri I 169 B3
Ittireddu I 178 B2
Íttiri I 178 B2
Itzehoe D 64 C2
Ivalo FIN 193 D11
Iván H 111 B3
Ivanava BY 13 B6
Ivančice CZ 97 B4
Ivančna Gorica SLO 123 B3
Iváncsa H 112 B2
Ivanec HR 124 A2
Ivanić Grad HR 124 B2
Ivanjska BIH 124 C3
Ivanka SK 98 C2
Ivankovo HR 125 B4
Ivano-Frankivsk UA 13 D6
Ivanovice na Hané CZ 98 B1
Ivanska HR 124 B2
Ivatsevichy BY 13 B6
Ivaylovgrad BG 183 B8
Iveland N 53 B3
Ivoz Ramet B 79 B5
Ivrea I 119 B4
İvrindi TR 186 C2
Ivry-en-Montagne F 104 B3
Ivry-la-Bataille F 90 C1
Ivybridge GB 42 B3
Iwaniska PL 87 B5
Iwiny PL 85 A3
Iwuy F 78 B3
Ixworth GB 45 A4
Izarra E 143 B4
Izbica Kujawska PL 76 B3
Izbište SRB 127 B3
Izeda P 149 A3
Izegem B 78 B3
Izernore F 118 A2
Izmayil UA 17 C8
İzmir TR 188 A2
İzmit = Kocaeli TR 187 B4
Iznájar E 163 A3
Iznalloz E 163 A4
Iznatoraf E 164 A1
İznik TR 187 B4
Izola SLO 122 B2
Izsák H 112 C3
Izsófalva H 99 C4
Izyaslav UA 13 C7

J

Jabalquinto E 157 B4
Jablanac HR 123 C3
Jablanica BIH 139 B3
Jablonec nad Jizerou CZ 84 B3
Jablonec nad Nisou CZ 84 B3
Jablonica SK 98 C1
Jablonka PL 99 B3
Jabłonna PL 77 B5
Jablonné nad Orlicí CZ 97 A4
Jablonne Podještědi CZ 84 B2
Jablonov nad Turňou SK 99 C4
Jabłonowo Pomorskie PL 69 B4
Jablúnka CZ 98 B1
Jablunkov CZ 98 B2
Jabučje SRB 127 C2
Jabugo E 161 B3
Jabuka SRB 127 C2
Jabukovac HR 124 B2
Jaca E 145 B3
Jáchymov CZ 83 B4
Jacobidrebber D 72 B1
Jade D 71 A5
Jäderfors S 50 B3
Jädraås S 50 B3
Jadraque E 151 B5
Jægerspris DK 61 D1
Jaén E 163 A4
Jagare BIH 124 C3
Jagel D 64 B2
Jagenbach A 96 C3
Jagodina SRB 127 D3
Jagodnjak HR 125 B4
Jagodzin PL 84 A3
Jagstheim D 94 B2
Jagstzell D 94 B2
Jahodna SK 111 A4
Jajce BIH 138 A3
Ják H 111 B3
Jakabszálbs H 112 C3
Jäkkvik S 195 D8
Jakobsnes N 193 C14
Jakovlje HR 124 B1
Jakšic HR 125 B3
Jakubany SK 99 B4
Jalance E 159 B2
Jalasjärvi FIN 8 A3
Jalhay B 80 B1
Jaligny-sur-Besbre F 117 A3
Jallais F 102 B1
Jalón E 159 C3
Jâlons F 91 C4
Jamena SRB 125 C5
Jamilena E 163 A4
Jämjö S 63 B3
Jamnička Kiselica HR 124 B1
Jamno PL 67 B5
Jamoigne B 92 B1
Jämsä FIN 8 B4
Jämshög S 63 B2
Jamu Mare RO 126 B3
Janakkala FIN 8 B4
Jandelsbrunn D 96 C1
Jänickendorf D 74 B2
Janikowo PL 76 B3
Janja BIH 125 C5
Janjina HR 138 C3
Janki, *Łódzkie* PL 86 A3
Janki, *Mazowieckie* PL 77 B5
Jankov CZ 96 B2
Jankowo Dolne PL 76 B2
Jánoshalma H 126 A1
Jánosháza H 111 B4
Jánoshida H 113 B4
Jánossomorja H 111 B4
Janovice nad Uhlavou CZ 96 B1
Janów PL 86 B3
Janowiec Wielkopolski PL 76 B2
Janowo PL 77 A5
Jänsmässholmen S 199 B10
Janville F 103 A3
Janzé F 101 B4
Jarabá SK 99 C3
Jaraczewo PL 76 C2
Jarafuel E 159 B2
Jaraicejo E 156 A2
Jaraíz de la Vera E 150 B2
Jarak SRB 127 C1
Jarandilla de la Vera E 150 B2
Jaray E 152 A1
Järbo S 50 B3
Jard-sur-Mer F 114 B2
Jaren N 48 B2
Jargeau F 103 B4
Jarkovac SRB 126 B2
Järlåsa S 51 C4
Jarmen D 66 C2
Järna S 57 A3
Jarnac F 115 C3
Järnäs S 200 C5
Järnforsen S 62 A3
Jarny F 92 B1
Jarocin PL 76 C2
Jaroměř CZ 85 B3
Jaroměřice nad Rokytnou CZ 97 B3
Jaroslav CZ 97 A4
Jaroslavice CZ 97 C4
Jarosław PL 12 C5
Jaroslawiec PL 68 A1
Jarošov nad Nežarkou CZ 96 B3
Järpås S 55 B3
Järpen S 199 B10
Jarrow GB 37 B5
Järso FIN 51 B6
Järvenpää FIN 8 B4
Jarvorník CZ 85 B4
Järvsö S 200 E2
Jarzé F 102 B1
Jaša Tomic SRB 126 B2
Jasenak HR 123 B4
Jasenica BIH 124 C2
Jasenice HR 137 A4
Jasenovac HR 124 B2
Jasenovo SRB 127 C3
Jasień PL 84 A3
Jasienica PL 84 A2
Jasło PL 12 D4
Jásova SK 112 B2
Jasseron F 118 A2
Jastarnia PL 69 A3
Jastrebarsko HR 123 B4
Jastrowie PL 68 B1
Jastrzębia-Góra PL 68 A3
Jastrzębie Zdrój PL 98 B2
Jászals-Lószentgyörgy H 113 B4
Jászapáti H 113 B4
Jászárokszállás H 113 B3
Jászberény H 113 B3
Jászdózsa H 113 B4
Jászfényszaru H 113 B3
Jászjakóhalma H 113 B4
Jászkarajenö H 113 B4
Jászkisér H 113 B4
Jászladány H 113 B4
Jászszentlászló H 113 C3
Jásztelek H 113 B4
Játar E 163 B4
Jättendal S 200 E3
Jatznick D 74 A2
Jaun CH 106 C2
Jausiers F 132 A2
Jávea E 159 C4
Jävenitz D 73 B4
Javerlhac F 115 C4
Javier E 144 B2
Javorani BIH 124 C3
Javorina SK 99 B4
Javron F 89 B3
Jawor PL 85 A4
Jaworzno PL 86 B3
Jaworzyna Śl. PL 85 B4
Jayena E 163 B4
Jażow PL 84 A2
Jebel RO 126 B3
Jebjerg DK 58 B2
Jedburgh GB 35 C5
Jedlinsk PL 87 A5
Jedlnia PL 87 A5
Jedlnia Letnisko PL 87 A5
Jednorożec PL 77 A6
Jedovnice CZ 97 B4
Jędrychow PL 69 B4
Jędrzejów PL 87 B4
Jedwabno PL 77 A5
Jeesiö FIN 197 B9
Jegłownik PL 69 A4
Jegun F 129 C3
Jēkabpils LV 8 D4
Jektevik N 46 C2
Jektvik N 195 D4
Jelcz-Laskowice PL 85 A5
Jelenec SK 98 C2
Jelenia Góra PL 85 B3
Jelgava LV 8 D3
Jelka SK 111 A4
Jelling DK 59 C2
Jels DK 59 C2
Jelsa HR 138 B2
Jelsa N 52 A2
Jelšava SK 99 C4
Jemgum D 71 A4
Jemnice CZ 97 B3
Jena D 82 B3
Jenaz CH 107 C4
Jenbach A 108 B2
Jenikow PL 75 A4
Jennersdorf A 111 C3
Jenny S 62 A4
Jerchel D 73 B4
Jeres del Marquesado E 164 B1
Jerez de la Frontera E 162 B1
Jerez de los Caballeros E 155 C4
Jerica E 159 B3
Jerichow D 73 B5
Jerka PL 75 B5
Jermenovci SRB 126 B3
Jerslev DK 58 A3
Jerte E 150 B2
Jerup DK 58 A3
Jerxheim D 73 B3
Jerzmanowice PL 87 B3
Jerzu I 179 C3
Jerzwałd PL 69 B4
Jesberg D 81 B5
Jesenice, *Středočeský* CZ 83 B5
Jesenice, *Středočeský* CZ 96 B2
Jesenice SLO 109 C5
Jeseník CZ 85 B5
Jesenké SK 99 C4
Jesolo I 122 B1
Jessen D 83 A4

Jessenitz D 73 A4
Jessheim N 48 B3
Jessnitz D 83 A4
Jesteburg D 72 A2
Jeumont F 79 B4
Jeven-stedt D 64 B2
Jever D 71 A4
Jevíčko CZ 97 B4
Jevišovice CZ 97 C3
Jevnaker N 48 B2
Jezerane HR 123 B4
Jezero BIH 138 A3
Jezero HR 123 B4
Jezów PL 87 A3
Jičín CZ 84 B3
Jičiněves CZ 84 B3
Jihlava CZ 97 B3
Jijona E 159 C3
Jilemnice CZ 84 B3
Jilové CZ 84 B2
Jilové u Prahy CZ 96 B2
Jimbolia RO 126 B2
Jimena E 163 A4
Jimena de la Frontera E 162 B2
Jimera de Libar E 162 B2
Jimramov CZ 97 B4
Jince CZ 96 B1
Jindřichovice CZ 83 B4
Jindřichův Hradec CZ 96 B3
Jirkov CZ 83 B5
Jistebnice CZ 96 B2
Joachimsthal D 74 B2
João da Loura P 154 C2
Jobbágyi H 112 B3
Jochberg A 109 B3
Jockfall S 196 C5
Jódar E 163 A4
Jodoigne B 79 B4
Joensuu FIN 9 A6
Joesjö S 195 E5
Jœuf F 92 B1
Jõgeva EST 8 C5
Johann-georgen-stadt D 83 B4
Johannishus S 63 B3
Johanniskirchen D 95 C4
Johansfors S 63 B3
John o'Groats GB 32 C3
Johnshaven GB 35 B5
Johnstone GB 34 C3
Johnstown IRL 30 B1
Jõhvi EST 8 C5
Joigny F 104 B2
Joinville F 91 C5
Jokkmokk S 196 C2
Jöllenbeck D 72 B1
Jomala FIN 51 B6
Jönåker S 56 B2
Jonava LT 13 A6
Jonchery-sur-Vesle F 91 B3
Jondal N 46 B3
Jondalen N 53 A5
Joniškis LT 8 D3
Jönköping S 62 A2
Jonkowo PL 69 B5
Jønnbu N 53 A5
Jonsberg S 56 B2
Jonsered S 60 B2
Jonstorp S 61 C2
Jonzac F 114 C3
Jorba E 147 C2
Jordanów PL 99 B3
Jordanów Ślaski PL 85 B4
Jordanowo PL 75 B4
Jordbro S 57 A4
Jordbrua N 195 D5
Jördenstorf D 66 C1
Jordet N 49 A4
Jordøse DK 59 C3
Jork D 72 A2
Jörlanda S 60 B1
Jormlien S 199 A10
Jormvattnet S 199 A11
Jörn S 200 A6
Jørpeland N 52 A2
Jorquera E 158 B2
Jošan HR 123 C4
Jošavka BIH 124 C3
Josipdol HR 123 B4
Josipovac HR 125 B4
Jössefors S 54 A3
Josselin F 101 B3
Jøssund N 199 A7
Jostedal N 47 A4
Jósvafö H 99 C4
Jou P 148 A2
Jouarre F 90 C3
Joué-lès-Tours F 102 B2
Joué-sur-Erdre F 101 B4
Joure NL 70 B2
Joutseno FIN 9 B6
Joutsijärvi FIN 197 C10
Joux-la-Ville F 104 B2
Jouy F 90 C1
Jouy-le-Châtel F 90 C3
Jouy-le-Potier F 103 B3
Joyeuse F 131 A3
Joze F 116 B3
Juan-les-Pins F 132 B3
Juankoski FIN 8 A6
Jübek D 64 B2
Jubera E 144 B1
Jubrique E 162 B2
Jüchsen D 82 B2
Judaberg N 52 A1
Judenburg A 110 B1
Juelsminde DK 59 C3
Jugon-les-Lacs F 101 A3
Juillac F 129 A4
Juillan F 145 A4
Juist D 71 A4
Jukkasjärvi S 196 B3
Jule N 199 A10
Julianadorp NL 70 B1
Julianstown IRL 30 A2
Jülich D 80 B2
Jullouville F 88 B2
Jumeaux F 117 B3
Jumièges F 89 A4
Jumilhac-le-Grand F 115 C5
Jumilla E 159 C2
Jumisko FIN 197 C11
Juncosa E 153 A4
Juneda E 147 C1
Jung S 55 B4
Jungingen D 93 C5
Junglingster L 92 B2
Juniville F 91 B4
Junosuando S 196 B5
Junqueira P 149 A2
Junsele S 200 C2
Juoksengi S 196 C6
Juoksenki FIN 196 C6
Juprelle B 80 B1
Jurata PL 69 A3
Jurbarkas LT 12 A5
Jurjevo HR 123 C3
Jūrmala LV 8 D3
Jurmu FIN 197 D10
Juromenha P 155 C3
Jursla S 56 B2
Jussac F 116 C2
Jussey F 105 B4
Jussy F 90 B3
Juta H 125 A3
Jüterbog D 74 C2
Juuka FIN 3 E11
Juuma FIN 197 C12
Juvigny-le-Terte F 88 B2
Juvigny-sous-Andaine F 89 B3
Juzennecourt F 105 A3
Jyderup DK 61 D1
Jyrkänkoski FIN 197 C12
Jyväskylä FIN 8 A4

K

Kaamanen FIN 193 C11
Kaamasmukka FIN 193 C10
Kaaresuvanto FIN 192 D6
Kaarssen D 73 A4
Kaatscheuvel NL 79 A5
Kaba H 113 B5
Kåbdalis S 196 C3
Kačarevo SRB 127 C2
Kács H 113 B4
Kadan CZ 83 B5
Kadarkút H 125 A3
Kadınhanı TR 189 A7
Kaduy RUS 9 C10
Kåfalla S 56 A1
Kåfjord N 192 C7
Kåfjordbotn N 192 C4
Kågeröd S 61 D3
Kahl D 93 A5
Kahla D 82 B3
Kainach bei Voitsberg A 110 B2
Kaindorf A 110 B2
Kainulasjärvi S 196 C5
Kairala FIN 197 B10
Kaisepakte S 192 D3
Kaisersesch D 80 B3
Kaiserslautern D 93 B3
Kaisheim D 94 C2
Kajaani FIN 3 D10
Kajárpéc H 111 B4
Kajdacs H 112 C2
Kakanj BIH 139 A4
Kakasd H 125 A4
Kaklik TR 189 B4
Kakolewo PL 85 A4
Kál H 113 B4
Kalajoki FIN 3 D8
Kalak N 193 B11
Kalamata = Kalamata GR 184 B3
Kalamata = Kalamata GR 184 B3
Kalambaka GR 182 D3
Kalamria GR 182 C4
Kalandra GR 183 D5
Kälarne S 200 D2
Kalavrita GR 184 A3
Kalbe D 73 B4
Kalce SLO 123 B3
Káld H 111 B4
Kale, *Antalya* TR 189 C4
Kale, *Denizli* TR 188 B3
Kalecik TR 23 A7
Kalefeld D 82 A2
Kalesija BIH 139 A4
Kalety PL 86 B2
Kalevala RUS 3 D12
Kalhovd N 47 B5
Kalí HR 137 A4
Kalimnos GR 188 C2
Kaliningrad RUS 69 A5
Kalinkavichy BY 13 B8
Kalinovac HR 124 A3
Kalinovik BIH 139 B4
Kalinovo SK 99 C3
Kalirachi GR 183 C6
Kaliska, *Pomorskie* PL 68 A3
Kaliska, *Pomorskie* PL 68 B3
Kalisko PL 86 A3
Kalisz PL 86 A2
Kalisz Pomorski PL 75 A4
Kalix S 196 D6
Kaljord N 194 B6
Kalkan TR 189 C4
Kalkar D 80 A2
Kalkım TR 186 C2
Kall D 80 B2
Kall S 199 B10
Källby S 55 B4
Kållered S 60 B2
Kållerstad S 60 B3
Kallinge S 63 B3
Kallmünz D 95 B3
Kallo FIN 196 B7
Kallsedet S 199 B9
Källvik S 56 B3
Kalmar S 63 B4
Kalmthout B 79 A4
Kalná SK 112 A2
Kalo Nero GR 184 B2
Kalocsa H 112 C2
Kalokhorio CY 181 B2
Kaloni GR 186 C1
Káloz H 112 C2
Kals A 109 B3
Kalsdorf A 110 C2
Kaltbrunn CH 107 B4
Kaltenbach A 108 B2
Kaltenkirchen D 64 C2
Kaltennordheim D 82 B2
Kalundborg DK 61 D1
Kalush UA 13 D6
Kalv S 60 B3
Kalvåg N 198 D1
Kalvehave DK 65 A5
Kalwang A 110 B1
Kalwaria-Zebrzydowska PL 99 B3
Kalyazin RUS 9 D10
Kam H 111 B3
Kaman TR 23 B7
Kamares GR 185 C5
Kambos CY 181 A1
Kamen D 81 A3
Kamenice CZ 97 B3
Kamenice nad Lipou CZ 96 B3
Kameničná SK 112 B2
Kamenný Most SK 112 B2
Kamenny Ujezd CZ 96 C2
Kamenska HR 124 B3
Kamensko HR 138 B2
Kamenz D 84 A2
Kamičak BIH 124 C2
Kamień PL 87 A4
Kamień Krajeński PL 76 A2
Kamień Pomorski PL 67 C3
Kamieniec Zabk PL 85 B4
Kamienka SK 99 B4
Kamienna Góra PL 85 B4
Kamieńsk PL 86 A3
Kamiros Skala GR 188 C2
Kamnik SLO 123 A3
Kamp-Lintfort D 80 A2
Kampen NL 70 B2
Kampinos PL 77 B5
Kampor HR 123 C3
Kamyanets-Podil's'kyy UA 13 D7
Kamyanka-Buz'ka UA 13 C6
Kamýk n Vltavou CZ 96 B2
Kanal SLO 122 A2
Kanalia GR 182 D4
Kandalaksha RUS 3 C13
Kandanos GR 185 D4
Kandel D 93 B4
Kandern D 106 B2
Kandersteg CH 106 C2
Kandıra TR 187 A5
Kandila GR 184 B3
Kandyty PL 69 A5
Kanfanar HR 122 B2
Kangasala FIN 8 B4
Kangos S 196 B5
Kangosjärvi FIN 196 B6
Kaniów PL 75 C3
Kanjiža SRB 126 A2
Kankaanpää FIN 8 B3
Kannus FIN 3 E8
Kanturk IRL 29 B3
Kapaklı TR 186 A2
Kapellen A 110 B2
Kapellen B 79 A4
Kapellskär S 57 A5
Kapfenberg A 110 B2
Kapfenstein A 110 C2
Kaplice CZ 96 C2
Kapljuh BIH 124 C2
Kápolna H 113 B4
Kápolnásnyék H 112 B2
Kaposfö H 125 A3
Kaposfüred H 125 A3
Kaposszekcsö H 125 A4
Kaposvár H 125 A3
Kapp N 48 B2
Kappel D 93 C3
Kappeln D 64 B2
Kappelshamn S 57 C4
Kappl A 107 B5
Kappstad S 55 A4
Kaprun A 109 B3
Kaptol HR 125 B3
Kapuvár H 111 B4
Karaadilli TR 189 A5
Karabiğa TR 186 B2
Karabük TR 187 A7
Karaburun TR 186 D1
Karacabey TR 186 B3
Karacaköy TR 186 A3
Karacaören TR 189 A5
Karacasu TR 188 B3
Karácsond H 113 B4
Karád H 112 C1
Karahallı TR 189 A4
Karaisali TR 23 C8
Karaman, *Balıkesir* TR 186 C3
Karaman, *Karaman* TR 23 C7
Karamanlı TR 189 B4
Karamürsel TR 187 B4
Karan SRB 127 D1
Karancslapujto H 113 A3
Karaova TR 188 B2
Karapınar TR 23 C7
Karasjok N 193 C9
Karasu TR 187 A5
Karataş, *Adana* TR 23 C8
Karataş, *Manisa* TR 188 A3
Karatoprak TR 188 B2
Karavostasi CY 181 A1
Karbenning S 50 B3
Kårberg S 55 B5
Kårböle S 199 D12
Karby D 64 B2
Karby DK 58 B1
Kårby, *Kalmar* S 62 A4
Karby, *Stockholm* S 57 A4
Karcag H 113 B4
Karczów PL 86 B1
Karczowiska PL 85 A4
Kardamena GR 188 C2
Kardamila GR 185 A7
Kardamili GR 184 C3
Kardašova Rečice CZ 96 B2
Kardis S 196 C6
Karditsa GR 182 D3
Kärdla EST 8 C3
Kardoskút H 113 C4
Karesuando S 192 D6
Kargı TR 23 A8
Kargopol RUS 9 B11
Kargowa PL 75 B4
Karigasniemi FIN 193 C9
Karise DK 65 A5
Karistos GR 185 A5
Karkkila FIN 8 B4
Karlholmsbruk S 51 B4
Karlino PL 67 B4
Karlobag HR 137 A4
Karlovac HR 123 B4
Karlovasi GR 188 B1
Karlovčic SRB 127 C2
Karlovice CZ 85 B5
Karlovo BG 17 D6
Karlovy Vary CZ 83 B4
Karłowice PL 86 B1
Karlsborg S 55 B5
Karlshamn S 63 B2
Karlshöfen D 72 A2
Karlshus N 54 A1
Karlskoga S 55 A5
Karlskrona S 63 B3
Karlsrud N 47 B5
Karlsruhe D 93 B4
Karlstad S 55 A4
Karlstadt D 94 B1
Karlstetten A 110 A2
Karlstift A 96 C2
Karlstorp S 62 A3
Karmacs H 111 C4
Karmin PL 85 A5
Kärna S 60 B1
Karnobat BG 17 D7
Karojba HR 122 B2
Karow D 73 A5
Karpacz PL 85 B3
Karpathos GR 188 D2
Karpenisi GR 182 E3
Karpuzlu TR 188 B2
Kärrbo S 56 A2
Karrebaeksminde DK 65 A4
Karshult S 60 B3
Karsin PL 68 B2
Kårsta S 57 A4
Karstädt D 73 A4
Kartal TR 186 B4
Kartitsch A 109 C3
Kartuzy PL 68 A3
Karungi S 196 C6
Karunki FIN 196 C7
Karup DK 59 B2
Karviná CZ 98 B2
Kås DK 58 A2
Kaş TR 189 C4
Kasaba TR 189 C4
Kašava CZ 98 B1
Kåseberga S 66 A3
Kasejovice CZ 96 B1
Kasfjord N 194 B7
Kashin RUS 9 D10
Kašina HR 124 B2
Kasina-Wielka PL 99 B4
Kaskinen FIN 8 A2
Kašperské Hory CZ 96 B1
Kassandrino GR 183 C5
Kassel D 81 A5
Kassiopi GR 182 D1
Kastamonu TR 23 A7
Kastav HR 123 B3
Kaštel-Stari HR 138 B2
Kaštel Zegarski HR 138 A1
Kasteli GR 185 D4
Kastellaun D 93 A3
Kastelli GR 185 D6
Kasterlee B 79 A4
Kastl D 95 B3
Kastlösa S 63 B4
Kastorf D 65 C3
Kastoria GR 182 C3
Kastorio GR 184 B3
Kastraki GR 185 C6
Kastrosikia GR 182 D2
Kastsyukovichy BY 13 B10
Kaszaper H 113 C4
Katakolo GR 184 B2
Katapola GR 185 C6
Katastari GR 184 B1
Katerbow D 74 B1
Katerini GR 182 C4
Kathikas CY 181 B1
Kätkesuando S 196 A6
Katlenburg-Lindau D 82 A2
Kato Achaia GR 184 A2
Káto Pyrgos CY 181 A1
Katouna GR 182 E3
Katovice CZ 96 B1
Katowice PL 86 B3
Katrineberg S 50 A3
Katrineholm S 56 B2
Kattarp S 61 C2
Kattavia GR 188 D2
Katthammarsvik S 57 C4
Kattilstorp S 55 B4
Katwijk NL 70 B1
Kąty Wrocławskie PL 85 A4
Katymár H 125 A5
Katzenelnbogen D 81 B3
Katzhütte D 82 B3
Kaub D 93 A3
Kaufbeuren D 108 B1
Kauhajoki FIN 8 A3
Kauhava FIN 8 A3
Kaukonen FIN 196 B7
Kauliranta FIN 196 C6
Kaulsdorf D 82 B3
Kaunas LT 13 A5
Kaunisvaara S 196 B6
Kaupanger N 47 A4
Kautokeino N 192 C7
Kautzen A 97 C3
Kavadarci MK 182 B4
Kavajë AL 182 B1
Kavakköy TR 186 B1
Kavaklı TR 186 A2
Kavaklıdere TR 188 B3
Kavala GR 183 C6
Kavarna BG 17 D8
Kävlinge S 61 D3
Kawcze PL 68 A1
Kaxås S 199 B10
Kaxholmen S 62 A2
Käylä FIN 197 C12
Kaymakçı TR 188 A3
Kaymaz TR 187 C6
Kaynarca TR 187 A5
Käyrämö FIN 197 C9
Kayseri TR 23 B8
Kaysersberg F 106 A2
Kazanlŭk BG 17 D6
Kazár H 113 A3
Kazimierza Wielka PL 87 B4
Kazincbarcika H 113 A4
Kaźmierz PL 75 B5
Kcynia PL 76 A2
Kdyně CZ 95 B5
Kea GR 185 B5
Keadow IRL 26 B2
Keady GB 27 B4
Kecel H 112 C3
Keçiborlu TR 189 B5
Kecskemét H 113 C3
Kėdainiai LT 13 A5
Kędzierzyn-Koźle PL 86 B2
Keel IRL 28 A1
Keenagh IRL 28 A4
Keerbergen B 79 A4
Kefalos GR 188 C1
Kefken TR 187 A5
Keflavík IS 190 C3
Kegworth GB 40 C2
Kehl D 93 C3
Kehrigk D 74 B2
Keighley GB 40 B2
Keila EST 8 C4
Keillmore GB 34 C2
Keiss GB 32 C3
Keith GB 33 D4
Kelankylä FIN 197 D10
Kelberg D 80 B2
Kelbra D 82 A3
Kelč CZ 98 B1
Kelchsau A 108 B3
Këlcyrë AL 182 C2
Keld GB 37 B4
Kelebia H 126 A1
Kelekçi TR 188 B4
Kelemér H 99 C4
Keles TR 186 C4
Kelheim D 95 C3
Kell D 92 B2
Kellas GB 32 D3
Kellinghusen D 64 C2
Kelloselkä FIN 197 C11
Kells GB 27 B4
Kells IRL 27 C4
Kelmis B 80 B2
Kelokedhara CY 181 B1
Kelottijärvi FIN 192 D6
Kelsall GB 38 A4
Kelso GB 35 C5
Kelsterbach D 93 A4
Keltneyburn GB 35 B3
Kelujärvi FIN 197 B10
Kemaliye TR 188 A3
Kemalpaşa TR 188 A2
Kematen A 108 B2
Kemberg D 83 A4
Kemer, *Antalya* TR 189 C5
Kemer, *Burdur* TR 189 B5
Kemer, *Muğla* TR 189 C4
Kemerkaya TR 187 D6
Kemeten A 111 B3
Kemi FIN 196 D7
Kemijärvi FIN 197 C10
Keminmaa FIN 196 D7
Kemnath D 95 B3
Kemnay GB 33 D4
Kemnitz, *Brandenburg* D 74 B1
Kemnitz, *Mecklenburg-Vorpommern* D 66 B2
Kempen D 80 A2
Kempsey GB 39 B4
Kempten D 107 B5
Kemptthal CH 107 B3
Kendal GB 37 B4
Kenderes H 113 B4
Kengyel H 113 B4
Kenilworth GB 44 A2
Kenmare IRL 29 C2
Kenmore GB 35 B4
Kennacraig GB 34 C2
Kenyeri H 111 B4
Kenzingen D 106 A2
Kepez TR 186 B1
Kępice PL 68 A1
Kępno PL 86 A2
Kepsut TR 186 C3
Keramoti GR 183 C6
Keräntöjärvi S 196 B6
Keratea GR 185 B4
Kerava FIN 8 B4
Kerecsend H 113 B4
Kerekegyhaza H 112 C3
Kerepestarcsa H 112 B3
Keri GR 184 B1
Kérien F 100 A2
Kerkafalva H 111 C3
Kerken D 80 A2
Kerkrade NL 80 B2
Kerkyra GR 182 D1
Kerlouan F 100 A1
Kernascléden F 100 A2
Kernhof A 110 B2
Kerns CH 106 C3
Kerpen D 80 B2
Kerrysdale GB 31 B3
Kerta H 111 B4
Kerteminde DK 59 C3
Kerzers CH 106 C2
Keşan TR 186 B1
Kesgrave GB 45 A5
Kesh GB 26 B3
Keskin TR 23 B7
Kesselfall A 109 B3
Kestenga RUS 3 D12
Keswick GB 36 B3
Keszthely H 111 C4
Kétegyháza H 113 C5
Kéthely H 111 C4
Kętrzyn PL 12 A4
Kettering GB 44 A3
Kettlewell GB 40 A1
Kęty PL 99 B3
Ketzin D 74 B1
Keula D 82 A2
Keuruu FIN 8 A4
Kevelaer D 80 A2
Kevermes H 113 C5
Kevi SRB 126 B1
Keyingham GB 41 B3
Keynsham GB 43 A4
Kežmarok SK 99 B4
Kharmanli BG 183 B7
Khaskovo BG 183 B7
Khimki RUS 9 E10
Khisinev = Chişinău MD 17 B8
Khmelnik UA 13 D7
Khmelnytskyy UA 13 D7
Khodoriv UA 13 D6
Kholm RUS 9 D7
Khotyn UA 13 D7
Khoyniki BY 13 C8
Khust UA 17 A5

La Galera E 153 B4
La Garde-Freinet F 132 B2
La Garnache F 114 B2
La Garriga E 147 C3
La Garrovilla E 155 C4
La Gaubretière F 114 B2
La Gineta E 158 B1
La Granadella, *Alicante* E 159 C4
La Granadella, *Lleida* E 153 A4
La Grand-Combe F 131 A3
La Grande-Croix F 117 B4
La Grande-Motte F 131 B3
La Granja d'Escarp E 153 A4
La Granjuela E 156 B2
La Grave F 118 B3
La Gravelle F 101 A4
La Guardia E 151 C4
La Guardia de Jaén E 163 A4
La Guerche-de-Bretagne F 101 B4
La Guerche-sur-l'Aubois F 104 C1
La Guérinière F 114 B1
La Haba E 156 B2
La Haye-du-Puits F 88 A2
La Haye-Pesnel F 88 B2
La Herlière F 78 B2
La Hermida E 142 A2
La Herrera E 158 C1
La Higuera E 158 C2
La Hiniesta E 149 A4
La Horcajada E 150 B2
La Horra E 143 C3
La Hulpe B 79 B4
La Hutte F 89 B4
La Iglesuela E 150 B3
La Iglesuela del Cid E 153 B3
La Iruela E 164 B2
La Javie F 132 A2
La Jonchère-St. Maurice F 116 A1
La Jonquera E 146 B3
La Lantejuela E 162 A2
La Línea de la Concepción E 162 B2
La Llacuna E 147 C2
La Londe-les-Maures F 132 B2
La Loupe F 89 B5
La Louvière B 79 B4
La Luisiana E 162 A2
La Machine F 104 C2
la Maddalena I 178 A3
La Mailleraye-sur-Seine F 89 A4
La Malène F 130 A2
La Mamola E 163 B4
La Manresana dels Prats E 147 C2
La Masadera E 145 C3
La Mata E 150 C3
La Mata de Ledesma E 149 A4
La Mata de Monteagudo E 142 B1
La Meilleraye-de-Bretagne F 101 B4
La Ménitré F 102 B1
La Mojonera E 164 C2
La Mole F 132 B2
La Molina E 147 B2
La Monnerie-le-Montel F 117 B3
La Morera E 155 C4
La Mothe-Achard F 114 B2
La Mothe-St. Héray F 115 B3
La Motte-Chalançon F 131 A4
La Motte-du-Caire F 132 A2
La Motte-Servolex F 118 B2
La Mudarra E 142 C2
La Muela E 152 A2
La Mure F 118 C2
La Nava E 161 B3
La Nava de Ricomalillo E 156 A3
La Nava de Santiago E 155 B4
La Neuve-Lyre F 89 B4
La Neuveville CH 106 B2
La Nocle-Maulaix F 104 C2
La Nuez de Arriba E 143 B3
La Paca E 164 B3
La Pacaudière F 117 A3
La Palma d'Ebre E 153 A4
La Palma del Condado E 161 B3
La Palme F 146 B4
La Palmyre F 114 C2
La Parra E 155 C4
La Pedraja de Portillo E 150 A3
La Peraleja E 152 B1
La Petit-Pierre F 93 C3
La Pinilla E 165 B3
La Plagne F 118 B3
La Plaza E 141 A4
La Pobla de Lillet E 147 B2
La Pobla de Vallbona E 159 B3
La Pobla Llarga E 159 B3
La Pola de Gordón E 142 B1
la Porta F 180 A2
La Pouëze F 102 B1
La Póveda de Soria E 143 B4
La Preste F 146 B3
La Primaube F 130 A1
La Puebla de Almoradie E 157 A4
La Puebla de Cazalla E 162 A2
La Puebla de los Infantes E 162 A2
La Puebla de Montalbán E 150 C3
La Puebla de Roda E 145 B4
La Puebla de Valdavia E 142 B2
La Puebla de Valverde E 152 B3
La Puebla del Río E 162 A1
La Pueblanueva E 150 C3
La Puerta de Segura E 164 A2
La Punt CH 107 C4
La Quintana E 162 A3
La Quintera E 162 A2
La Rábita, *Granada* E 164 C1
La Rábita, *Jaén* E 163 A3
La Rambla E 163 A3
La Reale I 178 A2
La Redondela E 161 B2
La Réole F 128 B2
La Riera E 141 A4
La Riera de Gaià E 147 C2
La Rinconada E 162 A1
La Rivière-Thibouville F 89 A4
La Robla E 142 B1
La Roca de la Sierra E 155 B4
La Roche CH 106 C2
La Roche-Bernard F 101 B3
La Roche-Canillac F 116 B1
La Roche-Chalais F 128 A3
La Roche Derrien F 100 A2
La Roche-des-Arnauds F 132 A1
La Roche-en-Ardenne B 80 B1
La Roche-en-Brénil F 104 B3
La Roche-Guyon F 90 B1
La Roche-Posay F 115 B4
La Roche-sur-Foron F 118 A3
La Roche-sur-Yon F 114 B2
La Rochebeaucourt-et-Argentine F 115 C4
La Rochefoucauld F 115 C4
La Rochelle F 114 B2
La Rochette F 131 A4
La Roda, *Albacete* E 158 B1
La Roda, *Oviedo* E 141 A4
La Roda de Andalucía E 162 A3
La Roque-Gageac F 129 B4
La Roque-Ste. Marguerite F 130 A2
La Roquebrussanne F 132 B1
La Rubia E 143 C4
La Sagrada E 149 B3
La Salceda E 151 A4
La Salle F 118 C3
la Salute di Livenza I 122 B1
La Salvetat-Peyralés F 130 A1
La Salvetat-sur-Agout F 130 B1
La Sarraz CH 105 C5
La Seca E 150 A3
La Selva del Camp E 147 C2
La Senia E 153 B4
La Serra E 147 C2
La Seu d'Urgell E 146 B2
La Seyne-sur-Mer F 132 B1
La Solana E 157 B4
La Souterraine F 116 A1
La Spézia I 134 A2
La Storta I 168 B2
La Suze-sur-Sarthe F 102 B2
La Teste F 128 B1
La Thuile I 119 B3
La Toba E 152 B2
La Toledana E 157 A3
La Torre de Cabdella E 146 B1
La Torre de Esteban Hambrán E 151 B3
La Torre del l'Espanyol E 153 A4
La Torresaviñán E 152 B1
La Tour d'Aigues F 132 B1
La Tour de Peilz CH 106 C1
La Tour-du-Pin F 118 B2
La Tranche-sur-Mer F 114 B2
La Tremblade F 114 C2
La Trimouille F 115 B5
La Trinité F 100 B2
La Trinité-Porhoët F 101 A3
La Turballe F 101 B3
La Uña E 142 A1
La Unión E 165 B4
La Vall d'Uixó E 159 B3
La Vecilla de Curueño E 142 B1
La Vega, *Asturias* E 141 A5
La Vega, *Asturias* E 142 A1
La Vega, *Cantabria* E 142 A2
La Velilla E 151 A4
La Velles E 150 A2
La Ventosa E 152 B1
La Victoria E 162 A3
La Vid E 151 A4
La Vilavella E 159 B3
La Vilella Baixa E 147 C1
La Villa de Don Fadrique E 157 A4
La Ville Dieu-du-Temple F 129 B4
La Villedieu F 115 B3
La Voulte-sur-Rhône F 117 C4
La Wantzenau F 93 C3
La Yesa E 159 B3
La Zubia E 163 A4
Laa an der Thaya A 97 C4
Laage D 65 C5
Laanila FIN 193 D11
Laatzen D 72 B2
Laban IRL 28 A3
Labastide-Murat F 129 B4
Labastide-Rouairoux F 130 B1
Labastide-St. Pierre F 129 C4
Lábatlan H 112 B2
Labenne F 128 C1
Labin HR 123 B3
Łabiszyn PL 76 B2
Lablachère F 131 A3
Lábod H 124 A3
Laboe D 64 B3
Labouheyre F 128 B2
Łabowa PL 99 B4
Labrit F 128 B2
Labros E 152 A2
Labruguière F 130 B1
Labrujo P 148 A1
L'Absie F 114 B3
Laç AL 182 B1
Lacalahorra E 164 B1
Lacanau F 128 B1
Lacanau-Océan F 128 A1
Lacanche F 104 B3
Lacapelle-Marival F 129 B4
Laćarak SRB 127 B1
Lacaune F 130 B1
Laceby GB 41 B3
Lacedónia I 172 A1
Láces I 108 C1
Lachania GR 188 D2
Lachen CH 107 B3
Lachendorf D 72 B3
Lachowice PL 99 B3
Łąck PL 77 B4
Läckeby S 62 B4
Läckö S 55 B4
Lacock GB 43 A4
Láconi I 179 C3
Lacq F 145 A3
Lacroix-Barrez F 116 C2
Lacroix-St. Ouen F 90 B2
Lacroix-sur-Meuse F 92 C1
Łącznik PL 86 B1
Lad H 125 A3
Ladbergen D 71 B4
Lądek-Zdrój PL 85 B4
Ladelund D 64 B2
Ladendorf A 97 C4
Ladignac-le-Long F 115 C5
Ladíspoli I 168 B2
Ladoeiro P 155 B3
Ladon F 103 B4
Ladushkin RUS 69 A5
Ladybank GB 35 B4
Laer D 71 B4
Lærdalsøyri N 47 A4
Lafkos GR 183 D5
Lafnitz A 111 B3
Lafrançaise F 129 B4
Lagan S 60 C3
Laganadi I 175 C1
Lagarde F 146 A2
Lagares, *Coimbra* P 148 B2
Lagares, *Porto* P 148 A1
Lagaro I 135 A4
Lagartera E 150 C2
Lågbol S 51 B5
Lage D 72 C1
Lägerdorf D 64 C2
Lagg GB 34 C2
Laggan GB 32 D2
Laggartorp S 55 A5
Łagiewniki PL 85 B4
Láglio I 120 B2
Lagnieu F 118 B2
Lagny-sur-Marne F 90 C2
Lago, *Calabria* I 175 B2
Lago, *Veneto* I 121 B5
Lagôa P 160 B1
Lagoaça P 149 A3
Lagonegro I 174 A1
Lagos GR 183 B7
Lagos P 160 B1
Lagosanto I 121 C5
Łagów, *Lubuskie* PL 75 B4
Łagów, *Świętokrzyskie* PL 87 B5
Lagrasse F 146 A3
Laguardia E 143 B4
Laguarres E 145 B4
Laguenne F 116 B1
Laguépie F 129 B4
Laguiole F 116 C2
Laguna de Duera E 150 A3
Laguna de Negrillos E 142 B1
Laguna del Marquesado E 152 B2
Lagundo I 108 C2
Lagunilla E 149 B3
Laharie F 128 B1
Lahden D 71 B4
Laheycourt F 91 C5
Lahnstein D 81 B3
Laholm S 61 C3
Lahr D 93 C3
Lahti FIN 8 B4
Laichingen D 94 C1
L'Aigle F 89 B4
Laignes F 104 B3
Laiguéglia I 133 B4
L'Aiguillon-sur-Mer F 114 B2
Laimbach am Ostrong A 97 C3
Laina E 152 A1
Lainio S 196 B5
Lairg GB 32 C2
Laissac F 130 A1
Laisvall S 195 D8
Láives I 121 A4
Lajkovac SRB 127 C2
Lajoskomárom H 112 C2
Lajosmizse H 112 B3
Lak H 99 C4
Lakenheath GB 45 A4
Lakitelek H 113 C4
Lakki GR 185 D4
Lakolk DK 64 A1
Łąkorz PL 69 B4
Lakšárska Nová Ves SK 98 C1
Lakselv N 193 B8
Laksfors N 195 E4
Laktaši BIH 124 C3
Lalapaşa TR 186 A1
L'Albagès E 153 A4
Lalbenque F 129 B4
L'Alcudia E 159 B3
L'Aldea E 153 B4
Lalín E 140 B2
Lalinde F 129 B3
Lalizolle F 116 A3
Lalley F 118 C2
Lalling D 95 C5
Lalm N 198 D6
L'Alpe-d'Huez F 118 B3
Laluque F 128 C1
Lam D 95 B5
Lama dei Peligni I 169 A4
Lama Mocogno I 135 A3
Lamadrid E 142 A2
Lamagistére F 129 B3
Lamarche F 105 A4
Lamarche-sur-Saône F 105 B4
Lamargelle F 105 B3
Lamarosa P 154 B2
Lamarque F 128 A2
Lamas P 148 B1
Lamas de Moaro P 140 B2
Lamastre F 117 C4
Lambach A 109 A4
Lamballe F 101 A3
Lamberhurst GB 45 B4
Lambesc F 131 B4
Lambia GR 184 B2
Lambley GB 37 B4
Lambourn GB 44 B2
Lamego P 148 A2
L'Ametlla de Mar E 153 B4
Lamia GR 182 E4
Lammhult S 62 A2
Lamothe-Cassel F 129 B4
Lamothe-Montravel F 128 B3
Lamotte-Beuvron F 103 B4
Lampertheim D 93 B4
Lampeter GB 39 B2
L'Ampolla E 153 B4
Lamprechtshausen A 109 B3
Lamsfeld D 74 C3
Lamspringe D 72 C3
Lamstedt D 72 A2
Lamure-sur-Azergues F 117 A4
Lana I 108 C2
Lanaja E 145 C3
Lanarce F 117 C3
Lanark GB 36 A3
Lancaster GB 37 B4
Lanchester GB 37 B5
Lanciano I 169 A4
Lancing GB 44 C3
Lancon-provence F 131 B4
Lancova Vas SLO 124 A1
Landau, *Bayern* D 95 C4
Landau, *Rheinland-Pfalz* D 93 B4
Landeck A 108 B1
Landen B 79 B5
Landerneau F 100 A1
Landeryd S 60 B3
Landesbergen D 72 B2
Landete E 158 B2
Landévant F 100 B2
Landévennec F 100 A1
Landivisiau F 100 A1
Landivy F 88 B2
Landl A 108 B3
Landön S 199 B11
Landos F 117 C3
Landouzy-le-Ville F 91 B4
Landquart CH 107 C4
Landrecies F 91 A3
Landreville F 104 A3
Landriano I 120 B2
Lands-berg D 83 A4
Landsberg D 108 A1
Landsbro S 62 A2
Landscheid D 92 B2
Landshut D 95 C4
Landskrona S 61 D2
Landstuhl D 93 B3
Lanesborough IRL 28 A4
Lanester F 100 B2
Lanestosa E 143 A3
Langå DK 59 B2
Langa de Duero E 151 A4
Langada GR 185 A7
Langadas GR 183 C5
Langadia GR 184 B3
Langangen N 53 A5
Långared S 60 A2
Långaröd S 61 D3
Långaryd S 60 B3
Långås S 60 C2
Långasjö S 63 B3
Langau A 97 C3
Langeac F 117 B3
Langeais F 102 B2
Langedijk NL 70 B1
Langeln D 73 C3
Langelsheim D 72 C3
Langemark-Poelkapelle B 78 B2
Langen, *Hessen* D 93 B4
Langen, *Niedersachsen* D 72 A1
Langenau D 94 C2
Langenberg D 81 A4
Langenbruck CH 106 B2
Langenburg D 94 B1
Längenfeld A 108 B1
Langenfeld D 80 A2
Langenhorn D 64 B1
Langenlois A 97 C3
Langenlonsheim D 93 B3
Langennaudorf D 83 A5
Langenneufnach D 94 C2
Langenthal CH 106 B2
Langenzenn D 94 B2
Langeoog D 71 A4
Langeskov DK 59 C3
Langesund N 53 A5
Langewiesen D 82 B2
Långflon S 49 A4
Langförden D 71 B5
Langhagen D 73 A5
Länghem S 60 B3
Langhirano I 120 C3
Langholm GB 36 A4
Langholt IS 191 D7
Långlöt S 62 B4
Langnau CH 106 C2
Langø DK 65 B4
Langogne F 117 C3
Langon F 128 B2
Langquaid D 95 C4
Långrådna S 56 B2
Langreo E 142 A1
Langres F 105 B4
Långsele S 200 C3
Långserud S 54 A3
Langset N 48 B3
Långshyttan S 50 B3
Langstrand N 192 B7
Långträsk S 196 D3
Langueux F 101 A3
Languidic F 100 B2
Längvik S 57 A4
Langwarden D 71 A5
Langwathby GB 37 B4
Langwedel D 72 B2
Langweid D 94 C2
Langwies CH 107 C4
Lanheses P 148 A1
Lanięta PL 77 B4
Lanildut F 100 A1
Lanjarón E 163 B4
Lanmeur F 100 A2
Lanna, *Jönköping* S 60 B3
Lanna, *Örebro* S 55 A5
Lännaholm S 51 C4
Lannavaara S 196 A4
Lannéanou F 100 A2
Lannemezan F 145 A4
Lanneuville-sur-Meuse F 91 B5
Lannilis F 100 A1
Lannion F 100 A2
Lanouaille F 115 C5
Lansjärv S 196 C5
Lanškroun CZ 97 B4
Lanslebourg-Mont-Cenis F 119 B3
Lanta F 129 C4
Lantadilla E 142 B2
Lanton F 128 B1
Lantosque F 133 B3
Lanusei I 179 C3
Lanúvio I 168 B2
Lanvollon F 100 A3
Lánycsók H 125 A4
Lanz D 73 A4
Lanza E 140 A2
Lanzada E 140 B2
Lanzahita E 150 B3
Lanžhot CZ 97 C4
Lanzo Torinese I 119 B4
Laole SRB 127 C3
Laon F 91 B3
Laons F 89 B5
Lapalisse F 117 A3
Łapczyna Wola PL 87 B3
Lapeyrade F 128 B2
Lapeyrouse F 116 A2
Lapford GB 42 B3
Lapithos CY 181 A2
Laplume F 129 B3
Lapoutroie F 106 A2
Lapovo SRB 127 C3
Läppe S 56 A1
Lappeenranta FIN 8 B6
Lappoluobbal N 192 C7
Lappträsk S 196 C6
Lapseki TR 186 B1
Lapua FIN 8 A3
L'Aquila I 169 A3
Laracha E 140 A2
Laragh IRL 30 A2
Laragne-Montéglin F 132 A1
l'Arboç E 147 C2
L'Arbresle F 117 B4
Lärbro S 57 C4
Larceveau F 144 A2
Larche, *Alpes-de-Haute-Provence* F 132 A2
Larche, *Corrèze* F 129 A4
Lårdal N 53 A4
Lardosa P 155 B3
Laredo E 143 A3
Largentière F 131 A3
L'Argentière-la-Bessée F 118 C3
Largs GB 34 C3
Lari I 134 B3
Lariño E 140 B1
Larino I 170 B2
Larisa GR 182 D4
Larkhall GB 36 A3
Larkollen N 54 A1
Larmor-Plage F 100 B2
Larnaca CY 181 B2
Larne GB 27 B5
Larochette L 92 B2
Laroque d'Olmes F 146 B2
Laroque-Timbaut F 129 B3
Laroquebrou F 116 C2
Larouco E 141 B3
Larraga E 144 B2
Larrau F 144 A3
Larrazet F 129 C4
Larsnes N 198 C2
Laruns F 145 A3
Larva E 164 B1
Larvik N 53 A6
Las Arenas E 142 A2
Las Cabezadas E 151 A4
Las Cabezas de San Juan E 162 B2
Las Correderas E 157 B4

Malczyce PL 85 A4
Maldegem B 79 A3
Maldon GB 45 B4
Małdyty PL 69 B4
Malè I 121 A3
Malemort F 129 A4
Malente D 65 B3
Mâlerås S 62 B3
Males GR 185 D6
Malesherbes F 90 C2
Malesina GR 183 E5
Malestroit F 101 B3
Maletto I 177 B3
Malexander S 56 B1
Malgrat de Mar E 147 C3
Malhadas P 149 A3
Mali Lošinj HR 137 A3
Malia CY 181 B1
Malia GR 185 D6
Malicorne-sur-Sarthe F 102 B1
Malijai F 132 A2
Malildjoš SRB 126 B1
Målilla S 62 A3
Malin IRL 27 A3
Málinec SK 99 C3
Malingsbo S 50 C2
Maliniec PL 76 B3
Malinska HR 123 B3
Maliq AL 182 C2
Maljevac HR 123 B4
Malkara TR 186 B1
Małki PL 69 B4
Malko Tŭrnovo BG 17 D7
Mallaig GB 34 A2
Mallaranny IRL 28 A2
Mallemort F 131 B4
Mallén E 144 C2
Malléon F 146 A2
Mallersdorf-Pfaffenberg D 95 C4
Málles Venosta I 108 C1
Malling DK 59 B3
Mallnitz A 109 C4
Mallow IRL 29 B3
Mallwyd GB 38 B3
Malm N 199 A8
Malmbäck S 62 A2
Malmberget S 196 B3
Malmby S 56 A3
Malmédy B 80 B2
Malmesbury GB 43 A4
Malmköping S 56 A2
Malmö S 61 D3
Malmon S 54 B2
Malmslätt S 56 B1
Malnate I 120 B1
Malo I 121 B4
Małogoszcz PL 87 B4
Maloja CH 120 A2
Małomice PL 84 A3
Måløy N 198 D2
Malpartida E 155 B4
Malpartida de la Serena E 156 B2
Malpartida de Plasencia E 150 C1
Malpas E 145 B4
Malpas GB 38 A4
Malpica P 155 B3
Malpica de Bergantiños E 140 A2
Malpica de Tajo E 150 C3
Malsch D 93 C4
Malšice CZ 96 B2
Malta A 109 C4
Maltat F 104 C2
Maltby GB 40 B2
Malung S 49 B5
Malungsfors S 49 B5
Maluszów PL 75 B4
Maluszyn PL 87 B3
Malva E 142 C1
Malvaglia CH 120 A1
Malveira P 154 C1
Malvik N 199 B7
Malyn UA 13 C8
Mamarrosa P 148 B1
Mamer L 92 B2
Mamers F 89 B4
Mamirolle F 105 B5
Mammendorf D 108 A2
Mámmola I 175 C2
Mamoiada I 178 B3
Mamonovo RUS 69 A4
Mamuras AL 182 B1
Maňa SK 112 A2
Manacor E 167 B3
Manavgat TR 189 C6
Mancera de Abajo E 150 B2
Mancha Real E 163 A4
Manchester GB 40 B1
Manching D 95 C3
Manchita E 156 B1
Manciano I 168 A1
Manciet F 128 C3
Mandal N 52 B3
Mandanici I 177 A4
Mándas I 179 C3
Mandatoríccio I 174 B2
Mandayona E 151 B5
Mandelieu-la-Napoule F 132 B2
Mandello del Lário I 120 B2
Mandelsloh D 72 B2
Manderfeld B 80 B2
Manderscheid D 80 B2
Mandino Selo BIH 138 B3
Mandoudi GR 183 E5
Mandra GR 185 A4
Mandraki GR 188 C2
Mandúria I 173 B3
Mane, *Alpes-de-Haute-Provence* F 132 B1
Mane, *Haute-Garonne* F 145 A4
Manérbio I 120 B3
Mañeru E 144 B2
Manetin CZ 96 B1
Manfredónia I 171 B3
Mangalia RO 17 D8
Manganeses de la Lampreana E 149 A4
Manganeses de la Polvorosa E 141 B5
Mangen N 48 C3
Manger N 46 B2
Mangiennes F 92 B1
Mangotsfield GB 43 A4
Mångsbodarna S 49 A5
Mangualde P 148 B2
Maniago I 122 A1
Manilva E 162 B2
Manisa TR 186 D2
Manises E 159 B3
Mank A 110 A2
Månkarbo S 51 B4
Manlleu E 147 C3
Manna DK 58 A2
Männedorf CH 107 B3
Mannersdorf am Leithagebirge A 111 B3
Mannheim D 93 B4
Manningtree GB 45 B5
Manoppello I 169 A4
Manorbier GB 39 C2
Manorhamilton IRL 26 B2
Manosque F 132 B1
Manowo PL 67 B5
Manresa E 147 C2
Månsarp S 62 A2
Månsåsen S 199 B11
Manschnow D 74 B3
Mansfeld D 82 A3
Mansfield GB 40 B2
Mansilla de Burgos E 143 B3
Mansilla de las Mulas E 142 B1
Manskog S 55 A3
Mansle F 115 C4
Manso F 180 A1
Manteigas P 148 B2
Mantel D 95 B4
Mantes-la-Jolie F 90 C1
Mantes-la-Ville F 90 C1
Manthelan F 102 B2
Mantorp S 56 B1
Mántova I 121 B3
Mänttä FIN 8 A4
Mäntyjärvi FIN 197 C10
Manuel E 159 B3
Manyas TR 186 B2
Manzanal de Arriba E 141 B4
Manzanares E 157 A4
Manzanares el Real E 151 B4
Manzaneda, *León* E 141 B4
Manzaneda, *Orense* E 141 B3
Manzanedo E 143 B3
Manzaneque E 157 A4
Manzanera E 153 B3
Manzanilla E 161 B3
Manzat F 116 B2
Manziana I 168 A2
Manziat F 117 A4
Maó E 167 B4
Maoča BIH 125 C4
Maqueda E 150 B3
Mara E 152 A2
Maramaraereğlisi TR 186 B2
Maraña E 142 A1
Maranchón E 152 A1
Maranello I 135 A3
Marano I 170 C2
Marano Lagunare I 122 B2
Marans F 114 B2
Maratea I 174 B1
Marateca P 154 C2
Marathokambos GR 188 B1
Marathonas GR 185 A4
Marathóvouno CY 181 A2
Marazion GB 42 B1
Marbach, *Baden-Württemberg* D 94 C1
Marbach, *Hessen* D 82 B1
Marbach F 92 C2
Marbäck S 60 B3
Mårbacka S 55 A4
Marbella E 162 B3
Marboz F 118 A2
Marburg D 81 B4
Marcali H 111 C4
Marčana HR 122 C2
Marcaria I 121 B3
Marcelová SK 112 B2
Marcenat F 116 B2
March GB 41 C4
Marchamalo E 151 B4
Marchaux F 105 B5
Marche-en-Famenne B 79 B5
Marchegg A 111 A3
Marchena E 162 A2
Marchenoir F 103 B3
Marcheprime F 128 B2
Marciac F 128 C3
Marciana Marina I 134 C3
Marcianise I 170 B2
Marcigny F 117 A4
Marcilla E 144 B2
Marcillac-la-Croisille F 116 B2
Marcillac-Vallon F 130 A1
Marcillat-en-Combraille F 116 A2
Marcille-sur-Seine F 91 C3
Marcilloles F 118 B2
Marcilly-le-Hayer F 91 C3
Marcinkowice PL 75 A5
Marciszów PL 85 B4
Marck F 78 B1
Marckolsheim F 106 A2
Marco de Canevezes P 148 A1
Mårdsele S 200 B5
Mårdsjö S 200 C1
Mareham le Fen GB 41 B3
Marek S 62 A3
Marennes F 114 C2
Maresquel F 78 B1
Mareuil F 115 C4
Mareuil-en-Brie F 91 C3
Mareuil-sur-Arnon F 103 C4
Mareuil-sur-Lay F 114 B2
Mareuil-sur-Ourcq F 90 B3
Margam GB 39 C3
Margariti GR 182 D2
Margate GB 45 B5
Margaux F 128 A2
Margerie-Hancourt F 91 C4
Margès F 117 B5
Margherita di Savóia I 171 B4
Margita SRB 126 B3
Margone I 119 B4
Margonin PL 76 B2
Marguerittes F 131 B3
Margut F 91 B5
Maria E 164 B2
Maria Neustift A 110 B1
Maria Saal A 110 C1
Mariager DK 58 B2
Mariana E 152 B1
Mariannelund S 62 A3
Marianópoli I 176 B2
Mariánské Lázně CZ 95 B4
Mariapfarr A 109 B4
Mariazell A 110 B2
Maribo DK 65 B4
Maribor SLO 110 C2
Marieberg S 56 A1
Mariefred S 56 A3
Mariehamn FIN 51 B6
Marieholm S 61 D3
Mariembourg B 91 A4
Marienbaum D 80 A2
Marienberg D 83 B5
Marienheide D 81 A3
Mariental D 73 B3
Mariestad S 55 B4
Marieux F 90 A2
Marigliano I 170 C2
Marignane F 131 B4
Marigny, *Jura* F 105 C4
Marigny, *Manche* F 88 A2
Marigny-le-Châtel F 91 C3
Marija Bistrica HR 124 A2
Marijampolė LT 13 A5
Marín E 140 B2
Marina HR 138 B2
Marina del Cantone I 170 C2
Marina di Acquappesa I 174 B1
Marina di Alberese I 168 A1
Marina di Amendolara I 174 B2
Marina di Árbus I 179 C2
Marina di Campo I 134 C3
Marina di Carrara I 134 A3
Marina di Castagneto-Donorático I 134 B3
Marina di Cécina I 134 B3
Marina di Gáiro I 179 C3
Marina di Ginosa I 173 B2
Marina di Gioiosa Iónica I 175 C2
Marina di Grosseto I 135 C3
Marina di Léuca I 173 C4
Marina di Massa I 134 A3
Marina di Nováglie I 173 C4
Marina di Pisa I 134 B3
Marina di Ragusa I 177 C3
Marina di Ravenna I 135 A5
Marina di Torre Grande I 179 C2
Marina Romea I 135 A5
Marinaleda E 162 A3
Marine de Sisco F 180 A2
Marinella I 176 B1
Marinella di Sarzana I 134 A3
Marineo I 176 B2
Marines F 90 B1
Maringues F 116 B3
Marinha das Ondas P 154 A2
Marinha Grande P 154 B2
Marinhas P 148 A1
Marino I 168 B2
Marjaliza E 157 A4
Markabygd N 199 B8
Markaryd S 61 C3
Markdorf D 107 B4
Markelo NL 71 B3
Market Deeping GB 40 C3
Market Drayton GB 38 B4
Market Harborough GB 40 C3
Market Rasen GB 40 B3
Market Warsop GB 40 B2
Market Weighton GB 40 B3
Markethill GB 27 B4
Markgröningen D 93 C5
Markhausen D 71 B4
Marki PL 77 B6
Markina-Xemein E 143 A4
Markinch GB 35 B4
Märkische Buchholz D 74 B2
Markitta S 196 B4
Markkleeberg D 83 A4
Marklohe D 72 B2
Marknesse NL 70 B2
Markneukirchen D 83 B4
Markopoulo GR 185 B4
Markovac, *Srbija* SRB 127 C3
Markovac, *Vojvodina* SRB 126 B3
Markowice PL 86 B2
Markranstädt D 83 A4
Marksuhl D 82 B2
Markt Allhau A 111 B3
Markt Bibart D 94 B2
Markt Erlbach D 94 B2
Markt-heidenfeld D 94 B1
Markt Indersdorf D 95 C3
Markt Rettenbach D 108 B1
Markt Schwaben D 108 A2
Markt-Übelbach A 110 B2
Marktbreit D 94 B2
Marktl D 95 C4
Marktleuthen D 83 B3
Marktoberdorf D 108 B1
Marktredwitz D 95 A4
Markusica HR 125 B4
Markušovce SK 99 C4
Marl D 80 A3
Marlborough, *Devon* GB 42 B3
Marlborough, *Wiltshire* GB 44 B2
Marle F 91 B3
Marlieux F 117 A5
Marlow D 66 B1
Marlow GB 44 B3
Marma S 51 B4
Marmagne F 104 C3
Marmande F 128 B3
Marmara TR 186 B2
Marmaris TR 188 C3
Marmelete P 160 B1
Marmolejo E 157 B3
Marmoutier F 93 C3
Marnay F 105 B4
Marne D 64 C2
Marnheim D 93 B4
Marnitz D 73 A4
Maroldsweisach D 82 B2
Marolles-les-Braults F 89 B4
Maromme F 89 A5
Marone I 120 B3
Maronia GR 183 C7
Maroslele H 126 A2
Maróstica I 121 B4
Marotta I 136 B2
Marpisa GR 185 B6
Marquion F 78 B3
Marquise F 78 B1
Marradi I 135 A4
Marrasjärvi FIN 197 C8
Marraskoski FIN 197 C8
Marratxi E 166 B2
Marrúbiu I 179 C2
Marrum NL 70 A2
Marrupe E 150 B3
Mars-la-Tours F 92 B1
Marsac F 129 C5
Marsac-en-Livradois F 117 B3
Marságlia I 120 C2
Marsala I 176 B1
Marsberg D 81 A4
Marsciano I 135 C5
Marseillan F 130 B2
Marseille = Marseilles F 131 B4
Marseille en Beauvaisis F 90 B1
Marseilles = Marseille F 131 B4
Mársico Nuovo I 172 B1
Marske-by-the-Sea GB 37 B5
Marsliden S 195 E6
Marson F 91 C4
Märsta S 57 A3
Marstal DK 65 B3
Marstrand S 60 B1
Marta I 168 A1
Martano I 173 B4
Martel F 129 B4
Martelange B 92 B1
Martfeld D 72 B2
Martfű H 113 B4
Martham GB 41 C5
Marthon F 115 C4
Martiago E 149 B3
Martigné-Briand F 102 B1
Martigné-Ferchaud F 101 B4
Martigne-sur-Mayenne F 102 A1
Martigny CH 119 A4
Martigny-les-Bains F 105 A4
Martigues F 131 B4
Martim-Longo P 160 B2
Martin SK 98 B2
Martin de la Jara E 162 A3
Martin Muñoz de las Posadas E 150 A3
Martina CH 108 C1
Martina Franca I 173 B3
Martinamor E 150 B2
Martinengo I 120 B2
Martinsberg A 97 C3
Martinšćica HR 123 C3
Martinshöhe D 93 B3
Martinsicuro I 136 C2
Martinszell D 107 B5
Mártis I 178 B2
Martofte DK 59 C3
Martonvásár H 112 B2
Martorell E 147 C2
Martos E 163 A4
Martres Tolosane F 146 A1
Martti FIN 197 B11
Marugán E 150 B3
Marúggio I 173 B3
Marvão P 155 B3
Marvejols F 130 A2
Marville F 92 B1
Marwałd PL 77 A4
Marykirk GB 35 B5
Marypark GB 32 D3
Maryport GB 36 B3
Marytavy GB 42 B2
Marzabotto I 135 A4
Marzahna D 74 C1
Marzahne D 73 B5
Marzamemi I 177 C4
Marzocca I 136 B2
Mas-Cabardès F 146 A3
Mas de Barberáns E 153 B4
Mas de las Matas E 153 B3
Masa E 143 B3
Máscali I 177 B4
Mascaraque E 157 A4
Mascarenhas P 149 A2
Mascioni I 169 A3
Masegoso E 158 C1
Masegoso de Tajuña E 151 B5
Masera I 119 A5
Masevaux F 106 B1
Masfjorden N 46 B2
Masham GB 37 B5
Masi N 192 C7
Maside E 140 B2
Maslacq F 144 A3
Maslinica HR 138 B2
Maşloc RO 126 B3
Maslovare BIH 138 A3
Masone I 133 A4
Massa I 134 A3
Massa Fiscáglia I 121 C5
Massa Lombarda I 135 A4
Massa Lubrense I 170 C2
Massa Marittima I 135 B3
Massa Martana I 136 C1
Massafra I 173 B3
Massamagrell E 159 B3
Massanassa E 159 B3
Massarosa I 134 B3
Massat F 146 B2
Massay F 103 B3
Massbach D 82 B2
Masseret F 116 B1
Masseube F 145 A4
Massiac F 116 B3
Massignac F 115 C4
Massing D 95 C4
Massmechelen B 80 B1
Masterud N 49 B4
Mästocka S 61 C3
Masty BY 13 B6
Masúa I 179 C2
Masueco E 149 A3
Masugnsbyn S 196 B5
Mašun SLO 123 B3
Maszewo, *Lubuskie* PL 75 B3
Maszewo, *Zachodnio-Pomorskie* PL 75 A4
Mata de Alcántara E 155 B4
Matala GR 185 E5
Matalebreras E 144 C1
Matallana de Torio E 142 B1
Matamala E 151 A5
Mataporquera E 142 B2
Matapozuelos E 150 A3
Mataró E 147 C3
Matarocco I 176 B1
Matélica I 136 B2
Matera I 172 B2
Mátészalka H 16 B5
Matet E 159 B3
Matfors S 200 D3
Matha F 115 C3
Mathay F 106 B1
Matignon F 101 A3
Matilla de los Caños del Rio E 149 B4
Matlock GB 40 B2
Matosinhos P 148 A1
Matour F 117 A4
Mátrafüred H 113 B3
Mátraterenye H 113 A3
Matre, *Hordaland* N 46 B2
Matre, *Hordaland* N 52 A1
Matrei am Brenner A 108 B2
Matrei in Osttirol A 109 B3
Matrice I 170 B2
Matsdal S 195 E6
Mattarello I 121 A4
Mattersburg A 111 B3
Mattighofen A 109 A4
Mattinata I 171 B4
Mattos P 154 B2
Mattsee A 109 B4
Mattsmyra S 50 A2
Måttsund S 196 D5
Matulji HR 123 B3
Maubert-Fontaine F 91 B4
Maubeuge F 79 B3
Maubourguet F 145 A4
Mauchline GB 36 A2
Maud GB 33 D4
Mauer-kirchen A 109 A4
Mauern D 95 C3
Mauguio F 131 B3
Maulbronn D 93 C4
Maule F 90 C1
Mauléon F 114 B3
Mauléon-Barousse F 145 B4
Mauléon-Licharre F 144 A3
Maulévrier F 114 A3
Maum IRL 28 A2
Maurach A 108 B2
Maure-de-Bretagne F 101 B4
Maureilhan F 130 B2
Măureni RO 126 B3
Mauriac F 116 B2
Mauron F 101 A3
Maurs F 116 C2
Maury F 146 B3
Maussane-les-Alpilles F 131 B3
Mautern A 97 C3
Mautern im Steiermark A 110 B1
Mauterndorf A 109 B4
Mauthausen A 110 A1
Mauthen A 109 C3
Mauvezin F 129 C3
Mauzé-sur-le-Mignon F 114 B3
Maxent F 101 B3
Maxey-sur-Vaise F 92 C1
Maxial P 154 B1
Maxieira P 154 C2
Maxwellheugh GB 35 C5
Mayalde E 149 A4
Maybole GB 36 A2
Mayen D 80 B3
Mayenne F 88 B3
Mayet F 102 B2
Maylough IRL 28 A3
Mayorga E 142 B1
Mayres F 117 C4
Mayrhofen A 108 B2
Mazagón E 161 B3
Mazaleón E 153 A4
Mazamet F 130 B1
Mazan F 131 A4
Mazara del Vallo I 176 B1
Mazarambroz E 157 A3
Mazarete E 152 B1
Mazaricos E 140 B2
Mazarrón E 165 B3

Moravče SLO 123 A3
Moravec CZ 97 B4
Moraviţa RO 126 B3
Morávka CZ 98 B2
Moravská Třebová CZ 97 B4
Moravské Budějovice CZ 97 B3
Moravské Lieskové SK 98 C1
Moravske Toplice SLO 111 C3
Moravský-Beroun CZ 98 B1
Moravský Krumlov CZ 97 B4
Moravský Svätý Ján SK 98 C1
Morawica PL 87 B4
Morawin PL 86 A2
Morbach D 92 B3
Morbegno I 120 A2
Morbier F 105 C5
Mörbisch am See A 111 B3
Mörbylånga S 63 B4
Morcenx F 128 B2
Morciano di Romagna I 136 B1
Morcone I 170 B2
Morcuera E 151 A4
Mordelles F 101 A4
Mordoğan TR 188 A1
Moréac F 100 B3
Morebattle GB 35 C5
Morecambe GB 36 B4
Moreda, *Granada* E 163 A4
Moreda, *Oviedo* E 142 A1
Morée F 103 B3
Moreles de Rey E 141 B5
Morella E 153 B3
Moreruela de los Infanzones E 149 A4
Morés E 152 A2
Móres I 178 B2
Morestel F 118 B2
Moret-sur-Loing F 90 C2
Moreton-in-Marsh GB 44 B2
Moretonhampstead GB 43 B3
Moretta I 119 C4
Moreuil F 90 B2
Morez F 105 C5
Mörfelden D 93 B4
Morgat F 100 A1
Morges CH 105 C5
Morgex I 119 B4
Morgongåva S 51 C3
Morhange F 92 C2
Morhet B 92 B1
Mori I 121 B3
Morialmé B 79 B4
Morianes P 160 B2
Moriani Plage F 180 A2
Mórichida H 111 B4
Moriles E 163 A3
Morille E 150 B2
Moringen D 82 A1
Morjärv S 196 C5
Morkarla S 51 B4
Mørke DK 59 B3
Mørkøv DK 61 D1
Morkovice-Slížany CZ 98 B1
Morlaàs F 145 A3
Morlaix F 100 A2
Morley F 91 C5
Mörlunda S 62 A3
Mormanno I 174 B1
Mormant F 90 C2
Mornant F 117 B4
Mornay-Berry F 103 B4
Morón de Almazán E 152 A1
Morón de la Frontera E 162 A2
Morović SRB 125 B5
Morozzo I 133 A3
Morpeth GB 37 A5
Morphou CY 181 A1
Mörrum S 63 B2
Morsbach D 81 B3
Mörsch D 93 C4
Mörsil S 199 B10
Morsum D 64 B1
Mørsvikbotn N 194 C6
Mortagne-au-Perche F 89 B4
Mortagne-sur-Gironde F 114 C3
Mortagne-sur-Sèvre F 114 B3
Mortágua P 148 B1
Mortain F 88 B3
Mortara I 120 B1
Morteau F 105 B5
Mortegliano I 122 B2
Mortelle I 177 A4
Mortemart F 115 B4
Mortimer's Cross GB 39 B4
Mortrée F 89 B4
Mörtschach A 109 C3
Mortsel B 79 A4
Morud DK 59 C3
Morwenstow GB 42 B2
Moryń PL 74 B3
Morzeszczyn PL 69 B3
Morzewo PL 69 B4
Morzine F 118 A3
Mosbach D 93 B5
Mosbjerg DK 58 A3
Mosby N 53 B3
Mosca P 149 A3
Moscavide P 154 C1
Moščenica HR 124 B2
Mošćenice HR 123 B3
Moščenicka Draga HR 123 B3
Mosciano Sant'Ángelo I 136 C2
Mościsko PL 85 B4
Moscow = Moskva RUS 9 E10
Mosina PL 75 B5
Mosjøen N 195 E4
Moskog N 46 A3
Moskorzew PL 87 B3
Moskosel S 196 D2
Moskuvarra FIN 197 B9
Moskva = Moscow RUS 9 E10
Moslavina Podravska HR 125 B3
Moşniţa Nouă RO 126 B3
Moso in Passíria I 108 C2
Mosonmagyaróvár H 111 B4
Mošorin SRB 126 B2
Mošovce SK 98 C2
Mosqueruela E 153 B3
Moss N 54 A1
Mossfellsbær IS 190 C4
Mössingen D 93 C5
Mosstrand N 47 C5
Most CZ 83 B5
Most na Soči SLO 122 A2
Mosta M 175 C3
Mostar BIH 139 B3
Mosterhamn N 52 A1
Mostki PL 75 B4
Móstoles E 151 B4
Mostová SK 111 A4
Mostowo PL 68 A1
Mostuéjouls F 130 A2
Mosty PL 75 A3
Mostys'ka UA 13 D5
Mosvik N 199 B7
Mota del Cuervo E 158 B1
Mota del Marqués E 150 A2
Motala S 55 B6
Motherwell GB 35 C4
Möthlow D 74 B1
Motilla del Palancar E 158 B2
Motnik SLO 123 A3
Motovun HR 122 B2
Motril E 163 B4
Motta I 121 B4
Motta di Livenza I 122 B1
Motta Montecorvino I 170 B3
Motta Visconti I 120 B1
Mottisfont GB 44 B2
Móttola I 173 B3
Mou DK 58 B3
Mouchard F 105 C4
Moudon CH 106 C1
Moudros GR 183 D7
Mougins F 132 B2
Mouilleron en-Pareds F 114 B3
Mouliherne F 102 B2
Moulinet F 133 B3
Moulins F 104 C2
Moulins-Engilbert F 104 C2
Moulins-la-Marche F 89 B4
Moulismes F 115 B4
Moult F 89 A3
Mount Bellew Bridge IRL 28 A3
Mountain Ash GB 39 C3
Mountfield GB 27 B3
Mountmellick IRL 30 A1
Mountrath IRL 30 A1
Mountsorrel GB 40 C2
Moura P 160 A2
Mourão P 155 C3
Mourenx F 145 A3
Mouriés F 131 B3
Mourmelon-le-Grand F 91 B4
Mouronho P 148 B1
Mourujärvi FIN 197 C11
Mouscron B 78 B3
Mousehole GB 42 B1
Moussac F 131 B3
Moussey F 92 C2
Mousteru F 100 A2
Moustey F 128 B2
Moustiers-Ste. Marie F 132 B2
Mouthe F 105 C5
Mouthier-Haute-Pierre F 105 B5
Mouthoumet F 146 B3
Moutier CH 106 B2
Moûtiers F 118 B3
Moutiers-les-Mauxfaits F 114 B2
Mouy F 90 B2
Mouzaki GR 182 D3
Mouzon F 91 B5
Møvik N 46 B2
Moville IRL 27 A3
Moy, *Highland* GB 32 D2
Moy, *Tyrone* GB 27 B4
Moycullen IRL 28 A2
Moyenmoutier F 92 C2
Moyenvic F 92 C2
Mózar E 141 C5
Mozhaysk RUS 9 E10
Mozirje SLO 123 A3
Mözs H 112 C2
Mozzanica I 120 B2
Mramorak SRB 127 C2
Mrčajevci SRB 127 D2
Mrkonjić Grad BIH 138 A3
Mrkopalj HR 123 B3
Mrocza PL 76 A2
Mroczeń PL 86 A1
Mroczno PL 69 B4
Mrzezyno PL 67 B4
Mšec CZ 84 B1
Mšeno CZ 84 B2
Mstów PL 86 B3
Mstsislaw BY 13 A9
Mszana Dolna PL 99 B4
Mszczonów PL 77 C5
Muć HR 138 B2
Múccia I 136 B2
Much D 80 B3
Much Marcle GB 39 C4
Much Wenlock GB 39 B4
Mücheln D 83 A3
Muchów PL 85 A4
Mucientes E 142 C2
Muckross IRL 29 B2
Mucur TR 23 B8
Muda P 160 B1
Mudanya TR 186 B3
Mudau D 93 B5
Müden D 72 B3
Mudersbach D 81 B3
Mudurnu TR 187 B6
Muel E 152 A2
Muelas del Pan E 149 A4
Muess D 73 A4
Muff IRL 27 A3
Mugardos E 140 A2
Muge P 154 B2
Mügeln, *Sachsen-Anhalt* D 83 A5
Mügeln, *Sachsen* D 83 A5
Múggia I 122 B2
Muğla TR 188 B3
Mugnano I 135 B5
Mugron F 128 C2
Mugueimes E 140 C3
Muhi H 113 B4
Mühlacker D 93 C4
Mühlbach am Hochkönig A 109 B4
Mühlberg, *Brandenburg* D 83 A5
Mühlberg, *Thüringen* D 82 B2
Mühldorf A 109 C4
Mühldorf D 95 C4
Muhleberg CH 106 C2
Mühleim D 107 A3
Muhlen-Eichsen D 65 C4
Mühlhausen, *Bayern* D 94 B2
Mühlhausen, *Thüringen* D 82 A2
Mühltroff D 83 B3
Muhos FIN 3 D10
Muhr A 109 B4
Muine Bheag IRL 30 B2
Muir of Ord GB 32 D2
Muirkirk GB 36 A2
Muirteira P 154 B1
Mukacheve UA 12 D5
Muker GB 37 B4
Mula E 165 A3
Mulben GB 32 D3
Mulegns CH 107 C4
Mules I 108 C2
Mülheim D 80 A2
Mulhouse F 106 B2
Muljava SLO 123 B3
Mullanys Cross IRL 26 B2
Müllheim D 106 B2
Mullhyttan S 55 A5
Mullinavat IRL 30 B1
Mullingar IRL 30 A1
Mullion GB 42 B1
Müllrose D 74 B3
Mullsjö S 60 B3
Mulseryd S 60 B3
Munaðarnes IS 190 A4
Munana E 150 B3
Muñás E 141 A4
Münchberg D 83 B3
Müncheberg D 74 B3
München = Munich D 108 A2
Munchen-Gladbach = Mönchen-gladbach D 80 A2
Münchhausen D 81 B4
Mundaka E 143 A4
Münden D 82 A1
Munderfing A 109 A4
Munderkingen D 107 A4
Mundesley GB 41 C5
Munera E 158 B1
Mungia E 143 A4
Munich = München D 108 A2
Muñico E 150 B2
Muniesa E 153 A3
Munka-Ljungby S 61 C2
Munkebo DK 59 C3
Munkedal S 54 B2
Munkflohögen S 199 B11
Munkfors S 49 C5
Munktorp S 56 A2
Münnerstadt D 82 B2
Muñopepe E 150 B3
Muñotello E 150 B2
Münsingen CH 106 C2
Münsingen D 94 C1
Munsö S 57 A3
Münster CH 106 C3
Münster, *Hessen* D 93 B4
Munster, *Niedersachsen* D 72 B3
Münster, *Nordrhein-Westfalen* D 71 C4
Munster F 106 A2
Muntibar E 143 A4
Münzkirchen A 96 C1
Muodoslompolo S 196 B6
Muonio FIN 196 B6
Muotathal CH 107 C3
Mur-de-Barrez F 116 C2
Mur-de-Bretagne F 100 A2
Mur-de-Sologne F 103 B3
Muradiye TR 186 D2
Murakeresztúr H 124 A2
Murán SK 99 C4
Murano I 122 B1
Muras E 140 A3
Murat F 116 B2
Murat-sur-Vèbre F 130 B1
Muratlı TR 186 A2
Murato F 180 A2
Murau A 109 B5
Muravera I 179 C3
Murazzano I 133 A4
Murça P 148 A2
Murchante E 144 B2
Murchin D 66 C2
Murcia E 165 B3
Murczyn PL 76 B2
Mureck A 110 C2
Mürefte TR 186 B2
Muret F 146 A2
Murg CH 107 B4
Murguia E 143 B4
Muri CH 106 B3
Murias de Paredes E 141 B4
Muriedas E 143 A3
Muriel Viejo E 143 C4
Murillo de Rio Leza E 143 B4
Murillo el Fruto E 144 B2
Murjek S 196 C3
Murlaggan GB 34 B2
Murmansk RUS 3 B13
Murmashi RUS 3 B13
Murnau D 108 B2
Muro E 167 B3
Muro F 180 A1
Muro de Alcoy E 159 C3
Muro Lucano I 172 B1
Murol F 116 B2
Muron F 114 B3
Muros E 140 B1
Muros de Nalón E 141 A4
Murowana Goślina PL 76 B2
Mürren CH 106 C2
Murrhardt D 94 C1
Murska Sobota SLO 111 C3
Mursko Središce HR 111 C3
Murtas E 164 C1
Murten CH 106 C2
Murter HR 137 B4
Murtiçi TR 189 C6
Murtosa P 148 B1
Murtovaara FIN 197 D12
Murvica HR 137 A4
Murviel-lès-Béziers F 130 B2
Mürzsteg A 110 B2
Murzynowo PL 75 B4
Mürzzuschlag A 110 B2
Musculdy F 144 A3
Muskö S 57 A4
Mušov CZ 97 C4
Musselburgh GB 35 C4
Musselkanaal NL 71 B4
Mussidan F 129 A3
Mussomeli I 176 B2
Musson B 92 B1
Mussy-sur-Seine F 104 B3
Mustafakemalpaşa TR 186 B3
Muszaki PL 77 A5
Muszyna PL 99 B4
Mut TR 23 C7
Muta SLO 110 C2
Muthill GB 35 B4
Mutné SK 99 B3
Mutriku E 143 A4
Muttalip TR 187 C5
Mutterbergalm A 108 B2
Muurola FIN 197 C8
Muxía E 140 A1
Muxilka-Ugarte E 143 A4
Muzillac F 101 B3
Mužla SK 112 B2
Muzzano del Turgnano I 122 B2
Mybster GB 32 C3
Myckelgensjö S 200 C3
Myennes F 104 B1
Myjava SK 98 C1
Myking N 46 B2
Mykland N 53 B4
Myra N 53 B5
Myrdal N 46 B4
Myre, *Nordland* N 194 A6
Myre, *Nordland* N 194 B6
Myresjö S 62 A2
Mýri IS 191 B8
Myrtou CY 181 A2
Mysen N 54 A2
Mysłakowice PL 85 B3
Myślenice PL 99 B3
Myślibórz PL 75 B3
Mysłowice PL 86 B3
Myszków PL 86 B3
Mytishchi RUS 9 E10
Mýtna SK 99 C3
Mýtne Ludany SK 112 A2
Mýto CZ 96 B1

N

N Unnaryd S 60 B3
Nå N 46 B3
Naaldwijk NL 79 A4
Naantali FIN 8 B2
Naas IRL 30 A2
Nabais P 148 B2
Nabbelund S 62 A5
Nabburg D 95 B4
Načeradec CZ 96 B2
Náchod CZ 85 B4
Nacław PL 68 A1
Nadarzyce PL 75 A5
Nadarzyn PL 77 B5
Nádasd H 111 C3
Nădlac RO 126 A2
Nádudvar H 113 B5
Nadvirna UA 13 D6
Nærbø N 52 B1
Næsbjerg DK 59 C1
Næstved DK 65 A4
Näfels CH 107 B4
Nafpaktos GR 184 A2
Nafplio GR 184 B3
Nagel D 95 B3
Nagele NL 70 B2
Naggen S 200 D2
Nagłowice PL 87 B4
Nagold D 93 C4
Nagore E 144 B2
Nagyatád H 124 A3
Nagybajom H 124 A3
Nagybaracska H 125 A4
Nagybátony H 113 B3
Nagyberény H 112 C2
Nagybörzsöny H 112 B2
Nagycenk H 111 B3
Nagycserkesz H 113 B5
Nagydorog H 112 C2
Nagyfüged H 113 B4
Nagyhersány H 125 B4
Nagyigmánd H 112 B2
Nagyiván H 113 B4
Nagykanizsa H 111 C3
Nagykáta H 113 B3
Nagykonyi H 112 C2
Nagykörös H 113 B3
Nagykörü H 113 B4
Nagylóc H 112 A3
Nagymágocs H 113 C4
Nagymányok H 125 A4
Nagymaros H 112 B2
Nagyoroszi H 112 A3
Nagyrábé H 113 B5
Nagyréde H 113 B3
Nagyszékely H 112 C2
Nagyszénás H 113 C4
Nagyszokoly H 112 C2
Nagytöke H 113 C4
Nagyvázsony H 111 C4
Nagyvenyim H 112 C2
Naharros E 152 B1
Nahe D 64 C3
Naila D 83 B3
Nailloux F 146 A2
Nailsworth GB 43 A4
Naintré F 115 B4
Nairn GB 32 D3
Najac F 129 B4
Nájera E 143 B4
Nak H 112 C2
Nakksjø N 53 A5
Nakło nad Notecią PL 76 A2
Nakskov DK 65 B4
Nalda E 143 B4
Nälden S 199 B11
Nálepkovo SK 99 C4
Nallıhan TR 187 B6
Nalliers F 114 B2
Nalzen F 146 B2
Nalžouské Hory CZ 96 B1
Namdalseid N 199 A8
Náměšt'nad Oslavou CZ 97 B4
Námestovo SK 99 B3
Namnå N 49 B4
Namsos N 199 A8
Namsskogan N 199 A10
Namur B 79 B4
Namysłów PL 86 A1
Nançay F 103 B4
Nanclares de la Oca E 143 B4
Nancy F 92 C2
Nangis F 90 C3
Nannestad N 48 B3
Nant F 130 A2
Nanterre F 90 C2
Nantes F 101 B4
Nanteuil-le-Haudouin F 90 B2
Nantiat F 115 B5
Nantua F 118 A2
Nantwich GB 38 A4
Naoussa, *Imathia* GR 182 C4
Naoussa, *Cyclades* GR 185 B6
Napajedla CZ 98 B1
Napiwoda PL 77 A5
Naples = Nápoli I 170 C2
Nápoli = Naples I 170 C2
Nar S 57 C4
Nara N 46 A1
Naraval E 141 A4
Narberth GB 39 C2
Narbonne F 130 B1
Narbonne-Plage F 130 B2
Narbuvollen N 199 C8
Narcao I 179 C2
Nardò I 173 B4
Narkaus FIN 197 C9
Narken S 196 C5
Narmo N 48 B3
Narni I 168 A2
Naro I 176 B2
Naro Fominsk RUS 9 E10
Narón E 140 A2
Narros del Castillo E 150 B2
Narta HR 124 B2
Naruszewo PL 77 B5
Narva EST 8 C6
Narvik N 194 B8
Narzole I 133 A3
Näs FIN 51 B7
Nås, *Dalarnas* S 50 B1
Näs, *Gotland* S 57 C4
Näsåker S 200 C2
Năsăud RO 17 B6
Nasavrky CZ 97 B3
Nasbinals F 116 C3
Näshull S 62 A3
Našice HR 125 B4
Nasielsk PL 77 B5
Naso I 177 A3
Nassau D 81 B3
Nassenfels D 95 C3
Nassenheide D 74 B2
Nassereith A 108 B1
Nässjö S 62 A2
Nastätten D 81 B3
Näsum S 63 B2
Näsviken S 199 B12
Natalinci SRB 127 C2
Nater-Stetten D 108 A2
Naters CH 119 A5
Nattavaara S 196 C3
Natters A 108 B2
Nattheim D 94 C2
Nättraby S 63 B3
Naturno I 108 C1
Naucelle F 130 A1
Nauders A 108 C1
Nauen D 74 B1
Naul IRL 30 A2
Naumburg D 83 A3
Naundorf D 83 B5
Naunhof D 83 A4
Naustdal N 46 A2
Nautijaur S 196 C2
Nautsi RUS 193 D13
Nava E 142 A1
Nava de Arévalo E 150 B3
Nava de la Asunción E 150 A3
Nava del Rey E 150 A2
Navacerrada E 151 B3
Navaconcejo E 149 B4
Navafriá E 151 A4
Navahermosa E 157 A3
Navahrudak BY 13 B6
Naval E 145 B4
Navalacruz E 150 B3
Navalcán E 150 B2
Navalcarnero E 151 B3
Navaleno E 143 C3
Navalmanzano E 151 A3
Navalmoral E 150 B3
Navalmoral de la Mata E 150 C2
Navalón E 159 C3
Navalonguilla E 150 B2
Navalperal de Pinares E 150 B3
Navalpino E 157 A3

Noresund N 48 B1
Norg NL 71 A3
Norheimsund N 46 B3
Norie S 63 B2
Norma I 169 B2
Nornäs S 49 A5
Norra Vi S 62 A3
Norrahammar S 62 A2
Norråker S 200 B1
Norrala S 51 A3
Nørre Åby DK 59 C2
Nørre Alslev DK 65 B4
Nørre Lyndelse DK 59 C3
Nørre Nebel DK 59 C1
Nørre Snede DK 59 C2
Nørre Vorupør DK 58 B1
Norrent-Fontes F 78 B2
Nørresundby DK 58 A2
Norrfjärden S 196 D4
Norrhed S 196 C3
Norrhult Klavreström S 62 A3
Norrköping S 56 B2
Norrskedika S 51 B5
Norrsundet S 51 B4
Norrtälje S 57 A4
Nors DK 58 A1
Norsbron S 55 A4
Norsholm S 56 B1
Norsjö S 200 B5
Nort-sur-Erdre F 101 B4
Nörten-Hardenberg D 82 A1
North Berwick GB 35 B5
North Charlton GB 37 A5
North Frodingham GB 40 B3
North Kessock GB 32 D2
North Molton GB 42 A3
North Petherton GB 43 A3
North Somercotes GB 41 B4
North Tawton GB 42 B3
North Thoresby GB 41 B3
North Walsham GB 41 C5
Northallerton GB 37 B5
Northampton GB 44 A3
Northeim D 82 A2
Northfleet GB 45 B4
Northleach GB 44 B2
Northpunds GB 33 B5
Northwich GB 38 A4
Norton GB 40 A3
Nortorf D 64 B2
Nörvenich D 80 B2
Norwich GB 41 C5
Norwick GB 33 A6
Nøsen N 47 B5
Nossa Senhora do Cabo P 154 C1
Nossebro S 55 B3
Nössemark S 54 A2
Nossen D 83 A5
Notaresco I 169 A3
Noto I 177 C4
Notodden N 53 A5
Nottingham GB 40 C2
Nottuln D 71 C4
Nouan-le-Fuzelier F 103 B4
Nouans-les-Fontaines F 103 B3
Nougaroulet F 129 C3
Nouvion F 78 B1
Nouzonville F 91 B4
Nova H 111 C3
Nová Baňa SK 98 C2
Nová Bystrica SK 99 B3
Nová Bystřice CZ 97 B3
Nova Crnja SRB 126 B2
Nova Gorica SLO 122 B2
Nova Gradiška HR 124 B3
Nova Levante I 108 C2
Nová Paka CZ 84 B3
Nova Pazova SRB 127 C2
Nová Pec CZ 96 C1
Nova Siri I 174 A2
Nova Topola BIH 124 B3
Nova Zagora BG 17 D6
Novaféltria I 135 B5
Nováky SK 98 C2
Novalaise F 118 B2
Novales E 145 B3
Novalja HR 137 A3
Novara I 120 B1
Novara di Sicília I 177 A4
Novate Mezzola I 120 A2
Novaya Ladoga RUS 9 B8
Nové Hrady CZ 96 C2
Nové Město SK 98 C1
Nové Město na Moravě CZ 97 B4
Nové Město nad Metují CZ 85 B4
Nové Město pod Smrkem CZ 84 B3
Nové Mitrovice CZ 96 B1
Nové Sady SK 98 C1
Nové Strašeci CZ 84 B1
Nové Zámky SK 112 B2
Novelda E 165 A4
Novellara I 121 C3
Noventa di Piave I 122 B1
Noventa Vicentina I 121 B4
Novés E 151 B3
Noves F 131 B3
Novés de Segre E 147 B2
Novgorod RUS 9 C7
Novi Bečej SRB 126 B2
Novi di Módena I 121 C3
Novi Kneževac SRB 126 A2
Novi Lígure I 120 C1
Novi Marof HR 124 A2
Novi Pazar BG 17 D7
Novi Pazar SRB 16 D4
Novi Sad SRB 126 B1
Novi Slankamen SRB 126 B2
Novi Travnik BIH 139 A3
Novi Vinodolski HR 123 B3
Novigrad, *Istarska* HR 122 B2
Novigrad, *Zadarsko-Kninska* HR 137 A4
Novigrad Podravski HR 124 A2
Noville B 92 A1
Novion-Porcien F 91 B4
Novo Mesto SLO 123 B4
Novo Miloševo SRB 126 B2
Novo Selo BIH 125 B3
Novohrad-Volynskyy UA 13 C7
Novorzhev RUS 9 D6
Novoselytsya UA 17 A7
Novosokolniki RUS 9 D6
Novoveská Huta SK 99 C4
Novovolynsk UA 13 C6
Novska HR 124 B2
Nový Bor CZ 84 B2
Nový Bydžov CZ 84 B3
Novy-Chevrières F 91 B4
Novy Dwór Mazowiecki PL 77 B5
Nový-Hrozenkov CZ 98 B2
Nový Jičín CZ 98 B2
Novy Knin CZ 96 B2
Nowa Cerekwia PL 86 B1
Nowa Dęba PL 87 B5
Nowa Karczma PL 68 A3
Nowa Kościoł PL 85 A3
Nowa Ruda PL 85 B4
Nowa Słupia PL 87 B5
Nowa Sól PL 85 A3
Nowa Wieś PL 69 B4
Nowa-Wieś Wielka PL 76 B3
Nowe PL 69 B3
Nowe Brzesko PL 87 B4
Nowe Grudze PL 77 B4
Nowe Kiejkuty PL 77 A6
Nowe Miasteczko PL 85 A3
Nowe Miasto, *Mazowieckie* PL 77 B5
Nowe Miasto, *Mazowieckie* PL 87 A4
Nowe Miasto Lubawskie PL 69 B4
Nowe Miasto nad Wartą PL 76 B2
Nowe Skalmierzyce PL 86 A2
Nowe Warpno PL 74 A3
Nowica PL 69 A4
Nowogard PL 75 A4
Nowogród Bobrzanski PL 84 A3
Nowogrodziec PL 84 A3
Nowosolna PL 86 A3
Nowy Dwór Gdański PL 69 A4
Nowy Korczyn PL 87 B4
Nowy Sącz PL 99 B4
Nowy Staw PL 69 A4
Nowy Targ PL 99 B4
Nowy Tomyśl PL 75 B5
Nowy Wiśnicz PL 99 B4
Noyal-Pontivy F 100 A3
Noyalo F 101 B3
Noyant F 102 B2
Noyelles-sur-Mer F 78 B1
Noyen-sur-Sarthe F 102 B1
Noyers F 104 B2
Noyers-sur-Cher F 103 B3
Noyers-sur-Jabron F 132 A1
Noyon F 90 B2
Nozay F 101 B4
Nuaillé F 102 B1
Nuaillé-d'Aunis F 114 B3
Nuars F 104 B2
Nubledo E 141 A5
Nuéno E 145 B3
Nuestra Señora Sa Verge des Pilar E 166 C1
Nueva E 142 A2
Nueva Carteya E 163 A3
Nuevalos E 152 A2
Nuits F 104 B3
Nuits-St. Georges F 105 B3
Nule I 178 B3
Nules E 159 B3
Nulvi I 178 B2
Numana I 136 B2
Numansdorp NL 79 A4
Nümbrecht D 81 B3
Nunchritz D 83 A5
Nuneaton GB 40 C2
Nunnanen FIN 196 A7
Nuñomoral E 149 B3
Nunspeet NL 70 B2
Nuorgam FIN 193 B11
Núoro I 178 B3
Nurallao I 179 C3
Nuremberg = Nürnberg D 94 B3
Nurmes FIN 3 E11
Nürnberg = Nuremberg D 94 B3
Nurri I 179 C3
Nürtingen D 94 C1
Nus I 119 B4
Nusnäs S 50 B1
Nusplingen D 107 A3
Nuštar HR 125 B4
Nuupas FIN 197 C9
Nyåker S 200 C5
Nyáregyháza H 112 B3
Nyarlörinc H 113 C3
Nyasvizh BY 13 B7
Nybble S 55 A5
Nybergsund N 49 A4
Nybøl DK 64 B2
Nyborg DK 59 C3
Nyborg S 196 D6
Nybro S 62 B3
Nybster GB 32 C3
Nyby DK 65 B5
Nye S 62 A3
Nyékládháza H 113 B4
Nyergesujfalu H 112 B2
Nyhammar S 50 B1
Nyhyttan S 55 A5
Nyirád H 111 B4
Nyirbátor H 16 B5
Nyíregyháza H 16 B4
Nyker DK 67 A3
Nykil S 56 B1
Nykirke N 48 B2
Nykøbing, *Falster* DK 65 B4
Nykøbing, *Vestsjællands Amt.* DK 61 D1
Nykøbing M DK 58 B1
Nyköping S 56 B3
Nykroppa S 55 A5
Nykvarn S 56 A3
Nykyrke S 55 B5
Nyland S 200 C3
Nylars DK 67 A3
Nymburk CZ 84 B3
Nynäshamn S 57 B3
Nyon CH 118 A3
Nyons F 131 A4
Nýřany CZ 96 B1
Nýrsko CZ 95 B5
Nyrud N 193 C13
Nysa PL 85 B5
Nysäter S 55 A3
Nyseter N 198 C5
Nyskoga S 49 B4
Nysted DK 65 B4
Nystrand N 53 A5
Nyúl H 111 B4
Nyvoll N 192 B7

O

O Barco E 141 B4
O Bolo E 141 B3
O Carballiño E 140 B2
O Corgo E 141 B3
Ö Lagnö S 57 A4
Ö Näsberg S 49 B5
O Páramo E 140 B3
O Pedrouzo E 140 B2
O Pino E 140 B2
O Porriño E 140 B2
O Rosal E 140 C2
Oadby GB 40 C2
Oakengates GB 38 B4
Oakham GB 40 C3
Oanes N 52 B2
Obalj BIH 139 B4
Oban GB 34 B2
Obbola S 200 C6
Obdach A 110 B1
Obejo E 156 B3
Ober Grafendorf A 110 A2
Ober-Morlen D 81 B4
Oberammergau D 108 B2
Oberasbach D 94 B2
Oberau D 108 B2
Oberawdorfo D 108 B3
Oberbruck F 106 B1
Oberdiessbach CH 106 C2
Oberdorf CH 106 B2
Oberdrauburg A 109 C3
Obere Stanz A 110 B2
Oberelsbach D 82 B2
Obergünzburg D 108 B1
Obergurgl A 108 C2
Oberhausen D 80 A2
Oberhof D 82 B2
Oberkirch D 93 C4
Oberkirchen D 81 A4
Oberkochen D 94 C2
Obermassfeld-Grimmenthal D 82 B2
Obermünchen D 95 C3
Obernai F 93 C3
Obernberg A 96 C1
Obernburg D 93 B5
Oberndorf D 93 C4
Oberndorf bei Salzburg A 109 B3
Obernkirchen D 72 B2
Oberort A 110 B2
Oberpullendorf A 111 B3
Oberriet CH 107 B4
Oberröblingen D 82 A3
Oberrot D 94 B1
Oberstaufen D 107 B5
Oberstdorf D 107 B5
Obertauern A 109 B4
Obertilliach A 109 C3
Obertraubling D 95 C4
Obertraun A 109 B4
Obertrubach D 95 B3
Obertrum A 109 B4
Oberursel D 81 B4
Obervellach A 109 C4
Oberviechtach D 95 B4
Oberwart A 111 B3
Oberwesel D 93 A3
Oberwinter D 80 B3
Oberwölzstadt A 110 B1
Oberzell D 96 C1
Obice PL 87 B4
Óbidos P 154 B1
Obing D 109 B3
Objat F 129 A4
Objazda PL 68 A2
Öblarn A 109 B5
Obninsk RUS 9 E10
Oborniki PL 75 B5
Oborniki Śląskie PL 85 A4
Obornjača SRB 126 B1
Obrenovac SRB 127 C2
Obrež SRB 127 C1
Obrigheim D 93 B5
Obrov SLO 123 B3
Obrovac HR 137 A4
Obrovac SRB 126 B1
Obrovac Sinjski HR 138 B2
Obruk TR 23 B7
Obrzycko PL 75 B5
Obudovac BIH 125 C4
Ocaña E 151 C4
Occhiobello I 121 C4
Occimiano I 119 B5
Očevlja BIH 139 A4
Ochagavía E 144 B2
Ochiltree GB 36 A2
Ochla PL 84 A3
Ochotnica-Dolna PL 99 B4
Ochotnica-Górna PL 99 B4
Ochsenfurt D 94 B2
Ochsenhausen D 107 A4
Ochtendung D 80 B3
Ochtrup D 71 B4
Ocieka PL 87 B5
Ockelbo S 50 B3
Öckerö S 60 B1
Ocniţa MD 17 A7
Očová SK 99 C3
Ócsa H 112 B3
Öcseny H 125 A4
Öcsöd H 113 C4
Octeville F 88 A2
Ocypel PL 69 B3
Ödåkra S 61 C2
Odby DK 58 B1
Odda N 46 B3
Odder DK 59 C3
Ödeborg S 54 B2
Odeceixe P 160 B1
Odechów PL 87 A5
Odeleite P 160 B2
Odemira P 160 B1
Ödemiş TR 188 A2
Ödensbacken S 56 A1
Odense DK 59 C3
Odensjö, *Jönköping* S 62 A2
Odensjö, *Kronoberg* S 60 C3
Oderberg D 74 B3
Oderzo I 122 B1
Odesa = Odessa UA 17 B9
Ödeshög S 55 B5
Odessa = Odesa UA 17 B9
Odiáxere P 160 B1
Odie GB 33 B4
Odiham GB 44 B3
Odintsovo RUS 9 E10
Odivelas P 160 A1
Odolanów PL 85 A5
Odón E 152 B2
Odorheiu Secuiesc RO 17 B6
Odrowaz PL 87 A4
Odry CZ 98 B1
Odrzywół PL 87 A4
Ødsted DK 59 C2
Odžaci SRB 126 B1
Odžak BIH 125 B4
Oebisfelde D 73 B3
Oederan D 83 B5
Oeding D 71 C3
Oegstgeest NL 70 B1
Oelde D 81 A4
Oelsnitz D 83 B4
Oer-Erkenschwick D 80 A3
Oerlinghausen D 72 C1
Oettingen D 94 C2
Oetz A 108 B1
Oeventrop D 81 A4
Offanengo I 120 B2
Offenbach D 81 B4
Offenburg D 93 C3
Offida I 136 C2
Offingen D 94 C2
Offranville F 89 A5
Ofir P 148 A1
Ofte N 53 A4
Ofterschwang D 107 B5
Oggiono I 120 B2
Ogihares E 163 A4
Ogliastro Cilento I 170 C3
Ogliastro Marina I 170 C2
Ogmore-by-Sea GB 39 C3
Ogna N 52 B1
Ogre LV 8 D4
Ogrodzieniec PL 86 B3
Ogulin HR 123 B4
Ögur IS 190 A3
Ohanes E 164 B2
Ohey B 79 B5
Ohlstadt D 108 B2
Ohrdorf D 73 B3
Ohrdruf D 82 B2
Ohrid MK 182 B2
Öhringen D 94 B1
Oia E 140 B2
Oiã P 148 B1
Oiartzun E 144 A2
Oijärvi FIN 197 D8
Oilgate IRL 30 B2
Oimbra E 148 A2
Oiselay-et-Grachoux F 105 B4
Oisemont F 90 B1
Oisterwijk NL 79 A5
Öja S 57 C4
Öje S 49 B5
Ojén E 162 B3
Ojrzeń PL 77 B5
Ojuelos Altos E 156 B2
Okalewo PL 77 A4
Okány H 113 C5
Okehampton GB 42 B2
Oklaj HR 138 B2
Økneshamn N 194 B6
Okoč SK 111 B4
Okoličné SK 99 B3
Okonek PL 68 B1
Okonin PL 69 B3
Okřisky CZ 97 B3
Oksa PL 87 B4
Oksbøl DK 59 C1
Oksby DK 59 C1
Øksfjord N 192 B6
Øksna N 48 B3
Okučani HR 124 B3
Okulovka RUS 9 C8
Ólafsfjörður IS 191 A7
Ólafsvík IS 190 C2
Olagüe E 144 B2
Oland N 53 B4
Olargues F 130 B1
Oława PL 85 B5
Olazagutia E 144 B1
Olbernhau D 83 B5
Ólbia I 178 B3
Olching D 108 A2
Old Deer GB 33 D4
Oldbury GB 43 A4
Oldcastle IRL 27 C3
Oldeberkoop NL 70 B3
Oldeboorn NL 70 A2
Olden N 198 D3
Oldenbrok D 71 A5
Oldenburg, *Niedersachsen* D 71 A5
Oldenburg, *Schleswig-Holstein* D 65 B3
Oldenzaal NL 71 B3
Olderdalen N 192 C4
Olderfjord N 193 B9
Oldersum D 71 A4
Oldervik N 192 C2
Oldham GB 40 B1
Oldisleben D 82 A3
Oldmeldrum GB 33 D4
Olea E 142 B2
Oleby S 49 B5
Olechów PL 87 A5
Oledo P 155 B3
Olèggio I 120 B1
Oleiros, *Coruña* E 140 A2
Oleiros, *Coruña* E 140 B1
Oleiros P 154 B3
Oleksandriya UA 13 C7
Olen B 79 A4
Ølen N 52 A1
Olenegorsk RUS 3 B13
Olenino RUS 9 D8
Olesa de Montserrat E 147 C2
Oleśnica PL 85 A5
Olešnice CZ 97 B4
Olesno PL 86 B2
Oletta F 180 A2
Olette F 146 B3
Olevsk UA 13 C7
Olfen D 80 A3
Olgiate Comasco I 120 B1
Olginate I 120 B2
Ølgod DK 59 C1
Olgrinmore GB 32 C3
Olhão P 160 B2
Olhava FIN 197 D8
Olhavo P 154 B1
Oliana E 147 B2
Olias del Rey E 151 C4
Oliena I 178 B3
Oliete E 153 B3
Olimbos GR 188 D2
Olite E 144 B2
Oliva E 159 C3
Oliva de la Frontera E 155 C4
Oliva de Mérida E 156 B1
Oliva de Plasencia E 149 B3
Olivadi I 175 C2
Olival P 154 B2
Olivar E 163 B4
Olivares E 161 B3
Olivares de Duero E 142 C2
Olivares de Júcar E 158 B1
Oliveira de Azeméis P 148 B1
Oliveira de Frades P 148 B1
Oliveira do Conde P 148 B2
Oliveira do Douro P 148 A1
Oliveira do Hospital P 148 B2
Olivenza E 155 C3
Olivet F 103 B3
Olivone CH 107 C3
Öljehult S 63 B3
Olkusz PL 86 B3
Ollerton GB 40 B2
Ollerup DK 65 A3
Olliergues F 117 B3
Ölmbrotorp S 56 A1
Ölme S 55 A4
Olmedilla de Alarcón E 158 B1
Olmedillo de Roa E 143 C3
Olmedo E 150 A3
Olmedo I 178 B2
Olmeto F 180 B1
Olmillos de Castro E 149 A3
Olmos de Ojeda E 142 B2
Olney GB 44 A3
Ołobok PL 86 A2
Olocau del Rey E 153 B3
Olofström S 63 B2
Olomouc CZ 98 B1
Olonets RUS 9 B8
Olonne-sur-Mer F 114 B2
Olonzac F 130 B1
Oloron-Ste. Marie F 145 A3
Olost E 147 C3
Olot E 147 B3
Olovo BIH 139 A4
Olpe D 81 A3
Olsberg D 81 A4
Olsene B 79 B3
Olserud S 55 A4
Olshammar S 55 B5
Olshanka UA 13 D9
Olszanica PL 85 A3
Olsztyn, *Śląskie* PL 86 B3
Olsztyn, *Warmińsko-Mazurskie* PL 69 B5
Olsztynek PL 77 A5
Olszyna PL 84 A3
Olszyny PL 77 A6
Oltedal N 52 B2
Olten CH 106 B2
Olteniţa RO 17 C7
Olula del Rio E 164 B2
Ølve N 46 B2
Olvega E 144 C2
Olvera E 162 B2
Olympia GR 184 B2
Olzai I 178 B3
Omagh GB 27 B3
Omalos GR 185 D4
Omegna I 119 B5
Omiš HR 138 B2
Omišalj HR 123 B3
Ommen NL 71 B3
Omodhos CY 181 B1
Omoljica SRB 127 C2
On B 79 B5
Oña E 143 B3
Onano I 168 A1
Oñati E 143 A4
Onda E 159 B3
Ondara E 159 C4
Ondarroa E 143 A4
Onesse-et-Laharie F 128 B1
Oneşti RO 17 B7
Onhaye B 79 B4
Onich GB 34 B2
Onil E 159 C3
Onis E 142 A2
Önnestad S 61 C4
Onsala S 60 B2
Ontinyent E 159 C3
Ontur E 158 C2

Palhaça P 148 B1
Palheiros da Tocha P 148 B1
Palheiros de Quiaios P 148 B1
Paliaopoli GR 185 B5
Palić SRB 126 A1
Palidoro I 168 B2
Palinuro I 172 B1
Paliouri GR 183 D5
Paliseul B 91 B5
Pallanza I 119 B5
Pallares E 161 A3
Pallaruelo de Monegros E 153 A3
Pallas Green IRL 29 B3
Pallerols E 146 B2
Palling D 109 A3
Palluau F 114 B2
Palma P 154 C2
Palma Campània I 170 C2
Palma de Mallorca E 166 B2
Palma del Río E 162 A2
Palma di Montechiaro I 176 B2
Palma Nova E 166 B2
Palmádula I 178 B2
Palmanova I 122 B2
Palmela P 154 C2
Palmerola E 147 B3
Palmi I 175 C1
Pälmonostora H 113 C3
Palo del Colle I 171 B4
Palojärvi FIN 192 D7
Palojoensuu FIN 196 A6
Palomares E 164 B3
Palomares del Campo E 158 B1
Palomas E 156 B1
Palombara Sabina I 168 A2
Palos de la Frontera E 161 B3
Palotaboszok H 125 A4
Palotás H 112 B3
Pals E 147 C4
Pålsboda S 56 A1
Paluzza I 109 C4
Pamhagen A 111 B3
Pamiers F 146 A2
Pamiętowo PL 76 A2
Pampaneira E 163 B4
Pamparato I 133 A3
Pampilhosa, *Aveiro* P 148 B1
Pampilhosa, *Coimbra* P 148 B2
Pampliega E 143 B3
Pamplona E 144 B2
Pampow D 73 A4
Pamukçu TR 186 C2
Pamukkale TR 188 B4
Pamukova TR 187 B5
Panagyurishte BG 17 D6
Pancalieri I 119 C4
Pančevo SRB 127 C2
Pancey F 91 C5
Pancorvo E 143 B3
Pancrudo E 152 B2
Pandino I 120 B2
Pandrup DK 58 A2
Panenský-Týnec CZ 84 B1
Panes E 142 A2
Panevėžys LT 8 E4
Pangbourne GB 44 B2
Panissières F 117 B4
Panki PL 86 B2
Pannes F 103 A4
Panningen NL 80 A1
Pannonhalma H 111 B4
Pano Lefkara CY 181 B2
Pano Panayia CY 181 B1
Panormos GR 185 B6
Panschwitz-Kuckau D 84 A2
Pansdorf D 65 C3
Pantano de Cíjara E 156 A3
Panticosa E 145 B3
Pantín E 140 A2
Pantoja E 151 B4
Pantón E 140 B3
Panxon E 140 B2
Páola I 174 B2
Paola M 175 C3
Pápa H 111 B4
Papasídero I 174 B1
Pápateszér H 111 B4
Papenburg D 71 A4
Paphos CY 181 B1
Pappenheim D 94 C2
Paprotnia PL 77 B5
Parábita I 173 B4
Paraćin SRB 127 D3
Parád H 113 B4
Parada, *Bragança* P 149 A3
Parada, *Viseu* P 148 B1
Paradas E 162 A2
Paradela E 140 B3
Parades de Rubiales E 150 A2
Paradinas de San Juan E 150 B2
Paradiso di Cevadale I 108 C1
Paradyż PL 87 A4
Parainen FIN 8 B3
Parakhino Paddubye RUS 9 C8
Parakka S 196 B4
Paralimni CY 181 A2
Parallo Astros GR 184 B3
Paramé F 88 B2
Paramithia GR 182 D2
Páramo E 141 A4
Páramo del Sil E 141 B4
Parandaça P 148 A2
Paravadella E 141 A3
Paray-le-Monial F 104 C3
Parceiros P 154 B2
Parcey F 105 B4
Parchim D 73 A4
Parciaki PL 77 A6
Parcice PL 86 A2
Pardilla E 151 A4
Pardubice CZ 97 A3
Paredes E 151 B5
Paredes P 148 A1
Paredes de Coura P 140 C2
Paredes de Nava E 142 B2
Paredes de Siguenza E 151 A5
Pareja E 151 B5
Parennes F 102 A1
Parenti I 175 B2
Parentis-en-Born F 128 B1
Parey D 73 B4
Parfino RUS 9 D7
Parga GR 182 D2
Pargny-sur-Saulx F 91 C4
Pari-Gagné F 117 A4
Parigné-l'Évêque F 102 B2
Parikkala FIN 9 B6
Paris F 90 C2
Parisot F 129 B4
Parkalompolo S 196 B5
Parkano FIN 8 A3
Parknasilla IRL 29 C2
Parla E 151 B4
Parlavá E 147 B4
Parma I 120 C3
Parndorf A 111 B3
Párnica SK 99 B3
Parnu EST 8 C4
Parolis E 164 A2
Paros GR 185 B6
Parrillas E 150 A2
Parsberg D 95 B3
Parstein D 74 B3
Partakko FIN 193 C11
Partanna I 176 B1
Parthenay F 102 C1
Partinico I 176 A2
Partizani SRB 127 C2
Partizánske SK 98 C2
Partney GB 41 B4
Påryd S 63 B3
Parzymiechy PL 86 A2
Paşcani RO 17 B7
Pasewalk D 74 A2
Pašina Voda CG 139 B5
Påskallavik S 62 A4
Pasłęk PL 69 A4
Pašman HR 137 B4
Passage East IRL 30 B2
Passail A 110 B2
Passais F 88 B3
Passau D 96 C1
Passegueiro P 148 B1
Passignano sul Trasimeno I 135 B5
Passo di Tréia I 136 B2
Passopisciaro I 177 B4
Passow D 74 A3
Passy F 118 B3
Pastavy BY 13 A7
Pástena I 170 B2
Pastrana E 151 B5
Pastrengo I 121 B3
Pasym PL 77 A5
Pásztó H 113 B3
Pata SK 98 C1
Patay F 103 A3
Pateley Bridge GB 40 A2
Paterek PL 76 A2
Paterna E 159 B3
Paterna de Rivera E 162 B2
Paterna del Campo E 161 B3
Paterna del Madera E 158 C1
Paternion A 109 C4
Paternò I 177 B3
Paternópoli I 170 C3
Patersdorf D 95 B4
Paterswolde NL 71 A3
Patitiri GR 183 D5
Patmos GR 188 B1
Patna GB 36 A2
Pątnow PL 76 B3
Patoniva FIN 193 C11
Patopirtti FIN 197 B12
Patos AL 182 C1
Patra = Patras GR 184 A2
Patras = Patra GR 184 A2
Patreksfjörður IS 190 B2
Patrickswell IRL 29 B3
Patrimonio F 180 A2
Patrington GB 41 B3
Pattada I 178 B3
Pattensen, *Niedersachsen* D 72 A3
Pattensen, *Niedersachsen* D 72 B2
Patterdale GB 36 B4
Patti I 177 A3
Páty H 112 B2
Pau F 145 A3
Pauillac F 128 A2
Paularo I 109 C4
Paulhaguet F 117 B3
Paulhan F 130 B2
Paulilátino I 178 B2
Paulistróm S 62 A3
Paullo I 120 B2
Paulstown IRL 30 B1
Pausa D 83 B3
Pauträsk S 200 B3
Pavia I 120 B2
Pavia P 154 C2
Pavias E 159 B3
Pavilly F 89 A4
Pāvilosta LV 8 D2
Pavullo nel Frignano I 135 A3
Pawłowice, *Opolskie* PL 86 A1
Pawlowice, *Śląskie* PL 98 B2
Paxi GR 182 D2
Payallar TR 189 C6
Payerne CH 106 C1
Paymogo E 161 B2
Payrac F 129 B4
Pazardzhik BG 183 A6
Pazaryeri TR 187 B4
Pazin HR 122 B2
Paziols F 146 B3
Pčelić HR 124 B3
Peal de Becerro E 164 B1
Peasmarsh GB 45 C4
Peć SRB 16 D4
Péccioli I 135 B3
Pécel H 112 B3
Pechao P 160 B2
Pechenga RUS 3 B12
Pechenizhyn UA 13 D6
Pecica RO 126 A3
Pećinci SRB 127 C1
Pecka SRB 127 C1
Peckelsheim D 81 A5
Pečory RUS 8 D5
Pécs H 125 A4
Pécsvárad H 125 A4
Peczniew PL 86 A2
Pedaso I 136 B2
Pedavena I 121 A4
Pedérobba I 121 B4
Pedersker DK 67 A3
Pedescala I 121 B4
Pedrafita E 141 B3
Pedrajas de San Esteban E 150 A3
Pedralba E 159 B3
Pedralba de la Praderia E 141 B4
Pedraza E 151 A4
Pedreguer E 159 C4
Pedrera E 162 A3
Pedro Abad E 157 C3
Pedro Bernardo E 150 B3
Pedro-Martinez E 164 B1
Pedro Muñoz E 158 B1
Pedroche E 156 B3
Pedrógão, *Beja* P 160 A2
Pedrógão, *Castelo Branco* P 149 B2
Pedrógão, *Leiria* P 154 B2
Pedrógão Grande P 154 B2
Pedrola E 144 C2
Pedrosa de Tobalina E 143 B3
Pedrosa del Rey E 150 A2
Pedrosa del Rio Urbel E 143 B3
Pedrosillo de los Aires E 150 B2
Pedrosillo el Ralo E 150 A2
Pędzewo PL 76 A3
Peebles GB 35 C4
Peel GB 36 B2
Peenemünde D 66 B2
Peer B 79 A5
Pega P 149 B2
Pegalajar E 163 A4
Pegau D 83 A4
Peggau A 110 B2
Pegli I 133 A4
Pegnitz D 95 B3
Pego E 159 C3
Pegões-Estação P 154 C2
Pegões Velhos P 154 C2
Pęgów PL 85 A4
Pegswood GB 37 A5
Peguera E 166 B2
Pehlivanköy TR 186 A1
Peine D 72 B3
Peisey-Nancroix F 118 B3
Peissenberg D 108 B2
Peiting D 108 B1
Peitz D 84 A2
Péjo I 121 A3
Pelagićevo BIH 125 C4
Pelahustán E 150 B3
Pełczyce PL 75 A4
Pelhřimov CZ 97 B3
Pélissanne F 131 B4
Pelkosenniemi FIN 197 B10
Pellegrino Parmense I 120 C2
Pellegrue F 128 B3
Pellérd H 125 A4
Pellestrina I 122 B1
Pellevoisin F 103 C3
Pellizzano I 121 A3
Pello FIN 196 C7
Pello S 196 C6
Peloche E 156 A2
Pelplin PL 69 B3
Pelussin F 117 B4
Pély H 113 B4
Pembroke GB 39 C2
Pembroke Dock GB 39 C2
Peña de Cabra E 149 B4
Peñacerrada E 143 B4
Penacova P 148 B1
Peñafiel E 151 A3
Penafiel P 148 A1
Peñaflor E 162 A2
Peñalba de Santiago E 141 B4
Peñalsordo E 156 B2
Penalva do Castelo P 148 B2
Penamacôr P 149 B2
Peñaparda E 149 B3
Peñaranda de Bracamonte E 150 B2
Peñaranda de Duero E 143 C3
Peñarroya de Tastavins E 153 B4
Peñarroya-Pueblonuevo E 156 B2
Peñarrubla E 141 B3
Penarth GB 39 C3
Peñas de San Pedro E 158 C2
Peñascosa E 158 C1
Peñausende E 149 A4
Penc H 112 B3
Pencoed GB 39 C3
Pendalofos GR 182 C3
Pendeen GB 42 B1
Pendine GB 39 C2
Pendueles E 142 A2
Penedono P 148 B2
Penela P 154 A2
Penhas Juntas P 149 A2
Peniche P 154 B1
Penicuik GB 35 C4
Penig D 83 B4
Penilhos P 160 B2
Peñíscola E 153 B4
Penistone GB 40 B2
Penkridge GB 40 C1
Penkun D 74 A3
Penmarch F 100 B1
Pennabilli I 135 B5
Penne I 169 A3
Penne-d'Agenais F 129 B3
Pennes I 108 C2
Pennyghael GB 34 B1
Peno RUS 9 D8
Penpont GB 36 A3
Penrhyndeudraeth GB 38 B2
Penrith GB 37 B4
Penryn GB 42 B1
Pentraeth GB 38 A2
Penybontfawr GB 38 B3
Penygroes, *Carmarthenshire* GB 39 C2
Penygroes, *Gwynedd* GB 38 A2
Penzance GB 42 B1
Penzberg D 108 B2
Penzlin D 74 A2
Pepinster B 80 B1
Peqin AL 182 B1
Pér H 111 B4
Pera Boa P 148 B2
Perachora GR 184 A3
Perafita P 148 A1
Peraleda de la Mata E 150 C2
Peraleda de San Román E 156 A2
Peraleda del Zaucejo E 156 B2
Perales de Alfambra E 152 B2
Perales de Tajuña E 151 B4
Perales del Puerto E 149 B3
Peralta E 144 B2
Peralta de la Sal E 145 C4
Peralva P 160 B2
Peralveche E 152 B1
Perama GR 185 D5
Peranka FIN 197 D12
Perbál H 112 B2
Perchtoldsdorf A 111 A3
Percy F 88 B2
Perdasdefogu I 179 C3
Perdiguera E 145 C3
Peredo P 149 A3
Peregu Mare RO 126 A2
Pereiro, *Faro* P 160 B2
Pereiro, *Guarda* P 149 B2
Pereiro, *Santarém* P 154 B2
Pereiro de Aguiar E 140 B3
Perelada E 147 B4
Perelejos de las Truchas E 152 B2
Pereña E 149 A3
Pereruela E 149 A4
Pérfugas I 178 B2
Perg A 110 A1
Pérgine Valsugana I 121 A4
Pérgola I 136 B1
Pergusa I 177 B3
Periam RO 126 A2
Periana E 163 B3
Périers F 88 A2
Périgueux F 129 A3
Perino I 120 C2
Perjasica HR 123 B4
Perkáta H 112 B2
Perković HR 138 B2
Perleberg D 73 A4
Perlez SRB 126 B2
Përmet AL 182 C2
Pernarec CZ 95 B5
Pernek SK 98 C1
Pernes P 154 B2
Pernes-les-Fontaines F 131 A4
Pernik BG 17 D5
Pernink CZ 83 B4
Pernitz A 110 B2
Pernu FIN 197 C10
Pero Pinheiro P 154 C1
Peroguarda P 160 A1
Pérols F 131 B2
Péronne F 90 B2
Péronnes B 79 B4
Perorrubio E 151 A4
Perosa Argentina I 119 C4
Perozinho P 148 A1
Perpignan F 146 B3
Perranporth GB 42 B1
Perranzabuloe GB 42 B1
Perrecy-les-Forges F 104 C3
Perrero I 119 C4
Perrignier F 118 A3
Perros-Guirec F 100 A2
Persan F 90 B2
Persberg S 55 A5
Persenbeug A 110 A2
Pershore GB 44 A1
Persön S 196 D5
Perstorp S 61 C3
Perth GB 35 B4
Pertisau A 108 B2
Pertoča SLO 111 C3
Pertuis F 131 B4
Perućac SRB 127 D1
Perúgia I 136 B1
Perušić HR 123 C4
Péruwelz B 79 B3
Pervomaysk UA 13 D9
Perwez B 79 B4
Pesadas de Burgos E 143 B3
Pesaguero E 142 A2
Pésaro I 136 B1
Pescantina I 121 B3
Pescara I 169 A4
Pescasséroli I 169 B3
Peschici I 171 B4
Peschiera del Garda I 121 B3
Péscia I 135 B3
Pescina I 169 A3
Pesco Sannita I 170 B2
Pescocostanzo I 169 B4
Pescopagano I 172 B1
Peshkopi AL 182 B2
Peshtera BG 183 A6
Pesmes F 105 B4
Pesnica SLO 110 C2
Peso da Régua P 148 A2
Pesquera de Duero E 142 C2
Pessac F 128 B2
Pestovo RUS 9 C9
Petäjäskoski FIN 197 C8
Petalidi GR 184 C2
Pétange L 92 B1
Petas GR 182 D3
Peteranec HR 124 A2
Peterborough GB 41 C3
Peterculter GB 33 D4
Peterhead GB 33 D5
Peterlee GB 37 B5
Petersfield GB 44 B3
Petershagen, *Brandenburg* D 74 B2
Petershagen, *Brandenburg* D 74 B3
Petershagen, *Nordrhein-Westfalen* D 72 B1
Petershausen D 95 C3
Peterswell IRL 28 A3
Pétervására H 113 A4
Petília Policastro I 175 B2
Petín E 141 B3
Pětipsy CZ 83 B5
Petkus D 74 C2
Petlovac HR 125 B4
Petlovača SRB 127 C1
Petőfiszallás H 113 C3
Petra E 167 B3
Petralia Sottana I 177 B3
Petrčane HR 137 A4
Petrella Tifernina I 170 B2
Petrer E 159 C3
Petreto-Bicchisano F 180 B1
Petrich BG 183 B5
Petrijevci HR 125 B4
Petrinja HR 124 B2
Petrodvorets RUS 9 C6
Pétrola E 158 C2
Petronà I 175 B2
Petronell A 111 A3
Petroşani RO 17 C5
Petrovac SRB 127 C3
Petrovaradin SRB 126 B1
Petrovice BIH 139 A4
Petrovice CZ 84 B1
Petrovo RUS 69 A5
Petrozavodsk RUS 9 B9
Pettenbach A 109 B5
Pettigo IRL 26 B3
Petworth GB 44 C3
Peuerbach A 96 C1
Peuntenansa E 142 A2
Peurasuvanto FIN 197 B9
Pevensey Bay GB 45 C4
Peveragno I 133 A3
Pewsey GB 44 B2
Pewsum D 71 A4
Peyrat-le-Château F 116 B1
Peyrehorade F 128 C1
Peyriac-Minervois F 146 A3
Peyrins F 117 B5
Peyrissac F 116 B1
Peyrolles-en-Provence F 132 B1
Peyruis F 132 A1
Pézarches F 90 C2
Pézenas F 130 B2
Pezinok SK 111 A4
Pezuls F 129 B3
Pfaffenhausen D 108 A1
Pfaffenhofen, *Bayern* D 94 C2
Pfaffenhofen, *Bayern* D 95 C3
Pfaffenhoffen F 93 C3
Pfäffikon CH 107 B3
Pfarrkirchen D 95 C4
Pfeffenhausen D 95 C3
Pfetterhouse F 106 B2
Pforzheim D 93 C4
Pfreimd D 95 B4
Pfronten D 108 B1
Pfullendorf D 107 B4
Pfullingen D 94 C1
Pfunds A 108 C1
Pfungstadt D 93 B4
Pfyn CH 107 B3
Phalsbourg F 92 C3
Philippeville B 79 B4
Philippsreut D 96 C1
Philippsthal D 82 B1
Pınarbaşı TR 186 C1
Pınarhisar TR 186 A2
Piacenza I 120 B2
Piacenza d'Adige I 121 B4
Piádena I 120 B3
Piana F 180 A1
Piana Crixia I 133 A4
Piana degli Albanesi I 176 B2
Piana di Monte Verna I 170 B2
Piancastagnáio I 135 C4
Piandelagotti I 134 A3
Pianella, *Abruzzi* I 169 A4
Pianella, *Toscana* I 135 B4
Pianello Val Tidone I 120 C2
Piano I 119 C5
Pianoro I 135 A4
Pians A 108 B1
Pías E 141 B4
Pias P 160 A2
Piaseczno PL 77 B6
Piasek PL 74 B3
Piaski PL 69 A4
Piastów PL 77 B5
Piaszcyna PL 68 A2
Piątek PL 77 B4
Piatra Neamţ RO 17 B7
Piazza al Sérchio I 134 A3
Piazza Armerina I 177 B3
Piazza Brembana I 120 B2
Piazze I 135 C4
Piazzola sul Brenta I 121 B4
Picassent E 159 B3
Piccione I 136 B1
Picerno I 172 B1
Picher D 73 A4
Pickering GB 40 A3
Pico I 169 B3
Picón E 157 A3
Picquigny F 90 B2

Riba-Roja de Turia E 159 B3
Riba-roja d'Ebre E 153 A4
Ribadavia E 140 B2
Ribadeo E 141 A3
Ribadesella E 142 A1
Ribaflecha E 143 B4
Ribaforada E 144 C2
Ribare SRB 127 C3
Ribe DK 59 C1
Ribeauvillé F 106 A2
Ribécourt-Dreslincourt F 90 B2
Ribeira da Pena P 148 A2
Ribeira de Piquín E 141 A3
Ribemont F 91 B3
Ribera I 176 B2
Ribera de Cardós E 146 B2
Ribera del Fresno E 156 B1
Ribérac F 129 A3
Ribes de Freser E 147 B3
Ribesalbes E 159 A3
Ribiers F 132 A1
Ribnica BIH 139 A4
Ribnica SLO 123 B3
Ribnica na Potorju SLO 110 C2
Ribnik HR 123 B4
Ribniţa MD 17 B8
Ribnitz-Damgarten D 66 B1
Ribolla I 135 C4
Říčany, *Jihomoravský* CZ 97 B4
Ričany, *Středočeský* CZ 96 B2
Ríccia I 170 B2
Riccione I 136 A1
Ricco Del Golfo I 134 A2
Richebourg F 105 A4
Richelieu F 102 B2
Richisau CH 107 B3
Richmond, *Greater London* GB 44 B3
Richmond, *North Yorkshire* GB 37 B5
Richtenberg D 66 B1
Richterswil CH 107 B3
Rickling D 64 B3
Rickmansworth GB 44 B3
Ricla E 152 A2
Riddarhyttan S 50 C2
Ridderkerk NL 79 A4
Riddes CH 119 A4
Ridjica SRB 125 B5
Riec-sur-Bélon F 100 B2
Ried A 109 A4
Ried im Oberinntal A 108 B1
Riedenburg D 95 C3
Riedlingen D 107 A4
Riedstadt D 93 B4
Riegersburg A 110 C2
Riego de la Vega E 141 B5
Riego del Camino E 149 A4
Riello E 141 B5
Riemst B 80 B1
Rienne B 91 B4
Riénsena E 142 A2
Riesa D 83 A5
Riese Pio X I 121 B4
Riesi I 177 B3
Riestedt D 82 A3
Rietberg D 81 A4
Rieti I 169 A2
Rietschen D 84 A2
Rieumes F 146 A2
Rieupeyroux F 130 A1
Rieux F 146 A2
Riez F 132 B2
Rīga LV 8 D4
Riggisberg CH 106 C2
Rignac F 130 A1
Rignano Gargánico I 171 B3
Rigolato I 109 C3
Rigside GB 36 A3
Rigutino I 135 B4
Riihimäki FIN 8 B4
Rijeka HR 123 B3
Rijen NL 79 A4
Rijkevorsel B 79 A4
Rijssen NL 71 B3
Rila BG 183 A5
Rilić BIH 138 B3
Rilievo I 176 B1
Rillé F 102 B2
Rillo de Gallo E 152 B2
Rimavská Baňa SK 99 C3
Rimavská Seč SK 99 C4
Rimavská Sobota SK 99 C4
Rimbo S 57 A4
Rimforsa S 56 B1
Rímini I 136 A1
Rîmnicu Sărat RO 17 C7
Rimogne F 91 B4
Rimpar D 94 B1
Rimske Toplice SLO 123 A4
Rincón de la Victoria E 163 B3
Rincón de Soto E 144 B2
Rindal N 198 B6
Rinde N 46 A3
Ringarum S 56 B2
Ringaskiddy IRL 29 C3
Ringe DK 59 C3
Ringebu N 48 A2
Ringkøbing DK 59 B1
Ringsaker N 48 B2
Ringsted DK 61 D1
Ringwood GB 44 C2
Rinkaby S 63 C2
Rinkabyholm S 63 B4
Rinlo E 141 A3
Rinn A 108 B2
Rinteln D 72 B2
Rio E 140 B3
Rio do Coures P 154 B2
Rio Douro P 148 A2
Rio Frio P 154 C2
Rio frio de Riaza E 151 A4
Rio Maior P 154 B2
Rio Marina I 134 C3
Rio Tinto P 148 A1
Riobo E 140 B2
Riodeva E 152 B2
Riofrio E 150 B3
Riofrio de Aliste E 149 A3
Riogordo E 163 B3
Rioja E 164 C2
Riola I 135 A4
Riola Sardo I 179 C2
Riolobos E 155 B4
Riom F 116 B3
Riom-ès-Montagnes F 116 B2
Riomaggiore I 134 A2
Rion-des-Landes F 128 C2
Rionegro del Puente E 141 B4
Rionero in Vúlture I 172 B1
Riopar E 158 C1
Riós E 141 C3
Rioseco E 142 A1
Rioseco de Tapia E 141 B5
Riotord F 117 B4
Riotorto E 141 A3
Rioz F 105 B5
Ripač BIH 124 C1
Ripacándida I 172 B1
Ripanj SRB 127 C2
Ripatransone I 136 C2
Ripley GB 40 B2
Ripoll E 147 B3
Ripon GB 40 A2
Riposto I 177 B4
Ripsa S 56 B2
Risan CG 16 D3
Risbäck S 200 B1
Risca GB 39 C3
Rischenau D 81 A5
Riscle F 128 C2
Risebo S 56 B2
Risnes N 46 A2
Rišňovce SK 98 C1
Risør N 53 B5
Risøyhamn N 194 B6
Rissna S 199 B12
Ritsem S 194 C3
Ritterhude D 72 A1
Riutula FIN 193 D10
Riva del Garda I 121 B3
Riva Lígure I 133 B3
Rivanazzano I 120 C2
Rivarolo Canavese I 119 B4
Rivarolo Mantovano I 121 B3
Rive-de-Gier F 117 B4
Rivedoux-Plage F 114 B2
Rivello I 174 A1
Rivergaro I 120 C2
Rives F 118 B2
Rivesaltes F 146 B3
Rivignano I 122 B2
Rivne UA 13 C7
Rívoli I 119 B4
Rivolta d'Adda I 120 B2
Rixheim F 106 B2
Rixo S 54 B2
Riza GR 183 C5
Rizokarpaso CY 181 A3
Rjukan N 47 C5
Rø DK 67 A3
Rö S 57 A4
Roa E 143 C3
Roa N 48 B2
Roade GB 44 A3
Roager DK 59 C1
Roaldkvam N 52 A2
Roanne F 117 A4
Röbäck S 200 C6
Robakowo PL 69 B3
Róbbio I 120 B1
Röbel D 73 A5
Roberton GB 35 C5
Robertsfors S 200 B6
Robertville B 80 B2
Robin Hood's Bay GB 37 B6
Robleda E 149 B3
Robledillo de Trujillo E 156 A2
Robledo, *Albacete* E 158 C1
Robledo, *Orense* E 141 B4
Robledo de Chavela E 151 B3
Robledo del Buey E 156 A3
Robledo del Mazo E 156 A3
Robledollano E 156 A2
Robles de la Valcueva E 142 B1
Robliza de Cojos E 149 B4
Robres E 145 C3
Robres del Castillo E 144 B1
Rocafort de Queralt E 147 C2
Rocamadour F 129 B4
Rocca di Mezzo I 169 A3
Rocca di Papa I 168 B2
Rocca Imperiale I 174 A2
Rocca Priora I 136 B2
Rocca San Casciano I 135 A4
Rocca Sinibalda I 169 A2
Roccabernarda I 175 B2
Roccabianca I 120 B3
Roccadáspide I 172 B1
Roccagorga I 169 B3
Roccalbegna I 135 C4
Roccalumera I 177 B4
Roccamena I 176 B2
Roccamonfina I 170 B1
Roccanova I 174 A2
Roccapalumba I 176 B2
Roccapassa I 169 A3
Roccaraso I 169 B4
Roccasecca I 169 B3
Roccastrada I 135 B4
Roccatederighi I 135 B4
Roccella Iónica I 175 C2
Rocchetta Sant'António I 172 A1
Rocester GB 40 C2
Rochdale GB 40 B1
Roche-lez-Beaupré F 105 B5
Rochechouart F 115 C4
Rochefort B 79 B5
Rochefort F 114 C3
Rochefort-en-Terre F 101 B3
Rochefort-Montagne F 116 B2
Rochefort-sur-Nenon F 105 B4
Rochemaure F 131 A3
Rocheservière F 114 B2
Rochester, *Medway* GB 45 B4
Rochester, *Northumberland* GB 37 A4
Rochlitz D 83 A4
Rociana del Condado E 161 B3
Rockenhausen D 93 B3
Rockhammar S 56 A1
Rockneby S 62 B4
Ročko Polje HR 123 B3
Ročov CZ 84 B1
Rocroi F 91 B4
Roda de Bara E 147 C2
Roda de Ter E 147 C3
Rodach D 82 B2
Rodalben D 93 B3
Rødberg N 47 B5
Rødby DK 65 B4
Rødbyhavn DK 65 B4
Rødding, *Sonderjyllands Amt.* DK 59 C2
Rødding, *Viborg Amt.* DK 58 B1
Rödeby S 63 B3
Rodeiro E 140 B3
Rødekro DK 64 A2
Roden NL 71 A3
Ródenas E 152 B2
Rodenkirchen D 72 A1
Rödental D 82 B3
Rödermark D 93 B4
Rodewisch D 83 B4
Rodez F 130 A1
Rodi Gargánico I 171 B3
Roding D 95 B4
Rödjebro S 51 B4
Rødkærsbro DK 59 B2
Rodolivas GR 183 C5
Rodoñá E 147 C2
Rødvig DK 65 A5
Roermond NL 80 A1
Roesbrugge B 78 B2
Roeschwoog F 93 C4
Roeselare B 78 B3
Roetgen D 80 B2
Roffiac F 116 B3
Röfors S 55 B5
Rofrano I 172 B1
Rogač HR 138 B2
Rogačica SRB 127 C1
Rogalinek PL 76 B1
Rogaška Slatina SLO 123 A4
Rogatec SLO 123 A4
Rogatica BIH 139 B5
Rogatyn UA 13 D6
Rogätz D 73 B4
Roggendorf D 65 C4
Roggiano Gravina I 174 B2
Roghadal GB 31 B2
Rogliano F 180 A2
Rogliano I 175 B2
Rognan N 195 C6
Rogne N 47 A6
Rognes F 131 B4
Rogny-les-7-Ecluses F 103 B4
Rogowo PL 76 B2
Rogoznica HR 138 B1
Rogoźnica PL 85 A4
Rogoźno PL 76 B1
Rohan F 101 A3
Röhlingen D 94 C2
Rohožnik SK 98 C1
Rohr D 82 B2
Rohr im Gebirge A 110 B2
Rohrbach A 96 C1
Rohrbach-lès-Bitche F 92 B3
Rohrberg D 73 B4
Röhrnbach D 96 C1
Roisel F 90 B3
Roja LV 8 D3
Rojales E 165 A4
Röjeråsen S 50 B1
Rojewo PL 76 B3
Rokiciny PL 87 A3
Rokietnica PL 75 B5
Rokiškis LT 8 E4
Rokitki PL 85 A3
Rokycany CZ 96 B1
Rolampont F 105 B4
Rold DK 58 B2
Røldal N 52 A2
Rolde NL 71 B3
Rolfs S 196 D6
Rollag N 47 B6
Rollán E 149 B4
Rolle CH 105 C5
Roma S 57 C4
Roma = Rome I 168 B2
Romagnano Sésia I 119 B5
Romagné F 88 B2
Romakloster S 57 C4
Roman RO 17 B7
Romana I 178 B2
Romanèche-Thorins F 117 A4
Romano di Lombardia I 120 B2
Romans-sur-Isère F 118 B2
Romanshorn CH 107 B4
Rombas F 92 B2
Rome = Roma I 168 B2
Romeán E 141 B3
Romenay F 105 C4
Romeral E 157 A4
Römerstein D 94 C1
Rometta I 177 A4
Romford GB 45 B4
Romhány H 112 B3
Römhild D 82 B2
Romilly-sur-Seine F 91 C3
Romont CH 106 C1
Romorantin-Lanthenay F 103 B3
Romrod D 81 B5
Romsey GB 44 C2
Rømskog N 54 A2
Rønbjerg DK 58 B1
Roncal E 144 B3
Ronce-les-Bains F 114 C2
Ronchamp F 106 B1
Ronchi dei Legionari I 122 B2
Ronciglione I 168 A2
Ronco Canavese I 119 B4
Ronco Scrivia I 120 C1
Ronda E 162 B2
Rønde DK 59 B3
Rone S 57 C4
Ronehamn S 57 C4
Rong N 46 B1
Rönnäng S 60 B1
Rønne DK 67 A3
Ronneburg D 83 B4
Ronneby S 63 B3
Rönneshytta S 55 B6
Rönninge S 57 A3
Rönnöfors S 199 B10
Rönö S 56 B2
Ronov nad Doubravou CZ 97 B3
Ronse B 79 B3
Roosendaal NL 79 A4
Roosky IRL 26 C3
Ropczyce PL 87 B5
Ropeid N 52 A2
Ropinsalmi FIN 192 D5
Ropuerelos del Páramo E 141 B5
Roquebilière F 133 A3
Roquebrun F 130 B2
Roquecourbe F 130 B1
Roquefort F 128 B2
Roquemaure F 131 A3
Roquesteron F 132 B3
Roquetas de Mar E 164 C2
Roquetes E 153 B4
Roquevaire F 132 B1
Røra N 199 B8
Rörbäcksnäs S 49 A4
Rørbæk DK 58 B2
Rore BIH 138 A2
Röro S 60 B1
Røros N 199 C8
Rorschach CH 107 B4
Rørvig DK 61 D1
Rørvik N 199 A8
Rörvik S 62 A2
Rosà I 121 B4
Rosa Marina I 173 B3
Rosal de la Frontera E 161 B2
Rosalina Mare I 122 B1
Rosans F 132 A1
Rosário P 160 B1
Rosarno I 175 C1
Rosbach D 81 B3
Rosche D 73 B3
Rościszewo PL 77 B4
Roscoff F 100 A2
Roscommon IRL 28 A3
Roscrea IRL 28 B4
Rosdorf D 82 A1
Rose I 174 B2
Rosegg A 109 C5
Rosehall GB 32 D2
Rosehearty GB 33 D4
Rosel GB 88 A1
Rosell E 153 B4
Roselló E 153 A4
Rosendal N 46 C3
Rosenfeld D 93 C4
Rosenfors S 62 A3
Rosenheim D 108 B3
Rosenow D 74 A2
Rosenthal D 81 A4
Rosersberg S 57 A3
Roses E 147 B4
Roseto degli Abruzzi I 169 A4
Roseto Valfortore I 170 B3
Rosheim F 93 C3
Rosia I 135 B4
Rosice CZ 97 B4
Rosières-en-Santerre F 90 B2
Rosignano Maríttimo I 134 B3
Rosignano Solvay I 134 B3
Roşiori-de-Vede RO 17 C6
Roskhill GB 31 B2
Roskilde DK 61 D2
Roskovec AL 182 C1
Röslau D 83 B3
Roslev DK 58 B1
Rosmaninhal P 155 B3
Rosnowo PL 67 B5
Rosolini I 177 C3
Rosova CG 139 B5
Rosoy F 104 A2
Rosporden F 100 B2
Rosquete P 154 B2
Rosrath D 80 B3
Ross-on-Wye GB 39 C4
Rossa CH 120 A2
Rossano I 174 B2
Rossas, *Aveiro* P 148 B1
Rossas, *Braga* P 148 A1
Rossdorf D 82 B2
Rossett GB 38 A4
Rosshaupten D 108 B1
Rossiglione I 133 A4
Rossignol B 92 B1
Rossla D 82 A3
Rosslare IRL 30 B2
Rosslare Harbour IRL 30 B2
Rosslau D 83 A4
Rosslea GB 27 B3
Rossleben D 82 A3
Rossön S 200 C2
Rossoszyca PL 86 A2
Rosswein D 83 A5
Röstånga S 61 C3
Roštár SK 99 C4
Rostock D 65 B5
Rostrenen F 100 A2
Røsvik N 194 C6
Rosvik S 196 D4
Rosyth GB 35 B4
Röszke H 126 A2
Rot S 49 A6
Rot am See D 94 B2
Rota E 161 C3
Rota Greca I 174 B2
Rotberget N 49 B4
Rotella I 136 C2
Rotenburg, *Hessen* D 82 B1
Rotenburg, *Niedersachsen* D 72 A2
Roth, *Bayern* D 94 B3
Roth, *Rheinland-Pfalz* D 81 B3
Rothbury GB 37 A5
Rothemühl D 74 A2
Rothenkempenow D 74 A3
Röthenbach D 95 B3
Rothenburg D 84 A2
Rothenburg ob der Tauber D 94 B2
Rothéneuf F 88 B2
Rothenstein D 94 C3
Rotherham GB 40 B2
Rothes GB 32 D3
Rothesay GB 34 C2
Rothwell GB 44 A3
Rotnes N 48 B2
Rotonda I 174 B2
Rotondella I 174 A2
Rotova E 159 C3
Rott, *Bayern* D 108 B1
Rott, *Bayern* D 108 B3
Rottach-Egern D 108 B2
Röttenbach D 94 B3
Rottenbuch D 108 B1
Rottenburg, *Baden-Württemberg* D 93 C4
Rottenburg, *Bayern* D 95 C4
Rottenmann A 110 B1
Rotterdam NL 79 A4
Rotthalmünster D 96 C1
Rottingdean GB 44 C3
Röttingen D 94 B1
Rottleberode D 82 A1
Rottne S 62 A2
Rottneros S 55 A4
Rottofreno I 120 B2
Rottweil D 107 A3
Rötz D 95 B4
Roubaix F 78 B3
Roudnice nad Labem CZ 84 B2
Roudouallec F 100 A2
Rouen F 89 A5
Rouffach F 106 B2
Rougé F 101 B4
Rougemont F 105 B5
Rougemont le-Château F 106 B1
Rouillac F 115 C3
Rouillé F 115 B4
Roujan F 130 B2
Roulans F 105 B5
Roundwood IRL 30 A2
Rousínov CZ 97 B4
Roussac F 115 B5
Roussennac F 130 A1
Rousses F 130 A2
Roussillon F 117 B4
Rouvroy-sur-Audry F 91 B4
Rouy F 104 B2
Rovanieman maalaiskunta FIN 197 C8
Rovaniemi FIN 197 C8
Rovato I 120 B2
Rovensko pod Troskami CZ 84 B3
Roverbella I 121 B3
Rovereto I 121 B4
Rövershagen D 65 B5
Roverud N 49 B4
Rovigo I 121 B4
Rovinj HR 122 B2
Rovišce HR 124 B2
Rów PL 74 B3
Rowy PL 68 A2
Royal Leamington Spa GB 44 A2
Royal Tunbridge Wells GB 45 B4
Royan F 114 C2
Royat F 116 B3
Roybon F 118 B2
Roybridge GB 34 B3
Roye F 90 B2
Royère-de-Vassivière F 116 B1
Røykenvik N 48 B2
Royos E 164 B2
Røyrvik N 199 A10
Royston GB 44 A3
Rozadas E 141 A4
Rozalén del Monte E 151 C5
Różańsko PL 75 B3
Rozay-en-Brie F 90 C2
Roždalovice CZ 84 B3
Rozdilna UA 17 B9
Rozental PL 69 B4
Rozhyshche UA 13 C6
Rožmitál pod Třemšínem CZ 96 B1
Rožňava SK 99 C4
Rožnov pod Radhoštěm CZ 98 B2
Rozoy-sur-Serre F 91 B4
Rozprza PL 86 A3
Roztoky CZ 84 B2
Rozvadov CZ 95 B4
Rozzano I 120 B2
Rrëshen AL 182 B1
Rrogozhine AL 182 B1
Ruanes E 156 A2
Rubbestadneset N 46 C2
Rubi E 147 C3
Rubiá E 141 B4
Rubiacedo de Abajo E 143 B3
Rubielos Bajos E 158 B1
Rubielos de Mora E 153 B3
Rubiera I 121 C3
Rubik AL 182 B1

Siorac-en-Périgord F 129 B3
Šipanska Luka HR 139 C3
Šipovo BIH 138 A3
Sira N 52 B2
Siracusa I 177 B4
Siret RO 17 B7
Sirevåg N 52 B1
Sirig SRB 126 B1
Sirkka FIN 196 B7
Sirmione I 121 B3
Sirniö FIN 197 D11
Sirok H 113 B4
Široké SK 99 C4
Široki Brijeg BIH 139 B3
Sirolo I 136 B2
Siruela E 156 B2
Sisak HR 124 B2
Sisante E 158 B1
Šišljavić HR 123 B4
Sissach CH 106 B2
Sissonne F 91 B3
Sistelo P 140 C2
Sisteron F 132 A1
Sistiana I 122 B2
Sistranda N 198 B5
Sitasjaurestugorna S 194 C8
Sitges E 147 C2
Sitia GR 185 D7
Sittard NL 80 A1
Sittensen D 72 A2
Sittingbourne GB 45 B4
Sitzenroda D 83 A4
Sivac SRB 126 B1
Sivaslı TR 189 A4
Siverić HR 138 B2
Sivrihisar TR 187 C6
Sixt-Fer-á-Cheval F 119 A3
Siziano I 120 B2
Sizun F 100 A1
Sjenica SRB 16 D3
Sjoa N 198 D6
Sjoåsen N 199 A8
Sjöbo S 61 D3
Sjøenden, *Hedmark* N 48 A3
Sjøenden, *Hedmark* N 48 B3
Sjøholt N 198 C3
Sjøli N 48 A3
Sjølstad N 199 A9
Sjölunda S 56 A1
Sjømarken S 60 B2
Sjørring DK 58 B1
Sjötofta S 60 B3
Sjötorp S 55 B4
Sjoutnäset S 199 A11
Sjøvegan N 194 B8
Sjuntorp S 54 B3
Skåbu N 47 A6
Skælskør DK 65 A4
Skærbæk DK 64 A1
Skafså N 53 A4
Skaftafell IS 191 D9
Skagaströnd IS 190 B5
Skagen DK 58 A3
Skagersvik S 55 B5
Skaiå N 53 B3
Skaidi N 193 B8
Skala GR 184 A1
Skała PL 87 B3
Skala Oropou GR 185 A4
Skala-Podilska UA 13 D7
Skaland N 194 A8
Skalat UA 13 D6
Skalbmierz PL 87 B4
Skålevik N 53 B4
Skalica SK 98 C1
Skalité SK 98 B2
Skällinge S 60 B2
Skalná CZ 83 B4
Skals DK 58 B2
Skalstugan S 199 B9
Skanderborg DK 59 B2
Skåne-Tranås S 61 D3
Skånes-Fagerhult S 61 C3
Skånevik N 52 A1
Skänninge S 55 B6
Skanör med Falsterbo S 66 A1
Skåpafors S 54 A3
Skąpe PL 75 B4
Skara S 55 B4
Skarberget N 194 B7
Skärblacka S 56 B1
Skarda S 200 B4
Skarð IS 190 B3
Skare N 46 C3
Skåre S 55 A4
Skärhamn S 60 B1
Skarnes N 48 B3
Skarp Salling DK 58 B2
Skärplinge S 51 B4
Skarpnatö FIN 51 B6
Skarrild DK 59 C1
Skarstad N 194 B7
Skärstad S 62 A2
Skarsvåg N 193 A9
Skarszewy PL 69 A3
Skårup DK 65 A3
Skärvången S 199 B11
Skarvsjöby S 195 F8
Skaryszew PL 87 A5
Skarżysko-Kamienna PL 87 A4
Skarzysko Ksiazece PL 87 A4
Skatøy N 53 B5
Skattkärr S 55 A4
Skattungbyn S 50 A1
Skatval N 199 B7
Skaulo S 196 B4
Skave DK 59 B1
Skawina PL 99 B3
Skebobruk S 51 C5
Skebokvarn S 56 A2
Skedala S 61 C2
Skedevi S 56 B1
Skedsmokorset N 48 B3
Skee S 54 B2
Skegness GB 41 B4
Skei N 46 A3
Skela SRB 127 C2
Skelani BIH 127 D1
Skellefteå S 2 D7
Skelleftehamn S 2 D7
Skelmersdale GB 38 A4
Skelmorlie GB 34 C3
Skelund DK 58 B3
Skender Vakuf BIH 138 A3
Skene S 60 B2
Skępe PL 77 B4
Skepplanda S 60 B2
Skeppshult S 60 B3
Skerries IRL 30 A2
Ski N 54 A1
Skiathos GR 183 D5
Skibbereen IRL 29 C2
Skibotn N 192 C4
Skidra GR 182 C4
Skien N 53 A5
Skierniewice PL 77 C5
Skillingaryd S 60 B4
Skillinge S 63 C2
Skillingmark S 49 C4
Skilloura CY 181 A2
Skinnardai S 57 A4
Skinnskatteberg S 50 C2
Skipmannvik N 195 C6
Skipness GB 34 C2
Skipsea GB 41 B3
Skipton GB 40 B1
Skiptvet N 54 A2
Skiros GR 183 E6
Skivarp S 66 A2
Skive DK 58 B2
Skjærhalden N 54 A2
Skjånes N 193 B12
Skjeberg N 54 A2
Skjeggedal N 46 B3
Skjeljanger N 46 B1
Skjeljavik N 46 C2
Skjern DK 59 C1
Skjervøy N 192 B4
Skjold, *Rogaland* N 52 A1
Skjold, *Troms* N 192 C3
Skjoldastraumen N 52 A1
Skjolden N 47 A4
Skjønhaug N 54 A2
Skjøtningsberg N 193 A11
Škocjan SLO 123 B4
Skoczów PL 98 B2
Skodborg DK 59 C2
Škofja Loka SLO 123 A3
Škofljica SLO 123 B3
Skog S 51 A3
Skoganvarre N 193 C9
Skogen S 54 A3
Skogfoss N 193 C13
Skoghall S 55 A4
Skogly N 193 C13
Skogn N 199 B8
Skognes N 192 C3
Skogstorp, *Halland* S 60 C2
Skogstorp, *Södermanland* S 56 A2
Skoki PL 76 B2
Skokloster S 57 A3
Sköldinge S 56 A2
Skole UA 13 D5
Skollenborg N 53 A5
Sköllersta S 56 A1
Skomlin PL 86 A2
Skonseng N 195 D5
Skopelos GR 183 D5
Skopje MK 182 A3
Skoppum N 54 A1
Skórcz PL 69 B3
Skorogoszcz PL 86 B1
Skoroszów PL 85 A5
Skorovatn N 199 A10
Skorped S 200 C3
Skørping DK 58 B2
Skotfoss N 53 A5
Skotniki PL 87 A3
Skotselv N 48 C1
Skotterud N 49 C4
Skottorp S 61 C2
Skovby DK 64 B2
Skövde S 55 B4
Skovsgård DK 58 A2
Skrad HR 123 B3
Skradin HR 138 B1
Skradnik HR 123 B4
Skråmestø N 46 B1
Škrdlovice CZ 97 B3
Skrea S 60 C2
Skreia N 48 B2
Skrolsvik N 194 A7
Skruv S 63 B3
Skrwilno PL 77 A4
Skrydstrup DK 59 C2
Skucani BIH 138 B2
Skudeneshavn N 52 A1
Skui N 48 C2
Skulsk PL 76 B3
Skultorp S 55 B4
Skultuna S 56 A2
Skuodas LT 8 D2
Skurup S 66 A2
Skute N 48 B2
Skuteč CZ 97 B3
Skutskär S 51 B4
Skutvik N 194 B6
Skvyra UA 13 D8
Skwierzyna PL 75 B4
Skýcov SK 98 C2
Skyllberg S 55 B5
Skyttmon S 200 C1
Skyttorp S 51 B4
Sládkovičovo SK 111 A4
Slagelse DK 61 D1
Slagharen NL 71 B3
Slagnäs S 195 E9
Slaidburn GB 40 B1
Slane IRL 30 A2
Slangerup DK 61 D2
Slano HR 139 C3
Slantsy RUS 8 C6
Slaný CZ 84 B2
Slap SLO 122 A2
Šlapanice CZ 97 B4
Slåstad N 48 B3
Slatina BIH 139 B3
Slatina HR 125 B3
Slatina RO 17 C6
Slatiňany CZ 97 B3
Slatinice CZ 98 B1
Slättberg S 50 A1
Slattum N 48 C2
Slavičin CZ 98 B1
Slavkov CZ 98 C1
Slavkov u Brna CZ 97 B4
Slavkovica SRB 127 C2
Slavonice CZ 97 C3
Slavonski Brod HR 125 B4
Slavonski Kobas HR 125 B3
Slavošovce SK 99 C4
Slavskoye RUS 69 A5
Slavuta UA 13 C7
Sława, *Lubuskie* PL 85 A4
Sława, *Zachodnio-Pomorskie* PL 67 C4
Slawharad BY 13 B9
Sławków PL 86 B3
Sławno, *Wielkopolskie* PL 76 B2
Sławno, *Zachodnio-Pomorskie* PL 68 A1
Sławoborze PL 67 C4
Sl'ažany SK 98 C2
Sleaford GB 40 C3
Sleðbrjótur IS 191 B11
Sledmere GB 40 A3
Sleights GB 37 B6
Slemmestad N 54 A1
Ślesin PL 76 B3
Sliač SK 99 C3
Sliema M 175 C3
Sligo IRL 26 B2
Slite S 57 C4
Slitu N 54 A2
Sliven BG 17 D7
Śliwice PL 68 B3
Slobozia RO 17 C7
Slochteren NL 71 A3
Slöinge S 60 C2
Słomniki PL 87 B4
Slonim BY 13 B6
Słońsk PL 75 B3
Slootdorp NL 70 B1
Slottsbron S 55 A4
Slough GB 44 B3
Slövag N 46 B2
Slovenj Gradec SLO 110 C2
Slovenska Bistrica SLO 123 A4
Slovenská L'upča SK 99 C3
Slovenská-Ves SK 99 B4
Slovenské Darmoty SK 112 A3
Slovenske Konjice SLO 123 A4
Słubice PL 74 B3
Sluderno I 108 C1
Sluis NL 78 A3
Šluknov CZ 84 A2
Slunj HR 123 B4
Słupca PL 76 B2
Słupia PL 87 A3
Słupiec PL 85 B4
Słupsk PL 68 A2
Slutsk BY 13 B7
Smålandsstenar S 60 B3
Smalåsen N 195 E4
Smardzewo PL 75 B4
Smarhon BY 13 A7
Smarje SLO 123 A4
Šmarjeta SLO 123 B4
Šmartno SLO 123 A3
Smečno CZ 84 B2
Smedby S 63 B4
Smědec CZ 96 C2
Smederevo SRB 127 C2
Smederevska Palanka SRB 127 C2
Smedjebacken S 50 B2
Smęgorzów PL 87 B5
Smeland N 53 B4
Smidary CZ 84 B3
Śmigiel PL 75 B5
Smilde NL 71 B3
Smiřice CZ 85 B3
Smithfield GB 36 B4
Śmitowo PL 75 A5
Smögen S 54 B2
Smogulec PL 76 A2
Smołdzino PL 68 A2
Smolenice SK 98 C1
Smolensk RUS 13 A10
Smolník SK 99 C4
Smolyan BG 183 B6
Smuka SLO 123 B3
Smygehamn S 66 A2
Smykow PL 87 A4
Snainton GB 40 A3
Snaith GB 40 B2
Snaptun DK 59 C3
Snarby N 192 C3
Snarum N 48 B1
Snåsa N 199 A9
Snedsted DK 58 B1
Sneek NL 70 A2
Sneem IRL 29 C2
Snejbjerg DK 59 B1
Snillfjord N 198 B6
Šnjegotina BIH 125 C3
Snøde DK 65 A3
Snøfjord N 193 B8
Snogebaek DK 67 A4
Snyatyn UA 13 D6
Soave I 121 B4
Sober E 140 B3
Sobernheim D 93 B3
Soběslav CZ 96 B2
Sobota, *Dolnośląskie* PL 85 A3
Sobota, *Łódzkie* PL 77 B4
Sobotište SK 98 C1
Sobotka CZ 84 B3
Sobótka, *Dolnośląskie* PL 85 B4
Sobótka, *Wielkopolskie* PL 86 A1
Sobra HR 139 C3
Sobrado, *Coruña* E 140 A2
Sobrado, *Lugo* E 141 B3
Sobral da Adica P 161 A2
Sobral de Monte Argraço P 154 C1
Sobreira Formosa P 154 B3
Søby DK 64 B3
Soca SLO 122 A2
Sochaczew PL 77 B5
Sochos GR 183 C5
Socodor RO 113 C5
Socol RO 127 C3
Socovos E 164 A3
Socuéllamos E 158 B1
Sodankylä FIN 197 B9
Soderåkra S 63 B4
Söderala S 51 A3
Söderås S 50 B2
Söderbärke S 50 B2
Söderby-Karl S 51 C5
Söderfors S 51 B4
Söderhamn S 51 A4
Söderköping S 56 B2
Söderö S 56 B1
Södertälje S 57 A3
Södingberg A 110 B2
Södra Finnö S 56 B2
Södra Ny S 55 A4
Södra Råda S 55 A5
Södra Sandby S 61 D3
Södra Vi S 62 A3
Sodražica SLO 123 B3
Sodupe E 143 A3
Soengas P 148 A1
Soest D 81 A4
Soest NL 70 B2
Sofades GR 182 D4
Sofia = Sofiya BG 17 D5
Sofikon GR 184 B4
Sofiya = Sofia BG 17 D5
Şofronea RO 126 A3
Sögel D 71 B4
Sogliano al Rubicone I 135 A5
Sogndalsfjøra N 46 A4
Søgne N 53 B3
Söğüt, *Bilecik* TR 187 B5
Söğüt, *Burdur* TR 189 B4
Söğütköy TR 188 C3
Söğütlu TR 187 B5
Soham GB 45 A4
Sohland D 84 A2
Sohren D 93 B3
Soignies B 79 B4
Soissons F 90 B3
Söjtör H 111 C3
Sokal' UA 13 C6
Söke TR 188 B2
Sokna N 48 B1
Sokndal N 52 B2
Soknedal N 199 C7
Soko BIH 125 C4
Sokolac BIH 139 B4
Sokółka PL 13 B5
Sokolov CZ 83 B4
Sokołów Podlaski PL 12 B5
Sokołowo PL 76 B3
Sola N 52 B1
Solana de los Barros E 155 C4
Solana del Pino E 157 B3
Solánas I 179 C3
Solares E 143 A3
Solarino I 177 B4
Solarussa I 179 C2
Solas GB 31 B1
Solber-gelva N 53 A6
Solberg S 200 C3
Solberga S 62 A2
Solbjørg N 46 B2
Solčany SK 98 C2
Solčava SLO 123 A3
Solda I 108 C1
Sölden A 108 C2
Solec Kujawski PL 76 A3
Soleils F 132 B2
Solenzara F 180 B2
Solera E 163 A4
Solesmes F 79 B3
Soleto I 173 B4
Solgne F 92 C2
Solheim N 46 B2
Solheimsvik N 52 A2
Solignac F 115 C5
Solihull GB 44 A2
Solin HR 138 B2
Solingen D 80 A3
Solivella E 147 C2
Solkan SLO 122 B2
Söll A 108 B3
Sollana E 159 B3
Sollebrunn S 54 B3
Sollefteå S 200 C3
Sollen-tuna S 57 A3
Sollenau A 111 B3
Sóller E 166 B2
Sollerön S 50 B1
Søllested DK 65 B4
Solliès-Pont F 132 B2
Sollihøgda N 48 C2
Solnechnogorsk RUS 9 D10
Solnice CZ 85 B4
Solofra I 170 C2
Solomiac F 129 C3
Solopaca I 170 B2
Solórzano E 143 A3
Solothurn CH 106 B2
Solre-le-Château F 79 B4
Solsona E 147 C2
Solsvik N 46 B1
Solt H 112 C3
Soltau D 72 B2
Soltsy RUS 9 C7
Soltszentimre H 112 C3
Soltvadkert H 112 C3
Solumsmoen N 48 C1
Solund N 46 A1
Solva GB 39 C1
Sölvesborg S 63 B2
Solymár H 112 B2
Soma TR 186 C2
Somain F 78 B3
Somberek H 125 A4
Sombernon F 104 B3
Sombor SRB 125 B5
Sombreffe B 79 B4
Someren NL 80 A1
Somero FIN 8 B3
Somersham GB 44 A3
Somerton GB 43 A4
Sominy PL 68 A2
Somma Lombardo I 120 B1
Sommariva del Bosco I 119 C4
Sommarøy N 192 C2
Sommarset N 194 C6
Sommatino I 176 B2
Somme-Tourbe F 91 B4
Sommeilles F 91 C4
Sommen S 55 B5
Sommepy-Tahure F 91 B4
Sömmerda D 82 A3
Sommerfeld D 74 B2
Sommersted DK 59 C2
Sommesous F 91 C4
Sommières F 131 B3
Sommières-du-Clain F 115 B4
Somo E 143 A3
Somogyfajsz H 111 C4
Somogyjád H 111 C4
Somogysámson H 111 C4
Somogysárd H 125 A3
Somogyszil H 112 C2
Somogyszob H 124 A3
Somogyvár H 111 C4
Somontin E 164 B2
Somosiero E 151 A4
Somosköújifalu H 113 A3
Sompolno PL 76 B3
Sompuis F 91 C4
Son N 54 A1
Son Bou E 167 B4
Son en Breugel NL 80 A1
Son Servera E 167 B3
Sonceboz CH 106 B2
Soncillo E 143 B3
Soncino I 120 B2
Sóndalo I 120 A3
Søndeled N 53 B5
Sønder Bjert DK 59 C2
Sønder Felding DK 59 C1
Sønder Hygum DK 59 C1
Sønder Omme DK 59 C1
Sønderborg DK 64 B2
Sønderby DK 64 B2
Sønderho DK 59 C1
Sondershausen D 82 A2
Søndersø DK 59 C3
Søndervig DK 59 B1
Søndre Enningdal Kappel N 54 B2
Sóndrio I 120 A2
Soneja E 159 B3
Songe N 53 B5
Songeons F 90 B1
Sonkamuotka FIN 196 A6
Sonkovo RUS 9 D10
Sönnarslöv S 61 D4
Sonneberg D 82 B3
Sonnefeld D 82 B3
Sonnewalde D 84 A1
Sonnino I 169 B3
Sonogno CH 120 A1
Sonsbeck D 80 A2
Sonseca E 157 A4
Sønsterud N 49 B4
Sonstorp S 56 B1
Sonta SRB 125 B5
Sontheim D 94 C2
Sonthofen D 107 B5
Sontra D 82 A1
Sopelana E 143 A4
Sopje HR 125 B3
Šoporňa SK 111 A4
Sopot PL 69 A3
Sopot SRB 127 C2
Sopotnica MK 182 B3
Sopron H 111 B3
Šor SRB 127 C1
Sora I 169 B3
Soragna I 120 C3
Söråker S 200 D3
Sorano I 168 A1
Sorbara I 121 C4
Sorbas E 164 B2
Sórbolo I 121 C3
Sörbygden S 200 D2
Sordal N 52 B3
Sordale GB 32 C3
Sore F 128 B2
Sörenberg CH 106 C3
Soresina I 120 B2
Sorèze F 146 A3
Sörforsa S 200 E3
Sorges F 115 C4
Sórgono I 179 B3
Sorgues F 131 A3
Sorgun TR 23 B8
Soria E 143 C4
Soriano Cálabro I 175 C2
Soriano nel Cimino I 168 A2
Sorihuela del Guadalimar E 164 A1
Sorisdale GB 34 B1
Sørkjosen N 192 C4
Sørli N 199 A10
Sormás H 111 C3
Sörmjöle S 200 C6
Sørmo N 194 B9
Sornac F 116 B2
Sorø DK 61 D1
Soroca MD 17 A8
Sørreisa N 194 A9
Sorrento I 170 C2
Sorsele S 195 E8
Sörsjön S 49 A5
Sorso I 178 B2
Sort E 146 B2
Sortavala RUS 9 B7
Sortino I 177 B4
Sortland N 194 B6
Sørum N 48 B2
Sørumsand N 48 C3
Sorunda S 57 A3
Sörup D 64 B2
Sørvær N 192 B6
Sørvågen N 194 C3
Sorvik S 50 B2
Sørvika N 199 C8
Sos F 128 B3
Sos del Rey Católico E 144 B2
Sösdala S 61 C3
Sošice HR 123 B4
Sośnica PL 75 A5
Sośnicowice PL 86 B2
Sośno PL 76 A2
Sosnovyy Bor RUS 9 C6
Sosnowiec PL 86 B3
Sospel F 133 B3
Šoštanj SLO 123 A4
Sotaseter N 198 D4
Sotillo de Adrada E 150 B3
Sotillo de la Ribera E 143 C3
Sotin HR 125 B5
Sotkamo FIN 3 D11
Soto de la Marina E 143 A3
Soto de los Infantes E 141 A4

Struer DK 58 B1
Struga MK 182 B2
Strugi Krasnyye RUS 9 C6
Strumica MK 182 B4
Strumien PL 98 B2
Struy GB 32 D2
Stružec HR 124 B2
Stryków PL 77 C4
Stryn N 198 D3
Stryy UA 13 D5
Strzałkowo PL 76 B2
Strzegocin PL 77 B5
Strzegom PL 85 B4
Strzegowo PL 77 B5
Strzelce PL 77 B4
Strzelce Krajeńskie PL 75 B4
Strzelce Kurowo PL 75 B4
Strzelce Opolskie PL 86 B2
Strzelin PL 85 B5
Strzelno PL 76 B3
Strzepcz PL 68 A3
Strzybnica PL 86 B2
Strzygi PL 77 A4
Stubbekøbing DK 65 B5
Stuben A 107 B5
Stubenberg A 110 B2
Stubline SRB 127 C2
Studená CZ 97 B3
Studenci HR 138 B3
Studenka CZ 98 B2
Studenzen A 110 B2
Studienka SK 98 C1
Studland GB 43 B5
Studley GB 44 A2
Studzienice PL 68 A2
Stuer D 73 A5
Stugudal N 199 C8
Stugun S 200 C1
Stuhr D 72 A1
Stukenbrock D 81 A4
Stülpe D 74 B2
Stupava SK 111 A4
Stupnik HR 124 B1
Stupsk PL 77 A5
Sturkö S 63 B3
Sturminster Newton GB 43 B4
Štúrovo SK 112 B2
Sturton GB 40 B3
Stuttgart D 94 C1
Stvolny CZ 96 A1
Stykkishólmur IS 190 B3
Styri N 48 B3
Stysö S 60 B1
Suances E 142 A2
Subbiano I 135 B4
Subiaco I 169 B3
Subotica SRB 126 A1
Subotište SRB 127 C1
Sučany SK 98 B2
Suceava RO 17 B7
Sucha-Beskidzka PL 99 B3
Suchacz PL 69 A4
Suchań PL 75 A4
Suchdol nad Lužnice CZ 96 C2
Suchedniów PL 87 A4
Suchorze PL 68 A2
Suchteln D 80 A2
Sucina E 165 B4
Suckow D 73 A4
Sućuraj HR 138 B3
Sudbury GB 45 A4
Suddesjaur S 195 E10
Suden D 64 B1
Süderbrarup D 64 B2
Süderlügum D 64 B1
Súðavík IS 190 A3
Suðureyri IS 190 A2
Sudoměřice u Bechyně CZ 96 B2
Sudovec HR 124 A2
Sueca E 159 B3
Suelli I 179 C3
Sugenheim D 94 B2
Sugères F 117 B3
Sugny B 91 B4
Suhl D 82 B2
Suhlendorf D 73 B3
Suho Polje BIH 125 C5
Suhopolje HR 124 B3
Şuhut TR 189 A5
Šuica BIH 138 B3
Suippes F 91 B4
Sukošan HR 137 A4
Sükösd H 125 A4
Suków PL 87 B4
Šul'a SK 99 C3
Suldalsosen N 52 A2
Suldrup DK 58 B2
Sulechów PL 75 B4
Sulęcin PL 75 B4
Sulęczyno PL 68 A2
Sulejów PL 87 A4
Süleymanlı TR 186 D2
Sulgen CH 107 B4
Sulibórz PL 75 A4
Sulina RO 17 C8
Sulingen D 72 B1
Suliszewo PL 75 A4
Sulitjelma N 195 C7
Sułkowice PL 99 B3
Süller TR 189 A4
Sully-sur-Loire F 103 B4
Sulmierzyce, *Łódzkie* PL 86 A3
Sulmierzyce, *Wielkopolskie* PL 85 A5
Sulmona I 169 A3
Süloğlu TR 186 A1
Sułoszowa PL 87 B3
Sulów PL 85 A5
Sulsdorf D 65 B4
Sultandağı TR 189 A6
Sülüklü TR 187 D7
Suluova TR 23 A8
Sulvik S 54 A3
Sülysáp H 112 B3
Sülz D 93 C4
Sulzbach, *Baden-Württemberg* D 94 B1
Sulzbach, *Baden-Württemberg* D 94 C1
Sulzbach, *Bayern* D 93 B5
Sulzbach, *Saarland* D 92 B3
Sulzbach-Rosenberg D 95 B3
Sülze D 72 B3
Sulzfeld D 82 B2
Sumartin HR 138 B2
Sumburgh GB 33 B5
Sümeg H 111 C4
Sumiswald CH 106 B2
Šumná CZ 97 C3
Šumperk CZ 97 B4
Šumvald CZ 98 B1
Sunbilla E 144 A2
Sünching D 95 C4
Sund FIN 51 B7
Sund S 54 A2
Sundborn S 50 B2
Sundby DK 58 B1
Sunde N 46 C2
Sunde bru N 53 B5
Sunderland GB 37 B5
Sundern D 81 A4
Sundhultsbrunn S 62 A2
Sundnäs S 195 D8
Sundom S 196 D5
Sunds DK 59 B2
Sundsfjord N 195 D5
Sundsvall S 200 D3
Sungurlu TR 23 A8
Suni I 178 B2
Sunja HR 124 B2
Sunnansjö S 50 B1
Sunnaryd S 60 B3
Sunndalsøra N 198 C5
Sunne S 49 C5
Sunnemo S 49 C5
Sunnersberg S 55 B4
Suolovuopmio N 192 C7
Suomussalmi FIN 3 D11
Suoyarvi RUS 9 A8
Super Sauze F 132 A2
Supetar HR 138 B2
Supetarska Draga HR 123 C3
Supino I 169 B3
Šuplja Stijena CG 139 B5
Surahammar S 56 A2
Šurany SK 112 A2
Surazh BY 13 A9
Surbo I 173 B4
Surčin SRB 127 C2
Surgères F 114 B3
Surhuisterveen NL 70 A3
Súria E 147 C2
Surin F 115 B4
Surka N 48 B2
Surnadalsøra N 198 C5
Sursee CH 106 B3
Surte S 60 B2
Surwold D 71 B4
Sury-le-Comtal F 117 B4
Susa I 119 B4
Šušara SRB 127 C3
Susch CH 107 C5
Susegana I 122 B1
Süsel D 65 B3
Sušice CZ 96 B1
Sušnjevica HR 123 B3
Sussen D 94 C1
Susurluk TR 186 C3
Susz PL 69 B4
Sütçüler TR 189 B5
Sutivan HR 138 B2
Sutjeska SRB 126 B2
Sutri I 168 A2
Sutton GB 44 B3
Sutton Coldfield GB 40 C2
Sutton-in-Ashfield GB 40 B2
Sutton-on-Sea GB 41 B4
Sutton-on-Trent GB 40 B3
Sutton Scotney GB 44 B2
Sutton Valence GB 45 B4
Suvaja BIH 124 C2
Suvereto I 135 B3
Suwałki PL 12 A5
Suze-la-Rousse F 131 A3
Suzzara I 121 C3
Svabensverk S 50 A2
Svalbarð IS 191 A10
Svalöv S 61 D3
Svanabyn S 200 B2
Svanberga S 51 C5
Svaneke DK 67 A4
Svanesund S 54 B2
Svängsta S 63 B2
Svannäs S 195 D9
Svanskog S 54 A3
Svanstein S 196 C6
Svappavaara S 196 B4
Svärdsjö S 50 B2
Svarstad N 53 A5
Svartå, *Örebro* S 55 A5
Svärta, *Södermanland* S 56 B3
Svartå, *Värmland* S 55 A4
Svartbyn S 196 C5
Svärtinge S 56 B2
Svartlå S 196 D4
Svartnäs S 50 B3
Svartnes N 195 C5
Svarttjärn S 195 E7
Svatsum N 48 A1
Svätý Jur SK 111 A4
Svätý Peter SK 112 B2
Svedala S 61 D3
Sveg S 199 C11
Sveindal N 52 B3
Sveio N 52 A1
Svejbæk DK 59 B2
Svelgen N 198 D2
Svelvik N 54 A1
Svendborg DK 65 A3
Svene N 53 A5
Svenljunga S 60 B3
Svennevad S 56 A1
Svenstavik S 199 C11
Svenstrup DK 58 B2
Švermov CZ 84 B2
Sveti Ivan Zabno HR 124 B2
Sveti Ivan Zelina HR 124 B2
Sveti Nikole MK 182 B3
Sveti Rok HR 137 A4
Světlá nad Sázavou CZ 97 B3
Svetlyy RUS 69 A5
Svetvinčenat HR 122 B2
Švica HR 123 C4
Švidník SK 12 D4
Švihov CZ 96 B1
Svilajnac SRB 127 C3
Svilengrad BG 183 B8
Svindal N 54 A2
Svinhult S 62 A3
Svinna SK 98 C2
Svinninge DK 61 D1
Svinninge S 57 A4
Sviritsa RUS 9 B8
Svishtov BG 17 D6
Svislach BY 13 B6
Svit SK 99 B4
Svitavy CZ 97 B4
Svodin SK 112 B2
Svolvær N 194 B5
Svortemyr N 46 A2
Svortland N 52 A1
Svratka CZ 97 B4
Svrčinovec SK 98 B2
Svullrya N 49 B4
Svyetlahorsk BY 13 B8
Swadlincote GB 40 C2
Swaffham GB 41 C4
Swanage GB 43 B5
Swanley GB 45 B4
Swanlinbar IRL 26 B3
Swansea GB 39 C3
Swarzędz PL 76 B2
Swatragh GB 27 B4
Świątki PL 69 B5
Świdnica, *Dolnośląskie* PL 85 B4
Świdnica, *Lubuskie* PL 84 A3
Świdnik PL 12 C5
Świdwin PL 67 C4
Świebodzice PL 85 B4
Świebodzin PL 75 B4
Świecie PL 76 A3
Świedziebnia PL 77 A4
Świeradów Zdrój PL 84 B3
Świerki PL 85 B4
Swierzawa PL 85 A3
Swierzno PL 67 C3
Swięta PL 74 A3
Swieta Anna PL 86 B3
Świętno PL 75 B5
Swifterbant NL 70 B2
Swindon GB 44 B2
Swineshead GB 41 C3
Swinford IRL 26 C2
Świnoujście PL 66 C3
Swinton GB 35 C5
Swobnica PL 74 A3
Swords IRL 30 A2
Swornegacie PL 68 B2
Sya S 56 B1
Syasstroy RUS 9 B8
Sycewice PL 68 A1
Sychevka RUS 9 E9
Syców PL 86 A1
Sycowice PL 75 B4
Sydnes N 52 A1
Syfteland N 46 B2
Syke D 72 B1
Sykkylven N 198 C3
Sylling N 48 C2
Sylte N 198 C4
Symbister GB 33 A5
Symington GB 36 A3
Symonds Yat GB 39 C4
Sypniewo, *Kujawsko-Pomorskie* PL 76 A2
Sypniewo, *Wielkopolskie* PL 68 B1
Syserum S 62 A4
Sysslebäck S 49 B4
Syväjärvi FIN 197 B8
Szabadbattyán H 112 B2
Szabadegyháza H 112 B2
Szabadszállás H 112 C3
Szadek PL 86 A2
Szajol H 113 B4
Szakály H 112 C2
Szakcs H 112 C2
Szakmár H 112 C3
Szalánta H 125 B4
Szałas PL 87 A4
Szalkszentmárton H 112 C3
Szalonna H 99 C4
Szamocin PL 76 A2
Szamotuły PL 75 B5
Szany H 111 B4
Szarvas H 113 C4
Szarvaskö H 113 B4
Szászvár H 125 A4
Százhalombatta H 112 B2
Szczawa PL 99 B4
Szczawnica PL 99 B4
Szczecin PL 74 A3
Szczecinek PL 68 B1
Szczekociny PL 87 B3
Szczerców PL 86 A3
Szczucin PL 87 B5
Szczuczarz PL 75 A5
Szczuki PL 77 B5
Szczurowa PL 87 B4
Szczyrk PL 99 B3
Szczytna PL 85 B4
Szczytno PL 77 A5
Szczyty PL 86 A2
Szécsény H 112 A3
Szederkény H 125 B4
Szedres H 112 C2
Szeged H 126 A2
Szeghalom H 113 B5
Szegvár H 113 C4
Székesfehérvár H 112 B2
Székkutas H 113 C4
Szekszárd H 125 A4
Szemplino Czarne PL 77 A5
Szemud PL 68 A3
Szendehely H 112 B3
Szendrö H 99 C4
Szentendre H 112 B3
Szentes H 113 C4
Szentgotthárd H 111 C3
Szentlászló H 125 A3
Szentlörinc H 125 A3
Szentmártonkáta H 113 B3
Szenyér H 111 C4
Szeremle H 125 A4
Szerencs H 113 A5
Szerep H 113 B5
Szigetszentmiklós H 112 B3
Szigetvár H 125 A3
Szikáncs H 126 A2
Szikszó H 113 A4
Szil H 111 B4
Szilvásvárad H 113 A4
Szklarska Poreba PL 84 B3
Szlichtyngowa PL 85 A4
Szob H 112 B2
Szolnok H 113 B4
Szombathely H 111 B3
Szorosad H 112 C2
Szpetal Graniczny PL 77 B4
Szprotawa PL 84 A3
Szreńsk PL 77 A5
Sztum PL 69 B4
Sztutowo PL 69 A4
Szubin PL 76 A2
Szücsi H 113 B3
Szulmierz PL 77 B5
Szulok H 124 A3
Szumanie PL 77 B4
Szwecja PL 75 A5
Szydłów, *Łódzkie* PL 86 A3
Szydłów, *Świętokrzyskie* PL 87 B5
Szydłowiec PL 87 A4
Szydlowo, *Mazowieckie* PL 77 A5
Szydłowo, *Wielkopolskie* PL 75 A5
Szymanów PL 77 B5
Szynkielów PL 86 A2

T

Tab H 112 C2
Tabanera la Luenga E 151 A3
Tabaqueros E 158 B2
Tábara E 149 A4
Tabenera de Cerrato E 142 B2
Taberg S 62 A2
Tabernas E 164 B2
Tabiano Bagni I 120 C3
Taboada E 140 B3
Taboadela E 140 B3
Tábor CZ 96 B2
Táborfalva H 112 B3
Taborište HR 124 B2
Tábua P 148 B1
Tabuaco P 148 A2
Tabuenca E 152 A2
Tabuyo del Monte E 141 B4
Täby S 57 A4
Tác H 112 B2
Tachov CZ 95 B4
Tadcaster GB 40 B2
Tadley GB 44 B2
Tafalla E 144 B2
Tafjord N 198 C4
Taganheira P 160 B1
Tågarp S 61 D2
Tággia I 133 B3
Tagliacozzo I 169 A3
Táglio di Po I 121 B5
Tagnon F 91 B4
Tahal E 164 B2
Tahitótfalu H 112 B3
Tahtaköprü TR 187 C4
Tailfingen D 107 A4
Taillis F 101 A4
Tain GB 32 D2
Tain-l'Hermitage F 117 B4
Taipadas P 154 C2
Taivalkoski FIN 197 D11
Takene S 55 A4
Takovo SRB 127 C2
Taksony H 112 B3
Tal E 140 B2
Tal-Y-Llyn GB 38 B3
Talachyn BY 13 A8
Talamello I 135 B5
Talamone I 168 A1
Talant F 105 B3
Talarrubias E 156 A2
Talaván E 155 B4
Talavera de la Reina E 150 C3
Talavera la Real E 155 C4
Talayuela E 150 C2
Talayuelas E 159 B2
Talgarth GB 39 C3
Talgje N 52 A1
Talhadas P 148 B1
Táliga E 155 C3
Talizat F 116 B3
Tálknafjörður IS 190 B2
Talla I 135 B4
Talladale GB 31 B3
Tallaght IRL 30 A2
Tallard F 132 A2
Tällberg, *Dalarnas* S 50 B1
Tallberg, *Norrbotten* S 196 C5
Tallinn EST 8 C4
Talloires F 118 B3
Tallow IRL 29 B3
Tallsjö S 200 B4
Tallvik S 196 C5
Talmay F 105 B4
Talmont-St. Hilaire F 114 B2
Talmont-sur-Gironde F 114 C3
Talne UA 13 D9
Talsano I 173 B3
Talsi LV 8 D3
Talvik N 192 B6
Talybont GB 39 B3
Tamajón E 151 B4
Tamame E 149 A4
Tamames E 149 B3
Tamarit de Mar E 147 C2
Tamarite de Litera E 145 C4
Tamariu E 147 C4
Tamási H 112 C2
Tambach-Dietharz D 82 B2
Tameza E 141 A4
Tammisaari FIN 8 B3
Tampere FIN 8 B3
Tamsweg A 109 B4
Tamurejo E 156 B3
Tamworth GB 40 C2
Tana bru N 193 B12
Tañabueyes E 143 B3
Tanakajd H 111 B3
Tananger N 52 B1
Tanaunella I 178 B3
Tancarville F 89 A4
Tandsjöborg S 199 D11
Tånga S 61 C2
Tangelic H 112 C2
Tangen N 48 B3
Tangerhütte D 73 B4
Tangermünde D 73 B4
Tanhua FIN 197 B10
Taninges F 118 A3
Tankavaara FIN 197 A10
Tann D 82 B2
Tanna D 83 B3
Tannadice GB 35 B5
Tannåker S 60 C3
Tännäs S 199 C9
Tannay, *Ardennes* F 91 B4
Tannay, *Nièvre* F 104 B2
Tannenbergsthal D 83 B4
Tännesberg D 95 B4
Tannheim A 108 B1
Tannila FIN 197 D8
Tanowo PL 74 A3
Tanum S 54 B2
Tanumshede S 54 B2
Tanus F 130 A1
Tanvald CZ 84 B3
Taormina I 177 B4
Tapa EST 8 C4
Tapfheim D 94 C2
Tapia de Casariego E 141 A4
Tapio F 146 A2
Tápióbicske H 112 B3
Tápiógyörgye H 113 B3
Tápióság H 112 B3
Tápiószecsö H 112 B3
Tápiószele H 113 B3
Tápiószentmárton H 113 B3
Tapolca H 111 C4
Tapolcafö H 111 B4
Tar HR 122 B2
Tarabo S 60 B2
Taradell E 147 C3
Taraklı TR 187 B5
Taramundi E 141 A3
Tarancón E 151 B4
Táranto I 173 B3
Tarare F 117 B4
Tarascon F 131 B3
Tarascon-sur-Ariège F 146 B2
Tarashcha UA 13 D9
Tarazona E 144 C2
Tarazona de la Mancha E 158 B2
Tarbena E 159 C3
Tarbert GB 34 C2
Tarbert IRL 29 B2
Tarbes F 145 A4
Tarbet GB 34 B3
Tarbolton GB 36 A2
Tarcento I 122 A2
Tarčin BIH 139 B4
Tarczyn PL 77 C5
Tardajos E 143 B3
Tardelcuende E 151 A5
Tardets-Sorholus F 144 A3
Tardienta E 145 C3
Tärendö S 196 B5
Targon F 128 B2
Târgovişte RO 17 C6
Târgu-Jiu RO 17 C5
Târgu Mureş RO 17 B6
Târgu Ocna RO 17 B7
Târgu Secuiesc RO 17 C7
Tarifa E 162 B2
Tariquejas E 161 B2
Tarján H 112 B2
Tárkany H 112 B2
Tarland GB 33 D4
Tarłów PL 87 A5
Tarm DK 59 C1
Tarmstedt D 72 A2
Tärnaby S 195 E6
Tarnalelesz H 113 A4
Tarnaörs H 113 B4
Târnăveni RO 17 B6
Tårnet N 193 C14
Tarnobrzeg PL 87 B5
Tarnos F 128 C1
Tarnów, *Lubuskie* PL 75 B3
Tarnów, *Małopolskie* PL 87 B4
Tarnowo Podgórne PL 75 B5
Tarnowskie Góry PL 86 B2
Tärnsjö S 51 B3
Tårnvik N 194 C6
Tarouca P 148 A2
Tarp D 64 B2
Tarquínia I 168 A1
Tarquínia Lido I 168 A1
Tarragona E 147 C2
Tärrajaur S 196 C2
Tàrrega E 147 C2
Tarrenz A 108 B1
Tårs, *Nordjyllands* DK 58 A3
Tårs, *Storstrøms* DK 65 B4
Tarsia I 174 B2
Tarsus TR 23 C8
Tartas F 128 C2
Tartu EST 8 C5
Tarves GB 33 D4
Tarvísio I 109 C4
Taşağıl TR 189 C6
Täsch CH 119 A4
Taşköprü TR 23 A8
Tasov CZ 97 B4
Tasovčići BIH 139 B3
Tåstrup DK 61 D2
Taşucu TR 23 C7
Tát H 112 B2
Tata H 112 B2
Tatabánya H 112 B2
Tataháza H 126 A1
Tatarbunary UA 17 C8
Tatárszentgyörgy H 112 B3
Tatranská-Lomnica SK 99 B4
Tau N 52 A1

Torrejón de la Calzada E 151 B4
Torrejón del Rey E 151 B4
Torrejon el Rubio E 156 A1
Torrejoncillo E 155 B4
Torrelaguna E 151 B4
Torrelapaja E 152 A2
Torrelavega E 142 A2
Torrelobatón E 150 A2
Torrelodones E 151 B4
Torremaggiore I 171 B3
Torremanzanas E 159 C3
Torremayor E 155 C4
Torremezzo di Falconara I 174 B2
Torremocha E 156 A1
Torremolinos E 163 B3
Torrenieri I 135 B4
Torrenostra E 153 B4
Torrenova I 168 B2
Torrent E 159 B3
Torrente de Cinca E 153 A4
Torrenueva, *Ciudad Real* E 157 B4
Torrenueva, *Granada* E 163 B4
Torreorgaz E 155 B4
Torreperogil E 157 B4
Torres E 163 A4
Torres-Cabrera E 163 A3
Torres de la Alameda E 151 B4
Torres Novas P 154 B2
Torres Vedras P 154 B1
Torresandino E 143 C3
Torrevieja E 165 B4
Torri del Benaco I 121 B3
Torricella I 173 B3
Torridon GB 31 B3
Torriglia I 134 A2
Torrijos E 151 C3
Tørring DK 59 C2
Torrita di Siena I 135 B4
Torroal P 154 C2
Torroella de Montgrì E 147 B4
Torrox E 163 B4
Torrskog S 54 A3
Torsåker S 50 B3
Torsang S 50 B2
Torsås S 63 B4
Torsby S 49 B4
Torsetra N 48 B2
Torshälla S 56 A2
Tórshavn FO 4 A3
Torslanda S 60 B1
Torsminde DK 59 B1
Törtel H 113 B3
Tórtoles E 150 B2
Tórtoles de Esgueva E 142 C2
Tortoli I 179 C3
Tortona I 120 C1
Tórtora I 174 B1
Tortoreto Lido I 136 C2
Tortorici I 177 A3
Tortosa E 153 B4
Tortosendo P 148 B2
Tortuera E 152 B2
Tortuero E 151 B4
Toruń PL 76 A3
Torup S 60 C3
Torver GB 36 B3
Tørvikbygde N 46 B3
Torviscón E 163 B4
Torzhok RUS 9 D9
Torzym PL 75 B4
Tosbotn N 195 E3
Toscelanor-Maderno I 121 B3
Tosno RUS 9 C7
Tossa de Mar E 147 C3
Tossåsen S 199 C10
Tosse F 128 C1
Tösse S 54 B3
Tossicía I 169 A3
Tostedt D 72 A2
Tosya TR 23 A8
Tószeg H 113 B4
Toszek PL 86 B2
Totana E 165 B3
Totebo S 62 A4
Tôtes F 89 A5
Tótkomlós H 113 C4
Totland N 198 D2
Tøtlandsvik N 52 A2
Totnes GB 43 B3
Tótszerdahely H 124 A2
Tøttdal N 199 A8
Totton GB 44 C2
Touça P 149 A2
Toucy F 104 B2
Toul F 92 C1
Toulon F 132 B1
Toulon-sur-Allier F 104 C2
Toulon-sur-Arroux F 104 C3
Toulouse F 129 C4
Tour de la Parata F 180 B1
Tourcoing F 78 B3
Tourlaville F 88 A2
Tournai B 78 B3
Tournan-en-Brie F 90 C2
Tournay F 145 A4
Tournon-d'Agenais F 129 B3
Tournon-St. Martin F 115 B4
Tournon-sur-Rhône F 117 B4
Tournus F 105 C3
Touro E 140 B2
Touro P 148 B2
Tourouvre F 89 B4
Tourriers F 115 C4
Tours F 102 B2
Tourteron F 91 B4
Tourves F 132 B1
Toury F 103 A3
Touvedo P 148 A1
Touvois F 114 B2
Toužim CZ 83 B4
Tovačov CZ 98 B1
Tovariševo SRB 126 B1
Tovarnik HR 125 B5
Tovdal N 53 B4
Towcester GB 44 A3
Town Yetholm GB 35 C5
Tråastølen N 47 B4
Trabada E 141 A3
Trabadelo E 141 B4
Trabanca E 149 A3
Trabazos E 149 A3
Traben-Trarbach D 92 B3
Trabia I 176 B2
Tradate I 120 B1
Trädet S 60 B3
Trafaria P 154 C1
Tragacete E 152 B2
Tragwein A 96 C2
Traiguera E 153 B4
Trainel F 91 C3
Traisen A 110 A2
Traismauer A 97 C3
Traitsching D 95 B4
Trákhonas CY 181 A2
Tralee IRL 29 B2
Tramacastilla de Tena E 145 B3
Tramagal P 154 B2
Tramariglio I 178 B2
Tramatza I 179 B2
Tramelan CH 106 B2
Tramonti di Sopra I 122 A1
Tramore IRL 30 B1
Trampot F 92 C1
Trana I 119 B4
Tranås S 55 B5
Tranbjerg DK 59 B3
Tranby N 54 A1
Trancoso P 148 B2
Tranebjerg DK 59 C3
Tranekær DK 65 B3
Tranemo S 60 B3
Tranent GB 35 C5
Tranevåg N 52 B2
Trängslet S 49 A5
Tranhult S 60 B3
Trani I 171 B4
Trans-en-Provence F 132 B2
Transtrand S 49 A5
Tranum DK 58 A2
Tranvik S 57 A4
Trápani I 176 A1
Trappes F 90 C2
Traryd S 61 C3
Trasacco I 169 B3
Trasierra E 156 B1
Träslövsläge S 60 B2
Trasmiras E 140 B3
Traspinedo E 150 A3
Trate SLO 110 C2
Trauchgau D 108 B1
Traun A 110 A1
Traunreut D 109 B3
Traunstein D 109 B3
Traunwalchen D 109 B3
Tråvad S 55 B4
Travemünde D 65 C3
Traversétolo I 120 C3
Travnik BIH 139 A3
Travnik SLO 123 B3
Travo F 180 B2
Travo I 120 C2
Trawsfynydd GB 38 B3
Trbovlje SLO 123 A4
Trbušani SRB 127 D2
Treban F 116 A3
Třebařov CZ 97 B4
Trebatsch D 74 B3
Trebbin D 74 B2
Třebechovice pod Orebem CZ 85 B3
Trebel D 73 B4
Třebenice CZ 84 B1
Trébeurden F 100 A2
Třebíč CZ 97 B3
Trebinje BIH 139 C4
Trebisacce I 174 B2
Trebitz D 83 A4
Trebnje SLO 123 B4
Třeboň CZ 96 B2
Třebovice CZ 97 B4
Trebsen D 83 A4
Trebujena E 161 C3
Trecastagni I 177 B4
Trecate I 120 B1
Trecenta I 121 B4
Tredegar GB 39 C3
Tredózio I 135 A4
Treffen A 109 C4
Treffort F 118 A2
Treffurt D 82 A2
Trefnant GB 38 A3
Tregaron GB 39 B3
Trégastel-Plage F 100 A2
Tregnago I 121 B4
Tregony GB 42 B2
Tréguier F 100 A2
Trégunc F 100 B2
Treharris GB 39 C3
Trehörningsjö S 200 C4
Tréia I 136 B2
Treignac F 116 B1
Treignat F 116 A2
Treignes B 91 A4
Treis-Karden D 80 B3
Trekanten S 63 B4
Trélazé F 102 B1
Trelech GB 39 C2
Trélissac F 129 A3
Trelleborg S 66 A2
Trélon F 91 A4
Trélou-sur-Marne F 91 B3
Tremblay-le-Vicomte F 89 B5
Tremés P 154 B2
Tremezzo I 120 B2
Třemošná CZ 96 B1
Tremp E 145 B4
Trenčianska Stankovce SK 98 C1
Trenčianska Turná SK 98 C2
Trenčianske Teplá SK 98 C2
Trenčianske Teplice SK 98 C2
Trenčín SK 98 C2
Trendelburg D 81 A5
Trengereid N 46 B2
Trensacq F 128 B2
Trent D 66 B2
Trento I 121 A4
Treorchy GB 39 C3
Trept F 118 B2
Trepuzzi I 173 B4
Trescore Balneário I 120 B2
Tresenda I 120 A3
Tresfjord N 198 C4
Tresigallo I 121 C4
Trešnjevica SRB 127 D3
Tresnurághes I 178 B2
Trespaderne E 143 B3
Třešť CZ 97 B3
Trestina I 135 B5
Tretower GB 39 C3
Trets F 132 B1
Tretten N 48 A2
Treuchtlingen D 94 C2
Treuen D 83 B4
Treuenbrietzen D 74 B1
Treungen N 53 A4
Trevelez E 163 B4
Trevi I 136 C1
Trevi nel Lázio I 169 B3
Treviana E 143 B3
Treviglio I 120 B2
Trevignano Romano I 168 A2
Treviso I 122 B1
Trévoux F 117 B4
Treysa D 81 B5
Trézelles F 117 A3
Trezzo sull'Adda I 120 B2
Trhová Kamenice CZ 97 B3
Trhové Sviny CZ 96 C2
Triacastela E 141 B3
Triaize F 114 B2
Trianda GR 188 C3
Triaucourt-en-Argonne F 91 C5
Tribanj Kruščica HR 137 A4
Triberg D 106 A3
Tribsees D 66 B1
Tribuče SLO 123 B4
Tricárico I 172 B2
Tricase I 173 C4
Tricésimo I 122 A2
Trie-sur-Baïse F 145 A4
Trieben A 110 B1
Triebes D 83 B4
Triepkendorf D 74 A2
Trier D 92 B2
Trieste I 122 B2
Triggiano I 173 A2
Triglitz D 73 A5
Trignac F 101 B3
Trigueros E 161 B3
Trigueros del Valle E 142 C2
Trikala GR 182 D3
Trikeri GR 183 D5
Trikomo CY 181 A2
Trilj HR 138 B2
Trillo E 152 B1
Trilport F 90 C2
Trim IRL 30 A2
Trimdon GB 37 B5
Trindade, *Beja* P 160 B2
Trindade, *Bragança* P 149 A2
Třinec CZ 98 B2
Tring GB 44 B3
Trinità d'Agultu I 178 B2
Trinitápoli I 171 B4
Trino I 119 B5
Trinta P 148 B2
Triora I 133 B3
Tripoli GR 184 B3
Triponzo I 136 C1
Triptis D 83 B3
Triste E 144 B3
Trittau D 72 A3
Trivento I 170 B2
Trivero I 119 B5
Trivigno I 172 B1
Trn BIH 124 C3
Trnava HR 125 B4
Trnava SK 98 C1
Trnovec SK 112 A1
Trnovo BIH 139 B4
Trnovska vas SLO 110 C2
Troarn F 89 A3
Trochtelfingen D 94 C1
Trödje S 51 B4
Trœnse DK 65 A3
Trofa P 148 A1
Trofaiach A 110 B2
Trofors N 195 E4
Trogir HR 138 B2
Trøgstad N 54 A2
Tróia I 171 B3
Troia P 154 C2
Troina I 177 B3
Trois-Ponts B 80 B1
Troisdorf D 80 B3
Troisvierges L 92 A2
Trojane SLO 123 A3
Troldhede DK 59 C1
Trollhättan S 54 B3
Trolog BIH 138 B2
Tromello I 120 B1
Tromøy N 53 B4
Tromsø N 192 C3
Trondheim N 199 B7
Tronget F 116 A3
Trönninge S 61 C2
Trönningeby S 60 B2
Trönö S 51 A3
Tronzano-Vercellese I 119 B5
Trôo F 102 B2
Troon GB 36 A2
Tropea I 175 C1
Tropy Sztumskie PL 69 B4
Trosa S 57 B3
Trösken S 50 B3
Trosly-Breuil F 90 B3
Trossingen D 107 A3
Trostberg D 109 A3
Trouville-sur-Mer F 89 A4
Trowbridge GB 43 A4
Troyes F 104 A3
Trpanj HR 138 B3
Trpinja HR 125 B4
Tršće HR 123 B3
Tršice CZ 98 B1
Trstená SK 99 B3
Trstenci BIH 125 B3
Trsteno HR 139 C3
Trstice SK 111 A4
Trstin SK 98 C1
Trubia E 141 A5
Trubjela CG 139 C4
Truchas E 141 B4
Trujillanos E 155 C4
Trujillo E 156 A2
Trumieje PL 69 B4
Trun CH 107 C3
Trun F 89 B4
Truro GB 42 B1
Trusetal D 82 B2
Truskavets' UA 13 D5
Trustrup DK 59 B3
Trutnov CZ 85 B3
Tryserum S 56 B2
Trysil N 49 A4
Tryszczyn PL 76 A2
Trzcianka PL 75 A5
Trzciel PL 75 B4
Trzcińsko Zdrój PL 74 B3
Trzebiatów PL 67 B4
Trzebiel PL 84 A2
Trzebielino PL 68 A2
Trzebień PL 84 A3
Trzebiez PL 74 A3
Trzebinia PL 86 B3
Trzebnica PL 85 A5
Trzebnice PL 85 A4
Trzeciewiec PL 76 A3
Trzemeszno PL 76 B2
Trzemeszno-Lubuskie PL 75 B4
Trzetrzewina PL 99 B4
Tržič SLO 123 A3
Tsamandas GR 182 D2
Tschagguns A 107 B4
Tschernitz D 84 A2
Tsebrykove UA 17 B9
Tsyelyakhany BY 13 B6
Tua P 148 A2
Tuam IRL 28 A3
Tubbergen NL 71 B3
Tubilla del Lago E 143 C3
Tübingen D 93 C5
Tubize B 79 B4
Tučapy CZ 96 B2
Tučepi HR 138 B3
Tuchan F 146 B3
Tüchen D 73 A5
Tuchola PL 76 A2
Tuchomie PL 68 A2
Tuchów PL 99 B5
Tuczno PL 75 A5
Tuddal N 53 A4
Tudela E 144 B2
Tudela de Duero E 150 A3
Tudweiliog GB 38 B2
Tuejar E 159 B2
Tuffé F 102 A2
Tufsingdalen N 199 C8
Tuhaň CZ 84 B2
Tui E 140 B2
Tukhkala RUS 197 D13
Tukums LV 8 D3
Tula I 178 B2
Tulcea RO 17 C8
Tul'chyn UA 13 D8
Tulette F 131 A3
Tuliszków PL 76 B3
Tulla IRL 28 B3
Tullamore IRL 30 A1
Tulle F 116 B1
Tullins F 118 B2
Tulln A 97 C4
Tullow IRL 30 B2
Tułowice PL 85 B5
Tulppio FIN 197 B12
Tulsk IRL 28 A3
Tumba S 57 A3
Tummel Bridge GB 35 B3
Tun S 55 B3
Tuna, *Kalmar* S 62 A4
Tuna, *Uppsala* S 51 B5
Tuna Hästberg S 50 B2
Tunçbilek TR 187 C4
Tunes P 160 B1
Tungelsta S 57 A4
Tunnerstad S 55 B5
Tunnhovd N 47 B5
Tunstall GB 45 A5
Tuohikotti FIN 8 B5
Tuoro sul Trasimeno I 135 B5
Tupadły PL 76 B3
Tupanari BIH 139 A4
Tupik RUS 9 E8
Tuplice PL 84 A2
Tura H 112 B3
Turanj HR 137 B4
Turany SK 99 B3
Turbe BIH 139 A3
Turbenthal CH 107 B3
Turcia E 141 B5
Turčianske Teplice SK 98 C2
Turcifal P 154 B1
Turckheim F 106 A2
Turda RO 17 B5
Turégano E 151 A4
Turek PL 76 B3
Tŭrgovishte BG 17 D7
Turgutlu TR 188 A2
Turi I 173 B3
Turin = Torino I 119 B4
Turis E 159 B3
Türje H 111 C4
Turka UA 12 D5
Túrkeve H 113 B4
Türkheim D 108 A1
Türkmenli TR 186 C1
Turku FIN 8 B3
Turleque E 157 A4
Turňa nad Bodvou SK 99 C4
Turnberry GB 36 A2
Turnhout B 79 A4
Türnitz A 110 B2
Turnov CZ 84 B3
Turnu RO 126 A3
Turnu Măgurele RO 17 D6
Turón E 164 C1
Turoszów PL 84 B2
Turowo PL 77 A5
Turquel P 154 B1
Turri I 179 C2
Turries F 132 A2
Turriff GB 33 D4
Tursi I 174 A2
Turtmann CH 119 A4
Turtola FIN 196 C6
Turze PL 86 A1
Turzovka SK 98 B2
Tusa I 177 B3
Tuscánia I 168 A1
Tuse DK 61 D1
Tušilovic HR 123 B4
Tuszyn PL 86 A3
Tutow D 66 C2
Tutrakan BG 17 C7
Tuttlingen D 107 B3
Tutzing D 108 B2
Tuzla BIH 125 C4
Tuzla TR 23 C8
Tuzlukçu TR 189 A6
Tvååker S 60 B2
Tvärålund S 200 B5
Tvärskog S 63 B4
Tvedestrand N 53 B4
Tveit, *Hordaland* N 47 B4
Tveit, *Rogaland* N 52 A2
Tver RUS 9 D9
Tverrelvmo N 192 D3
Tversted DK 58 A3
Tving S 63 B3
Tvrdošin SK 99 B3
Tvrdošovce SK 112 A2
Twardogóra PL 85 A5
Twatt GB 33 B3
Twello NL 70 B3
Twimberg A 110 C1
Twist D 71 B4
Twistringen D 72 B1
Tworóg PL 86 B2
Twyford, *Hampshire* GB 44 B2
Twyford, *Wokingham* GB 44 B3
Tyachiv UA 17 A5
Tychówka PL 67 C5
Tychowo PL 67 C5
Tychy PL 86 B2
Tydal N 199 B8
Týec nad Labem CZ 97 A3
Tyfors S 49 B6
Tygelsjö S 61 D2
Tylldal N 199 C7
Tylstrup DK 58 A2
Tymbark PL 99 B4
Tymowa PL 99 B4
Týn nad Vltavou CZ 96 B2
Tyndrum GB 34 B3
Týnec nad Sázavou CZ 96 B2
Tynemouth GB 37 A5
Tyngsjö S 49 B5
Týniště nad Orlicí CZ 85 B4
Tynset N 199 C7
Tyresö S 57 A4
Tyringe S 61 C3
Tyrislöt S 56 B2
Tyristrand N 48 B2
Tyrrellspass IRL 30 A1
Tysnes N 46 B2
Tysse N 46 B2
Tyssebotn N 46 B2
Tyssedal N 46 B3
Tystberga S 56 B3
Tysvær N 52 A1
Tywyn GB 39 B2
Tzermiado GR 185 D6
Tzummarum NL 70 A2

U

Ub SRB 127 C2
Ubby DK 61 D1
Úbeda E 157 B4
Überlingen D 107 B4
Ubidea E 143 A4
Ubli HR 138 C2
Ubrique E 162 B2
Ucero E 143 C3
Uchaud F 131 B3
Uchte D 72 B1
Uckerath D 80 B3
Uckfield GB 45 C4
Ucklum S 54 B2
Uclés E 151 C5
Ucria I 177 A3
Udbina HR 137 A4
Uddebo S 60 B3
Uddeholm S 49 B5
Uddevalla S 54 B2
Uddheden S 49 C4
Uden NL 80 A1
Uder D 82 A2
Udiča SK 98 B2
Údine I 122 A2
Udvar H 125 B4
Ueckermünde D 74 A3
Uelsen D 71 B3
Uelzen D 73 B3
Uetendorf CH 106 C2
Uetersen D 72 A2
Uetze D 72 B3
Uffculme GB 43 B3
Uffenheim D 94 B2
Ugarana E 143 A4
Ugento I 173 C4
Ugerldse DK 61 D1
Uggerby DK 58 A3
Uggerslev DK 59 C3
Uggiano la Chiesa I 173 B4
Ugíjar E 164 C1
Ugine F 118 B3
Uglejevik BIH 125 C5
Uglenes N 46 B2
Uglich RUS 9 D11
Ugljane HR 138 B2
Ugod H 111 B4
Uherské Hradiště CZ 98 B1
Uherský Brod CZ 98 B1
Uherský Ostroh CZ 98 C1
Uhingen D 94 C1
Uhlířské-Janovice CZ 96 B3
Uhřiněves CZ 96 A2
Uhyst D 84 A2
Uig GB 31 B2
Uitgeest NL 70 B1
Uithoorn NL 70 B1
Uithuizen NL 71 A3
Uithuizermeeden NL 71 A3
Uivar RO 126 B2
Ujazd, *Łódzkie* PL 87 A3
Ujazd, *Opolskie* PL 86 B2
Ujezd u Brna CZ 97 B4
Ujhartyán H 112 B3
Újkígyós H 113 C5
Ujpetre H 125 B4
Ujście PL 75 A5
Ujsolt H 112 C3
Újszász H 113 B4

Újszentmargita H 113 B5
Ujué E 144 B2
Ukanc SLO 122 A2
Ukmergė LT 13 A6
Ukna S 56 B2
Ula TR 188 B3
Ul'anka SK 99 C3
Ulaş TR 186 A2
Ulássai I 179 C3
Ulbjerg DK 58 B2
Ulbster GB 32 C3
Ulceby GB 40 B3
Ulcinj CG 16 E3
Uldum DK 59 C2
Ulefoss N 53 A5
Uleila del Campo E 164 B2
Ulëz AL 182 B1
Ulfborg DK 59 B1
Uljma SRB 127 B3
Ullånger S 200 C4
Ullapool GB 32 D1
Ullared S 60 B2
Ullatti S 196 B4
Ullatun N 52 A2
Ulldecona E 153 B4
Ulldemolins E 147 C1
Ullerslev DK 59 C3
Ullervad S 55 B4
Üllés H 126 A1
Üllö H 112 B3
Ullvi S 56 A2
Ulm D 94 C1
Ulme P 154 B2
Ulmen D 80 B2
Ulnes N 47 B6
Ulog BIH 139 B4
Ulricehamn S 60 B3
Ulrichstein D 81 B5
Ulrika S 56 B1
Ulriksfors S 200 C1
Ulrum NL 71 A3
Ulsberg N 198 C6
Ulsta GB 33 A5
Ulsted DK 58 A3
Ulsteinvik N 198 C2
Ulstrup, *Vestsjællands Amt.* DK 59 C3
Ulstrup, *Viborg Amt.* DK 59 B2
Ulsvåg N 194 B6
Ulubey TR 188 A4
Uluborlu TR 189 A5
Ulukışla TR 23 C8
Ulverston GB 36 B3
Ulvik N 46 B3
Umag HR 122 B2
Uman UA 13 D9
Umba RUS 3 C14
Umbértide I 135 B5
Umbriático I 174 B2
Umčari SRB 127 C2
Umeå S 200 C6
Umgransele S 200 B4
Umhausen A 108 B1
Umka SRB 127 C2
Umljanovic HR 138 B2
Umnäs S 195 E7
Umurbey TR 186 B1
Unaðsdalur IS 190 A3
Unapool GB 32 C1
Unari FIN 197 B8
Unbyn S 196 D4
Uncastillo E 144 B2
Undenäs S 55 B5
Undersaker S 199 B10
Undredal N 46 B4
Unešić HR 138 B2
Úněšov CZ 96 B1
Ungheni MD 17 B7
Unhais da Serra P 148 B2
Unhošt CZ 84 B2
Unichowo PL 68 A2
Uničov CZ 98 B1
Uniejów PL 76 C3
Unisław PL 76 A3
Unkel D 80 B3
Unken A 109 B3
Unna D 81 A3
Unnaryd S 60 C3
Unquera E 142 A2
Unter Langkampfen A 108 B3
Unter-steinbach D 94 B2
Unterach A 109 B4
Unterägeri CH 107 B3
Unterammergau D 108 B2
Unterhaching D 108 A2
Unteriberg CH 107 B3
Unterkochen D 94 C2
Unterlaussa A 110 B1
Unterlüss D 72 B3
Untermünkheim D 94 B1
Unterschächen CH 107 C3
Unterschleissheim D 95 C3
Unterschwaningen D 94 B2
Untersiemau D 82 B2
Unterweissenbach A 96 C2
Unterzell D 95 B4
Upavon GB 44 B2
Úpice CZ 85 B4
Upiłka PL 68 B2
Upphärad S 54 B3
Uppingham GB 40 C3
Upplands-Väsby S 57 A3
Uppsala S 51 C4
Uppsjøhytta N 48 A1
Upton-upon-Severn GB 39 B4
Ur F 146 B2
Uras I 179 C2
Uraz PL 85 A4
Urbánia I 136 B1
Urbino I 136 B1
Urçay F 103 C4
Urda E 157 A4
Urdax E 144 A2
Urdilde E 140 B2
Urdos F 145 B3
Urk NL 70 B2
Úrkút H 111 B4
Urla TR 188 A1
Urlingford IRL 30 B1
Urnäsch CH 107 B4
Urnes N 47 A4
Uroševac SRB 16 D4
Urracal E 164 B2
Urries E 144 B2
Urroz E 144 B2
Ursensollen D 95 B3
Urshult S 63 B2
Uršna Sela SLO 123 B4
Urszulewo PL 77 B4
Ury F 90 C2
Urziceni RO 17 C7
Urzulei I 178 B3
Usagre E 156 B1
Uşak TR 187 D4
Usedom D 66 C2
Useldange L 92 B1
Uséllus I 179 C2
Ushakovo RUS 69 A5
Usingen D 81 B4
Usini I 178 B2
Usk GB 39 C4
Uskedal N 46 C2
Üsküdar TR 186 A4
Uslar D 82 A1
Úsov CZ 97 B5
Usquert NL 71 A3
Ussássai I 179 C3
Ussé F 102 B2
Usséglio I 119 B4
Ussel, *Cantal* F 116 B2
Ussel, *Corrèze* F 116 B2
Usson-du-Poitou F 115 B4
Usson-en-Forez F 117 B3
Usson-les-Bains F 146 B3
Ust Luga RUS 8 C6
Ustaoset N 47 B5
Ustaritz F 144 A2
Uštěk CZ 84 B2
Uster CH 107 B3
Ústi CZ 98 B1
Ústi nad Labem CZ 84 B2
Ústi nad Orlicí CZ 97 B4
Ustikolina BIH 139 B4
Ustiprača BIH 139 B5
Ustka PL 68 A1
Ustroń PL 98 B2
Ustronie Morskie PL 67 B4
Ustyuzhna RUS 9 C10
Uszód H 112 C2
Utåker N 52 A1
Utansjö S 200 D3
Utebo E 152 A3
Utena LT 13 A6
Utery CZ 95 B5
Uthaug N 198 B6
Utiel E 159 B2
Utne N 46 B3
Utö S 57 B4
Utrecht NL 70 B2
Utrera E 162 A2
Utrillas E 153 B3
Utsjoki FIN 193 C11
Utstein kloster N 52 A1
Uttendorf A 109 B3
Uttenweiler D 107 A4
Utterslev DK 65 B4
Uttoxeter GB 40 C2
Utvälinge S 61 C2
Utvorda N 199 A7
Uusikaarlepyy FIN 3 E8
Uusikaupunki FIN 8 B2
Uvaly CZ 96 A2
Uvdal N 47 B5
Uza F 128 B1
Uzdin SRB 126 B2
Uzdowo PL 77 A5
Uzein F 145 A3
Uzel F 100 A3
Uzerche F 116 B1
Uzès F 131 A3
Uzhhorod UA 12 D5
Uzhok UA 12 D5
Užice SRB 127 D1
Uznach CH 107 B3
Üzümlü, *Konya* TR 189 B6
Üzümlü, *Muğla* TR 188 C4
Uzunköprü TR 186 A1

V

Vaalajärvi FIN 197 B9
Vaas F 102 B2
Vaasa FIN 8 A2
Vaasen NL 70 B2
Vabre F 130 B1
Vác H 112 B3
Vacha D 82 B2
Váchartyán H 112 B3
Väckelsång S 63 B2
Vacqueyras F 131 A3
Vad S 50 B2
Vada I 134 B3
Väddö S 51 C5
Väderstad S 55 B5
Vadheim N 46 A2
Vadillo de la Sierra E 150 B2
Vadillos E 152 B1
Vadla N 52 A2
Vado I 135 A4
Vado Lígure I 133 A4
Vadsø N 193 B13
Vadstena S 55 B5
Vadum DK 58 A2
Vaduz FL 107 B4
Væggerløse DK 65 B4
Vafos N 53 B5
Vág H 111 B4
Vågåmo N 198 D6
Vaggeryd S 62 A2
Vaghia GR 184 A4
Vaglia I 135 B4
Váglio Basilicata I 172 B1
Vagney F 106 A1
Vagnhärad S 57 B3
Vagnsunda S 57 A4
Vagos P 148 B1
Vai GR 185 D7
Vaiano I 135 B4
Vaiges F 102 A1
Vaihingen D 93 C4
Vaillant F 105 B4
Vailly-sur-Aisne F 91 B3
Vailly-sur-Sauldre F 103 B4
Vairano Scalo I 170 B2
Vaison-la-Romaine F 131 A4
Vaite F 105 B4
Väjern S 54 B2
Vajszló H 125 B3
Vaksdal N 46 B2
Vál H 112 B2
Val de San Lorenzo E 141 B4
Val de Santo Domingo E 150 B3
Val d'Esquières F 132 B2
Val-d'Isère F 119 B3
Val-Suzon F 105 B3
Val Thorens F 118 B3
Valaam RUS 9 B7
Valada P 154 B2
Vålådalen S 199 B10
Valadares P 148 A1
Valado P 154 B1
Valandovo MK 182 B4
Valaská SK 99 C3
Valaská Belá SK 98 C2
Valaská Dubová SK 99 B3
Valašská Polanka CZ 98 B1
Valašské Klobouky CZ 98 B2
Valašské Meziříčí CZ 98 B1
Valberg F 132 A2
Välberg S 55 A4
Valbo S 51 B4
Valbom P 148 A1
Valbondione I 120 A3
Valbonnais F 118 C2
Valbuena de Duero E 142 C2
Vălcani RO 126 B2
Valdagno I 121 B4
Valdahon F 105 B5
Valdaracete E 151 B4
Valday RUS 9 D8
Valdealgorfa E 153 B3
Valdecaballeros E 156 A2
Valdecabras E 152 B1
Valdecarros E 150 B2
Valdeconcha E 151 B5
Valdeflores E 161 B3
Valdefresno E 142 B1
Valdeganga E 158 B2
Valdelacasa E 150 B2
Valdelacasa de Tajo E 156 A2
Valdelarco E 161 B3
Valdelosa E 149 A4
Valdeltormo E 153 B4
Valdelugeros E 142 B1
Valdemanco de Esteras E 156 B3
Valdemarsvik S 56 B2
Valdemorillo E 151 B3
Valdemoro E 151 B4
Valdemoro Sierra E 152 B2
Valdenoceda E 143 B3
Valdeobispo E 149 B3
Valdeolivas E 152 B1
Valdepeñas E 157 B4
Valdepeñas de Jaén E 163 A4
Valdepiélago E 142 B1
Valdepolo E 142 B1
Valderas E 142 B1
Valdérice I 176 A1
Valderrobres E 153 B4
Valderrueda E 142 B2
Valdestillas E 150 A3
Valdetorres E 156 B1
Valdetorres de Jarama E 151 B4
Valdeverdeja E 150 C2
Valdevimbre E 142 B1
Valdieri I 133 A3
Valdilecha E 151 B4
Valdobbiádene I 121 B4
Valdocondes E 143 C3
Valdoviño E 140 A2
Vale de Açor, *Beja* P 160 B2
Vale de Açor, *Portalegre* P 154 B3
Vale de Agua P 160 B1
Vale de Cambra P 148 B1
Vale de Lobo P 160 B1
Vale de Prazeres P 148 B2
Vale de Reis P 154 C2
Vale de Rosa P 160 B2
Vale de Santarém P 154 B2
Vale de Vargo P 160 B2
Vale do Peso P 155 B3
Valea lui Mihai RO 16 B5
Valega P 148 B1
Valéggio sul Mincio I 121 B3
Valeiro P 154 C2
Valença P 140 B2
Valençay F 103 B3
Valence, *Charente* F 115 C4
Valence, *Drôme* F 117 C4
Valence d'Agen F 129 B3
Valence-d'Albigeois F 130 A1
Valence-sur-Baise F 129 C3
Valencia E 159 B3
Valencia de Alcántara E 155 B3
Valencia de Don Juan E 142 B1
Valencia de las Torres E 156 B1
Valencia de Mombuey E 161 A2
Valencia del Ventoso E 161 A3
Valenciennes F 79 B3
Valensole F 132 B1
Valentano I 168 A1
Valentigney F 106 B1
Valentine F 145 A4
Valenza I 120 B1
Valenzuela E 163 A3
Valenzuela de Calatrava E 157 B4
Våler, *Hedmark* N 48 B3
Våler, *Østfold* N 54 A1
Valera de Abajo E 158 B1
Valeria E 158 B1
Valestrand N 52 A1
Valestrandsfossen N 46 B2
Valevåg N 52 A1
Valfabbrica I 136 B1
Valflaunes F 131 B2
Valga EST 8 D5
Valgorge F 131 A3
Valgrisenche I 119 B4
Valguarnera Caropepe I 177 B3
Valhelhas P 148 B2
Valjevo SRB 127 C1
Valka LV 8 D4
Valkeakoski FIN 8 B4
Valkenburg NL 80 B1
Valkenswaard NL 79 A5
Valkó H 112 B3
Vall d'Alba E 153 B3
Valla S 56 A2
Vallada E 159 C3
Vallado E 141 A4
Valladolid E 150 A3
Vallåkra S 61 D2
Vallata I 172 A1
Vallberga S 61 C3
Valldemossa E 166 B2
Valle N 52 A3
Valle Castellana I 136 C2
Valle de Abdalajís E 163 B3
Valle de Cabuérniga E 142 A2
Valle de la Serena E 156 B2
Valle de Matamoros E 155 C4
Valle de Santa Ana E 155 C4
Valle Mosso I 119 B5
Valledolmo I 176 B2
Valledoria I 178 B2
Vallelado E 150 A3
Vallelunga Pratameno I 176 B2
Vallendar D 81 B3
Vallentuna S 57 A4
Valleraås S 49 B5
Valleraugue F 130 A2
Vallermosa I 179 C2
Vallet F 101 B4
Valletta M 175 C3
Valley GB 38 A2
Vallfogona de Riucorb E 147 C2
Valli del Pasúbio I 121 B4
Vallo della Lucánia I 172 B1
Valloire F 118 B3
Vallombrosa I 135 B4
Vallon-Pont-d'Arc F 131 A3
Vallorbe CH 105 C5
Vallouise F 118 C3
Valls E 147 C2
Vallset N 48 B3
Vallsta S 50 A3
Vallstena S 57 C4
Valmadrid E 153 A3
Valmiera LV 8 D4
Valmojado E 151 B3
Valmont F 89 A4
Valmontone I 169 B2
Valö S 51 B5
Valognes F 88 A2
Valonga P 148 B1
Valongo P 148 A1
Válor E 164 C1
Valoria la Buena E 142 C2
Valøy N 199 A7
Valozhyn BY 13 A7
Valpaços P 148 A2
Valpelline I 119 B4
Valpiana I 135 B3
Valpovo HR 125 B4
Valras-Plage F 130 B2
Valréas F 131 A3
Vals CH 107 C4
Vals-les-Bains F 117 C4
Valsavarenche I 119 B4
Vålse DK 65 B4
Valsequillo E 156 B2
Valsjöbyn S 199 A11
Valsonne F 117 B4
Valstagna I 121 B4
Valtablado del Rio E 152 B1
Valþjofsstaður IS 191 B11
Valtice CZ 97 C4
Valtiendas E 151 A4
Valtierra E 144 B2
Valtopina I 136 B1
Valtorta I 120 B2
Valtournenche I 119 B4
Valverde E 144 C2
Valverde de Burguillos E 155 C4
Valverde de Júcar E 158 B1
Valverde de la Vera E 150 B2
Valverde de la Virgen E 142 B1
Valverde de Llerena E 156 B2
Valverde de Mérida E 156 B1
Valverde del Camino E 161 B3
Valverde del Fresno E 149 B3
Valvträsk S 196 C4
Vamberk CZ 85 B4
Vamdrup DK 59 C2
Våmhus S 50 A1
Vamlingbo S 57 D4
Vammala FIN 8 B3
Vamos GR 185 D5
Vámosmikola H 112 B2
Vámosszabadi H 111 B4
Vanault-les-Dames F 91 C4
Vandel DK 59 C2
Vandenesse F 104 C2
Vandenesse-en-Auxois F 104 B3
Vandóies I 108 C2
Väne-Ås aka S 54 B3
Vänersborg S 54 B3
Vänersnäs S 54 B3
Vang N 47 A5
Vänge S 51 C4
Vangsnes N 46 A3
Vänjaurbäck S 200 B4
Vännacka S 54 A3
Vannareid N 192 B3
Vännäs S 200 C5
Vannes F 101 B3
Vannsätter S 51 A3
Vannvåg N 192 B3
Vansbro S 49 B6
Vanse N 52 B2
Vantaa FIN 8 B4
Vanttauskoski FIN 197 C9
Vanviken N 199 B7
Vanyarc H 112 B3
Vaour F 129 B4
Vapnyarka UA 13 D8
Vaprio d'Adda I 120 B2
Vaqueiros P 160 B2
Vara S 55 B3
Varacieux F 118 B2
Varades F 101 B4
Varages F 132 B1
Varaldsøy N 46 B2
Varallo I 119 B5
Varangerbotn N 193 B12
Varano de'Melegari I 120 C3
Varaždin HR 124 A2
Varaždinske Toplice HR 124 A2
Varazze I 133 A4
Varberg S 60 B2
Vardal N 48 B2
Varde DK 59 C1
Vårdö FIN 51 B7
Vardø N 193 B15
Vardomb H 125 A4
Varejoki FIN 196 C7
Varel D 71 A5
Varėna LT 13 A6
Vårenes N 52 A1
Varengeville-sur-Mer F 89 A4
Varenna I 120 A2
Varennes-en-Argonne F 91 B5
Varennes-le-Grand F 105 C3
Varennes-St. Sauveur F 105 C4
Varennes-sur-Allier F 117 A3
Varennes-sur-Amance F 105 B4
Vareš BIH 139 A4
Varese I 120 B1
Varese Ligure I 134 A2
Vârfurile RO 16 B5
Vårgårda S 60 A2
Vargas E 143 A3
Vargas P 154 B2
Vargön S 54 B3
Varhaug N 52 B1
Variaş RO 126 A2
Variaşu Mic RO 126 A3
Varilhes F 146 A2
Varín SK 98 B2
Väring S 55 B4
Váriz P 149 A3
Varkaus FIN 8 A5
Varmahlíð IS 190 B6
Varmaland IS 190 C4
Värmlands Bro S 55 A4
Värmskog S 55 A3
Varna BG 17 D7
Varna SRB 127 C1
Värnamo S 60 B4
Varnhem S 55 B4
Varnsdorf CZ 84 B2
Värö S 60 B2
Varoška Rijeka BIH 124 B2
Városlöd H 111 B4
Várpalota H 112 B2
Varreddes F 90 C2
Vars F 118 C3
Varsi I 120 C2
Varsseveld NL 71 C3
Vårsta S 57 A3
Vartdal N 198 C3
Vartofta S 55 B4
Vårvik S 54 A3
Várvölgy H 111 C4
Varzi I 120 C2
Varzjelas P 148 B1
Varzo I 119 A5
Varzy F 104 B2
Vasad H 112 B3
Väse S 55 A4
Vašica SRB 125 B5
Vasilevichi BY 13 B8
Väskinde S 57 C4
Vaskút H 125 A4
Vaslui RO 17 B7
Vassbotn N 53 B4
Vassenden N 47 A6
Vassieux-en-Vercors F 118 C2
Vassmolösa S 63 B4
Vassy F 88 B3
Västansjö S 195 E6
Västanvik S 50 B1
Västerås S 56 A2
Västerby S 50 B2
Västerfärnebo S 50 C3
Västergarn S 57 C4
Västerhaninge S 57 A4
Västervik S 62 A4
Vasto I 170 A2
Västra Ämtervik S 55 A4
Västra-Bodarne S 60 B2
Västra Karup S 61 C2
Vasvár H 111 B3
Vasylkiv UA 13 C9
Vát H 111 B3
Vatan F 103 B3
Väte S 57 C4
Vathia GR 184 C3
Vatican City = Città del Vaticano I 168 B2
Vatili CY 181 A2
Vatin SRB 126 B3
Vatland N 52 B3
Vatnar N 53 A5
Vatnås N 48 C1
Vatne N 53 B3
Vatnestrøm N 53 B4
Vätö S 51 C5
Vatra-Dornei RO 17 B6
Vatry F 91 C4
Vattholma S 51 B4
Vättis CH 107 C4
Vauchamps F 91 C3
Vauchassis F 104 A2
Vaucouleurs F 92 C1
Vaudoy-en-Brie F 90 C3
Vaulen N 52 B1
Vaulruz CH 106 C1
Vaulx Vraucourt F 90 A2
Vaumas F 104 C2
Vausseroux F 115 B3
Vauvenargues F 132 B1

Vrhovine HR 123 C4
Vrhpolie SRB 127 C1
Vriezenveen NL 71 B3
Vrigne-aux-Bois F 91 B4
Vrigstad S 62 A2
Vrlika HR 138 B2
Vrnograč BIH 124 B1
Vron F 78 B1
Vroomshoop NL 71 B3
Vroutek CZ 83 B5
Vrpolje HR 125 B4
Vršac SRB 126 B3
Vrsar HR 122 B2
Vrsi HR 137 A4
Vrtoče BIH 124 C2
Vrútky SK 98 B2
Všeruby CZ 95 B4
Všestary CZ 85 B3
Vsetín CZ 98 B1
Vučkovica SRB 127 D2
Vught NL 79 A5
Vuillafans F 105 B5
Vukovar HR 125 B5
Vuku N 199 B8
Vulcan RO 17 C5
Vulcaneşti MD 17 C8
Vuoggatjålme S 195 D7
Vuojärvi FIN 197 B9
Vuolijoki FIN 3 D10
Vuollerim S 196 C3
Vuotso FIN 197 A10
Vuzenica SLO 110 C2
Vy-lès Lure F 105 B5
Vyartsilya RUS 9 A7
Vyborg RUS 9 B6
Výčapy CZ 97 B3
Výčapy-Opatovce SK 98 C2
Východna SK 99 B3
Vydrany SK 111 A4
Vyerkhnyadzvinsk BY 13 A7
Vyhne SK 98 C2
Vylkove UA 17 C8
Vynohradiv UA 17 A5
Vyshniy Volochek RUS 9 D9
Vyškov CZ 97 B5
Vysoká nad Kysucou SK 98 B2
Vysoké Mýto CZ 97 B4
Vysokovsk RUS 9 D10
Vyšší Brod CZ 96 C2
Vytegra RUS 9 B10

W

Waabs D 64 B2
Waalwijk NL 79 A5
Waarschoot B 79 A3
Wabern D 81 A5
Wąbrzeźno PL 69 B3
Wąchock PL 87 A5
Wachow D 74 B1
Wachów PL 86 B2
Wächtersbach D 81 B5
Wackersdorf D 95 B4
Waddington GB 40 B3
Wadebridge GB 42 B2
Wadelsdorf D 84 A2
Wädenswil CH 107 B3
Wadern D 92 B2
Wadersloh D 81 A4
Wadlew PL 86 A3
Wadowice PL 99 B3
Wagenfeld D 72 B1
Wageningen NL 70 C2
Waghäusel D 93 B4
Waging D 109 B3
Wagrain A 109 B4
Wągrowiec PL 76 B2
Wahlsdorf D 74 C2
Wahlstedt D 64 C3
Wahrenholz D 73 B3
Waiblingen D 94 C1
Waidhaus D 95 B4
Waidhofen an der Thaya A 97 C3
Waidhofen an der Ybbs A 110 B1
Waimes B 80 B2
Wainfleet All Saints GB 41 B4
Waizenkirchen A 96 C1
Wakefield GB 40 B2
Wałbrzych PL 85 B4
Walchensee D 108 B2
Walchsee A 109 B3
Wałcz PL 75 A5
Wald CH 107 B3
Wald-Michelbach D 93 B4
Waldaschaff D 94 B1
Waldbach A 110 B2
Waldböckelheim D 93 B3
Waldbröl D 81 B3
Waldeck D 81 A5
Waldenburg D 83 B4
Waldfischbach-Burgalben D 93 B3
Waldheim D 83 A5
Waldkappel D 82 A1
Waldkirch D 106 A2
Waldkirchen D 96 C1
Waldkirchen am Wesen A 96 C1
Waldkraiburg D 109 A3
Waldmohr D 93 B3
Waldmünchen D 95 B4
Waldring A 109 B3
Waldsassen D 95 A4
Waldshut D 106 B3
Waldstatt CH 107 B4
Waldwisse F 92 B2
Walenstadt CH 107 B4
Walentynów PL 87 A5
Walichnowy PL 86 A2
Walincourt F 90 A3
Walkenried D 82 A2
Walkeringham GB 40 B3
Wallasey GB 38 A3
Walldürn D 94 B1
Wallenfells D 82 B3
Wallenhorst D 71 B5
Wallers F 78 B3
Wallersdorf D 95 C4
Wallerstein D 94 C2
Wallingford GB 44 B2
Wallitz D 74 A1
Walls GB 33 A5
Wallsbüll D 64 B2
Walmer GB 45 B5
Walsall GB 40 C2
Walshoutem B 79 B5
Walsrode D 72 B2
Waltenhofen D 107 B5
Waltershausen D 82 B2
Waltham Abbey GB 45 B4
Waltham on the Wolds GB 40 C3
Walton-on-Thames GB 44 B3
Walton-on-the-Naze GB 45 B5
Wamba E 142 C2
Wanderup D 64 B2
Wandlitz D 74 B2
Wanfried D 82 A2
Wangen im Allgäu D 107 B4
Wangerooge D 71 A4
Wangersen D 72 A2
Wängi CH 107 B3
Wanna D 64 C1
Wansford GB 40 C3
Wantage GB 44 B2
Wanzleben D 73 B4
Waplewo PL 77 A5
Wapnica PL 75 A4
Wapno PL 76 B2
Warburg D 81 A5
Wardenburg D 71 A5
Ware GB 44 B3
Waregem B 79 B3
Wareham GB 43 B4
Waremme B 79 B5
Waren D 74 A1
Warendorf D 71 C4
Warga NL 70 A2
Warin D 65 C4
Wark GB 37 A4
Warka PL 87 A5
Warkworth GB 37 A5
Warlubie PL 69 B3
Warminster GB 43 A4
Warnemünde D 65 B5
Warnow D 65 C4
Warnsveld NL 70 B3
Warrenpoint GB 27 B4
Warrington GB 38 A4
Warsaw = Warszawa PL 77 B6
Warsingsfehn D 71 A4
Warsow D 73 A4
Warstein D 81 A4
Warszawa = Warsaw PL 77 B6
Warta PL 86 A2
Wartberg A 110 B1
Warth A 107 B5
Warwick GB 44 A2
Warza D 82 B2
Wasbister GB 33 B3
Washington GB 37 B5
Wąsosz PL 85 A4
Wasselonne F 93 C3
Wassen CH 107 C3
Wassenaar NL 70 B1
Wasserauen CH 107 B4
Wasserburg D 108 A3
Wassertrüdingen D 94 B2
Wassy F 91 C4
Wasungen D 82 B2
Watchet GB 43 A3
Waterford IRL 30 B1
Watergrasshill IRL 29 B3
Waterloo B 79 B4
Waterville IRL 29 C1
Watford GB 44 B3
Wathlingen D 72 B3
Watten F 78 B2
Watten GB 32 C3
Wattens A 108 B2
Watton GB 41 C4
Wattwil CH 107 B4
Waunfawr GB 38 A2
Wavignies F 90 B2
Wavre B 79 B4
Wearhead GB 37 B4
Węchadlow PL 87 B4
Wedel D 72 A2
Wedemark D 72 B2
Weedon Bec GB 44 A2
Weener D 71 A4
Weert NL 80 A1
Weesp NL 70 B2
Weeze D 80 A2
Weferlingen D 73 B4
Wegeleben D 82 A3
Weggis CH 106 B3
Węgierska-Górka PL 99 B3
Węgliniec PL 84 A3
Węgorzyno PL 75 A4
Węgrzynice PL 75 B4
Wegscheid D 96 C1
Wehdel D 72 A1
Wehr D 106 B2
Weibersbrunn D 94 B1
Weichering D 95 C3
Weida D 83 B4
Weiden D 95 B4
Weidenberg D 95 B3
Weidenhain D 83 A4
Weidenstetten D 94 C1
Weierbach D 93 B3
Weikersheim D 94 B1
Weil D 108 A1
Weil am Rhein D 106 B2
Weil der Stadt D 93 C4
Weilburg D 81 B4
Weilerswist D 80 B2
Weilheim, *Baden-Württemberg* D 94 C1
Weilheim, *Bayern* D 108 B2
Weilmünster D 81 B4
Weiltensfeld A 110 C1
Weimar D 82 B3
Weinberg D 94 B2
Weinfelden CH 107 B4
Weingarten, *Baden-Württemberg* D 107 B4
Weingarten, *Baden-Württemberg* D 93 B4
Weinheim D 93 B4
Weinstadt D 94 C1
Weismain D 82 B3
Weissbriach A 109 C4
Weissenbach A 108 B1
Weissenberg D 84 A2
Weissenbrunn D 82 B3
Weissenburg D 94 B2
Weissenfels D 83 A3
Weissenhorn D 94 C2
Weissenkirchen A 97 C3
Weissensee D 82 A3
Weissenstadt D 83 B3
Weisskirchen im Steiermark A 110 B1
Weisstannen CH 107 C4
Weisswasser D 84 A2
Weitendorf D 65 C5
Weitersfeld A 97 C3
Weitersfelden A 96 C2
Weitnau D 107 B5
Wéitra A 96 C2
Weiz A 110 B2
Wejherowo PL 68 A3
Welkenraedt B 80 B1
Wellaune D 83 A4
Wellin B 91 A5
Wellingborough GB 44 A3
Wellington, *Somerset* GB 43 B3
Wellington, *Telford & Wrekin* GB 38 B4
Wellingtonbridge IRL 30 B2
Wells GB 43 A4
Wells-next-the-Sea GB 41 C4
Wels A 109 A5
Welschenrohr CH 106 B2
Welshpool GB 38 B3
Welver D 81 A3
Welwyn Garden City GB 44 B3
Welzheim D 94 C1
Welzow D 84 A2
Wem GB 38 B4
Wembury GB 42 B2
Wemding D 94 C2
Wenden D 81 B3
Wendisch Rietz D 74 B3
Wendlingen D 94 C1
Weng A 109 A4
Weng bei Admont A 110 B1
Wengen CH 106 C2
Wenigzell A 110 B2
Wennigsen D 72 B2
Wenns A 108 B1
Wenzenbach D 95 B4
Weppersdorf A 111 B3
Werben D 73 B4
Werbig D 74 C2
Werdau D 83 B4
Werder D 74 B1
Werdohl D 81 A3
Werfen A 109 B4
Werkendam NL 79 A4
Werl D 81 A3
Werlte D 71 B4
Wermelskirchen D 80 A3
Wermsdorf D 83 A4
Wernberg Köblitz D 95 B4
Werne D 81 A3
Werneck D 94 B2
Werneuchen D 74 B2
Wernigerode D 82 A2
Wertach D 108 B1
Wertheim D 94 B1
Wertingen D 94 C2
Weseke D 80 A2
Wesel D 80 A2
Wesenberg D 74 A1
Wesendorf D 73 B3
Wesołowo PL 77 A5
Wesselburen D 64 B1
Wesseling D 80 B2
West Bridgford GB 40 C2
West Bromwich GB 40 C2
West Haddon GB 44 A2
West Kilbride GB 34 C3
West Linton GB 35 C4
West Lulworth GB 43 B4
West Mersea GB 45 B4
West-Terschelling NL 70 A2
West Woodburn GB 37 A4
Westbury, *Shropshire* GB 38 B4
Westbury, *Wiltshire* GB 43 A4
Westbury-on-Severn GB 39 C4
Westendorf A 108 B3
Westensee D 64 B2
Westerbork NL 71 B3
Westerburg D 81 B3
Westerhaar NL 71 B3
Westerholt D 71 A4
Westerkappeln D 71 B4
Westerland D 64 B1
Westerlo B 79 A4
Westerstede D 71 A4
Westheim D 94 B2
Westhill GB 33 D4
Westkapelle B 78 A3
Westkapelle NL 79 A3
Westminster GB 44 B3
Weston GB 40 C1
Weston-super-Mare GB 43 A4
Westport IRL 28 A2
Westruther GB 35 C5
Westward Ho! GB 42 A2
Wetheral GB 37 B4
Wetherby GB 40 B2
Wetter, *Hessen* D 81 B4
Wetter, *Nordrhein-Westfalen* D 80 A3
Wetteren B 79 A3
Wettin D 83 A3
Wettringen D 71 B4
Wetzikon CH 107 B3
Wetzlar D 81 B4
Wewelsfleth D 64 C2
Wexford IRL 30 B2
Weybridge GB 44 B3
Weyer Markt A 110 B1
Weyerbusch D 81 B3
Weyersheim F 93 C3
Weyhe D 72 B1
Weyhill GB 44 B2
Weymouth GB 43 B4
Weyregg A 109 B4
Węzyska PL 75 B3
Whalton GB 37 A5
Whauphill GB 36 B2
Wheatley GB 44 B2
Whickham GB 37 B5
Whipsnade GB 44 B3
Whitburn GB 35 C4
Whitby GB 37 B6
Whitchurch, *Hampshire* GB 44 B2
Whitchurch, *Herefordshire* GB 39 C4
Whitchurch, *Shropshire* GB 38 B4
White Bridge GB 32 D2
Whitegate IRL 29 C3
Whitehaven GB 36 B3
Whitehead GB 27 B5
Whithorn GB 36 B2
Whitley Bay GB 37 A5
Whitstable GB 45 B5
Whittington GB 38 B4
Whittlesey GB 41 C3
Wiązów PL 85 B5
Wick GB 32 C3
Wickede D 81 A3
Wickford GB 45 B4
Wickham GB 44 C2
Wickham Market GB 45 A5
Wicklow IRL 30 B2
Wicko PL 68 A2
Widawa PL 86 A2
Widdrington GB 37 A5
Widecombe in the Moor GB 42 B3
Widemouth GB 42 B2
Widnes GB 38 A4
Widuchowo PL 74 A3
Więcbork PL 76 A2
Wiefelstede D 71 A5
Wiehe D 82 A3
Wiehl D 81 B3
Wiek D 66 B2
Większyce PL 86 B1
Wielbark PL 77 A5
Wiele PL 68 B2
Wieleń PL 75 B5
Wielgie, *Kujawsko-Pomorskie* PL 77 B4
Wielgie, *Łódzkie* PL 86 A2
Wielgie, *Mazowieckie* PL 87 A5
Wielgomłyny PL 87 A3
Wielichowo PL 75 B5
Wieliczka PL 99 B4
Wielka Łąka PL 76 A3
Wielowies PL 86 B2
Wieluń PL 86 A2
Wien = Vienna A 111 A3
Wiener Neustadt A 111 B3
Wiepke D 73 B4
Wierden NL 71 B3
Wieren D 73 B3
Wieruszów PL 86 A2
Wierzbica, *Mazowieckie* PL 77 B6
Wierzbica, *Mazowieckie* PL 87 A5
Wierzbie PL 86 A2
Wierzbięcin PL 75 A4
Wierzchowo PL 75 A5
Wierzchucino PL 68 A3
Wierzchy PL 86 A2
Wies A 110 C2
Wiesau D 95 B4
Wiesbaden D 93 A4
Wieselburg A 110 A2
Wiesen CH 107 C4
Wiesenburg D 73 B5
Wiesenfelden D 95 B4
Wiesensteig D 94 C1
Wiesentheid D 94 B2
Wiesloch D 93 B4
Wiesmath A 111 B3
Wiesmoor D 71 A4
Wietmarschen D 71 B4
Wietze D 72 B2
Wigan GB 38 A4
Wiggen CH 106 C2
Wigston GB 40 C2
Wigton GB 36 B3
Wigtown GB 36 B2
Wijchen NL 80 A1
Wijhe NL 70 B3
Wijk bij Duurstede NL 70 C2
Wil CH 107 B4
Wilamowice PL 99 B3
Wilczęta PL 69 A4
Wilczkowice PL 77 B4
Wilczna PL 76 B3
Wilczyn PL 76 B3
Wildalpen A 110 B1
Wildbad D 93 C4
Wildberg, *Baden-Württemberg* D 93 C4
Wildberg, *Brandenburg* D 74 B1
Wildegg CH 106 B3
Wildendürnbach A 97 C4
Wildeshausen D 72 B1
Wildon A 110 C2
Wilfersdorf A 97 C4
Wilhelmsburg A 110 A2
Wilhelmsburg D 74 A2
Wilhelmsdorf D 107 B4
Wilhelmshaven D 71 A5
Wilków PL 77 B5
Willebadessen D 81 A5
Willebroek B 79 A4
Willgottheim F 93 C3
Willhermsdorf D 94 B2
Willich D 80 A2
Willingen D 81 A4
Willington GB 37 B5
Willisau CH 106 B3
Wilmslow GB 40 B1
Wilsdruff D 83 A5
Wilster D 64 C2
Wilsum D 71 B3
Wilton GB 44 B2
Wiltz L 92 B1
Wimborne Minster GB 43 B5
Wimereux F 78 B1
Wimmenau F 93 C3
Wimmis CH 106 C2
Wincanton GB 43 A4
Winchcombe GB 44 B2
Winchelsea GB 45 C4
Winchester GB 44 B2
Windermere GB 36 B4
Windisch-eschenbach D 95 B4
Windischgarsten A 110 B1
Windorf D 96 C1
Windsbach D 94 B2
Windsor GB 44 B3
Wingene B 78 A3
Wingham GB 45 B5
Winkleigh GB 42 B3
Winklern A 109 C3
Winnenden D 94 C1
Winnica PL 77 B5
Winnigstedt D 73 B3
Winnweiler D 93 B3
Winschoten NL 71 A4
Winsen, *Niedersachsen* D 72 A3
Winsen, *Niedersachsen* D 72 B2
Winsford GB 38 A4
Wińsko PL 85 A4
Winslow GB 44 B3
Winsum, *Friesland* NL 70 A2
Winsum, *Groningen* NL 71 A3
Winterberg D 81 A4
Winterfeld D 73 B4
Winterswijk NL 71 C3
Winterthur CH 107 B3
Wintzenheim F 106 A2
Winzer D 95 C5
Wipperdorf D 82 A2
Wipperfürth D 80 A3
Wirksworth GB 40 B2
Wisbech GB 41 C4
Wischhafen D 64 C2
Wishaw GB 35 C4
Wisła PL 98 B2
Wisła Wielka PL 98 B2
Wislica PL 87 B4
Wismar D 65 C4
Wisniewo PL 77 A5
Wiśniowa PL 99 B4
Wissant F 78 B1
Wissembourg F 93 B3
Wissen D 81 B3
Witanowice PL 99 B3
Witham GB 45 B4
Withern GB 41 B4
Withernsea GB 41 B4
Witkowo PL 76 B2
Witmarsum NL 70 A2
Witney GB 44 B2
Witnica PL 75 B3
Witonia PL 77 B4
Witry-les-Reims F 91 B4
Wittdün D 64 B1
Wittelsheim F 106 B2
Witten D 80 A3
Wittenberge D 73 A4
Wittenburg D 73 A4
Wittenheim F 106 B2
Wittichenau D 84 A2
Wittighausen D 94 B1
Wittingen D 73 B3
Wittislingen D 94 C2
Wittlich D 92 B2
Wittmannsdorf A 110 C2
Wittmund D 71 A4
Wittorf D 72 A2
Wittstock D 73 A5
Witzenhausen D 82 A1
Wiveliscombe GB 43 A3
Wivenhoe GB 45 B4
Władysławowo PL 69 A3
Wleń PL 84 A3
Włocławek PL 77 B4
Włodawa PL 13 C5
Włodzimierzów PL 87 A3
Włosień PL 84 A3
Włostow PL 87 B5
Włoszakowice PL 75 C5
Włoszczowa PL 87 B3
Wöbbelin D 73 A4
Woburn GB 44 B3
Wodzisław PL 87 B4
Wodzisław Śląski PL 98 B2
Woerden NL 70 B1
Wœrth F 93 C3
Wohlen CH 106 B3
Woippy F 92 B2
Wojcieszow PL 85 B3
Wojkowice Kościelne PL 86 B3
Wojnicz PL 99 B4
Woking GB 44 B3
Wokingham GB 44 B3
Wola Jachowa PL 87 B4
Wola Niechcicka PL 86 A3
Wolbórz PL 87 A3
Wolbrom PL 87 B3
Wołczyn PL 86 A2
Woldegk D 74 A2
Wolfach D 93 C4
Wolfegg D 107 B4
Wolfen D 83 A4
Wolfenbüttel D 73 B3
Wolfersheim D 81 B4
Wolfhagen D 81 A5
Wolfratshausen D 108 B2
Wolf's Castle GB 39 C2
Wolfsberg A 110 C1
Wolfsburg D 73 B3
Wolfshagen D 74 A2
Wolfstein D 93 B3
Wolfurt A 107 B4
Wolgast D 66 B2
Wolhusen CH 106 B3
Wolin PL 67 C3
Wolka PL 87 A4
Wolkenstein D 83 B5
Wolkersdorf A 97 C4
Wöllersdorf A 111 B3
Wollin D 73 B5
Wöllstadt D 81 B4
Wolmirstedt D 73 B4
Wolnzach D 95 C3
Wołów PL 85 A4
Wolsztyn PL 75 B5
Wolvega NL 70 B2